INTRODUCTION TO COMPUTERS

With BASIC

INTRODUCTION TO COMPUTERS
With BASIC

FRED G. HAROLD
Florida Atlantic University

WEST PUBLISHING COMPANY
St. Paul   New York   San Francisco   Los Angeles

This Book is Dedicated to My Wife Nancy

COPYRIGHT © 1984 By WEST PUBLISHING CO.
50 West Kellogg Boulevard
P.O. Box 3526
St. Paul, Minnesota 55165

1st Reprint—1984

Library of Congress Cataloging in Publication Data

Harold, Frederick.
    Introduction to computers.

    Includes index.
    1. Computers.   I. Title.
QA76.H2836   1984   001.64   83-23501
ISBN 0-314-77910-8

Compositor: Clarinda
Artwork: Editing, Design and Production
Copyeditor: Mary Berry

Cover Photo
© Brett H. Froomer. Reprinted with the permission of the Image Bank.

Text Photo Credits

Chapter 1 Courtesy of Quotron Systems, Inc. **Fig. 1-1** Courtesy of AT&T, Bell Laboratories. **Fig. 1-2** Courtesy of Chase Manhattan Archives. **Fig. 1-3** Courtesy of Commodore Computer Systems Division. **Fig. 1-4** Courtesy of Commodore Computer Systems Division. **Fig. 1-5** Courtesy of Federal Bureau of Investigation. **Fig. 1-6** Courtesy of The Office of the Assistant Secretary of Defense. **Chapter 2** Courtesy of AT&T. **Fig. 2-1** Reprinted by permission of International Business Machines Corporation. **Fig. 2-2** Courtesy of The Science Museum, London. **Fig. 2-3** Reprinted by permission of International Business Machines Corporation. **Fig. 2-4** Reprinted by permission of International Business Machines Corporation. **Fig. 2-5** Crown copyright, The Science Museum, London. **Fig. 2-6** Reprinted by permission of International Business Machines Corporation. **Fig. 2-7** Courtesy of Burroughs Corporation. **Fig. 2-8** Reprinted by permission of International Business Machines Corporation. **Fig. 2-9** Reprinted by permission of International Business Machines Corporation. **Fig. 2-10** Reprinted by permission of International Business Machines Corporation and Harvard University, Craft Photo Lab. **Fig. 2-11** Courtesy of Iowa State of Science and Technology. **Fig. 2-12** Courtesy of Sperry Corporation. **Fig. 2-13** Courtesy of The Institute for Advanced Study. **Fig. 2-14** Courtesy of The Department of the Navy. **Fig. 2-15** Courtesy of The MIT Museum. **Fig. 2-16** Courtesy of AT&T, Bell Laboratories. **Fig. 2-17** Reprinted by permission of International Business Machines Corporation. **Fig. 2-18** Courtesy of Texas Instruments. **Fig. 2-19** Photography by Mark Leet. **Fig. 2-20** Courtesy of Intel Corporation. **Fig. 2-21** Courtesy of Dartmouth College, Hanover, NH 03755. **Fig. 2-22** Photo courtesy of Cray Research, Inc. **Fig. 2-23** Courtesy of Radio Shack, a Division of Tandy Corporation. **Fig. 2-24** Courtesy of Apple Computer, Inc.; courtesy of Unuson. **Fig. 2-25** Reprinted by permission of International Business Machines Corporation. **Fig. 2-26** Diana Walker / TIME Magazine. **Fig. 2-27** Courtesy of The MIT Museum. **Chapter 3** Courtesy of Informatics General Corporation. **Fig. 3-1** Courtesy of Sperry Univac, a division of the Sperry Rand Corporation. **Fig. 3-2** Reprinted by permission of International Business Machines Corporation. **Fig. 3-3** Reprinted by permission of International Business Machines Corporation. **Fig. 3-4** Reprinted by permission of International Business Machines Corporation. **Fig. 3-5** Courtesy of AT&T, Bell Laboratories. **Chapter 4** Courtesy of Xerox Corporation. **Fig. 4-3** Reprinted by permission of International Business Machines Corporation. **Fig. 4-4** Courtesy of Inforex, Inc. **Fig. 4-10** Courtesy of NCR Corporation. **Fig. 4-11** Photo by Norma Morris. **Fig. 4-13** Courtesy of NCR Corporation. **Fig. 4-14** Printed with permission of Anderson, Jackson, Inc. **Fig. 4-15** Courtesy of The Firestone Tire & Rubber Company. **Fig. 4-16** Courtesy of Intel Corporation. **Chapter 5** Courtesy of Boise Cascade Corporation. **Fig. 5-6** Reprinted by permission of International Business Machines Corporation. **Fig. 5-7** Courtesy of AT&T, Bell Laboratories. **Fig. 5-8** Courtesy of National Semiconductor. **Fig. 5-9** Courtesy of Intel. **Chapter 6** Courtesy of Dysan Corporation. **Fig. 6-5** Courtesy of Honeywell Inc. **Fig. 6-7** Courtesy of Shugart Corporation. **Fig. 6-8** Courtesy of BASF Systems Corporation. **Fig. 6-10** Courtesy of BASF Systems Corporation. **Fig. 6-12** Courtesy of Armco, Inc. **Fig. 6-14** Courtesy of Intel Corporation. **Fig. 6-15** Reprinted by permission of International Business Machines Corporation. **Fig. 6-16** Courtesy of Eastman Kodak Company. **Chapter 7** The Mt. Sinai Medical Center, Cleveland, Ohio. **Fig. 7-2** Courtesy of Qume. **Fig. 7-4** Courtesy of Dataproducts Corporation. **Fig. 7-6** Courtesy of Dataproducts Corporation. **Fig. 7-10** Courtesy of DataGraphix, Inc. **Fig. 7-11** Ampex Corporation, Computer Products Division. **Fig. 7-12** Courtesy of Form & Substance, Inc. **Fig. 7-13** Photo courtesy of CalComp (California Computer Products, Inc.), Anaheim CA. **Chapter 8** Photo courtesy of Hewlett-Packard Company. **Chapter 9** Courtesy of National Semiconductor. **Chapter 10** Courtesy of Nixdorf Corporation. **Chapter 11** Courtesy of Control Data Corporation. **Chapter 12** Photo courtesy of NASA. **Fig. 12-3** Courtesy of Novation, Inc. **Fig. 12-4** Courtesy of Novation, Inc. **Chapter 13** Courtesy of The Atchison, Topeka, and the

Credits are continued following the index.

CONTENTS-IN-BRIEF

CONTENTS

OVERVIEW OF COMPUTER SYSTEMS 53

HARDWARE 79

4
INPUT 81

5
PROCESSING 103

6
STORAGE   129

7
USER-DIRECTED OUTPUT   151

PART III

SOFTWARE 171

PROGRAMMING LOGIC 173

11
OPERATING SYSTEMS   253

PART IV

SYSTEMS   273

12
TELECOMMUNICATIONS AND DISTRIBUTED COMPUTING   275

13
DATA DESIGN AND FILE STRUCTURE   303

14
SYSTEMS ANALYSIS AND DESIGN   323

15
MANAGEMENT INFORMATION SYSTEMS 349

PART V

COMPUTER IMPACT   365

16
COMPUTER SYSTEMS   367

APPENDIX B
RANDOMIZING TECHNIQUES 475

APPENDIX C
FLOWCHARTING COMMON PROBLEM
SOLUTIONS 481

BASIC PROGRAMMING SUPPLEMENT 491

THE PORTFOLIOS

PREFACE

Many introductory computing and data processing textbooks have appeared during the past few years to meet the rapidly increasing demand for beginning courses in the computer discipline. Most of these books are oriented towards one of three primary audiences: business students, computer science students or the general "computer literacy" audience. This textbook, while making no claims to serve all three of these groups, attempts to strike a balance between the first two. It does not focus exclusively on the business context (although many of its examples and illustrations address business situations). Neither does it present the highly theoretical and mathematical approach typical of introductory computer science texts (although some of its topics – particularly those in Chapters 11–13 and BASIC Supplement Sections VI and VII – address material usually covered in computer science courses).

The content includes complete and contemporary coverage of the primary topics in computing, for either the computer major or the serious survey course enrollee. The organization of the subjects is rather traditional, with an overview section addressing applications, history, and a comprehensive look at computer *systems* in their most global form followed by four other sections dealing with hardware, software, systems (more constrained than in the opening section) and the impact of computers. An extensive BASIC programming supplement is also provided, which provides BASIC instruction in a modified structured fashion.

Key features of the book include:
● Coverage of computing history that focuses on the *people* who have constituted the driving force behind hardware and software technology.
● Emphasis throughout on the structured approaches to both applications system and program design, without adopting any specific set of "cookbook" rules.
● Concentration on microcomputers (including a full chapter on *Microprocessors and Personal Computing* plus a Highlight box in each chapter) without omission of important information regarding minicomputers, mainframes, and even supercomputers.

- Inclusion of four *Highlight* boxes in each chapter, focusing on micro-computers, society, business, and the future. Each of these is a brief discussion of a technology or application selected for its appeal to the student.
- Full color *portfolios* interspersed throughout the text, address a specific application area of current importance.
- Three appendices covering numbering systems, randomizing or hashing techniques for direct-access files, and flowchart logic for common problems.

Supplementary Materials

- An instructor's manual containing teaching strategies plus an average of more than 50 multiple-choice questions per chapter. Answers to end-of-chapter review questions are also provided.
- A computerized testing system for the multiple-choice questions from the instructor's manual (available to qualified adopters for main-frames or popular microcomputers).
- A complete study guide to assist the student in using the text.
- A software sampler *(Your First Computer Experience)* available on diskette to qualified adopters in versions for the Apple IIe, IBM PC, Tandy TRS–80, or Commodore 64. This software is licensed for unlimited classroom reproduction. Documentation and teaching guidelines are included.

Acknowledgments

Many people were directly and indirectly involved in the development of this book. Particular thanks go to Norma Morris, who coordinated the creation of the book, and to Candy Streeter for her efforts in collecting and selecting the photographs and other illustrations used, as well as for her substantive research. The following researchers also contributed materially to the book, the study guide, and the instructor's manual:

Doug Avery	Edgar Hoge
Nan Barnett	Bob Szymanski
Bill Brandon	Russ Thompson
Donna Cavanaugh	Garnet Topper
Devendra Gulati	Denise Weldon-Sivey

Many thanks also to Linda Cupp for the typing and paste-up of camera-ready study guide copy.

The exemplary copy editing services of Mary Berry deserve special mention; her professional work added greatly to the cohesiveness of the book.

At West Publishing Company in St. Paul, John Orr was tireless in his role as Senior Production Editor responsible for the actual manufacture of the book. John had an extremely tight schedule under which to work but was always most supportive. At the West offices in Westlake Village, California, Editor-in-Chief Clyde Perlee was very helpful, as was Carole Grumney. My particular thanks go to Carole for her guidance in the development of the instructor's manual.

Finally, I'd like to express my appreciation for the professional criticism and helpful suggestions of the following reviewers:

Barbara Denison
Wright State University, Ohio

Lois Graff
George Washington University, Washington D.C.

Douglas W. Knight
University of Southern Colorado

Margaret U. Miller
Skyline College, California

Marvin Schlichting
Triton College, Illinois

Gene Seelbach
Foothill College, California

William A. Suter
Lima Technical College, Ohio

R. Kenneth Walter
Weber State College, Utah

David Y. Wen
Diablo Valley College, California

Fred G. Harold
Boca Raton, Florida
February, 1984

PART 1

UNDERSTANDING COMPUTERS

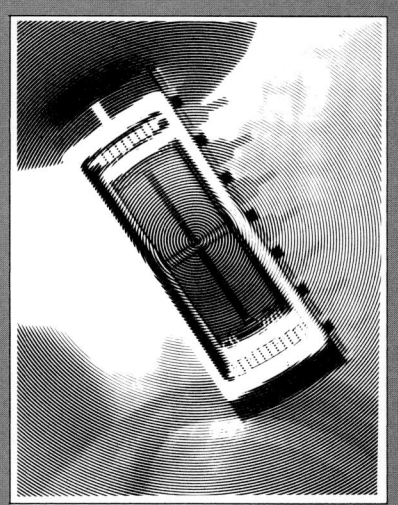

THE WORLD OF COMPUTERS

LEARNING OBJECTIVES

After reading this chapter, you will understand the roles played by computers in multiple segments of our environment in:

☐ Our lives.
☐ The home.
☐ Our schools.
☐ Our country.
☐ The world.

Chapter 1

INTRODUCTION

Computers affect people on five different levels: (1) They cause subtle changes—many times without people's realization—in daily life. (2) They affect the way people view their homes through the widespread and constantly accelerating growth of home computer systems. (3) In schools, they are preparing children for the technological world to come—with many of its features already here. (4) On a national level, they are beginning to control the way large segments of the country operate. (5) Finally, on a global level, they are revolutionizing communication and interaction between nations.

Willing or not, we are being escorted rapidly into a new era of technological advancement. Whether we dominate this area or are intimidated by it will depend—to a large extent—on whether we truly understand the ways in which computers are influencing the world at all five levels.

COMPUTERS IN OUR LIVES

As children, your parents probably sat for hours watching space movies brimming with mad scientists, aliens, and computers—literally tons of computers, each one typically filling an entire room jammed with swirling tapes, flashing lights, and the clickety-clack of great quantities of printed output being spewed into the laboratory air. These movies more recently have evolved into films with the sophistication of the **Star Wars** series and its lovable robots, which make the computers of those early movies more alien to us today than were the hordes of Martians they defeated every Saturday afternoon. The computer has shrunk drastically. No longer requiring a room, the computer now fits in the palm of a hand. The parts of the computer that actually do the computing (or processing, more accurately)—the chips—are now no bigger than the fingernail on a little finger (see Figure 1–1); some are even smaller. Reels of tape have given way to smaller and faster means of storage. Those flashing lights, while still present on large computers, are now overshadowed visually by precise, multicolored, high-resolution graphic displays. Most of all, the computer has stepped out of the movies and into everyday life.

Almost everyone everywhere is affected by computers—every day. They are a part of life. In a single day, you come into contact with computers more often than you would think:

● Even before you awake, a small chip in your coffee maker starts the machine. The mail you pick up in the morning has been sorted and processed by computer to get it to you as quickly as possible. Even the junk mail you receive is there because one company sold its computerized mailing list to another.

Figure 1—1 Relative Size of a Computer Chip

- As you leave the house, you know to take an umbrella because the computer at the National Weather Service has alerted your local weather forecaster to the probability of rain.
- As you drive to work or school, the computer chip in your car's engine controls the emissions from your exhaust.
- On the way to work or school, you stop at a traffic signal that is part of a computerized traffic control system.
- At the end of the day, you stop at the electronic bank teller (see Figure 1–2) location to get money for the weekend.
- The newspaper you read has been written, edited, and typeset using a computer.
- The television news program you watch receives information from an elaborate computer-controlled communications network.
- Many of the commercials you see on television use sophisticated computer graphics to attract your attention and convey their messges.
- Even the book you read for a homework assignment or to prepare for a meeting has been written with the aid of a word processor; this book is no exception.

Every day people are constantly affected by computers. They are a constant, yet ever-changing, part of life. As they become more common, they are having an even greater effect on how people live, entertain themselves, and view the world.

The effects of the pervasive computer presence are not uniformly

Figure 1–2 Electronic Bank Teller

good; the near addiction of many children (and some adults) to video games is a cause for social concern. Organized crime is reputed to use computers in the management of global criminal activities. We all have been subjected to the dehumanization of many activities that becomes possible when computer applications are developed with more concern for productivity than for humanity. The invasion of personal privacy has become more common through the power of interconnected computer systems and centralized data bases.

These characteristics of computers—both helpful and detrimental to society—make it essential that people understand the current technology and its implications for them as individuals and as participants in society. Only with a grasp of computing can people hope to harness and exploit this growing resource while still imposing controls over its application. Technology, it has been said, is neutral. Skilled and conscientious professionals are required to insure the responsible use of the computing tool, whether it is applied in pioneering artificial intelligence (AI) research or the mundane record keeping of an inventory control system. The computer is a sophisticated tool, yet in many ways it is still more a high-speed moron than an electronic brain.

COMPUTERS IN OUR HOMES AND DAILY LIVES

Consumers encounter computers daily. Most shopping and banking transactions are now computerized. In addition, we are experiencing the effects of computers in our recreational activities. As home computer sales continue to increase, consumers will have even greater opportunities to use computer technology for home control systems, personal hobbies, recordkeeping, and educational and recreational interests.

1. Football scoreboards are computer-controlled. **2.** Here, a New York Yankees Baseball Operations Department official uses an Apple Computer at Yankee Stadium. During the games, he records every pitch, hit, and play for later analysis.

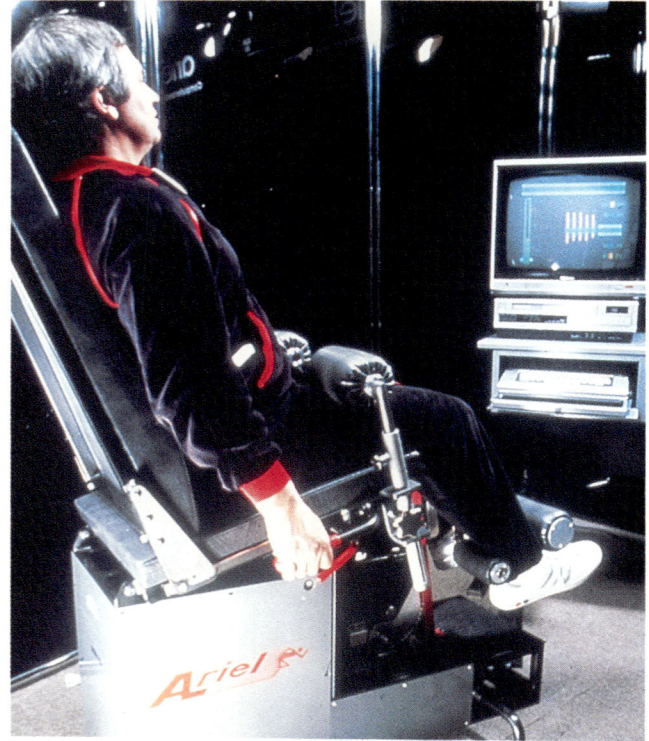

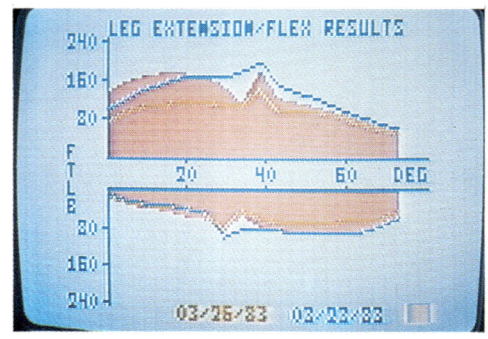

Daily Life and Home—continued. **3.** Physical fitness is taking on increased significance in our society. Through the use of high-tech equipment, The Coto Research Center in California has implemented one of the most effective exercise and training programs in the country. The ARIEL 4000, shown here, uses a computer to monitor and produce instant feedback on an individual's performance. **4.** This is sample output produced by the ARIEL 4000. This particular analysis compares current performance to training goals. **5.** Bowling, one of the most popular participant sports in the world, is now benefiting from computer technology.

6

7

6. Automated teller machines use
increasingly sophisticated software to
link customers and their home banks.
7. Have a Coke and a "thank you" is
what customers will get when they
purchase Coke from the new "Talking
Vendor," a coin-operated vending
machine that talks to customers
through a computerized voice
synthesizer. **8.** Point-of-sale terminals
are commonplace in retail outlets.
"Wraparound" light rays of a
supermarket scanner read UPC stripes
on merchandise held in various
positions. This speeds service by
allowing checkout personnel more
freedom in guiding goods over the
scanning window.

8

Daily Life and Home—continued. **9.** The Smarthome I home control system may be used to control household appliances and lighting. This is a display screen showing the TomorrowHouse home control system. **10.** Homes are now being designed to accommodate the option of a personal computer as part of the modern decor.

11. The Apple computer is popular among personal computer users. **12.** IBM PCjr is well suited for the application of school children's homework. **13.** IBM PC in home environment.

14

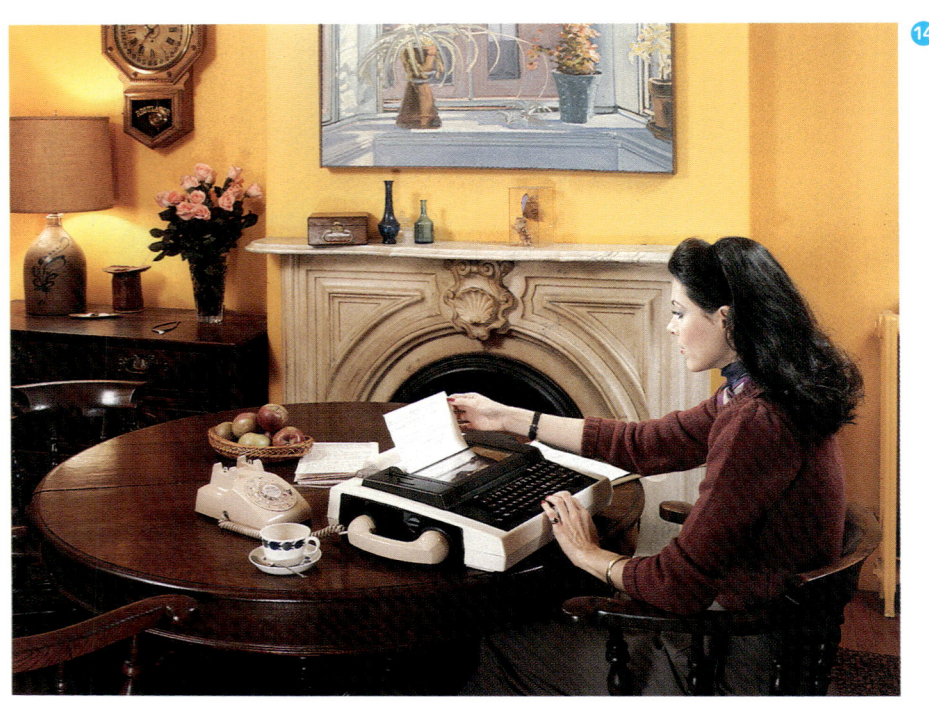

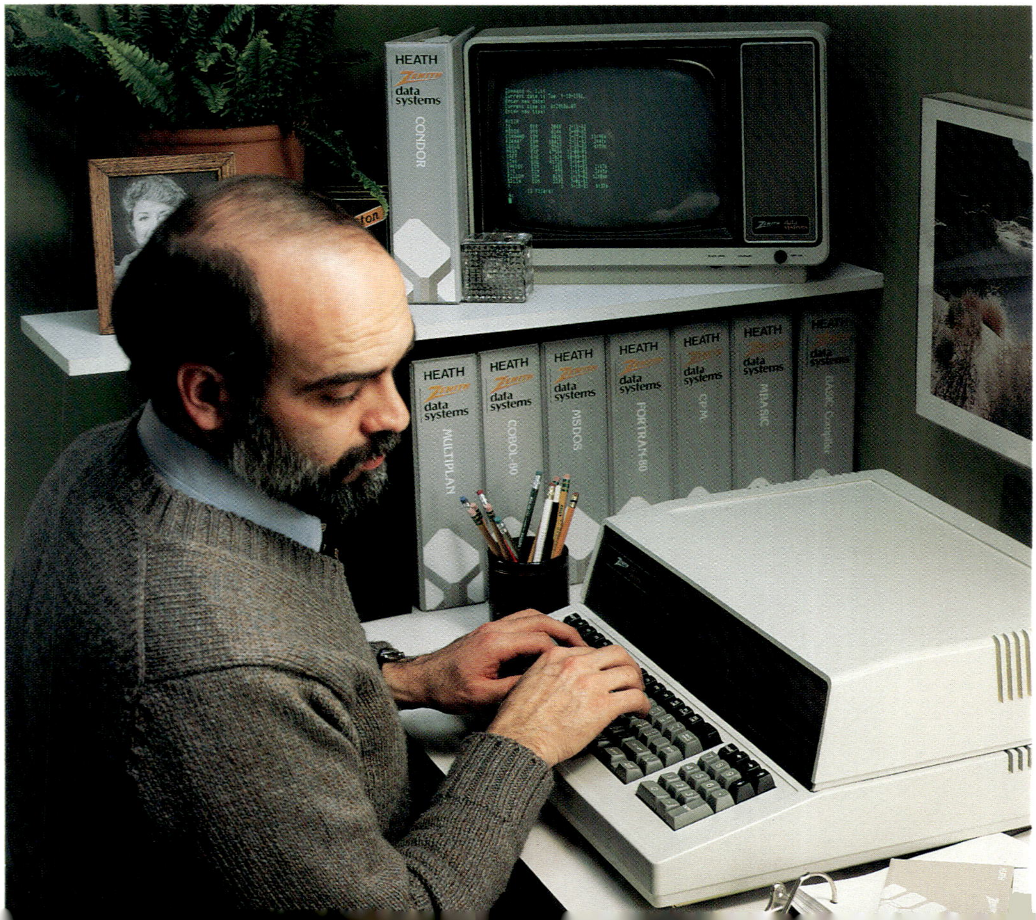
HEATH
data systems
CONDOR
MULTIPLAN
COBOL-80
MSDOS
FORTRAN-80
CP/M
MBASIC
BASIC Compiler

15

Daily Life and Home—continued. **14.** As a result of telecommuting, new job opportunities have been created for those working at home. Shown here is a DEC "correspondence," portable terminal. **15.** Educational games are popular among home computer users. **16.** This couple uses their Residence Energy Management terminal to keep track of how much electricity and natural gas they have used in their home. **17.** Microcomputers are enabling more people to work from their home. Here a real estate agent uses a computerized online multiple listing system and computer-generated photo listing books to provide more efficient and accurate service to prospective buyers. **18.** Financial management software is popular among home computer users.

Daily Life and Home—continued. **19, 20, 21, and 22.** Video Games are still one of the most common uses of personal computers.

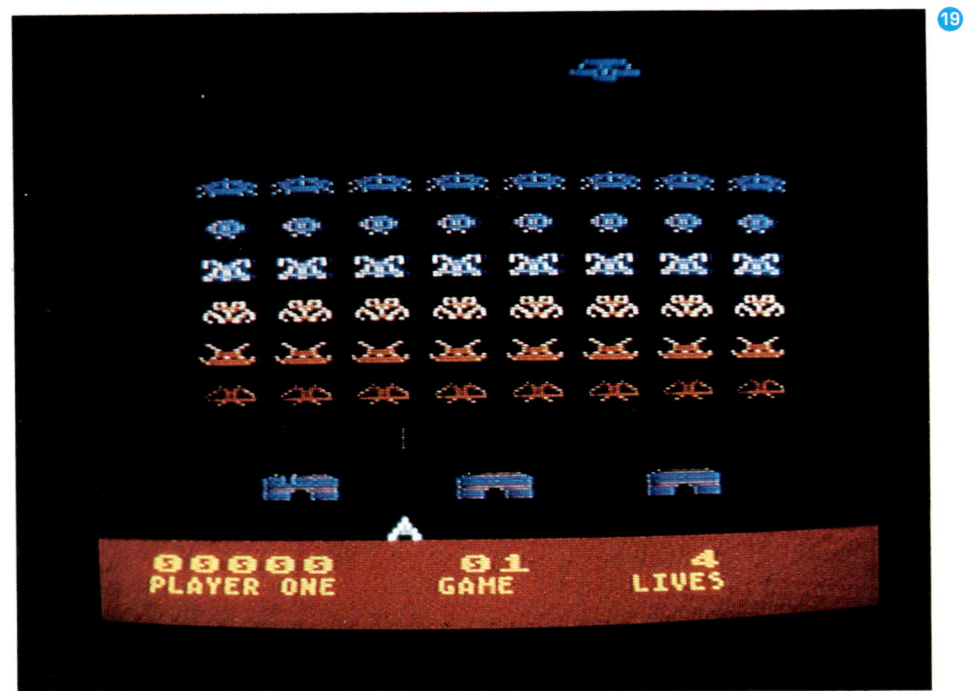

COMPUTERS IN THE HOME

The number of home or personal computers (microcomputers) is expanding at an unbelievable rate; the microcomputer market is predicted to generate sales of twenty-five billion dollars by the 1990s. As computers move into the personal market, they affect the way people view their homes. Although most computers in homes were purchased primarily for entertainment, families now are realizing that they can do much more than just play games with their personal computers. The availability of "canned" software—programs available to help the individual in areas ranging from financial management (see Figure 1–3) to menu planning—underlines the computer's role as a general-purpose machine.

Many home computers are becoming educational and entertainment centers for the entire family. Grolier, Inc., which publishes more encyclopedias and reference books than any other company in the world, is developing a computerized encyclopedia that will be geared to the home. The system is tailored to benefit the entire family by adjusting the level of its responses to the age of the inquirer. In this way, the system can be equally useful to parents and children.

Computers also are bringing families together, and this has not escaped public notice. A Georgia legislator recently proposed a bill to give home computer owners a tax credit for their purchases. His reasoning was based not on the educational or business applications of the sys-

Figure 1–3 Financial Management Software is Popular Among Home Computer Users

Micro Decor

Interior designers are delving into the area of "micro decor"—developing convenient and attractive quarters for home computers. One group of these, the Bernita Designers, designs a variety of settings for computers. These designers claim that "form and function are most important in home design today."

Proper form may include unobtrusive work stations with colors and lines that blend into the general atmosphere of the room. Systems may or may not be enclosed within shelves or hidden behind doors, depending on the extent to which the systems are used. This is the functional aspect.

Space is also a consideration. Although some people have a spare room to devote to their computers, most do not. Many computer stations are designed to blend into the corners of living rooms or bedrooms. Some even wheel into the closet.

The style is also the client's choice. High tech sleekness or drab beige is by no means required. Brightly colored Formica has been found to work very well. Some clients even prefer the eclectic approach, arranging heirlooms, terminals, antiques, and disk drives side by side.

tems, but on the fact that they are an excellent way to bring families together—and they do. Today's computers are commanding the attention of the entire family. They provide the means to process business information and to categorize and keep records of household expenditures. They provide word-processing capabilities for latent and professional writers (this chapter was written using a word-processing program) and educational programs for both children and adults. Programs are available that teach a foreign language, do income tax returns, and "learn" about animals as family members quiz each other (and the computer) about unusual creatures. Even an electronically based Bible is available. The opportunities and capabilities seem endless.

Today's personal computers are having the same effect that television sets did when they were introduced: they tend to become the focal point in the home. They are turning spare rooms and dens into areas of great activity. Some architects and interior designers now take this phenomenon into account in their plans. The computer has had a great effect on the way people view their homes. Just as family activity moved from the dinner table to the living room with the advent of television, some families now are retiring to the computer room for their evening discussions.

COMPUTERS IN SCHOOLS

Computers are not only a part of the world; through education, they also are affecting the way people view the world. Today's children are becoming familiar with computers at progressively earlier ages, and this technological knowledge may influence the way they view the rest of society. It has been said that within ten years, adults who are not computer literate will be at a great disadvantage. It is therefore important to look at the effects of computers on school children, who by necessity will be exposed to the technology early in their formal education (see Figure 1–4).

More and more schools in the United States are recognizing the importance of computer literacy. Computer education has been listed as the most important curriculum change issue in the country. Many high schools, such as Nolan Catholic High School in Fort Worth, Texas, now require computer literacy as a prerequisite to graduation.

In the United States, there is an average of one computer per 250 elementary and secondary school students. Unfortunately, the distribution is not even. Wealthy school districts have more systems available than do poorer districts and inner city schools, which have difficulty acquiring funds for such equipment. This problem is currently being examined by the government because of the concern that if the situation is not remedied, it may create a new class system based on those who are computer literate and those who are not.

Figure 1– 4
Computer-Assisted Instruction

Some progress is being made in this area thanks to the interests of private industry. Eighty-four public and private schools in New York, California, and Florida are receiving a total of 1,500 personal computers courtesy of IBM; this donation is accompanied by an intensive summer curriculum for the teachers who will be using these computers in the schools. IBM has allocated eight million dollars to improve computer education in secondary schools through this program. In addition, the California school system will be receiving ten thousand Apple II computers as a gift from Apple Computer, Inc.

Naturally, the companies do have ulterior motives—primarily tax credits and the familiarization of young people with their products. It should be noted that the states receiving free computers are those that allow the greatest tax credit benefits. In states with less generous tax structures, finding funds for computer education is a problem. The "Apple Bill," a law currently being considered by Congress, is a proposal to allow U.S. computer manufacturers to double the usual tax benefits for donations to educational institutions. Its name is derived from Apple Computer, Inc., which originated the idea.

The best point at which to introduce computing into the schools has yet to be determined. Many educators argue that computers belong primarily in the higher educational circuit—colleges and universities, trade schools, and so on. It is also difficult to determine what effects computer training will have on children in primary and secondary schools. Although the systems are obviously useful for education, some educators feel they have an adverse effect on socialization if introduced into the child's world too early. However, would it not be easier for the child to learn the basic concepts at an early age, before any type of computer phobia or anxiety could develop? These and other questions will be difficult, if not impossible, to answer for many years. Computers have not been used in early education long enough to provide some of the answers.

Most parents, it seems, feel that early computer education is important. At the Lawton Elementary School in Ann Arbor, Michigan, fourth and fifth graders are being introduced to computers by using a Commodore PET. Each teacher at these two levels has at least one computer available at all times; according to school officials, the arrangement is working wonderfully. The children are generally interested in the computer, which seems to make learning more fun for them. The truly interesting aspect of the program is that it was implemented because of parental pressure. Parents want their children to become computer literate early in their schooling.

Computer software manufacturers also are aware of the youth market. More educational programs are being produced, and more of these are aimed at a young audience. For example, Spinnaker Software now offers a package called KinderComp; it contains six educational games designed for children three to eight years old.

A look at all the uses in, as well as effects of computers on, education indicates that computers—when used properly—are of great benefit to children. As long as they are used to supplement teachers rather than

replace them, and as long as computer lessons are supported by sufficient human comment and interaction, they will prepare children for
life in a technological world without interrupting the socialization process. Exposing children to computers at an early age enables them to
bypass the computer phobia that affects so many adults, as well as to
grasp the fundamentals of the field; thus, when they enter the work
place or the higher education circuit, computer use will be as natural to
them as fundamental math and reading skills are now. This is particularly important, because today's children are maturing in a society in
which computers are not only familiar, but commonplace. They will be
entering a job market in which computer literacy will not merely be
expected—it will be demanded.

COMPUTERS IN THE UNITED STATES

Computers not only affect individuals, families, and schools; they also
affect the United States as a whole. This country is becoming a technological wonderland; our Alice is seeing a world being radically
changed by computers, whose applications are becoming more and more
curious. As the impact of computers continues to grow, it is important
that we examine that impact and its effect on people in the United
States. Let us examine how different areas of U.S. government are being
affected.

In a highly visible way, computers are helping to stamp out corrup-
tion and fraud as they take over the record keeping and billing functions
for social services. One prime example of such applications was seen in
Pennsylvania when the Department of Welfare computerized the claims
services for its 1.1 million Medicaid recipients in July 1980. The computerized system had greater capabilities for storage, cross-referencing,
and validation of claims. By 1982 over twelve million dollars had been
saved through a reduction in the number of duplicate, fraudulent, and
otherwise incorrect claims. The savings were great enough to permit the
department to reimburse physicians at a 50 percent increase, raising
rates from eight to twelve dollars per patient.

On the same dramatic level, the Federal Bureau of Investigation (FBI)
has installed three new systems—OCIS, ISIS, and FCIS—to help reduce
crime on a national level (see Figure 1–5). The Organized Crime Information System (OCIS) has terminals located in twenty-nine areas
known to have extensive criminal activity; it contains information on
approximately fifty thousand known criminals. The Investigative Support Information System (ISIS), located in twenty field offices, is used to
help with especially complex investigations. It is specifically designed
to assist in cases with literally thousands of leads. Perhaps the most
intriguing of the three is the Foreign Counter-Intelligence System
(FCIS). This system records the movements and U.S. contacts of sus-
pected foreign spies and international terrorists.

Although computers are powerful tools in the fight against crime,
they have unfortunately made possible a whole new area of white–collar
crime. Computer fraud and theft—crimes committed with the aid of

Computer Skills for the Unemployed

The Minneapolis/St. Paul area has an excellent offering for its unemployed: the Twin Cities Opportunities Industrialization Center (TCOIC). The TCOIC is a school that offers free training in computer programming and operations. Taken under the wing of IBM, TCOIC offers modern equipment and qualified instructors (many of whom are on leave from IBM). Instructors claim that TCOIC offers more state-of-the-art computer facilities than many expensive vocational/technical schools.

How can TCOIC offer all that tuition-free? The answer is free enterprise: "The list of the training center's benefactors reads like a Who's Who of Twin City corporations." In TCOIC's first year, Northwestern National Bank of Minneapolis alone donated twenty thousand dollars to help the school.

Job training specialists predict that free schools like TCOIC will proliferate across the United States, reflecting technological changes and helping workers whose jobs have been phased out by a changing economy.

computers—range from embezzlement to unauthorized access to sensitive information. The 1983 movie **War Games** and the subsequent very real exploits of a group of high school students who infiltrated, among other facilities, the Sloan Kettering Cancer Institute's computer system highlight the potential for computer "snooping." While not always done

Figure 1–5 FBI's NCIC Magnetic Tape Drives

with criminal intent, such violations of supposedly secure computer facilities dramatize the need for tighter controls over computer access.

On a much more public level, computers are being used by politicians as campaign tools. During a candidate's run for office, computers can be used to generate thousands of fund-raising letters, as well as to record campaign contributions and report them to the Federal Election Commission (FEC). Systems of these types were used extensively by both candidates in the 1982 Kennedy versus Shamie senatorial race in Massachusetts. Shamie alone used his system to generate two thousand letters to supporters per week.

Many people are opposed to these new campaign systems, but not for their word-processing capabilities. Some candidates have programmed their systems to gauge public reactions and opinions and enable them to stay on the public's better side. Demographic analysis, furthermore, permits a candidate to tailor the content of both speeches and mailings to the prevailing attitudes in a particular region of the country. The possibility that such systems might enable candidates to tailor campaigns simply to what the computer claims will facilitate their elections—rather than to their actual positions on the issues—is frightening. Most people in the United States feel that there are enough games being played by politicians already; computerization offers the potential to compound this problem.

On the lighter side of computers in government, the Oregon legislature has implemented a computer-based information system for its residents. The system enables computer-owning constituents to look up anything from the status of a bill and the dates of public hearings on that bill to state laws and even public opinion. Although the principal users of the system at this time are lobbyists, the system has great potential as a future information service.

Computers are being used to inform people of their representatives' views and interests, and vice versa. Word processors produce thousands of letters and questionnaires for legislators and tabulate responses to surveys. Although these systems are instrumental in keeping both sides informed, they also incur massive costs because of the free mailing privileges extended to representatives. When the free postal privilege was implemented, hordes of secretaries with quill pens and ink could not do much damage; today the annual cost of complimentary postage runs into the millions of dollars.

In the executive branch of government, computers are used to support many traditional recordkeeping functions, as well as state-of-the art systems. The majority of applications are in the Department of Defense, where command and control systems and communications links are controlled by computers (see Figure 1–6).

As computers become more involved with U.S. government, government becomes more involved with computers. Legislators are trying to become more familiar with this tool by attending seminars and even computer camps. They are interested in becoming more familiar with existing and potential applications. Each year more computer-related legislation reaches lawmakers, and it is becoming more important that

Figure 1–6 A USAF Sergeant Operates the Washington Terminal of the Washington-Moscow Direct Communications Link

they gain a knowledge of the area and its implications. In the next few years, they will be making monumental decisions concerning this new technology. They will examine the role of computers in education, the area of computer literacy, the need for laws to prevent computers from becoming a means by which to invade personal privacy, and the possibilities of tax credits and exemptions related to computers. Decisions in these areas will affect the development of this emerging technology. Consequently, it is imperative that U.S. representatives make informed decisions.

Communication by Touch

The telephones of London's Williams & Glyn's Bank have a radically different dialing system. The system is the City Business System (CBS) computer, equipped with touch control dialing. The CBS gives Williams & Glyn an advantage in the foreign trade market, where prices are constantly fluctuating and time is of the essence. The CBS puts the world market at finger's end.

The CBS stores fifty pages of information. Each page consists of a matrix of sixty-four boxes. Its use is very simple: If operators need to speak with a broker at Chase Manhattan, they simply touch the box labeled **Chase Manhattan.** Within seconds the box flashes, indicating that a broker at Chase has answered

the call, and the operators pick up their telephones.

Incoming calls also are handled by the CBS. An appropriately labeled box flashes, and any operator may touch that box and have the call sent to his or her headphones.

Each page also contains boxes marked **Exchange Line.** These are used to dial numbers that are not stored in the computer. When the Exchange Line box is touched, a matrix of the numbers 0 to 9 appears on the screen. The operators then "dial" the numbers as they would on a touch tone telephone.

The CBS also can manipulate standard computer input; it is even possible to split the screen—to have computer data on the top half and boxes on the bottom.

As we examine the profound effect computers are having on the United States, we must recognize that ours is not an isolated case. Rather, we are part of a worldwide market that is undergoing a computerized global revolution.

Computers are radically changing the world by supporting a global communications network that allows simplified technological information exchange between nations. Communications satellites built using computer technology and deposited in space by one of the space shuttles are one example. These devices figuratively shrink the size of the globe. Today you can transmit electronic mail from New York to London in much less time than it would have taken your great-great-grandmother to write a short letter with her quill and ink. The effect of this technology is to reduce the effective distance between foreign neighbors in our "global village." Time barriers to travel and communications in business and diplomacy are being broken by computer-designed supersonic jets, computer-monitored air travel, and computer-based communications systems.

One of the most obvious effects of computers on global affairs is a developing cultural oneness. Computers are standardizing business

Computer Tunes

The U.S. music industry has encountered the worst slump in its history, and one of the tools it hopes to use to crawl out of that depression is the computer. Computers can help the music industry in many ways. Computer synthesizers can mimic the sounds of a wide spectrum of musical instruments, thus eliminating the costs of professional musicians in recording complex songs that call for many instruments. Computers can be used to help composers who are more adept with invention than they are with instruments. They also can help with the especially difficult task of reproducing sounds that simply are not within the range of traditional instruments, for example, the sounds of breaking glass or ghoulish screams.

Even after a song has been written and recorded, the computer can be used to analyze and alter it. Computers can merge several takes of a song, producing a composite version containing the best sections of the recordings.

All these capabilities are available today. However, the real effects of computers on the music industry will be seen in the future as these techniques are applied in an organized, consistent manner. When used together, they very well may change our concepts and expectations of music.

transactions around the world, as well as enabling nations to share cultural and entertainment traditions through electronic transmission of visual and auditory information. A quick summary of computers worldwide should highlight these effects.

In Japan, advanced computer technology has been embraced with amazing speed and determination. While the United States is striving to maintain its supremacy in the marketplace, its robotics technology already has been surpassed by Japan's. It is estimated that about half of the approximately ten thousand industrial robots in use worldwide are in Japan.

In addition, Japanese researchers are working on what they call the fifth generation computer, which will create a revolutionary expansion in the communications market. This computer will be designed for use with AI applications. When refined, such systems will allow the computer to "think" or reason in much the same way humans do. It is predicted that the new family of Japanese computers will be able to analyze mounds of information for relevant facts, make inferences from what they find, and even help program themselves. Their major use will be in breaking the language barrier; using 100,000-word vocabularies in each of several languages, they will be capable of translating among these languages with about 90 percent accuracy. Strong financial and moral support from the Japanese government points to eventual success for this ambitious project.

The technological revolution has had a profound effect on the Japanese. As business and trade with the West have grown, U.S. culture and tastes have infiltrated Japan. Rockabilly (1950s U.S.–style) clothing and music are a recent fad. In April 1983, extensive graphics, video, and audioanimatronics invaded Japan as Mickey-san moved into the new Tokyo Disneyland.

China also is involved with U.S. computer systems. In 1979 the Chinese government approached the United Nations for some unusual statistical advice: they wanted to know how they could count, record, and analyze the number, educational level, family size, and mobility of their over one billion citizens. The answer was straightforward—computerize the process, as the United States had done in the early 1950s. The United Nations assisted by providing a structure for the process and some support funding.

To facilitate the counting, China bought twenty-nine computers made in the United States. The actual counting required only ten days, from July 1 through July 10, 1982. However, the coding and analysis of that much data, even with computers, will require two years.

The computerized census was a big step for China, whose last census (in 1964) was done mostly by abacus. Because of the demographic details required to feed and clothe a nation of one billion people, the census involved over ten billion answers on over 200 million questionnaires. The twenty-nine U.S. computers purchased for the census have been installed in computer centers around the country to enable the Chinese to continue computerization advances.

In France, the videotex computerized home information system has made national and international waves. People using the service have home terminals hooked to various data banks by telephone. People have computer access to a variety of services: financial and banking transactions; electronic mail, mail order catalogs, and telephone directories; travel, entertainment, and restaurant guides; and educational lessons and games.

France's success with videotex has been so impressive that it has spread to the United States. In 1982 the First Bank System, Inc., of Minneapolis/St. Paul introduced France's Teletel Videotex system into several South Dakota farming communities.

The Instrumentation Control and Automation Division at London's Unilever Company has used the computer to design a bottle that requires less material than conventional designs for the same volume, yet yields a container of greater strength than traditional bottles. The program, developed by Andy Polydorou, produced a bottle that weighed 3.6 grams less than the original and had more than twice the strength. This bottle design process was so successful that it has since been adopted by companies in the United States, Japan, West Germany, Italy, and the Netherlands.

Canada has taken the computer "culture" concept to its logical conclusion by cataloging all the artifacts in the country's 250 major museums with the aid of a computer system. As other countries have cataloged their currency and libraries, the National Museums of Canada have filed away references for over thirty-five million artifacts. While information is readily available to all museums and qualified researchers, an elaborate security system keeps potential thieves from gaining information on the location of valuable items.

In reading about the effects of advances in computing in various countries, it becomes apparent that most technological developments have a global effect. Developments in the United States affect China and Japan, Japanese and French developments affect the United States and Europe, and so on.

The international aspects of computer technology are solidifying people's knowledge of relationships with foreign neighbors. If trade and communications networks continue to expand people's contacts with and understanding of different cultures, a world citizenry may evolve in the future—maintaining a single common culture for communications purposes while still retaining national and regional identities.

SUMMARY POINTS

- Computers have a significant impact on our lives in many ways: in our homes, our schools, our nation, and the world.
- In our homes, computers not only provide vehicles for the playing of sophisticated electronic games; they also help by providing an information resource and by bringing families together in common activities around the computer.
- School children are being exposed to computers in the early years of their education. Computer literacy is becoming an important educational issue.
- Computer manufacturers are supporting primary and secondary schools through equipment donations and training programs.
- Software is being developed for young users; packages are now available for children in the three to eight year age range.
- Government at all levels makes use of computers for both mundane and unique applications. Crime prevention, welfare tracking, and political campaigns are all supported by computer applications. The Department of Defense uses computers for sophisticated command and control applications as well as for traditional record keeping.
- Japanese research will propel us into the fifth generation of computer technology—a period in which artificial intelligence (AI) will come into its own. The Chinese government has applied computer technology (using American hardware) to its latest census of the world's most populous nation.
- The French introduced the videotex concept—the notion of a true computer utility providing access to a variety of services from banking to electronic mail, computerized shopping, and computer-based education. Videotex services are now available in several areas of the United States.
- The computer may contribute to the development of a world citizenry, which will create a single common culture for communication purposes without the blurring of national and regional identities.

1. List all the ways in which your life is affected by computers during an average day.

2. Assume you have a home computer. List at least one potential use for each member of your family.

3. In what ways is the home computer similar to the television set?

4. What are the reactions of parents and educators to the use of computers in education?

5. What is one current problem with the use of computers in education?

6. Why are many schools requiring computer literacy?

7. Name one of the FBI's three new computer systems, and explain what it does.

8. Give two examples of ways computers are being used by the U.S. government to keep people informed.

9. How are computers being used in government to save money?

10. How do computers affect people's global perspective, or the way they view the world?

11. Give two examples of how computer developments in one country have affected people or businesses in another country.

12. List the five levels on which computers affect people.

13. List three ways in which computer applications can be destructive to, rather than supportive of, our society.

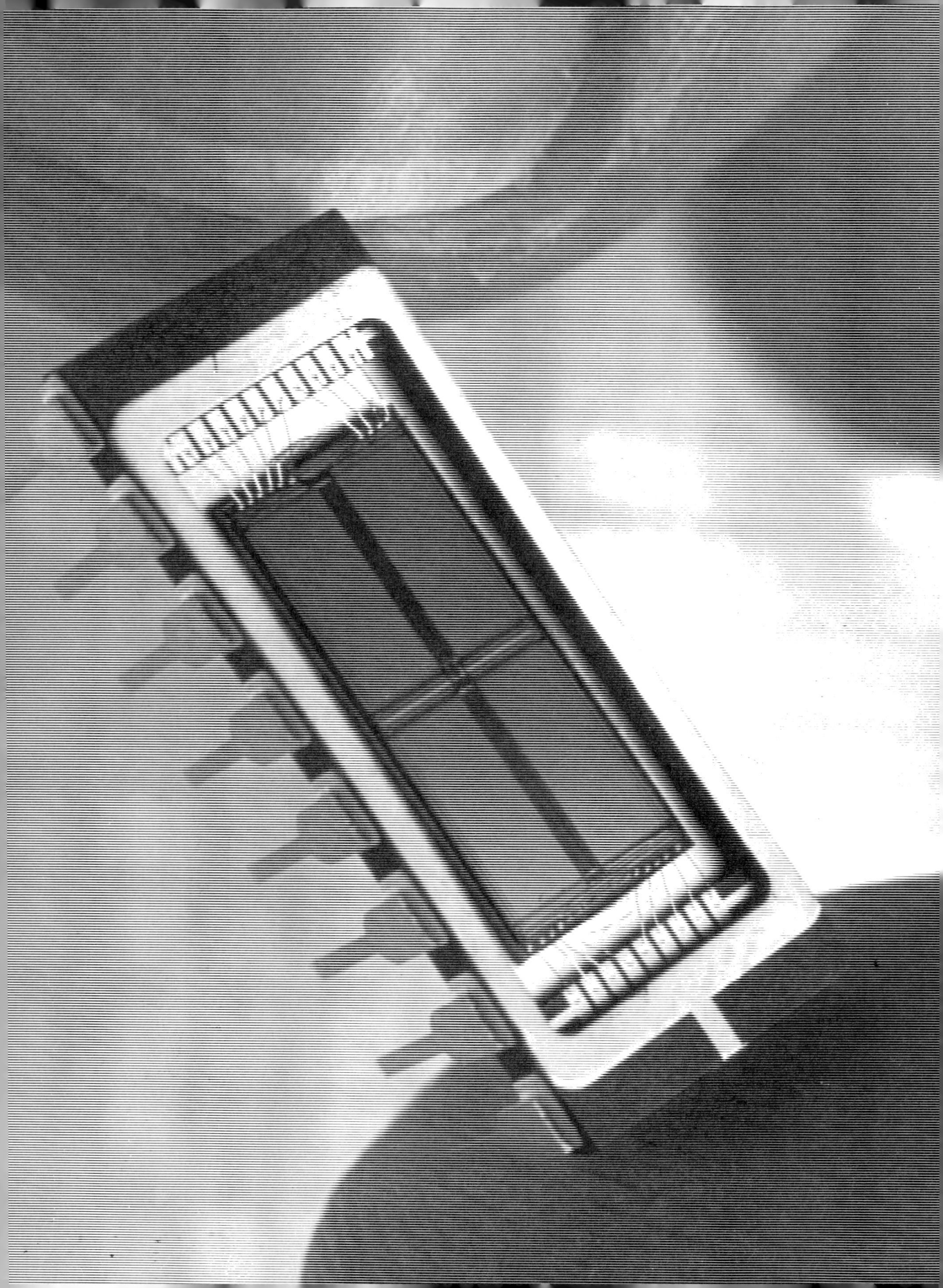

ROOTS

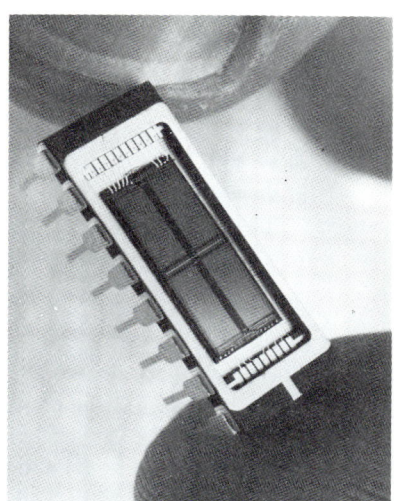

LEARNING OBJECTIVES

After reading this chapter, you will be able to do the following:

☐ Trace the evolution of computers.
☐ Identify major technological advancements and understand their impact.
☐ Recognize people who shaped the industry.
☐ Learn how leading computer businesses were formed.

Chapter 2

INTRODUCTION

This chapter traces the evolution of the computer from early calculating methods to state-of-the-art technology. It describes the progress of technology by combining traditional history with brief profiles of people who contributed to the field of computers. Throughout the chapter it will become obvious that these people shared an enthusiasm for and dedication to the field. Their ingenious ideas and enterprising skills are largely responsible for the invention's impact on society. In addition, the backgrounds of some leading computer companies are presented.

The chapter is divided into time frames that closely parallel the computer generations discussed in Chapter 3. Through this structure, it is clear how the specific discoveries in hardware, software, memory and storage devices, input/output methods, and languages were classified into their respective generations.

THEORISTS

The need for computational methods was evident in early civilizations, when people depended on knots tied in rope, stones used as counters, and notches carved in sticks to keep records of herds of animals or values of traded merchandise. The **abacus** (see Figure 2–1), one of the earliest known computational devices, dates back to the Chinese in 2600 B.C. The Chinese, and later other groups, found that using beads strung on wires to represent values was an easy way of handling problems that involved addition and subtraction.

The abacus, along with hand calculations, seemed to be an adequate method for computation until the early 1600s, when **John Napier** (1550–1617) developed a table of numbers to aid in multiplication and division

Figure 2–1 The Abacus

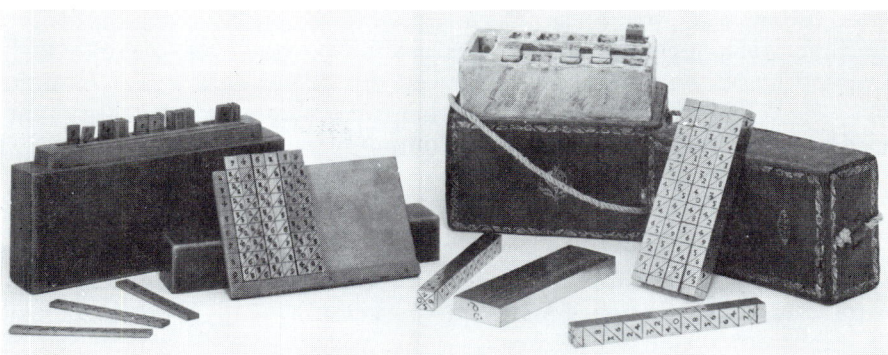

Figure 2–2 Napier's Bones

(See Figure 2–2). This primitive slide rule, referred to as **Napier's Bones** (or **Napier's Rods**), indicated the need for permanent, accessible solutions.

Blaise Pascal

The first successful attempt to automate computational methods was made by **Blaise Pascal** (1623–1662). Pascal, a French scientist and philosopher (perhaps inspired by his father, a respected mathematician and tax collector), developed a machine capable of adding and subtracting (see Figure 2–3). **Pascal's adding machine,** developed in 1642, operated on the principal of gears. Each gear had ten teeth—one for each numeric digit (0 through 9); a carry from the value represented by one gear acti-

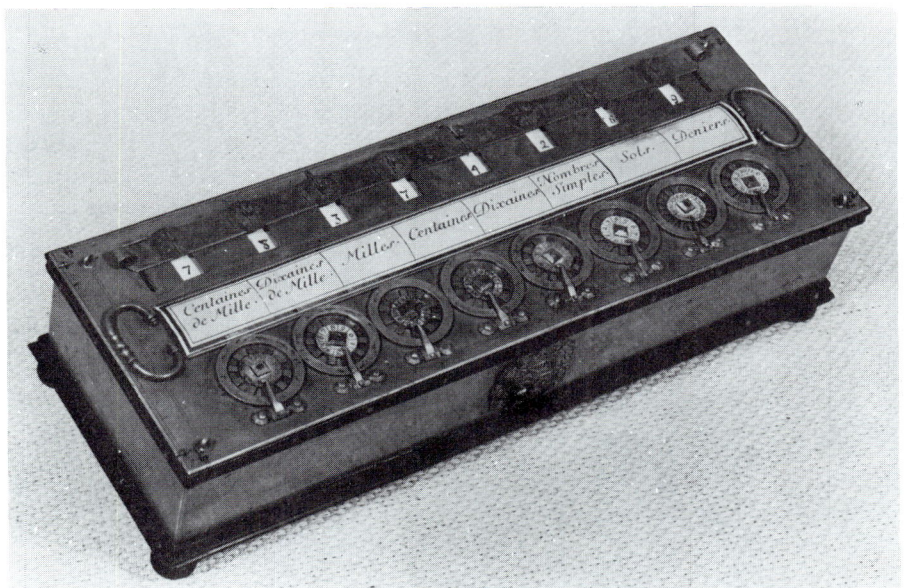

Figure 2–3 Blaise Pascal and His Adding Machine

vated the next decimal place. At the age of nineteen Pascal had invented the first **mechanical calculator.** The calculator, however, was not well received by the tax clerks, who viewed the device as a threat to their jobs. Pascal's invention made mechanical calculation a reality and opened the doors to state-of-the-art computer technology.

Gottfried Wilhelm von Leibniz

Pascal's calculator remained a one-of-a-kind device until about fifty years later, when **Gottfried Wilhelm von Leibniz** (1646–1716) developed an improved model (see Figure 2–4). Leibniz's machine, completed in 1694, was capable of not only addition and subtraction, but also multiplication, division, and finding square roots. Although the machine was intended to free scientists from time-consuming hand calculations, it did not become widely used.

Joseph Marie Jacquard

Joseph Marie Jacquard (1752–1834) made a most unexpected contribution to the computer industry—job automation. Jacquard was a native of France who wove rugs on a loom. In 1801 he improvised a device to automate weaving through the use of coded punched cards (see Figure 2–5). His device became extremely popular, and by 1812 he was receiving royalties on the eleven thousand looms in use. Although Jacquard's invention changed the entire weaving industry and earned him much fame and respect, several contemporaries feared the results of widespread automation.

Charles Babbage and Ada Augusta Byron, Countess of Lovelace

The first person to propose the concept of the modern computer was **Charles Babbage** (1791–1871), a man truly ahead of his time. Babbage was a professor of mathematics at Cambridge University, as well as an inventor. As a mathematician, he realized the time-consuming and boring nature of constructing mathematical tables (squares, logarithms,

Figure 2–4 Gottfried Wilhelm von Leibniz and His Mechanical Calculator

Figure 2–5 The Jacquard Loom

sines, cosines, and so on). Since the calculators developed by Pascal and Leibniz could not provide the calculations required for these more complex tables, Babbage proposed the idea of building a machine that could compute the various properties of numbers, accurate to twenty digits. With a grant from the British government, he designed and partially built a simple model of the **difference engine** (see Figure 2–6). However, the lack of technology in the 1800s prevented him from making a working model. Discouraged by his inability to materialize his ideas, Babbage imagined a better version, which would be a general-purpose, problem-solving machine—the **analytical engine.**

The similarities between the analytical engine and the modern computer are amazing. Babbage's analytical engine, which was intended to

Figure 2–6 Charles Babbage and His Difference Engine

be a steam-powered device, had four components: (1) a "mill" that manipulated and computed the data; (2) a "store" that held the data; (3) an "operator," or system that carried out instructions; and (4) a separate device that entered data and received processed information via punched cards.

After spending many years sketching variations and improvements for this new model, Babbage received some assistance in 1842. **Ada Augusta Byron, Countess of Lovelace** (1815–1852), became interested in Babbage's efforts when translating a paper on the analytical engine from French to English. Upon meeting Babbage, she began the task of writing an original paper. Through the process, she documented Babbage's ideas and made it possible to understand Babbage's original intentions. Over time, she became a full collaborator on the project, correcting some errors and suggesting the use of the binary system of storage rather than the decimal. Lady Lovelace's most important contribution was her concept of a loop. She observed that a repetition of a sequence of instructions often was necessary to perform a single calculation. Thus, she discovered that by using a single set of cards and a conditional jump facility, the calculation could be performed with a fraction of the effort. This idea has earned her the distinction of being the first programmer.

After Lady Lovelace's tragic death from cancer, Babbage was again alone to continue his labor. At his death in 1871, thousands of sketches existed. Both of these pioneers are better remembered now than they were in the first half of this century: Babbage is recognized as the father of the computer, and the latest state-of-the-art programming language, Ada, was named in honor of Countess Lovelace's achievements.

FOUNDING FATHERS

William Seward Burroughs

The first commercially successful adding machine was invented by **William Seward Burroughs** (see Figure 2–7). Employed as a bookkeeper, Burroughs, who was born in 1857, wanted to make his job easier and more efficient. As a result, he invented a crank-operated, key-driven machine that not only calculated numbers, but also printed them. Many of the features incorporated in his initial model are still relevant today. With a patent granted in 1888, Burroughs formed the Burroughs Adding Machine Company (a direct ancestor of Burroughs Corporation) to produce his invention for commercial use.

Figure 2-7 William S. Burroughs

Herman Hollerith

Herman Hollerith (1860–1929), a graduate of Columbia University's School of Mines, was hired by the U.S. Census Bureau at the age of nineteen. The 1880 census took seven and a half years to complete, and the 1890 census was predicted to take longer. Hollerith was assigned the responsibility of developing a mechanical method of tabulating the census data. In 1887 Hollerith introduced his **census machine** (see Figure 2–8). There were four parts to the machine: a punched paper card that represented data using a special code (**Hollerith code**); a hand-operated card punch; a tabulator that read the punched cards, causing appropriate counting dials to increment; and a sorting machine with twenty-four compartments. Hollerith adapted the idea of the punched card from Jacquard; whereas Jacquard encoded control information in his cards, Hollerith recorded data. The size of Hollerith's cards—still the same in today's versions as in the machines originally used—is identical to that of dollar bills in the late nineteenth century. Hollerith needed precision dies to stamp his blank cards from cardboard stock and found them through a friend at the Treasury Department.

The efficiency of Hollerith's equipment and techniques was demonstrated by the fact that tabulation of 1890 census data was completed

Figure 2—8 Herman Hollerith and His Census Machine

three times faster than that of the 1880 census—despite a population increase of twelve million.

Pleased with his success, Hollerith formed the Tabulating Machine Company in 1896 and began supplying the equipment to census takers in western Europe and Canada. The U.S. Census Bureau continued to be the major user of the tabulating equipment through the 1900 census. A disagreement with the census director, however, caused Hollerith to lose business with the Census Bureau and forced him to find new markets for the equipment. Meanwhile, his successor at the Census Bureau, James Powers, redesigned the tabulating machines and eventually formed his own company—later to become Remington Rand and Sperry Univac.

Hollerith, while cautious in implementing the equipment in outside applications, was nevertheless a dynamic businessman in pursuit of commercial success. He energetically solicited new clients and found them. The railroad industry was the first to implement his tabulating machines, and soon mercantile and manufacturing clients followed. In 1911 Hollerith sold his company, which later combined with twelve others to form the Computing-Tabulating-Recording (CTR) Company, a direct ancestor of International Business Machines (IBM).

Thomas J. Watson, Sr.

Three years after Hollerith sold his company, **Thomas J. Watson, Sr.** (1874–1956), was hired for a sales position with CTR. Watson had stud-

ied accounting and business at the Miller School of Commerce in El-
mira, New York. He worked briefly as a bookkeeper in a meat market.
Looking for a greater challenge, he joined a traveling salesman and
worked fifteen years for National Cash Register (NCR). A conflict with
the president at NCR brought him to CTR.

Figure 2–9 Thomas
J Watson

Promoted to general manager in 1915, Watson served in that position
until the death of CTR's president in 1924. At the age of fifty, he assumed the position of chief executive and changed the company name
to International Business Machines Corporation (IBM). Watson is shown
in Figure 2–9.

The U.S. Congress passed legislation in 1935 for setting up the Social
Security System. Despite problems of the Great Depression, Watson's
preparedness won IBM the contract to provide the machines needed for
this massive accounting and payment distribution system.

Watson and his company also were actively involved in the record
keeping related to World War II. Tabulating centers were established to
keep track of the prisoners of war, and employees collected intelligence
information from offices in enemy or occupied territory. It has been suggested that the tabulators even helped break the Japanese code at Pearl
Harbor. Because of these and other efforts, IBM became highly recognized, and the company's profits more than tripled.

The military needed improved calculating machines to compute firing
tables for artillery weapons. Watson was asked to finance two projects
with IBM resources––one for a huge mechanical computing device proposed by Howard H. Aiken and the other for an electronic computer
device proposed by John W. Mauchly and J. Presper Eckert. Watson
chose to finance only Aiken's project, a mistake that resulted in the
establishment of a leading competitor.

Howard H. Aiken

The project of **Howard H. Aiken** was made possible with IBM's $500,000
investment and engineering support. The Mark I (also called the Automatic Sequence Controlled Calculator) was the first **large-scale digital
computer.** Built at IBM's Endicott plant and dedicated to Harvard University in 1944, the Mark I was capable of storing seventy-two words
and performing three additions a second (see Figure 2–10).

John Vincent Atanasoff and Clifford Berry

The next two events appear to have taken place simultaneously. For a
long time, John W. Mauchly and J. Presper Eckert were credited with
inventing the first **electronic digital computer.** However, a 1973 federal
court ruling set history straight, and that honor now belongs to **John
Vincent Atanasoff.**

Atanasoff, after receiving a doctorate in theoretical physics at the University of Wisconsin, joined the Iowa State faculty in the early 1930s.
There he experienced the computational difficulties involved in solving
complex mathematical equations with several variables. Since the avail-

Figure 2–10 Howard
Aiken and the Mark I

able calculating machines were inadequate in both speed and precision,
he decided in 1935 that something had to be done to remedy the situation. Recalling Pascal's and Babbage's inventions and applying principles
from his hobby of radio electronics, he set forth in his task.

Solving the problems involved in building a machine were even more
complex than the mathematical calculations; many decisions had to be
made in the planning stage, including the type of memory to be used,
the method of input, and the logic design. In 1937 at a tavern 189 miles
from the university, Atanasoff finally reached a conclusion incorporat-
ing several innovative ideas, the most visionary being the use of the
binary code.

He spent the next year finalizing the details. With a $650 grant from
the Iowa State Research Council, Atanasoff purchased the materials
needed to build a prototype model and hired a part-time assistant, **Clifford Berry,** a graduate student in engineering. Two additional grants and
a donation from a private foundation totaling $6,640 enabled Atanasoff
and Berry to complete their project—the **Atanasoff-Berry Computer
(ABC)**—by the fall of 1939 (see Figure 2–11).

Although Atanasoff attempted to publicize his machine by filing a
patent, contacting influential scientists for support, and negotiating a
marketing contract with IBM, all these efforts failed. Atanasoff also
wanted to improve the prototype model but was diverted by the war
effort.

John W. Mauchly and J. Presper Eckert

John W. Mauchly, born in Chevy Chase, Maryland, in 1907, had an early
interest in calculating machines. While working toward his physics de-

Figure 2–11 John Atanasoff, Clifford Berry and the Atanasoff-Berry Computer

gree at Johns Hopkins University, he also worked as a research assistant for his father, a physicist at Carnegie Institute of Washington. Mauchly's need for calculating power for both school and his job led him to experiment briefly with methods of faster calculation. After accepting a position as head of the physics department at Ursinus College near Philadelphia in 1933, Mauchly specialized in researching atmospheric electricity. To do this, however, he needed extensive weather statistics; the graduate students employed to compile these statistics were unable to generate the substantial amount of information with the speed Mauchly required.

Meanwhile, Mauchly was developing a theory involving the use of vacuum tube devices. His colleagues were experimenting with these vacuum tubes in atomic research, and Mauchly reasoned that the vacuum tubes could be used to electronically speed up computations. Because of limited funds, he built a small analog computer and planned to deliver a paper on his theory at the American Association for the Advancement of Science (AAAS) in December 1940. There Mauchly met Atanasoff and learned of the ABC.

Mauchly accepted Atanasoff's invitation to see the machine and spent five days in June 1941 carefully observing the operation and construction of the ABC, which was capable of solving twenty-nine simultaneous equations with twenty-nine variables. Mauchly undoubtedly was influenced by this demonstration and returned to Pennsylvania with increased enthusiasm for developing his previous theory. He enrolled in a course at the University of Pennsylvania's Moore School of Engineering—a governmental program designed to train engineers in electronics in the hope of recruiting prospective researchers. **J. Presper Eckert,** a young graduate student, was the laboratory instructor of the course.

After completing the course at the Moore School, Mauchly left Ursinus College and joined the staff of the Moore School in 1941. This move proved to be most advantageous to Mauchly, since the school was engaged in a joint project with the U.S. Army Ordnance Department's Aberdeen Proving Ground. Aberdeen specialized in ballistics research, or the process of computing artillery firing tables using such factors as gravity, air movement, and the size and material of the weapons.

Mauchly and Eckert seized the opportunity for involvement in the project and were determined to find a more precise and efficient method of generating the tables. Mauchly circulated his ideas (some of which were based on Atanasoff's machine) among the faculty and requested research funds from IBM. IBM felt the venture was too risky, but the ideas were well received by Herman Goldstine, the liaison between Aberdeen and the Moore School. Goldstine convinced the Ordnance Department to fund Mauchly and Eckert's proposal.

Mauchly and Eckert officially began work in April 1943. The finished machine (see Figure 2–12), the **Electronic Numerical Integrator and**

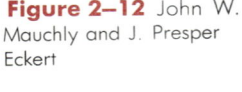 **Figure 2–12** John W. Mauchly and J. Presper Eckert

Computer (ENIAC), was introduced in June 1946. The ENIAC, costing over $480,000, could perform a calculation in three-thousandths of a second. This machine, the first **operational electronic digital computer,** was a huge device consisting of over eighteen thousand vacuum tubes; it was controlled by external switches and control panels (plugboards) that required changing for every new series of computations. Unlike the ABC, the ENIAC used the decimal code and was a general-purpose machine.

John von Neumann

Herman Goldstine inspired **John von Neumann** (1903–1957) to apply his mathematical knowledge to the computer field. Von Neumann was born and educated in Europe. In addition to being a superb mathematician, he held degrees in chemistry and physics. As a faculty member at the Institute for Advanced Study in Princeton, New Jersey, von Neumann was one of the most highly regarded citizens of the community.

Figure 2–12 (cont'd) The ENIAC

Serving as a consultant at Aberdeen, von Neumann learned of the ENIAC project during a conversation with Goldstine in the summer of 1944. Intrigued, he became a consultant to the ENIAC project and discussed with Mauchly and Eckert the building of a second machine—the **Electronic Discrete Variable Calculator (EDVAC)**—that would correct some of the unsolved problems of the ENIAC.

Von Neumann (see Figure 2–13) was referring in particular to the problems encountered with the plugboards. Programming was accomplished by plugging and replugging six thousand switches. Whenever a mistake was made in setting even one switch, the program would be incorrect. Von Neumann and others believed there had to be a way of storing the program internally.

Von Neumann's concept was more clearly defined in a one hundred–page paper, "First Draft of a Report on the EDVAC." A landmark in computing theory, this paper emphasized the logical functions of the computer rather than the electrical engineering aspects. The most important idea presented in the paper, however, was von Neumann's suggestion for storing programs and data in computer memory—**the stored-program concept.** It is the ability to store a program that distinguishes a computer from a calculator. Von Neumann was able to implement what Babbage had proposed a century earlier.

Von Neumann also is considered the father of flowcharting. While involved with the ENIAC project, he and two coauthors (Herman Goldstine and Arthur W. Burks) described the use of **flow diagrams** in a 1946 report written for the U.S. Army, "Preliminary Discussion of the Logical Design of an Electronic Computing Instrument." These flow diagrams, intended as a tentative aid in the programming process, have become an

Figure 2–13 John von Neumann and the EDVAC

important tool commonly used in programming preparation and documentation.

Early Commercial Machines

The first operational computer to incorporate the stored-program concept was the **Electronic Delay Storage Automatic Computer (EDSAC)**, built under the direction of **Maurice V. Wilkes** at Cambridge University in 1949.

Completion of the EDVAC was delayed by other priorities. In 1946 Mauchly and Eckert founded the Electronic Controls Corporation, which later was renamed the Eckert-Mauchly Computer Corporation. Their company had two major projects: the BINAC for Northrop Corporation and the **Universal Automatic Computer (UNIVAC) I** for the National Bureau of Standards' use in the U.S. Census Bureau.

Two years later the BINAC was delivered but refused, because it did not meet Northrop's needs. After suffering a financial loss, Eckert and Mauchly turned to Remington Rand Corporation, a company specializing in typewriters and office equipment; there they found much-needed financial backing.

The inventors subsequently focused their efforts on developing the UNIVAC I; they delivered it to the Census Bureau in June 1951. Representing the beginning of the "first generation" of computers, the UNIVAC I was the first commercially successful electronic computer designed for business purposes. Until IBM's strong entry into the computer business in the mid-1950s, the term **UNIVAC** was used generically to mean computer, much as Kleenex and Jell-O are informally used to represent tissues and gelatin desserts of any brand.

After multiple mergers, the company that Eckert and Mauchly formed and that later was taken over by Remington Rand has become Sperry Univac.

INVENTORS

The first generation of computers, mentioned in connection with the UNIVAC I, was characterized by machines whose processing capabilities were based on vacuum tube electronics. These computers were large, slow, and unreliable, requiring significant cooling capabilities to dissipate the heat generated by thousands of tubes. Advances made in the next decade—in both the use of computers and their circuitry—led to the second generation. This section presents some of the more important innovators and their achievements.

Grace Murray Hopper

A major nonelectronic area demanding attention was that of communicating with the computer. The first person to recognize the inefficiency

History in Review

Computers have had a tremendous impact on society. One way of learning more about computers—especially the historical aspect—was made possible through the establishment of the Computer Museum.

Opened to the public in 1982 and housed in the lobby of Digital Equipment Corporation's (DEC's) complex in Marlborough, Massachusetts, the Computer Museum has exhibits dating from Napier's Bones to the more recent experimental robots. The idea for the museum can be attributed to DEC's founder and current president, Kenneth Olsen.

Olsen had worked on the Whirlwind computer project at MIT in the early 1950s. When he learned that MIT was disposing of the Whirlwind in 1974, he hurried to rescue it. Olsen, however, had no real use for the machine, so he stored the computer in a warehouse. During the following years, Olsen and a friend, Bob Everett, the founder of Mitre Corporation, began acquiring other computer artifacts.

By 1980 the warehouse was overflowing with computer memorabilia, and the two men decided that something worthwhile should be done with their collection. They organized the collection and founded the Computer Museum. Almost every significant machine of the computer revolution is represented in the display. There are approximately fifty calculating machines, fifteen complete computers, and parts from about fifty other computers. In addition, there are photographs, computer-generated murals, a library of film clips, and periodic lectures by pioneers such as Maurice Wilkes and John Vincent Atanasoff.

Supported by DEC and private donations, the museum is open to the public without an admission charge.

of using the binary machine language strings of 0s and 1s was **Commodore Grace Murray Hopper.**

A living legend, Hopper was born in New York City in 1906, was schooled at Vassar College and Harvard University, and served as an associate professor of mathematics at Vassar. When Hopper entered the Naval Reserve in December 1943, her first assignment with the Bureau of Ordnance's project at Harvard introduced her to the world of computers. There she became the third programmer on the first U.S. computer (the Mark I), and she has been taming computers ever since.

By 1949 her attention was directed to Mauchly and Eckert's work on the UNIVAC. In 1952 Hopper and her staff developed the first compiler (program to translate other programs into machine language). This was developed while she was employed at Remington Rand following her first period of Navy service. This mathematical translator represented a landmark achievement in referencing machine language codes through English abbreviations. Hopper took this concept one step further as the leader in the development of FLOW-MATIC, the first operational high-level language for business applications. FLOW-MATIC strongly influenced the development of COBOL, which was the result of a cooperative effort of competing computer vendors, government, and business users. Although not directly involved in the development of COBOL, Hopper was instrumental in calling the first meetings leading to its creation, and served as an advisor to the group supervising COBOL development.

Figure 2–14
Commodore Grace
Murray Hopper

John Backus

In 1957 a group of IBM engineers led by **John Backus** designed **FORTRAN (FORmula TRANslation),** the first algebralike programming language. FORTRAN was oriented toward the mathematical and scientific communities.

Backus, after graduating from Columbia University, was one of the few programmers during the first three years of the computer industry. As his involvement with programming languages continued, he developed a formal notation for describing the structure of a programming language, known as **Backus Normal Form.** He applied this notation, or syntax, when he participated in developing Algol, another programming language. Backus's new project with IBM remains undisclosed, but it is likely to deal with programming languages.

Jay W. Forrester

The U.S. government's continued support of computer development was evidenced by the Whirlwind I Computer project, headquartered at the Massachusetts Institute of Technology's (MIT's) Digital Computer Laboratory. The Whirlwind's purpose was to experiment with real-time aircraft simulation; therefore, speed and reliability were essential. The laboratory chief, **Jay W. Forrester** (see Figure 2–15), devised a new internal memory—the **magnetic core**—to accomplish this objective. Magnetic cores proved to be a successful memory medium that soon replaced the magnetic drums of earlier computers.

Following his discovery, Forrester became absorbed in a new effort in the late 1950s—using computers to solve problems (system dynamics). System dynamics uses computer simulations to study human social systems by analyzing factors behind economic conditions and resource utilization; unemployment, inflation, tax policies, energy, and pollution are examples of analyses. Still involved in this work today, Forrester has written several highly regarded books that incorporate these analyses.

Figure 2–15 Jay W.
Forrester

William Shockley

William Shockley improved electronic circuitry through the development of the **transistor.** After earning his doctorate in physics at MIT in 1936, Shockley was hired by Bell Labs. The invention of the transistor,

Figure 2–16 William Shockley (foreground) and the co–inventors of the transistor.

publicly announced in June 1948, did not receive much attention until Shockley and two coinventors (John Bardeen and Walter Braittain) were awarded the Nobel Prize in 1956 (see Figure 2–16).

Within a short time, this "invention of the century" became a big business. Transistors, which were faster and more reliable than vacuum tubes, also were much smaller, thereby reducing computer size. They also generated comparatively little heat, permitting more modest air-handling devices to replace the massive air-conditioning systems necessary for first generation machines.

Shockley eventually joined Beckman Instruments, where he set up his own semiconductor laboratory; this was regarded as the first "Silicon Valley" company (the designation applied to chip-manufacturing and related high technology companies that have located in the valley area south of San Franciso). Shockley is appropriately considered the father of solid state electronics.

One other significant development had its origins in World War II. The Germans used huge steel tapes (two feet in diameter and weighing two hundred pounds) for sound recording during the war. Plastic magnetic tapes—scaled-down replicas of the German metal tapes—were adapted for use in data recording and playback by the mid-1950s, becoming the standard input/output and storage medium used with large volumes of computer data. These were followed by magnetic disks, called **random access devices** because of their ability (similar to that of jukeboxes) to selectively access recorded data without passing by all previously recorded information (as would be necessary with magnetic tape).

Transistors, magnetic tapes, and magnetic disks represent the major advances in hardware that led to the second computer generation.

CORPORATE GIANTS

Thomas J. Watson, Jr., led IBM into the electronic age by the late 1950s (see Figure 2–17). He was also responsible for establishing the company's image and standards of quality that prevail today. Although IBM expanded to dominate the computer industry, other companies emerged during the 1960s and gradually became competitors. These competitors, collectively known as the Seven Dwarfs (IBM being Big Brother), included Sperry Rand, Control Data Corporation, Honeywell, RCA, NCR, General Electric (GE), and Burroughs. (Xerox and Digital Equipment Corporation replaced GE and RCA by the end of the decade; Xerox then left the computer business, and the allusion was dropped.) Because of this new competitiveness, the technological improvements tended to be more corporate, as opposed to the earlier individual accomplishments.

Although COBOL and FORTRAN remained the predominant languages and magnetic cores, the primary internal storage medium, significant progress was made in developing new electronic circuitry.

Figure 2–17 Thomas Watson, Jr.

Jack S. Kilby

Jack S. Kilby (see Figure 2–18), the pioneer who introduced the **integrated circuit** (or **silicon chip**) in September 1958, earlier worked for an electronics firm in Milwaukee. In 1952 Kilby had the opportunity of attending a Bell Labs transistor seminar. Fascinated by this field, Kilby transferred to Texas Instruments. Assigned to the Micro-Module project,

VisiCalc: The Original Electronic Spreadsheet

VisiCalc is a software package that helps businesses in their financial planning by showing the overall results of various shifts in capital. This electronic spreadsheet was created by Daniel Bricklin to simplify such manipulations and minimize the kinds of errors that are common when calculations are done manually.

Bricklin, who had worked with computers since his teens, came up with the idea for VisiCalc in 1978, while he was a student at the Harvard Business School. He and his friend Robert Frankston actually developed the software. (Its name stands for **visible calculator.**)

As useful as VisiCalc was, its invention earned little attention and even less excitement in the business and computer communities until Daniel Fylstra was put in charge of marketing. In 1982 Bricklin's company, Software Arts, of Wellesley, Massachusetts, had sales of seven million dollars. By early 1983 approximately 400,000 copies of VisiCalc were in consumer hands, and many competing packages had appeared on the market.

he was in charge of interconnecting electrical components; his input on altering the layout made the integrated circuit more cost effective. Kilby, a diversified inventor, also developed an early hand-held electronic calculator, as well as a solar energy collection and conversion system.

Figure 2—18 Jack S. Kilby and the first integrated circuit.

Other major engineering improvements included Digital Equipment Corporation's introduction of the **minicomputer** and IBM's development of **removable magnetic disks.** These achievements, along with the silicon chip, characterized the beginning of the third computer generation.

TECHNOLOGY TREND SETTERS

Hardware compatibility (that is, interchangeability of computers and input/output devices) and miniaturization were two key characteristics leading to the fourth generation of computers. The people behind these discoveries are examined in this section.

Gene Amdahl

Gene Amdahl (see Figure 2–19) served as chief designer of the IBM 704 and 7030 computers. He also created an architectural revolution in designing the IBM System/360 series. This series offered both scientific and business applications, improved compatibility between mainframes (processing equipment) and peripherals (input/output devices), and the introduction of disk-oriented operating systems (control programs stored on magnetic disks).

Figure 2–19 Gene Amdahl

In 1970 Amdahl founded Amdahl Corporation and introduced industry-compatible mainframes that were smaller, faster, and less expensive than the corresponding IBM models. After a disagreement with other owners, he resigned from Amdahl Corporation and established Trilogy Corporation, a company that also promotes competitive, compatible mainframes.

Ted Hoff

Ted Hoff (see Figure 2–20) improved the integrated circuit by designing the **microprocessor.** Hoff, an engineer from Stanford University employed at Intel, was given the responsibility of designing a series of chips for the calculator company. His efforts resulted in the microprocessor (or "computer on a chip"), introduced in 1971. The 4004 microprocessor had all the components of a full-sized central processing unit (CPU) on one chip.

John G. Kemeny

A new wave of user-oriented programming languages was initiated by the work of **John G. Kemeny** (see Figure 2–21). Born in Hungary in 1926, Kemeny immigrated to the United States in 1940. As an undergraduate at Princeton University, Kemeny served on the U.S. Army's Manhattan Project, where he helped design the first atomic bomb. He also worked as a research assistant for Albert Einstein while earning his doctorate.

Figure 2–20 Ted Hoff

Figure 2–21 John G. Kemeny

Upon graduation, Kemeny taught mathematics at Princeton University and Dartmouth College.

An early advocate of computer literacy, Kemeny developed an introductory computer course at Dartmouth in 1963 and soon realized the inadequacy of the existing punched card–oriented batch-processing systems for course assignments. With a team of assistants, Kemeny developed the first prototype **time-sharing system,** which permitted multiple independent users to interact concurrently through terminals with a central computer.

Next Kemeny and colleague Thomas Kurtz developed the **BASIC (Beginner's All-Purpose Symbolic Instruction Code)** language, the most common language used on microcomputers today. Until recently the president of Dartmouth, Kemeny has published several books on computers and BASIC.

Seymour Cray

Figure 2–22 Seymour Cray

Seymour Cray (see Figure 2–22) was an exception to the miniaturization trends typical of this period. He developed large, very fast scientific computers.

Hired by Control Data Corporation, Cray convinced the company president to build powerful computers. Cray's first project was such a success that a private laboratory was built in his home town for designing future projects.

Rather than continue with Cray's project, Control Data Corporation became more service and peripheral oriented by 1972. Therefore, Cray gathered investors and formed Cray Research in 1976. In 1980 he released the Cray-1 supercomputer; other models include the Cray X-MP and the Cray-2.

MICRO MEN

The microcomputer industry has produced several success stories. The following people have achieved great fame and represent the driving force behind five of the major microcomputers.

First, however, mention should be made of the man associated with starting the microcomputer revolution—one of the most unrecognized people in the business—**Lester Solomon.** Solomon, the technical editor of **Popular Electronics** (now **Computers and Electronics**), featured the MITS Altair, the first do-it-yourself computer kit, in the January 1975 issue of the magazine. Enormous interest was generated by the debut of the Altair. Little marketing time was wasted; three major microcomputer manufacturers emerged in 1977—Radio Shack, Commodore, and Apple.

Microcomputers in the Classroom

Computers are being introduced into classrooms at an accelerating rate, and school systems are investing in both equipment and curricula in order to help their students achieve computer literacy. The Logo programming language, created by Seymour Papert with the collaboration of countless other people including computer scientists, classroom teachers, and even the students themselves, is designed as a learning environment in which people easily progress not only to computer literacy, but computer *fluency*.

Papert points out that children easily learn French when they live in France. Logo is designed as a "Mathland" where children (and adults) can just as easily learn a variety of mathematical concepts—concepts that, like French, children find difficult to learn using the "formal" methods usually employed in schools. Logo's Turtle Geometry allows children to use their own bodily movements to create sophisticated computer programs.

Papert studied mathematics and philosophy in his native South Africa, at Cambridge University in England, and in Paris, France. There he met Jean Piaget, beginning a long and fruitful interaction which focused his interest in the influence of environment on learning. Following five years which he spent in Geneva with Piaget, Papert came to MIT in 1963, and became Co-Director with Marvin Minsky of the Artificial Intelligence Laboratory in 1967. At this time, he began designing a computer language that would be suitable for children. The first implementation of the language was done at the research firm of Bolt, Beranek and Newman, with subsequent implementations at MIT where the language grew into its modern form. Logo was shown to be an exciting and effective means of transforming abstract and thus difficult-to-learn ideas into concrete, readily explored and mastered ones.

The past dozen years have seen many expansions and refinements of Logo, as well as the development of microcomputers both powerful enough to use Logo and inexpensive enough to allow school systems to provide each child with a microcomputer within the foreseeable future. Papert's book *Mindstorms*, published in 1980, describes both Logo and the philosophies which led to its development. Because Logo is especially well-suited to learning environments, it is very likely to replace BASIC as the best means of introducing students (of all ages) to computer programming.

John V. Roach

Tandy Corporation's Radio Shack division released the first official microcomputer—the **TRS-80**—in September 1977. The quick action was due largely to **John V. Roach** (see Figure 2–23), the manager most interested in and supportive of the microcomputer movement.

Figure 2–23 John V. Roach

Originally hired by Charles Tandy as general manager of Tandy Computer Services, Roach was promoted to vice-president of Radio Shack Manufacturing in 1975. Roach persuaded Tandy to enter the microcomputer market and followed the project through in less than a year.

Synonymous with the first personal computers, the TRS-80 resulted in immediate profits. Roach now serves as chairman of Tandy Corporation.

Jack Tramiel

Commodore Business Machines also entered the personal computer market in 1977. **Jack Tramiel**, the founder and president of Commodore International, has maintained company growth even over some rough times.

Starting with a job in a typewriter repair business in Brooklyn, Tramiel expanded the business to one that assembled and sold adding machines, first to Canada and later to the United States.

By the mid-1970s, calculators were the main product for Commodore. Commodore bought two companies—one of which was MOS Technology, a semiconductor manufacturer in the process of developing the 6502 microprocessor (a promising computer chip). Tramiel provided additional funds for this project, and his insight proved to be most rewarding: the 6502 microprocessor is used in the Apple and Atari 400 and 800 microcomputers and, of course, in his own release, the Commodore PET microcomputer.

The **Commodore PET,** the largest-selling personal computer in Europe, was introduced in January 1977. Tramiel's insistence on offering a more affordable model for home users resulted in the **VIC 20.** The company subsequently has produced other small computers, such as the **Commodore 64.**

Steven Paul Jobs and Stephen Wozniak

Perhaps the most publicized computer success story to date concerns the adventurous duo who founded Apple Computer, Inc.—**Steven Paul Jobs** and **Stephen Wozniak** (see Figure 2–24). Jobs has been a primary advocate of the microcomputer business and the chief marketing wizard behind Apple Computer, Inc. Technology interested Jobs early in high school; he attended lectures at Hewlett-Packard and attracted enough attention from the president to get a summer job. Jobs attended Reed College in Oregon for a semester after high school, and for the next three years, he remained in the campus community.

Returning home in 1974, Jobs worked for a short time at Atari, then in its second year of operation. In 1975, he and some friends, including Stephen Wozniak, began attending meetings of the Homebrew Computer Club. While working at Hewlett-Packard, Wozniak built a small computer using state-of-the-art technology scaled down for the small user. Jobs, impressed by the invention, believed that marketing the

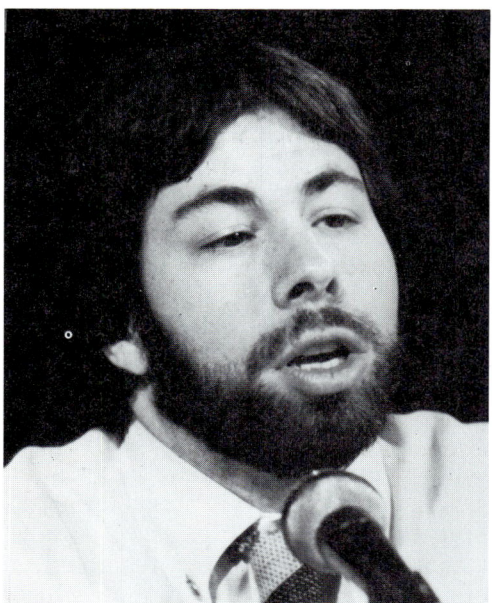

Figure 2–24 Steven Wozniak (left) and Steven Paul Jobs (right).

product would be profitable. After persuading Wozniak to leave Hewlett-Packard, Jobs sold his Volkswagen and Wozniak's scientific calculator to raise $1,300 to build the first Apples.

The **Apple II** was officially unveiled in 1977, and by 1982 Apple Computer, Inc. had collected revenues of $401 million. In 1983 Jobs, currently chairman of the board at Apple, introduced two new microcomputer models—the **Apple IIe** and **Lisa.** Initial responses look very good for Jobs, who already has a net worth of $210 million. Wozniak, although still a major stockholder in the company, left Apple to return to college and develop other interests.

John Opel

The three companies that initially entered the microcomputer market were experiencing overwhelming success. IBM followed this positive direction under the leadership of **John Opel** (see Figure 2–25).

After receiving his master in business administration degree in 1949, Opel was hired by IBM in his home town of Jefferson City, Missouri. Ten years of outstanding sales records promoted him to the corporate headquarters in Armonk, New York. There he quickly rose to president in 1974 and then chief executive officer in 1981. The **IBM Personal Computer (PC)** was announced in August 1981. The success of the PC can be attributed to both Opel and **Philip D. Estridge,** manager of the PC endeavor and now the president of IBM's Entry Systems Division. The PCjr, announced in November 1983, is IBM's latest entry in the microcomputer market.

Figure 2–25 John Opel

Figure 2–26 Adam Osborne

Figure 2–26 Adam Osborne

Adam Osborne

Born in Bangkok, **Adam Osborne** (see Figure 2–26) earned his doctorate from the University of Delaware and worked as an engineer for two companies. Neither engineering job provided the satisfaction for which Osborne was searching. Osborne's need to be his own boss led him to establish a company that provided programming and technical writing services. Technical writing assignments informed Osborne of new developments in microprocessors and prepared him for his next role—as microprocessor consultant. To differentiate himself from other consultants, Osborne wrote a book that brought him much success: **An Introduction to Microcomputers** (McGraw-Hill; 1980). In 1976 he started writing a column for **Interface Age.** This enabled him to observe the strengths and weaknesses of the microcomputer revolution. Osborne's chief criticism was that microcomputers could not satisfy the average consumer's need. His solution was obvious—produce an inexpensive product that was industry compatible both in hardware and software.

In four months he built a prototype, the **Osborne 1,** released in 1981. The portable microcomputer was compact and affordable. Another version, the Osborne Executive, was unveiled in April 1983. The **Executive** has improved features, including a screen that is two inches larger; the price is also proportionately higher. Despite the problems experienced by Osborne's organization in the latter part of 1983, Adam Osborne's contribution to microcomputer development was of real significance.

IDEALISTS

Throughout this chapter you have discovered the key people behind the progress of computer technology. The trends of increasing speed and accuracy and diminishing size and cost have brought computers into the reach of businesses and individuals. As computers become more widely used, their impact will be more widely felt. Continued refinements in hardware, input and output methods, storage devices, and languages are inevitable in the future.

The major areas of advancement, however, will focus on improving two areas—software compatibility and effectiveness, and **artificial intelligence (AI).** Computer vendors already market some of their products as "intelligent" or "smart," but true AI involves more than the ability to mimic analytical procedures or control self-regulating functions. The two founders of AI are John McCarthy and Marvin Minsky. This section will focus on the accomplishments of the former.

Figure 2–27 John McCarthy

John McCarthy

John McCarthy (see Figure 2–27), after receiving a doctorate at Princeton University, accepted a job teaching mathematics at Dartmouth College in 1956. A year later he moved to MIT and by 1963 had accepted an offer to head his own department at Stanford University.

Life after Pong

Nolan Bushnell, the entrepreneur who introduced Pong in 1972, now is involved in projects that may have equal or greater influence in the commercial market of the future. Bushnell, a creative genius, grew up in Clearfield, Utah. His interest in science and technology was evident in childhood experiments and pranks. Games, too, had an important role in Bushnell's life. He supported himself through college by directing the games department at a Salt Lake City amusement park. With five hundred dollars he founded Atari in 1971 and began marketing Pong, the first commercially successful video game. When Bushnell sold the company to Warner Communications for twenty-eight million dollars in 1976, he also signed a contract restraining him from competing against Atari for seven years.

Since games were temporarily out of his life, Bushnell began developing other ideas—robotics, in particular. In 1977 he opened the first Pizza Time Theatre Restaurant in San Jose, California. Besides an arcade of coin-operated games and miniature amusement park rides, the real attraction of the restaurant was entertainment provided by Muppet-like robots. Like Pong, Pizza Time became an instant hit, with two hundred franchises by 1983.

Meanwhile, Bushnell also established Catalyst Technologies, an organization to provide facilities and financial support for entrepreneurial companies including Androbot, which recently introduced a series of the first personal robots—perhaps creating the next revolution in the home market. He also formed Sente Technologies to develop second generation video games by using the most advanced technologies available.

Whatever computer-related products are marketed for consumers in the future, Nolan Bushnell is likely to be involved.

In the computer field, McCarthy created the programming language LISP, which later was to be instrumental in his AI research. He also developed the concept of interactive computing at MIT; this method of time sharing permits multiple terminals to be connected to a central computer, each appearing to have complete dominance over the central computer.

McCarthy's most outstanding achievement, however, is associated with AI. In fact, he coined the term artificial intelligence when organizing the first conference on the subject in 1956. Two of the three world-famous AI laboratories were founded by McCarthy: MIT laboratory in 1957 and Stanford Laboratory in 1963. (The third is part of Carnegie-Mellon University.)

Artificial intelligence involves programming computers with qualities of creativity, judgment, and intuition, which are unique to humans. The major challenge of installing commonsense characteristics in computers seems to be in the way the information is organized. The computer must be able to mix and match pieces of information and form permanent links. Both McCarthy and Minsky agree that machines will not reach the human intelligence level in the near future—perhaps not until scientists determine how the human brain works.

- The abacus and Napier's Bones were the earliest computational aids.
- Blaise Pascal introduced the first automated computational tool; his adding machine was developed in 1642 and was capable only of adding and subtracting.
- In 1694 Gottfried Wilhelm von Leibniz developed a machine capable of addition, subtraction, multiplication, division, and finding square roots.
- Job automation dates back to France in 1801. There, Joseph Marie Jacquard improvised a device to control weaving using a series of coded punched cards.
- The true father of the computer is Charles Babbage. His efforts with the difference engine and the analytical engine were too advanced for the technology of his time.
- Ada Augusta Byron, Countess of Lovelace, assisted Babbage in designing and documenting the analytical engine; she is recognized as the first computer programmer.
- William Seward Burroughs invented the first commercially successful adding machine and founded the current Burroughs Corporation.
- In 1887 Herman Hollerith devised a mechanical method for tabulating census data. Hollerith established a company and a commercial market for the tabulating machine. He is most famous for Hollerith code, a method of representing data on punched cards.
- Thomas J. Watson, Sr., became employed at Computing-Tabulating-Recording (CTR) Company, which was formed by merging several companies (including Hollerith's). Watson became the president in 1924, renamed the company International Business Machines (IBM), and led it to be a dominant company.
- With IBM funds, Howard H. Aiken invented the first large-scale digital computer in 1944. The Mark I was capable of performing three additions a second.
- The first electronic digital computer, the Atanasoff-Berry Computer (ABC), was introduced by John Vincent Atanasoff and Clifford Berry in 1939. This machine, built at a cost of $6,640, could solve twenty-nine simultaneous equations with twenty-nine variables.
- Influenced by Atanasoff's demonstration of the ABC, John W. Mauchly teamed up with J. Presper Eckert at the Moore School on a government project. They invented the ENIAC at a cost of $480,000. This first operational electronic digital computer was capable of performing a calculation in three-thousandths of a second.
- John von Neumann introduced the stored-program concept, as well as the idea of flowcharting.

- The Electronic Delay Storage Automatic Computer (EDSAC) was the first operational stored-program computer, built under the direction of Maurice V. Wilkes at Cambridge University in 1949.
- Remington Rand bought Mauchly and Eckert's company. Here the inventors designed the UNIVAC I, the first commercially successful electronic computer. The UNIVAC I, sold to the U.S. Census Bureau, represented the beginning of the first generation of computers.
- Commodore Grace Murray Hopper is a computer pioneer. She invented the first compiler in 1952 and was instrumental in developing the COBOL language in 1959. She also found the first computer bug.
- FORTRAN was developed by a group under John Backus at IBM in 1957.
- Jay W. Forrester developed the magnetic core, an internal memory device that replaced magnetic drums. He is also a leader in system dynamics.
- The transistor was invented in 1948 by Nobel prizewinner William Shockley. Shockley also established the first "Silicon Valley" computer company.
- Magnetic tapes were developed as a major input/output and storage medium; larger tapes were used during World War II.
- Thomas J. Watson, Jr., led IBM into the electronic age. IBM was the dominant company during the 1960s; the others were referred to as the Seven Dwarfs. The original Dwarfs included Sperry Rand, Control Data Corporation, Honeywell, RCA, NCR, GE, and Burroughs.
- The integrated circuit (silicon chip) was first developed by Texas Instruments' Jack S. Kilby in 1958. This chip soon replaced the transistor.
- Other contributions leading to the third generation of computers include minicomputers and removable magnetic disks.
- Gene Amdahl promoted the concept of hardware compatibility.
- Ted Hoff introduced the microprocessor in 1971; all the components of the central processing unit were included on a single chip.
- John G. Kemeny is most noted for leading the development of BASIC, a high-level, user-oriented programming language.
- Seymour Cray is recognized for designing supercomputers—huge mainframes that operate at incredibly fast speeds.
- Lester Solomon started the microcomputer revolution by arranging for the publishing of an article on the MITS Altair computer kit in 1975.
- Three microcomputers debuted in 1977. John V. Roach was responsible for the first microcomputer, the TRS-80. Jack Tramiel introduced the Commodore PET, the largest-selling personal computer in Europe. Stephen Wozniak built the first Apple, and Steven Paul Jobs marketed the product; together they founded Apple Computer, Inc.
- Under the leadership of John Opel, IBM developed a microcomputer, the IBM PC.
- In 1981 Adam Osborne invented a portable microcomputer, the Osborne 1.
- The future promises advancements in software compatibility and effectiveness, as well as in artificial intelligence (AI). John McCarthy is a pioneer of AI who founded two famous research laboratories.

1. Name the first person to automate computational methods. What was his invention?

2. Who is regarded as the father of the computer? Briefly describe his work.

3. What contribution did Herman Hollerith make to the computer industry?

4. Who designed the Mark I computer?

5. What was the name of the first electronic digital computer? Who invented it?

6. Describe the efforts of John W. Mauchly and J. Presper Eckert throughout their careers.

7. Who introduced the stored-program concept? Why was it important?

8. Name the developers of COBOL and FORTRAN, and provide a brief profile of each person.

9. Who won a Nobel Prize for his invention? Identify the invention.

10. Name the original Seven Dwarfs of computer manufacturers.

11. Describe the major contributions of each of the following people: (1) Gene Amdahl, (2) Tedd Hoff, (3) John G. Kemeny, and (4) Seymour Cray.

12. What was the name of the first microcomputer?

13. List the five major microcomputer inventors, and briefly describe the history of each.

14. What is John McCarthy known for?

OVERVIEW OF COMPUTER SYSTEMS

LEARNING OBJECTIVES

After reading this chapter, you will be able to do the following:

☐ Describe the characteristics of each generation of computers.
☐ Explain what hardware is.
☐ Identify and describe the components of the central processing unit (CPU).
☐ Explain what software is.
☐ Discuss the evolution in methods of software development.
☐ Distinguish between systems and applications programs.
☐ Identify the three levels of programming languages.
☐ Define a *system*.
☐ Discuss information systems and systems analysis and design.

Chapter 3

INTRODUCTION

We have become a computerized society. Business corporations, government agencies, and other organizations depend on the computer to process data and make information available for decision making. Home computers also will become a more integral part of daily life as the cost and size of computer equipment continue to decrease. People in the United States soon may be banking, shopping, and taking care of a multitude of other needs through the convenience of a home computer. Because of the proliferation of computers, it is becoming essential that people gain a basic understanding of them.

This chapter presents an introductory description of computer hardware, software, and systems to give the reader general insight into the world of computers. The section on hardware discusses computer generations and information flow in data processing, as well as some general hardware features. The software section provides an overview of how software development has evolved and offers brief discussions of programming and programming languages. The final section introduces the reader to systems. Information systems and system analysis and design are touched upon. Each of these subject areas will be expanded in subsequent chapters.

HARDWARE

Computer Generations

With the coming of the computer age, enhancements in computer technology were primarily in the areas of size, speed, and cost. These developments can conveniently (if somewhat artificially) be classified into four chronological categories, or "generations."

First Generation: 1951 to 1958 The first commercial computer, the **UNIVAC I** (Universal Automatic Computer), was delivered to the U.S. Census Bureau in June 1951 and marked the beginning of the first generation of computers (see Figure 3–1). The **first generation computers** used large numbers of vacuum tubes, which generated a great deal of heat and used a great deal of power. The heat problem required precise climate control and temperature regulation. Additionally, the vacuum tubes had to function simultaneously for reasonable time periods, and this led to frequent burnouts. Input and output operations also were quite slow because of the use of paper tape and punched cards.

Second Generation: 1959 to 1964 The transistor was developed in 1948, and it became obvious that vacuum tubes would eventually become obsolete. Solid state transistors were much smaller than vacuum tubes, required very little power, and were faster and more reliable. The development of the transistor preceded its incorporation in electronic devices by more than a decade; even in the 1960's and 1970's some television

Figure 3–1 First Generation Computer— UNIVAC I

sets still contained vacuum tubes. By the late 1950's, however, solid–state computers were a reality. Through the replacement of vacuum tubes by transistors, **second generation computers** operated much faster, with greater reliability, and with greatly reduced space requirements in comparison to their first generation counterparts (see Figure 3–2).

Solid state electronics led to the modular, or building-block, approach to the design of computer systems. Various components were built individually; these modules could be replaced in case of malfunctions, thus reducing downtime. Computer systems also could be expanded by adding additional modules instead of replacing the entire computer.

Other significant developments occuring in the late first generation and refined in the second generation computers were the use of **magnetic cores** for **primary** (internal) **storage** and **magnetic tape** for **auxiliary** (external) **storage.** With magnetic tape, input/output (I/O) operations could be performed at least fifty times faster than with punched cards. **Disk storage** also was refined during this period, allowing data to be

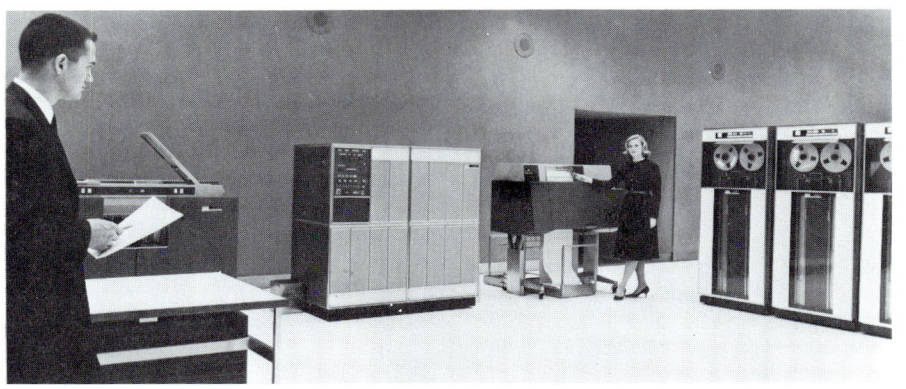

Figure 3–2 Second Generation Computer System—IBM 7070

accessed directly (or randomly) rather than sequentially. These terms will be defined in subsequent chapters but will be introduced in this chapter.

The programming of second generation computers was done in high-level languages, which are much closer to English than machine or symbolic coding. This freed programmers from struggling with the complexities of the coding process, enabling them to focus on problem solving.

Third Generation: 1965 to 1971 **Third generation computers** were characterized by the replacement of the transistor with miniature circuits, known as **integrated circuits (ICs).** By etching circuits on **silicon wafers,** manufacturers could include hundreds of electronic components on a **chip** less than one-eighth of an inch square (see Figure 3–3). The chip as a replacement for entire circuit board of transistors was first introduced by IBM in its System/360 series of computers. Other manufacturers, such as Honeywell, Burroughs, NCR and Univac, soon followed with

Figure 3–3 First, Second and Third Generation Components

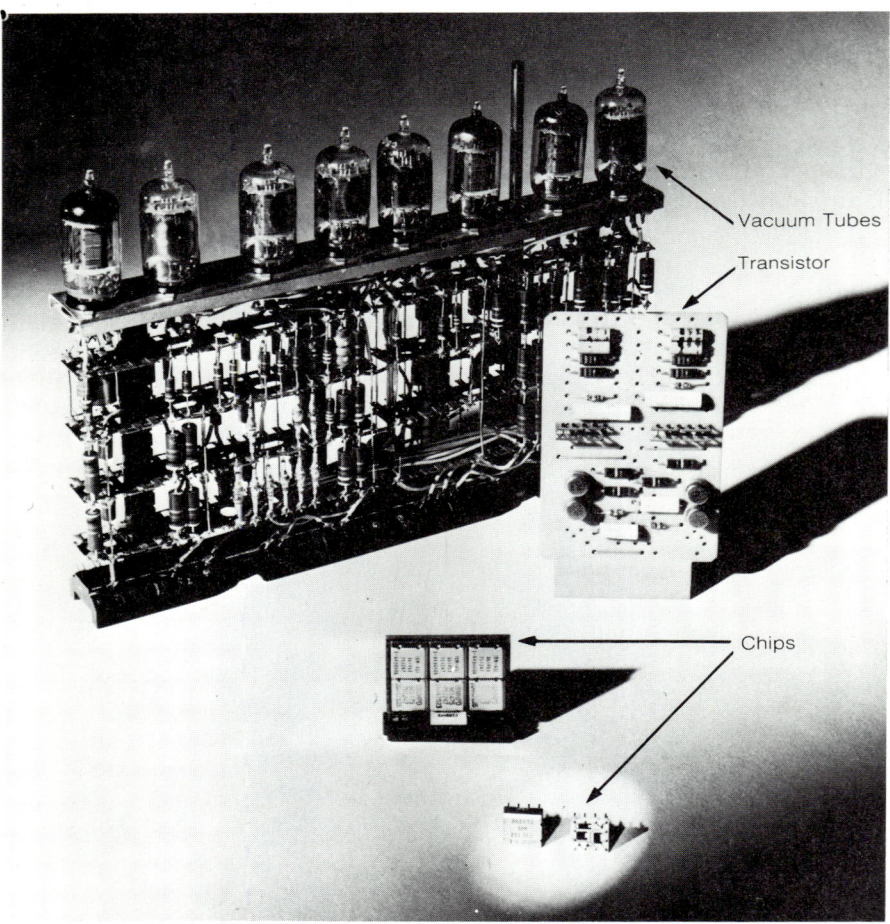

Vacuum Tubes

Transistor

Chips

Shortage of Silicon?

If the popularity of computers continues to grow, there may be a shortage of silicon in the future. To prevent this, accurate estimates of future demands for high-grade silicon must be made now.

The process used to produce high-grade silicon from sand takes four days. First, the sand is treated with carbon to remove the oxygen. The sand then is chlorinated and heated to 1,300 degrees Fahrenheit to remove any impurities. The resultant silicon is deposited onto tiny rods. The equipment used in this process is both intricate and costly.

Because of the significant investment required for such equipment, any increases in silicon needs must be predicted well in advance, or shortages will occur. Only ten companies in the world today produce enough silicon to satisfy their own needs with excess left to sell; only two of these companies are located in the United States.

Another factor contributing to a possible silicon shortage could be the chemical tricholosilane (or trichlor). Although this substance is necessary for the production of silicon, in the United States a single company provides 40 percent of the trichlor. When the microcomputer market blossomed in the late 1970s, that company was unable to meet increased demands, and a temporary shortage ensued. With the explosive nature of the computer market, it is possible that such a situation may occur again. Perhaps next time it will not be so temporary.

Whether or not there will ever be a silicon shortage is simply guesswork at this stage of the game. Some experts predict its occurrence, and others consider it nonsense. But considering that the world's communications and information networks depend on silicon, the possibility of a shortage certainly demands attention.

Figure 3—4 Third Generation Computer System

their own systems (see Figure 3–4). The major features of the IC revolution were as follows:

- **Smaller size.** Because of the small size of the silicon chip, electric signals had to travel far shorter distances, increasing operating speed. Computer size also was reduced dramatically.
- **Reliability.** Integrated circuits were manufactured under rigid quality control procedures. Consequently, the ICs that were used in computers were extremely reliable and rarely failed.
- **Low cost.** Mass production techniques combined with the miniature size of the ICs enabled the manufacturers to achieve drastic reductions in unit costs of the silicon chips.

Other related developments, such as increased storage capacity, multiprogramming (the ability to process several programs concurrently), and teleprocessing (which allowed a computer to be accessed by a remote terminal hundreds of miles away), all enhanced the ability of the computer to store and process data.

Fourth Generation: From 1971 In the early 1970s computers were introduced that were smaller, faster, and even more powerful. Refinements incorporated in these **fourth generation computers** included monolithic (available in a single compact unit) semiconductor memories, self-diagnostic capabilities, and **large-scale integration (LSI) circuits.** Telecommunications abilities were further improved, and data-entry equipment was developed to capture data at the point of origin in a form suitable for direct computer processing. Examples of such devices are magnetic-ink character readers (commonly used by banks for check processing) and optical scanners (used at many grocery stores). Many of these computers are "user friendly"; that is, they are much simpler to use and operate. These improvements, coupled with modular design and increased compatability between different types of equipment, have provided the user with greater flexibility and increased computing power at a lower cost.

The new, more densely packed LSI circuits also have marked the advent of the **microprocessor.** Microprocessors are entire computers on one tiny silicon chip (see Figure 3–5). These microprocessor chips have all the components of a large computer but are somewhat slower and vastly cheaper. Microprocessors have taken the computer industry by storm and are the vanguard of the booming small business and home computer market. In 1982 **Time** chose the computer as man of the year, and it is becoming quite apparent that computers will play an increasingly important role in human affairs during the coming years.

Digital and Analog Computers

Up to now the computers discussed have been of the digital type. The other type of computer is an analog computer. The distinction between the two types is based on the data representation method used in each.

Hardware on the High Seas

Microcomputers have made such a splash everywhere else that somehow it does not seem unreasonable to picture them on sailboats. And it is not. A new group of microcomputer enthusiasts now is offering computer workshops on a Caribbean cruise. The group, enthusiastically dubbed the "Micro People," consists of William Trayfois, Noel Berge, and Nancy Berge, from Washington, D.C. The Micro People offer a cruise from Florida to the Virgin Islands, complete with gourmet meals, tropical rum, and computer lessons.

Although the number of students is determined by the size of the sailboat, the cruise has been quite a success. In fact, the Micro People have worked their way up to a seventy-foot sailboat. Their students also seem very pleased with the computer cruise. As noted in the August, 1983 edition of **Popular Computing** student John Grierson felt the setting was more than appropriate: "We worked in splendid isolation from the twentieth century. No phones, no traffic, no telexes—the setting enabled us to immerse ourselves in the twenty-first century" (p. 21).

In a **digital computer,** data is represented by discrete "on" and "off" states. Numbers, letters, and other special symbols can be represented by a unique code of 1s (on) and 0s (off). This is referred to as **binary notation** (see Appendix A). The digital computer must convert all its input to binary form and after processing the data, output the results in the same form. The 1 and 0 states used for both numeric and alphabetic data are represented by holes in punched cards or paper tape, as well as by magnetic spots on tapes and disks. This binary data can be converted to regular print for the computer user.

Unlike digital computers, **analog computers** represent data by measuring physical or electrical quantities such as pressure, temperature, voltage, or current. The analog computer converts a physical quantity into a symbolic representation that is a measure of that quantity. An exam-

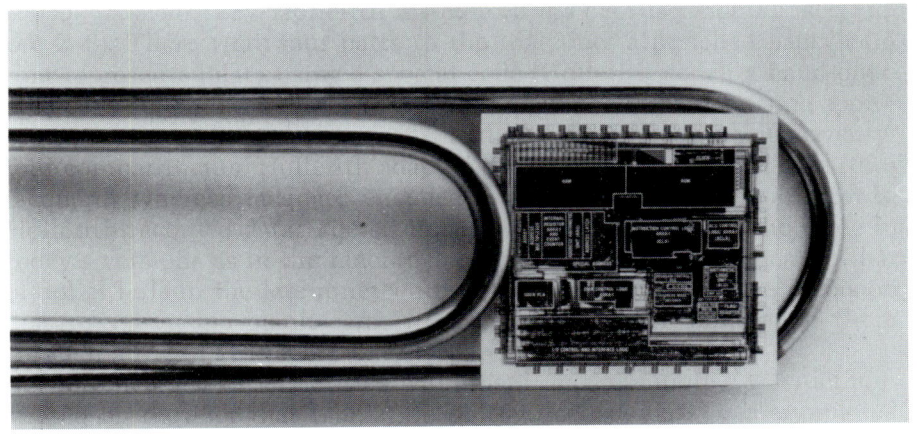

Figure 3–5
Microprocessor

ple of an analog computer is the tachometer, which measures the revolutions per minute of the automobile engine and then converts this into numeric form by the movement of a needle on a graduated scale. Thus, although analog computers can provide numeric results, these are obtained indirectly. Because of this, analog computers are usually less accurate than digital computers. Analog machines also have no memory units; information is obtained by reading a dial or observing a signal on a video screen.

Analog computers are mostly special-purpose machines and have been used as controlling devices in continuous processes such as crude-oil refining. Since digital computers are much more general purpose and are commonly used for both scientific and business data processing, and increasingly in control applications as well, we will confine our discussion to this type in the remainder of the book.

Information Flow in Data Processing

Just as a person can drive an automobile without having the faintest notion as to how the internal combustion engine operates, it is also possible to use a computer without knowing how the internal circuitry works. Nevertheless, a basic understanding of the components of a computer and the functions they perform is just as important as an automobile driver's knowledge about the difference between the gas pedal and the brake. The diagram in Figure 3–6 illustrates the principal components of a computer.

To begin, **data**—usually referred to as the **input**—is entered into the computer, where it is processed (that is, it undergoes some manipulation). The result is useful information, or **output.** Before data can be manipulated, or processed, it is held in the **primary storage unit** (internal storage, or main memory) of the computer. Thus, the information flow in any data-processing application can be represented by the following three steps (see Figure 3–7):

- Input.
- Processing ⇌ Storage (arrows imply the transfer of both data and control functions between units).
- Output.

Figure 3–6
Components of a Computer

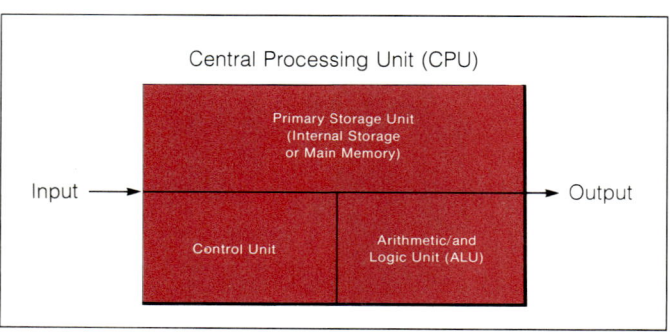

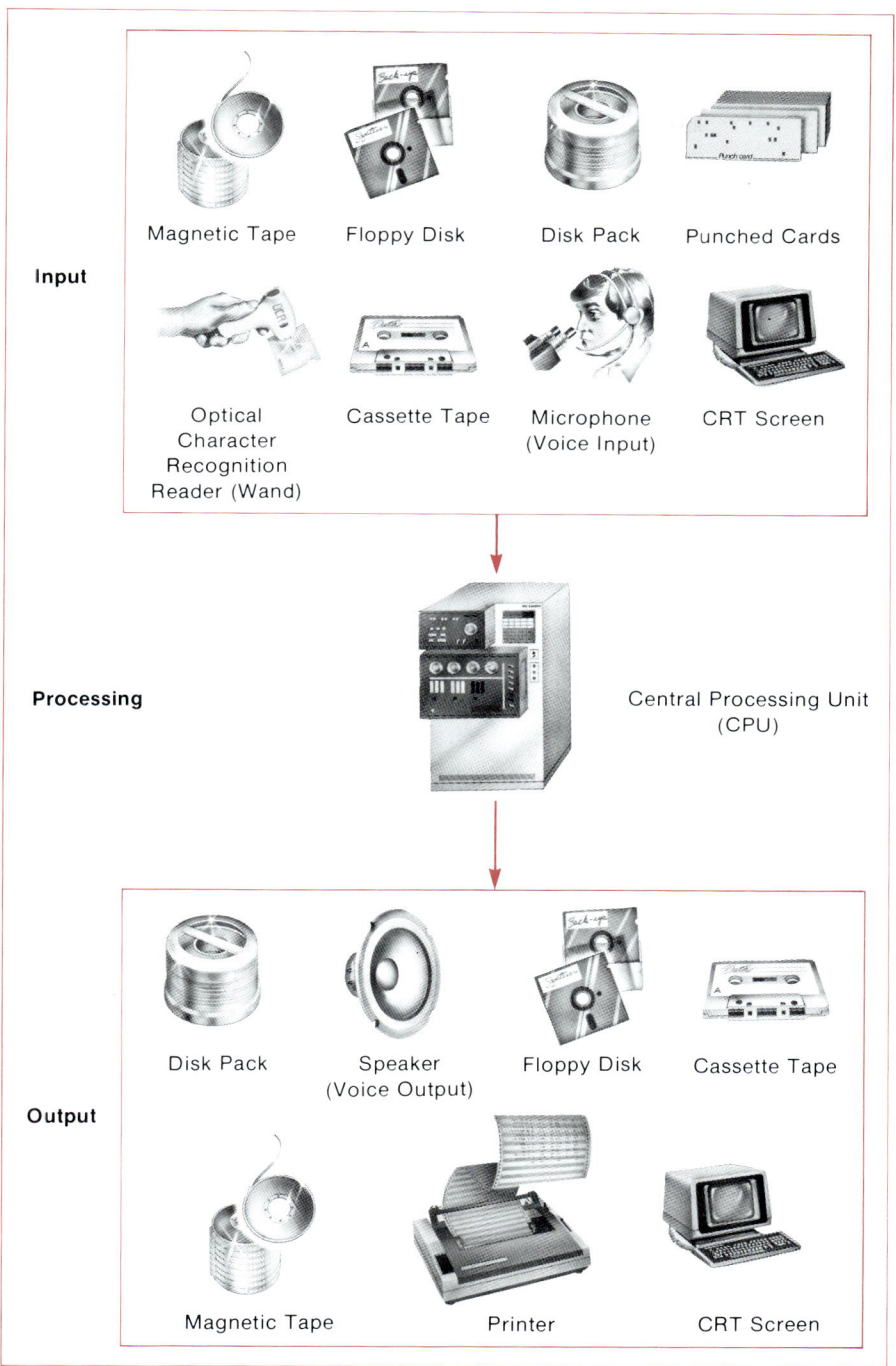

Figure 3—7 Data Flow

Input The input to the computer consists of (1) the instructions, or program, that the computer will follow to process the data and (2) the data itself that is to be manipulated. The input can be entered into the computer in various ways. Common forms of data entry are punched cards, magnetic tape, typewriterlike terminals, optical scanners, and magnetic disks. (These and other input devices will be discussed in detail in Chapter 6.)

Processing $\rightleftharpoons$ Storage The processing and storage of the data is done by the **central processing unit (CPU),** which is the brains of any computer system. The CPU has three major components: (1) the **control unit,** which directs and controls the activities of all other units; (2) the **arithmetic and logic unit (ALU),** which performs the arithmetic and logical operations; and (3) the **primary storage unit** (internal storage), where both instructions and data are held until needed for processing. These will be discussed in more detail in Chapter 5.

Output The final step in processing of data is the transfer of information to the user via the output device. Printers and television-type visual display units are two output devices that provide information in a form people can read. Other media, such as punched cards, magnetic tape, and magnetic disks, provide output that can be read only by machines. (All these devices will be fully discussed in Chapter 7.)

Features of Hardware

The physical devices that make up the computer system are designated the **hardware.** The programs, or instructions, that are written to direct the operation of the hardware are called **software.** Both hardware and software are necessary for a computer system to function.

What makes a computer **efficient** is the hardware, that is, the raw power that depends on the speed and accuracy of the CPU and the input and output (or peripheral) devices. In contrast, what makes a computer system **effective**—that is, how well it serves the needs of the user—is the software. If the appropriate programs for an application are not available, what good is the most powerful machine?

During the first three generations of the computer, what distinguished one generation from the next were the revolutionary changes in the speed, accuracy, memory capacity, and cost of the hardware. The time needed to execute an instruction decreased from milliseconds (thousandths of a second) to nanoseconds (billionths of a second). Vacuum tubes, which failed on an average of one every fifteen minutes, were replaced by ICs, whose failure may occur only once in thirty to thirty-five million hours of operation. Main storage capacities have gone up from thousands of characters to billions of characters, and the cost of memory has plummeted from $100,000 per million characters in first generation computers to $500 per million characters in today's machines.

The improvements in the last two generations have not only been in hardware, but also in software. Tremendous progress had been made in the software through such developments as time sharing, virtual storage, multiprogramming, self-diagnostic operating systems, and sophisticated applications programs for microcomputers (all terms to be defined later). It is obvious that with the microprocessor occupying center stage in the 1980s, we are in the midst of an information revolution—a revolution that sees the productive capabilities of society increasingly engaged in the creation and manipulation of information rather than manufactured goods.

SOFTWARE

Software Development

In the most general sense, software is needed to allow a computer to perform its intended function. Remember, **hardware** refers to the physical components of a computer, whereas **software** refers to the programs written for execution by the computer. A **program** is a series of step-by-step instructions organized in a logical sequence to direct the computer in solving a particular task. Each instruction typically specifies an action and the location of the data to be involved in that action. Programs must be logical in that the computer must be told in detailed terms not only what actions are to take place, but in what specific order they are to occur.

Programmers are the individuals who develop programs to accomplish specific tasks. Programmers design and implement **algorithms,** or detailed specifications for the solution of a problem in a finite sequence of steps. The development of a sound algorithm is, of course, more demanding than the conversion of that algorithm to a programming language implementation.

Early Programming Programming on early computers was an arduous task. Wired control panels containing instructions were plugged into the computer at the start of every job, or punched cards were read in at various intervals during processing. These machines did not have a memory that could store all the instructions and data needed to solve a programming problem. It was necessary for human operators to step in to read additional cards into the computer or to plug in more control panels to allow processing to continue. This human intervention slowed processing considerably. A great deal of time was lost in continually having to stop and set up in order to resume processing.

Stored-Program Concept After the development in 1949 of the first stored-program computer, the EDSAC, data along with the instructions needed to manipulate that data could be stored within the computer. The **stored-program concept** eliminated the need for outside assistance, thus allowing the computer to perform operations at speeds far greater

$$$Software$$$

The business of writing computer software is challenging and extremely lucrative. Consider the case of Paul Lutus.

Paul Lutus writes computer software packages. Some of the ones he has written are Apple Writer, Appleworld, Graforth, and Musicomp. As an indication of Lutus's success, he recently bought a $240,000 home situated on thirty-two acres—and paid for it in cash. Although he claims that he is still basically a hermit, Lutus is a very rich hermit. In 1982 he made over one million dollars on Apple Writer alone.

Lutus has incorporated himself, forming Walden Software, Inc. Now he gives away money to charity, has formed his own foundation to fund worthy causes, and tries to avoid funding the Internal Revenue Service. Perhaps success stories like Lutus's are one reason so many people are studying computer programming.

than were previously possible. Whole programs could be executed in a fraction of a second, approaching even the speed of light. The data-processing function also was made more efficient by the reduction of unnecessary labor costs and, most important, by the distribution of information on a more timely basis.

Today's computers are primarily stored-program computers. Programs are input into the computer and assigned individual memory locations. Each instruction is placed in a storage location adjacent to the instruction that directly precedes it in the written program sequence. The order in which instructions actually are executed, however, varies according to the logic of the program.

The computer will begin executing instructions in sequential order until, for example, a certain instruction calls for control to jump back to a previous point in the program. In this case, the logic of the program requires that an earlier instruction or set of instructions be executed again. The characteristic of memory that allows the same instructions or data to be read repeatedly without alteration or destruction is known as **nondestructive read, destructive write.** A computer's memory functions in a manner similar to a tape recorder, since the same data and instructions can be reused over and over until new data and instructions are stored over them; only then are the previous contents erased.

Structured Programming Ideally, a program should be written so that the logic is as simple and straightforward as possible. When the flow of processing is continually altered by branching, which transfers control to other segments of the program in any sequence, the logic becomes complex and confusing. The program also becomes more difficult and costly in terms of the time required for program maintenance and modification to be completed. To minimize complexity at the start, when programmers are first beginning to develop software, structured programming is the approach that has become widely accepted.

Structured programming involves first clearly understanding the problem to be solved and then breaking it down into independent modules, each performing only one function (the "divide and conquer" concept). Each module is small and has just one entry and exit point (see Figure 3–8). The use of the GO TO statement, which causes the flow of execution to be altered, is kept to a minimum when writing the program so that control of execution passes from one module to another in a top-down design. The manufacturing notion of replacement parts applies here to module changes in programming. Programs are easier to read not only by the original programmer, but also by anyone else who uses the program. In addition, a significant savings can be realized in the amount of time and costs involved in program development, maintenance, and modification. The concepts of structured programming will be further elaborated in Chapter 8. The following chart is an example of how a diagram similar to an organization chart can depict the structure inherent in a computer application.

Programs

As earlier described, a program is actually a series of step-by-step instructions that direct the computer in solving a problem. Program complexity varies according to the level of difficulty of the problem and the

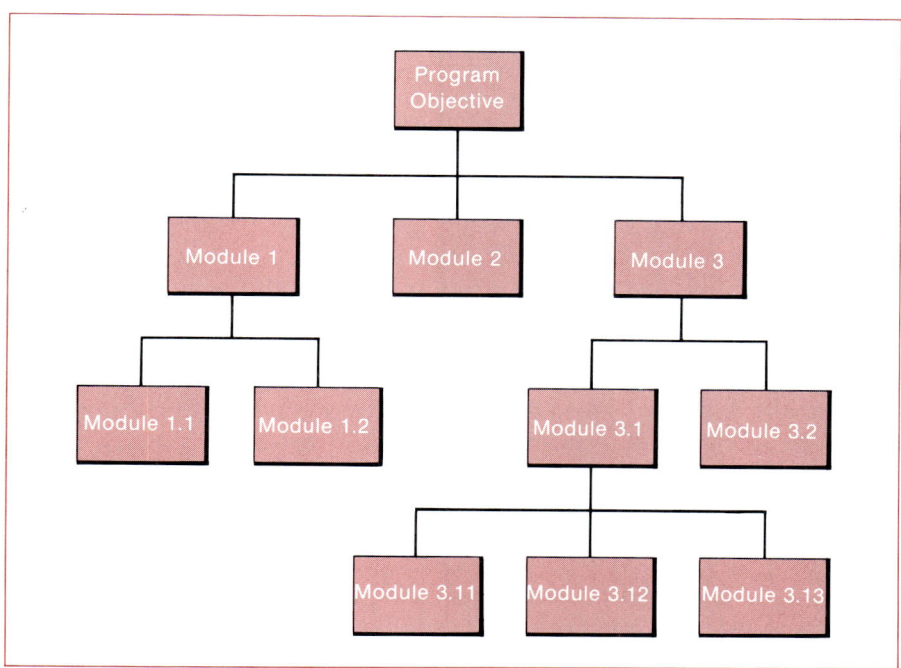

Figure 3—8 Structure Chart

Computers Fight Forest Fires

Computers now are being used to protect U.S. national parks and timberlands from forest fires. The system used to safeguard these natural resources was designed by the Federal Bureau of Land Management (covering the western United States) and uses Hewlett-Packard personal computers.

Because 45 percent of all Western forest fires are caused by lightning strikes, the personal computers operate in conjunction with the Automatic Lightning Detection System (ALDS). In the ALDS, lightning sensors are placed approximately every 250 miles throughout the western United States. When lightning is detected, it is reported to the computer. The computer then prints out the location of the probable fire, and it notifies the nearest ranger station and fire company. Currently, the system monitors 95 percent of the parks and timberlands in eleven Western states and Alaska.

This computerized fire-fighting system saves a great deal of forest from destruction by reducing the time lost between combustion and the arrival of the fire fighters. The time lag between the lightning strike and the computer printout is only six minutes. This response time is of invaluable assistance to rangers, who may be looking over hundreds of miles of timberland for signs of fire.

type, as well as number, of objectives to be met by that particular program. There are two basic types of programs: (1) **systems programs,** which coordinate the capabilities of the computer itself, and (2) **applications programs,** which solve individual user problems.

Systems Programs The sizes and capabilities of computers in existence today differ greatly. Major differences are found in the speed of processing, the storage space available in primary memory, the manner in which data is stored, and the types of operations that can be performed. Systems programs provide an individual computer's capability to utilize its hardware to capacity and insure the system's quick and efficient operations. Systems programs are machine specific: the programs written reflect a particular computer's characteristics and cannot be transferred to a different type of computer without some modification.

When a computer is first purchased, the general systems programs needed to operate it can be obtained from the vendor or through a specialized programming firm. Since each person or organization owning a computer has specific needs and objectives, the systems programs can then be tailored to mesh more closely with individual user requirements.

A specialized collection of systems programs is referred to as an **operating system.** The operating system allows the computer to manage its own operations and can be thought of as the "agent" between the hardware, the software, and the user. All the resources available to the computer, including the CPU, the I/O devices, and the software, are managed collectively by the operating system. These programs can be written by systems programmers or purchased as standard packages from software firms; in the 1980s, increasingly sophisticated applications in packaged "off-the-shelf" form are available.

The need for human intervention is minimized through the use of an operating system. It is not necessary for human operators to monitor computer operations and perform such tasks as loading programs into storage for execution, preparing I/O devices to be used for each program, or determining the order in which submitted programs are to be run. A system of control instead is provided through the use of an operating system, which performs these functions in addition to numerous other responsibilities.

A major benefit of an operating system is software compatibility. Software written in a high-level language usually is structured to communicate with a particular operating system, which in turn communicates with the computer hardware. As long as the operating system is the same, applications programs can be written that can be transferred to a different hardware configuration or to a different computer entirely.

Applications Programs Programs written to solve a particular user problem are referred to as **applications programs.** These programs also can be written by the user of a computer system, or they can be purchased from software firms. There are numerous types of applications programs ranging from educational, games, inventory control, record keeping, and word processing programs to almost any type of application that can be thought of. Many applications programs can be purchased as prewritten packages from software firms.

The applications programmer should understand the computer language or languages that can be used on a system without needing to have an in-depth understanding of the computer's internal operations. The major concern of the applications programmer is writing the appropriate series of instructions in a suitable computer programming language to solve the specific problem at hand.

Languages

Just as humans have developed words to represent objects, actions, and ideas, a computer also must have a method of accepting words (or symbols) that it can understand in order for processing to take place. People communicate by producing words or symbols with their voices, whereas the computer communicates by using symbols in the form of on and off states of electricity. A computer language consists of written symbols, as does a human language, so it can be read and understood by programmers; these symbols, however, then must be translated into pulses that tell the computer what function it is to perform.

There are numerous languages spoken around the world, and there are numerous computer languages as well. Basically, computer languages can be divided into three levels according to their complexity. These levels are machine language, assembly language, and high-level language.

Machine Language **Machine language** consists of a series of 1s and 0s that represent symbols as on and off states of electricity; these symbols are commonly referred to as **binary digits.** It is the only language the computer can execute directly; therefore, it is referred to as the **language of the computer** (see Figure 3–9).

Each type of computer has its own machine language, which is not transferable to another type of computer. Each machine language instruction must specify not only what operation is to be performed, but also the storage location of data items needed. Because of these requirements and the nature of the language itself, machine language programming is extremely complex, tedious, and time consuming. Therefore, other languages have been developed.

Assembly Language One of the major problems with using machine language is that every internal computer instruction is a long string of 1s and 0s. The machine language code in Figure 3–9 has been converted to more compact hexadecimal form, but it still represents binary 1s and 0s (see Appendix A). To make these internal instructions more understandable, **assembly languages** were developed. These languages are one step removed from machine language and are more easily understood by humans. Each instruction is assigned a symbolic name, called a **mnemonic,** which replaces the 0 and 1 groupings of machine language. For example, STO may stand for "store" and TRA, for "transfer." While assembly language is easier to use than machine language, it is still machine dependent, and programming with it is still a long and tedious process (see Figure 3–10).

High-Level Languages **High-level languages** were developed to allow the user to work in a language that is closer to English or mathematical notation, thus improving efficiency and simplifying the communications process to the computer. Such languages are both procedure and problem oriented, allowing the programmer to be concerned mainly with the problem to be solved rather than with details of computer op-

Figure 3–9 Machine Language (Binary Represented in Hexadecimal Notation)

⁻STANDARD-	ROUTINE						
	000778						
MULTIPLY	000778	F2	71	D	1E8	7	010
	00077E	F2	73	D	1F0	7	012
	000784	FC	42	D	1EB	D	1E5
	00078A	F3	43	6	000	D	1EC
	000790	96	F0	6	004		
	000794	58	10	D	21C		
	000798	07	F1				

```
* THIS PROGRAM CALCULATES THE AVERAGE OF THREE TEST SCORES FOR FIVE
* STUDENTS AND ASSIGNS A LETTER GRADE
              BALR   12,0               SET UP BASE REGISTER
              USING  *,12
              LA     3,5                LOAD REGISTER 3 WITH A 5
              XPRNT  HEADER,27          PRINT HEADING
              XPRNT  PRTOUT-1,31        PRINT BLANK LINE
LOOP          XREAD  NAME,30            READ IN DATA CARD
              XDECI  4,TEST1            CONVERT TEST1 TO BINARY AND PUT IN REG 4
              XDECI  5,TEST2            CONVERT TEST2 TO BINARY AND PUT IN REG 5
              XDECI  6,TEST3            CONVERT TEST3 TO BINARY AND PUT IN REG 6
              AR     5,4                ADD CONTENTS OF REG 4 TO REG 5
              AR     5,6                ADD CONTENTS OF REG 6 TO REG 5
              SR     4,4                ZERO OUT REG 4
              L      6,=F'3'            LOAD REG 6 WITH CONSTANT 3
              DR     4,6                DIVIDE CONTENTS OF REG 4 BY REG 6
              MVC    PRTOUT(15),NAME    MOVE NAME TO PRINT AREA
              C      5,=F'90'           COMPARE AVERAGE IN REG 5 TO 90
              BM     B                  IF MINUS (AVERAGE < 90) BRANCH TO B
              MVI    PRTOUT+23,C'A'     MOVE LETTER GRADE A TO PRINT AREA
              B      PRINT              BRANCH TO PRINT
B             C      5,=F'80'           COMPARE AVERAGE TO 80
              BM     C                  IF AVERAGE < 80 BRANCH TO C
              MVI    PRTOUT+23,C'B'     MOVE LETTER GRADE B TO PRINT AREA
              B      PRINT              BRANCH TO PRINT
C             C      5,=F'70'           COMPARE AVERAGE TO 70
              BM     D                  IF AVERAGE < 70 BRANCH TO D
              MVI    PRTOUT+23,C'C'     MOVE LETTER GRADE C TO PRINT AREA
              B      PRINT              BRANCH TO PRINT
D             C      5,=F'60'           COMPARE AVERAGE TO 60
              BM     F                  IF AVERAGE < 60 BRANCH TO F
              MVI    PRTOUT+23,C'D'     MOVE LETTER GRADE D TO PRINT AREA
              B      PRINT              BRANCH TO PRINT
F             MVI    PRTOUT+23,C'F'     MOVE LETTER GRADE F TO PRINT AREA
PRINT         XPRNT  PRTOUT-1,31        PRINT NAME AND GRADE
              BCT    3,LOOP             BRANCH BACK TO READ AGAIN
              BR     14                 STOP
* DECLARE VARIABLES
HEADER        DC     C'1 STUDENT NAME        GRADE'
NAME          DS     CL15
TEST1         DS     CL5
TEST2         DS     CL5
TEST3         DS     CL5
              DC     C' '
PRTOUT        DC     CL30' '
              END
                     =F'3'
                     =F'90'
                     =F'80'
                     =F'70'
                     =F'60'



    STUDENT NAME          GRADE

    JOANN WEISS             A
    TOM FARR                D
    ANN BLASS               B
    BOB WILLS               F
    JANIS MAYS              C
```

Figure 3–10 Assembly Language

erations. The time and effort needed to write a program are reduced, and programs are easier to correct and modify.

High-level languages are so called because they have high user orientation and are farthest removed from the hardware. Whereas one assembly language instruction corresponds to one machine language instruction, one high-level language statement can represent a half-dozen or more machine language instructions, mainly because the addresses for many of the required storage locations are handled automatically, without having to be specified. Some of the more commonly used high-level languages are BASIC, COBOL, FORTRAN, and Pascal (see Figure 3–11).

SYSTEMS

In today's fast-paced world, we are faced with a multitude of complex and changing conditions that can affect our decision making. In the past, decision making typically focused only on the particular problem in question. However, as the complexity of the variables involved has increased, a broad systems look has become popular. The approach of

Figure 3–11 High-Level Language

```
C THIS PROGRAM CALCULATES THE AVERAGE OF THREE TEST SCORES FOR FIVE
C STUDENTS AND ASSIGNS A LETTER GRADE
        INTEGER TEST1, TEST2, TEST3, I
        REAL  AVG
        CHARACTER  NAME*15, GRADE
        WRITE (6,100)
  100   FORMAT ('1',1X,'STUDENT NAME',7X,'GRADE')
        WRITE (6,200)
  200   FORMAT (' ')
        DO 500 I = 1, 5
        READ (5,300) NAME, TEST1, TEST2, TEST3
  300   FORMAT (A15,3I3)
        AVG = (TEST1 + TEST2 + TEST3) / 3.0
        IF (AVG .GE. 90) GRADE = 'A'
        IF ((AVG .GE. 80) .AND. (AVG .LT. 90)) GRADE = 'B'
        IF ((AVG .GE. 70) .AND. (AVG .LT. 80)) GRADE = 'C'
        IF ((AVG .GE. 60) .AND. (AVG .LT. 70)) GRADE = 'D'
        IF (AVG .LT. 60) GRADE = 'F'
        WRITE (6,400) NAME, GRADE
  400   FORMAT (1X,A15,7X,A1)
  500   CONTINUE
        STOP
        END



    STUDENT NAME          GRADE

    JOANN WEISS            A
    TOM FARR              D
    ANN BLASS            B
    BOB WILLS            F
    JANIS MAYS          C
```

COMPUTERS IN EDUCATION

Dramatic changes are taking place in the educational system as a result of increasing computer use. Schools are expanding the curricula to include courses on computer awareness and programming in an effort to prepare upcoming generations with the necessary skills to interact with computers. In addition, computer-assisted instruction (CAI) is used to supplement teaching methods through drill and practice, tutorial, and simulation activities.

1. Computer-assisted instruction (CAI) is gaining in popularity among U.S. school systems.

Computers in Education—continued. **2.** Several colleges are predicting that each student will be required to have a computer in order to complete coursework. **3.** In Hampton, Virginia, high school students have developed a daily dialogue with a computer to widen their academic horizons. **4.** Typical of the student population, these children are enthusiastic about computer programming courses. **5.** *FAIR BREAK®* Centers use Control Data's PLATO® computer-based education system to offer training for future employment to the disadvantaged, unemployed, and underemployed.

Computers in Education—continued. **6.** A classroom with computer-assisted instruction, using Tektronix 4006 graphics terminals. **7.** The summer program at this school offers a computer class for six-year-olds. **8.** A day at computer camp means waking up in a college dormitory, slipping into a t-shirt and shorts, eating breakfast and turning on a computer. **9.** Teaching students computer skills so they will be prepared for the world in which they will live and work, has brought educators to the forefront of the computer revolution. **10.** Demonstrating the parts of a computer, and the general function of each, is an important element of computer education.

8

9

10

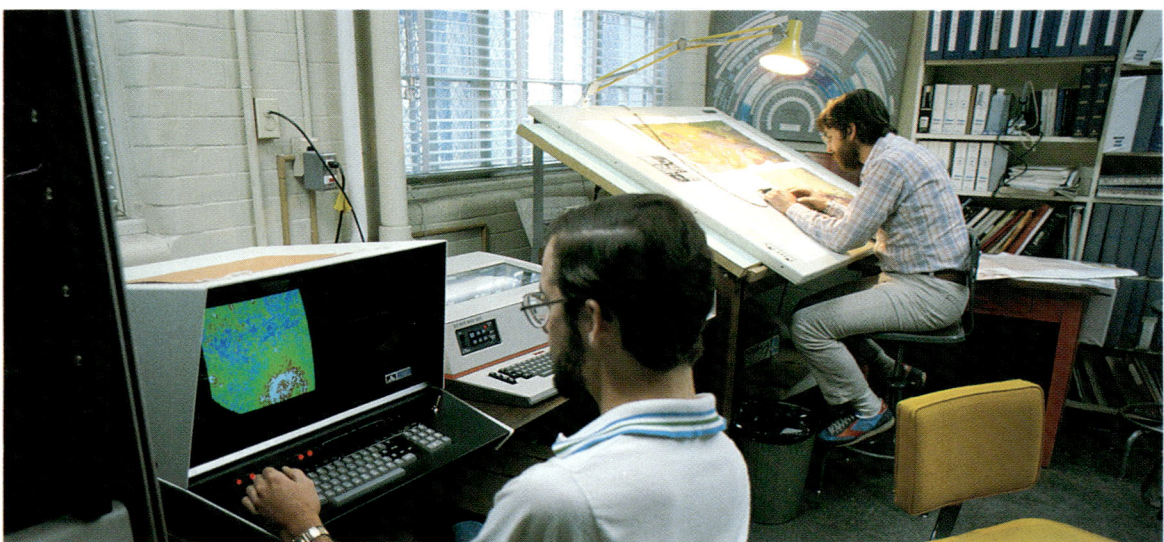

11

Computers in Education—continued.
11. Geology students at Brown University in Rhode Island use computers to analyze crater distribution on earth's moon and to study NASA images of the planets. Brown is the NASA data center for New England and has datasets from almost all NASA missions.
12. Colleges recommend an introductory computer course for many of their programs.

12

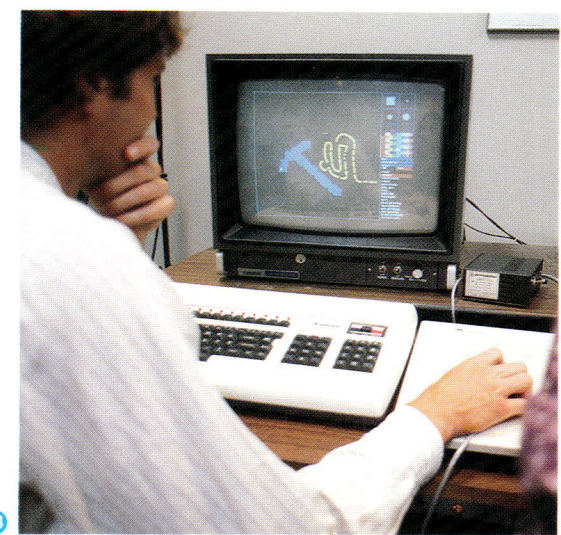

13. PLATO® courses in mathematics, science, foreign languages and computer concepts are now available. **14.** A workroom in Brown University's new Gould Laboratory provides computer science students with a variety of equipment, including high-resolution color monitors for computer graphics projects. **15.** Faculty member explains an image to a student in color video studio at the School of Film/Video, California Institute of the Arts.

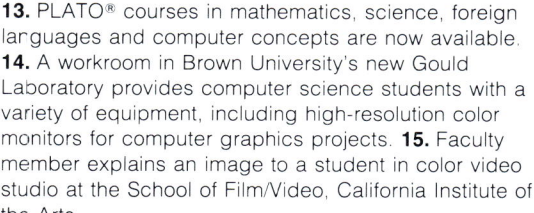

Computers in Education—continued. **16.** A researcher accesses DIALOG's computer at a terminal to obtain information from over 180 databases on subjects ranging from business and finance to science and technology.
17. CLSI's Public Access Catalog provides a library's users with access to up-to-date bibliographic, holdings, location, and status information via keyboard terminals or touch-sensitive browsing terminals. The touch terminal permits patrons to browse through the library's catalog simply by touching the screen.

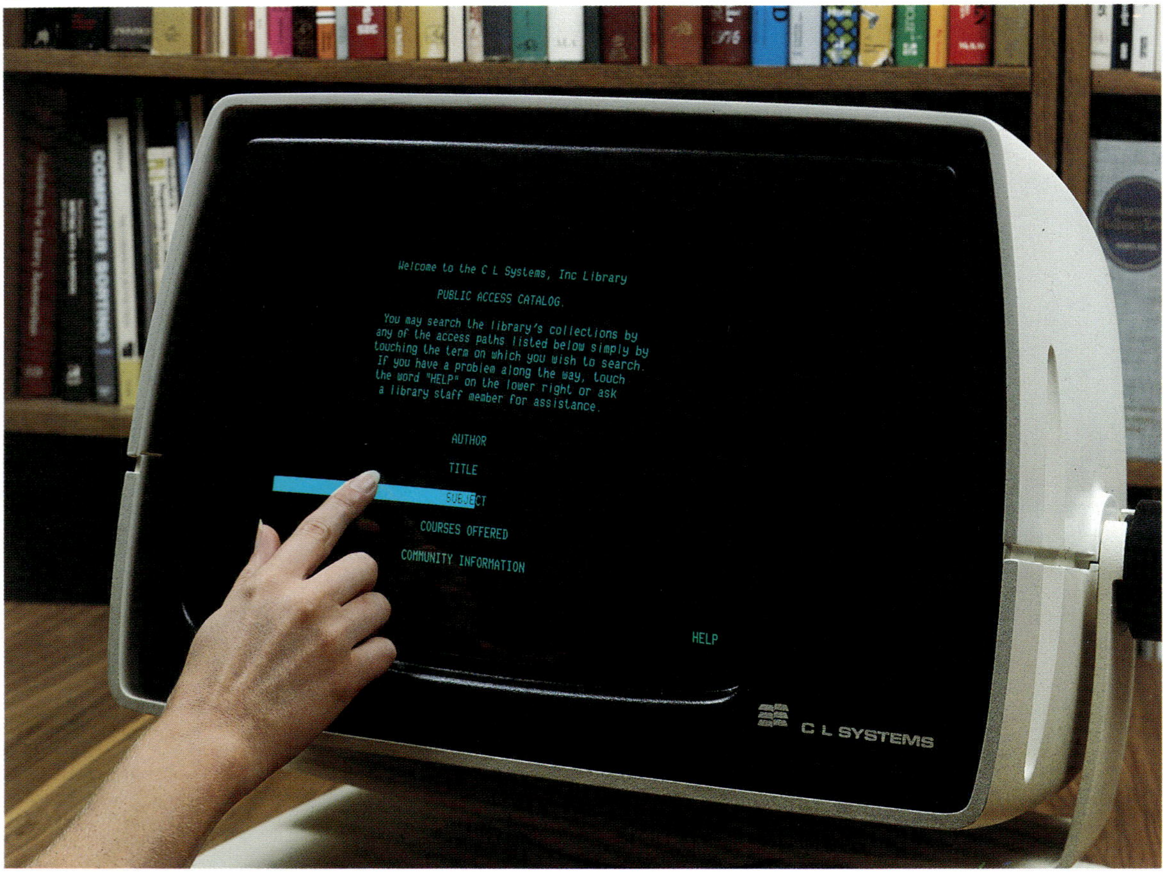

viewing the system as a whole has been termed the **systems approach.** It contrasts with the analytical method, which is the process of segmenting the whole into smaller parts. Although the analytical method has its merits and may be fine for noncomplex situations, many believe that because of the mutual interaction of the parts of a system, the whole takes on distinctive properties that would be lacking if one of those parts were removed. Systems thinking does not do away with analytical thinking, however, but rather supplements it. The necessity of integrating both approaches was noted by Blaise Pascal some 300 years ago when he wrote: "I find as impossible to know the parts without knowing the whole, as knowing the whole, without specifically knowing the parts."

To isolate the system in question from all other systems and from its environment, the parts and their interrelationships must be defined. To do this we employ the analytical method. We must be careful, however, that in the process of isolating the system for study, the essential interrelationships existing among the various components are not ignored or cut out. The systems analyst concentrates on the process that links the parts together.

What Is a System?

The term **system** is derived from the Greek word **systema,** which refers to an organized, functioning relationship among units or components. We will define a **system** as a group of related elements that work together toward a common goal. **Element** may refer to physical parts or components (such as the steering wheel or tires of an automobile), interrelated steps (such as those of managerial planning, organizing, supervising, staffing, and controlling), or a subsystem made up of its own elements (such as the nervous, circulatory, and muscular systems that make up the human body).

A system is composed of inputs, processes, and outputs (see Figure 3–12). Inputs may be matter, energy, humans, or information, depending on the type of system. The process is that which transforms the input into an output. Outputs are the results of the operations of the process or, alternatively, the purpose for which the system exists.

A number of points are of concern when talking about systems. What are the goals or objectives of the system, and how is the performance of

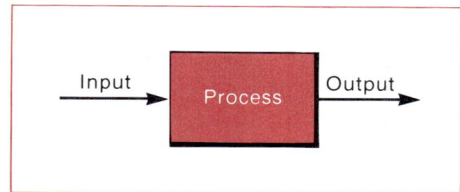

Figure 3–12 Simple System

the system measured? What is the system environment (all that is outside the system that has an effect on the system) like? What resources
are available to the system for the execution of the activities necessary
for goal realization? What are the components (jobs, activities, and so
on, that the system must perform to realize its objectives) of the system? Finally, how is the system managed (planned and controlled)?

Everyone deals with numerous systems every day. Some are more
readily identifiable than others, depending on the level at which the
system is viewed. For example, we all are part of the solar system—a
system not so readily observable. In contrast, many systems such as the
city's transportation system, the school system, or the governmental
system are more easily identifiable. People are composed of many systems, including the nervous, circulatory, muscular, and respiratory systems, among a great many others.

To illustrate some points about systems, let us look at the human
body—a system in its own right—and some of the subsystems the body
comprises. In the respiratory system, for example, oxygen is taken into
the lungs (input). The oxygen then is bound to the red blood cells (process) and transported by the circulatory system (another system) to the
various parts of the body where the oxygen is needed. There the red
blood cells deposit the oxygen and bind to carbon dioxide (another process), and the circulatory system is called upon again to transport the
red blood cells back to the lungs, where the carbon dioxide is exhaled
(output).

This example greatly simplifies the actual processes but illustrates a
number of interesting points about systems. One of these is the concept
of **feedback.** Feedback is used as a check on the system to see whether
the predetermined objectives of the system are being met. There are
numerous feedback systems within the body, but one of the more obvious is the increase in breathing rate that takes place because of a
buildup of carbon dioxide concentration. Everyone has experienced this
phenomenon after strenuous activity. It is one of the body's feedback
mechanisms indicating that corrections in the input (increase the respiratory rate) are needed to facilitate the exchange of gases (carbon dioxide and oxygen), in order to allow the body to return to normal functioning conditions. This involves yet another system, the nervous system.
It feeds back the message to the respiratory control center of the brain,
which then takes corrective measures in the form of increasing the respiratory rate.

There are two forms of feedback in any system: internal and external.
Internal feedback is generated within the system itself. External feedback is obtained from the environment. Both are used to monitor the
output and make the appropriate corrections in input whenever the system deviates from the established goals. The process that increases the
respiratory rate would be a form of internal feedback, whereas the analysis of a machine that indicates lung capacity would be a form of external feedback (from the environment).

This example also illustrates another very important point about the
systems environment. It is sometimes very difficult to define the bound-

aries between systems or to identify the elements of a system that could stand alone as systems themselves. At some points, such as the exchange of gases in the muscles, it is hard to pinpoint exactly what system the process belongs to, or if in fact a system in its own right. We have seen that the respiratory system intricately interacts with the circulatory, muscular, and nervous systems, among others. All these systems in turn are subsystems of a larger system we call the human body. Most systems are collections of subsystems and are themselves subsystems in larger systems. The fact that we have this hierarchy of systems is an important concept in systems theory, because it implies that there is interaction among systems.

The previous example is what could be called a **naturally occurring system.** There are, however, systems that humans contrive themselves. One example that lends itself particularly well to the concepts of the systems approach is the business organization. Figure 3–13 depicts a typical organization as a system that incorporates internal and external feedback from the environment. Within the organization there are groups of related elements, (departments and employees) working toward a common goal (profit and survival). Here, again, the interacting of systems can be seen. The accounting, sales, finance, purchasing, and production departments—all systems themselves—interact to form a larger system, which is the organization itself.

This business organization also can be seen as part of a larger system, the economic system of today's business world. In this situation, the organization is affected by external environmental factors outside its control, such as governmental regulation, the economy, and competition. Internal factors also affect an organization. Examples include departmental relationships, internal communications channels, and the quality of the organization's managers. Both the internal and external

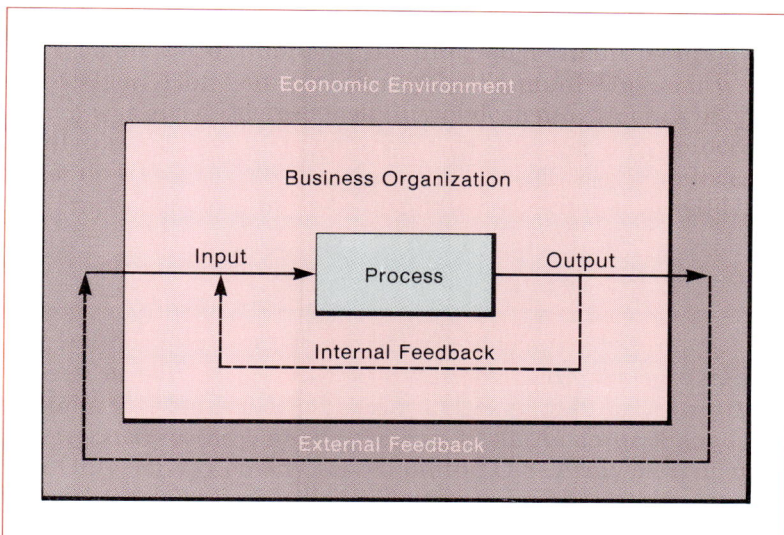

Figure 3–13 System with Feedback

environmental factors must be taken into consideration when determining the information needs of the organization. To organize and determine the effects of all these different factors, an information system should be designed. With the number of factors involved, it becomes obvious that it would be easier to understand and evaluate them by designing an information system based on the systems approach rather than on an analytical approach, which may misinterpret or fail to include components that would be vital to the organization's well-being.

Information Systems

An **information system** consists of the methods and channels used to gather and distribute information within an organization. **Information** is data that has been processed into a form that is useful to the user in making decisions. One person's information may be another's garbage. The paths that the flow of information takes within an organization are called **information channels.**

The analyst is concerned with both the information channels being used and the information that is being provided by these channels. All organizations have some form of information system; whether they are properly managed is another matter. Is the user getting the information needed, too much information, or perhaps even the wrong information? Today's world offers an environment where conditions, and thus the information needs of managers, are constantly changing. To keep abreast of these changes, an **effective** information system must be designed to provide managers with the information needed to make timely and accurate decisions. An ineffective information system may lull a manager into a false sense of security while providing misleading, incorrect, or tardy information. People also must be wary of a system that provides an overabundance of information. A new problem that has arisen out of the computer age is information overload. Managers often overlook important facts because they get lost in a multitude of forms and reports.

Because of the complexity involved in studying most real-world events, the analyst needs tools to help break down these complexities in order to better understand and evaluate them. One way in which this is accomplished is by using the systems approach to information systems analysis. Using this model, an analyst attempts to mirror events in the real world while reducing the complexity of the activities involved in those events. The systems model is intended to show overall patterns rather than accurately represent the individual components of the system. From the overall patterns, the analyst can gather the important factors, patterns, and flows of the system under study. An information system may be either manual or computerized. During the systems analysis and design process it is the responsibility of the systems analyst to insure that the final design conforms to the needs of the user; otherwise, it will be unused and soon outdated as informal replacement systems arise.

Systems Analysis and Design

Because of the large amount of time and money involved in systems analysis and design, some type of process must monitor its development to insure that the system is efficient, meets the user's needs, and stays within the constraints placed upon it by management. This requires that communications channels remain open between the systems analyst, management, and the user.

The **systems life cycle** approach to systems analysis and design is a widely used method that helps insure that these conditions are met. It is defined as a step-by-step approach to systems development, beginning with logical design (what should be done and how it should be done) and gradually moving to physical design (the actual coding of programs, printing of forms, and so on). One of the requirements is that specific documentation be prepared at the end of each step. This documentation helps facilitate communication between the analyst, management, and the user. The output documentation of one step also serves as the input to the next step.

The systems analyst is expected to complete the requirements of each step before moving on to the next. Management approval is the key factor in proceeding to the next step. The user, however, holds the ultimate fate of the system in his or her hands. As was stated earlier, if a system is implemented that does not satisfy the user's needs, it soon will be replaced by informal systems. This also means that much time and money have been wasted. The systems life cycle approach attempts to avoid these problems by requiring the analyst to submit clear and consisely written documents so that both the user and management can be assured that they all are viewing the problem and the solution design on the same scope. This also helps insure that the project will remain within its predetermined organizational constraints. This saves time and money, since it eliminates having to repeat steps already completed because of a misunderstanding about the nature or scope of the problem. One view of the steps in the systems life cycle approach is listed here:

1. Problem definition.
2. Feasibility study.
3. Analysis.
4. General system design.
5. Detailed system design.
6. Implementation.
7. Maintenance.

Each of these steps will be discussed in detail in Chapter 13.

Despite the detailed sequence of steps in systems life cycle development, one current approach to the building of systems attempts to compress the number of steps. This approach is called **prototyping,** a methodology used for many years in the development of physical (manufactured) products. Based on initial, sometimes incomplete, specifications provided by the customer or user, the systems specialist develops a "quick and dirty" version of the application. The user then critiques this preliminary product on the assumption that agreement on final specifications can be reached more quickly if a sample system and its output exist. Recently introduced high-level languages and other software tools make this approach attractive because of the speed with which prototypes can be generated.

- First generation computers were characterized by large numbers of vacuum tubes, slow input and output operations, and the use of paper tape and punched cards.
- Second generation computers were characterized by solid state transistors, magnetic cores, primary (internal) storage, and magnetic tape for auxiliary (external) storage. Disk storage and use of high-level programming languages also were refined.
- Third generation computers were characterized by the use of integrated circuits (ICs), which led to smaller size, greater reliability, and lower costs.
- Fourth generation computers are characterized by the use of LSI circuits.
- Digital computers represent data by discrete on and off states, known as binary notation.
- Analog computers represent data by measuring physical or electrical quantities such as pressure, temperature, voltage, or current.
- The information flow in any data-processing application can be represented by the following three steps:

   Input.
   Processing ⇌ Storage.
   Output.

- The three major components of the central processing unit (CPU) are the control unit, which directs and controls the activities of all other units; the arithmetic and logic unit (ALU), which performs the arithmetic and logical operations; and the primary storage unit, where both instructions and data are held until needed for processing.
- Hardware refers to the physical devices that make up the computer system.
- A program is a series of step-by-step instructions organized in a logical sequence to direct the computer in solving a particular task.
- The stored-program concept allowed data and instructions to be stored within the computer. It increased the speed of processing, since it eliminated the need for human intervention.
- Ideally, a program should be written so that the logic is as simple and straightforward as possible. Structured programming is the approach that minimizes complexity and makes programs easier to read, maintain, and modify.

● There are two general categories of programs: (1) systems programs, which coordinate the operation of computer circuitry, and (2) applications programs, which solve individual user problems.

● When a computer is first purchased, the general systems programs needed to operate it can be obtained from the vendor or through a specialized programming firm.

● An operating system allows the computer to manage its own operations and can be thought of as the "agent" between the hardware, the software, and the user.

● A major benefit of an operating system is software compatibility. As long as the operating system is the same, applications programs can be written that can be transferred to a different hardware configuration or to a different computer entirely.

● There are numerous types of applications programs ranging from educational, games, inventory control, record keeping, and word processing programs to almost any type of application that can be conceived.

● A computer language consists of written words or symbols, which then are translated into on and off states of electricity that indicate what functions are to be performed.

● Computer languages can be divided into three levels according to their complexity: machine language, assembly language, and high-level language.

● A system is a group of related elements that work together toward a common goal.

● A system is composed of inputs, processes, and outputs.

● Element may refer to physical parts or components, interrelated steps, or a subsystem made up of its own elements.

● There are two forms of feedback: Internal feedback is generated from within the system; external feedback is generated from outside the system.

● A group of subsystems may interact with each other to form a larger system.

● An information system consists of the methods and channels used to gather and distribute information within an organization.

● Information is data that has been processed into a form that is useful to the user. Information channels are the paths that the flow of information takes within an organization.

● The systems life cycle approach is composed of the following or similar steps: problem definition, feasibility study, analysis, general system design, detailed system design, implementation, and maintenance.

---

1. What characteristics identify a computer as a first generation computer? A second? A third? A fourth?

2. Describe the difference between a digital and an analog computer.

3. Identify the three steps of information flow in any data-processing application.

REVIEW QUESTIONS

4. Name and describe the three major components of a CPU.
5. Define *hardware*.
6. Explain the difference between software and hardware.
7. Define the meaning and importance of the stored-program concept.
8. What is program logic? How does the computer approach solving a programming problem?
9. What is the significance of the nondestructive read, destructive write characteristic of memory?
10. Discuss the structured programming approach. List some advantages to this methodology.
11. There are two basic types of programs. List each type and several functions each performs.
12. What is the significance of an operating system? Give examples of the tasks it can perform.
13. Distinguish between the three levels of programming languages: machine, assembly, and high level.
14. Define a system and give an example. Describe any subsystems within the system. Does the system belong to a larger system?
15. Define the two types of feedback, and give examples of each.
16. What is information? Give an example of and describe an information channel.
17. What advantages can you see in using the systems life cycle approach to systems analysis and design?
18. List the steps of the systems life cycle approach.

PART II

HARDWARE

INPUT

LEARNING OBJECTIVES

This chapter deals with the most fundamental prerequisite for using a computer: getting the data into the computer in the first place. In studying this chapter, you will learn the following:

☐ What the traditional input devices are, how they work, and what their advantages and disadvantages are.

☐ What source-data automation is, and how it is used.
☐ The differences between types of remote terminals and how these terminals are being used.
☐ The uses and effectiveness of specialized input devices such as light pens and voice-recognition systems.

Chapter 4

Input has traditionally been a bottleneck for computer systems. In terms of both the time required to generate it and the errors encountered during its creation, the input process has been problematic. Most input has required a keying operation to convert human-readable data to computer-readable form.

This chapter examines all aspects of the input process, concentrating on discussions of traditional input media, source-data automation, remote terminals, and advances in specialized input devices and media.

Data **input** is the process of capturing data about an event and then transforming that data ino a language, or coded repesentation, the computer can understand. This transformation process is very important: it is the interface, or interpreter, between human and machine. If this interpretation process does not transmit data in its proper form or with correct values, the possibility of effective communication decreases rapidly. Historically, the data input process has been extremely slow compared with the speed at which the CPU can process that data.

There are three main reasons for the input process's being slow; the first is the method by which the data is captured. Data input commonly has required a two-step process before the actual entry of data into the CPU for processing. The first step consists of rewriting or recording data from a **source document** (such as an employee's time card, a magazine subscription order, or even a tax return) onto an input medium in a language the computer can understand. Some of these media include punched cards, magnetic tape, or sheets of paper with blocks that are filled in with a heavy lead pencil similar to those used for multiple-choice tests. This rewriting of data is a duplication of effort and is time consuming, because a second person must again record data that already has been accumulated. The second step requires the use of a reading device that transmits the data written on the input medium to the computer for processing.

The second reason for data input's being relatively slow is the amount of mechanization involved in both the process of writing on an input medium such as punched cards or magnetic tape and the process of reading from that input medium. A CPU is limited in the speed at which it can process data, that limit being the speed of electricity, or approximately the speed of light. During the input process, machines that write on input media (such as keypunches) and machines that read the data from those input media (such as card readers) are limited in the speed at which they are able to operate. This limiting speed is equal to the speed of the slowest electromechanical operation performed by that particular machine. This limiting concept is similar to the adage a chain is only as strong as its weakest link.

The third reason that input is relatively slow is the process of error control. In any type of system—computerized or manual—error-free data is essential if the final results are to be used for any significant decision making. If the data used to produce the needed information is unreliable, the resulting information also could be unreliable. This concept, known as **garbage in–garbage out (GIGO),** applies to many things, including hot dogs. If the input is garbage, the output cannot possibly be a gourmet meal.

During the input process, error control involves comparing the data to be input to a general rule of how that data should look. For example, if the computer expects a person's Social Security number but receives four letters and five numbers, it will assume an error has been made and reject that piece of data. Rejected data is not just forgotten; it must be manually corrected and sent through the entire system a second time. Although error control techniques can be much more sophisticated than this example, the possibility of errors being entered into the system still exists. Most so-called computer errors are actually data-entry errors.

The use of error control checks slows the data input process, but the cost of detecting errors before the data has been processed by the computer is much less than after processing has occurred. It has been estimated that the cost of correction before processing by the computer can be as little as ten cents per character in error, as compared with two dollars per character in error after the data has been processed. Because of the need for error-free data and costs of correcting data already processed by the computer, most computer applications perform some type of error detection before the data is processed.

Although technology has advanced rapidly in computer equipment during the last several years, most of the advancement has been in the area of data processing and data storage, not data input. With this increasing technology, costs of data processing and data storage decrease while leaving data input costs relatively the same. It has been estimated that 30 to 50 percent of all expenses associated with the computer are related to data entry. These expenses stem from the large amounts of labor required to rewrite the already captured data into a format the computer can understand, as well as the time required to detect and correct errors in data.

As data-entry technology progresses, it will be necessary either to shorten or eliminate these three delays in the data-entry process. **Source-data automation** is one advance in data-entry technology that eliminates duplication of effort in the data-capturing process. Source-data automation involves specialized input devices, usually located near the scene of an event, to record data about that event in machine language. This process eliminates the duplication of effort associated with traditional input practices.

TRADITIONAL INPUT MEDIA

Historically, the main devices used for input have included punched cards, magnetic tape, and magnetic disks. All three of these input media require two steps to complete the data-input process. The first step requires that data be placed on the medium in a notation the computer can understand. The second step requires the use of a reading device that reads the data contained on the medium and then passes that data on to the computer. Each of these input media and its corresponding reading device will be discussed here.

Punched Cards

The eighty-column **punched card,** also known as the **Hollerith card** after its developer Herman Hollerith, is the most common punched card in use today. Each card is divided into eighty columns, with each column capable of containing one character (letter, number, or punctuation symbol). When a character is formed in any column, both the human-readable form and the machine-readable form appear in that particular column (see Figure 4–1).

The other, less common punched card in use today is the IBM punched card, which is used primarily with small computers. This card is smaller than the eighty-column card but is capable of containing 20 percent more data. This IBM card, also known as the ninety-six–column card, uses three rows of data with thirty-two characters in each row. As characters are formed on the card, both the human-readable form and the machine-readable form appear automatically (see Figure 4–2).

Much time is spent keying in data from **source documents** to the punched card with the use of a **keypunch** (see Figure 4–3). This machine is similar to a typewriter, except that in addition to printed symbols, the keypunch places combinations of holes representing characters into a designated area of the card. The keypunch automatically feeds, advances, and stacks the cards.

Figure 4–1 Eighty-Column Punched Card

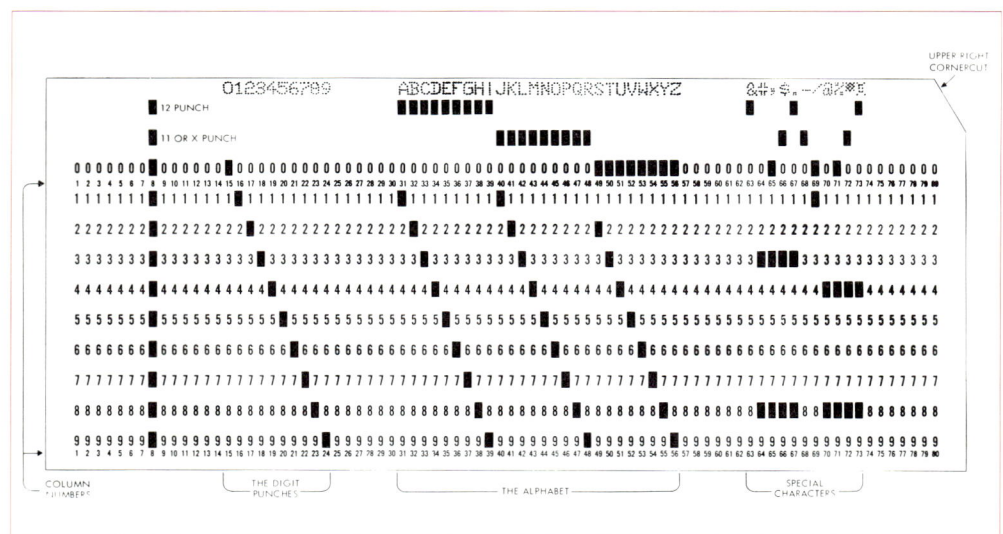

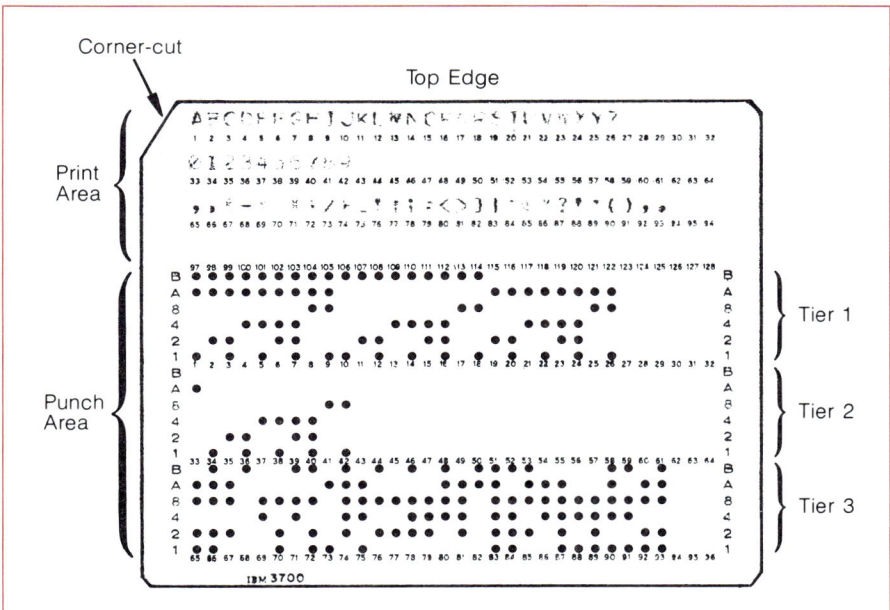

Figure 4—2 Ninety-Six—Column Punched Card

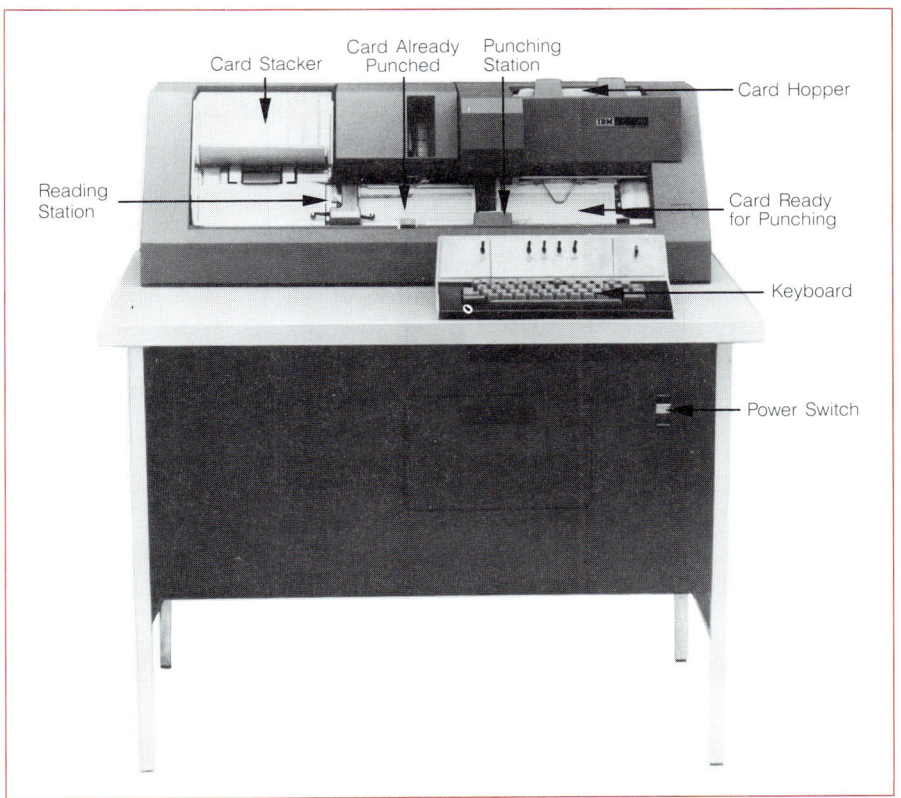

Figure 4—3 Keypunch

Terminal Strain

With the widespread use of word processors, business has begun to show the strain. To be specific, terminal strain. Terminal strain is eye soreness, a slight headache, a literal pain in the neck, or all three. It always is caused by spending too much time in one place: in front of a computer terminal.

Ergonomics—the study of the relationship between people and machines—can help reduce terminal strain. Ergonomic research has indicated several ways to avoid terminal strain. Avoid wearing tinted glasses or bifocals. Tinted glasses distort the light level. People who wear bifocals tend to lean forward and raise their heads to read through the bottom part of their glasses. This causes neck kinks. People who wear any type of glasses are more susceptible to terminal strain, because in terminal use the distance from the eye to the reading surface is eighteen inches, as opposed to twelve inches in ordinary reading. People who wear bifocals are especially susceptible.

Lighting is also an important factor in terminal strain. The lighting level of the office should be reduced by one-third when a terminal is installed. The most important consideration, however, is time spent in front of the terminal. Therefore, the most successful way to avoid terminal strain is to spend at least ten minutes every hour away from the terminal.

Experienced keypunch operators can enter data at a rate of up to ten thousand characters per hour. However, no matter how competent the operator, every card should be checked for accuracy. This checking can be done visually or with the use of a **key verifier.** A key verifier resembles a keypunch, but instead of creating holes, it senses existing holes. The process requires the data to be keyed a second time; if any keyed character does not agree with the corresponding column of the previously punched card, a red light will appear. Frequently, the same unit can be used for both keypunching and key verifying. The time-consuming duplication of keying necessary for the verification of punched card data is a major drawback of this input medium.

After the cards have been verified, a **card reader** is used to transfer the recorded data to the computer. There are two main types of card readers in use today: the brush reader and the photoelectric reader. The brush reader uses tiny metal brushes, which pass over the card and sense the location of a punched hole. The photoelectric reader uses a light source on one side of the card and a light sensor on the opposite side to determine the locations of punched holes. These card readers automatically feed, scan, and stack the cards and involve much mechanization. Although there are many moving parts, they are able to process six hundred to two thousand cards per minute.

Card readers are designed to read and transfer data from only one card at a time. This is designated the **unit record concept,** a **record** being a collection of related data values or fields and the **unit** implying that one card should contain a single record. Since punched cards are confined to eighty or ninety-six columns, a record that requires more than this hinders the processing of data and makes computer operation inefficient. Also, if a record requires less space, parts of the card are wasted. A final disadvantage of punched cards is people who "fold, staple, spindle, and mutilate" punched cards or who drop a box full of cards that must be kept in order. These problems create total chaos during the input process.

Key-to-Magnetic Media

A more technologically advanced method of keyboard data entry requires magnetic media, specifically magnetic tape and magnetic disks. These media allow data to be input up to twenty-five times faster than with punched cards and they require much less data storage space. (For example, 1,600 characters or more can be stored on one inch of magnetic tape.) Both tape and disks are similar in the way data is entered through the use of a keyboard and then stored as magnetic particles on the respective medium. Because of these similarities, these two **key-to-magnetic media** will be discussed together.

As mentioned earlier, the first step of data input is to place data on the medium in a format and notation the computer can understand. When data is entered from a source document onto magnetic media, it is first keyed via a keyboard—much like one used for punched cards—into a small memory compartment located within the computer, called a **buffer.** The data then is analyzed by the computer and checked for any obvious errors using error control techniques mentioned earlier. If the data appears to be correct, it then is recorded on the magnetic medium in the form of magnetic iron oxide particles, which can be stored indefinitely, because the particles retain their magnetism until they are erased and reused for new information. If data items are found to contain errors, they are displayed on a cathode-ray tube (CRT) screen for investigation and correction by the keyboard operator.

There are two types of configurations, or hardware designs, in use today for the key-to-magnetic media devices. The first is known as a **stand-alone key-to-tape** or **stand-alone key-to-disk device.** This configuration is a self-contained unit complete with a keyboard, a buffer used to temporarily hold the data just entered by the keyboard, memory for the stored-program instructions (used for error control), and the magnetic medium. If several of these configurations are used, the data usually is collected from all tapes or disks and "pooled" onto one reel of magnetic tape or one magnetic disk.

The second configuration is known as the **clustered key-to-tape** or **clustered key-to-disk** device; it also is known as the **key-to-central-tape** or **key-to-central-disk** device (see Figure 4–4). In this configuration, all keyboards are connected to a minicomputer, which edits all data and then writes onto a single tape or disk. This type of configuration elimi-

Figure 4—4 Custered Key-to-Magnetic Disk Configuration

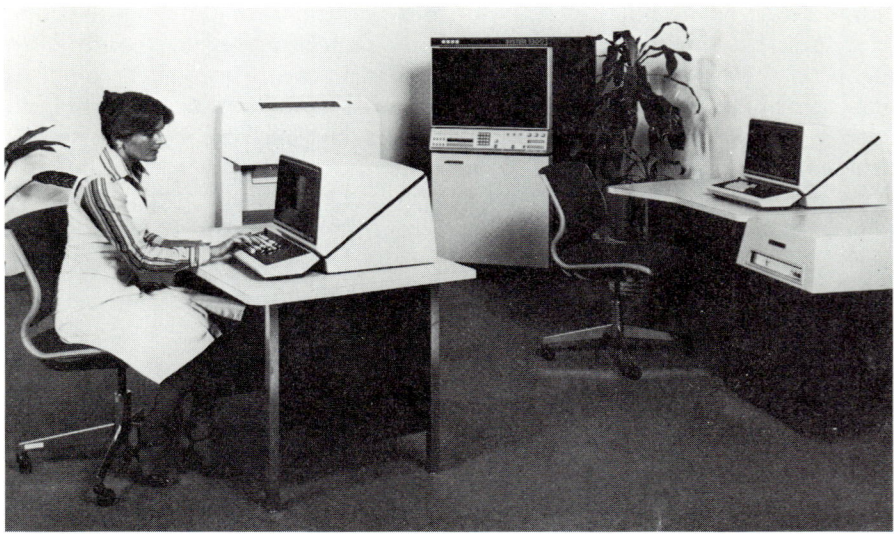

nates the pooling needed with stand-alone devices. This configuration is best suited for applications where most entries are of similar data.

Key-to-magnetic media have several advantages over punched cards that make them attractive, but they also have one major disadvantage. The advantages of key-to-magnetic media include the smaller space required, the ability to correct errors, faster processing speeds, and reusability. It is possible to rewrite or record data on magnetic media via a keyboard at speeds up to eighteen thousand characters per hour, whereas punched cards allow only ten thousand characters per hour because of the mechanical characteristics of the keypunch. Data then can be transferred to the computer twenty-five times faster with magnetic media than with cards. Reusability, speed, ease of handling, and space requirements thus are advantages to the use of magnetic media, but its cost is not. The price tag of hardware to be used with magnetic media is significantly higher than hardware for use with punched cards. As a general rule, the greater the volume of data to be entered and processed, the more desirable magnetic media become.

SOURCE-DATA AUTOMATION

Source-data automation is the latest trend in data input designed to eliminate the wasted effort associated with preparing already recorded data for input. For all input devices previously discussed, data must be rewritten from a source document onto the input medium through the use of a keyboard. Usually, this keying in of data takes place at a later time than that of original data capture; technically, therefore, all records in the computer never can be updated to this very minute. With the use of specialized input devices, source-data automation helps eliminate both this time lag and the undesirable duplication of efforts.

Specialized input devices usually are located at the scene of an event and used to collect and record data about that event in a language and format the computer can understand. Since these devices automatically prepare the data about an event when the event occurs, the speed, accuracy, and efficiency of the data-processing operation are enhanced. The need for such input devices has existed since the invention of the computer; however, the lack of advanced technology made these devices too cumbersome to work with and too expensive to afford until recent years. Research and development in source-data automation has been recognized as critical and is advancing rapidly. The following sections offer present uses and new possibilities for source-data automation (see Figure 4–5).

One of the first steps toward data-input automation was **magnetic-ink character recognition (MICR).** This system uses particles of iron oxide placed in certain sections of a seventy-section matrix to represent different characters (see Figure 4–6). These characters can then be read by a **magnetic-ink character reader** and translated into machine language. Since the characters printed in the matrices are written in a language that humans can read, no translation devices are needed. Although magnetic-ink characters must be printed very carefully, once they are written, eventual smudging and overprinting by pen or pencil will not affect the accuracy of the reading.

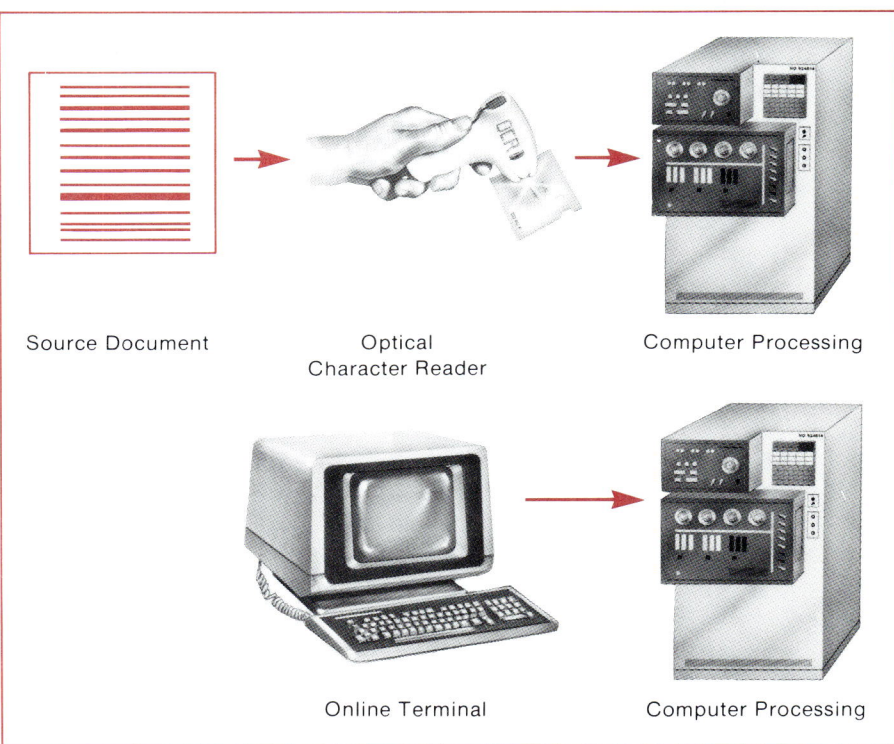

Source Document   Optical   Computer Processing
                     Character Reader

Online Terminal   Computer Processing

Figure 4–5 Typical Methods of Source-Data Automation

Figure 4–6 Matrix Patterns for Magnetic-Ink Characters

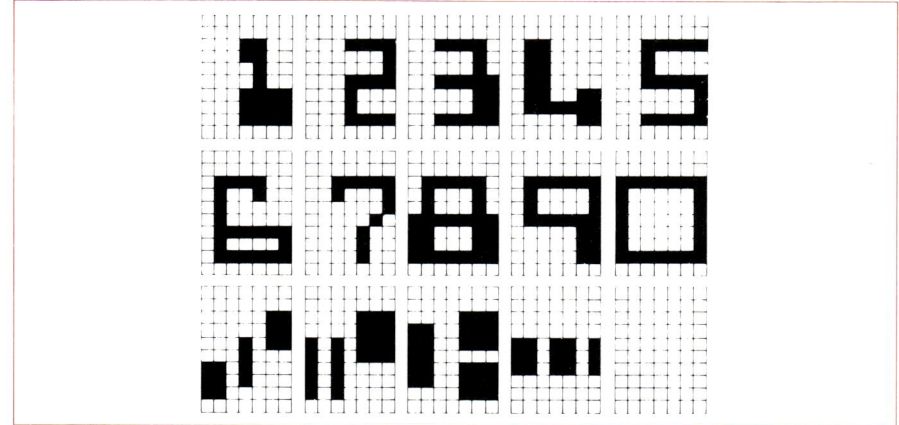

The banking industry began to use MICR in the late 1950s to aid in check processing and sorting (see Figure 4–7). Located at the bottom of each check is a bank number designating what bank is holding the money to cover this check, as well as an account number designating the identity of the person or organization originating the check. The bank number is located in an area called the Transit, or FRABA, Field, and the account number is located in an area called the On Us Field. Each of these fields begins and ends with special characters known as Q-codes to aid the computer in determining where the matrices begin and end. After a check has been written, a data-entry operator at the bank uses an MICR inscriber to record the amount of the check in an amount field. These checks then are processed through an MICR reader/ sorter and returned to the account holder with a statement.

Optical recognition was the next advancement over MICR, since this process did not require specialized magnetic-ink inscribers to record the

Figure 4–7 Sample Check with Magnetic-Ink Characters

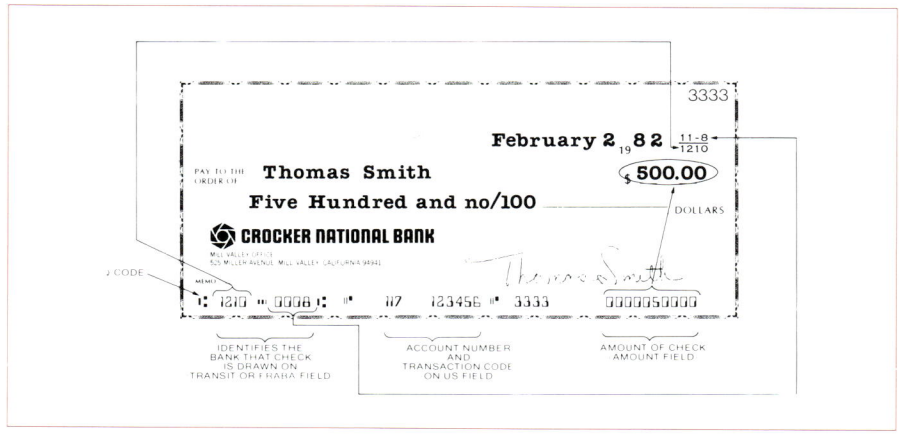

Name Student No.
Subject Teacher
Date Hour

Scores	
Part 1	
Part 2	
Total	

Directions:
Use a No. 2 pencil to fill in completely the lettered box corresponding to your answer. For example, if you believe the correct answer relates to box c, fill in box c as follows:
Example:
To change your answer, erase completely and re-mark.

Error
Do not mark in this shaded area. It is reserved for the error-indicating function of the Test Scorer.

Rescore
T F Part 1
Visual Products Division/3M
Number Correct
Feed

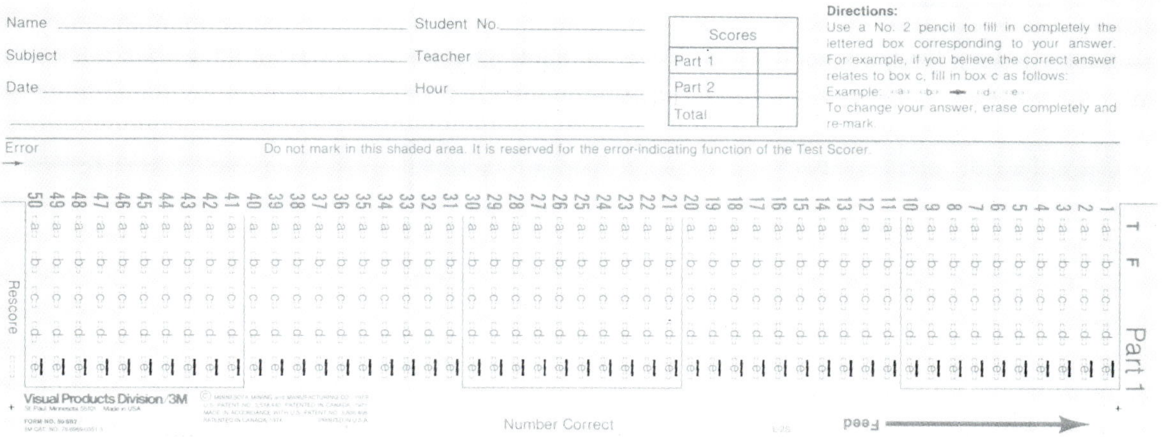

Figure 4–8 Optical-Mark Recognition: A Multiple-Choice Examination

data on some type of document. The most popular type of optical recognition is **optical-mark recognition (OMR),** or **mark sensing.** This method is widely used for multiple-choice examinations, surveys, and even the census, where marks are made with a heavy lead pencil in preprinted boxes on standardized forms (see Figure 4–8). These forms then are read by being passed under a light source, which is reflected by the presence of a mark. These light reflections then are transformed into machine format. Up to two thousand forms can be processed per hour using an optical-mark page reader.

Another type of optical-mark recognition uses **bar codes** and **bar-code readers.** Bar codes usually represent sets of numbers by using vertical bars of different widths (see Figure 4–9). The codes are read by being passed over a light source located in a hand-held **wand reader** or a **fixed scanning device** (see Figure 4–10). These codes usually begin and end with a set of specialized bars used for determining the positioning of the code by the computer and for error control. Bar codes have been used for several applications, including keeping track of railroad cars, airport baggage handling, and grocery store automation.

The **Universal Product Code (UPC)** is a standardized bar code found on almost every type of food in a grocery store (see Figure 4–11). Each food product is assigned a different code, which identifies the product name and manufacturer but not the price; the price is stored in the computer's memory at the store to facilitate price changes. Since the checker only has to pass the code over a light source, training is made easier, checkouts are faster, and human error is reduced.

A more understandable code was developed soon after the bar code for the process of **optical-character recognition (OCR).** This process enabled typed alphabetic characters (see Figure 4–12) to be read with hand-held wand readers or other devices much like bar-code readers. Most OCR readers can read typefaces of only a certain size and script, but some can

Figure 4—9 Bar Codes

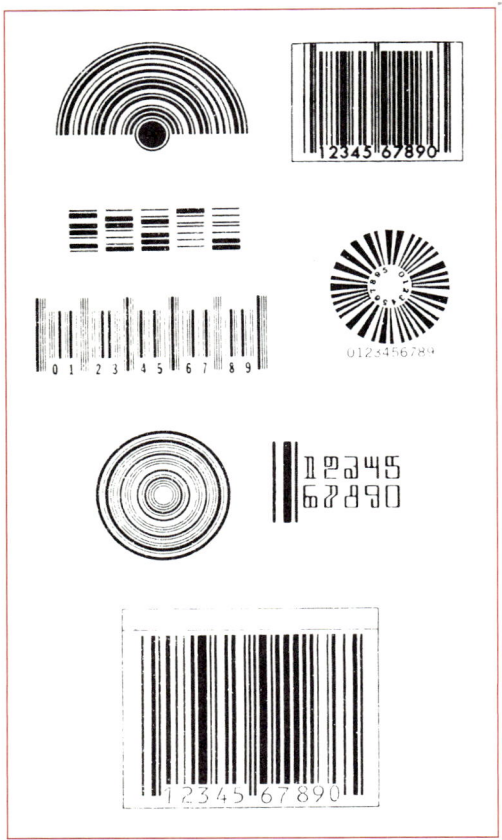

Figure 4—10
Scanning Device

Figure 4—11
Universal Product Code
(UPC)

read many different typefaces, including handwritten characters. This type of optical recognition differs from all previously mentioned, because these characters are recognized by their shape rather than the positioning of light reflections within preprinted boxes or seventy-section matrices.

REMOTE TERMINALS

As technology becomes more advanced, basic pieces of hardware such as input devices become so sophisticated that they are difficult to name. This problem arises when two or more pieces of hardware are joined to form a single piece of equipment. For example, if a CRT screen is added to a wand reader, is it difficult to say that piece of equipment is an input device exclusively, since it has some output device qualities (namely, the CRT screen). The category of **terminal** has become the common name used to describe these hybrid devices that are linked in some manner to the main computer. When the main computer and terminal are

Figure 4—12 Optical-
Character Recognition
(OCR) Characters

ABCDEFGHIJKLMN
OPQRSTUVWXYZ,.
$/*-1234567890

What Is a Mouse?

A mouse is an input device that is held in the hand. It is used to control the position of a cursor or pointer on a terminal screen. Most useful for visual designs, a mouse can interact directly with the computer when combined with the right software.

The first mouse was designed in 1964 by Doug Englebart. In fact, when Englebart began the research that led to the development of the mouse, there were only four computers in the entire United States.

Today the computer is everywhere, and so is the mouse. Many of the personal computers entering the market in the eighties use mice. Because of the rapid increase of the mouse population, 1983 was declared by **Time** to be "the year of the mouse."

located in different buildings, cities, or states, the terminals are referred to as **remote terminals.**

With the addition of small memories, terminals are able to store small amounts of programmed instructions, giving them limited "intelligence." These terminals can be broken down into categories by the amount of intelligence each possesses. **Dumb terminals,** on the one hand, have very little memory and typically are used only for a specific purpose. **Smart terminals** and **intelligent terminals,** on the other hand, have a larger amount of internal memory and can perform many functions, including error control, editing, communication functions, and even some data processing. Adding this intelligence to the terminals reduces the amount of time the computer and terminal must interact and, as a result, improves efficiency in computer processing.

Dumb terminals usually are connected directly to the computer or a data storage medium and transfer data items exactly as they are entered. Since these data items usually are entered intermittently (that is, with a pause between characters), the use of such dumb terminals with a computer is inefficient—during these pauses, the computer does nothing but wait. If a dumb terminal is connected to a data storage device, this too is inefficient, because the device that writes on the input medium must start and stop at each pause. To help eliminate some of this inefficiency, small amounts of memory, known as **buffers,** have been added to store a specified number of characters. These terminals accumulate the data that has been entered until the buffer becomes full; then they forward the entire buffer to the computer and start over.

With the addition of a buffer, the dumb terminal is more efficient; nevertheless, it is still dumb, because it does not interact with the user on a two-way level. Smart terminals and intelligent terminals have larger internal memories that store instructions, or programs, to be used by the terminal. These terminals have a display of some type to allow interaction between the terminal and the user for the editing of input data. The difference between a smart terminal and an intelligent terminal is the number and scope of different functions the terminal can perform. This line separating smart and intelligent terminals is obscure, but a smart terminal is thought of as being able to perform only a few processing activities, whereas the capabilities of an intelligent terminal could range from performing multiple processing activities to being a small computer linked to a larger computer, but capable of doing significant processing on its own.

Point-of-sale (POS) terminals are one example of intelligent terminals. Such electronic cash registers are used by many businesses, including grocery and department stores (see Figure 4–13). These registers receive data entered through an input device such as a bar-code reader or keyboard and perform error control checks on that data. If the data are error-free, the register may interact with the main computer to determine the

Figure 4–13 POS Terminal

price and description of goods and enter that information on the customer's bill. A POS terminal can record all necessary sales information until the end of the day, if needed, and then transfer that data to a main computer.

Touch-tone devices are remote terminals used to collect and temporarily store data about an event until that data can be forwarded to a central computer. These touch-tone devices include push-button telephones, as well as portable hand-held devices with a cassette tape for data storage (see Figure 4–14). They use tones and combinations of tones to represent different characters and transmit them over public telephone lines. Devices of this type are used by salespeople to transmit orders to the home office, as well as by bank-at-home services, in which the telephone is used to pay bills and transfer funds from the comfort of home.

Remote terminals can be used in many applications, all of which are concerned with achieving the same goals: to reduce paperwork, reduce the time lag between event and computer processing, and increase productivity.

SPECIALIZED INPUT

Some of the most technologically advanced input devices are used for designing clothes, buildings, and automobiles, and even in medicine. **Computer-aided design (CAD)** involves displaying an object on the screen of a CRT for visual inspection (see Figure 4–15). This object can be rotated; magnified; reduced; and most impressively of all, altered

Figure 4–14 Touch-Tone Device

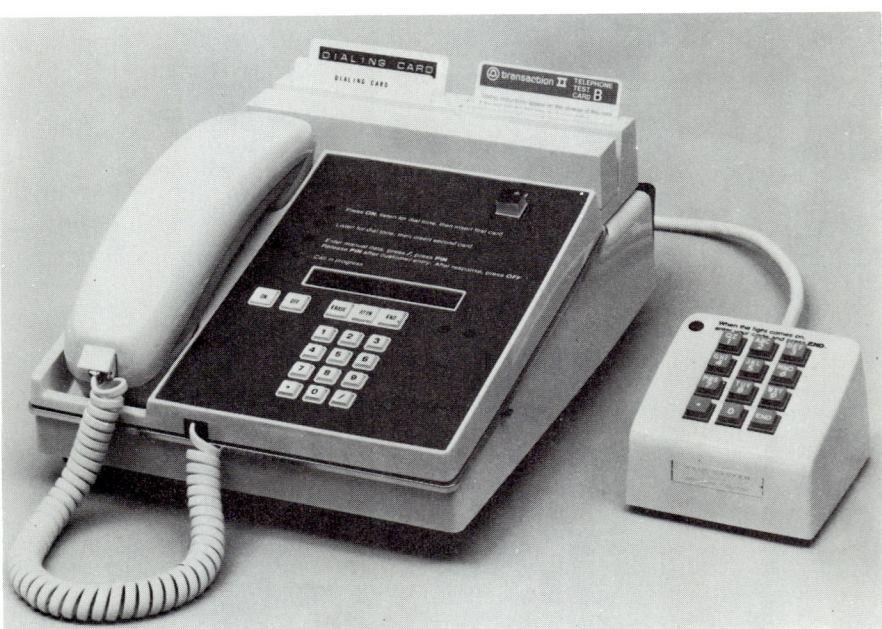

Computerized Drawing

Many microcomputer makers now offer sketch pads that allow users to enter graphic images into the computer simply by drawing them freehand on a computerized tablet. One of these tablets is the Digikitizer, put out by Talos Systems. This tablet is built from a kit and is easily hooked up to the Apple II or Radio Shack TRS-80. When used with the Apple II, this tablet allows the user to draw in either six colors in high-resolution mode or sixteen colors in low-resolution mode. One of the Talos BASIC programs even allows the user to change background and drawing colors simply by pressing the "pen" to the appropriately colored box at the bottom of the screen.

Perhaps the most versatile aspect of the graphics tablet is that this method of input requires no programming at all. The user simply sketches on the computerized tablet, and the drawing materializes on the terminal screen.

Figure 4–15
Computer-Aided Design

with the use of a **light pen.** This alteration can be temporary or permanent, and all new specifications about a requested change are figured by
the computer. Light pens are used exactly like pencils to draw on the
screen or as erasers to erase from the screen. With CAD, an object can
be created and analyzed to determine feasibility without even manufacturing a prototype. These CAD systems probably will make traditional
drafting equipment obsolete.

A **voice-recognition system** is an input method that recognizes spoken
words. This type of input is twice as fast as input entered through a
keyboard and has a 91 percent accuracy rate (superior to that of manual
data entry). Voice-recognition devices recognize either isolated words or
entire simple sentences, depending on the sophistication of the equipment. Some such devices are speaker dependent; that is, the device
must be trained to recognize each particular user's voice. This is done
by having the user repeat several words over and over so that the device
knows that user's voice only. Speaker-independent voice-recognition devices are capable of understanding almost anyone and are much more
versatile. These speaker-independent devices are trained by having several people say the same word over and over so that the computer recognizes several versions (see Figure 4–16).

Voice-recognition devices can be used in several applications but are
best suited for situations in which users are unable to enter data manually because their eyes and hands must remain in contact with the task
being performed. Although voice recognition is much faster than manual data entry, two possible problems can arise through its use. Voice
recognition can fail in two ways. The first way is misinterpretation of a
word as an alternate word. This type of error has serious implications,

Figure 4–16 Voice-
Recognition System
used for Voice Data
Entry

Talkies

Silent computers soon will be going the way of silent movies. Instead of typing away at our terminals, we will simply tell our computers what we want them to do.

The technology for speech recognition is already in use, but there are still a few bugs that need to be worked out. The largest problem is vocabulary. The computers on the market that are capable of understanding spoken input are equipped with relatively small vocabularies because of memory constraints. Another problem is that we can completely change the meaning of a sentence by placing emphasis on a particular word. Before unrestricted spoken input can become practical, computers will have to be programmed to recognize and interpret these inflections.

The results should be well worth the effort. In addition to making input much easier, the use of voice-recognition systems will greatly strengthen security. Because people's voice patterns are as distinctive as their fingerprints, it will become nearly impossible to access someone else's account. As the use of spoken input becomes widespread, we very well may see the voice replace the signature as the primary means of identification.

especially if the two words have very different meanings. The second way is failure to recognize a valid word. This problem, although not as serious, is still annoying. Uses for voice-recognition input range from changing radio frequencies for the pilot of an airplane to the control of various equipment and appliances for the handicapped.

Advances in state-of-the-art data-input techniques such as voice recognition eventually may make the conventional keyboard data-entry terminal obsolete.

● Historically, data input has been slow compared with the speeds at which a computer can process that data. This slow speed has been due to the methods by which data is captured, as well as the mechanization involved in most traditional input devices.

● The traditional input media are punched cards, magnetic tape, and magnetic disks.

● There are two types of punched cards in use today: (1) the eighty-column Hollerith card and (2) the ninety-six—column IBM punched card. Key verifiers are used to check the cards for errors.

● There are two types of card readers: the brush reader and the photoelectric reader.

● Magnetic tape and disks are key-to-magnetic media that require less space and are up to twenty-five times faster than punched cards.

● There are two types of hardware designs for key-to-magnetic media devices: (1) stand-alone key-to-tape or stand-alone key-to-disk devices and (2) key-to-central-tape or key-to-central-disk devices. The first requires a buffer to temporarily save the data, and if data items are entered from more than one keyboard, they must be collected and then pooled onto a single tape or disk. The latter device, key-to-central, eliminates the need to pool data, because all keyboards are connected to a single minicomputer.

● Source-data automation is a method of data entry that eliminates the doubling of effort during data capturing by recording data about an event in machine format at the scene of a data origination event.

● Two types of source-data automation are magnetic-ink character recognition (MICR) and optical-mark recognition (OMR). The MICR type uses particles of iron oxide placed within a seventy-section matrix for character representation. The OMR type reads standard typed characters or shaded boxes (as on an examination) by the position of reflections.

● Remote terminals are devices used to collect data at the scene of an event.

● Dumb terminals have no memory, whereas smart terminals and intelligent terminals have some memory, as well as processing capabilities of some type.

● Intelligent terminals eliminate some unnecessary mechanization and help relieve the computer of simple, recurring tasks.

● With the progress in data-entry technology in the fields of voice recognition and computer-aided design (CAD), keyboards and drafting equipment may become collectible antiques.

REVIEW QUESTIONS

1. What are the three main reasons why the data input process historically has been considered slow?
2. Explain the GIGO concept.
3. What are the two types of punched cards, and how do they differ?
4. What are the two types of card readers, and how do they differ?
5. In what ways are punched cards expensive and inefficient?
6. What are the advantages of using key-to-magnetic media?
7. What are the two types of hardware design for key-to-magnetic media devices, and how do they differ?
8. What is the difference between MICR and OMR?
9. How is OMR being used today?
10. How do dumb, smart, and intelligent remote terminals differ?
11. What are light pens, and what are they used for?
12. What is the current scope of computer-aided design (CAD) applications? What are some future uses you can envision for CAD?
13. What are the advantages of voice-recognition systems?

PROCESSING

LEARNING OBJECTIVES

This chapter summarizes the central function of the computer—processing. After "processing" the information in this chapter, you will know the following:

☐ What the CPU is.
☐ What the main units of the CPU are and how they function.
☐ What the functional components of the CPU are and what they do.
☐ What a machine cycle is and what it consists of.
☐ How data is stored in memory.
☐ Methods by which data is represented.

Chapter 5

INTRODUCTION

Information is required in virtually every field of human endeavor. For data to be converted into information and become meaningful, it has to be analyzed, sorted, and classified into some order and then communicated to the user. Processing data into useful information is obviously not a new activity, but one that has been done since the Babylonians first used clay tablets and cuneiform symbols to record business transactions. However, with the introduction of electronic digital computers in the mid-1900s, data-processing activities truly have been revolutionized.

The essential components of the digital computer were described briefly in Chapter 3; this chapter will take a closer look at how these components interact to process raw data into meaningful information.

CENTRAL PROCESSING UNIT

All data processing is done by the **central processing unit (CPU),** which is the workhorse of the entire computer system. Processing raw data to convert it to meaningful information may require arithmetic computations, logical operations, and movement of data to appropriate locations. All these operations are performed by the CPU. Furthermore, the CPU also controls and supervises all the input/output (I/O) devices.

The CPU is made up of three subunits, which are all contained in a single enclosure referred to as the **mainframe** (although through usage this term has come to mean primarily large computers). The three units are the following (see Figure 5–1):

- The control unit.
- The arithmetic and logic unit (ALU).
- The primary storage unit (sometimes separated from the CPU in systems that allow access to the same storage unit by more than one computer).

This section will examine the functions of each of these units in more detail.

Figure 5–1 Central Processing Unit (CPU) Operations (Arrows Indicate Data Flow)

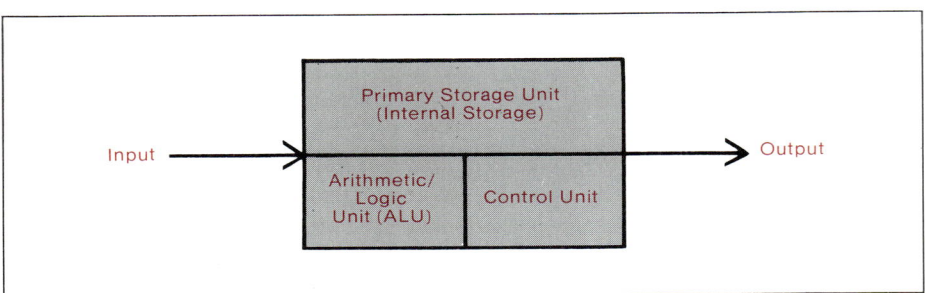

Control Unit

The **control unit** coordinates and controls all the activities in the CPU, just as a band conductor leads and blends different sections of the band into a coordinated musical performance. Based on the program instructions, the control unit is capable of performing the following functions:

- Isolating or picking up (fetching) a program instruction from main memory.
- Interpreting a program instruction.
- Entering and retrieving data from main memory or auxiliary storage.
- Transfering data between the ALU and main storage.
- Controlling input and output devices.

All these operations require precise timing, which is provided with the help of an internal clock. The clock consists of an electronic circuit containing a quartz crystal that oscillates so accurately and consistently that it can be used to control the activities going on inside the CPU.

Arithmetic and Logic Unit

The **arithmetic and logic unit (ALU)** contains the electronic circuitry necessary for performing arithmetic computations and logical operations. The ALU only manipulates data; it cannot store it. A computer that is able to handle both scientific and business applications should be capable of handling arithmetic operations with three types of numbers, all represented in fundamentally binary form: (1) integer numbers, (2) fixed-point numbers, and (3) floating-point numbers.

Integer numbers do not contain decimal points (that is, they do not involve fractions). Both fixed-point and floating-point numbers can be used to represent fractions. However, when fixed-point numbers are being manipulated, the programmer has to keep track of the decimal point. In the case of floating-point numbers, the CPU keeps track of the decimal position.

Logical operations involve making comparisons, testing for various conditions during processing, or both. The three basic relationships between two like items are (1) equal to, (2) less than, and (3) greater than. Based on the results of such a logical comparison, the sequence in which instructions are being executed may be changed. All processing involves arithmetic computations, logical comparisons, or both. Consequently, the speed and efficiency of the CPU depend largely on the capabilities of the ALU.

Primary Storage Unit

The **primary storage unit** is the section of the CPU that holds data and instructions.* The program that is being executed and a portion of the

---

*NOTE: In preceding and following discussions, the terms **storage** and **memory** are used interchangeably when preceded by **internal, main,** or **primary.**

associated data have to be in primary storage before execution can begin. Primary storage is usually supplemented by **secondary** (or auxiliary) **storage,** which is outside the CPU. The main advantage of primary storage is that time required to retrieve data, referred to as the **access time,** is much shorter for primary storage than for secondary storage. Data must be in primary storage to be accessed by the other CPU components—in other words, to be processed.

The wires or cables internally connecting the primary storage unit, control unit, ALU, and I/O devices are collectively designated a **bus.** A bus exists for communication of control information, data transfer, and the provision of addresses to those components needing them.

Initially, the program is transferred to primary storage from an input device. For some programs requiring very small quantities of input data, this data is entered into main memory along with the program; a more typical scenario requires that the program itself, after beginning execution, specify when and from what device the input data is to be read. Processing then begins, and intermediate and final results as developed by the ALU are transferred back to primary, or main, storage. At certain points in the processing, the program may request additional data from one or more input devices. At intervals during processing (or, for applications generating only small quantities of output, when program execution is complete), results are transmitted from main memory to an output unit.

Operational Units

In addition to the three major subunits that make it up, the CPU also contains the following functional elements (which may be individual components or be integrated into the control unit or the ALU): registers, the instruction decoder, and the program counter.

Registers A **register** is a device that can receive data from other subunits, hold it temporarily, and transfer it very quickly under the direction of the control unit. There are various types of registers, and they usually are classified by the function they perform. The most common types follow:

- **Accumulator.** A register that accumulates the results of computations such as additions.
- **Storage register.** A register that temporarily holds data being sent to or retrieved from main storage.
- **Address register.** A register that holds the address of a data item.
- **General-purpose register.** A register that can be used for storage, keeping addresses, or as an accumulator. Not all computers have general-purpose registers.

The number and size of registers vary from one computer to another. However, the basic purpose of all registers is to act as temporary storage

Computerized Wedding Gifts

Engaged couples who want to avoid receiving duplicate wedding gifts may now do so through computerized gift processing. A forerunner in this area, Hudson's department stores have computerized the bridal registries in several outlets. The computer keeps track of which requested items have been purchased—even if the purchase was not made at the outlet where the registry was filed. To provide even more accuracy, brides are cross-referenced with grooms, gift wishes, and purchases. This novel application of computer power exemplifies the range of unique tasks in which computers have been found effective.

areas, facilitate the processes carried out by the ALU, and speed up the transfer of data and instructions within the CPU. Note that both the instruction decoder and the program counter are sometimes viewed as forms of registers (see the following sections).

Instruction Decoder Program instructions are stored in main storage in a form that may not be understood by the CPU. The **instruction decoder** contains circuitry that provides signals to the control unit of the CPU indicating the operation to be performed based on the instruction being decoded.

Program Counter The CPU does its job by sequentially executing a list of instructions (the program) in its memory. The function of the **program counter** is to see which instruction is being completed and point to the location of the next instruction to be executed.

STORED-PROGRAM CONCEPT

A better understanding of the components of the CPU can be obtained if we look at the flow of data and instructions through the central processor. The sequence of instructions according to which the CPU processes the data is called the **program.** Each instruction in a program has the same format: an **operation code (op code)** and one or more **operands** (sometimes called **addresses**). The op code tells the control unit what to do (add, divide, compare, and so on), and the operand or operands tell the machine on what data elements the operation has to be performed.

The sequence of instructions is executed in order by the computer unless otherwise indicated. An analogy that illustrates this processing is that of a train moving along a track; each railroad tie represents an instruction. The only time the sequential crossing of ties is interrupted is when a switch has been thrown, resulting in the train's diversion to a siding or an alternate route. The switch inside a computer occurs when an instruction tests data for a certain condition and initiates a

Consulting Computers

In the future, computers are expected to have excellent career prospects as consultants in the field of diagnostic medicine. Two such consulting computers are already in use and appear to be working with great success.

The largest of the two is SUMEX-AIM (Stanford University Medical Experimental Computer—Artificial Intelligence in Medicine). The purpose of the machine is to help the physician match symptoms to possible diagnoses. The system also contains information about drugs and side effects.

According to Stanford's Edward Shortliffe, one of SUMEX-AIM's better points is that it attempts to imitate the physician's reasoning. This includes avoiding the simple diagnosis in favor of listing all possibilities.

The potential of these computers is amazing. The system housed at the University of Pittsburgh, CADUCEUS, has proved this beyond a doubt. CADUCEUS recently passed a section of the internal medicine board examination.

Although they will never replace the family doctor, these diagnostic computers definitely are going to grow in popularity. Among other qualities, they never forget and are always in the office. What they lack in bedside manner, they make up for in memory and availabilty.

sequential flow of instruction execution at another location in the program if that condition is present.

For each instruction, the computer goes through the following cycle (see Figure 5–2):

A. The control unit fetches (gets) the instruction from main storage.
B. The instruction is decoded by the instruction decoder, and the control unit then knows what operation has to be performed and on what data.

Figure 5–2 Machine Cycle

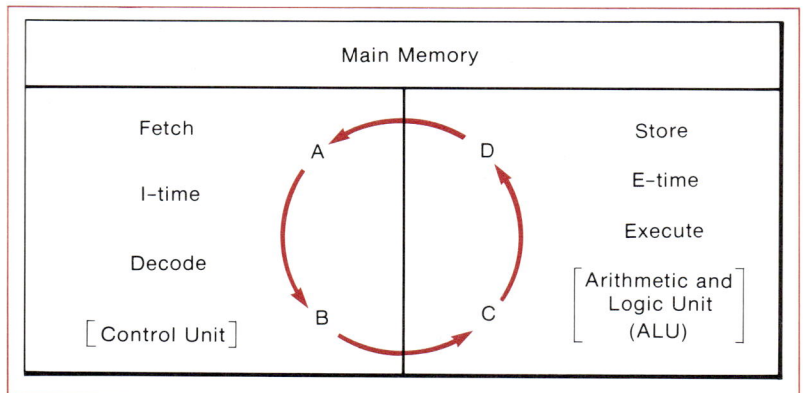

C. The control unit then passes control to the ALU, which performs the necessary operations on the required data.

D. The results of the operation are placed back in memory, and the control unit is ready to fetch the next instruction.

These four steps required to process a single instruction in a program are referred to as a **machine cycle.** A machine cycle is made up of instruction time, or I-time, followed by one or more execution cycles, or E-time. I time involves fetching the instruction and decoding it (the first two steps). E-time involves executing the instruction and storing the results in main memory (the last two steps). E-time may require a few or several execution cycles, depending on the complexity of the operation. For example, addition requires fewer execution cycles than division. The machine cycle for fourth generation computers is measured in **nanoseconds** (a nanosecond is one-billionth of a second; see Figure 5–3).

A major feature of the electronic computer is the fact that the program is stored in the primary storage unit of the CPU. In early computers, instructions had to be wired on control panels and plugged in before a job could be processed. The idea of putting the instructions in main memory—the **stored-program concept**—is particularly effective, because once the program is in storage, it can be executed by the computer with no human intervention, and can interact with the data also in primary storage. The program that is stored in the computer's memory in electronic form now can be processed at electronic speeds, since no mechanical motion is involved.

Entering a new program into primary storage of a computer permits the same computer to be used to perform a new job. In fact, modern computers can store a variety of programs in main memory at the same time and thus perform many different tasks. This general-purpose nature of the digital computer is one of its most significant features.

PRIMARY STORAGE

The primary storage unit already has been discussed under the heading "Central Processing Unit." The variety and importance of primary storage, however, merit a more complete coverage here.

Figure 5–3 Computer Speeds

1 Millisecond	(msec)	= 1/1,000 second
1 Microsecond	(μsec)	= 1/1,000,000 second
1 Nanosecond	(nsec)	= 1/1,000,000,000 second
1 Picosecond	(psec)	= 1/1,000,000,000,000 second

Primary storage is the holding area in which instructions and data are kept within the CPU. For the control unit of the CPU to control and coordinate all processing activity, it must be able to locate each instruction and data item in storage. How does the control unit find the appropriate instruction or data item? To understand this, we can view primary storage as a collection of mailboxes. Each mailbox has a unique address and represents a location in memory (see Figure 5–4). Like the mail in a mailbox, the contents of the storage location can change, but the address always remains the same. With this arrangement, a particular instruction or data item that is held in main storage can be located by knowing its address. It is the responsibility of the programmer to keep track of the address of the storage location of each data item, and this usually is done through the assignment of descriptive names to data items (symbolic or mnemonic names).

In general, primary storage devices are classified according to the type of magnetic or electronic principle used to store data. Some of the common types of storage media used in today's computers are magnetic core storage, semiconductor storage, and bubble storage.

Magnetic Core Storage

Although magnetic core storage is no longer in common use, this section will discuss it in some detail, because its concepts are easily described and apply generally to the more integrated semiconductor and bubble forms of internal storage. **Magnetic core storage** is composed of tiny doughnut-shaped rings made of ferrite and strung on a grid of very thin wires. Each ring is about the size of a pinhead. Since data in computers is stored in binary (base two) form, a two-state device is needed to represent the two binary digits, (sometimes abbreviated to **bits**) 0 (off) and 1 (on). In core storage, each ferrite ring can represent a 0 or 1 bit, depending on its magnetic state. A core magnetized in one direction represents a 1 bit, whereas a core magnetized in the opposite direction represents a 0 bit. Cores are magnetized by sending an electric current through the wires on which the core is strung. The direction in which a core gets magnetized depends on whether the current is sent one way or the other (see Figure 5–5).

Computer Forecasts

The weather affects everyone everywhere. One of the ways that computers affect everyone is through the National Weather Service (NWS). Meteorologists in almost every section of the United States are being given accurate, up-to-date information twice a day by the NWS computer.

Over the last fifteen years, the use of computers has revolutionized the science of weather prediction. New advancements in technology increase the accuracy of weather forecasts by one-half of a percent each year.

The amount of information processed by the NWS computer is both astounding and enlarging. In the summer of 1983, the NWS supercomputer sprang into action—doubling the accuracy of daily forecasts. This system combines the temperatures, weather maps, and so on from over 100,000 separate stations—weather balloons, satellites, airplanes, and ships, as well as 10,000 land-based stations. The system then integrates the information from all these stations.

All in all, we are provided with the most in-depth and accurate analysis of the earth's weather in history: According to the August 2, 1983, issue of Time, "The new machine should by decade's end make eight-day forecasts as accurate as four-day forecasts are today." Just imagine the forecasts by the end of the century!

Core storage is relatively fast, because data can be transferred at rates that vary between two million and four million characters per second. However, semiconductor storage can store more data in less space and is faster, more reliable, and less costly than magnetic core storage; consequently, it has virtually eliminated the use of core storage in today's machines.

Semiconductor Storage

Semiconductor memory consists of hundreds of thousands of tiny electronic circuits etched on a silicon chip. Each of these electronic circuits is referred to as a **bit cell;** it can be in either an off state or an on state

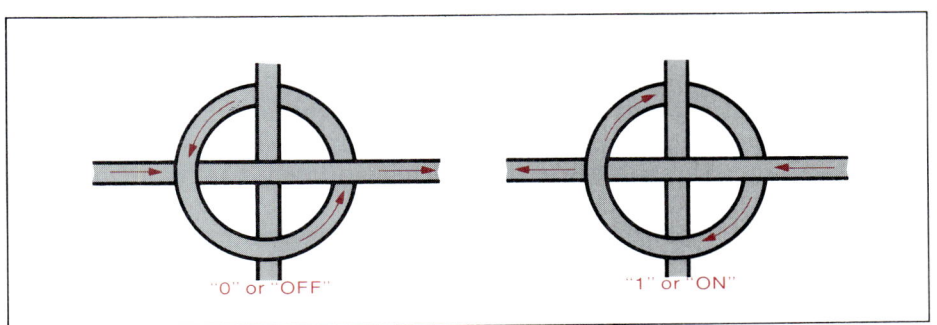

Figure 5–5
Magnetizing a Core

"0" or "OFF"   "1" or "ON"

to represent a 0 bit or 1 bit, depending on whether current is flowing in that cell. Semiconductor memory chips are also called **integrated circuits (ICs)** and are manufactured by processes that are almost completely automated (see Figure 5–6). In recent years, because of mass production and high automation, the cost of semiconductor storage has dropped significantly, so it is now the most widely used primary storage medium. Developments in technology have led to **large-scale integration (LSI)**, which means that more circuits can be squeezed onto the same silicon chip. Today there is **very large scale integration (VLSI)**, which means even further miniaturization.

The advantages of semiconductor storage are speed, reliability, low power consumption, high density, and low cost. However, such storage also has a disadvantage: It is **volatile**, which means it requires a constant power source. If the power fails and there is no backup system, all the stored data is lost. In magnetic core storage, data in main storage is retained even if there is a breakdown, as cores store data in the form of magnetic charges rather than electric current.

With mass production techniques, the cost of a single IC has dropped from around one hundred dollars to less than one dollar, and each chip can hold up to 256,000 bits of information. With the increasing demand

Figure 5–6
Semiconductor Memory Chip

for these chips, costs are expected to go down even farther while even higher packing densities probably will be achieved.

Bubble Storage

One of the most recent technological developments in storage media is the introduction of **bubble memory.** This innovation has taken the microminiaturization of semiconductor storage one step farther, making bubble memory chips the densest chips now manufactured. Bubble memory consists of a very thin crystal of semiconductor material; the molecules of this special crystal act as tiny magnets. The polarity of these molecules, or "magnetic domains," can be switched in an opposite direction by passing a current through a control circuit imprinted on top of the crystal. Data can be stored by changing the polarity of the magnetic domains. Since the principle involved is the same as for magnetic core storage, bubble memories are nonvolatile (data is retained even if there is a power failure). Also, the process of reading from bubble memory is nondestructive. In other words, the data is still present after being read (unlike the data in core storage, which must be electronically regenerated after being read). The magnetic domains, if viewed under a powerful microscope, look like tiny bubbles, giving the memory its name (see Figure 5–7).

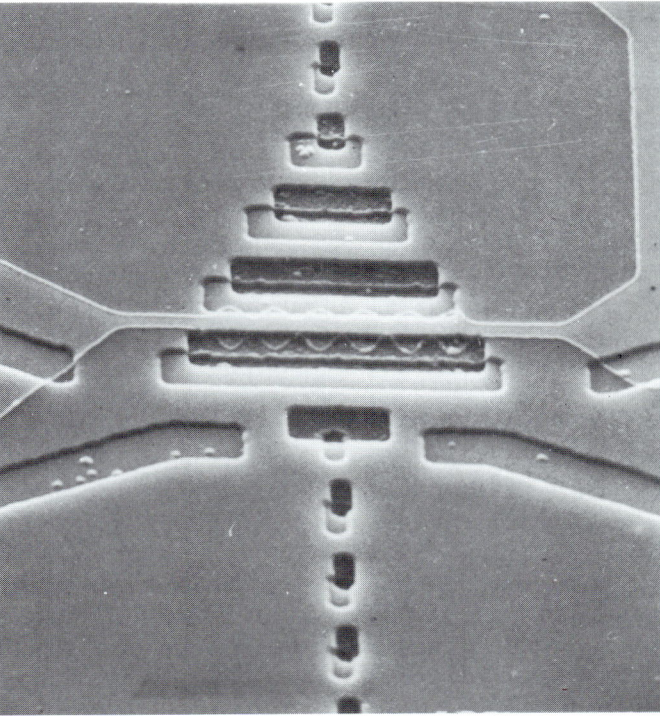

Figure 5–7 Bubble Memory Section Magnified 1,500 Times

Bubbles are much smaller than magnetic cores and consequently can store much more data in a smaller area. Early bubble memories had bubbles about one-tenth the width of a human hair, and a module the size of a quarter could store nearly twenty thousand characters of data (see Figure 5–7). If production problems and high costs can be overcome, bubble memory soon may be a widely used medium not only for main storage, but also for secondary storage.

Until now we have characterized main memory according to the physical principle involved in storing data. Another useful way to classify primary storage is functionally, that is, by what operational features it has. Functional primary storage classifications include the following categories: (1) random-access memory (RAM), (2) read-only memory (ROM), (3) programmable read-only memory (PROM), and (4) erasable programmable read-only memory (EPROM).

Random-Access Memory (RAM)

Random-access memory (RAM) would be better titled read/write random access, since all memories previously mentioned are random access—any location in the memory can be accessed without having to go through all the locations before it. Data can be read (retrieved) and written (stored) into RAM routinely just by giving the computer the correct address of the location where the data is to be stored or retrieved. When data previously stored in such a memory is not needed, the user can just write over it. Core, semiconductor, and bubble storage all have random-access capability (see Figure 5–8).

Read-Only Memory (ROM)

Read-only memory (ROM) is similar to RAM except that the computer user cannot write into it. Instead, in ROM, data or programs are permanently installed (written) into the device by the manufacturer and can never be changed. Consequently, users cannot put any of their own data or programs into ROM, but they can always read whatever is already there. Many complex functions, such as routines to extract square roots, evaluate exponents, and the like, can be placed in ROM. Entire high-level language translators and operating systems often are implemented in ROM for microcomputers. Since these instructions are hard wired, they will be performed quickly and accurately. Another advantage of ROM is that users can order programs tailored for their needs and have them permanently installed in ROM by the manufacturer. Such programs are called microprograms or **firmware.** Microprogramming allows the user to access not only the standard features of a particular machine, but also certain options that otherwise would not be available (see Figure 5–8).

Figure 5–8
Microcomputer with CPU Chip, ROM Chip, and RAM Chip

Programmable Read-Only Memory (PROM)

An alternative to ROM is **programmable read-only memory (PROM),** which can be purchased already programmed by the manufacturer or in a blank state. By receiving a blank memory, the user can enter any programs into the memory. However, once the PROM has been written into, it can never be altered. Thus, the user has the advantage of ROM with the additional flexibility of being able to program the memory so that it meets a unique need. The main disadvantage of PROM is that if a mistake is made and entered into memory, it cannot be corrected. A special device is required to "burn" the program into the PROM.

Erasable Programmable Read-Only Memory (EPROM)

To overcome the drawback of PROM, **erasable programmable read-only memory (EPROM)** has been developed (see Figure 5–9). Like PROMs, EPROMs also can be purchased blank from the manufacturer and programmed locally, again requiring special equipment. The significant feature of the EPROM is that such a memory can be erased. Data and programs can be retrieved over and over without destroying the contents of memory. However, if the user desires, the information stored can be erased by exposing the unit to strong ultraviolet light. This means that a mistake while programming the EPROM is not fatal; the EPROM can

Figure 5–9 EPROM
Chip

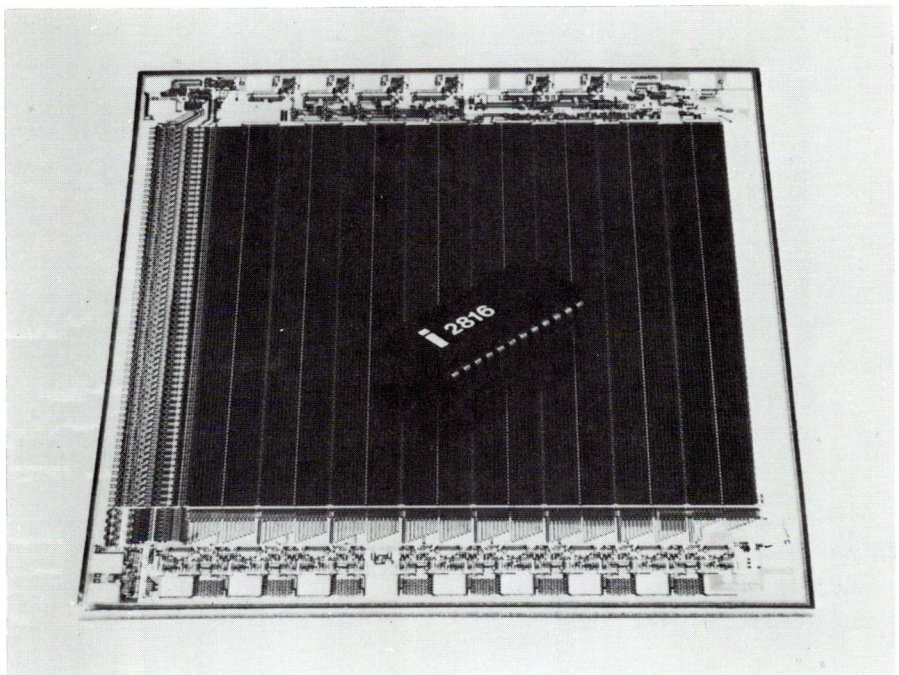

Figure 5–9 EPROM
Chip

be erased and the corrected information entered. Also, EPROMs allow
the user the flexibility of changing programs stored in them if enhanced
versions of those programs become available.

DATA REPRESENTATION

A unique characteristic of the human mind is its ability to construct
and use symbols for communication. Symbols such as the letters making up the English language are combined to form words and sentences,
which then are used to express ideas or convey messages. Communicating with computers also involves symbols. In contrast to the human
brain, which can understand and employ thousands of symbols, the
modern digital computer can understand only two symbols or states: off
(0) and on (1). Thus, all data in a digital computer has to be represented
in this two-state, or binary, form.

Binary Representation

To understand how numbers are represented in binary form, we will
start with the familiar decimal number system. Let us begin by looking
at the number 7,012 and breaking it down into the value of each digit:

$$
\begin{array}{llll}
7 & 0 & 1 & 2 \\
\end{array}
$$

$$
\begin{aligned}
2 \times 10^0 &= 2 \\
1 \times 10^1 &= 10 \\
0 \times 10^2 &= 0 \\
7 \times 10^3 &= \underline{7{,}000} \\
&\ \underline{7{,}012}
\end{aligned}
\quad \text{or} \quad
\begin{array}{cccc}
7 & 0 & 1 & 2 \\
\times & \times & \times & \times \\
10^3 & 10^2 & 10^1 & 10^0
\end{array}
$$

$$7000 + 0 + 10 + 2 = \underline{7{,}012}$$

Thus, each digit in a number has a special meaning that depends on its position, or "place value." Each position represents a certain power of 10, the **base** of the decimal system. The extreme right position is the units position; the next position to the immediate left is the 10s position; and as we keep moving toward the left, each position represents an incremental power of 10. This is illustrated here:

10^5	10^4	10^3	10^2	10^1	10^0
100,000	10,000	1,000	100	10	1

The decimal system has ten symbols—0 through 9—to represent all numbers. It is a base 10 system. The **binary system** has only two symbols—0 and 1—to represent all numbers, and it is therefore a base 2 system. The principle of representing numbers is the same, except that each position now represents a power of 2 rather than 10. Let us consider the binary number 11011 and analyze it to see what decimal number it represents:

$$
\begin{array}{lllll}
1 & 1 & 0 & 1 & 1 \\
\end{array}
$$

$$
\begin{aligned}
1 \times 2^0 &= 1 \\
1 \times 2^1 &= 2 \\
0 \times 2^2 &= 0 \\
1 \times 2^3 &= 8 \\
1 \times 2^4 &= \underline{16} \\
&\ \underline{27}
\end{aligned}
\quad \text{or} \quad
\begin{array}{ccccc}
1 & 1 & 0 & 1 & 1 \\
\times & \times & \times & \times & \times \\
2^4 & 2^3 & 2^2 & 2^1 & 2^0
\end{array}
$$

$$16 + 8 + 0 + 2 + 1 = \underline{27}$$

Thus, the binary number 11011 is equivalent to the decimal number 27. Place values in the binary system are as follows:

2^6	2^5	2^4	2^3	2^2	2^1	2^0
64	32	16	8	4	2	1

The following is another example, the binary equivalent of the decimal number 182, which turns out to be 10110110.

$$
\begin{array}{llllllll}
1 & 0 & 1 & 1 & 0 & 1 & 1 & 0 \\
\end{array}
$$

$$
\begin{aligned}
0 \times 2^0 &= 0 \\
1 \times 2^1 &= 2 \\
1 \times 2^2 &= 4 \\
0 \times 2^3 &= 0 \\
1 \times 2^4 &= 16 \\
1 \times 2^5 &= 32 \\
0 \times 2^6 &= 0 \\
1 \times 2^7 &= \underline{128} \\
&\ \underline{182}
\end{aligned}
\quad \text{or} \quad
\begin{array}{cccccccc}
1 & 0 & 1 & 1 & 0 & 1 & 1 & 0 \\
\times & \times & \times & \times & \times & \times & \times & \times \\
2^7 & 2^6 & 2^5 & 2^4 & 2^3 & 2^2 & 2^1 & 2^0
\end{array}
$$

$$128 + 0 + 32 + 16 + 0 + 4 + 2 + 0 = \underline{182}$$

Although the binary number system may seem awkward to us, it is perfect for digital computers, as it employs only two binary digits (or bits), 0 and 1, and this is compatible with the on/off logic of electrical circuits.

Hexadecimal Representation

The **hexadecimal** (base 16) **number system** is used by many large computers, including those in the IBM System/370 series, to show the contents of memory (the **core dump** or **memory dump**). A programmer may want to look at what is stored in memory at different locations if a program is not being executed properly because of some error (see Figure 5–10). If the core dump or memory dump is printed in binary form, the way the data actually is stored, the programmer would have a difficult time locating the error, staring at a seemingly unending list of 1s and 0s.

Listing the memory contents in hexadecimal notation has the following advantages:

- Printing time and space requirements are reduced by about three-fourths.
- Hexadecimal notation is simpler to read than binary notation.

Figure 5–10 Memory or Core Dump

9000D203	9000C11E	41330004	4650C05A
0010E020	C1220064	E020C186	006407FE
40F0F740	40F0F840	4040F540	40F2F340
40404040	40404040	40F2F340	40F2F340
40F4F640	40F2F540	40F1F240	40F2F440
4040F640	40F6F640	40F8F540	40404040
40F0F840	40F2F540	40F3F140	4040F540
F2F5F640	F7F8F940	F1F2F540	F6F2F440
00000005	00000005	00000006	00000007
0000000F	00000010	00000015	00000017
00000018	00000018	00000019	00000019
00000035	00000035	00000037	00000038
00000055	00000055	00000060	0000007D
0000022B	0000022B	0000022B	0000022B
0000022B	00000315	F0E3C8C5	40E4D5E2
E2D6D9E3	C5C440C1	D9D9C1E8	F1F5F5F5
F5F5F5F5	F5F5F5F5	F5F5F5F5	F5F5F5F5
F5F5F5F5	F5F5F5F5	F5F5F5F5	F5F5F5F5

THE CHIP MAKING PROCESS

Integrated circuitry, synonymous with silicon chips, is the technology responsible for making computers perform faster and more economically. The chip making process requires sophisticated engineering and manufacturing techniques. The following photographs show many of the steps involved in this complex process.

1. Traditionally, the design phase started with circuit designers drafting huge (8 sq. ft.) "blueprint-like diagrams" of the circuit. The diagram contains thousands of intricate lines that represent the circuit's electrical pathways. This hand-drawn information was then converted into computer memory by a process known as digitizing. The movable vertical device shown here optically scans the diagram and translates each line into a form recognizable by the computer. **2.** Today, experimental systems are being used to design circuitry directly on the computer. This is made possible by computer-assisted design (CAD) technology. Here, engineers examine a portion of an integrated circuit on a color graphics display terminal.

Chip Making Process—continued. **3.** The model generated by the digitized or CAD process is then stored on tape and used to prepare a photomask. The reduced negative shown here is a photomask; it contains the same intricate lines as the hand-drawn diagram. Employees who work with the chip making process wear protective clothing called "bunny suits" in a specially created environment called a "clean room." **4.** The photomask is scaled down even further in this step. The final photomask is the size of a single chip—1/100 of a square inch. The photomask will be used in a highly refined photoengraving process that "etches" the circuitry onto a silicon wafer. **5.** After the wafers are bathed in a type of photographic emulsion, called *photoresist,* the scaled down photomasks are placed over each wafer. Shown here is a worker carefully aligning the mask over the wafer using a high-powered microscope to ensure perfect registration. Once the mask is in place, the wafer is exposed to ultraviolet light. The ultraviolet light causes the patterns from the photomask to be etched onto the wafer.

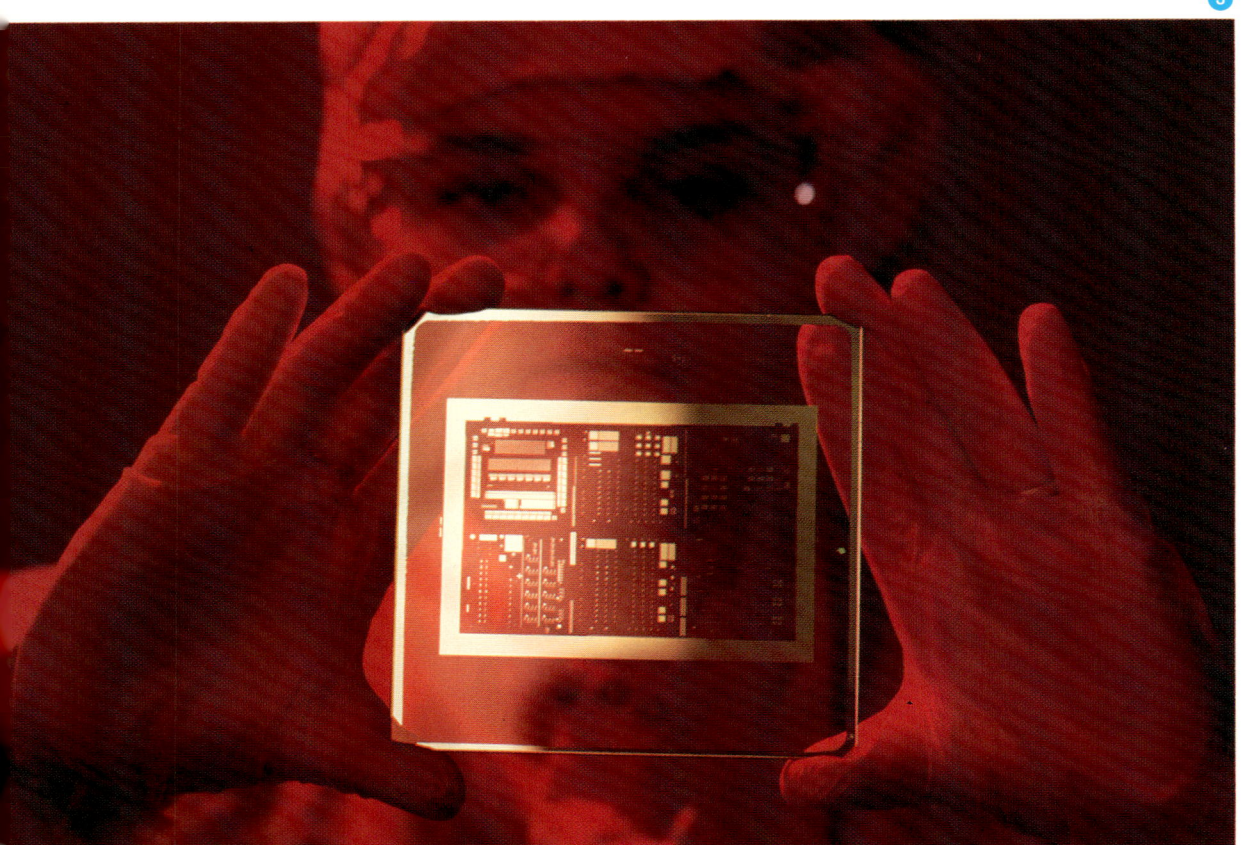

④

⑤

The Chip Making Process—continued. **6.** The next step is the acid bath. At this step, parts not exposed to the ultraviolet light are washed away, leaving the layer of elements formed by the photomask. **7.** The process is continued, alternating photomasks and acid baths until the layering process is completed. The choice of elements and the sequence in which they are applied creates the chip's electronic properties.

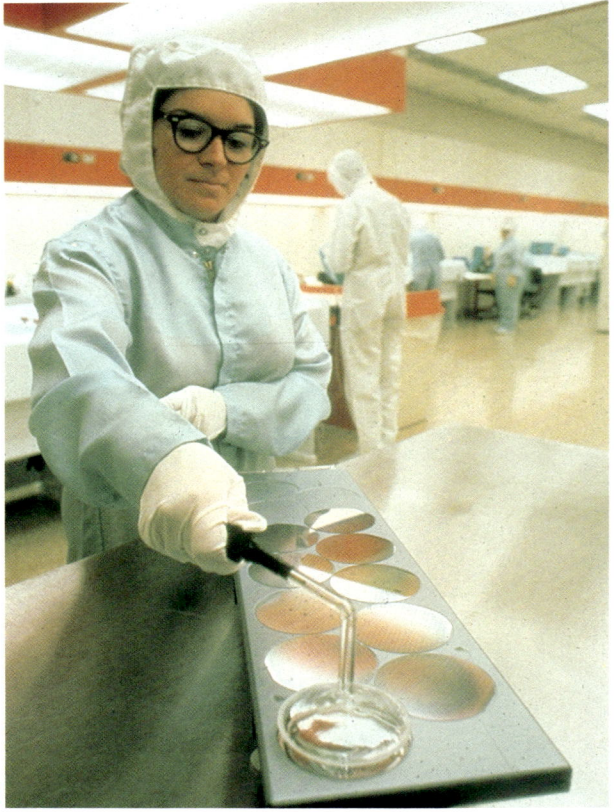

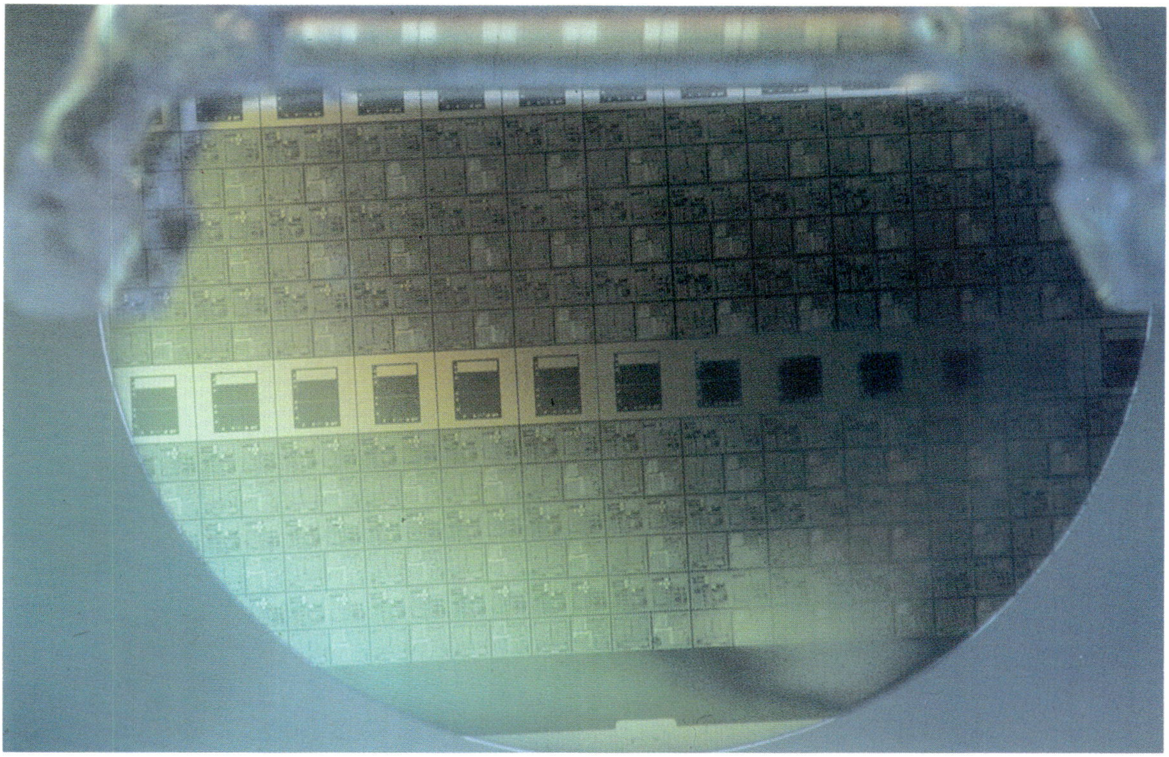

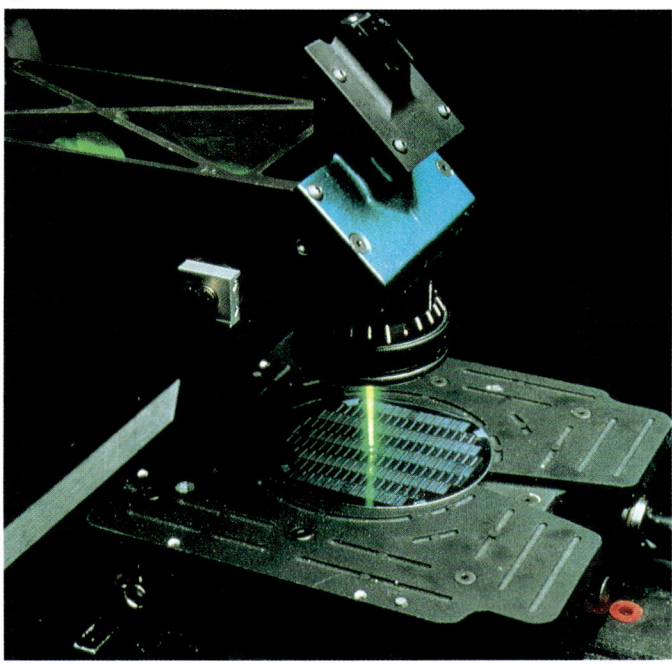

8. Here is a completed wafer containing three hundred chips. Upon close examination, you can see that each square has been engraved with circuitry. **9.** Next, the wafer is cut apart into individual chips by a laser process. Laser beams are used for the necessary cutting precision.

The Chip Making Process—continued. **10.** Here, selected chips have been cut from the wafer. **11.** Now the chip is mounted onto a carrier. The gold wires surrounding the chip connect it to other chips and circuitry. **12.** This is a RAM chip.

The Chip Making Process—continued. **13.** Finally, the chips (in their carriers) are assembled according to function onto circuit boards.

● The conversion from hexadecimal to binary notation and vice versa is much easier and quicker than the equivalent conversion between decimal and binary notation.

● Conversion from hexadecimal to decimal notation is somewhat more convenient than from binary to decimal notation.

Since the hexadecimal system is a base 16 system, it requires sixteen digits—0 through 15—to represent data. The letters A through F represent the values 10 to 15 as single symbols to distinguish the hexadecimal, or "hex," from the decimal system. Each position in hexadecimal notation represents a power of 16, which is the same as 2^4; consequently, four binary digits can be represented by a single hexadecimal number. This allows for easy conversion from binary to hexadecimal notation and vice versa (see Figure 5–11). Hexadecimal is a compressed, or shorthand, notation for binary notation.

See Appendix A for a more detailed discussion of numbering systems, including guidelines for converting between different bases.

Binary System (Place Values) 8 4 2 1	Hexadecimal Equivalent	Decimal Equivalent
0 0 0 0	0	0
0 0 0 1	1	1
0 0 1 0	2	2
0 0 1 1	3	3
0 1 0 0	4	4
0 1 0 1	5	5
0 1 1 0	6	6
0 1 1 1	7	7
1 0 0 0	8	8
1 0 0 1	9	9
1 0 1 0	A	10
1 0 1 1	B	11
1 1 0 0	C	12
1 1 0 1	D	13
1 1 1 0	E	14
1 1 1 1	F	15

Figure 5–11 Binary, Hexadecimal, and Decimal Equivalent Values

Processing in Chinese

Processing information in English-like statements is relatively easy. Processing information in Chinese-like statements is quite another matter. Until January 1983 it was immensely impractical to do word processing or effectively use high-level languages in Chinese. The problem stemmed from the fact that the Chinese language is composed of twenty-two thousand characters. In turn, each of these characters is composed of several strokes. Because of the complexity of the alphabet, it would take thirty-two bytes to store a single character. The amount of memory needed to accommodate that size of storage per character made the use of microcomputers nearly impossible.

All of that has changed now because of Taiwan's Chinese Character Controller. It is composed of two parts: (1) the Dragon Coding System, which codes specific strokes to save memory, and (2) the Dragon Character-Generating System, which decodes those same strokes for the printer. The Chinese Character Controller, made for the Microprofessor II Chinese (MPF-II-C) computer, allows its 64K memory to be used as effectively as that of its Western counterparts.

Computer Codes

Digital computers use the binary system for representing numbers, but different coding schemes become necessary for handling both individual numeric and alphabetic (alphanumeric) characters. Since most business applications require the manipulation of alphanumeric data, modern computers use such different codes to represent data. Three popular codes are the binary coded decimal (BCD) system, the Extended Binary Coded Decimal Interchange Code (EBCDIC), and the American Standard Code for Information Interchange (ASCII).

Binary Coded Decimal (BCD) System In the **binary coded decimal (BCD)** system, each alphanumeric character is represented by six bits. The two leftmost bits are called **zone bits,** and the remaining four bits are the **numeric bits.** Different combinations of the zone and numeric bits are used to represent the digits 0 through 9; the letters **A** through **Z;** and special characters like the period, comma, and so on.

The letters A through I are assigned zone bits 11; the letters J through R are assigned zone bits 10; and the letters S through Z have the zone bits 01. The numbers 0 through 9 all have the zone bits 00, followed by the four-bit binary representation of the number except for 0. The six-bit BCD code for 0 is 001010, because the code 000000 is used for the "blank" character. The six-bit BCD code for the alphabet and numbers is shown in Figure 5–12.

A	11 0001
B	11 0010
C	11 0011
D	11 0100
E	11 0101
F	11 0110
G	11 0111
H	11 1000
I	11 1001
J	10 0001
K	10 0010
L	10 0011
M	10 0100
N	10 0101
O	10 0110
P	10 0111
Q	10 1000
R	10 1001
S	01 0010
T	01 0011
U	01 0100
V	01 0101
W	01 0110
X	01 0111
Y	01 1000
Z	01 1001
0	00 1010
1	00 0001
2	00 0010
3	00 0011
4	00 0100
5	00 0101
6	00 0110
7	00 0111
8	00 1000
9	00 1001

Figure 5–12 Six-Bit BCD Code

Extended Binary Coded Decimal Interchange Code (EBCDIC) The six-bit BCD code can represent a maximum of 2^6, or sixty-four, different characters. To represent more than sixty-four characters it is necessary to have more than six bits. The **Extended Binary Coded Decimal Interchange Code** (EBCDIC), developed by IBM, uses eight bits and permits 2^8, or 256, different combinations. Whereas the six-bit BCD code could be used to represent only uppercase alphabetic characters because of the limited combinations, eight-bit EBCDIC allows both uppercase and lowercase letters to be represented, as well as even some additional special characters such as the quotation mark. The leftmost four bits of the eight-bit EBCDIC code are the zone bits, and the other four bits are the numeric bits. The EBCDIC code for uppercase letters and numbers is shown in Figure 5–13. A variant on EBCDIC, called the **packed decimal code,** is sometimes used to represent decimal digits in four bits, permitting two such digits to be contained in one eight-bit byte. A byte is the number of bits required to represent any character in a computer code–usually eight bits.

Figure 5–13 EBCDIC and ASCII-8 Codes

Character	EBCDIC Binary	ASCII-8 Binary
A	1100 0001	1010 0001
B	1100 0010	1010 0010
C	1100 0011	1010 0011
D	1100 0100	1010 0100
E	1100 0101	1010 0101
F	1100 0110	1010 0110
G	1100 0111	1010 0111
H	1100 1000	1010 1000
I	1100 1001	1010 1001
J	1101 0001	1010 1010
K	1101 0010	1010 1011
L	1101 0011	1010 1100
M	1101 0100	1010 1101
N	1101 0101	1010 1110
O	1101 0110	1010 1111
P	1101 0111	1011 0000
Q	1101 1000	1011 0001
R	1101 1001	1011 0010
S	1110 0010	1011 0011
T	1110 0011	1011 0100
U	1110 0100	1011 0101
V	1110 0101	1011 0110
W	1110 0110	1011 0111
X	1110 0111	1011 1000
Y	1110 1000	1011 1001
Z	1110 1001	1011 1010
0	1111 0000	0101 0000
1	1111 0001	0101 0001
2	1111 0010	0101 0010
3	1111 0011	0101 0011
4	1111 0100	0101 0100
5	1111 0101	0101 0101
6	1111 0110	0101 0110
7	1111 0111	0101 0111
8	1111 1000	0101 1000
9	1111 1001	0101 1001

American Standard Code for Information Interchange (ASCII) The
American Standard Code for Information Interchange (ASCII) is a seven-
bit code developed through the cooperation of several computer manufacturers for use in the transmission and processing of data. Since most
computers are designed to handle eight-bit codes, ASCII-8—an eight-bit
version of ASCII—is more popular. The ASCII bit pattern for uppercase
letters and numbers is shown in Figure 5–13 alongside the EBCDIC notation.

Bits and Bytes

A **bit** is a single binary digit and represents the smallest unit of data.
Computers do not usually operate on single bits but manipulate a fixed
number of adjacent bits. Commonly, the smallest unit on which a computer operates has eight bits, and this is called a **byte.** We know that the
EBCDIC and ASCII-8 codes use eight bits—that is, one byte—to represent a character. Thus, computers can manipulate individual bytes (single characters), and these eight-bit groupings are the basic units of memory. Main storage capacity usually is indicated in bytes, and the symbol
K is used when memory size is quite large. One K is 2^{10}, or 1,024, units;
thus, if a computer has 128K bytes of main storage, it can hold 128 ×
1,024, or 131,072 characters of data in memory. Microcomputers may
have as little as 2K of main storage, whereas large mainframes can have
more than 1,000K. In reality, the capacity of primary storage is very
limited and used primarily to hold program instructions rather than
data. In activities requiring the processing of large quantities of data, a
small portion of main memory is allocated to hold data and is replen-
ished from an input device when necessary.

Code Checking

Computers are not infallible machines, as some people might believe;
malfunctions do occur. When data is being transmitted within the CPU,
or from the CPU to a remote terminal or vice versa, information bits
can get lost. The loss may be due to environmental conditions like dust,
moisture, or magnetic fields, or it may be due to equipment failure. A
technique used to detect such errors is the **parity check.** To an eight-bit
code such as EBCDIC or ASCII-8, a ninth bit—called the **parity bit,** or
check bit—is added.

A computer may be designed for odd parity or even parity. In the case
of odd parity, an odd number of 1 bits is used to represent every character, whereas under even parity, an even number of 1 bits represents
each character. The parity bit is set internally to either 0 or 1 so that
the coded character will contain an odd or even number of 1 bits, as
required.

To insure that data is being transmitted correctly, the internal circuitry of the computer constantly checks that each character has the
correct number of 1 bits. For example, the letter A in EBCDIC code

would be represented by 0 1100 0001 under odd parity (the total number of 1 bits is 3, which is odd, so the parity bit is 0). If a 1 bit were lost during transmission, the number of 1 bits would be 2, which is even; the computer would know that an error had occurred and would retransmit the character. However, an error where two 1 bits were lost would not be detected as the total number of 1 bits would remain odd. However, the loss of two 1 bits occurs rarely, and there are multicharacter checks capable of detecting such a loss.

At this point, it also should be pointed out that the computer cannot detect the use of incorrect input, such as entering the number 67 instead of 76. Billing mistakes by computers almost always are attributable to incorrect input, or in computer jargon, to GIGO.

● The central processing unit (CPU), the workhorse of a computer system, processes all data. It is composed of three units: the control unit, the arithmetic and logic unit (ALU), and the primary storage unit. The control unit supervises and coordinates all activity in the CPU; the ALU performs arithmetic and logical operations, and the primary storage unit holds all data and instructions for processing.

● Other functional components of the CPU are registers, the program counter, and the instruction decoder. Registers are used for quick transfer of data and as temporary holding areas. The instruction decoder decodes instructions for the CPU, and the program counter keeps track of which instruction is to be executed next.

● All instructions are placed in consecutive locations in memory and are executed sequentially. The complete steps required to process a single instruction are referred to as the machine cycle. A machine cycle consists of I-time (the time required to fetch and decode an instruction) and E-time (the time required to execute an instruction).

● The stored-program concept involves storing both instructions and data in primary storage so that processing can be accomplished without human intervention.

● Each location in storage has a unique address and can be located by the control unit of the CPU during processing. The programmer also should know the symbolic or mnemonic address of each data item stored in memory.

● Data can be stored in memory by using magnetic cores that can be set to on and off states by the passage of electric current. The most common form of storage is semiconductor memory, which uses electronic circuits etched on a silicon chip. Semiconductor storage is denser and faster than core memory but requires a constant power source. Bubble memory consists of magnetized spots resting on a thin film of semiconductor material. Very high storage densities are possible, and the bubbles retain their magnetism even if there is a power loss.

● Random-access memory (RAM) allows data to be accessed without having to search all locations sequentially. Read-only memory (ROM) is similar to RAM except that data stored in it cannot be changed. Microprograms are instructions built into ROM to carry out complex functions that otherwise would be directed by stored program instructions at a much slower speed.

- Programmable read-only memory (PROM) can be programmed by either the manufacturer or the user to meet special requirements. Since PROMs cannot be corrected, erasable programmable read-only memories (EPROMs) have been developed to provide maximum flexibility.

- Data is represented in the computer in a two-state, or binary, form. A 1 in a given position indicates the presence of a power of 2; 0 indicates its absence. Hexadecimal, or base 16, notation is used to represent binary data in a concise form. Memory contents are printed in hexadecimal notation and used by programmers to locate programming errors.

- The six-bit binary coded decimal (BCD) system permits sixty-four unique bit combinations and is used to represent alphabetic, numeric, and twenty-eight special characters. Both EBCDIC and ASCII-8 are eight-bit coding systems capable of representing up to 256 different characters.

- Bits represent the smallest unit of data. Computers usually do not manipulate bits, but bytes. A byte commonly has eight bits, and main storage capacity is most often expressed in bytes.

- Parity bits, or check bits, are used to detect errors during the transmission of data.

1. What are the three major components of the CPU? Briefly discuss the function of each.

2. Name the operational units of the CPU other than the three major components. Explain the function of each of these.

3. What are the two components of an instruction? Explain the function of each.

4. What are the four steps required to process a single instruction? Distinguish between I-time and E-time.

5. Explain what is meant by the stored-program concept. Discuss why it is important in electronic data processing.

6. Name three types of primary storage technologies. What are the significant features of each, and what impact have these had on modern computers?

7. Explain the concept of read-only memory. How does it relate to microprogramming?

8. What are PROMs and EPROMs? What advantage do they offer over ROMs?

9. What are the features of a binary number system? Why is it particularly suitable for digital computers?

10. What is the relationship between the hexadecimal number system and the binary number system? Give one common use of hexadecimal representation.

11. Why are computer codes necessary? Briefly discuss the six-bit BCD code.

12. Briefly describe the EBCDIC and ASCII codes. What advantage do the EBCDIC and ASCII-8 codes have over the six-bit BCD code?

13. Distinguish between bits and bytes. What is the smallest unit on which the CPU can operate?

14. What is a parity check? Why is it necessary?

15. What is the parity of 0 1100 1010?

16. Convert HELLO to five ASCII-8 bytes.

STORAGE

LEARNING OBJECTIVES

This chapter concerns itself with storage devices and how the data on them can be accessed. After carefully examining it, you will know the following:

☐ The difference between primary and secondary storage devices.
☐ How each device stores data.
☐ The advantages and disadvantages of each medium.
☐ The difference between sequential and direct access, as well as the advantages and disadvantages of each.
☐ What mass storage is, along with how and why it used.

Chapter 6

INTRODUCTION

In Chapter 5 the concept of primary storage was discussed. Primary storage, however, typically requires the support of larger capacity *secondary storage* or memory in order to function effectively. This chapter examines the elements of data for which secondary storage is necessary and then addresses the most common forms of secondary storage devices: magnetic tape and magnetic disk. Brief discussions of semiconductor, bubble, and mass storage as secondary memory are also included.

Data can be entered into the computer by many different methods. This data then is processed into information and displayed in some form of output to the user. A mechanical adding machine follows this same sequence of events: input, processing, and output; however, a mechanical adding machine is limited in speed by the person pushing the buttons. The features that separate a mechanical adding machine from a computer are the computer's smaller amount of mechanization and, more important, the computer's ability to automatically retrieve information when needed and store it for future use. This recall ability, or "memory" (data storage), allows the computer to work at speeds much faster than those of a mechanical adding machine, because data is entered electronically rather than manually.

There are several data storage devices available today, the majority of which already have been discussed as input devices and which also fall into the output device category. A data storage device can fall into either of these categories, depending upon what use the current computer application makes of it; however, when the device sits idle, with no interaction between it and the computer, it retains data and is therefore a data storage device (see Figure 6–1). When the computer needs data from the storage device, it reads and obtains the data, and the device functions as an input medium. After the data has been processed and the results are to be saved for future use, the information is written on the device, now being employed as an output medium. (We actually are using the terms **device** and **medium** somewhat loosely here. The device really consists of the electronic and mechanical components necessary to transmit data between the computer and the medium on which the data is recorded. A tape drive—or unit or transport, as it is sometimes called—is a device; the magnetic tape itself is the medium).

DATA HIERARCHY

Before we can intelligently discuss storage devices, we must introduce the units of data that we record on, and retrieve from, these devices. Some of the following will be a review of information discussed earlier; some will be new.

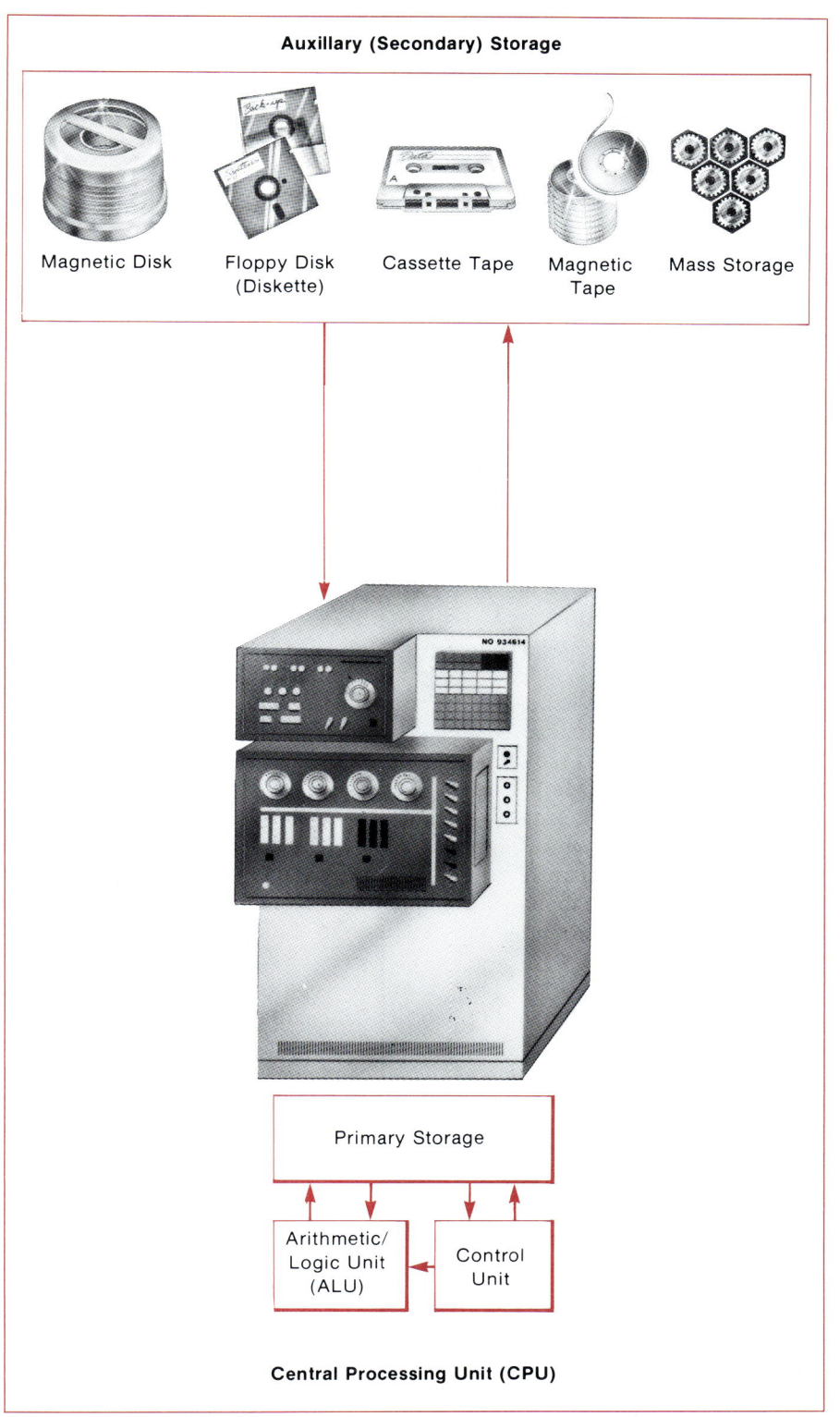

Auxillary (Secondary) Storage

Magnetic Disk Floppy Disk (Diskette) Cassette Tape Magnetic Tape Mass Storage

Primary Storage

Arithmetic/ Logic Unit (ALU) Control Unit

Central Processing Unit (CPU)

Figure 6—1
Secondary (Auxiliary) Storage for a Computer System

The data hierarchy, presented in increasing order of size, consists of the **bit, character (byte), field, record,** and **file.** The concept of **data base** (presented in Chapter 13) sometimes is included in the data hierarchy following **file;** we will omit it from discussion at this time. Each component of the data hierarchy usually is composed of a related grouping of the previous component in the list:

1. **Bit.** The smallest element of data, described as **bistable** because it can represent only one of two possible values (generally coded as 0 and 1) at any time. The word **bit** is a contraction of the words **bi**nary digi**t.**

2. **Character.** A group of related bits (usually eight in today's computing environment) representing a letter, number, or other symbol (such as a punctuation mark). All characters in computer storage devices are represented as **bytes,** although bytes can be used to represent other things besides characters.

3. **Field.** One or more related characters conveying a unit of information. Fields, also known as **data items, data elements,** and **data attributes,** may be alphabetic, numeric, or alphanumeric; they also may be of fixed or variable length. A Social Security number, for example, is a fixed-length (nine-digit) numeric field; a person's last name is a variable-length alphabetic field.

4. **Record.** A group of related fields all pertaining to the same person, thing, or event. An inventory record, for example, might consist of fields for part number, item name, item description, price, supplier, quantity on hand, and warehouse location.

5. **File.** A collection of related records, usually all in the same format. All the subscriber records for a magazine would constitute that publication's subscriber file.

SECONDARY (AUXILIARY) STORAGE

Primary versus Secondary Storage

Storage devices are divided into two main categories: primary storage and secondary storage. Primary storage, composed of all storage devices considered to be part of the CPU, contains all procedures and instructions used by the computer to carry out programs and perform certain functions. Primary storage was discussed in Chapter 5. Secondary (auxiliary) storage devices, which will be discussed in this chapter, are considered to be all storage devices that are not part of the CPU. These auxiliary devices include magnetic tape, disks, external semiconductor and bubble memory, and several different types of mass storage such as high-density magnetic tapes and disks. Most secondary storage devices are connected to the CPU by a set of small wires (similar to an electrical extension cord) that plug into each device. Storage devices connected to the CPU in this manner are referred to as being **soft wired.** Some storage devices, in contrast, are attached to the CPU in a more permanent manner: the storage device and the CPU appear to be the same piece of equipment, but they are really two separate pieces packaged together. When a secondary storage device is connected to a CPU in this manner, it is referred to as being **hard wired.** No matter which type of connection the secondary storage device uses, the CPU and the secondary storage device are considered separate devices.

Primary storage is capable of storing and retrieving information at very high speeds, because no mechanization is involved. The size of this data storage area has been limited, however, because of extremely high costs and the current level of technology. Because of this limitation, secondary storage devices are used to supply the desired information to the CPU at a speed relatively slower than primary storage, but still faster than any human could enter it by keypunching. These secondary storage devices are much cheaper than primary storage devices and can store much larger quantities of data. Secondary storage devices include the traditional devices of magnetic tape and magnetic disk, as well as the more sophisticated semiconductor memory known as **micro chips.**

Traditional Storage Devices

Historically, the most common secondary storage devices have been magnetic media, including **magnetic tape, magnetic disks (hard disks),** and **floppy disks (diskettes).** Data can be stored indefinitely as magnetized spots arranged on the surface of the medium or can be erased and reused if desired. Because of the differences in physical design, the methods by which magnetic tapes and magnetic disks process and access data are different. Magnetic tapes must rewind or advance the tape to read a particular piece of information, much like a cassette or reel-to-reel audio tape must advance or rewind to play a requested song. Since data must be read or scanned in the sequence in which it was recorded, the magnetic tape is known as a **sequential-access storage device (SASD).** A magnetic disk, in contrast, can access data at random, much like any song can be played on a record by placing the needle in the appropriate groove before the song. Because of this ability to access data anywhere, magnetic disks are referred to as being random-access or **direct-access storage devices (DASDs).**

Magnetic Tape Magnetic tape is made of plastic with a coating of iron oxide that can be magnetized in particular areas to represent data. A typical tape is 0.5 inch wide and 2,400 feet long and sells for less than twenty-five dollars. The amount of data or the number of characters that can be represented in an inch of tape is known as the tape's **density.** Some average tape densities are 800, 1,600, and 6,250 bytes per inch (bpi); this last density is equivalent to seventy-eight punched cards on one inch of tape. Figure 6–2 shows how data records are recorded electronically on magnetic tape. The read/write head magnetically senses (reads) or records (writes) coded data under direction of the CPU.

Each record on the tape is separated from the next by a relatively large section of blank tape. These blank areas in the tape, called **interrecord**

Figure 6—2 Recording
on a Magnetic Tape

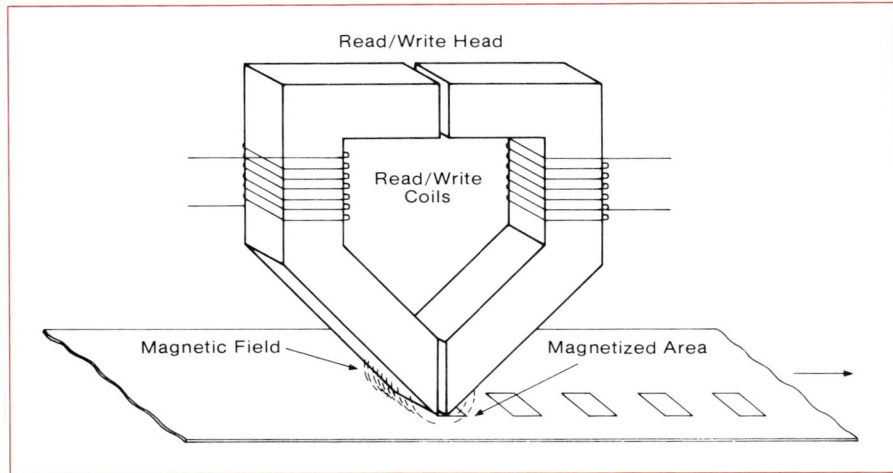

gaps **(IRGs),** signal to the CPU where a record starts and stops (see Figure 6–3). If the records are of different lengths, they are known as **variable-length records,** and if all the record lengths are equal, they are known as **fixed-length records.** The blank sections on each end of a record are usually only fractions of an inch wide but can be as large as three-fourths of an inch. If the records are small, as much as one-half of the entire tape can be wasted because of excessive IRGs. To eliminate some of the wasted space, blocked records were designed (see Figure 6–4).

Blocked records are groups of records joined together in blocks of equal size, with each block separated by an **interblock gap (IBG).** These blocked records can be read into the computer a block at a time, whereas unblocked records must be read one at a time. Each time the tape device reads data from the tape, a delay is caused by IRGs and IBGs, because the device must start and stop each time one is encountered. Therefore, blocked records have two advantages over unblocked records: (1) the elimination of wasted space and (2) increased data entry speeds (see Figure 6–4). Blocked records are also called **physical records** (a name also used for individual records recorded on tape without blocking). **Logical records** are individual data records, several of which may be grouped

Figure 6—3 Magnetic
Tape with Interrecord
Gaps

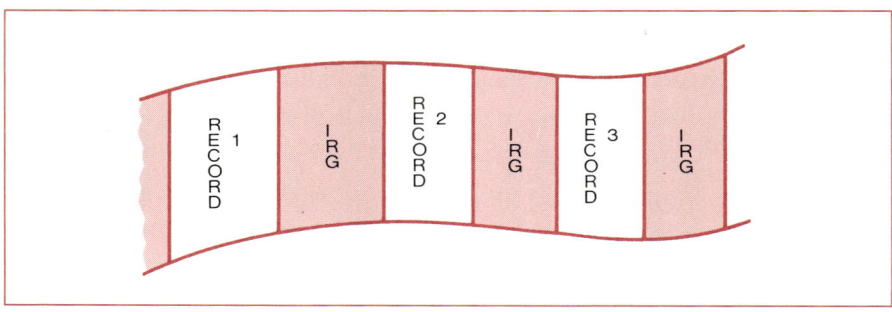

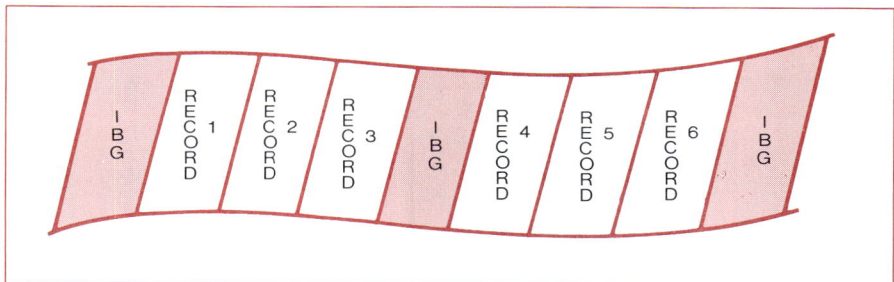

Figure 6—4 Magnetic Tape with Interblock Gaps

to form a block. Typically, logical records are processed one at a time, and software is used to separate individual logical records from a block.

When magnetic tapes are processed, there are usually at least two tapes involved—one used as input and one used as output. To change any information on a tape, the tape device must change directions several times for an item to be read and then rewritten. Magnetic tapes are capable of reading and writing at speeds of twenty-five to two hundred inches of tape per second; if the tape device is continuously changing directions, this speed and the computer's efficiency are reduced drastically (see Figure 6–5). Small variations in gap size also make it difficult to modify data on a tape. An advantage to using a system of multiple tapes is that in case of emergencies—such as a tape's being destroyed or accidentally erased—there is always a backup tape available. These backup tapes often are saved until the information they contain has been updated at least twice, or for two generations. When a tape is updated, the newly created tape is known as the **son,** and the tape that was used to create the son is known as the **father.** When the son is used to create another updated tape, a new generation is formed in which the father becomes a **grandfather,** the son becomes a father, and the newly created tape is the new son. These three generations of tapes usually are retained for backup use in emergencies, and any tapes older than a grandfather are erased and reused **(scratched).**

Magnetic tape drives, the devices which permit recording on and reading from magnetic tapes, are similar in concept to reel-to-reel audio tape decks. They are, however, designed to work at higher speeds and to start and stop with greater precision.

Sequential Access Since processing with magnetic tapes is accomplished sequentially, most applications use **batch mode processing,** where transaction records (records modifying the information already on tape) are arranged in the same order as the information on the main (master) magnetic tape. In batch mode a transaction record is read, and then the master tape is read until the desired record is found. The data from the old record is read and combined with the data on the transaction record, and the resulting information is placed on the new magnetic tape. After this information has been written onto the new tape, another transaction record is read, and the process starts over. In batch mode processing the magnetic tape is never required to rewind, because the

Figure 6–5 Magnetic
Tape Drive

transaction records are arranged in the same order as the master tape, and each medium is advanced through a file simultaneously. Transactions can be recorded on punched cards, disks, floppy disks, or magnetic tape.

If the transaction records contain a record not found on the tape, this new record can be inserted in the proper location. Since the files are arranged in a sorted sequence (for example, by part number), the tape will advance until it gets to the record that would appear after the new record. For example, if the transaction record contained part 632 and the master record contained parts 600, 615, 630, 640, and 650, the tape would advance to part 630 and advance again, because part 632 should appear after this. When the program encountered part 640, it would realize it had passed the location where part 632 should appear and would insert the record on the output tape.

Sequential-access storage devices and batch mode processing are traditional data-processing concepts, but they still provide a very efficient method of updating and storing data when there is a high volume of transactions to be processed (see Figure 6–6). If there are only a few transaction records to be processed, this efficiency decreases rapidly. Sequential-access storage devices are also most effectively used where exact, up-to-the-minute reports are not needed. Airline reservations are an excellent sample of an application for which sequential access would not be suitable. Payroll processing, however, can be accomplished efficiently using sequential access.

Figure 6–6 Master File Updating Via Batch Mode Processing

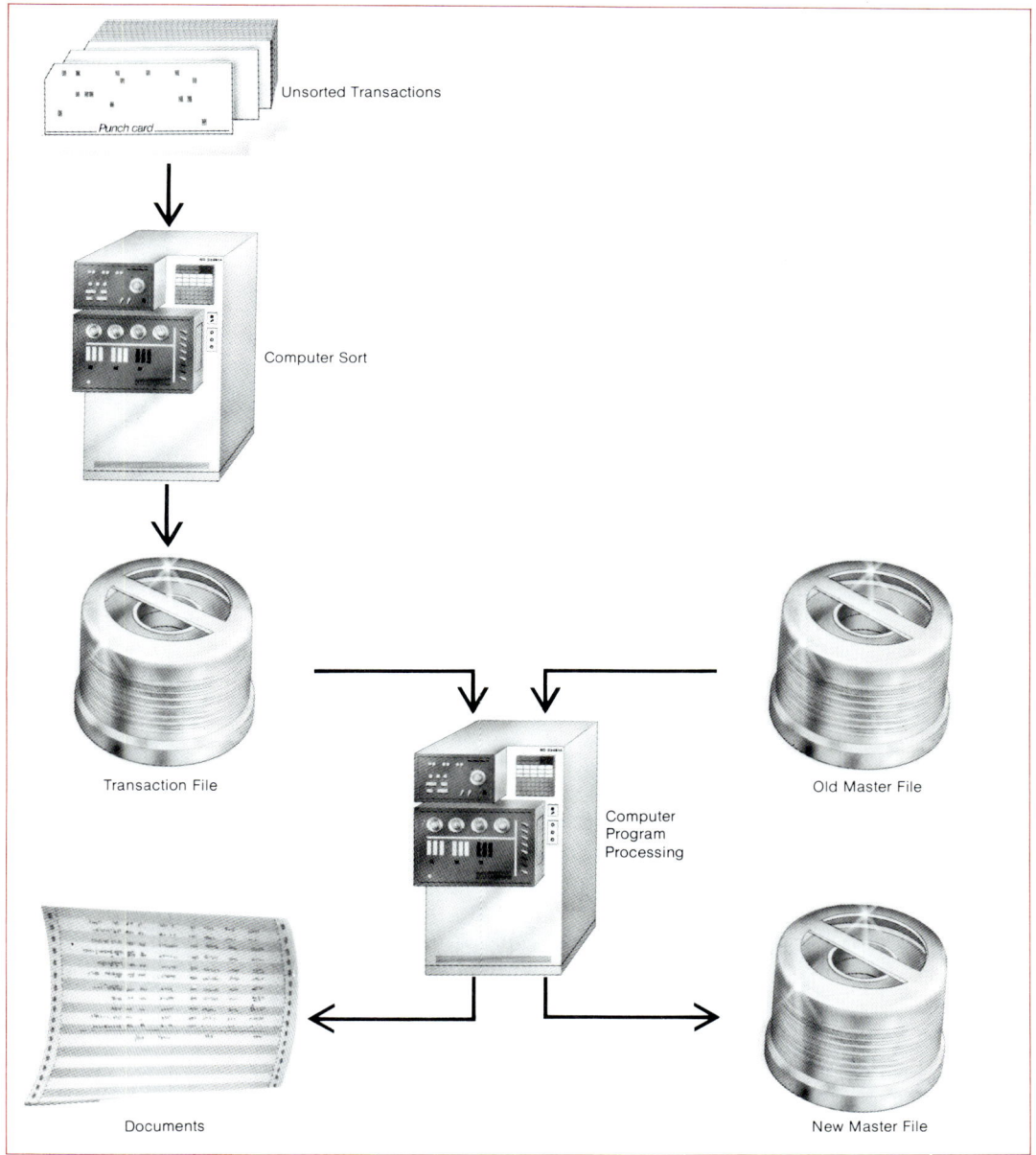

Figure 6–7 Cutaway View of Two Different Fixed Hard Disks

Figure 6–7 Cutaway View of Two Different Fixed Hard Disks

Magnetic Disks Magnetic disks are DASDs, because they can locate and read any record desired without having to search the entire disk. There are two types of magnetic disks produced today: **hard disks** and **floppy disks (diskettes).** Hard disks traditionally have been used for large mainframes and minicomputers; with increasing technology and decreasing costs, however, they now are available for **microcomputers,** or **personal computers** (see Figure 6–7). Floppy disks, in contrast, are most commonly used for microcomputers (see Figure 6–8). The diskette 5¼

Figure 6–8 Floppy Disks

A Floppy Is Not a Floppy Is Not a Floppy . . .

Contrary to popular belief, all floppies are not created equal. There are three sizes of floppies currently on the market: floppies, minifloppies, and microfloppies.

The "basic" floppy is an 8-inch diskette that holds up to three million bytes of information. This was the original floppy size. If you have used floppies, though, you probably have not used the 8-inch floppy.

Most microcomputers are equipped with disk drives that accommodate the 5¼-inch floppy, referred to as the **minifloppy.** It is the most popular size of floppy and holds up to one million bytes of information.

Microfloppies are relatively new. They generally are defined as being under 4-inches in diameter. So far, they come in 3-, 3½-, and 3⁹⁄₁₀-inch sizes. The amount of information they will hold varies greatly because of the variations in size.

The trend in floppy use is toward smaller diskettes. However, the use of microfloppies will not become widespread until their size is standardized (probably at 3½ inches).

---

inches in diameter that is typically used with microcomputers can hold up to 1 million bytes.

A magnetic disk stores information in the form of magnetized particles of iron oxide on its surface. Each disk if made up of several concentric circles, called **tracks,** which are numbered from the outer track to the center beginning with track 0 (see Figure 6–9). Each disk also is divided into areas called **sectors,** which resemble pieces of a pie. With the knowledge of on what track and on what sector a piece of information is located, the computer can find it easily, as the disk rotates and positions the data close to a magnetic **read/write head.**

Hard disks often are grouped in **packs** of as many as sixteen platterlike disks stacked on top of each other with a small space between each for read/write access (see Figure 6–10). A common pack size is eleven disks. Both the upper and lower surfaces of each disk can hold data, although the top surface of the upper disk and the bottom surface of the lower disk usually are not used. For a pack of eleven disks, recording surfaces are numbered from 0 to 19, beginning with the bottom surface of the top disk. As mentioned earlier, tracks are the concentric circles on which data is recorded.

Although the inner concentric circle on a disk surface has a smaller circumference than the outer circle, it is capable of holding as many bytes, because timing considerations dictate the recording density on a track. The corresponding tracks on each surface of a disk pack form a **cylinder.** Data is recorded on a complete cylinder before different tracks on a single surface are used; this approach is taken because the read/write mechanisms used for each surface of a disk pack all move together (they are attached to a comblike mechanism) and can access data on all

Figure 6—9 Top View of Disk Showing Tracks and Sectors

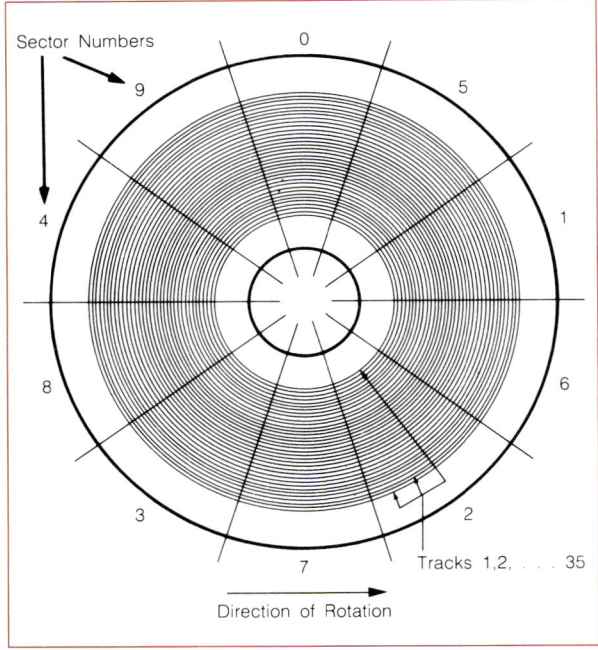

Figure 6—10 Disk Pack

tracks of one cylinder with a single positioning (seek) movement (see Figure 6–11). A more costly disk structure, providing faster access, provides one read/write head for each track of the pack; when information from a specific track is needed, the read/write head assigned to that track is electronically activated. This approach gives speeds similar to those available with **magnetic drums,** cylindrical devices whose outer circumference contains data in tracks, each of which is provided with a read/write head. Although still used in some large systems, drums generally have been replaced by disks.

The device which reads from and records on disk packs is generally called a disk drive or disk storage unit (see Figure 6–12). One of the most important features of this device type is the removable nature of the disk packs used; they can be stored in libraries like magnetic tapes and mounted in the disk storage unit when needed.

Direct (Random) Access Direct (random) access file organization uses a **key field,** such as a part number, and performs a mathematical calculation on that field to generate the address (surface, track, and sector) of that information. This method, known as **randomizing** or **hashing,** allows all records to be accessed quickly and directly (see Chapter 13 and Appendix B). A disadvantage of this type of addressing technique is that some space may be unused because that address is never calculated. Another disadvantage of this system of addressing is that all processing must be done on a record-by-record basis; no sequential processing is possible. Payroll, for example, would be most appropriately set up to

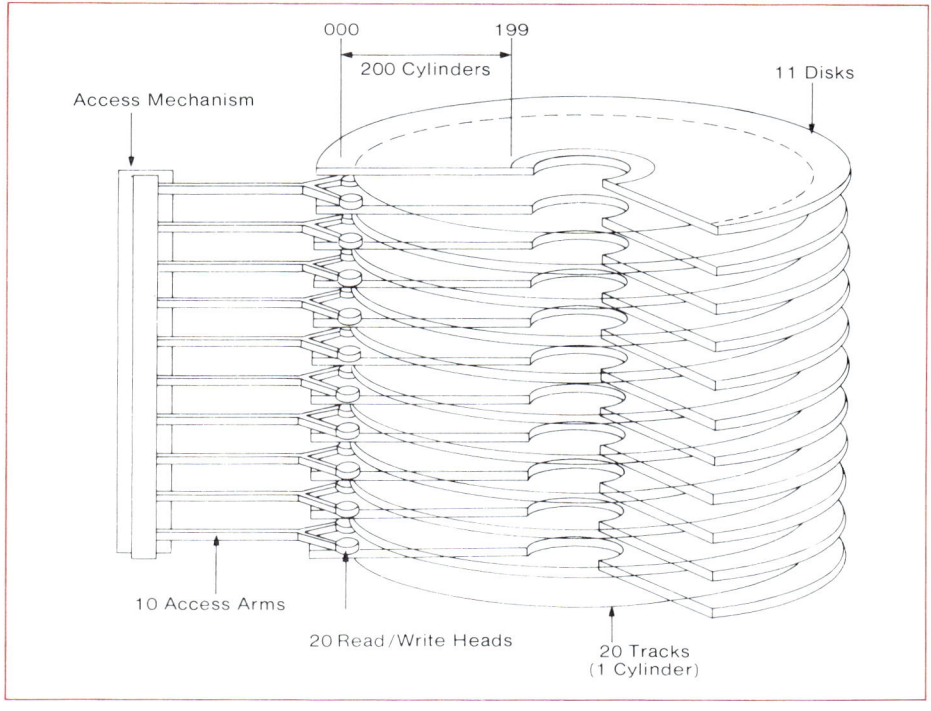

Figure 6–11 Disk Pack Showing Read/Write Heads

Figure 6–12 Disk pack with removable disk packs.

display each employee's name on a screen automatically so that his or her hours could be entered. In a direct-access environment, each employee's record must be specifically requested, which would be time consuming and inefficient for applications such as payroll (see Figure 6–13).

Indexed-Sequential Access To gain the advantages of both sequential and direct access without their limitations, **indexed-sequential access** was developed. This system uses an index containing two columns of data similar to the index found at the back of any book. The first column of this index includes the name of the record or **key field,** such as a part number or name. These key fields (and the corresponding records) are arranged in some order, such as numerically or alphabetically. The second column of the index contains the disk address of each particular record. See Chapter 13 for more details.

This type of design allows direct access to any records desired by using the index to determine the address of that record. The time required to access a record using the index method is slightly longer than with randomizing, but the ability to process sequentially is now available. This sequential processing is achieved by beginning at the top of the index and accessing each record in index order. An additional disadvantage of indexed-sequential access design on disks is that much more direct-access storage area is required because of the storage requirements of the indexes. In most indexed-sequential systems *sparse indexing* is used. In this approach, because the data is sorted by key, only the key of the last (highest) record on a track is present in the index entry. If, for example, ten records could fit on a track, only ten percent of the keys would appear as index entries.

Direct-access storage devices—particularly magnetic disks—have much more flexibility than magnetic tape, which can be used only in sequential-access applications. Magnetic disks are capable of being used

Computerized Microfilm

Computer output microfilm (COM) got its start in business when people began to realize that it was becoming much too expensive to store everything on disks. Disks have a habit of filling up quickly, and a cheaper alternative is outputting important (but space-consuming) documents onto microfilm or microfiche. With COM this is done by using a special type of printer that uses microfilm rather than paper.

Computer-assisted retrieval (CAR) makes this system practical. If people had to personally sort through all the microimages to find a document, they might as well go back to paper. With CAR, the computer keeps inventory of the microimages. Upon request, the system will provide either the address

or the location of the image a person is searching for. If the person wants to retrieve the image, the computer will display it (on a screen or a hard copy printer) within a few seconds.

Naturally, there is a catch to this simplicity. A computer-assisted microimage retrieval system would cost the average business somewhere between thirty thousand and forty thousand dollars. Therefore, the amount of paper processing that would be eliminated and the savings in disk space and office space determine whether or not CAR would be cost effective for a particular business. For the present banking is the biggest market for computerized microimages because of the large number of cash transactions that must be recorded daily.

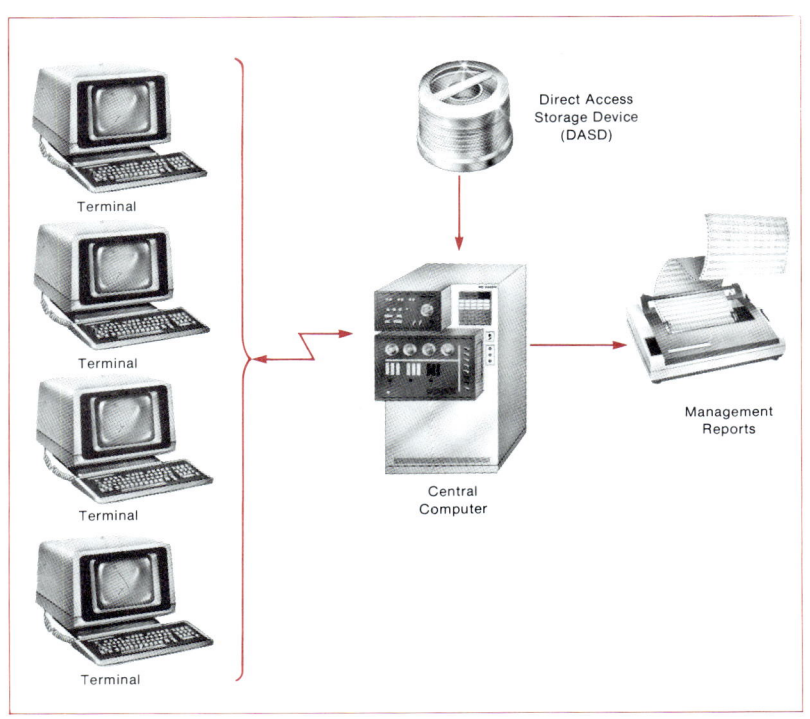

Terminal

Terminal

Terminal

Terminal

Direct Access
Storage Device
(DASD)

Central
Computer

Management
Reports

Figure 6–13
Direct-Access Processing

in both direct- and random-access applications, as well as in a sequential-access environment. Magnetic tapes do have one advantage in emergency situations: when magnetic tape is updated, an entirely new tape is created, allowing the old tape to be saved. Magnetic disk applications, in contrast, generally do all updating over the original disk data, thus eliminating any backup copy. This approach is called **updating in place.** Special precautions must be followed in both cases to insure that the recovery of all information is possible in disaster situations.

Semiconductor Storage

Another type of secondary storage device is small ceramic chips with printed circuits, referred to as **semiconductors. Random-access memory (RAM) chips** are the most popular of these micro chips. These RAM chips can store large amounts of data in the form of electrical circuits; this data can be accessed at speeds much faster than data on magnetic disks, because there is no mechanization involved. Some RAM micro chips are capable of holding as much information as a floppy disk and are being created for use specifically with personal computers. A minor disadvantage with RAM semiconductor storage devices is that if there is a power failure, all the memory is lost. This is, however, a minor problem, because if the data is stored periodically on tape or disks, it can be reentered after a power failure (see Figure 6–14).

Bubble Memory

Bubble memory is similar to RAM micro chips except the data is stored as tiny bubbles on the surface of a garnet (silicate) wafer. These bubbles can be moved on the surface of the chip to form strings of bubbles and, as a result, data. The advantage of bubble memory is that a continuous

Figure 6–14
Random-Access
Memory (RAM) Chip

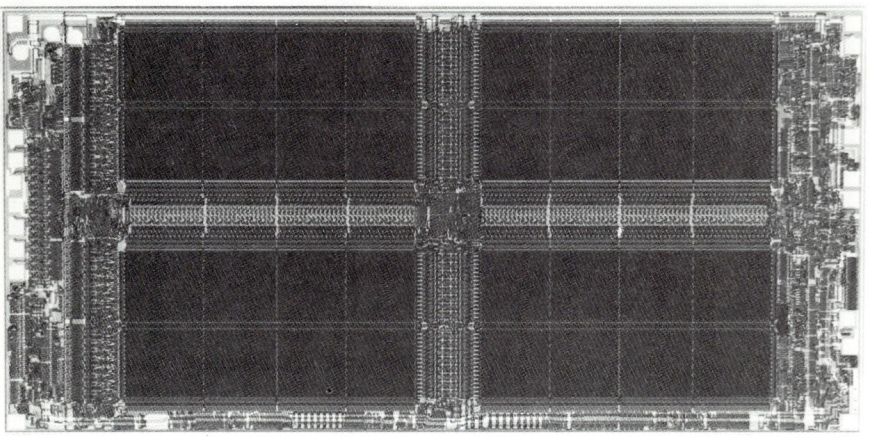

Prices Bubble Down

Prices in the computer industry are infamous for great fluctuations and nosedives. Many times it proves wiser to wait until a product has been on the market a few years before buying it. This is because society determines the prices the technology sells for. The more demand there is for a product, the cheaper it will be. Brand-new technologies are generally very expensive, because they have not yet developed a market.

One dramatic example of this was seen in the price of bubble memories. When Intel introduced its 7110 Bubble Storage System in April 1979, the units sold for as high as $2,500 each. By March 1983, that price had dropped to only $300 per unit. Intel now predicts that by 1986 its bubble memories will be selling for under $100 each. That will amount to a price reduction of 96 percent in only seven years.

Sometimes the smartest consumer is the one who waits.

supply of power is not necessary for the retention of stored data. The disadvantage, however, is its price—relatively high at three hundred dollars for a one-megabyte (one million byte) chip (about ten times the cost of RAM). This price is expected to drop to less than one hundred dollars by 1986.

Mass Storage

Even though the cost of primary and secondary storage has been steadily decreasing, it becomes relatively expensive to try to put all types of information generated within an organization onto some type of secondary storage device. Rarely used information on a secondary storage device wastes space that could be better used for more important information not available on the storage device.

To eliminate the inefficient use of secondary storage devices but retain the accessibility of the infrequently used data, **mass storage devices** have been developed. Mass storage devices allow data to be stored on high-density magnetic tape or disks requiring about 90 percent less storage area than traditional magnetic media (fifty megabytes can be held on a fist-sized tape cartridge offered by IBM). These tapes or disks are kept in a library controlled by the computer. When requested by a user, the computer automatically mounts and scans the records for the requested information. This type of system typically requires several seconds for response time—slow, but still much faster than the time generally required for a human operator to mount a reel of tape and have the computer access the information on that tape (see Figure 6–15). One use of such devices is to provide backup storage for disk packs.

A recent entry in the mass storage market is the *optical disk* or *videodisc*. (See Highlight on the Future on the next page of this chapter). Optical disk storage is becoming popular as a medium for films and

HIGHLIGHT
ON THE
FUTURE

Videodiscs

Interactive videodiscs are the storage of the future. It would take five thousand double-density floppy disks to store the information contained in a single videodisc, which is the size of an ordinary record album. Each side of a videodisc will hold over two gigabytes (two billion bytes) of digital data.

In addition to the bonus of having all that storage available in such a small space, videodiscs have an extra plus for software manufacturers; it would be extremely difficult and costly to illegally copy the entire contents of a videodisc.

Even in their infancy, videodiscs have found obscure applications. The National Aeronautic and Space Administration (NASA) Jet Propulsion Laboratory (JPL) in Pasadena, California, has cataloged over 100,000 planetary images on a single videodisc. Not one to let all those pictures go to waste, JPL's Mike Martin attached the videodisc player to an Apple II and joystick. Using the joystick to control the speed, Mike's BASIC program allows players to either meander or race through our solar system.

Cataloging (probably things other than planets) will be one of the first extremely important areas in videodisc technology. Videodiscs already are gaining a foothold in the catalog divisions of museums, art galleries, and some government agencies. Why? **Popular Computing** in its April, 1983 issue, said it well when they noted: "Every painting in the New York Metropolitan Museum can be catalogued on a single [video] disc" (p. 79). Just imagine what videodiscs could do for the paper mounds of government in the future.

Figure 6–15 Mass Storage Device

other visual information, but its compactness makes this medium attractive as well for mass storage of digital data. At present this medium is used for permanent (non-volatile) storage only, because of the cost and complexity of the recording process. (See Figure 6–16).

As technology continues to progress in the data storage field, the separation between mass storage and secondary storage devices will begin to disappear. If access time can be reduced for high-density tapes and disks, the user who needs the information will be unaware of the physical method by which data is stored in secondary or mass storage devices. The user will be concerned only about getting needed information quickly.

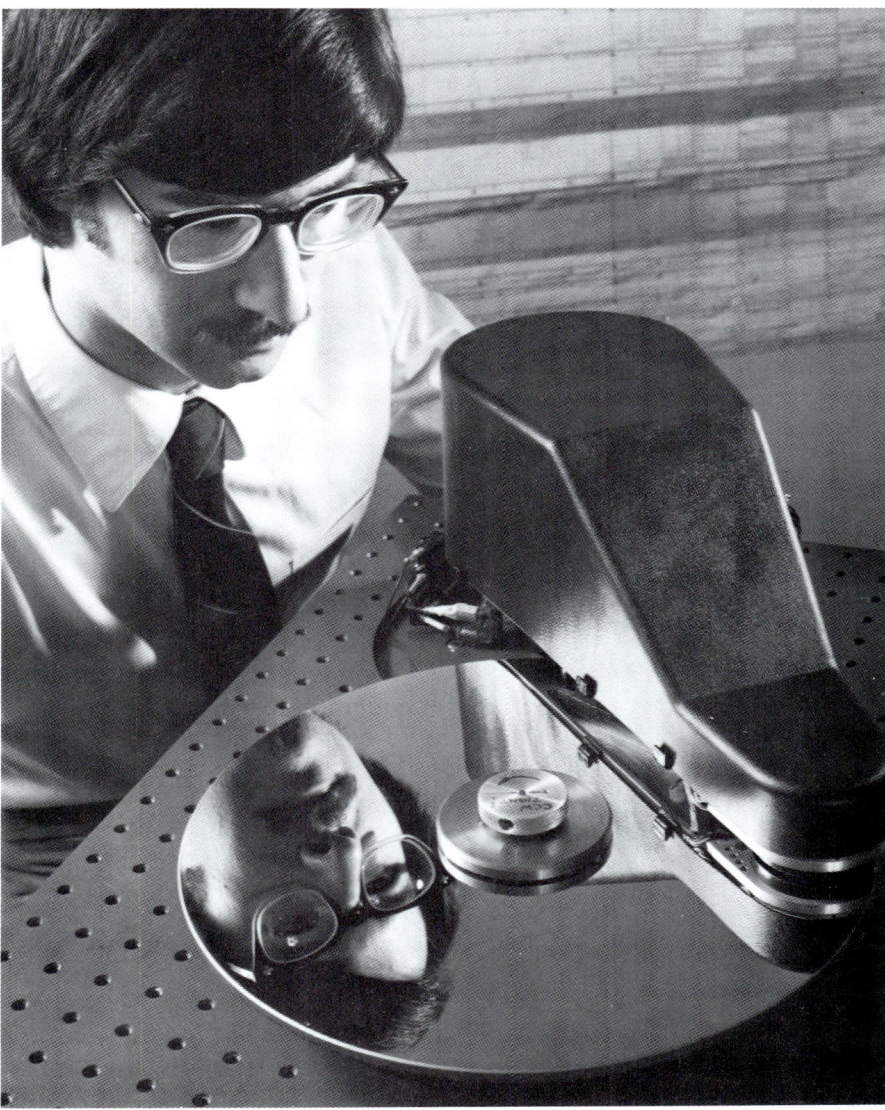

Figure 6–16 Optical Disk Storage

SUMMARY
POINTS

- There are two main categories of storage devices: primary and secondary (auxiliary). Primary storage is contained in the CPU; secondary storage is not.
- Secondary storage devices include magnetic tape, magnetic disk, semiconductor storage, bubble memory, and mass storage devices.
- Traditional secondary storage devices are magnetic tape, magnetic disks, and floppy disks (diskettes).
- Secondary storage devices may be divided into two types: sequential-access storage devices (SASDs) and direct-access storage devices (DASDs). The SASD must be read sequentially, in order. The DASD can access data randomly.
- Files also may use indexed-sequential access. This is used to permit both random and sequential processing.
- Random-access memory (RAM) chips are a type of semiconductor storage. The RAM chips are capable of storing large amounts of data and allow fast access time. However, if there is a power shortage, RAM memory is lost.
- Bubble memories store data on the surface of a silicate wafer and do not require power to retain the data. Unfortunately, they are very expensive.
- Mass storage devices are used for data that is not frequently accessed. Data is stored on high-density magnetic tape cartridges or disks that are stored in computer-controlled libraries.

REVIEW
QUESTIONS

1. What is the difference between primary and secondary storage?
2. List five examples of secondary storage devices.
3. What are the traditional secondary storage devices?
4. What is the difference between an SASD and a DASD?
5. What is indexed-sequential access?
6. What is semiconductor storage? Give an example.
7. How does a bubble memory work?
8. What is the biggest disadvantage of RAM chips?
9. What is an IRG? Where would you find one? Why would it be there?
10. What is a block, and why are blocks used?
11. How does a magnetic disk store information?
12. What is mass storage? How and why is it used?

USER-DIRECTED OUTPUT

LEARNING OBJECTIVES

This chapter examines the types of human-oriented output and printers. After studying this material, you will know the following:

☐ The differences in type and use between hard copy and soft copy.
☐ The types of output reports generated.
☐ The kinds of paper used for computer output.
☐ The difference between impact and nonimpact printers, including the types available, speed, and efficiency.
☐ The uses and types of plotters.
☐ The kinds of special-purpose output devices available, as well as their applications.

Chapter 7

INTRODUCTION

Output is perhaps the most important part of computer processing. Regardless of how fast or how efficiently a computer solves our problem, that work would be worthless if we were not provided with usable results.

This chapter examines all aspects of the output process: hard and soft copy; types of paper, reports, and printers; and the techniques used in different printers (specialized output). An examination of these areas will enable us to best decide which methods will provide the most useful output in a variety of situations.

SOFT COPY VERSUS HARD COPY

Computers originally were invented to process data into information and then provide the results, or feedback, to a user. If the computer were unable to communicate to the user, it would be similar to a one-sided conversation, and its uses would be severely limited or even nonexistent. This feedback, known as **output,** can be presented in two forms: soft or hard copy. **Hard copy** is the information recorded on paper; the user can touch and handle the printed record of information. **Soft copy,** in contrast, is feedback or output from the computer that is displayed on a screen; it only can be viewed by the user, not handled. Soft copy usually can be displayed at much higher speeds than hard copy can be printed because of the mechanization involved in hard copy printers.

Types of Output Reports

Output containing different types of information can be presented to many different users and issued at different time intervals. Most output reports are designed for people external to the computer room or even the organization. These **external reports** are generally very neat in appearance, with symmetrical spacing and easy-to-read print. Other reports, for limited use within the company or computer room, are more motivated by the timeliness and accuracy of the data than by its appearance. These are known as **internal reports.**

Output reports also can be issued at various time intervals, depending on what function the report serves and the speed with which the information contained in the report changes. Some reports are issued on a regular basis; these **periodic reports** are used to process or monitor routine activities such as payroll (see Figure 7–1), the number of cars produced in a manufacturing plant, or the printing of bills to customers by electric companies. **Demand reports** can be issued on demand when specialized inquiries need to be answered, such as the number of hamburgers sold by McDonald's on a certain day.

Output reports also can be classified by content. **Detailed listings** usually contain a review of each piece of data entered and processed during

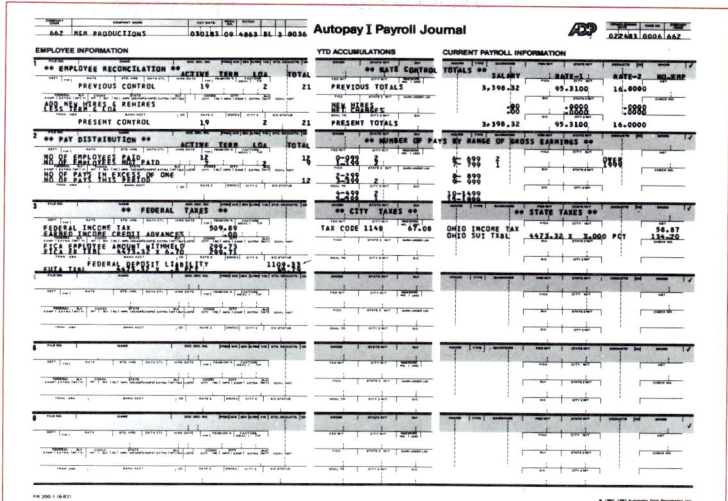

Figure 7–1 Periodic Report

a specified period of time, such as a bank statement. **Summary listings** contain just an overview of all computer activities, such as the number of data items entered and processed or the total number of cars produced this year. These summary reports do not list individual items that make up the total. **Exception listings** contain data that does not conform to a predefined rule. These exceptions to the rule could be overdrawn checking accounts, past-due bills, or credit cards with balances exceeding the credit line. Managers frequently make use primarily of exception information in controlling their organizations.

Types of Output Paper

The paper used for computer-printed output can be of various sizes, colors, and qualities; paper type usually is determined by what the output will be used for and who the end user will be. **Continuous forms** are the most common type of paper used today because of their self-feeding ability (see Figure 7–2). This paper can be preprinted with headings and easily separated by perforations between forms. **Bursting** is the process of separating these forms or pages of output. Output paper also can be layered with sheets of carbon paper to facilitate the production of multiple copies from one output run. The separation of carbon paper from the copies is called **decollating.** Both bursting and decollating can be done either manually or by machine. A special type of paper called **NCR** (no-carbon-required) **paper** now is used in many different applications to eliminate the waste and mess associated with carbon paper.

Turnaround Documents

Some output reports used today also are used as input. These **turnaround documents** are widely used by utility and major gasoline companies. The computer generates output in the form of bills by printing on

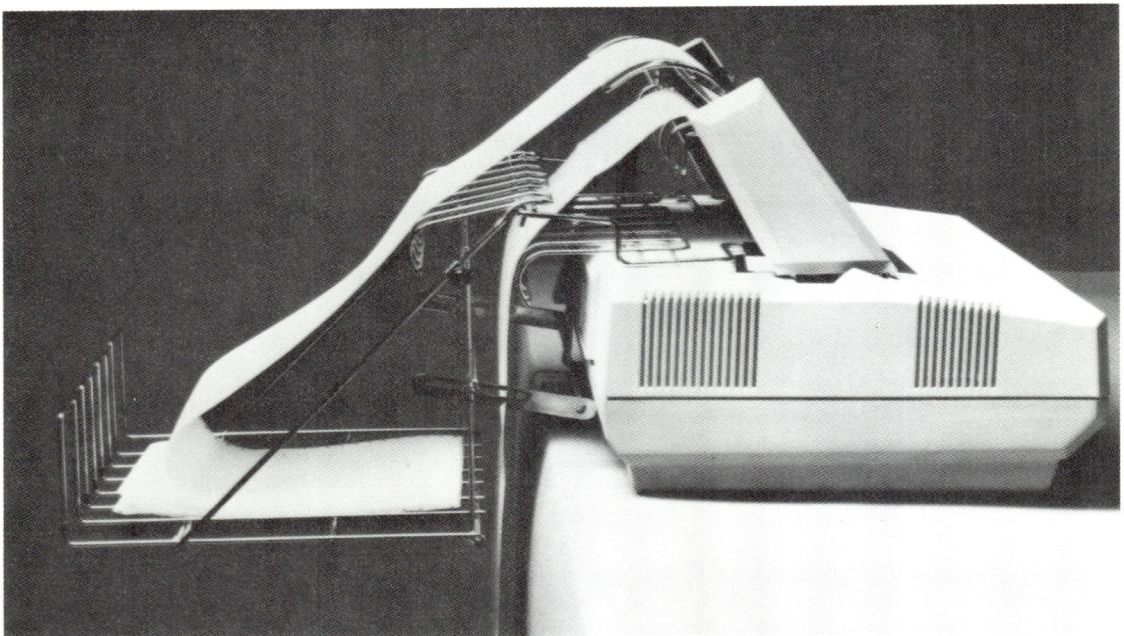

Figure 7–2
Continuous Forms

punched cards or thick paper with special characters that OCR devices can read. These output forms contain the customer's name, address, amount owed, and account number in a form easily read by humans. When the customer pays the bill, this form is returned with the payment and entered into the processing system as input. These forms, already coded in machine language, thus reduce the work needed to prepare data for entry into the processing system (see Figure 7–3).

OUTPUT—HISTORICALLY, A SLOW PROCESS

Historically, the process of computer output has been slow compared with the speed at which the CPU can process the data. The reason for this slow output speed is the same one that causes slow input: the mechanization in the equipment used during the process. Soft copy, as mentioned earlier, is computer output displayed on a viewing device such as a televisionlike screen known as a **cathode-ray tube (CRT).** These devices function through electrical pulses and do not require the use of mechanical equipment. Hard copy is computer output that has been printed on paper by a mechanical device such as a printer. This mechanization places a constraint on the speed at which the printer can operate. The optimum goal, or objective, of computer technology is to approach the speed of electricity, which is the speed of light. Therefore, if faster printer speeds are to be obtained, the mechanization that inhibits speed must be reduced or eliminated.

Braille Output

Like everyone else, Larry Wos's life has been greatly affected by computers. Unlike most of us, Wos has greatly affected the life of the computers. Blind since birth, Wos has never seen a computer. However, through the use of a braille computer terminal and braille computer output, Wos has become one of the most prominent computer scientists of this decade.

For the last ten years, Wos has worked with a team of computer scientists at the Argonne National Laboratory in Illinois. The result of this dedication is AURA, short for **AUtomated Reasoning Assistant.** According to Wos, AURA is "a program that automates the process known as reasoning." AURA provides the computer with the rules of logic and problem solving—basically, teaching the computer how to think.

During the output process, the computer transmits electrical signals to the output device so that characters can be displayed on a screen or printed on paper. These electrical signals, however, can be transmitted only at the speed the particular output device operates, or more slowly. If these electrical pulses are transmitted at a rate faster than that at which the output device operates, the information becomes lost. This is similar to a teacher who talks faster than a student can take notes: much of the information is lost. Because of this limitation, the computer often finds itself waiting for the output device to catch up with the CPU. This is inefficient use of the computer, because no processing is accomplished during this waiting time.

Figure 7–3
Turnaround Document

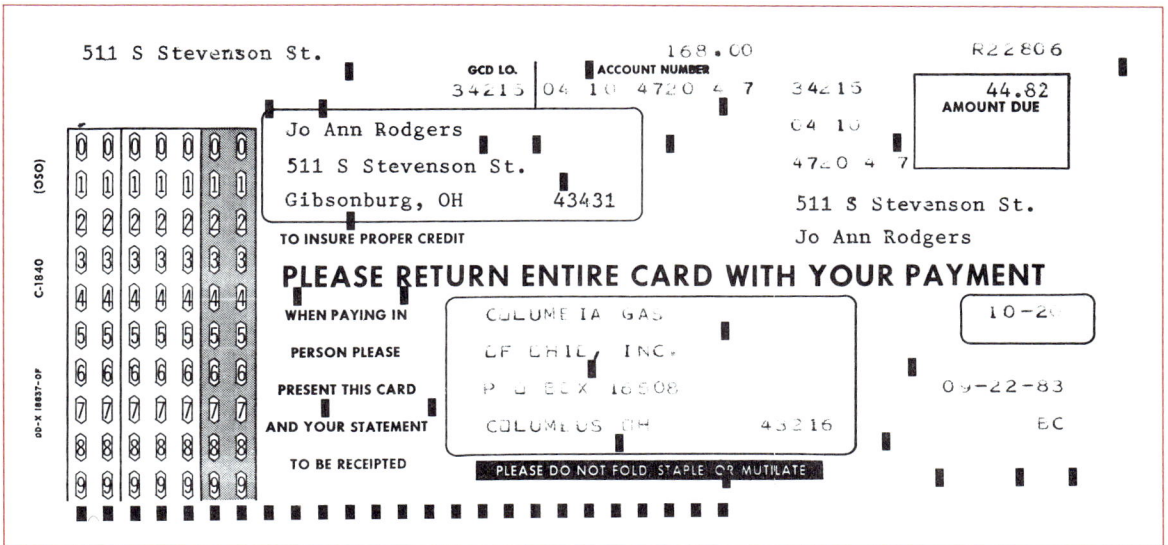

To eliminate the waiting-time inefficiency caused by the slower output device, memory devices called **buffers** have been connected onto many output devices. These buffers are designed to hold electrical signals from the CPU temporarily and transfer them to the output device at the proper speed. The efficiency of computer processing is increased, because characters in the form of electrical pulses can be transferred to buffers as fast as the computer can transmit them. After data has been entered into the buffer, the CPU is available to process more data, because it thinks the output has been displayed or printed. With buffers, therefore, it is possible (and even desirable) to have the CPU and output device working at 100 percent of their ability on two different sets of data. With such overlap, the system can be generating output for record **n** while processing record **n** + 1 and reading record **n** + 2.

OUTPUT DEVICES

Output devices serve a fundamental purpose—as interpreters between computers and humans. These devices transform information (processed data) from combinations of electrical pulses into a language humans can understand. This information can be displayed at varying speeds on a CRT or paper in the form of pictures or characters; if screens and paper are unnecessary or inappropriate, the information now can be "spoken" by the computer. This section will discuss the different output devices available today, beginning with the printer, since it is the most common type.

There are two basic classes of printers: impact printers and nonimpact printers. An **impact printer** forms characters by striking a device against an inked ribbon, causing a character to be imprinted onto the paper in a way similar to the way a typewriter forms characters. A **nonimpact printer** forms characters using a method other than impact, such as using heat-sensitive paper, using laser beams, or spraying magnetized ink onto the paper. These two classes are merely general descriptions of printer methods for forming characters on the paper; to get a more detailed description, each printer must be examined separately. Table 7–1 shows the difference in print speeds of the various types of impact and nonimpact printers.

Impact Printers

Character-at-a-Time Printers Some impact printers are similar to typewriters, because they can print on any type of paper, they print only one character per stroke, and they complete an entire line before beginning a new line. These printers, known as **character-at-a-time printers,** can print at speeds of 50 to 160 characters per second. Printers in this group include the printer-keyboard, dot matrix printer, and daisy wheel printer.

A **printer-keyboard** looks like an electric typewriter but actually is controlled by the computer. This device usually has a print element

Table 7–1 PRINTER TYPES AND TYPICAL SPEEDS

Printer Type	Representative Printing Capability
Impact Printers	
Character at a time:	
Daisy wheel	50 characters per second
Printer-keyboard	50 characters per second
Dot matrix (wire matrix)	160 characters per second
Line at a time:	
Print wheel	150 lines per minute
Chain	2,000 lines per minute
Drum	3,000 lines per minute
Nonimpact Printers	
Ink jet	300 characters per second
Electrosensitive	6,600 characters per second
Xerographic	4,000 lines per minute
Electrothermal	5,000 lines per minute
Electrostatic	5,000 lines per minute
Laser	More than 20,000 lines per minute

shaped like a golf ball, which is able to twist and turn in order to strike the inked or carbon transfer ribbon and paper at different angles. Every character is placed on the ball in a specific area so that when different points of the ball come in contact with the ribbon, a different character can be formed. This printer is relatively slow, printing only 50 characters per second; it generally is used only when the required output volume is low (see Figure 7–4).

Figure 7–4 Printer-Keyboard

The **dot matrix printer** (also known as the **wire matrix printer**) creates characters much like a scoreboard creates numbers. Typically, each character is formed by a vertical bar containing seven pins or hammers moving across a page; each hammer contacts the paper at specified moments to form a character usually within a five-by-seven or nine-by-eleven matrix. This printer can print up to 160 characters per second (see Figure 7–5).

The **daisy wheel printer** offers the typeface that is most professional and pleasing to the eye of the printers in the character-at-a-time impact printer class. This type of printer usually is used with word processors because of the crisp, sharp, high-quality (**letter quality**) characters it produces. The daisy wheel printer uses one round disk with characters located near the ends of petallike projections, similar to the petals of a daisy (see Figure 7–6). This disk rotates until the proper character is in position to be struck by a single hammer, causing that character to be printed on the paper. After that character is printed, the daisy wheel moves to the next print space and follows the same procedure until the line is completed. These printers are able to type at speeds of up to fifty characters per second.

Line-at-a-Time Printers Some impact printers use a process that enables them to print an entire line at the same time. These **line-at-a-time printers** include print wheel printers, drum printers, and chain printers.

Print wheel printers usually have 120 to 132 print wheels with forty-eight characters on each wheel. They resemble the wheels on slot machines except that there are 120 or more wheels, and none of the characters are duplicated on a single wheel. As data is transmitted to the

Figure 7–5 (A) Dot Matrix Patterns; (B) Dot Matrix Character Set

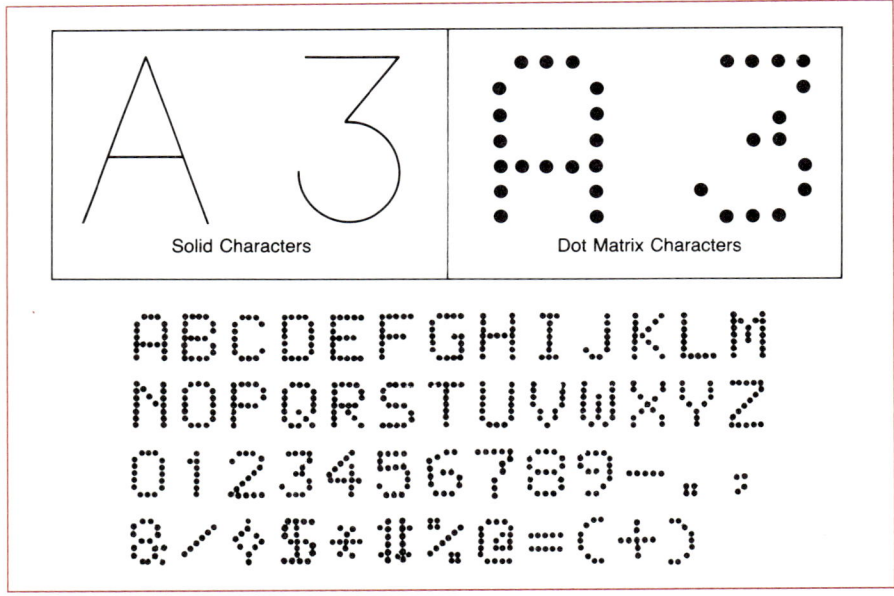

Figure 7–6 Daisy Wheel

printer, each wheel spins and positions the appropriate character for that column in front of the paper (see Figure 7–7). When all print wheels have been positioned, the paper is forced against the print wheels, and the entire line is printed at once. These printers are relatively slow and can rarely produce more than 150 lines per minute.

A **drum printer** is similar to a print wheel printer, except all wheels are connected to form a cylinder or drum (see Figure 7–8). In a drum printer, when one wheel turns, all wheels must turn at the same time

Figure 7–7 Print
Wheel of a Print Wheel
Printer

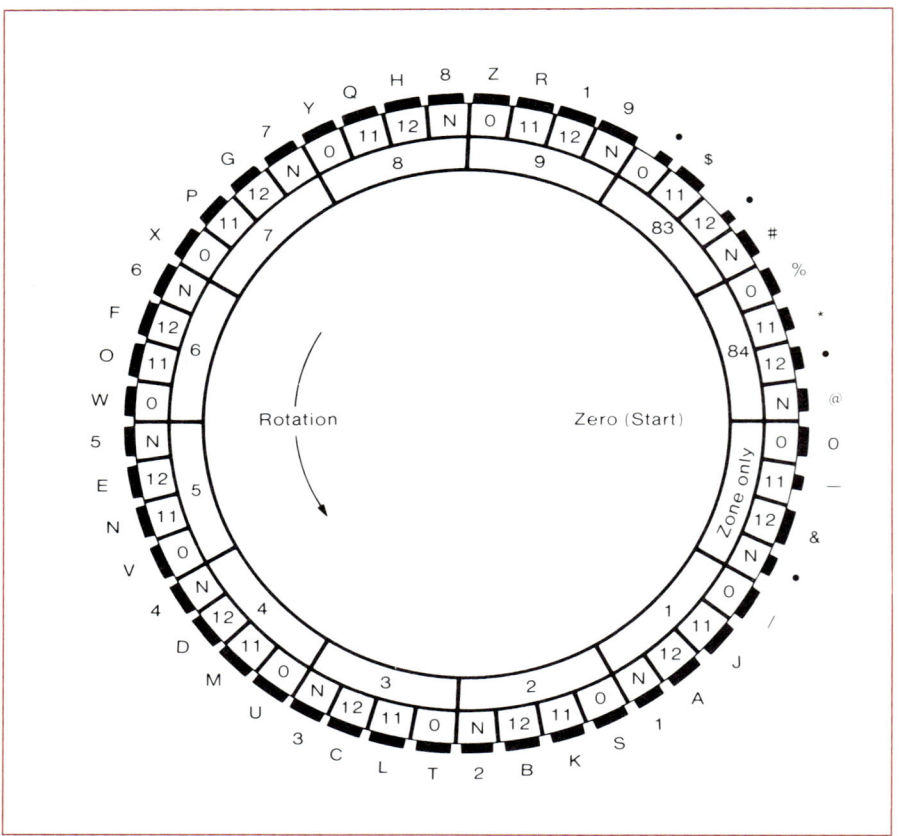

Figure 7–8 Drum of
a Drum Printer

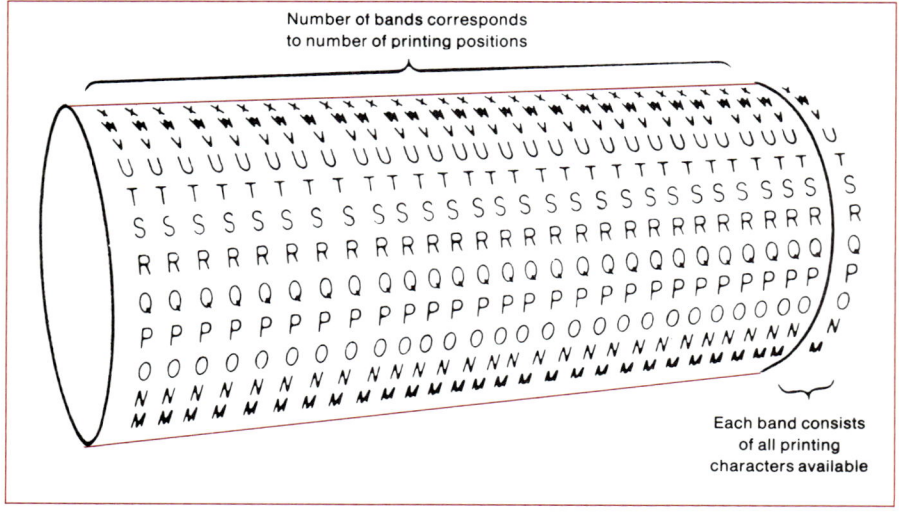

and the same speed. As the drum rotates, characters are imprinted on the paper by hammers that are located in each of the 120 to 135 print positions. One line of print is created by each revolution of the drum, because all forty-eight characters will have passed the hammer in any given column. These printers are capable of producing up to three thousand lines per minute.

Chain printers, like print wheel printers and drum printers, use several sets of characters. Unlike these printers, however, each set of characters is not used exclusively for one print column. Chain printers normally use five sets of characters, with each character laid side by side and connected into a loop. This chain of characters passes in front of the paper and rotates on gears located at each end of the print line. Each print column has a hammer that strikes the paper at the moment the appropriate character passes by. One set of characters is able to create an entire line of print, because each character will pass every column on the page. Since there are five sets of characters per chain, five lines of data can be printed per revolution of the chain (see Figure 7–9). These printers can produce up to two thousand lines per minute.

Nonimpact Printers

Nonimpact printers generally have the advantage of being faster and quieter than impact printers; however, they also cost more and are capable of creating only one copy. This inability to create carbon copies, however, could be meaningless if two nonimpact copies could be produced during the same time an impact copy was produced. Nonimpact

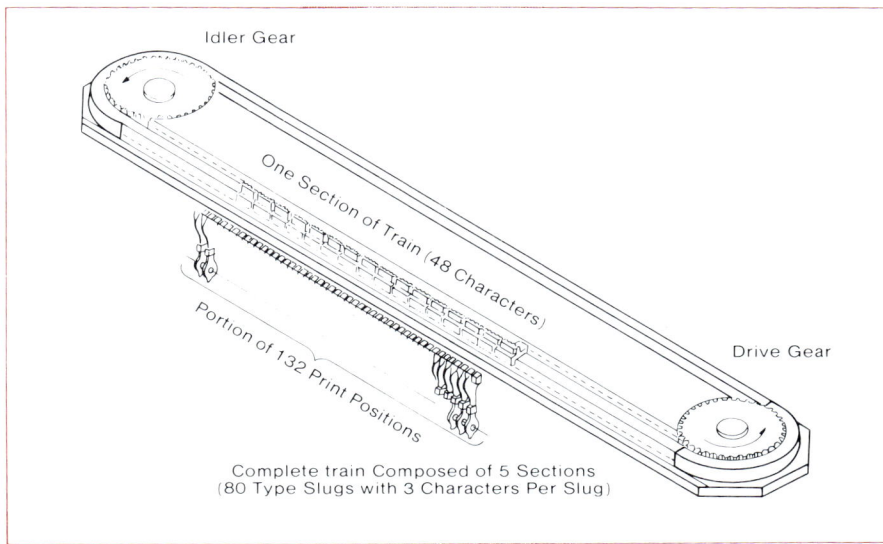

Idler Gear

One Section of Train (48 Characters)

Portion of 132 Print Positions

Drive Gear

Complete train Composed of 5 Sections
(80 Type Slugs with 3 Characters Per Slug)

Figure 7–9 Chain of a Chain Printer

Coffee Break

As U.S. businesses become more familiar with the workings of computers, they also become more amazed at what the machines can do. One of the most effective reminders of this is the analogy of the coffee break.

Imagine that you are an employee of a large company with a mainframe computer. You are taking your coffee break. As you lean back in your chair, your elbow knocks the coffee cup off the table.

According to Thomas R. Billadeau, president of Automated Office

Systems, before that coffee hits the floor, your company's computer could do all of the following:

□ Post two thousand checks to three hundred bank accounts.
□ Process payroll for one thousand employees.
□ Analyze one hundred electrocardiograms.
□ Grade three thousand examinations, each consisting of fifty questions—while examining whether or not the questions themselves are effective.

It is no wonder that computers have become so popular with the business community.

---

printing uses several techniques, including electrothermal, ink jet, electrosensitive, xerographic, electrostatic, and laser.

Electrothermal printers require the use of heat-sensitive paper and create characters by heating wires or pins in a matrix format as they pass over the paper. This heat-sensitive paper changes color upon the introduction of heat, allowing the characters to become visible. These printers cannot use preprinted forms because of the special nature of the paper, and as the paper gets older, the characters begin to fade. These printers are used in some calculators, as well as for computer output. They can print up to five thousand lines per minute.

Ink jet printers operate in a way similar to a can of spray paint and stencils. A spray of electrically charged ink is shot toward the paper, but before reaching the paper, the ink passes through an electrical field that forms the letters much as a stencil would. The print resulting from this process consists of high-quality characters that are fairly easy to read. These printers can produce up to three hundred characters per second.

Electrosensitive printers use a special metallic-coated paper that is silver before any printing is done. As the paper moves through the printer, tiny wires are selectively applied with voltage, causing the metallic coating to burn away. Such printers are relatively fast, but the quality of the characters is poor; the result is black characters on silver paper. Printers of this type can produce up to 6,600 characters per second.

Xerographic printers use printing methods similar to those used in common copier machines like Xerox's. These printers can operate at speeds of up to four thousand lines per minute.

Electrostatic printers use a special photographic paper, with characters etched onto the paper using a stylus. This paper then is passed through a toner solution to develop the characters, much as a photograph is developed. This toner-and-developing stage is very messy but is done inside the machine. These printers can be used for both printing and plotting (printing graphic output) and can produce up to five thousand lines per minute.

Laser printers also use photographic paper, but characters are formed by beams of light passing through a rotating disk containing a full set of characters. The paper then is developed and used to make copies. The output from this type of process consists of sharp, clean images that are pleasing to the eye. This process, often used to print books, can generate more than twenty thousand lines per minute (see Figure 7–10).

Special-Purpose Output

Impact and nonimpact printers are the two major hard copy output devices used today, but several other devices exist that are increasing in popularity as technology becomes more advanced. Most of these other devices allow direct interaction between the computer and the user, thus qualifying as both input and output devices. The output functions of each device will be covered in this section, since their input functions have been covered in Chapter 4.

Visual Display Terminals (VDTs) A **visual display terminal (VDT)** is a common type of output device that uses a CRT to display the data. The CRT supplies a user with soft copy, which is only a temporary presentation of information. This type of terminal is most desirable in applications where direct inquiries and responses are required to answer a single question, such as an account balance query in a savings account.

Figure 7–10 High-Speed Laser Printer

Books by Computer

No, computers will not actually be writing books. However, they will be doing just about everything else. Although different parts of the book-publishing process already are computerized, in the future the entire process—complete, integrated, and efficient—will be done by computer.

The first stage will be writing the book. Of course, this will be done on a word processor. Editorial changes and updates also will be handled through the word processor, eliminating the manual editing and the need to retype.

Once the writing and editing processes have been completed, the typesetting also will be done on computer. The typeset copy is the semifinal version of the book, all prepared for production and awaiting the author's approval. Currently, changes by the author at this stage account for 25 percent of the cost of typesetting. With the computerized process, this will be cut to a mere fraction of the original cost.

Finally, the book itself will be printed using a high-speed laser printer at the rate of one book every five minutes or less. This speed will enable the publisher to print the books as they are ordered, eliminating the costs incurred by stockpiling slow-moving books or running short of those in high demand. In addition to the savings in cost, the time required to publish a book will be slashed by more than 50 percent.

Typically, a CRT screen measures nine or twelve inches diagonally; some are as small as five inches (see Figure 7–11).

Features available in most VDTs include scrolling, paging, highlighting, and windowing. **Scrolling** is the ability to move lines of information up or down; it is similar to the process of reading a scroll. **Paging** is a faster method of obtaining different information whereby an entirely new screen of information is displayed. **Highlighting** is the ability to underscore certain information, to increase intensity in certain areas of information, to display blinking letters, and to reverse the color of the letters and the background (reverse video). **Windowing** is similar to using the zoom lens of a camera; it enables the user to magnify selected areas of the output display.

Visual display terminals are much faster and quieter than printers; they can display up to ten thousand characters per second. If a permanent copy of the displayed information is desired, it usually is possible to attach a printer to the CRT terminal, allowing a hard copy to be printed.

Another type of VDT is the **graphic display device,** typically used to display drawings, charts, and even animation. Many graphic display devices are used in conjunction with a hand-held **light pen,** which enables the user to alter certain areas of the screen as desired. With the aid of

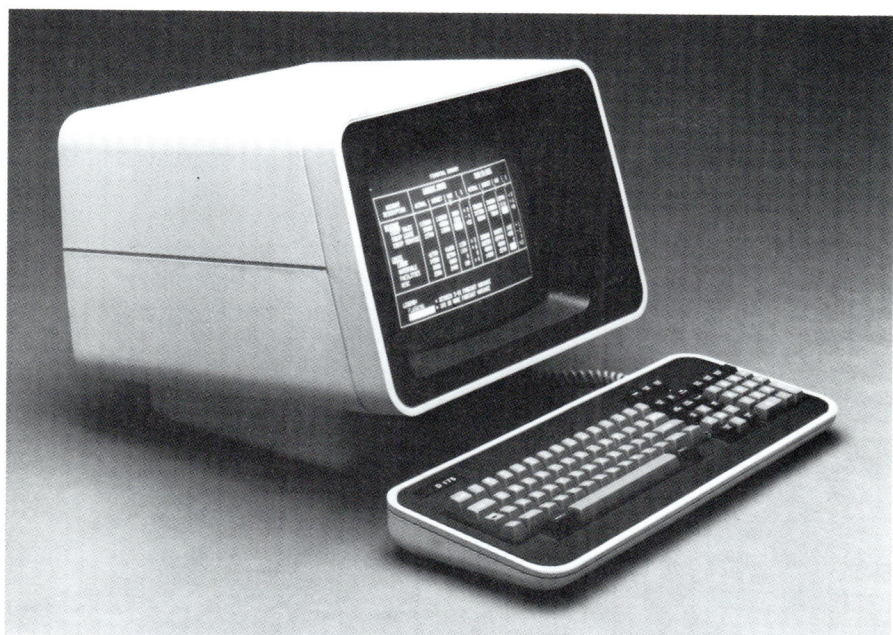

Figure 7–11 Visual Display Terminal (VDT)

windowing, the user can draw detailed designs of an object; with the press of a button, the exact specifications of that object can be calculated by the computer, as in computer-aided design (CAD). Furthermore, stress tests and other vital engineering safety tests can be conducted on the drawing to determine if the product is safe and reliable without ever having to build a test model. Thus, money is spent on flexible computer simulation rather than on more costly physical models (see Figure 7–12). Hard copy output from these graphic display devices can be obtained if needed from a specialized output device called a **plotter.**

Plotters Plotters are another type of hard copy printer; they prepare a permanent record of drawings and charts rather than print characters. There are two main types of plotters—flat bed and drum plotters—with the main difference lying in the method used to draw the pictures. Both types of plotters prepare drawings from the graphic display device using colored pens and ordinary paper. These plotters can draw complex shapes and irregular curves, as well as form characters (see Figure 7–13).

A **flat bed,** or **x-y, plotter** uses a flat tabletop to actually draw the output. Drawing markers are connected to arms that have the mobility to go from top to bottom and side to side over the entire paper. When a drawing is completed, it is simply lifted off the table and ready for use.

A **drum plotter** uses a sheet of paper wrapped around a drum that can rotate in either direction. A marker is attached to an arm that can go only from side to side. When the drum rotates as the arm moves, diagonal lines can be drawn.

HIGHLIGHT ON MICRO-COMPUTERS

Musical Microcomputers

For people whose creative inclinations are found in the musical realm, a personal computer may prove indispensable. It is now possible to compose, edit, and perform complete musical scores—without ever leaving the chair parked in front of a home computer.

Computerized music is beginning to gain popularity. In addition to helping professional composers, it shows great promise in the field of music education.

There are two possible methods of outputting music from a

microcomputer. The first and least expensive is to use a simple voice synthesizer. Although the sound will appear primitive to the professional, for the beginner it will provide sufficient range and tonal values for elementary compositions.

The second method is to wire in a synthesizer board. This is considerably more expensive, but its capabilities are considerably more advanced. For example, with the Apple Super Music Synthesizer board, musical output with up to sixteen "voices," drums, and sound effects can be produced—all in quadraphonic sound.

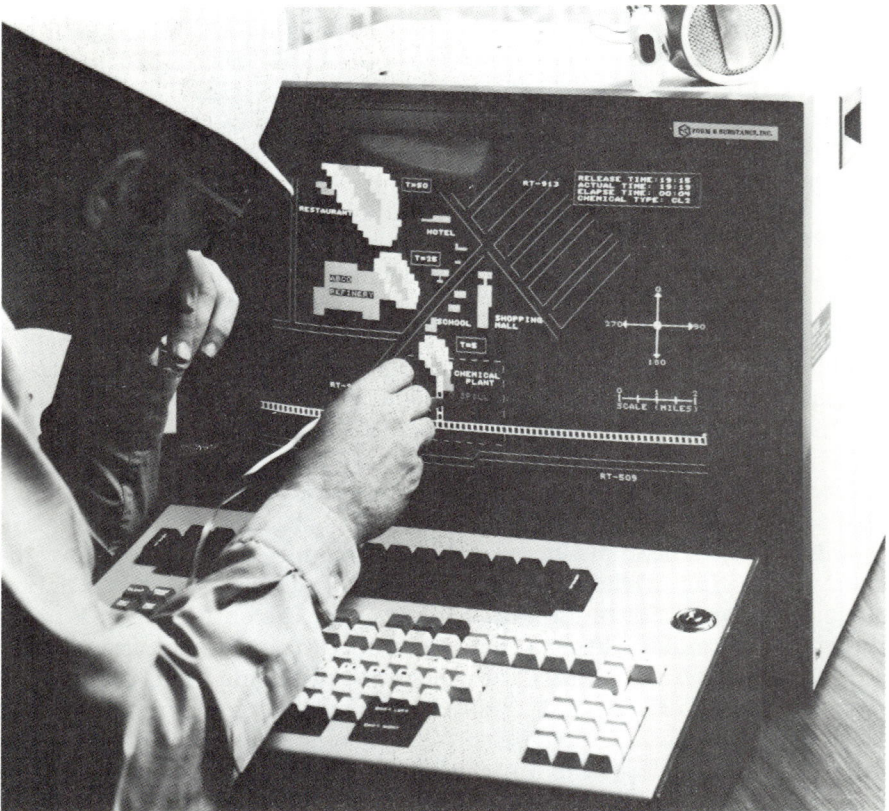

Figure 7–12 Graphic Display Device with Light Pen

COMPUTER AIDED DESIGN (CAD)
COMPUTER AIDED MANUFACTURING (CAM)

Computer-aided design and computer-aided manufacturing (CAD/CAM) are highly effective methods of using computer capabilities in industry.

In the CAD stage, engineers design products directly on a graphics display terminal. The design can be analyzed and revised prior to manufacturing either the prototype or final product.

The CAM stage involves machine directed processes to simulate, control, or monitor the manufacturing process.

1. This photograph shows three stages in the design of an automobile at Chrysler Corporation: a computer-generated line drawing on a terminal; a small, ⅜ size model; and the full-size model. **2.** Cyberman was developed from a graphics software program and is used in the CAD/CAM operation to evaluate interior pedal, angle of the steering column. **3.** Tires begin as a collection of data which is fed into computers and analyzed. Preliminary drawings are created and automatically appear on the display tube.

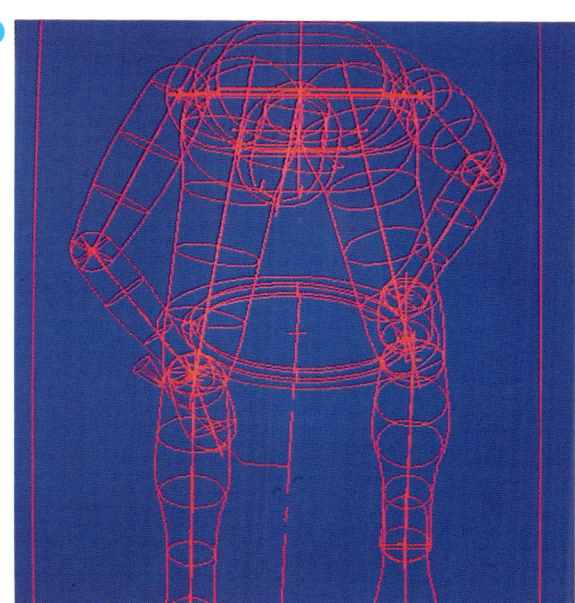

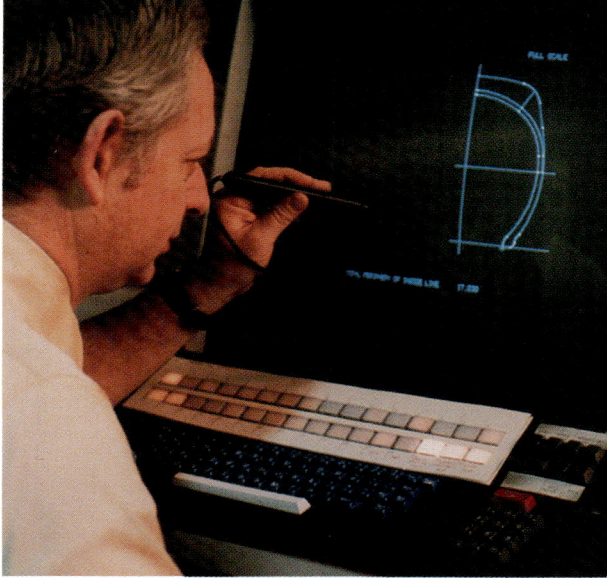

4

AY

5

Command:
F01 ADD
F02 DICTIONARY
F03 DIMENSION
F04 EXIT
F05 INFO
F06 LIBRARIAN
F07 LIST
F08 MODIFY
F09 SPECIFY
F10 TEXT
F11 USER
F12 VIEW
F13 WINDOW
QUIT
BACKUP
HELP
DONE
LINE 18
SCR2
S:0 R:0
E:0 O:0

6

7

8

calma

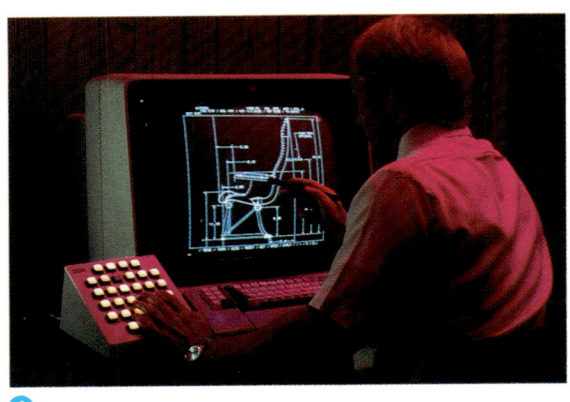

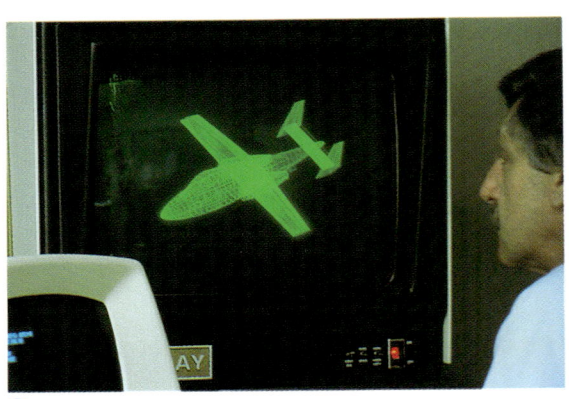

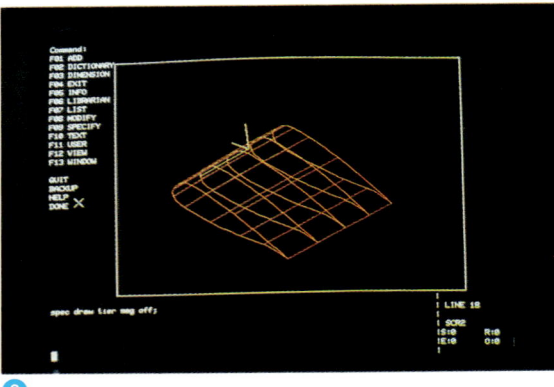

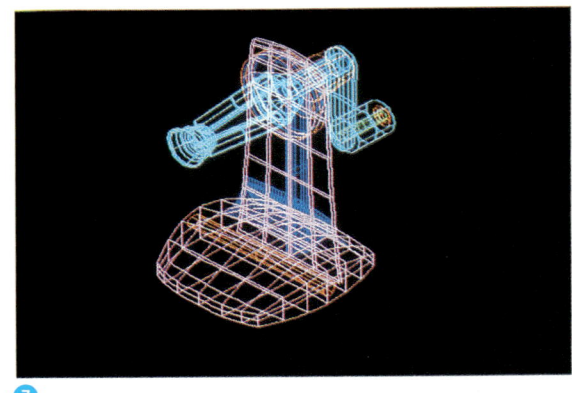

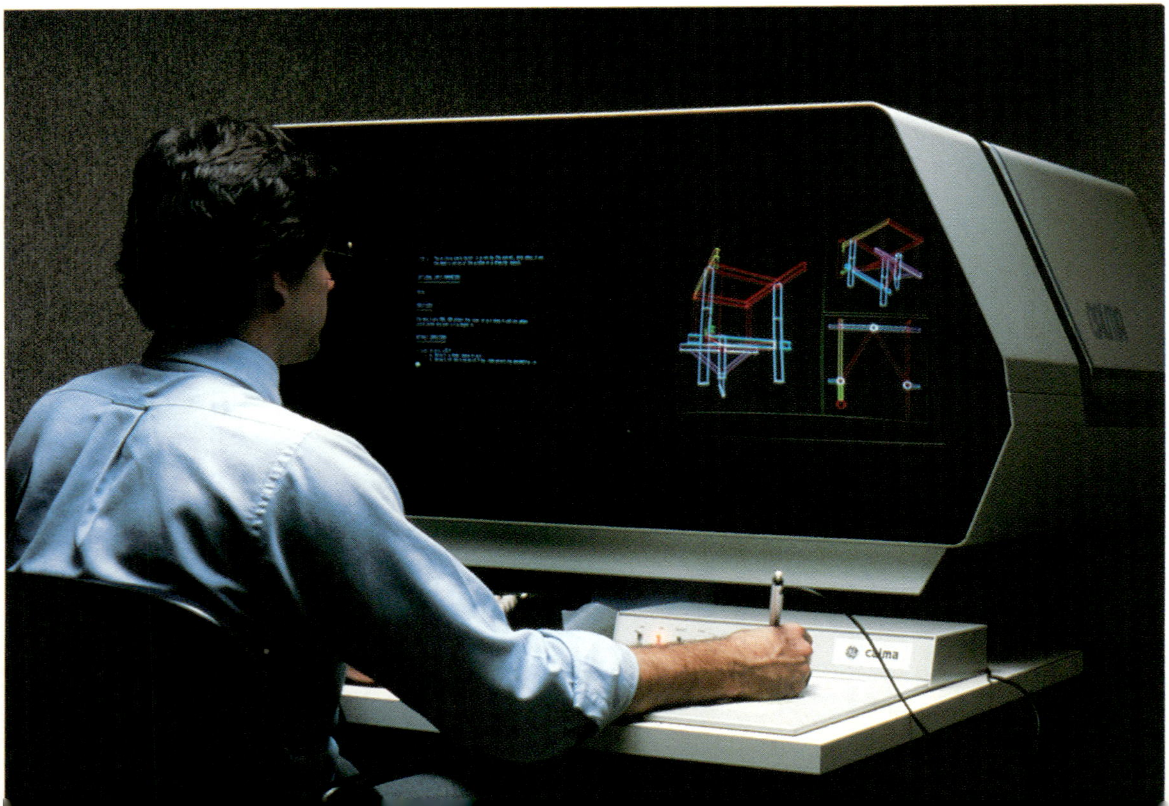

CAD/CAM–continued. **4.** Computerization is an integral part of aircraft seat design and manufacture at the Fairchild Burns Company division of Fairchild Industries, Inc. **5.** CADAM is being used extensively in the design of the new Air Force T-46A trainer that Fairchild Industries, Inc. is developing. **6.** Applicon's Surface Modeling Package combines mathematical algorithms with a VAX-based CAD/CAM system to create and manipulate surface geometry at interactive speeds. Here an early stage of the process shows the base of the pencil sharpener. **7.** Completed design of pencil sharpener. **8.** Calma applications engineer Todd Sherman designs an offshore platform using Calma's application package for architects, engineers and constructors, DIMENSION III. **9.** Cincinnati Milacron's new electric industrial robot uses an automatic screwdriver to insert screws into a workpiece. **10.** The automobile industry is one of the largest users of robotics. Here, a Cincinnati Milacron robot is used to finish spot welding a Ford Sierra car body.

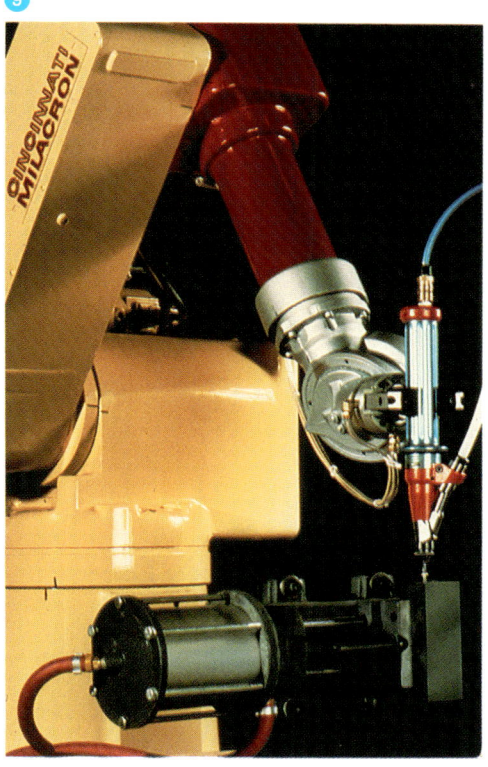

9

10

CAD/CAM—continued.
11. The entire steel rolling operation of this Bethlehem mill is supervised and monitored from this computerized control center. **12.** This manufacturing facility includes an automatic system for inserting components into circuit boards. The system accurately inserts 7,000

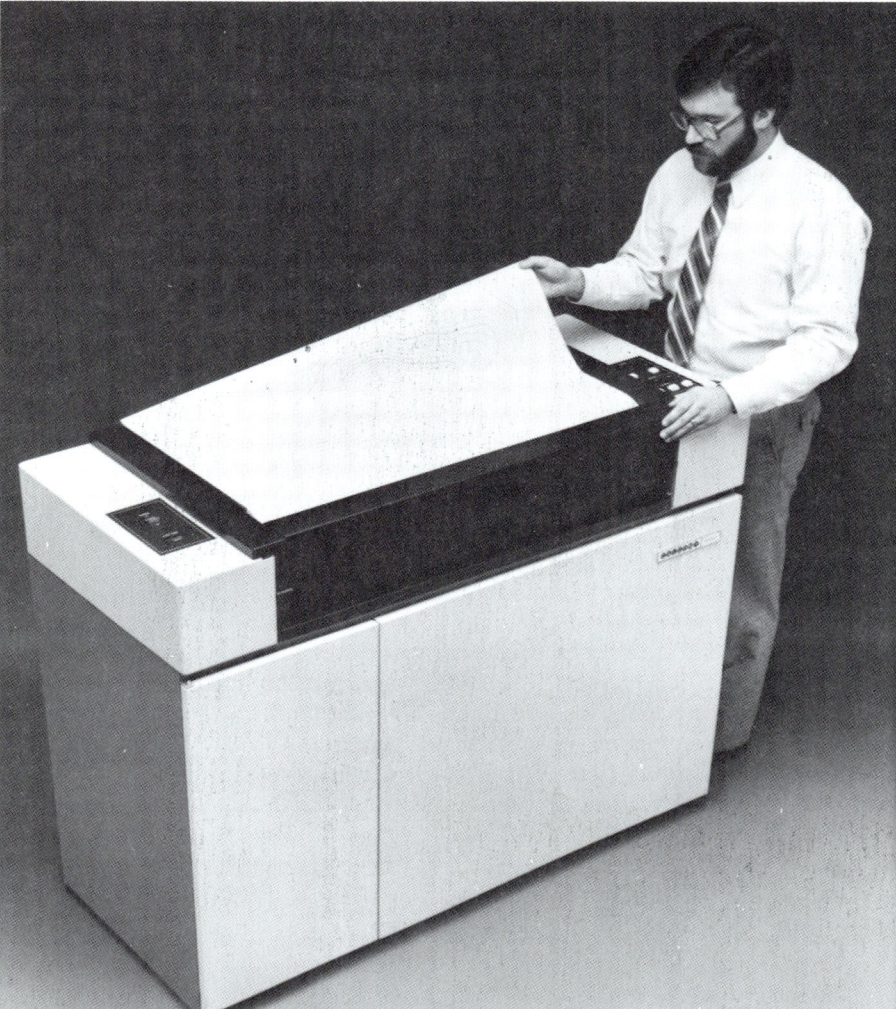

Figure 7–13 Plotter

Pictures drawn by plotters are extremely accurate, because the markers can be positioned in up to forty-five thousand points in each square inch of paper and can draw in as many as eight colors. Plotters and graphic display devices are useful and important output tools because of the ease in communicating information through the use of pictures.

Computer Output Microfilm (COM) In applications where a large volume of information is generated yearly, weekly, or even daily, it becomes impractical to store this information on magnetic media and impossible to retrieve it if stored on printed output. Because of this storage problem, **computer output microfilm (COM)** was developed to enable information to be placed on rolls of microfilm or four-by-six-inch microfiche cards. Information can be recorded on microform media up to twenty-five times faster than on traditional printing devices, and the resultant hard copy requires much less storage space than paper or magnetic media. Computer output microfilm can be used to store reports, drawings, photographs, and even reproductions of fingerprints used by the FBI. With the increase in technology, costs of reproducing a microfiche card or a roll of microfilm are being reduced continuously, thus increasing the feasibility of COM systems.

Voice-Response Output Sometimes printed output is impractical and VDTs are impossible; such is the case when we reach a nonworking number by telephone. When we dial a nonworking number, we hear a voice read the number we called in words that seem to be clipped at the very end of each word or number. This is actually a computer speaking by arranging half-second recordings of voice sounds (called **phonemes**) into a full sentence. In some applications, no prerecorded phonemes are used; a completely artificial voice is synthesized from electronic signals. This type of computer output, known as **audio output** or **voice response,** is gaining popularity and is used in everything from automobiles to pinball and video games to grocery stores.

Voice-response output has advantages over other types of output because it offers a second set of eyes to a user who must concentrate on viewing something other than the output device. Voice-response output, coupled with voice-recognition input, breaks many barriers in any task that requires constant eye and hand devotion and yet an occasional inquiry as to the status of something. Commercial airline pilots currently are using these capabilities to perform routine functions such as changing radio frequencies and receiving weather reports.

SUMMARY POINTS

● There are two major types of output: hard copy and soft copy. Hard copy is printed output; soft copy is displayed on the terminal screen.
● Turnaround documents are forms that first are output (usually in billing) and then are input again (when the bill is paid and being processed).
● Buffers are internal (primary) memory devices that temporarily hold data while it is being transferred from the CPU to the printer. Buffers speed operation by allowing the CPU to process something else while the output is waiting to be printed.
● There are two classes of printers: impact and nonimpact.
● Impact printers are either character-at-a-time or line-at-a-time printers. Character-at-a-time printers are the printer-keyboard, dot matrix printer, and daisy wheel printer. They print 50 to 160 characters per second. Impact printers, which print one line at a time, are the print wheel printer, drum printer, and chain printer, which print between 150 and 3,000 lines per minute.
● Nonimpact printers are faster and quieter than impact printers. Techniques used in nonimpact printing are electrothermal, ink jet, electrosensitive, xerographic, electrostatic, and laser. Their print speeds vary greatly—from 300 to 6,600 characters per second, and from 4,000 to more than 20,000 lines per minute.

- Special-purpose output devices include visual display terminals (VDTs) and graphic display devices.
- Plotters are used to print graphic output. The two types of plotters are flat bed plotters and drum plotters.
- Computer output microfilm (COM) and voice response are other types of output used in specialized applications.

1. Explain the difference between hard and soft copy.
2. List five different types of reports.
3. Define continuous forms, bursting, and NCR paper.
4. What is a turnaround document?
5. What is the function of buffers in data output?
6. What are the two classes of printers?
7. Name three types of nonimpact printers.
8. What are the differences between printer-keyboards, dot matrix printers, and daisy wheel printers?
9. What is the fastest and/or most efficient method of nonimpact printing, and how does it work?
10. What is the least permanent type of nonimpact printing, and why?
11. Name two special-purpose output devices, and explain their uses.
12. Explain the differences between flat bed plotters and drum plotters.
13. What is COM, and how is it used?
14. List some common uses of voice-response output.

PART III

SOFTWARE

PROGRAMMING LOGIC

LEARNING OBJECTIVES

After reading this chapter, you will be able to do the following:

☐ List the five steps of the program development process.
☐ Describe in detail the first two steps of the program development process.
☐ Identify the four basic logic patterns.
☐ Explain the flowcharting symbols.
☐ Develop a flowchart and write a pseudocode solution for a problem.
☐ Describe the benefits of structured programming.

Chapter 8

Ever since the first electronic digital computer, the ENIAC, was invented, it has been necessary for people to develop methods for communicating program instructions to the computer. Programmers of the early machines were required to have extensive knowledge of the system's internal circuitry and operations, which very few people possessed. Communicating with these early computers, as you can imagine, was extremely difficult and time consuming.

Programming today's computers has become much less complicated. In fact, even children in elementary schools are learning to write computer programs. It is important, however, that the programmer follow a logical series of steps in developing a program solution. This chapter will discuss the first two steps of the program development process: defining the problem and designing a solution.

COMPUTER PROBLEM SOLVING

The computer does not approach problem solving in the same manner people do. People solve problems through reason, intelligence, and intuition, whereas computers solve problems by following sets of instructions implementing algorithms provided by programmers. The instructions must be ordered in a logical sequence, guiding the computer in solving a particular problem step by step. As described earlier, the computer is extremely accurate, and the speed at which it can operate is incredibly fast; however, the computer is dependent on the skills and creativity of the programmer to exploit its capabilities. Computers do not possess any independent intelligence and are, in fact, dumb machines (high-speed morons).

The tasks that computers are able to perform are in some ways limited; it also can be argued, however, that computer capabilities are constrained only by the programmer's ability to break down a problem into steps that the computer can follow. As economist Leo Cherne suggested, "The computer is incredibly fast, accurate, and stupid. Man is unbelievably slow, inaccurate, and brilliant. The marriage of the two is a force beyond calculation."

PROBLEM-SOLVING PROCESS

Programming today involves more than it did when computers were first developed. There are now numerous languages to choose from, as well as various storage devices, processing techniques, and printing media from which to select. As a result, a structured approach to computer problem solving and program development is highly recommended.

Solving a problem through a structured approach involves following five major steps. It is important to clearly understand the problem first, so the initial step is **defining the problem.** The input, output, and pro-

Computerphobia

Even in today's computer-filled world, many people are plagued by computerphobia—the fear of computers. The area has commanded much attention lately, because it is increasingly clear that computers will become an integral part of our future. But will computerphobia as well?

Early indications say yes, but not to the same degree as it exists today. The reasons for this are the same reasons that cause computerphobia in the first place: fear of looking stupid, fear of breaking the machine, and poor documentation.

The first two reasons are fairly self-explanatory. Executives do not want to acknowledge publicly that they cannot use the machine that their children use to do their homework. By the same token (fear of the unknown),

people who have never used a computer are genuinely afraid that they will do the wrong thing and break the entire machine. The third reason—poor documentation—means that even people who want to use the machine become frustrated and develop a fear of it simply because they cannot understand the directions that explain how it is used.

Luckily, the first two reasons for computerphobia will not be as noticeable in the future, because children are being exposed to computers at a much earlier age than in the past. The documentation problem already is being solved by the emphasis on user-friendly manuals. However, just as math anxiety and fear of flying have not been completely eliminated, there always will be at least a few people with computerphobia.

cessing to be performed all must be identified. The second step is **designing a solution** to the problem through the use of a **flowchart** or **pseudocode**. A flowchart graphically represents the solution to the problem with the use of special symbols, whereas pseudocode is a written description of the processing steps to take place.

It is only after the problem is clearly defined and a viable solution is planned that the third step—**writing the program**—takes place. A program, as described earlier, is a series of step-by-step instructions written to direct the computer in solving a problem. A programming language must first be chosen; instructions can then be written by a programmer who is familiar with the commands and syntax (or grammatical rules) of that particular language. Regardless of the language chosen, however, the programmer should attempt to follow a structured approach in writing the program instructions. Program logic should be as simple and straightforward as possible, thus making the program easier to read, maintain, and modify.

The fourth step of the programming process involves **translating, debugging, and testing the program.** Testing can be accomplished through several methods, each one instrumental in detecting errors in program logic. Once errors have been corrected and the program debugged, the last step—**documenting the program**—can be completed.

Following the five steps described makes programming a more efficient process than it would be without this structured framework. Some steps will take longer than others; however, the programmer's valuable time will be used as productively as possible. We will now look at the first two steps involved in the programming process—defining the problem and designing a solution—in more detail. The last three steps will be discussed in the next chapter.

DEFINING THE PROBLEM

One of the most important steps in the programming process is the definition of the problem. Unless the problem and its objectives are clearly understood, a program cannot be written that will adequately meet requirements. Even if a program can be rewritten after the appropriate changes have been recognized, usually considerable time and effort will have been needlessly wasted.

A thorough problem definition consists of determining the desired output content and format, the data needed as input, and the types of calculations or processing that must take place. The definition should reflect the objectives at that particular time; however, modifications can be made if requirements change later. In defining the problem, the main concern is what needs to be done rather than how it will be accomplished. Programmers must be good communicators if they are to be effective at the problem definition stage.

Output

The objectives of a problem to be solved can be determined by analyzing the output requirements of users for a specific report. Analysts and programmers then can prepare a report mock-up that visually illustrates the items to be included in the report and their format. Users then can examine the report and can, for example, add other items they would like included, suggest a change in the structure of headings, or make any other requests for adjustments to the report. In this way, the analyst/programmer can detect any errors or omissions at the start and can be assured that the report will be satisfactory to users.

Input

Once the output has been appropriately specified, it is necessary to see what input data is needed to produce the required output. This can be accomplished by reviewing current systems to determine what data is presently available and deciding what new data items must be obtained so that the required information can be produced. If new data is to be collected, potential sources must be identified.

Processing

Once the output specifications have been clearly defined and the input necessary to achieve that desired output has been established, the processing requirements must be determined. After these requirements are known, the analyst/programmer can proceed to the next step in the programming process, which is to plan a solution.

DESIGNING A SOLUTION

Designing a solution requires the use of the information obtained in the first step—defining the problem. There are numerous ways in which a particular problem can be solved, but the analyst/programmer should attempt to find a method that will provide a solution in the least complicated manner. The solution will frequently (although less often than in the past because of the availability of packaged software) require the development of one or more new programs. Before the programmer can design a program, the logic and detailed steps necessary to achieve the desired objectives must be determined.

In designing a program, the programmer (designated simply as such now that the analyst portion of the job is done) takes each of the processing steps specified during problem definition and constructs a tentative flow of the tasks needed to complete that particular segment. The **program logic** (the precise sequence and specification of operations to be performed) is determined, that is, what needs to be done first in a program, what second, and so on. The individual steps needed to solve the problem and their order of execution must be clearly thought through by the programmer. By approaching each segment separately, the programmer can concentrate on developing a solution that is both efficient and logical for that individual segment.

It is not necessary to know in what programming language the program will be written in order to develop a tentative logic flow. The emphasis in planning a solution is on how the problem will be solved without specifying a language, although reviewing the processing requirements can indicate which programming language will be most appropriate. A programmer needs to know only the four basic logic patterns used by the computer.

Basic Logic Patterns

A number of different types of problems can be solved using the computer. Although the objectives of the programs written to solve these problems may vary, the logic patterns found within each program are quite similar. In fact, any computer problem can be solved through the repeated use of only four basic logic patterns. Three of these patterns— simple sequence, selection, and loop—are in accordance with **structured programming concepts** (which are discussed later). The branch logic pattern, which does not support the structured programming approach, also will be discussed. These basic logic patterns are illustrated in Figure 8–1.

Simple Sequence Logic Pattern The **simple sequence logic pattern** involves sequentially executing one statement after another. It is the most straightforward logic pattern, because there is no test or decision involved that could alter the flow of processing. In fact, the computer assumes that all statements within the program will be executed according to this pattern unless it is told otherwise.

Selection Logic Pattern The **selection logic pattern** requires a test condition that results in one of two alternate paths to be followed, depending on the result of the test. A selection is made on the basis of a test to see if a condition is true or false. Frequently this is expressed through the comparison of two data items for equality, greater than, or less than situations. Although these are the only three comparisons a computer can make, a sequence of comparisons can make selection quite complex. The selection logic pattern also is referred to as an **IF-THEN-ELSE pattern.**

Loop Logic Pattern The **loop logic pattern** allows a series of statements to be executed more than once within a program, thus eliminating the need for the programmer to rewrite the same set of statements again and again. A test condition also is needed in the loop pattern. As long as the test condition is true, the statements within the loop will be reexecuted. As soon as the test condition becomes false, control is sent to the first statement outside the loop.

Figure 8–1
Computer's Basic Logic Patterns

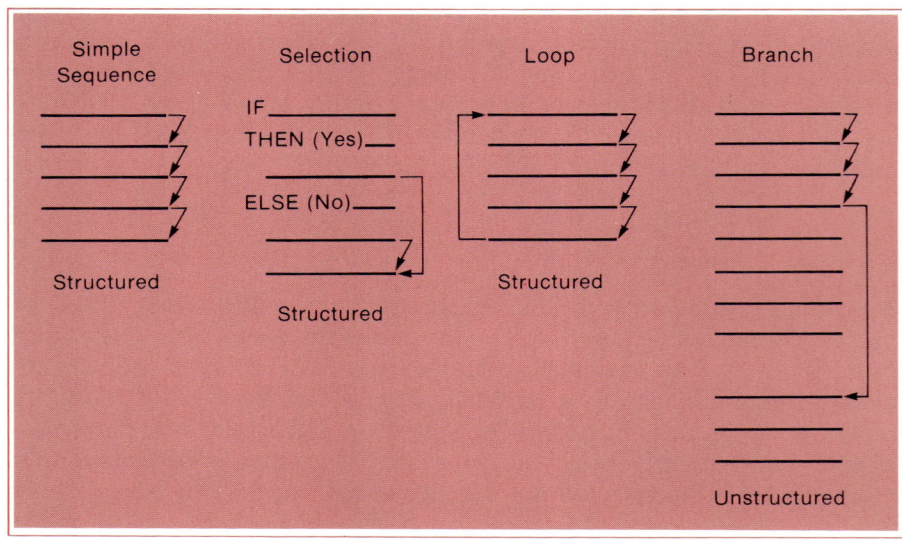

Branch Logic Pattern The last and most controversial pattern is the **branch logic pattern.** Depending on the result of a test condition, control can be transferred to a different part of the program, thus leaving a statement or series of statements unexecuted. Extensive use of the branch within a program can make the logic complicated and difficult for other programmers to follow. Programs written with excessive use of the branch are sometimes referred to as "spaghetti code." In addition, program maintenance becomes more time consuming and complex. Although not recommended, because it is not in accordance with structured programming concepts, the pattern is still used by some programmers. (When used, it should be restricted to the forward transfer of control within a short distance of the branch.)

Planning a solution to a problem involves knowledge of not only the capabilities of a computer, but its limitations as well. The programmer must work creatively, especially around the computer's limitations. The solution must be structured in such a way that it can be implemented by a series of simple sequence instructions; selections; loops; and, in some cases, branches. Comparisons that are to be made must be stated in terms of one item being less than, equal to, or greater than another.

It is quite possible that the first solution developed to solve a problem may not be the most efficient one. The programmer can easily make omissions or logic errors. As an aid to the programmer in spotting such omissions and errors early—before the program is actually written—pseudocode and flowcharting techniques can be used. The most efficient solution may never be found, but these techniques will be instrumental in developing one that is well planned and as efficient as feasible.

Pseudocode

Pseudocode is basically a written description of the processing steps that need to be performed within a program. The instructions are written in abbreviated form and are listed in the order they would be executed by the computer. There are no standardized rules to follow, and the programmer does not have to be concerned with phrasing instructions in a computer language. Pseudocode is, instead, concisely written in a human language such as English or French. Programmers following a structured approach to programming often choose pseudocode to plan a program solution, since it is simple to prepare and modify.

An example of pseudocode to calculate the average monthly rainfall is shown in Figure 8–2. Notice how the logic patterns just discussed are illustrated in this example. Correctly written, each pseudocode phrase will correspond to one or more programming statements. Pseudocode is becoming increasingly popular as a useful method of expressing programming logic in a clear, yet concise, manner.

Flowcharts

A program **flowchart,** sometimes referred to as a **block diagram** or a **logic diagram,** graphically illustrates the processing steps in a program.

Figure 8—2
Pseudocode

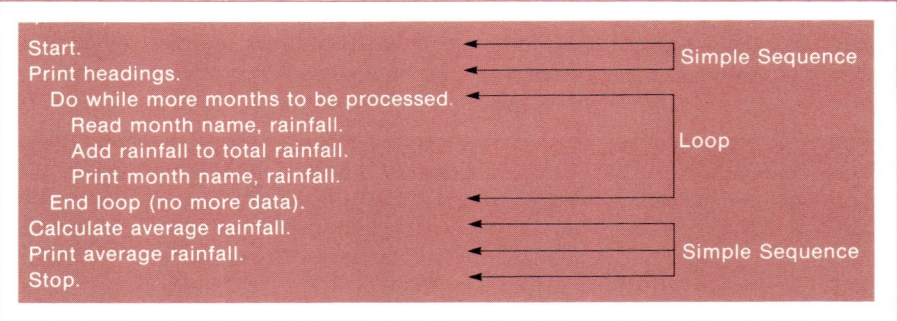

A flowchart consists of a series of special symbols, each representing a particular function. The programmer draws a symbol to represent each processing step and then briefly writes the instruction to be performed within the symbol. The symbols are arranged in the same logical sequence in which the corresponding instructions appear in the program and are interconnected by flow lines. Flowcharts should be arranged in a top-down fashion, with flow lines directing the flow of control from top to bottom and from left to right.

A beneficial characteristic of flowcharts is that they provide excellent documentation of a program. The flowchart is a useful tool in program maintenance, since it guides programmers in locating statements that may require modification. Once the necessary changes have been made in the flowchart to correspond to the changes made in the original program, good documentation of the revised program is provided. Because of their potential value, flowcharts should be kept up-to-date, complete, and easy to read. To help achieve the latter objective, the American National Standards Institute (ANSI) has adopted a set of standard flowcharting symbols that are commonly accepted by programmers.

Symbols Flowcharting requires the use of only a few symbols to represent various processing functions. Figure 8–3 shows some of the most commonly used ANSI flowchart symbols. The symbol $\bigcirc$ represents the start or termination of a program and so appears at the start and end of a program flowchart. The symbol $\square$ shows a process step such as addition, subtraction, division, or moving data into a storage location. Most of the data manipulation performed in a program is represented by process symbols. A comparison, or decision, is represented by the symbol $\diamond$, which represents in the program the location of a test or comparison; one of the specified alternative processing paths will be followed, based on the results of the comparison. If the result of the comparison is true, one path is executed; if the result is false, the other is taken. The symbol $\square$ indicates data to be made available for input or output. Data can be entered from a keyboard, punched cards, or secondary storage devices. Output from programs can be directed to CRT screens, printers, or secondary storage devices. Also included in Figure 8–3 is the symbol $\bigcirc$, used when initializing variables (setting variables to beginning values) in a program. When a flowchart extends across multiple pages, the symbol ▽ is used to specify where one part of the flowchart ends on one page and where it continues on another. There are other methods of flowcharting than the one illustrated here. Some of these are HIPO, Nassi-Shneiderman, and Chapin charts. Each has its advocates.

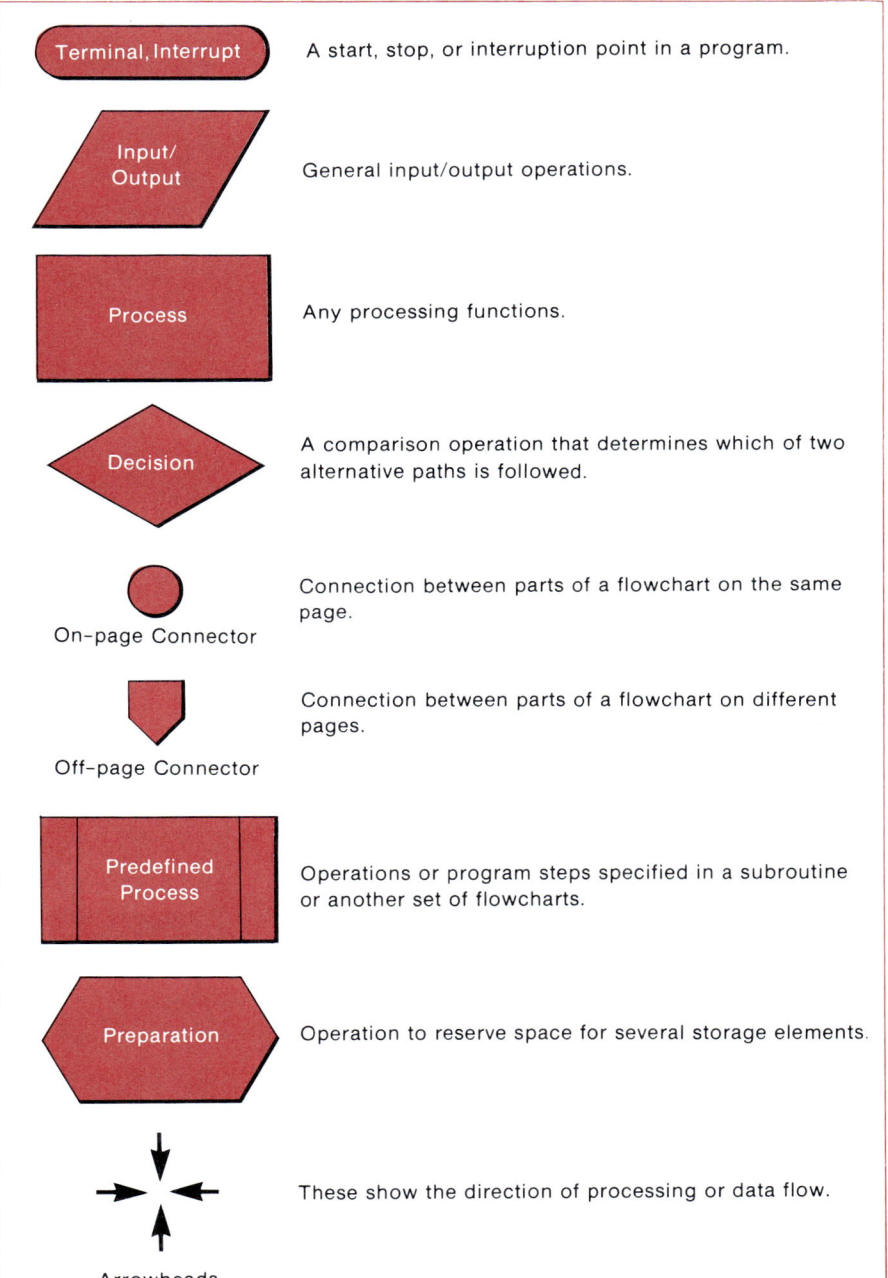

Figure 8—3 Flowchart Symbols

Terminal, Interrupt — A start, stop, or interruption point in a program.

Input/Output — General input/output operations.

Process — Any processing functions.

Decision — A comparison operation that determines which of two alternative paths is followed.

On-page Connector — Connection between parts of a flowchart on the same page.

Off-page Connector — Connection between parts of a flowchart on different pages.

Predefined Process — Operations or program steps specified in a subroutine or another set of flowcharts.

Preparation — Operation to reserve space for several storage elements.

Arrowheads — These show the direction of processing or data flow.

Figure 8–4 shows the rainfall example described in pseudocode form in Figure 8–2 now in ANSI flowchart form. The flowchart illustrates the logic required to calculate the average monthly rainfall and then display that result. The instructions are individually written within special symbols and interconnected by flow lines. Notice that the direction of the arrowheads indicates the flow of logic to be executed from top to bottom and left to right except as explicitly indicated in returning to the beginning of the loop.

The basic logic patterns earlier described can now be illustrated through flowcharting symbols, as shown in Figure 8–5. The first pattern shows one processing step followed by another to be executed in a simple sequence. The second pattern, selection, uses the decision symbol to indicate that a test is to be made. The flow line in the third pattern, the loop, illustrates that every time a loop has been executed, control will be sent back up to the decision block. As long as the test result is true, the loop will be reexecuted; otherwise, control will be sent outside the loop. The last pattern, the branch, shows that the flow of processing can be interrupted by transferring control to another point in the program. The location of the transfer is referenced by a number within a small circle, ○, called a **connector symbol.** In addition to indicating where transfer is to be made, the same connector symbol also labels the reentry location.

Figure 8–4 Flowchart

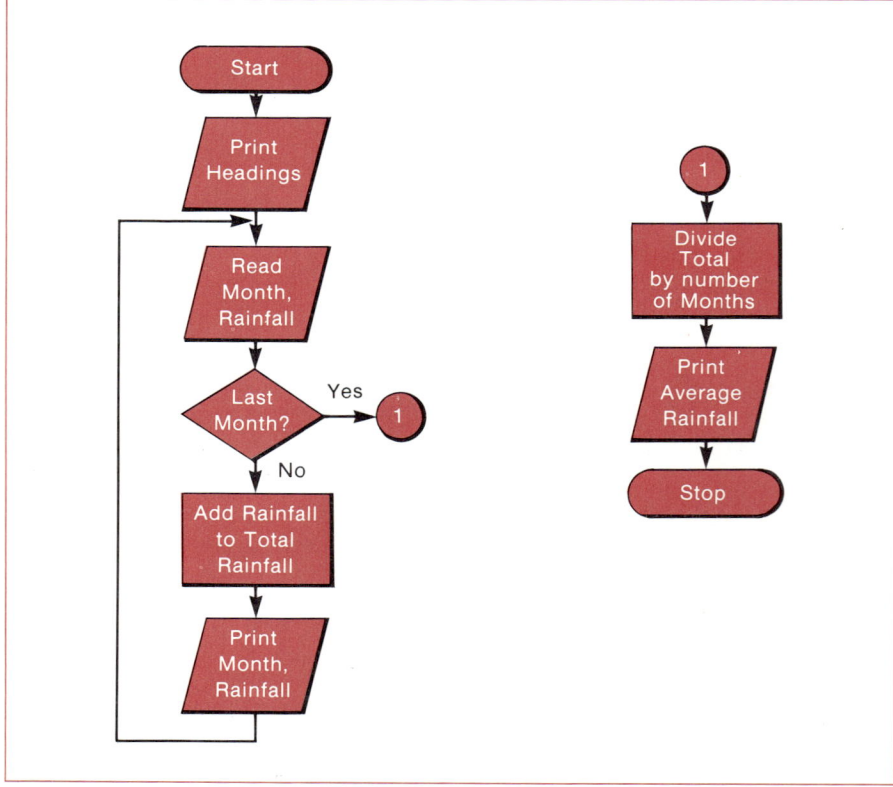

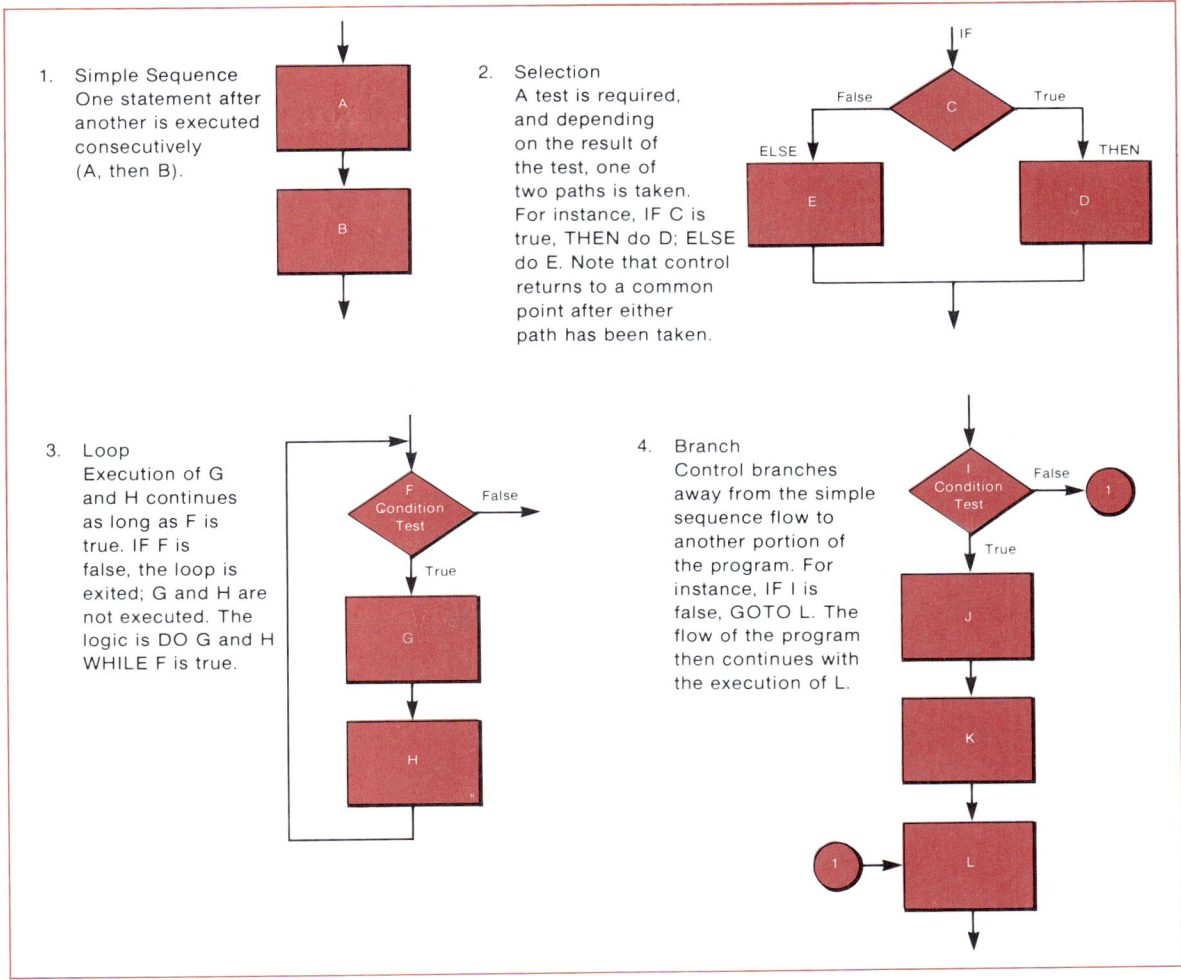

1. Simple Sequence
   One statement after another is executed consecutively (A, then B).

2. Selection
   A test is required, and depending on the result of the test, one of two paths is taken. For instance, IF C is true, THEN do D; ELSE do E. Note that control returns to a common point after either path has been taken.

3. Loop
   Execution of G and H continues as long as F is true. IF F is false, the loop is exited; G and H are not executed. The logic is DO G and H WHILE F is true.

4. Branch
   Control branches away from the simple sequence flow to another portion of the program. For instance, IF I is false, GOTO L. The flow of the program then continues with the execution of L.

Figure 8–5 Four Program Logic Patterns

Levels of Flowcharts Two levels of flowcharts can be developed. One level is distinguished from the other by the amount of detail shown. If just a general description of the major processing steps needs to be represented, a **macroflowchart,** or modular flowchart, can be constructed. The major segments of the program are called **modules.** Each module then can be treated as a separate entity and programmed individually. In this way a difficult problem can be broken down into manageable parts. The programming process is made less complex, in keeping with structured programming concepts.

If more detail is required than is shown in the macroflowchart, a **microflowchart,** or detail flowchart, can be developed. A microflowchart breaks down a general processing step found within a macroflowchart into more specific tasks. Several microflowcharts, then, can be prepared for each macroflowchart. A one-to-one correspondence often can be found between flowchart blocks and program statements. Figure 8–6 shows both macroflowcharts and microflowcharts needed to calculate library fines.

Flowcharts have several advantages, as well as disadvantages, as aids in programming analysis. As discussed earlier, they provide useful documentation. They function somewhat as road maps do in describing the necessary steps to follow in arriving at a desired destination. Through their symbolic representation of processing steps, relationships can more easily be seen and communicated to others. Programmers are better able to write, debug, and test a program by following an efficiently written flowchart.

Flowcharts have several disadvantages. The major one is that they can be difficult and time consuming to construct and modify when there are a large number of decisions required within a program. Also, depending on the level of detail specified, flowcharts may become complex and

Figure 8–6
Macroflowchart and
Microflowchart

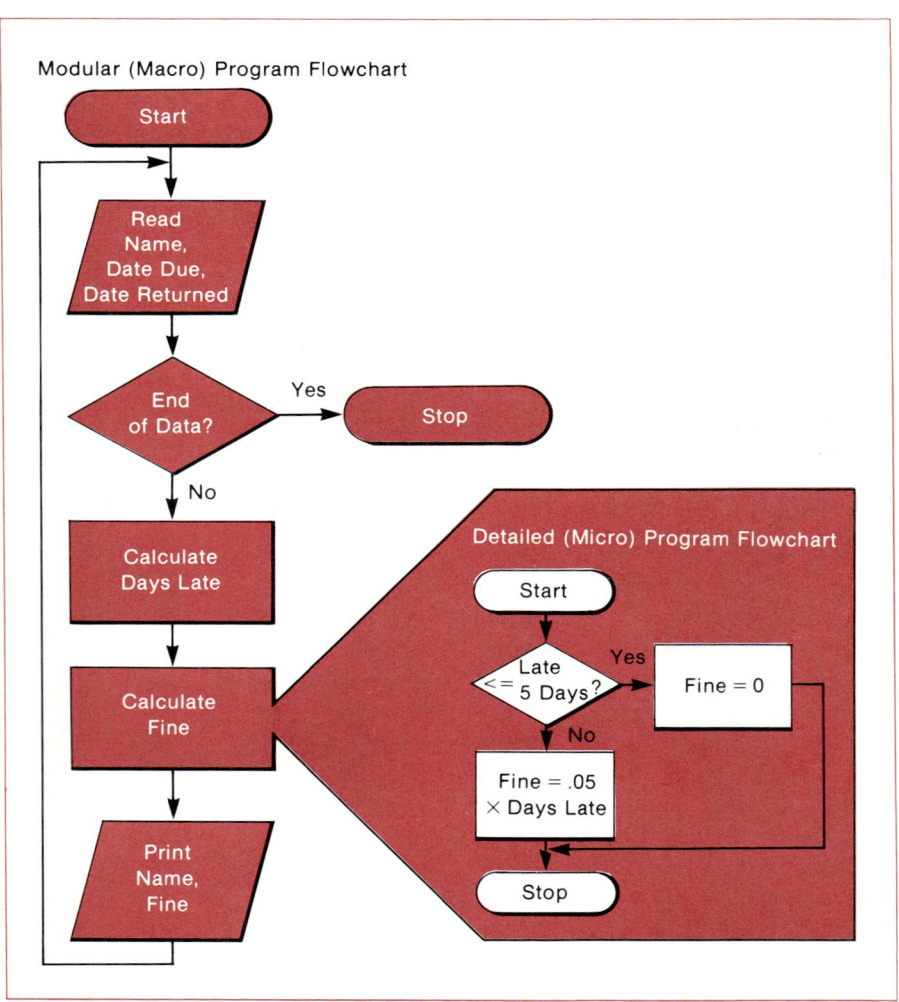

difficult to follow, especially if the branch pattern is used frequently. In such a case, pseudocode would be a less complicated alternative.

Special Considerations in Solution Design

In planning a solution to a problem, computer programmers must consider a number of factors. The programmer must be aware of (1) how the program will receive data as input, (2) the need for data to be verified for accuracy during processing and for potential errors to be identified, and (3) the form in which output will be generated.

Input There are numerous methods of entering data into a program. As Chapter 6 discussed, data can be stored on a variety of different storage devices. The programmer, however, must know what input devices will be used before finalizing a solution design. For example, if input is in the form of magnetic tape, the program must be structured in such a way that data can be input in the same format as it is stored on the tape. If a data base (see Chapter 13) provides the input, the program may need to actively search and retrieve data from the data base.

Processing To guard against errors in processing, the programmer needs to implement some type of check or control to insure accuracy. **Edit checks** are processing statements designed to identify potential errors in the input data. There are several different kinds of edit checks. For example, a "reasonableness" check analyzes a data item to see if its stated value is possible, given the type of data it represents. A "range" check evaluates the data item to see if its value lies within an established range. Another check, known as a "type" check, verifies that numeric data is not entered where there should be alphabetic data and vice versa. A number of other edit checks can be selected; the number and type of edit checks implemented in a specific program depend on what is thought to be sufficient by those involved in the solution design.

Output The output from a program can take several forms. It can be a hard copy, where a physical copy on paper is obtained, or it can be in soft copy form, where results are viewed from a VDT. A third alternative—in which the output from one program is used as input to another—is also possible. Programs can be interdependent, with each program performing a specific function. The programmer must insure that output from one program is in a format acceptable as input to another. In addition, if the output is in hard copy or soft copy form, the programmer must see that reports are in a format that is not confusing to read and understand.

STRUCTURED PROGRAMMING

Throughout the discussion of the programming process so far, the idea of following a structured approach has been stressed repeatedly. Why is

Meeting Management Needs

The "War Room King" is a title sometimes given to W. Robert Widener, a man who has made a career of designing offices and briefing rooms for management. Widener's career took this turn while he was working for Bell Telephone; he was chosen to design a presentation room for the the Bell System Business Communications Seminar. Widener's resulting design—a conference room for the modern executive—was futuristic, yet practical. The modern executive, à la Widener, had no use for paper; information needs were to be met instantly by keyboard. Thus, the room could be adapted to comfortable communications exchanges and not to paperwork processing.

So believable was Widener's design that he has since designed more than sixty briefing rooms for major corporations, and he now markets a computerized decision support system. He has these words of advice for those who design for management needs: Contrary to popular belief, managers need less, not more, information. Their specialized information requirements must be filled by practical summaries and condensed figures, not necessarily by the newest gadgets in town.

structured programming so important? One of the main reasons is that it provides a standardized method of attacking a problem, which, in turn, decreases the time necessary to determine an appropriate solution and to prepare the necessary instructions within a program. The costs associated with program maintenance are decreased as well (although some experts feel that structured programs execute somewhat more slowly than their unstructured equivalents).

Structured programming basically has four objectives:

1. To reduce testing time.
2. To increase programmer productivity.
3. To increase clarity by reducing complexity.
4. To decrease maintenance time and effort.

Structured programming is one element of **software engineering,** a discipline that has evolved since the late 1960s in an effort to make software development more rational.

When a structured approach to defining a problem and designing a solution is followed, the third step of the process—writing the program—simply involves coding the processing steps into a computer language. The logic of the program will have been thought out carefully to avoid complexity. Development of programs that users find easy to read and understand is encouraged by using only three basic logic patterns: simple sequence, selection, and loop. Through the avoidance of the branch pattern, the sequential flow of processing is not interrupted to

The Changing Shape of Robots

Contrary to recent publicity, the only currently practical application for robots is in heavy, repetitive, industrial labor. Although several companies recently introduced domestic models, the household robots of science fiction are still years away.

Today's home robots seem to create more problems than they solve. Their primitive optic fibers require an extensive amount of programming just to keep them from bouncing off the walls (or walking through them, depending on their size). Massive amounts of structured programming are required to teach these domestic robots even simple chores—how to pour a cup of coffee or run the vacuum cleaner, for example. Even if a robot could be programmed to do all the chores around the house, it would not have enough memory to hold more than a few programmed chores at a time. To get around this, it could be hooked up to a home computer, but this would only add to the complexity. We could no longer just look at Fred the Robot and say, "Coffee please, Fred." We would have to go to the computer, type in the proper command sequence, retrieve the right file, and so on.

Practical versions of household robots are sure to develop in the not-too-distant future. For the present, though, it is easier—and a few thousand dollars cheaper—just to pour our own coffee.

such an extent that the logic becomes tricky and confusing to program users and even to the original programmer.

The branch pattern, characterized by the GOTO statement, causes an unconditional branch from one part of the program to another. Excessive use of the GOTO statement not only makes the logic difficult to understand, but it also makes the program difficult to modify. Control can be transferred through a branch to totally different logical sections of the program, making the programmer uncertain how a change in one part of the program will affect the processing of other segments. Because of such problems, the GOTO statement is not advocated in structured programming. (In fact, structured programming is often improperly called "GOTO-less" programming.)

Basic to the concept of structured programming is the use of program modules. Each module is an independent program segment that performs only one function. Modules should be small to facilitate programming and later debugging. The programmer should attempt to construct each module so that there is only one entry and one exit point per block, allowing the flow of processing to be smooth and easy to follow (see Figure 8–7). To obtain these and other objectives of structured programming, the GOTO statement does not have to be avoided completely; if it needs to be used, however, transfers should be made from one part of a module to another forward location in the same module. Branching should never occur outside a particular module.

Computer Trees

More and more microcomputer owners are visiting via modem to discuss relevant issues such as hardware, software, conferences, workshops, life, religion, and the universe. For facts and amusement, these people are plugging into free information services known as trees.

Trees are known as trees because they are built in a treelike structure. Upon entering the network, users arrive at the main trunk. There they are provided with branching options. They might find categories such as computer news, new software, politics, religion, or jokes. If they decide on jokes, they may get to choose from other branches, such as animal jokes or riddles. At each branch the users either branch further to other branches or back to the main trunk.

Trees are an extension of electronic bulletin boards. However, whereas bulletin boards mainly provide subscribers with information, trees are designed for a two-way exchange. Most trees are accessed with a minimum of commands, generally READ, BROWSE, and ADDTO. After users have read through a branch, they may add their own comments, questions, or answers by using the ADDTO command.

Structured programming techniques are more easily implemented in some languages than in others. Pascal, Ada, PL/I, and ALGOL are well suited to structured programming; COBOL is moderately suited to structured techniques; and BASIC and FORTRAN are poorly designed for structured programming (although the current version of FORTRAN—FORTRAN 77—is greatly improved). The GOTO statement has been difficult to avoid in BASIC and FORTRAN because of specific characteristics of these two languages. Careful planning and well-placed GOTOs, however, can result in programs that meet the objectives of structured programming in even the most troublesome languages. Structured **design** methodology, which precedes structured programming, will be discussed in the next chapter.

PROGRAMMING EXAMPLE: CALCULATION OF STUDENT TUITION FEES

Colleges and universities use the computer extensively in a number of student, faculty, staff, operational, and related applications. A common application of the computer is the calculation of the fees each student is required to pay per quarter or semester. Imagine the time and effort involved if this were to be accomplished manually for several thousand students!

The problem in this example is to generate a bill for the university listing the total tuition fees to be paid per student this semester. In addition, the university would like to receive a report listing some sta-

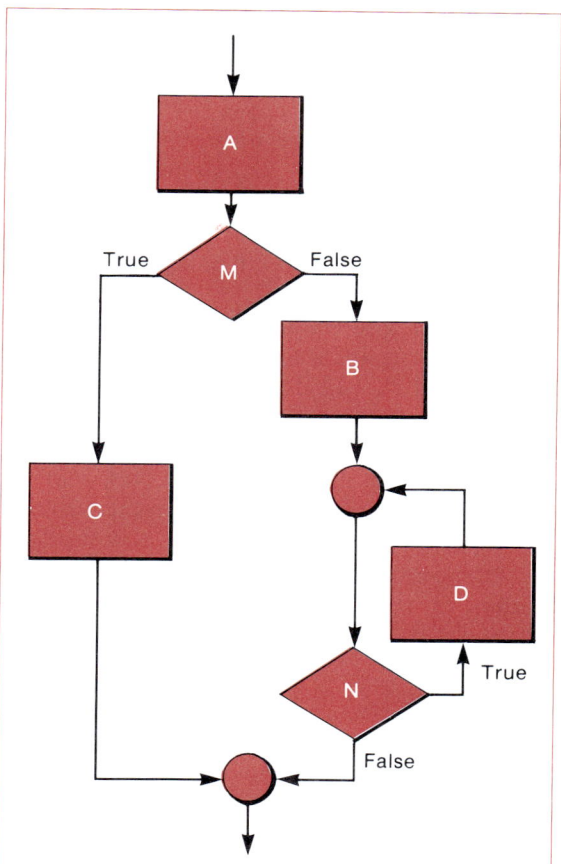

Figure 8–7
Flowchart of Structured Programming

tistics concerning the students enrolled during the current semester. We will follow the structured approach described in the chapter and begin by defining the problem. The input, processing, and output all must be described before the second step—designing a solution—can be accomplished. The last three steps in the development process will be described in the next chapter.

Defining the Problem

As discussed earlier, unless the problem is clearly defined, whatever program is written will most likely not successfully meet requirements. In defining the problem for calculating student tuition we know we must generate a list of items included in a student's total tuition fees; however, what other factors must we consider?

Output   The output will consist of a number of bills, each reflecting the amount to be paid by an individual student. In addition, an informational report will be generated. The structure of the output must be examined carefully to determine not only the items to be included, but also the format of these items. Figure 8–8 illustrates through a report mock-up the contents of the student tuition fee bill.

Input Next, the input needed to obtain the output specified can be determined. The main input will be the student registration card, which contains the student's name, number, class, college, major, residency status, and credit hours. Other input concerning the general fee and the amount charged per credit hour is supplied within the program.

Processing Once the ouput and input requirements are determined, the processing steps needed to obtain the desired results must be specified. These steps should describe, in general terms, the processing that will take place.

First, the general fee amount must be determined based on the residency status of the student. Second, instructional fees are to be calculated. Third, total tuition fees then will be calculated so that the last step—printing the bill—can be accomplished. Totals must be kept of the number of resident and nonresident students, as well as the total amount in tuition fees charged by the university that semester. These totals will be used to generate the statistical report. Once the problem has been defined to this level of detail, the analyst/programmer can proceed to develop a structured solution to the problem.

Planning a Solution

The first step in planning a solution is to take each of the processing steps outlined in the definition stage and construct a tentative program flow. First, to determine the general fee, the student's residency status must be examined. If the student is a resident, the general fee will be two hundred dollars; otherwise, the fee will be five hundred dollars for a nonresident. Next, the instructional fees will be calculated by multiplying the number of credit hours by thirty-five dollars for both resident and nonresident students. Third, a total payment-due figure is determined by adding together the general fee and the instructional fee. The bill then is printed, and the calculations are repeated for the next student. When all the student bills have been processed, the statistical report is printed.

Figure 8–8 Student Tuition Fee Bill

```
                    Fall Tuition Fees

  Smith, John R.
  287-40-4661

     General Fee  . . . . . . . . . . . . . . . . . . . . . . . . .   XXX
     Instructional Fee . . . . . . . . . . . . . . . . . . . . .   XXX
     Amount Due                                           $XXXX
```

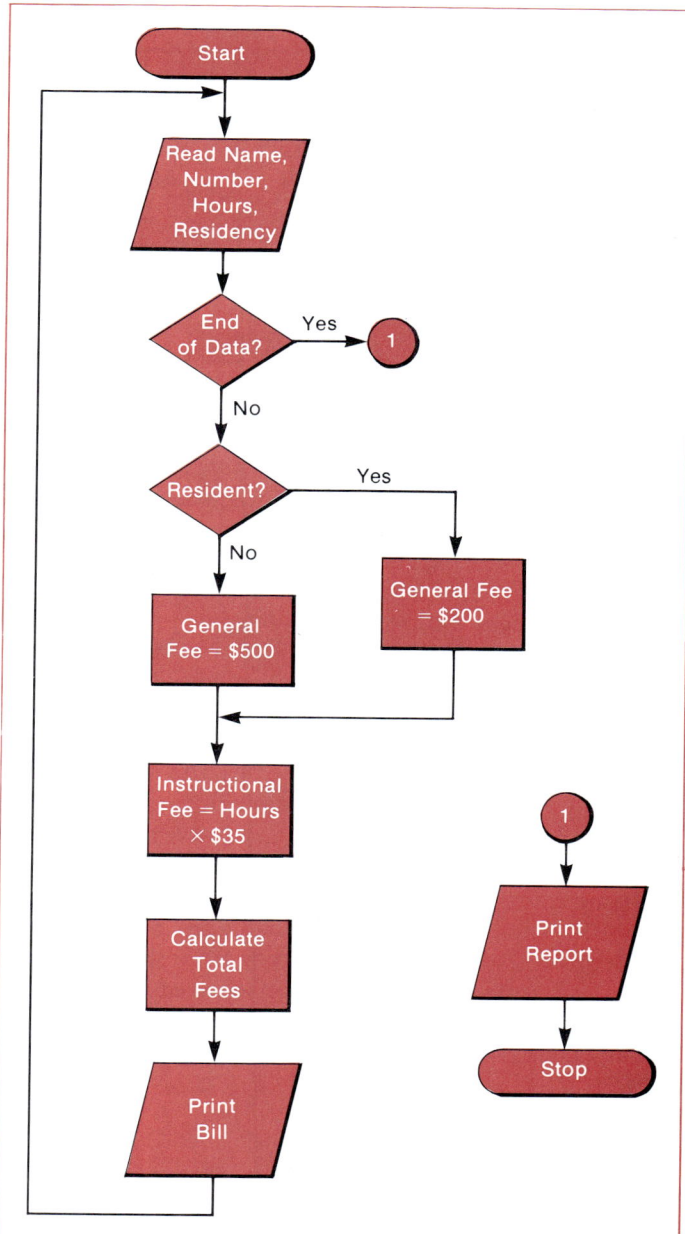

Figure 8–9
Macroflowchart for
Tuition Fees Program

A macroflowchart representing these steps without the accumulation of totals for the statistical report is illustrated in Figure 8–9. Pseudocode describing the processing functions also can be developed, as shown in Table 8–1. The first statement requires input of data and is represented by the symbol ▭. The next statement involves a decision; if there are no more students, skip the processing section of the program, and in-

Table 8–1   PSEUDOCODE FOR TUITION FEES PROGRAM

While more students, process student data:
   Read student name, number, hours, residency.
   If student is a resident, general fee = $200.
     Otherwise general fee = $500.
   Multiply credit hours by $35 to get instructional fee.
   Add general and instructional fees to get total fees.
   Print bill.
   Go process another set of student data.
Print report.

stead print the report. This statement is represented by a decision block, $\diamond$, with a branch that goes past the processing statements when the end of the data is reached. Next is another decision symbol asking the residency status of the student. Depending on the result of that test, one of two general fee amounts will be assigned, as represented by the processing symbol, $\square$. The next two statements—regarding the calculation of instructional fees and total fees—also are represented by the symbol $\square$. Printing a student bill requires output of data and is represented by the symbol $\square$. The statement sending processing back to the read statement is a loop, which will repeat until the last student's data has been processed. The final portion of the program requires output of data in the form of a report and is represented by the symbol $\square$.

Usually the calculation of student tuition fees involves more than has been described. For example, many universities charge more for graduate students than undergraduate students and less per credit hour for full-time than part-time students. Our example can be expanded as shown by the macroflowchart in Figure 8–10. A microflowchart illustrates the calculation of undergraduate resident fees in greater detail. A similar microflowchart can be constructed to illustrate the specific steps needed to calculate undergraduate resident and graduate tuition fees. Pseudocode for the expanded version of the problem is represented in Table 8–2.

Accumulators

The loop is a powerful tool not only for reducing the number of program statements required to perform a task or series of tasks, but also for accumulating totals. For example, as each student's total tuition fees are calculated, they can be added to the overall total of fees that the university should receive that semester. An **accumulator** is a programmer-supplied storage location that maintains a running total of values during processing. The total of resident and nonresident students can be accumulated, as well as any other desired value. When each student's data has been processed, these totals can be printed on summary reports required by the university. An important point to remember, however, is

Figure 8—10 Enhanced Fee-Processing Program

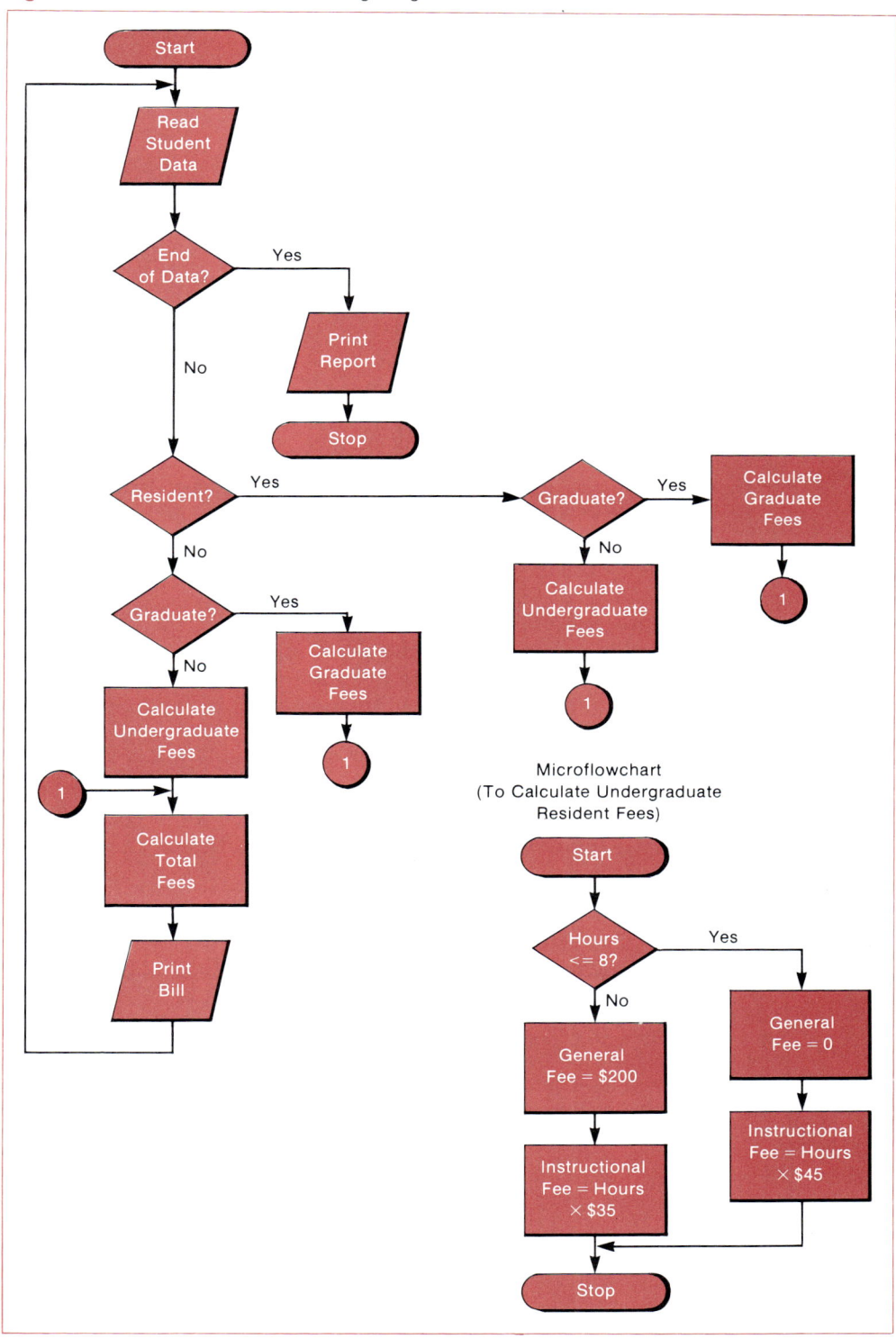

Table 8–2 PSEUDOCODE FOR ENHANCED FEE-PROCESSING PROGRAM

While more students, process student data:
   Read student name, number, hours, residency.
   If student is a resident
     And if student is a graduate
       Calculate graduate fees.
     Else calculate undergraduate fees.
   Else student is a nonresident.
     If student is a graduate
       Calculate graduate nonresident fees.
     Else calculate undergraduate nonresident fees.
   Calculate total fees.
   Print bill.
   Go process another set of student data.
Print report.

that these totals can be used only after all the student data has been read and processed. Although the accumulators are positioned within the loop, the displaying of their final values must occur outside the loop after it has been executed the required number of times (unless intermediate subtotals have been requested).

To accumulate totals in a program that uses a loop, the programmer must do three things. First, he or she must initially set the storage location to 0 to insure that there are no previous values stored in that location. Second, statements must be included within the loop to accumulate the desired totals. It is important to place these statements in the correct logical positions within the loop. For example, a statement accumulating the total of all university fees should appear directly after the statement that calculates the total tuition fees for a student, not before it. Finally, the programmer must provide for the printing or stor-

Table 8–3 PSEUDOCODE WITH ACCUMULATORS

Read student name, number, hours, residency.
If no more students, print report.
If student is a resident, general fees = $200.
Add 1 to total of all resident students.
   Else general fees = $500.
   Add 1 to total of non-resident students.
Multiply credit hours by $35 to get instructional fees.
Add general and instructional fees to get total fees.
Add total to total fees of all students.
Print bill.
Go process another set of student data.
Print report.

ing of the total outside the loop once the loop has been executed the desired number of times. The student fee-processing example without enhancements is written in pseudocode in Table 8–3 to describe the steps necessary to accumulate the total of all student tuition fees, as well as the number of resident and nonresident students enrolled.

- Computers are dependent on the skills and creativity of programmers to utilize their capabilities.
- A structured approach to problem solving involves following these five steps: (1) defining the problem; (2) designing a solution; (3) writing the program; (4) translating, debugging, and testing the program; and (5) documenting the program.
- Defining the problem consists of determining the output, input, and processing requirements.
- The logic and steps to follow in solving the problem can be planned with the use of flowcharts or pseudocode.
- Computer problems are solved through the repeated use of four basic logic patterns: simple sequence, selection, loop, and branch.
- Flowcharting the basic logic patterns requires the use of standardized ANSI symbols, whereas pseudocode involves written descriptions of processing steps.
- Two levels of flowcharts can be developed: macroflowcharts and microflowcharts. Each macroflowchart can include more than one microflowchart detailing specific steps.
- In planning a solution to a problem, programmers must consider how the program will receive data as input, the need for accuracy controls, and output requirements.
- Structured programming provides a standardized method of problem solving. Following this approach decreases testing time, as well as maintenance time and effort. Complexity is reduced, thus improving clarity.
- The branch pattern is not recommended by structured programming advocates, because it interrupts the sequential flow of logic.

1. In a structured approach to problem solving, the programmer follows five steps. List and briefly explain each step.

2. Why is it so important to clearly define the problem as the first step in computer problem solving? Name the three items defined in this step.

3. The computer solves a problem by following a set of logical instructions. What is meant by program logic?

4. List the four basic logic patterns. Which pattern does not involve a test condition?

5. Which of the basic logic patterns is not in accordance with structured programming, and why?

6. What is pseudocode? How does it differ from flowcharting?

7. Discuss the advantages and disadvantages of flowcharting. When would pseudocode be a more beneficial alternative?

8. Name the two levels of flowcharts and how they can be distinguished from one another.

9. The programmer must know ahead of time from what devices—such as magnetic tape, cards, disks, and so on—data will be entered. Why is this so important?

10. What can the programmer do to protect accuracy throughout processing?

11. Hard copy is just one of the forms that output can take. List two other ways in which output can be generated.

12. What is the significance of structured programming? Discuss the benefits of this approach as opposed to an unstructured approach.

13. List the four objectives of structured programming. Why is the term GOTO-less programming often associated with this approach?

PROGRAM DESIGN

LEARNING OBJECTIVES

After studying this chapter, you will be able to do the following:

☐ Explain top-down design and the importance of structured design methodology.
☐ List the desirable qualities that should be present in a program.
☐ Understand the importance of documentation and be familiar with the items that should be documented.
☐ Explain the chief programmer team (CPT) organization and the benefits that can be realized from such an approach.

Chapter 9

INTRODUCTION   Numerous possible solutions can be developed for any programming problem. There is a major difference, however, between a workable program solution and a good program solution. Even though a program may function without errors and produce the correct output, it is not necessarily a good solution. This chapter discusses structured design methodology, which can be applied to both program and system design. The purpose of structured design methodology, as will be described, is to aid the programmer or analyst in developing a solution that has a number of important characteristics.

This chapter also continues the discussion of the program development process: writing the program; translating, debugging, and testing the program; and documenting the program.

STRUCTURED DESIGN METHODOLOGY

Structured programming was discussed in the last chapter to emphasize the need to take a systematic and efficient approach in developing problem solutions. Especially when a problem is complex, the process of dividing it into a series of modules, each performing one function, becomes extremely important. Each functional step is written as an independent module, known as a **subroutine.** An **executive routine** (the controlling module) then accesses these subroutines as they are needed. The programmer's job is then greatly simplified, since the problem is broken down into more manageable parts. The modular approach is also useful when a programming team develops the solution, since the work involved can be easily subdivided among several programmers.

The use of modules facilitates solution planning. The various modules, or subroutines, must be organized in a way that shows how they are related to one another. **Top-down design** is a frequently used method of organizing a solution by defining it in terms of major functions to be performed and then further breaking down these major functions into subfunctions.

The top-down approach begins by the programmer viewing the problem in the most general way. The broadest overall description of the steps to be followed in the solution process is known as the **main control logic.** More and more detail is then introduced as these steps are further subdivided. Depending on the complexity of the problem, several levels of modules may be required, with the lowest-level modules containing the greatest amount of detail.

The structure of the problem solution is represented visually by arranging the modules in a hierarchical manner, much like an organization chart. The relationships existing between the different modules can easily be seen in this graphic representation, also referred to as a **structure chart.** Figure 9–1 shows a portion of such a chart for calculating grade point average. At the highest level in the hierarchy is the main

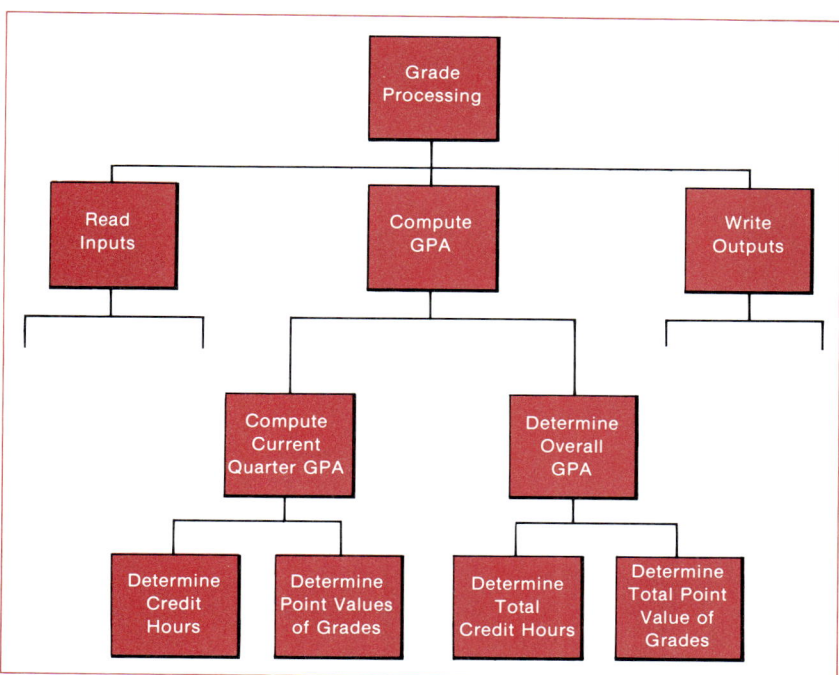

Figure 9–1 Partial Structure Chart: Grade Processing

control module, represented in Figure 9–1 by the block labeled "Grade Processing." This module, the executive routine mentioned earlier, is further broken down into lower-level modules that correspond to the grade-processing application's three basic functions: reading a student's master grade record and a current-quarter grade card, computing the grade point average (GPA), and writing an updated master file and student grade reports. The "Compute GPA" module can be further divided into "Compute Current-Quarter GPA" and "Determine Overall GPA" modules. These two modules are then even further subdivided to show that credit hours and point values of grades received must be determined in both cases.

The structure chart is arranged in a top-down format to show how the pieces of a program can be linked together. The flow of control passes downward from one module to another. In other words, each module has control of the modules directly below it and is controlled by the module directly above it. The higher-level modules are both processing modules and control modules; they describe processes and also control modules below them in the hierarchy. At the lowest level, modules involve only processing. The complete structure chart for the grade-processing application is shown in Figure 9–2.

Certain rules must be followed when top-down design is used. For instance, each module should perform only one logical function and

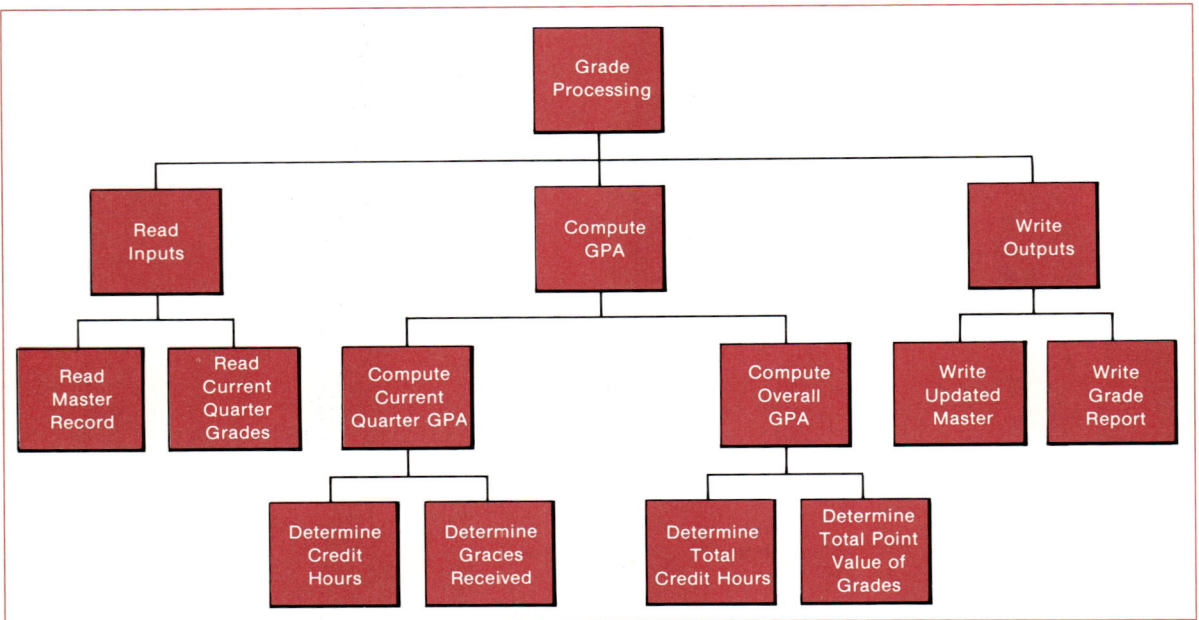

Figure 9–2 Complete Structure
Chart: Grade Processing

should be independent of other modules. A module should be executed only when control is passed to it from the module directly above. In addition, once a module has been executed, control should be passed back to the module directly above it. The return process continues until the main control module is reached.

To make the translation into program statements as simple as possible, each module should be relatively small. Normally, a module consists of no more than fifty or sixty lines of code so that only a single page of computer printout is necessary for listing module statements. Testing and debugging, as well as maintenance procedures, are simplified when module size is limited in this manner.

Frequently, the requirements for a system may change before it has been completed. The structure of the top-down design allows changes or alterations to be made to a solution plan without great difficulty. Each module should have only one exit and one entrance point, a requirement that not only makes the basic flow easy to follow, but also permits easy modification of program logic to accommodate system changes.

Another benefit of top-down design is that modules can be written and tested as they are completed without waiting for the entire program to be coded. To accomplish this, programmers create dummy modules and use them in place of the lower-level modules for testing purposes. A calling program (a form of executive program which requests execution of subroutines) is used to pass control from one module to another. Significant errors in higher-level modules can be isolated by observing

Documentation

As business progresses in the area of user-friendly systems and software, the need for user-friendly documentation also grows. Rising to meet these needs is a new group of specialists known as **technical writers** (or **documentation teams**). Technical writing provides the opportunity to combine a technical and liberal arts background into a profitable future in our high tech–oriented society. Technical writers must have a good background in computer science or management information systems and the ability to write in a clear, concise manner. They are responsible for writing the instructions, descriptions, and explanations that constitute the user's manuals that accompany new products.

The need for technical writers will continue to grow as businesses realize that no matter how good their products are, if their customers cannot understand how to use them, they will not be coming back for more. Some of the major companies that now employ technical writers are IBM, DEC, and Bell Laboratories.

whether control is correctly transferred between the high-level modules and the dummy modules. As the lower-level modules are designed and coded, they can replace the dummy modules and be tested in a similar manner. Thus, by the time the lower-level modules have been coded, all other modules already have been tested and debugged.

Documentation and Design Tools

One of the most important aspects of program design and system design is the preparation of accurate, easy-to-understand descriptions of processing steps and procedures that must be followed. These written and graphic descriptions are known as **documentation.** Structure charts provide a good form of documentation; however, they show only functions, their relationships, and the flow of control. To gain a better understanding of the processing flow, the order of execution, and the transfer of control to and from each module, programmers use other techniques to supplement structure charts. Program flowcharts, record layouts (discussed in Chapter 14), system charts, and pseudocode are a few of the commonly used techniques. Another useful documentation and design tool is known as **HIPO.**

HIPO The term **HIPO** (Hierarchy plus Input-Process-Output) describes a series of diagrams that serve as visual aids in supplementing structure charts. Structure charts emphasize only structure and function, whereas HIPO diagrams show other aspects, such as the inputs and outputs of program modules.

A typical HIPO package consists of three types of diagrams that show varying degrees of detail. The **visual table of contents (VTOC)** illustrates

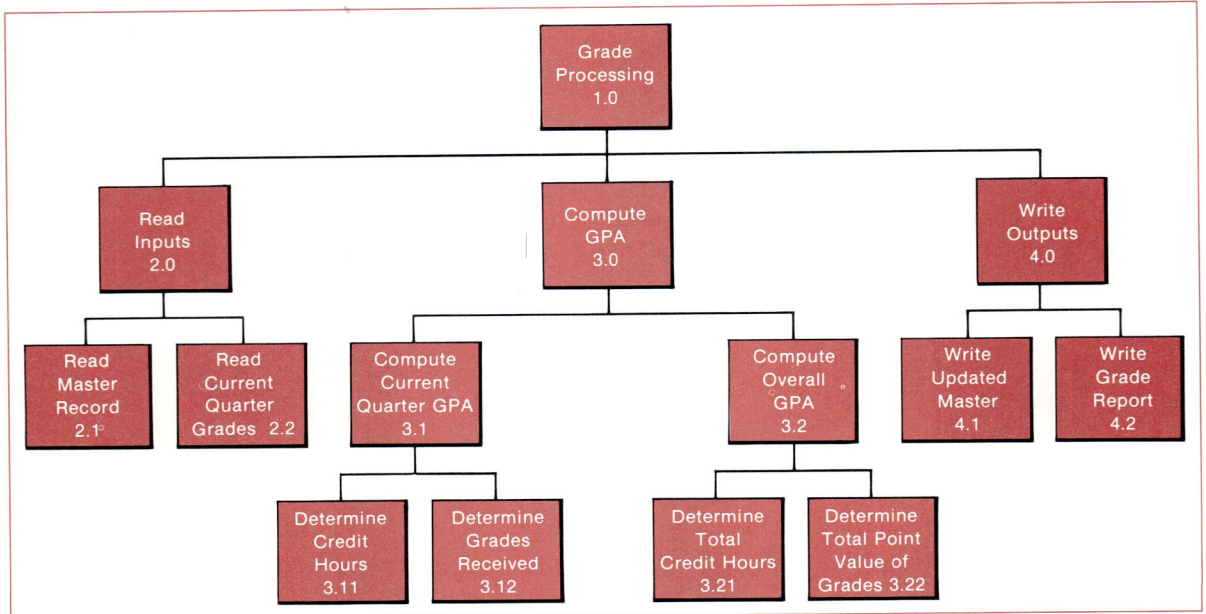

Figure 9–3 Visual
Table of Contents
(VTOC): Grade Pro-
cessing

the functions of the program in the most general and concise manner. Although the VTOC and the structure chart are very similar in appearance, the former technique includes some additional information that outlines the order of processing. Each module in the VTOC is given one identification number. The numbers serve to indicate the sequence of processing, as well as to reference each individual module. Figure 9–3 shows a VTOC for the grade-processing application introduced in Figure 9–1.

A second HIPO diagram, known as an **overview diagram,** can be used to show more detail about the main functions of a program illustrated in the VTOC. An overview diagram illustrates a module's input, output, and processing, as well as how one module is related to the next. The reference number shown in the overview diagram corresponds to the number assigned in the VTOC. An overview diagram for the grade-processing "Read Inputs" module (2.0) is shown in Figure 9–4.

The third type of HIPO diagram that can be used is the **detail diagram.** Just as the name implies, a detail diagram shows the greatest amount of detail about a particular function or subfunction. The amount of detail shown will depend on the complexity of the problem to be solved. Generally, enough detail should be included to enable a programmer to understand the functions, develop a flowchart or pseudocode, and then write the code to perform those functions. A major benefit of detail diagrams is that as more detail is established, flaws in the program design can be uncovered and corrected before too much programming time has been wasted.

HIPO diagrams are excellent documentation and communication tools. The varying degrees of detail described—from very general in the

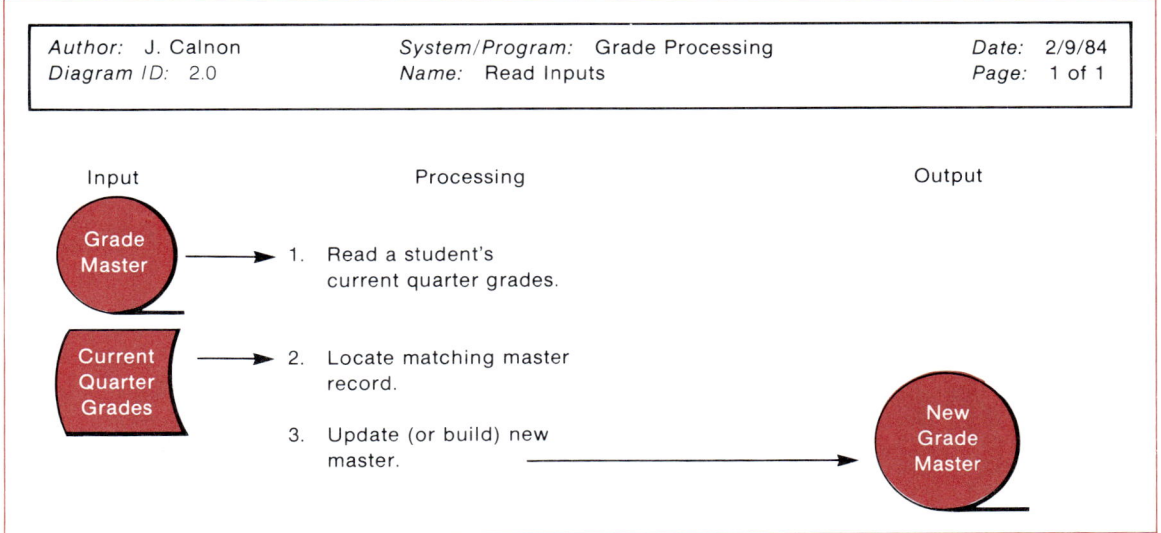

| Author: J. Calnon | System/Program: Grade Processing | Date: 2/9/84 |
| Diagram ID: 2.0 | Name: Read Inputs | Page: 1 of 1 |

Figure 9—4 HIPO Overview Diagram for the "Read Inputs" Module

VTOC to very specific in the detail diagrams—allows HIPO to provide documentation to individuals at different levels of technical understanding. Management and systems people, as well as programmers, all can comprehend at least one HIPO diagram.

PROGRAM DEVELOPMENT REVISITED

As Chapter 8 discussed, a program is developed by following a series of steps in a structured approach to problem solving. The following five steps make up this approach:

1. Define the problem.
2. Design a solution.
3. Write the program.
4. Translate, debug, and test the program.
5. Document the program.

The first two steps were covered in the last chapter. In discussing structured design methodology, parts of the last three steps—writing and testing the program—were just mentioned. We will now examine these last three steps in greater detail.

WRITING THE PROGRAM

Writing the program involves converting the processing steps outlined in the flowchart or pseudocode into lines of step-by-step instructions.

Computer Warfare

The army has invented a new video game, Janus. The design of the program is said to be excellent, and Janus obviously has impressed the big brass. The Pentagon claims that Janus is the world's most advanced combat simulator.

Players are armed with tanks, jets, artillery, personnel carriers, helicopters, chemical agents, and nuclear weapons. To get a good idea of their situations, players can call up a detailed topographical map of any fifteen-square-mile section of the earth's surface. Once the "war" has begun, Janus will keep in mind everything from flight time and reloading time to temperature, humidity, and wind speed. All of this contributes to the calculation of the most accurate estimate of casualties and damages possible.

The army currently is using Janus to train combat officers at the U.S. Army War College in Carlisle, Pennsylvania. Although the results of the war games are classified, the army has admitted that its officers tend to reach for the nuclear button too quickly. The army claims to use Janus to show potential officers this tendency. Army officials feel that presenting officers with accurate casualty estimates through Janus will provide the United States with officers who will be much less likely to rush for the nuclear button in a real combat situation.

This process is referred to as **coding.** Each programming language has its own rules, known as language **syntax,** for the programmer to follow in coding. The instructions, written according to the syntax of the language chosen, should direct the computer in solving the problem in the same sequence specified by the programmer in the solution design. The programmer must be certain, however, to follow the language syntax precisely. A program may be unable to execute properly if even a single coding error is made. If errors are made, the time necessary to develop an efficient and well-functioning program is needlessly extended. It is therefore of great importance that close attention be given to coding a program that is well structured and error-free.

The programmer can consider numerous programming languages when selecting an appropriate language. A number of considerations are weighed, but the choice of one particular language over another usually is made on the basis of the type of application to be solved. For example, FORTRAN is a language designed primarily for scientific applications; COBOL is normally used for business applications; and Ada is generally used for applications involving a computer embedded in a larger electronic or electromechanical system, such as a weapons system. Other considerations include the size and capabilities of the computer to be used (since some languages require larger amounts of storage space than others) or the ease of coding and readability of a language. Regardless of the language chosen, instructions must be written to direct the computer, step by step, in solving the problem. Programming languages will be discussed in more detail in Chapter 10.

Types of Statements

Programming languages consist of a number of different types of **statements** (instructions) that specify various types of operations to be performed by the computer. Although the structure and syntax can vary greatly from one language to another, most high-level languages have instructions that fall into the general categories of comments, declarations, input/output (I/O) statements, computations, transfers of control, and comparisons.

Comments The type of statement known as the **comment,** or remark, is not executed within the program. Comments are inserted at key points in the program as documentation notes to anyone reading the program to explain the purposes of program segments. For example, if a series of statements sorts a list of names into alphabetical order, the programmer may want to include a remark to explain that process: "This segment sorts names in ascending alphabetical order."

Declarations The programmer uses **declarations** to define data items used in the program. Examples include definitions of files, records, initial values of counters, accumulators, reusable functions, constants, and so on.

Input/Output (I/O) Statements Communication between the CPU and the I/O devices is permitted through the use of **input/output (I/O) statements.** Input statements bring data into main storage for use by the program. Output statements transfer data from main storage to output media such as hard copy printouts or displays on VDTs. These statements differ considerably in form (although not so much in function) from one programming language to another.

Computations Computational instructions perform arithmetic operations: addition, subtraction, multiplication, division, and exponentiation. These **computations** are common to all programming languages but can vary in structure and format according to the language.

Transfers of Control Another type of instruction, the **transfer of control,** allows the sequence of execution to be altered by transferring control. A conditional transfer of control alters the sequence only when a certain condition is met. An unconditional transfer always changes the sequence of execution.

Comparisons The final type of statement is the **comparison,** which allows two items to be compared to determine whether one item is less than, greater than, or equal to another. Based on the result of the comparison, transfer of control might occur. Note: You will be exposed to specific examples of each statement type when you study the BASIC supplement to this book or learn another language.

Desirable Program Qualities

Regardless of the language chosen or the different types of statements that can be used within that particular language, the programmer should strive to produce a well-structured program. When the problem has been coded, it should be as easy to read and understand as possible. Even though a program can produce the correct output, it is not necessarily a good program if the logic is needlessly complex. Not only will the program be difficult to read; it will also be difficult to maintain and modify. To develop high-quality programs, programmers should firmly adhere to the following standards:

● Programs should be easy to read and understand. The data names selected should be descriptive of the data that is represented. Statements should be arranged in a format that is easy to read and understand. For example, certain statements could be indented to improve readability and to make a particular segment more understandable to the reader.
● Programs should be reliable. They should consistently produce the correct output. All formulas and computations, as well as logic tests and transfers of control, must be accurate.
● Programs should work under all conditions (they should be "robust"). Programs should include statements that will give the correct response to a given test or comparison. Consider, for example, a program that uses the days of the week as input to determine the flight schedule for a particular day. If an error is made in spelling—say, Tuesday is spelled **Tusday**—a response should be given that requests data to be reentered until the spelling is corrected.
● Programs should be maintainable. They should be easy to update and modify. Programs should be written in independent modules, each performing a single logical function. Maintenance then is easier, since a change in one module does not require changes to be made in the entire program. The costs of changes over the life of a program frequently exceed the costs of initial program development, so ease of maintenance in a program is very important to overall costs.
● Programs should be efficient. Another reason behind making program logic simple when designing the solution is that execution time will undoubtedly be reduced. Statements should be written that will implement the solution in as little time as possible. The CPU time is an expensive resource, especially if the user is charged hundreds of dollars for just one minute of CPU time from the company renting computer time. An efficiently written program could save the user thousands of dollars a year.

Figure 9–5 illustrates a program segment written two different ways. Although both methods will produce the same result, the example using good coding standards is more easily read and understood.

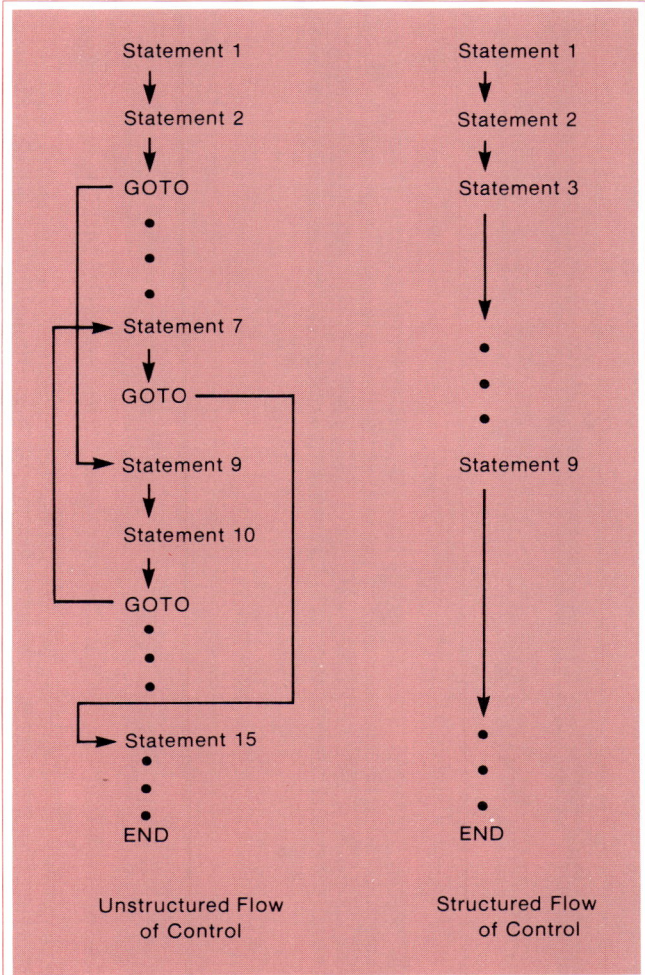

Figure 9–5 Structured Versus Unstructured Program Design

Program Development Aids

A programmer can use special coding forms when writing a program. The COBOL coding form shown in Figure 9–6 was designed to allow the programmer to write a COBOL program according to the standard rules of the language, such as column and space restrictions. Each line of the coding sheet can be keypunched onto one standard eighty-column card or entered as one line of code on a terminal. Similar coding forms are available for other programming languages.

Instead of using special forms, the programmer can enter coding directly through a VDT with an attached keyboard. It is much faster to enter statements from such a terminal than from a keypunch machine, and errors are more easily corrected. Programming statements entered on the terminals can be checked for errors in grammar and syntax, thereby helping reduce later debugging time. Program development is

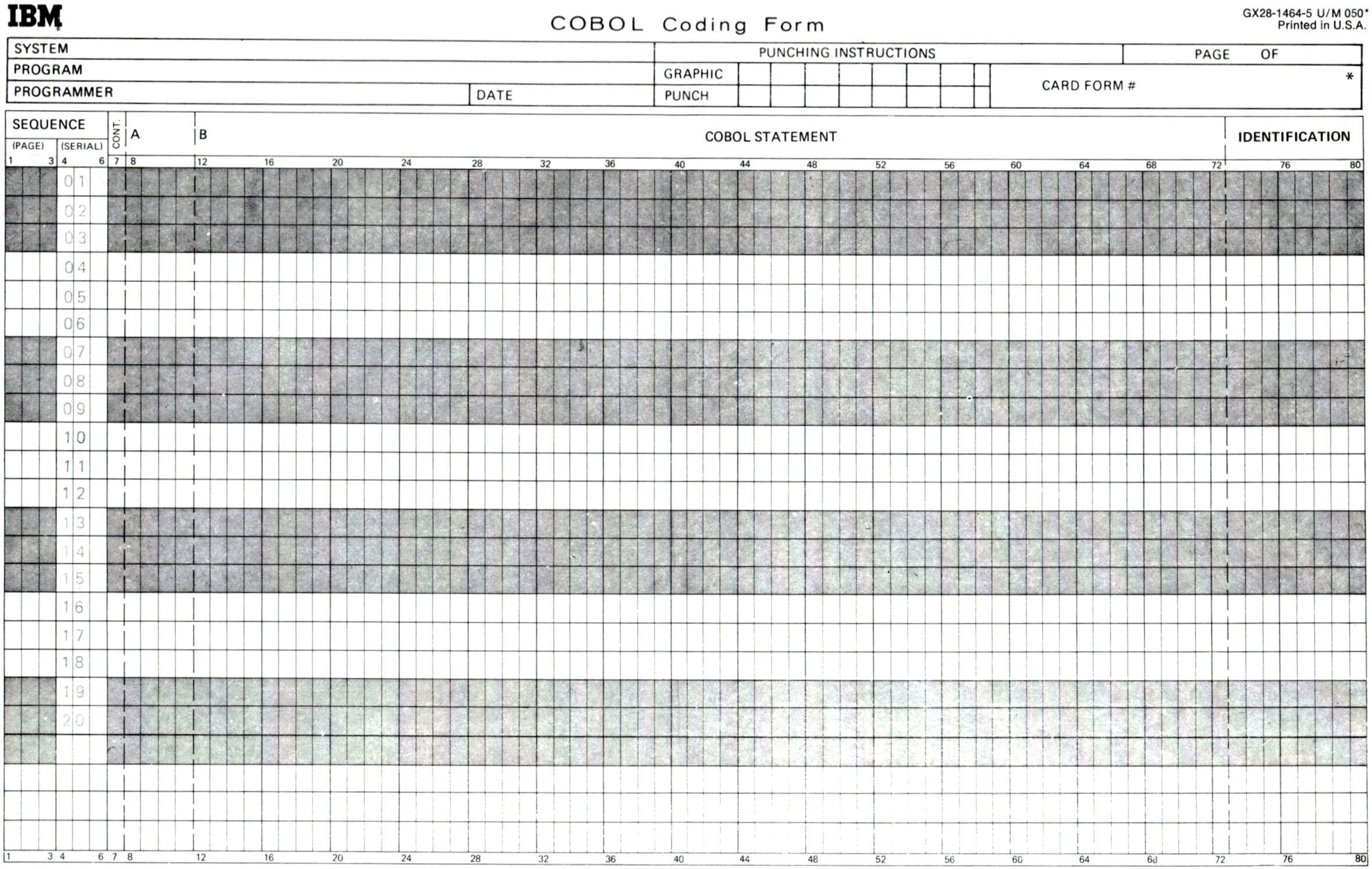

*A standard card form, IBM Electro C61897, is available for punching source statements from this form. Instructions for using this form are given in any IBM COBOL reference manual. Address comments concerning this form to IBM Corporation, LDS Publishing, Dept. J04, 1501 California Ave., Palo Alto, Ca. 94304

*No. of forms per pad may vary slightly

Figure 9–6 Cobol Coding Form

highly labor intensive, and even modest amounts of automation can generate benefits in the form of increased productivity.

After the program has been written, it is submitted to the computer via cards, tape, or disks, or by typing directly onto a terminal. Once the program has been entered into the computer, it must be translated into a form the computer can understand. Although a program can be written in a language such as COBOL or BASIC, which is much easier for the programmer to write than machine language, it then must be converted (compiled) to a series of 1s and 0s. During translation, syntax errors are located and subsequently corrected by the programmer. Language translation will be discussed in greater detail in the next chapter.

Debugging the Program

Although the computer can locate and list errors made in spelling and syntax, it cannot determine logic errors. Such errors may result when the programmer does not clearly understand the problem or is not aware of the statements that must be written to produce a desired result.

Only very rarely will a program execute correctly the first time it is run. Errors in programs are referred to as **bugs,** and the process of locating and correcting such errors is referred to as **debugging.** The amount of time spent on debugging varies according to the programmer's skill level and the quality of the program. It is not uncommon, however, for one-third to one-half of a programmer's time to be spent on debugging (although the programmer usually is engaged in other parallel activities such as documentation during these debugging periods).

Testing the Program

When the syntax errors found during translation have been corrected, the program is ready to be tested. The objective of testing the program is to determine whether accurate results are produced when the program is run. Sample test data is submitted, and the output is compared with manually prepared results from the same set of data. It is important that test data reflect all possible conditions to insure that there are no logic errors. For example, incorrect or inappropriate data should be entered along with correct data to test whether the program is capable of both processing correct data and appropriately handling errors.

An approach frequently used in testing is to break the program into modules and test each module separately. This procedure is especially appropriate when a structured approach to program development has been followed. Each module is coded and tested before the entire program is tested. By running each module separately with test data, errors can be isolated and corrected more easily. Modules can be run and rerun until all errors have been corrected.

Another technique that can be used in detecting errors or omissions is **desk checking,** or "playing computer." In this procedure, the programmer pretends to be the computer by reading each instruction in the logical sequence specified and simulating how the computer would respond. In this way flaws in program logic can be detected. If the programmer still has difficulty in locating errors, the program can be given to another programmer to test. Sometimes, after spending a great deal of time in debugging, the original programmer tends to overlook errors or assumes a clarity that may not exist. When another person tests the program, errors in logic are often easily identified.

Despite the amount of time a programmer spends in locating and attempting to correct errors, a program may continually fail to execute properly. In such cases two commonly used diagnostic procedures usually are available to the programmer: dump programs and trace programs.

A **dump program** is run to print out the contents of primary storage and registers. The dump is printed in hexadecimal notation (see Figure 9–7); the programmer examines the listing in this notation to determine whether data and instructions have been stored correctly in the proper locations. Trying to understand a dump can be a cumbersome procedure at first; however, once it has been learned, dump reading can be a very useful debugging technique. Because of advances in software tools, applications programmers use dump programs less than they did in the past.

A **trace program** is much easier to analyze than is a dump program. The trace lists each step of the program in the order actually executed by the computer. Sometimes a trace program generates a listing of only the line numbers of the statements in the sequence they are executed. The trace is often used in combination with desk checking to determine whether the flow of processing is occurring as intended by the programmer. The values of selected variables also can be displayed by a trace program to help determine whether necessary calculations have been performed correctly.

Once the program has been tested without errors resulting, it is ready to be run on a scheduled basis. Before actually implementing the program, however, a few finishing touches are added.

Figure 9–7 Dump

```
                              CORE ADDRESSES SPECIFIED-      000002  0 0001F6
000000   05C0E020 C0880021 E020C0B5 001E4130   00031B66 1B77E000 C0A9000C D208C0B6   *............................K...*
000020   C0A9D201 C0C5C0B3 5350C0B2 1A651844   D508C0A9 C1024770 C0405C40 C0F647F0   *..K..E...........N...A..... .6.0*
000040   C056D508 C0A9C108 4770C052 5C40C0FA   47F0C056 5C40C0FE 1A755250 C0C8E020   *..N...A...... ...O.... .....H..*
000060   C0B5001F 4630C014 D204C0B6 C0D35260   C0D95270 C0E6E020 C0D3001F E1600000   *.........K....L...R...W...L.....*
000080   0000E060 C00001F4 07FEF140 C1C3E3C9   E5C9E3E8 40404040 D4C9D5E4 E3C5E240   *.......4..1 ACTIVITY    MINUTES *
0000A0   404040C3 C1D3D6D9 C9C5E2E2 E6C9D4D4   C9D5C740 40F3F040 F0E3D6E3 C1C9D5C7   *   CALORIESSWIMMING  30 OTOTAING*
0000C0   40404040 404040F3 F0404040 40404040   404040F3 F3F0E3D6 E3C1D340 40404040   *        30        330TOTAL      *
0000E0   40404040 40F9F540 40404040 40404040   F1F0F7F0 F5F5F5F5 00000008 00000013   *        95        10705555........*
000100   0000000B C2C9C3E8 C3D3C9D5 C7D9E4D5   D5C9D5C7 4040F5F5 F5F5F5F5 00000000   *....BICYCLINGRUNNING  555555....*
000120   F5F5F5F5 F5F5F5F5 F5F5F5F5 F5F5F5F5   F5F5F5F5 F5F5F5F5 F5F5F5F5 F5F5F5F5   *555555555555555555555555555555555*
```

DOCUMENTING THE PROGRAM

Documentation consists of written descriptions and explanations of programs and other materials associated with an organization's data-processing system. It is one of the most important, yet often neglected, components of the programming process. Documentation that records important information concerning each program must be prepared in a format that can be easily read and understood by those using the program.

The programmer develops documentation on two levels. First, appropriate comments are placed within the program itself explaining to the reader the objective of the program, the definitions of variables used, or any special processing steps. Programs containing documentation often highlight comments (which are not actually executed by the computer) with asterisks, making the program easier to read (see Figure 9–8). Second, documentation is prepared for users of the program. The following items should be included for users other than the original programmer:

- A general description of the objective or objectives of the program.
- A program flowchart or pseudocode.
- A complete description of the contents and formats of all data inputs, outputs, and files to be used.
- A listing of the source program, (the program written in a language such as COBOL or BASIC) along with a listing of the program output generated by test data.
- A statement of the hardware requirements for running the program, such as magnetic tape drives, disk drives, and card readers, as well as the estimated processing time and storage requirements.
- A statement of the software requirements, such as utility programs (standard programs to sort, merge, copy, and reformat data) and library programs (programs used frequently in the organization); this statement also may identify the programming language to be used and list the reasons for choosing it.
- An operator's manual, sometimes known as a **run book.** This contains instructions to the operator that specify how the program is to be run on that type of computer system.

```
10 REM ***********************************************
20 REM ***  THIS PROGRAM COMPUTES MONTHLY         ***
30 REM ***  PAYMENTS FOR MORTGAGES                ***
40 REM ***  MI = MONTHLY INTEREST RATE            ***
50 REM ***  I  = INTEREST RATE                    ***
60 REM ***  M = MORTGAGE MULTIPLICATION FACTOR    ***
70 REM ***  MP = MONTHLY PAYMENT                  ***
80 REM ***  MA = MORTGAGE AMOUNT                  ***
90 REM ***  Y  = NUMBER OF YEARS FOR THE MORTGAGE ***
95 REM ***********************************************
```

Figure 9–8 Program Documentation in Comment Form

**Making the Most
of Manuals**

Try as they might, computer
manufacturers have a difficult time
producing manuals that tell users
exactly what they want to know, in the
order they want. Part of the problem
is that different users use different
applications of the same software on
different systems. Often, the
information that is most useful to one
user may be buried under pages and
pages of the information most useful
to someone else.

There are several ways to
customize your manual, making it

easier for you to use. Underline or
highlight the sections you use most
often. This will make them easier to
spot as you leaf through the pages.
Use paper clips to mark the
beginnings of the most important
chapters. As you read through the
manual, scribble explanatory notes in
the margins. Even write a few
additional references in the margin of
the table of contents. When you find a
section that you constantly refer to,
you may even want to tape a strip of
paper to the top of the page and
label it. That way you can locate the
section without even opening the
book.

● A user's manual containing documentation designed to aid people not
familiar with running a program. For example, the user's manual will
explain how to first establish contact with the computer and then specify the procedures that should be followed to enter and execute a program, along with other information that may be useful.

Once a program has been developed, it must be maintained on a continuing basis. If modifications become necessary, the documentation
previously prepared serves as a reference guide for analysts and programmers making the change. Without it, a programmer might have to spend
days or weeks to fully understand what a program does and how it accomplishes its objectives. Documentation is also useful in evaluating
the effectiveness of applications; it helps determine whether procedures
are efficient and, if they are not, where changes need to be made. The
success of any program or system requires that documentation be complete and up to date. Not one program change should be permitted without corresponding documentation updates.

A program, along with the required documentation, has been written
to solve the programming problem begun in Chapter 8 (see Figure 9–9).
Instructions are written in the BASIC language to generate a listing of
each student's tuition fees, in addition to a summary of the number of
resident and nonresident students and the total tuition fees charged by
the university. The output of the program is shown in Figure 9–10.

MANAGEMENT OF SYSTEM PROJECTS

Throughout this chapter and Chapter 8, a great deal of emphasis has
been placed on following a structured approach in the development of a

Figure 9–9 Basic
Program with Sample
Data for Case Study

```
100 REM ***** CALCULATION OF STUDENT FEES *****
105 REM *                                      *
110 REM *     MAJOR VARIABLES:                 *
120 REM *         STUDENT$ = STUDENT NAME      *
130 REM *         NUM$ = STUDENT NUMBER        *
140 REM *         HOURS = CREDIT HOURS         *
145 REM *         STATUS$ = RESIDENCY STATUS   *
148 REM ****************************************
150 READ STUDENT$,NUM$,HOURS, STATUS$
155 PRINT:PRINT:PRINT
160 IF STUDENT$ = "LAST" THEN PRINT "TOTAL RESIDENTS = ";RESIDENTS:
            PRINT "TOTAL NONRESIDENTS = ";NONRESIDENTS:
            PRINT "TOTAL FEES = $ ";FEES:STOP
210 IF STATUS$ = "RESIDENT" THEN GENERAL = 200:
            RESIDENTS = RESIDENTS + 1
    ELSE GENERAL = 500: NONRESIDENTS = NONRESIDENTS + 1
240 INSTRUCTION = HOURS * 35
250 TOTAL = GENERAL + INSTRUCTION
260 FEES = TOTAL + FEES
270 PRINT:PRINT
275 PRINT TAB(5);"FALL TUITION FEES"
276 PRINT
280 PRINT STUDENT$
290 PRINT NUM$
300 PRINT:PRINT
330 PRINT "GENERAL FEE";TAB(27);GENERAL
340 PRINT "INSTRUCTIONAL FEE";TAB(27);INSTRUCTION
350 PRINT TAB(25);"-------"
360 PRINT TAB(5);"AMOUNT DUE";TAB(26);"$";TOTAL
370 GOTO 150
380 DATA "DEBARR, MARK M.",256-83-3454,16,RESIDENT
390 DATA "LINDBURG, SALLY",342-87-8452,17,NONRESIDENT
400 DATA "SCHULER, MELISSA R.",435-83-8234,15,RESIDENT
410 DATA LAST,0,0,0
500 END
```

Figure 9–10 Output
for Case Study

```
        FALL TUITION FEES

    DEBARR, MARK M.
    256-83-3454


    GENERAL FEE              200
    INSTRUCTIONAL FEE        560
                         -------
        AMOUNT DUE        $ 760




        FALL TUITION FEES

    LINDBURG, SALLY
    342-87-8452


    GENERAL FEE              500
    INSTRUCTIONAL FEE        595
                         -------
        AMOUNT DUE        $ 1095




        FALL TUITION FEES

    SCHULER, MELISSA R.
    435-83-8234


    GENERAL FEE              200
    INSTRUCTIONAL FEE        525
                         -------
        AMOUNT DUE        $ 725



    TOTAL RESIDENTS =   2
    TOTAL NONRESIDENTS =   1
    TOTAL FEES = $   2580
```

problem solution. Different techniques, such as top-down design, modular design, HIPO diagrams, pseudocode, and structured programming, are all beneficial in designing an efficient, easy-to-maintain system in a minimal amount of time. However, even the most organized and well-structured system may contain errors and omissions that can render it useless. To avoid such a situation, a system must be reviewed periodically at various stages of development. Although errors can surface after a system becomes operational (sometimes even months or years later), such problems can be minimized with careful planning and review. Effective coordination of the efforts involved in the development process is also essential.

Chief Programmer Team (CPT)

The **chief programmer team (CPT)** organization was first used by certain divisions of IBM. In this approach, a small number of programmers are placed under the supervision of a chief programmer. The goals of the CPT approach are to produce a software product that is easy to maintain and modify, to improve programmer productivity, and to increase system reliability. The CPT approach has the advantage of producing fewer mistakes; thus, the implementation of projects is not delayed. In addition, through coordination of programming efforts, communication is improved and a better-trained staff emerges.

The chief programmer is an experienced programmer who is responsible for the overall coordination and development of the software system, as well as for its overall success. A lead analyst works with the chief programmer in large-system projects. In such cases, the lead analyst may supervise the general system design effort while the chief programmer concentrates on the technical development of the project.

Another member of the CPT is the backup programmer. This very technically oriented programmer assists the chief programmer in the development, testing, and evaluation of alternative designs. The chief programmer and the backup programmer normally code the most critical parts of the overall system. Separate modules of the system are programmed and tested by different programmers. The chief and backup programmers then work with one or more other programmers to integrate all parts into a complete system. This approach uses both structured programming and top-down design.

The CPT also uses a librarian to collect and organize documentation associated with the project. The information collected is useful when evaluating the project at different intervals to determine possible flaws, omissions, or inconsistencies. The librarian also relieves the team programmers of many clerical tasks they otherwise would have to perform. The librarian's duties include the following:

- Preparing computer input from coding forms completed by programmers.
- Submitting inputs and distributing computer output to programmers.

- Maintaining up-to-date source program listings in archives available to all programmers.
- Updating test data and implementing changes in programs and job control statements as required.
- Maintaining up-to-date documentation.

The librarian role frequently is filled by a programmer trainee or by an individual with a clerical background who is just entering the computing field.

Structured Review and Evaluation

The earliest approach to programming defined the programmer's task as one that was completed on an individual basis. Many programmers viewed their work as private creations and would not allow others to see their creations until they were finished.

Numerous problems resulting from this traditional approach isolated programmers from one another and thus limited communication. For instance, programs often contained errors and were not well structured. In 1971 Gerald Weinberg of Ethnotech, Inc., wrote **The Psychology of Computer Programming** (Van Nostrand Reinhold), a book that advocated the concept of "egoless" programming. Egoless programming requires that programmers not view their programs as personal possessions, but rather as products to be shared with others for suggestions of improvement or change.

Weinberg's idea caught on. In response to this change in attitude toward programming, structured reviews and evaluations evolved. An **informal design review** now is used in the early phases of system development to allow selected managers, analysts, and programmers to study the system design documentation. Each person responds with suggestions for additions, deletions, and modifications before the actual coding of program modules. A **formal design review**, called a **structured walkthrough** or **design inspection**, sometimes is conducted after the detailed parts of the system have been sufficiently documented. A review team of two to four members (**not** including any managers) discusses the overall completeness, accuracy, and quality of the design with program designers.

SOURCES OF PROGRAMS

There are several methods of acquiring needed software. If programmers are employed on a permanent basis within an organization, programs are said to be developed **in-house.** This approach has the advantages of allowing programming creativity while satisfying user requirements. A problem that results, however, is that payroll expenditures tend to be high for the programming staff. In addition, programming effort may be needlessly duplicated, since programs to accomplish the same objectives may already have been written by other organizations. Software development can account for the greatest percentage of a data-processing department's budget. If programs can be acquired at costs below those required for in-house development, additional savings can be realized in conservation of scarce resources such as programming time and talent.

An alternate approach to program development is to hire contract programmers. These programmers are temporary employees who are hired, or contracted, to complete specific programming tasks. Contract programmers work either independently or for firms that locate programming work for them.

There are several advantages, as well as disadvantages, to hiring contract programmers as opposed to developing programs solely in house. If programming assignments must be completed on a short-term basis, it would be economical to employ programmers only on those occasions. Even if an in-house staff is already employed, contract programmers can be hired temporarily to complete large programming tasks more quickly. Since many contract programmers work independently (often at home), away from the distractions of the normal work environment, high-quality programs often are produced. The opposite situation, unfortunately, also can occur: programs can be developed that are not well documented or easily maintained. Since contract programmers are hired only on a temporary basis, they may not have the incentive to produce efficient, well-structured programs. Thus, a firm should exercise caution when employing contract programmers.

SOFTWARE PACKAGES

Many different types of programs can be purchased as prewritten packages from software firms. A **software package** is a standardized set of programs designed to solve a particular type of problem. The most obvious benefit of purchasing such a package is that a significant amount of time and labor is saved by not having to develop programs in-house. The major disadvantage is that packages may not always fit the user's needs and may require tailoring to the user's individual requirements. Proprietary software packages are designed and owned by an organization but sold or leased to many users. Software packages have been written to solve numerous types of problems; costs of such packages range from $15 or less to more than $100,000.

There are two general categories of software packages. **Systems packages** are responsible for making the computer operate more efficiently, whereas **applications packages** solve particular programming problems. Systems packages exist in many forms; examples include operating systems, data base management systems, report generators, compilers, and I/O control routines. Applications packages have long been available for engineering and scientific applications; the Statistical Package for the Social Sciences (SPSS) and General Purpose Systems Simulator (GPSS) are examples. One of the most popular types of applications

Digital Diets

The first of the fad diet floppies already have appeared: menu planners, calorie counters, and nutritional analyzers. Like so many areas, the problem with computerized dieting is not that the applications programs do not exist; they simply are not integrated.

The possibilities for integration (linking existing programs) could be especially effective in providing total diet treatment. Kitchen inventory programs could be linked with diet programs to provide a list of possibilities for dinner that fall within both dieters' caloric quotas and the contents of their cupboards. Of course, the nutritional contents would be analyzed beforehand to insure that the dieters received proper nourishment, and the appropriate recipes would be printed out from electronic recipe files. Linked exercise programs could even suggest suitable after-dinner activities. Perhaps, in the distant future, such a system even could be accompanied by a domestic robot of the proper temperament to enforce the regimen.

packages used on microcomputers allows the computer to lay out spreadsheets. A spreadsheet is a form with rows and columns used to present and evaluate numeric information useful in business planning, report generation, forecasting, and other areas. Other applications packages range from educational programs used in computer-assisted instruction to games, inventory control, word processing, and almost any other application that can be thought of.

- Top-down design involves organizing a solution in terms of the functions to be performed and then breaking the functions into subfunctions.
- A structure chart shows the relationships existing between the different functions of a solution by arranging them in a hierarchical manner.
- HIPO diagrams serve as visual aids in supplementing structure charts by showing the inputs and outputs of modules.
- Writing a program involves choosing a programming language and translating the flowchart or pseudocode prepared earlier into lines of code.
- The choice of programming language entails weighing several factors. The type of application to be implemented is one of the prime considerations.
- In writing a program, the programmer should try to incorporate desirable qualities such as making the program easy to read and understand, efficient, reliable, able to work under all conditions, and maintainable.
- After the program is written, it must be compiled, tested, and debugged.

- Compiling involves translating the program into machine code so it can be executed by the computer.
- Debugging the program can take up a large part of the programmer's time, since logic errors not identified in compilation must be located and corrected.
- In testing the program, sample data—which includes correct as well as incorrect data—is used as input.
- Desk checking, dump programs, and trace programs are all used to locate errors.
- Documentation is one of the most important, yet most neglected, parts of the programming process.
- The chief programmer team (CPT) concept was developed to insure the development of a well-structured, error-free program in a minimal amount of time.

REVIEW QUESTIONS

1. Explain top-down design. How can the relationships existing between the different parts of a program or system design be visually represented?

2. List three rules that must be followed in top-down design.

3. What are the three types of HIPO diagrams, and what does each illustrate?

4. When writing a program, you should attempt to incorporate several desirable qualities. What are these qualities?

5. Explain several reasons for the inclusion of comment statements in a program. Where in the program are they placed?

6. What is the objective of testing a program? What characteristics should test data include?

7. When a structured approach to program development has been followed, how is testing performed?

8. List and explain two diagnostic procedures for aiding programmers in detecting logic errors.

9. What is documentation, and why is it so important?

10. List at least three items that are included in documentation for the users of programs.

11. What are the goals of a CPT?

12. Who makes up the CPT, and what are the responsibilities of each member?

13. What is meant by the term egoless programming?

14. Why were structured reviews and evaluations created?

15. List three potential sources of programs, along with advantages and disadvantages of each.

10

PROGRAMMING LANGUAGES

LEARNING OBJECTIVES

After reading this chapter, you will be able to do the following:

☐ Identify and describe the three levels of computer language.
☐ Explain language translation through the use of assemblers, compilers, interpreters, and pseudocompilers.
☐ Distinguish between machine-oriented, procedure-oriented, and problem-oriented programming languages.
☐ List advantages and disadvantages of each programming language described.
☐ Understand when it would be appropriate to choose one specific language over another.

Chapter 10

INTRODUCTION   As described in the last chapter, once the solution for a problem has been planned, the programmer must write the instructions necessary to direct the computer in solving the problem. The first step, however, is for the programmer to select a language. This may seem a difficult decision at first, considering the fact that there are at least two hundred programming languages from which to select!

This chapter will describe some of the most popular programming languages and their advantages and disadvantages. The same program example will be illustrated for most languages discussed so that the differences in structure from one language to another can be seen. This application tabulates the calories burned by three different physical fitness activities: bicycling, running, and swimming. The per-minute expenditure of calories is 8.2 for bicycling, 19.0 for running, and 11.4 for swimming. The program reads the minutes associated with each mode of exercise along with the name of the activity, and it calculates and outputs minutes and calories for each, plus total minutes spent and calories expended for all three.

LEVELS OF LANGUAGE

When computers were first developed they could perform only simple, repetitive tasks. The instructions required to execute those tasks, however, were extremely difficult and complicated for the programmer to write. Computer capabilities and programming languages today have taken opposite paths in terms of complexity. Modern-day computers can perform tasks that are much more complex; however, the programming languages designed to communicate with these computers have become much more user oriented. The increasing complexity of computer applications can, in fact, be attributed more to the increased usability of programming languages than to advances in computer hardware.

There are numerous computer languages in existence today, and they can be divided into three levels according to their degree of complexity. These levels are machine language, assembly language, and high-level language. Assembly languages and high-level languages are referred to as **source** languages to distinguish them from binary machine language.

Machine Language

Machine language was the first language programmers used to write computer programs. It consists of a combination of 1s and 0s indicating on and off states of electricity. Data and instructions are represented in binary form, which is the only form the computer can understand.

Every computer has its own machine language, which cannot be transferred to another type of computer. Each machine language instruction indicates both the function to be performed and the location of the data and instructions to be manipulated. Coding programs in machine

Babbage

Tony Karp of **Datamation's** Reader Forum has developed a satirical imaginary "perfect" computer language for the future—Babbage. Babbage is named for Charles Babbage, the man who desperately tried to develop the first computer and instead lived in poverty for many years. Thus, it is dedicated to the first "systems designer to fall behind schedule and go over budget."

Babbage is an all-purpose language that encompasses many functions not available with current languages. For example, the conditional statements are much more inclusive. Instead of the simple IF/THEN/ELSE, Babbage gives us the WHAT IF, the OR ELSE, and the WHY NOT. GOTOs are replaced with the GOING GOING GONE. This produces completely random branches and is equivalent to the effect of ten GOTOs.

Babbage eliminates the DO WHILE loop and, in its place, contributes a barrage of more useful loop structures: DON'T DO WHILE NOT, DIDN'T DO, CAN'T DO, WON'T DO, and MIGHT DO. And, of course, for the systems operator, the DO UNTO OTHERS.

CASE statements also are expanded in function. Babbage allows for the JUST IN CASE, the BRIEF CASE, the OPEN AND SHUT CASE, the IN ANY CASE, and the ever-persistent BASKET CASE.

Naturally, the complexity of Babbage requires a sophisticated operating system: the Virtual Time Operation System (VTOS). The VTOS enables the CPU to process an infinite number of jobs concurrently. This is done with a slight illusion and, although all of the jobs seem to be running right now, some of them actually are running next week.

language can take months because of such detail requirements, making programming a very expensive and tedious procedure. Because of the difficulty involved in using machine language, other languages were developed to simplify the programming process.

Assembly Language

Assembly language allows **mnemonics,** which are symbolic codes, to be used in place of the 1s and 0s required in machine language. The programmer's task was made less difficult when assembly language was developed, since convenient abbreviations, such as M for **multiply** or ST for **store,** could be used instead of binary representation. Programmers have to designate mnemonics not only for operations to be performed in assembly language, but also for the storage locations to be accessed. A symbolic name is given to a particular data item or instruction as well as to a numeric address; once this assignment has been made, the programmer can refer to the symbolic name rather than the address throughout the remainder of the program. Although assembly language is more user oriented than is machine language, it is still quite complex to work with.

Figure 10–1 One
Basic Statement and
Corresponding Ma-
chine Language In-
structions

> High-Level Language (Applesoft Basic):
> C = A + B
> Machine Language (6502 Machine Language) Represented in
> Hexadecimal Notation:
> 0C02 A0 00 0D
> 0C05 AD 0E 0D
> 0C08 79 60 0C
> 0C0A D8
> 0C0D 8D 3E 0C

High-Level Languages

High-level languages have the highest degree of user orientation. Because the programmer is not required to have an in-depth understanding of computer operations, programming becomes much easier. Many high-level languages are English-like and allow the use of common mathematical terms and symbols. The time and effort required to write a program are reduced, and programs are easier to correct and modify.

High-level languages are so called because they are farthest removed from the hardware; they least resemble the 0 and 1 combinations of machine language. In assembly language, one instruction corresponds to one machine instruction; with high-level languages, however, one instruction frequently corresponds to several machine instructions. Figure 10–1 illustrates one statement written in the high-level language BASIC and the machine language instructions corresponding to it. High-level language statements are more concise, since it is not necessary to specify the addresses of many required storage locations; they are handled automatically.

A major benefit of high-level languages is that they are not machine dependent. Many high-level languages are standardized, allowing programs written for one machine to be transferred to another type of machine. Those languages that are not standardized usually require only minor modifications in order to be made "portable" from one machine to another; thus, programming expense is greatly reduced when new equipment is purchased.

LANGUAGE TRANSLATION

Most programmers would gladly choose to code programs in high-level or assembly languages rather than machine language. The only language the computer can understand, however, is machine language, so these artificial languages must be translated into machine-usable code after they are entered into the computer. The instructions written by the programmer are referred to as the **source program.** These instructions are converted by a **language translator** into an **object program** in machine-executable form. Note that language translators are themselves programs, not hardware.

Assemblers and Compilers

The language translator for an assembly language is called an **assembler** program. Most high-level language translators are called **compiler** programs. Both assemblers and compilers are designed for specific machines and languages. For example, a compiler that translates a source program written in FORTRAN into an object program can translate only FORTRAN (see Figure 10–2), and into only a specific machine language.

Assembly language is translated into machine language in a shorter amount of time than is high-level language. Each assembly language command is translated directly into a machine language command, whereas each high-level language command must be translated into multiple commands. Even though the computer may be executing thousands of instructions per second, it may take several minutes for a program written in high-level language to be compiled.

During assembly, or compilation, the object program is generated along with a descriptive listing of program statements (the **source listing**) and errors **(diagnostics).** The errors are usually violations of the rules associated with the programming language. For example, a syntax

Figure 10–2
FORTRAN Program
Translation

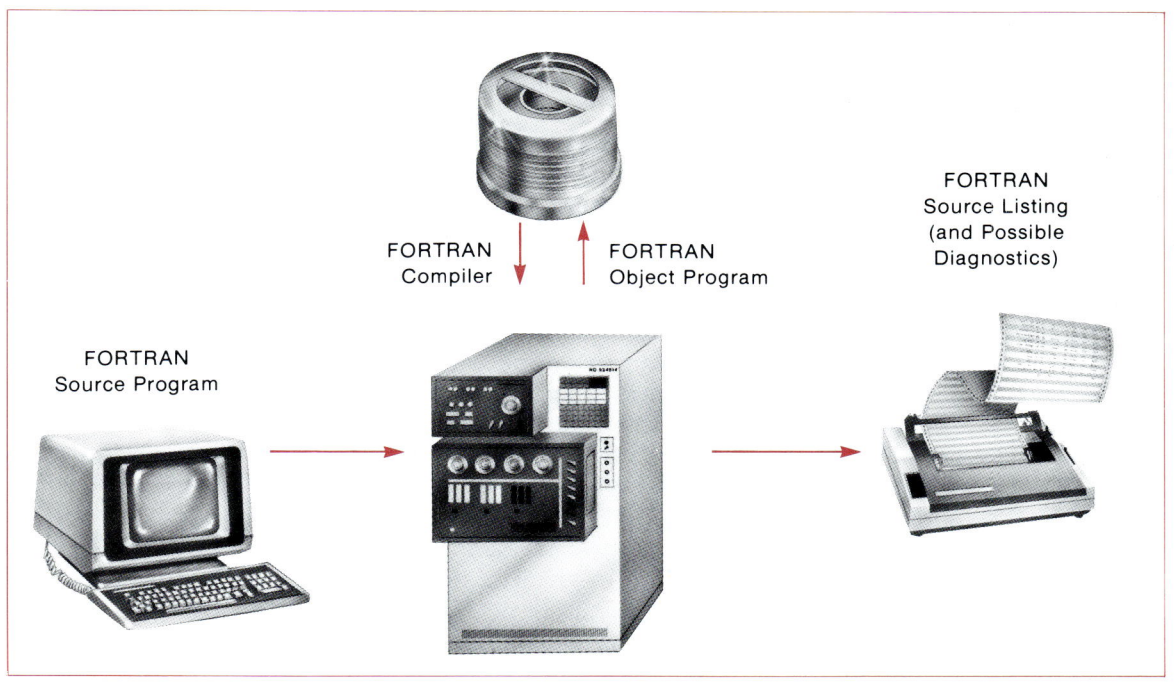

FORTRAN
Compiler

FORTRAN
Object Program

FORTRAN
Source Listing
(and Possible
Diagnostics)

FORTRAN
Source Program

The Origin of the Compiler

FLOW-MATIC, which led to COBOL, the computer language used in most business applications, was designed primarily by Commodore Grace Murray Hopper. At the time, Commodore Hopper was in the navy working on the United States' first computer—the Mark I. All the programming for the Mark I was being done in octal code (base 8). Commodore Hopper began to notice that it was very easy to make mistakes in copying and recopying octal code.

To take the tedium out of the job, Commodore Hopper made a library of the pieces of code that she had found to work. She assigned each piece a name and had the computer put the pieces together and copy them into octal code (or machine language). That was the first compiler, and it made all of today's high-level languages possible. Subsequent developments under Commodore Hopper's leadership led to a language called FLOW-MATIC, an important precursor to COBOL.

error will result if commands such as READ or WRITE are spelled incorrectly or if required punctuation is omitted. When all syntax errors have been corrected, the object program is ready to be executed with test data.

Interpreters

Another method can be used to process source statements in place of a compiler. Instead of compiling the source program into an object program and then executing the program once it is in machine-executable form, each line in the source program is executed immediately by an interpreter, sometimes resulting in printed output before the next line is executed. An **interpreter** is a program stored either in primary memory or read-only memory (ROM) that reads, interprets, and executes one statement from a source program at a time. Rather than generate an object program, the interpreter reads an instruction and carries out the functions specified according to a resident vocabulary of key words.

The use of an interpreter eliminates the waiting time required to compile an entire program into machine language before execution. There are several disadvantages in using interpreters, however. First, many errors made in the coding of a source program are not found until the program is being executed. Second, the interpreter requires significantly more time to read and execute source statements than would be required to execute object statements. In addition, if a statement is to be executed several times—within a loop pattern, for example—the interpreter must retranslate the same statement every time it goes through the loop. As a result, interpreters can operate very slowly. Interpreters for BASIC are commonly used on microcomputers. Figure 10–3 summarizes the two primary methods of program translation.

A **pseudocompiler** is another method of language translation that first translates a program into one- or two-byte data values referred to as **tokens.** These values, called **pseudocode** or **intermediate code,** then must be translated into machine code. This process is achieved by another part of the pseudocompiler known as the **pseudocode interpreter** or **code generator.** One benefit of using a pseudocompiler is that it is not necessary to retranslate a statement repeatedly, as must be done with an interpreter. Another benefit is the ability to use the pseudocompiler portion on a variety of machines, requiring only a new pseudocode interpreter or code generator for different hardware. A pseudocompiler generating an intermediate code called **P-code** is commonly used when working with Pascal. A corresponding intermediate form of Ada is called DIANA (Descriptive Intermediate Attributed Notation for Ada).

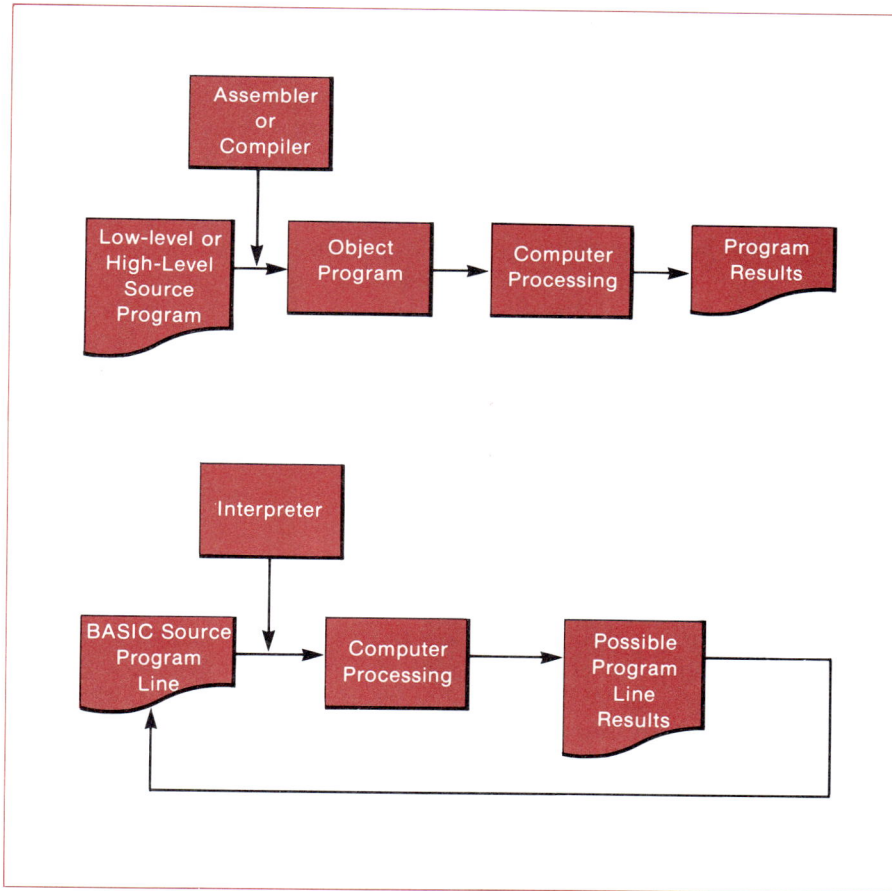

Figure 10–3 Two Methods of Program Translation

BATCH-ORIENTED VERSUS INTERACTIVE PROGRAMMING LANGUAGES

Batch-oriented Programming Languages

Batch-oriented programming languages are used to solve problems that recur periodically. For example, payroll processing usually is done in batch mode, since the same payroll processing functions must be performed each week or month. A batch program submitted to the computer contains all the instructions and data necessary to process payroll. Once the instructions and data have been put into the CPU, processing takes place without intervention from programmers or users.

Several different batch programs can be submitted to the same computer at different times. Instead of being executed as soon as they are entered into the CPU, several programs will be stored together on an auxiliary storage device. Each program, or job, is assigned a priority based on the urgency of its completion, and the programs then are executed by the computer in priority order. Several jobs may be read in at the same time but processed at different times during the day or night, depending on their priorities.

There are three categories of batch-oriented programming languages: machine-oriented, procedure-oriented, and problem-oriented languages. **Machine-oriented languages** are so named because they have the least amount of user orientation. Programming in a machine-oriented language requires a great deal of technical knowledge about the internal operations of the particular computer used. The statements written in machine language correspond to actual machine operations.

In response to the difficulty associated with programming in machine-oriented languages, high-level languages were developed (as described earlier in the chapter). There are two categories of high-level languages: procedure oriented, and problem oriented. **Procedure-oriented languages,** such as COBOL, FORTRAN, and PL/I, focus on the computational and logical procedures required to solve a problem. A **problem-oriented language,** such as RPG, describes the problem and solution without detailing the necessary computational procedures.

Interactive Programming Languages

With an **interactive programming language,** a programmer can communicate directly with the computer. Unlike batch-oriented languages, interactive languages allow processing to be interrupted for data to be entered by the programmer via a terminal. Inquiries can be made from local or remote terminals, and results can be returned in seconds. (In contrast, programs submitted in a batch mode may be delayed several hours before they are executed and the results returned to the user.) The three major interactive programming languages discussed in this chapter are BASIC, Pascal, and APL.

Numerous languages have been developed to allow programmers to communicate with the computer. Each language has characteristics that

COMPUTERS IN SCIENCE

Scientists were among the first to use computers for enormous number-crunching operations. The scientific community continues to rely on some of the most sophisticated computers for research and development, simulation and modeling, and experimental activities in such fields as meteorology, geophysics, atomic and nuclear physics, biology, chemistry, and astronomy.

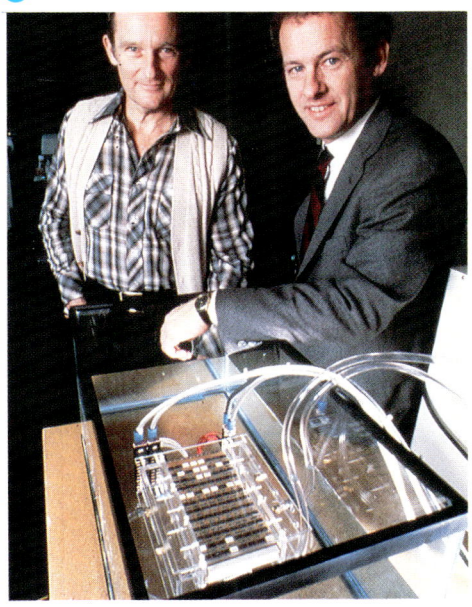

1. The field of space exploration relies on computer technology. Numerous computer devices are shown in this "fish-eye" lens view of the flight deck of the Space Shuttle Orbiter 102 Columbia. Each crewmember has his hand-controller to his immediate front for controlling the spacecraft. Between the two positions for the crewmembers are the flight computer and navigation aid console. Immediately in front of the console are the three cathode ray tubes (CRTs) used to display computer data and information for the crew. **2.** Considerable research is being done to increase computer capabilities. This Bell Laboratories scientist places a high-speed Josephson junction circuit in an ultra-cold liquid helium bath. Faster and smaller than conventional silicon circuits, such devices could be the basic elements in "supercomputers" of the future. **3.** Inventor Seymour Cray and Cray Research president, John Rollwagen, left, pose with the Cray 2 computer as it sits in a tank of liquid coolant. So dense are the machine's circuits that the fluid must be used to dissipate heat generated during operation.

Computers in Science—continued. **4.** One goal of artificial intelligence experts is to design robots that are able to simulate the thinking process. A step in that direction has been made by Odetics, Inc. Odex I, the first functionoid is capable of walking and working on any terrain. Its applications are vast. Research is already underway for its possible use in other commercial applications such as agriculture, forestry, construction, material handling, nuclear power plants and utilities, medicine, firefighting and prevention, and law enforcement.

5. Geophysicists of Marathon Oil Company examine a computer-generated contour map of a three-dimensional plot of the earth's interior. Geophysicists use special tools and techniques to remotely sense and measure characteristics below the surface. Computers such as this have magnified the geophysicists' ability to interpret remote measurements.

4

5

6. This three-dimensional computerized model of earth's layers aids the geologist in the interpretation of earth exploration data. **7.** Aero Service uses an IDIMS (Interactive Digital Image Manipulation System) computer to interactively integrate diverse exploration data and remote sensing imagery. **8.** Computers are used for data acquisition and processing in petroleum exploration. A computer analysis of the nature and content of geological layers at a potential petroleum exploration site is shown here.

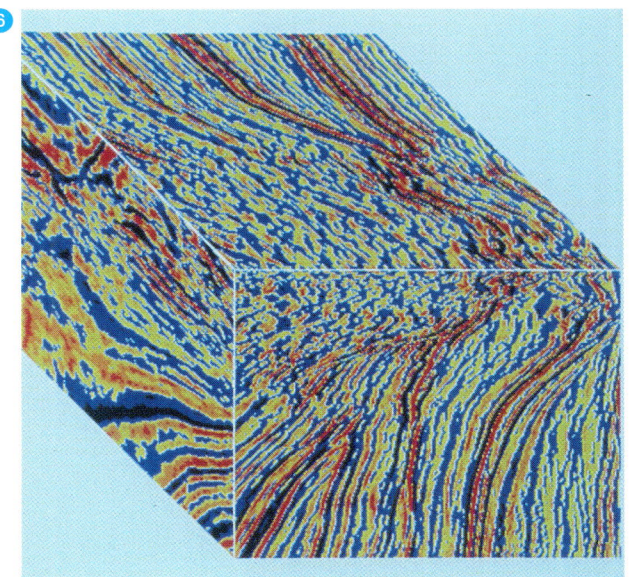

Computers in Science—continued. **9.** A topographical map made of color-coded contour lines is an easy task for computers. Color-elevation relations plus an accompanying key replace the small numbers printed on the contour lines of conventional maps. Graphic representations such as this provide scientists with a clearer understanding of the mathematical relationships of the variables under analysis. **10.** With use of a micro-probe electron microscope and a computer, metal samples can be evaluated for measurements of specific elements such as copper.

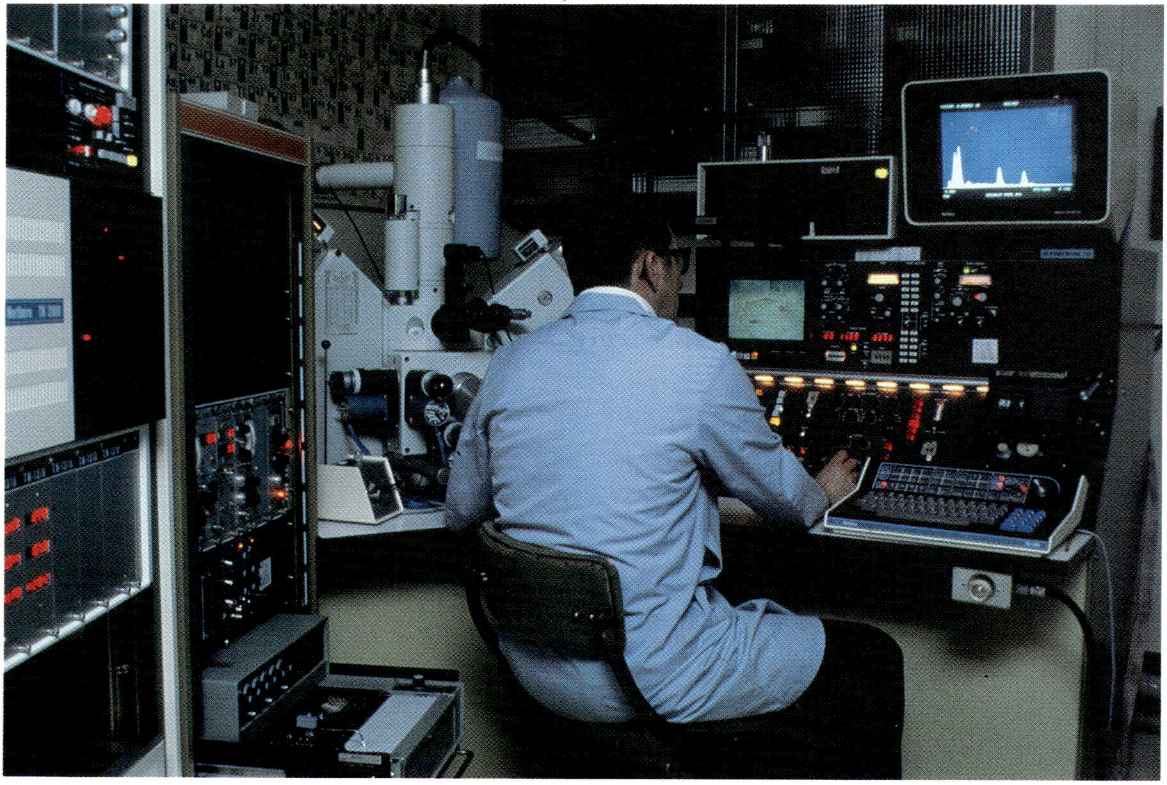

11. Geologists used computers to analyze the compound elements found in rocks.
12. From 570 miles above Tokyo, Japan, this computer-generated Landsat picture defines subtle details in surface geology. Urban areas appear as light blue surrounding the dark blue area—Tokyo Bay. Land under cultivation appears in red.

Computers in Science—continued.
13. Computers are used in the field of astronomy for several purposes, including the analysis of planetary orbits. **14.** A single frame from a computer-generated movie. This movie is an astronomical study of a complex double galaxy, M51. The height represents brightness; the different colors represent different levels of intensity; the two peaks represent the centers of the two galaxies; and the spikes represent the light intensities of individual stars.

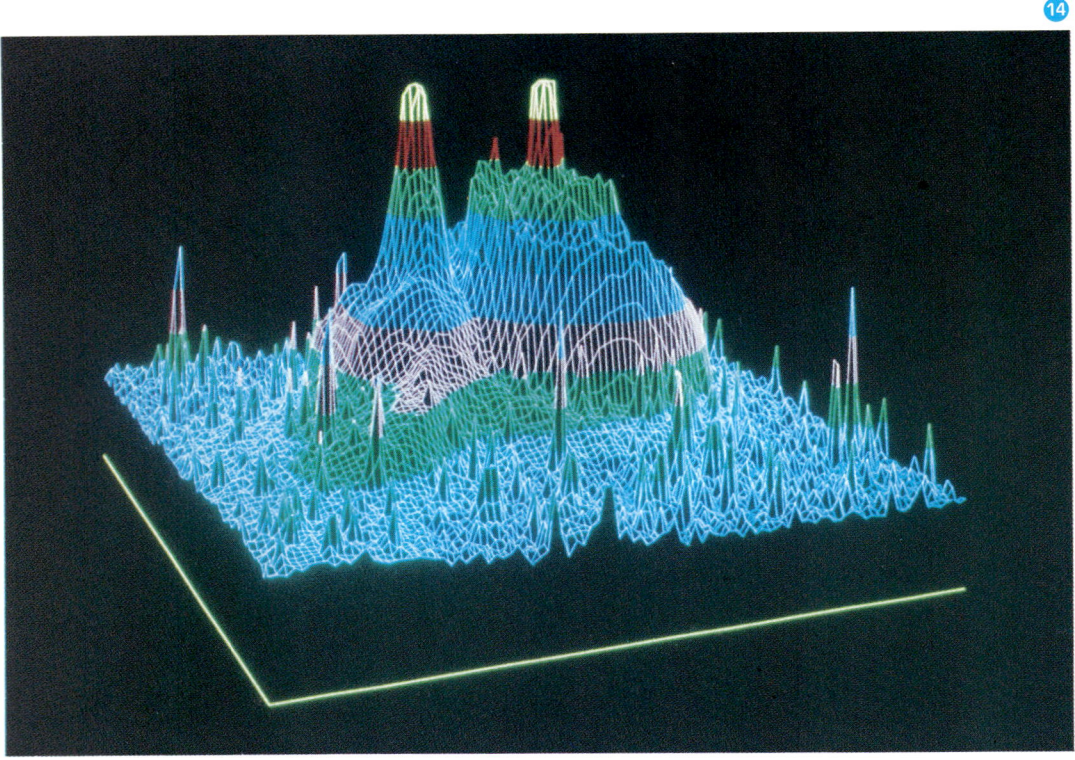

15. Forecasters in NOAA's National Weather Service provide nearly two million predictions per year to the public and commercial interests. This meteorologist is operating a new, computerized communications system designed to speed weather data handling. **16.** Computers are used by scientists in research and development aspects of new substances, for storage and analysis, and plotting of data. **17.** In search of new polymers for GE's engineered materials business, scientists are using computer graphics to study a polymer's molecular structure in order to judge its properties.

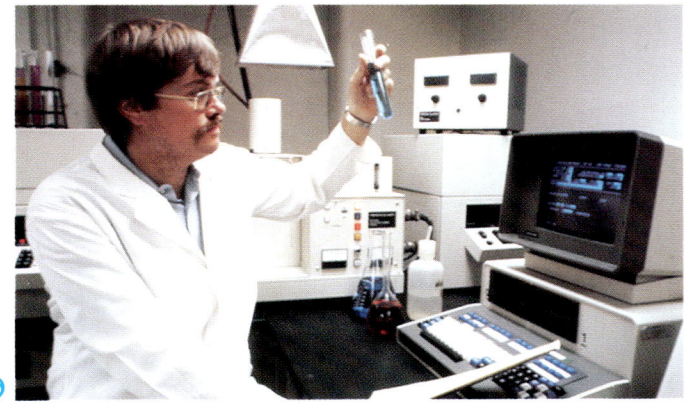

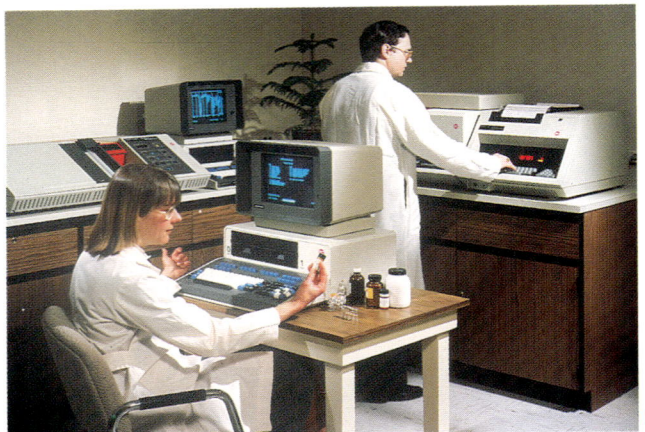

Computers in Science—continued.
18. Computer-aided chemistry harnesses digital electronics and computer technology and puts them to work for the chemist and laboratory manager. **19.** A laboratory technician uses an Apple computer for entry and storage of laboratory data. **20.** A chemist uses an Apple computer in the laboratory for recording data gathered from experiments. **21.** A biologist places vials in a counter to determine the radioactivity of human cell DNA that has been damaged by coal conversion products.

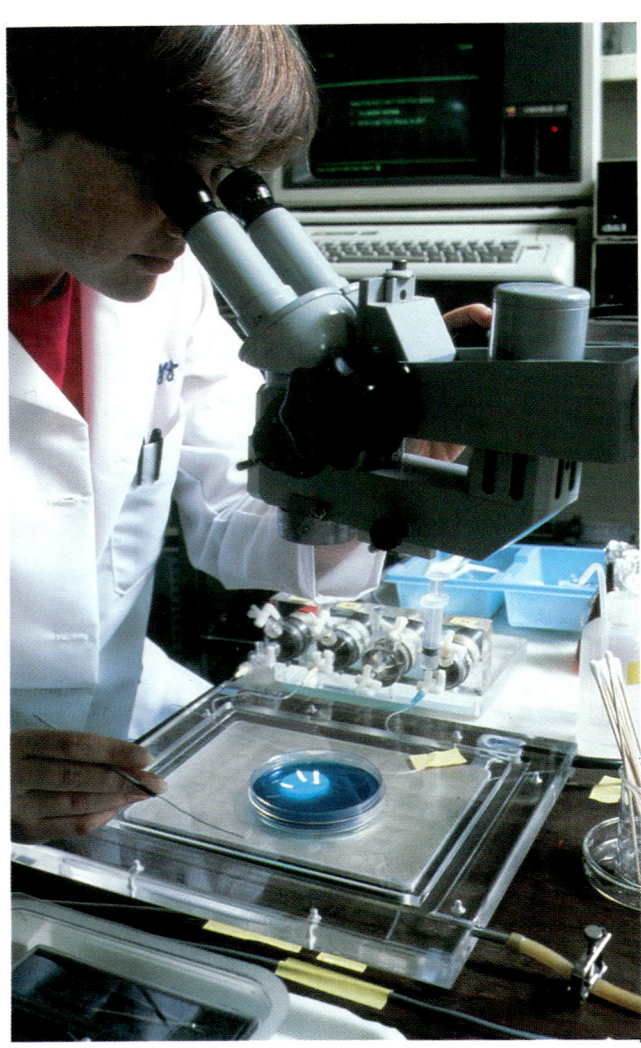

make it more suitable for some types of applications than for others. The different programming languages will be discussed throughout the remainder of this chapter along with their advantages and disadvantages.

MACHINE-ORIENTED LANGUAGES

Machine Language

As described earlier, machine languge was the first language programmers used to communicate with the computer. It is the only language a computer can understand. Although instructions can be written in high-level programming languages, they must be translated into object programs, which only then are machine executable. There are two parts to a machine language instruction: an op code and one or more operands. The **op code** (short for **operation code**) tells the computer what function to perform. The **operands** specify the locations of the data needed for that function to be performed. Figure 10–4 shows an example of machine language instructions.

Advantages and Disadvantages Since a program written in machine language does not require translation before it is executed, processing time is very fast. In addition, machine language is most efficient in storage area use.

The main disadvantage of machine language is that it is inconvenient for programmers to work with. It requires a thorough knowledge of the computer, including the most intricate details. Since a machine language program written for one computer so closely reflects that computer's operations, it cannot be transferred to another type of computer without extensive rewriting. Machine language programs are not standardized; in other words, they are highly inflexible.

Assembly Language

Assembly language is easier to read and understand than is machine language, but it is still difficult to work with. Each assembly instruction corresponds to one machine operation, so the programmer is still required to have extensive technical understanding of the particular computer being used.

Symbolic names called **mnemonics** are used to specify machine operations. Figure 10–5 shows some common arithmetic operations coded in an assembly language and in binary code. There are three parts to an assembly language instruction: an op code, an operand, and (sometimes) a label. The **label** is a programmer-supplied name used to refer to an instruction without having to specify the numeric address of that instruction. The op code and operand function in a manner similar to that in machine language; however, they are now in mnemonic, or symbolic, form. Figure 10–6 shows an example of an assembly program.

Figure 10—4 Machine Language Instructions Expressed in the Hexadecimal Number System

```
000000  05C0
000002
000002  E020  C07C  0021  0007E
000008  E020  C0A9  001E  000AB
00000E  4130  0003            00003
000012  1B66
000014  1B77
000016  E000  C09D  000C  0009F
00001C  D208  C0AA  C09D  000AC  0009F
000022  D201  C0B9  C0A7  000BB  000A9
000028  5350  C0A6            000A8
00002C  1A65
00002E  1844
000030  D508  C09D  C0F2  0009F  000F4
000036  4770  C040            00042
00003A  5C40  C0E6            000E8
00003E  47F0  C056            00058
000042  D508  C09D  C0FB  0009F  000FD
000048  4770  C052            00054
00004C  5C40  C0EA            000EC
000050  47F0  C056            00058
000054  5C40  C0EE            000F0
000058  1A75
00005A  5250  C0BC            000BE
00005E  E020  C0A9  001F  000AB
000064  4630  C014            00016
000068  D204  C0AA  C0C7  000AC  000C9
00006E  5260  C0CD            000CF
000072  5270  C0DA            000DC
000076  E020  C0C7  001F  000C9
00007C  07FE

00007E  F140C1C3E3C9E5C9
00009F
0000A8
0000AB  40
0000AC  4040404040404040

0000C9  FDE3D6E3C1D3
0000CF
0000DB  40
0000DC

0000E8  00000008
0000EC  00000013
0000F0  00000008
0000F4  C2C9C3E8C3D3C9D5
0000FD  D9E4D5D5C9D5C740
```

Figure 10–5
Assembly Language
Mnemonic Codes and
Corresponding Binary
Codes

Operation	Typical Assembly-Language Mnemonic Code	Typical Binary Op Code
Add memory to register	A	01011010
Add register to register	AR	00011010
Compare register to memory	CPY	10010111
Divide register	DR	00011101
Load from memory into register	L	01011000
Multiply register	MR	00011100
Store accumulator in memory	STA	01001001
Subtract memory from accumulator	SBC	10110011

Advantages and Disadvantages Like machine language, assembly language is very efficient in terms of storage space and processing time. Because of its efficiency, assembly language often is used in writing operating systems. In addition, certain checking functions can be performed and error messages generated that are useful in debugging.

The major disadvantage of assembly language is that it is cumbersome to use and thus requires a high level of skill to program effectively. As is true of machine language, assembly language is also machine dependent. Thus, equipment changes may require substantial reprogramming.

PROCEDURE-ORIENTED LANGUAGES

COBOL

COBOL, which initially stood for **COmmon Business Oriented Language,** is the standard language used for business data-processing today. The term **common** refers to the fact that commands used to instruct the computer are written in common, English-like sentences. People with little or no background in computers can read a COBOL program and generally deduce what the instructions mean. Approximately 80 percent of all government and industrial programming today is done in COBOL. A COBOL program is divided into four units, called **divisions.** The **identification division** contains the program name; other information, such as the author's name and the date the program was written, is optional. The second division of a COBOL program is the **environment division,** which identifies the type of computer being used and the devices on which the files needed within the program are stored. The third division of a COBOL program is the **data division.** In this division, all the necessary fields, records, and files are given programmer-supplied names and descriptions. The **procedure division,** the last division of a COBOL program, contains the instructions needed to direct the computer in solving a particular problem. These four divisions then can be further

```
* THIS PROGRAM CALCULATES THE NUMBER OF CALORIES FOR A
* GIVEN TIME SPENT BICYCLING, RUNNING, AND SWIMMING
              BALR   12,0                   SET UP BASE REGISTER
              USING  *,12
              XPRNT  HEADER,33              PRINT HEADING
              XPRNT  PRTOUT-1,30            PRINT BLANK LINE
              LA     3,3                    LOAD REGISTER 3 WITH A 3
              SR     6,6                    CLEAR REG 6 FOR TOTAL TIME
              SR     7,7                    CLEAR REG 7 FOR TOTAL CALORIES
LOOP          XREAD  ACTIV,12               READ IN DATA CARD
              MVC    PRTOUT(9),ACTIV        MOVE ACTIVITY TO PRINT AREA
              MVC    PRTOUT+15(2),MIN+1     MOVE MINUTES TO PRINT AREA
              XDECI  5,MIN                  CONVERT MIN TO BINARY IN REG 5
              AR     6,5                    ADD MIN TO TOTAL TIME
              SR     4,4                    CLEAR REG 4 FOR MULTIPLICATION
              CLC    ACTIV(9),=C'BICYCLING' CHECK IF ACTIVITY IS BICYCLING
              BNE    RUN                    IF NOT EQUAL, BRANCH TO RUN
              M      4,=F'8'                MULTIPLY MINUTES BIKING BY 8
              B      PRINT                  BRANCH TO PRINT
RUN           CLC    ACTIV(9),=C'RUNNING  ' CHECK IF ACTIVITY IS RUNNING
              BNE    SWIM                   IF NOT EQUAL, BRANCH TO SWIM
              M      4,=F'19'               MULTIPLY MINUTES RUNNING BY 19
              B      PRINT                  BRANCH TO PRINT
SWIM          M      4,=F'11'               MULTIPLY MINUTES SWIMMING BY 11
PRINT         AR     7,5                    ADD CALORIES TO TOTAL CALORIES
              XDECO  5,PRTOUT+18            CONVERT CAL; PUT IN PRINT AREA
              XPRNT  PRTOUT-1,31            PRINT ACTIVITY, MINUTES, CALORIES
              BCT    3,LOOP                 BRANCH BACK TO READ AGAIN
              MVC    PRTOUT(5),TOTAL        MOVE TOTAL READING TO PRINT AREA
              XDECO  6,TIME                 CONVERT AND MOVE MINUTE TOTAL
              XDECO  7,CAL                  CONVERT AND MOVE CALORIE TOTAL
              XPRNT  TOTAL,31               PRINT TOTALS
              BR     14                     STOP
*DECLARE VARIABLES
HEADER        DC     C'1 ACTIVITY       MINUTES        CALORIES'
ACTIV         DS     CL9
MIN           DS     CL3
              DC     C' '
PRTOUT        DC     CL29' '
TOTAL         DC     C'0TOTAL'
TIME          DS     CL12
              DC     C' '
CAL           DS     CL12
              END
                     =F'8'
                     =F'19'
                     =F'11'
                     =C'BICYCLING'
                     =C'RUNNING  '
```

ACTIVITY	MINUTES	CALORIES
BICYCLING	45	360
RUNNING	20	380
SWIMMING	30	330
TOTAL	95	1070

Figure 10—6 Assembly Program

Figure 10—7 COBOL Program

```
        IDENTIFICATION DIVISION.
        PROGRAM-ID.  EXERCISE.
 *      THIS PROGRAM CALCULATES THE NUMBER OF CALORIES BURNED
 *      FOR A GIVEN TIME SPENT BICYCLING, RUNNING, AND SWIMMING

        ENVIRONMENT DIVISION.
        CONFIGURATION SECTION.
        SOURCE-COMPUTER.  IBM-370.
        OBJECT-COMPUTER.  IBM-370.
        INPUT-OUTPUT SECTION.
        FILE-CONTROL.
            SELECT CARD-FILE ASSIGN TO UR-S-SYSIN.
            SELECT PRINT-FILE ASSIGN TO UR-S-SYSOUT.

        DATA DIVISION.
        FILE SECTION.
        FD  CARD-FILE
            LABEL RECORDS ARE OMITTED
            RECORD CONTAINS 80 CHARACTERS
            DATA RECORD IS ACT-INFO.
        01  ACT-INFO.
            02  ACTIVITY        PIC A(9).
            02  MINUTES         PIC 999.
            02  FILLER          PIC X(68).
        FD  PRINT-FILE
            LABEL RECORDS ARE OMITTED
            RECORD CONTAINS 133 CHARACTERS
            DATA RECORD IS PRINT-REC.
        01  PRINT-REC.
            02  CR              PIC X.
            02  OUT-LINE        PIC X(132).
        WORKING-STORAGE SECTION.
        77  CALORIES            PIC 999V9.
        77  TOTALTIME           PIC 999 VALUE ZERO.
        77  TOTALCAL            PIC 9999V9 VALUE ZERO.
        77  HEADING1            PIC X(29) VALUE
                                'ACTIVITY    MINUTES    CALORIES'.
        01  BLANK-LINE          PIC X(133) VALUE SPACES.
        01  LINE-FORM.
            02  CR              PIC X.
            02  ACTIV           PIC X(9).
            02  FILLER          PIC X(4).
            02  MIN             PIC 99.
            02  FILLER          PIC X(7).
            02  CAL             PIC Z999.9.

        PROCEDURE DIVISION.
        BEGIN.
            OPEN INPUT CARD-FILE
                 OUTPUT PRINT-FILE.
            DISPLAY HEADING1.
            WRITE PRINT-REC FROM BLANK-LINE AFTER ADVANCING 1 LINES.
            PERFORM WORK-LOOP 3 TIMES.
            PERFORM TOTALS.
            PERFORM FINISH.
        WORK-LOOP.
            READ CARD-FILE
                AT END PERFORM FINISH.
            IF ACTIVITY IS NOT EQUAL TO 'BICYCLING' THEN
                IF ACTIVITY IS NOT EQUAL TO 'RUNNING  ' THEN
                    MULTIPLY MINUTES BY 11.4 GIVING CALORIES
                ELSE MULTIPLY MINUTES BY 19.0 GIVING CALORIES
            ELSE MULTIPLY MINUTES BY 8.2 GIVING CALORIES.
            ADD MINUTES TO TOTALTIME.
            ADD CALORIES TO TOTALCAL.
            MOVE ACTIVITY TO ACTIV.
            MOVE MINUTES TO MIN.
            MOVE CALORIES TO CAL.
            WRITE PRINT-REC FROM LINE-FORM AFTER ADVANCING 1 LINES.
        TOTALS.
            MOVE 'TOTAL' TO ACTIV.
            MOVE TOTALTIME TO MIN.
            MOVE TOTALCAL TO CAL.
            WRITE PRINT-REC FROM LINE-FORM AFTER ADVANCING 2 LINES.
        FINISH.
            CLOSE CARD-FILE
                  PRINT-FILE.
            STOP RUN.
```

ACTIVITY	MINUTES	CALORIES
BICYCLING	45	369.0
RUNNING	20	380.0
SWIMMING	30	342.0
TOTAL	95	1091.0

subdivided into sections, paragraphs, or both. An example of a COBOL program is shown in Figure 10–7.

Advantages and Disadvantages Several advantages of COBOL make it a useful language for business applications. As mentioned earlier, COBOL statements are very English-like. Programs are relatively easy to read and understand, thereby reducing the amount of additional documentation needed. The language also has the capability of manipulating large data files, which most major business applications require. Finally, COBOL is standardized and is thus machine independent. Programs can be transferred to different computers having COBOL compilers with very little modification required.

There are several disadvantages to COBOL as well. First, because statements are so self-explanatory, programs tend to be wordy and rather long. Second, the language has limited computational abilities, which makes it inappropriate for applications requiring rigorous calculations. Finally, COBOL requires a sophisticated compiler program to translate source statements into object statements. The more English-like or user oriented a language is, the more complex the translating program will be. Certain subsets of COBOL can be used on small systems or on microcomputers. If the full version of COBOL is required, much storage space will be needed for the compiler program, thus limiting its use to only medium-sized or large systems.

FORTRAN

The language FORTRAN—short for **FORmula TRANslation**—was the first high-level language to be developed. At the time of FORTRAN's development in 1957, the primary users of computers were scientists and engineers. As a result, the language was geared toward applications involving rigorous computations.

By the early 1960s several different versions of FORTRAN existed. In response, a committee was formed to attempt to develop a standardized version of the language. Nearly four years later, ANSI made two standard versions of FORTRAN available: ANSI FORTRAN and basic FORTRAN. A group from the University of Waterloo in Ontario developed a subset of FORTRAN, known as WATFOR (for **WATerloo FORTRAN**), specifically for the beginning programmer. Improvements were made, and the enhanced version was called **WATFIV**. The most recent version of FORTRAN, FORTRAN 77, has incorporated many features of structured programming.

The basic unit of a FORTRAN program is a statement; the following four types of statements are used: control statements, arithmetic statements, input/output (I/O) statements, and specification statements. **Control statements** determine the sequence in which operations will be performed, whereas **arithmetic statements** direct the computer in solving computations. Data is read from or written to an I/O device according to the instructions contained in **input/output (I/O) statements. Spec-**

ification statements tell FORTRAN how to interpret data from an input device and how to write data to an output device. An example of a program written in FORTRAN is shown in Figure 10–8.

Advantages and Disadvantages FORTRAN today is still a language with strong mathematical capabilities, so it remains useful for scientific applications. It also can be used for certain types of business applications (for example, in quantitative analysis involving techniques such as linear programming and regression analysis).

One of the major disadvantages of FORTRAN is that it is not well suited for most business-oriented data processing. Programs cannot eas-

Figure 10–8
FORTRAN Program

```
C THIS PROGRAM CALCULATES THE NUMBER OF CALORIES BURNED FOR A GIVEN
C TIME SPENT BICYCLING, RUNNING, AND SWIMMING
        INTEGER I, MIN, TOTIM
        REAL CAL, TOTCAL
        CHARACTER ACTIV*9
        WRITE(6,100)
100     FORMAT ('1', 'ACTIVITY', 3X, 'MINUTES', 3X, 'CALORIES')
        WRITE(6,200)
200     FORMAT (' ')
        TOTIM = 0
        TOTCAL = 0
        DO 500 I = 1,3
        READ(5,300) ACTIV, MIN
300     FORMAT (A9,I3)
        IF (ACTIV .EQ. 'BICYCLING') CAL = MIN * 8.2
        IF (ACTIV .EQ. 'RUNNING  ') CAL = MIN * 19.0
        IF (ACTIV .EQ. 'SWIMMING ') CAL = MIN * 11.4
        TOTIM = TOTIM + MIN
        TOTCAL = TOTCAL + CAL
        WRITE(6,400) ACTIV, MIN, CAL
400     FORMAT (1X, A9, 4X, I2, 8X, F5.1)
500     CONTINUE
        WRITE(6,600) TOTIM, TOTCAL
600     FORMAT ('0', 'TOTAL', 8X, I2, 7X, F6.1)
        STOP
        END
```

ACTIVITY	MINUTES	CALORIES
BICYCLING	45	369.0
RUNNING	20	380.0
SWIMMING	30	342.0
TOTAL	95	1091.0

ily be written in FORTRAN for file maintenance, editing of data, or
production of documents, which are all-important in business applications.

PL/I

In the early 1960s, PL/I (short for **Programming Language I**) was developed by IBM to combine the best features of both COBOL and FOR-

Figure 10—9 PL/I
Program

```
ACTIVE:  PROCEDURE OPTIONS (MAIN);
/* THIS PROGRAM CALCULATES THE NUMBER OF CALORIES BURNED FOR */
/* A GIVEN TIME SPENT BICYCLING, RUNNING, AND SWIMMING       */
DECLARE (I, MINUTES, TOTALTIME) FIXED DECIMAL (3);
DECLARE (CALORIES, TOTALCAL) FIXED DECIMAL (6,1);
DECLARE (ACTIVITY) CHARACTER (9);
DECLARE (DUMMY) CHARACTER (68);
PUT PAGE LIST ('ACTIVITY   MINUTES   CALORIES');
PUT SKIP;
TOTALTIME = 0;
TOTALCAL = 0;
DO I = 1 TO 3;
  GET EDIT (ACTIVITY, MINUTES) (A(9), F(3));
  GET EDIT (DUMMY) (A(68));
  IF ACTIVITY = 'BICYCLING' THEN
    IF ACTIVITY = 'RUNNING  ' THEN
      CALORIES = MINUTES * 11.4;
    ELSE CALORIES = MINUTES * 19.0;
  ELSE CALORIES = MINUTES * 8.2;
  TOTALTIME = TOTALTIME + MINUTES;
  TOTALCAL = TOTALCAL + CALORIES;
  PUT SKIP EDIT (ACTIVITY, '     ', MINUTES,'          ', CALORIES)
    (A(9), A(4), F(2), A(8), F(5,1));
END /* DO */;
PUT SKIP;
PUT SKIP EDIT ('TOTAL        ', TOTALTIME, '        ', TOTALCAL)
  (A(12), F(3), A(7), F(6,1));
END;




ACTIVITY    MINUTES    CALORIES

BICYCLING    45         369.0
RUNNING      20         380.0
SWIMMING     30         342.0

TOTAL        95        1091.0
```

TRAN. IBM had developed the IBM System/360 computer, for use in business as well as scientific applications. Some of the applications required by business and scientific users reflected similarities, so it seemed appropriate to develop a new programming language (in addition to new equipment) that would be useful to both types of users.

PL/I is a language with few of the coding restrictions found in COBOL or FORTRAN. The basic element in a PL/I program is the statement, each of which must be followed by a semicolon. The language was designed for use by novice as well as expert programmers. Basic features of the language are easy to learn, but as the skill level of the programmer increases, more powerful features of PL/I can be utilized. PL/I combines the strong computational abilities of FORTRAN with the file manipulation ability of COBOL. Figure 10–9 illustrates a program written in PL/I.

The PL/I compiler has certain **default** features and also contains several **built-in functions.** A default provides the language with the capability of selecting a course of action from alternatives when one has not been explicitly specified by the programmer. Built-in functions, such as SQRT (for taking square roots), greatly simplify programming; the programmer need only refer to the function name, and the corresponding built-in program will perform the necessary steps. Many of the built-in functions are found in FORTRAN, but none are available in COBOL.

Several subsets of PL/I containing portions of the full language have been developed. Just as WATFIV, a subset of FORTRAN, is geared toward educational use, PL/C, a subset of PL/I developed at Cornell University, serves the same purpose.

Advantages and Disadvantages The greatest advantage of PL/I is its flexibility in handling both business and scientific applications. Another advantage is that structured programming concepts are enhanced when writing programs in PL/I. A program can be broken into individual modules, making coding, testing, and debugging much simpler. In addition, PL/I is less wordy than COBOL and has few coding restrictions.

The main disadvantage of PL/I is that it requires a lengthy, sophisticated compiler program. The use of PL/I is therefore limited primarily to large computer systems. Further, many programmers experienced in FORTRAN and COBOL have resisted learning a new language, making the future use of PL/I uncertain.

PROBLEM-ORIENTED LANGUAGES

RPG

RPG (short for **Report Program Generator**), a problem-oriented language, was designed to allow reports to be easily generated. To write programs in RPG, programmers do not have to be concerned with the logic involved; instead, they merely fill out a number of forms that specify file descriptions as well as input, output, and calculations to be made. Entries are made in predefined columns on the forms, which then are converted to a machine-readable format. The language processor then generates a program from these coded specifications to produce the desired report. As compared with COBOL, FORTRAN, and PL/I, RPG does not require a high level of skill from the programmer. Figure 10–10 shows the RPG instructions and forms necessary to produce a particular report.

RPG was developed in the late 1960s, a time when small computer systems were becoming increasingly more popular. The language originally was designed to be used on small computer systems using punched card equipment. Now RPG is used for processing files on tape or disk, as well as for preparing printed output.

A number of other improvements have been made to RPG. In the early 1970s, IBM introduced a new version—RPGII—for use on its System/3 computers. This version of RPG has replaced the original version and has become widely accepted by most computer manufacturers. A third version—RPGIII—was developed in 1979 to provide the capability of processing data stored in a data base.

Advantages and Disadvantages   One of the primary advantages of RPG is that it is relatively easy to learn and use, since the programmer need not specify the program logic involved. Because the language has file-processing capabilities and does not require a large amount of storage space for the compiler, it can be used on small systems, including mini-computers and microcomputers. Thus, computers that do not have the memory space to support COBOL still can have file-processing capabilities with RPG.

RPG also has several disadvantages. First, computational abilities such as looping, branching, and decision capabilities are limited. In addition, RPG is not standardized, so extensive rewriting may be required if programs are to be executed on different types of computers.

INTERACTIVE PROGRAMMING LANGUAGES

BASIC

BASIC—short for **Beginner's All-Purpose Symbolic Instruction Code**—was developed in 1965 at Dartmouth College for use in a time-sharing environment. As an interactive language it permits programmers to communicate with the computer in a conversational manner. Because BASIC is fairly easy to learn, people with little or no programming experience can begin to write programs in BASIC after just a few hours of instruction. Figure 10–11 shows our sample program written in BASIC.

With the increased use of time-sharing systems and the growth in microcomputer popularity, BASIC has become more widely used. Although originally intended for instructional use by colleges and universities, BASIC now is used by many businesses for their data-processing needs.

Advantages and Disadvantages   Two of the biggest advantages of BASIC are its flexibility and ease of use. It is easy to learn and can be used on

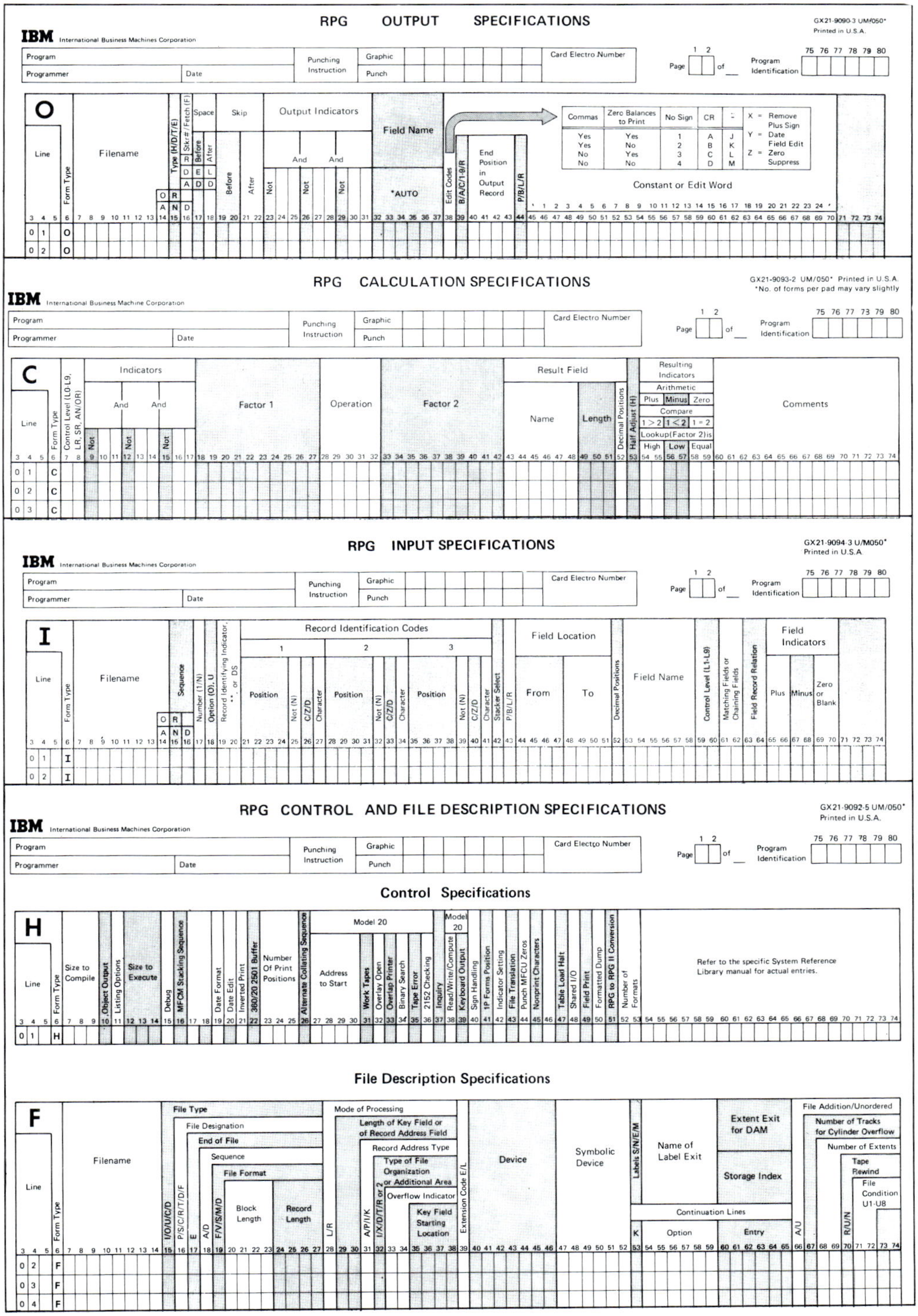

Figure 10–10 RPG Specification Forms

```
10 REM THIS PROGRAM CALCULATES THE NUMBER OF CALORIES BURNED
20 REM FOR A GIVEN TIME SPENT BICYCLING, RUNNING, AND SWIMMING
30 TOTALTIME = 0
40 TOTALCAL = 0
50 FOR I = 1 TO 3
60    PRINT
70    INPUT "ENTER ACTIVITY: ";ACTIVITY$
80    INPUT "ENTER MINUTES OF ACTIVITY: ";MINUTES
90    IF ACTIVITY$ = "BICYCLING" THEN CALORIES = MINUTES * 8.2 ELSE
         IF ACTIVITY$ = "SWIMMING" THEN CALORIES = MINUTES * 11.4 ELSE
            IF ACTIVITY$ = "RUNNING" THEN CALORIES = MINUTES * 19
140 TOTALTIME = TOTALTIME + MINUTES
150 TOTALCAL = TOTALCAL + CALORIES
160 PRINT "TOTAL CALORIES USED = ";CALORIES
170 NEXT I
180 PRINT
190 PRINT "TOTAL MINUTES OF EXERCISE = ";TOTALTIME
200 PRINT "TOTAL CALORIES USED = ";TOTALCAL
210 END



RUN

ENTER ACTIVITY: ? BICYCLING
ENTER MINUTES OF ACTIVITY: ? 45
TOTAL CALORIES USED =  369

ENTER ACTIVITY: ? RUNNING
ENTER MINUTES OF ACTIVITY: ? 20
TOTAL CALORIES USED =  380

ENTER ACTIVITY: ? SWIMMING
ENTER MINUTES OF ACTIVITY: ? 30
TOTAL CALORIES USED =  342

TOTAL MINUTES OF EXERCISE =  95
TOTAL CALORIES USED =  1091
```

Figure 10–11 BASIC
Program

large as well as small systems. In addition, BASIC can be used as both an interactive and a batch language. In BASIC's interactive form, the interpretive mode of translation and execution permits quick and easy debugging.

Although several extensions have been made to the language since it was developed, it is still somewhat limited in terms of its computational abilities. Different versions of BASIC are available for use on different types of computers. As a result, modifications must be made if programs are to be used on more than one type of machine. Another disadvantage of BASIC is that many versions of the language do not conform to structured programming, often making it difficult to avoid the use of the GOTO statement. BASIC is also somewhat slow on most machines when run interpretively.

Basically BASIC?

If you are thinking of buying a BASIC system for your microcomputer, you should know several things. First, many people are under the mistaken conception that BASIC is basically BASIC. In reality, there is ROM BASIC, DEC BASIC, Extended BASIC, E-BASIC, CBASIC, MBASIC, Applesoft BASIC, and BASIC+2—just to name a few.

The most common form of BASIC is ROM BASIC. This is an interpreter language rather than a compiler language (as most high-level languages are). An interpreter language "interprets" each line as it is entered; a compiler language "compiles" the entire program at once when it is run. Compiler BASIC is available and is faster, but it lacks the instant feedback and quick-change capability of interpreter BASIC.

The ideal form of BASIC is a combination of interpreter and compiler BASIC. This form of BASIC allows you to write and debug your program in the interpreter mode, which facilitates your making quick changes in the program. Once your program has been perfected, you can enter the compiler mode. This means that a compiled version of the program will be stored, so when you run the program in the future, it will not have to be reinterpreted. This approach will yield a much faster run time.

The most important factor to consider when purchasing a BASIC package is what type of microcomputer you own. All BASICs are not compatible with all home computers. Make sure that the BASIC you have decided to buy is available for your computer. After all, BASIC is not basically BASIC.

Pascal

Pascal is named after the mathematician Blaise Pascal, who invented the first mechanical adding machine. Niklaus Wirth, a computer scientist in Zurich, developed Pascal in 1968; three years later, the first Pascal compiler became operational. Figure 10–12 illustrates our program written in Pascal.

Each Pascal program has two basic parts: a heading (in which definitions and declarations are made) and a body (in which input, processing, and output are accomplished). Data names can be of any length in Pascal, and a number of control statements are available, which makes it possible to avoid the use of the GOTO statement.

Advantages and Disadvantages Pascal's popularity is still increasing, particularly in the educational environment. As is true of BASIC, Pascal is fairly easy to learn; however, Pascal is a more powerful language (capable of a richer variety of data manipulations than BASIC). The availability of Pascal on microcomputers allows greater programming capabilities on small computers than are possible with BASIC. Pascal also has very good graphics capabilities, which provides the programmer with the capability of creating intricate, detailed objects on properly

Figure 10–12
Pascal Program

```
PROGRAM EXERCISE;
(* THIS PROGRAM CALCULATES THE NUMBER OF CALORIES BURNED   *)
(* FOR A GIVEN TIME SPENT BICYCLING, RUNNING, AND SWIMMING *)
VAR
   ACTIVITY: STRING;
   I,MINUTES,TOTALTIME: INTEGER;
   CALORIES,TOTALCAL: REAL;
BEGIN
   TOTALTIME := 0;
   TOTALCAL := 0;
   FOR I := 1 TO 3 DO
   BEGIN
     WRITELN;
     WRITELN ('ENTER ACTIVITY:  ');
     READLN (ACTIVITY);
     WRITELN ('ENTER MINUTES OF ACTIVITY:  ');
     READLN (MINUTES);
     IF ACTIVITY <> 'BICYCLING' THEN
       IF ACTIVITY <> 'RUNNING' THEN
         CALORIES := MINUTES * 11.4
       ELSE CALORIES := MINUTES * 19.0
     ELSE CALORIES := MINUTES * 8.2;
     WRITELN ('CALORIES USED = ',CALORIES:5:1);
     TOTALTIME := TOTALTIME + MINUTES;
     TOTALCAL := TOTALCAL + CALORIES
   END;
   WRITELN;
   WRITELN ('TOTAL MINUTES OF EXERCISE = ', TOTALTIME);
   WRITELN ('TOTAL CALORIES USED = ', TOTALCAL:6:1);
END.


Running...

ENTER ACTIVITY:
BICYCLING
ENTER MINUTES OF ACTIVITY:
45
CALORIES USED =  369.0

ENTER ACTIVITY:
RUNNING
ENTER MINUTES OF ACTIVITY:
20
CALORIES USED =  380.0

ENTER ACTIVITY:
SWIMMING
ENTER MINUTES OF ACTIVITY:
30
CALORIES USED =  342.0

TOTAL MINUTES OF EXERCISE = 95
TOTAL CALORIES USED =  1091.0
```

The First Bug

One of the ways that all trends affect society is through language, and the computer trend is no exception. An example of this is in the term **debug.**

In 1945 early computer scientists were constructing the Mark II. Suddenly, for no apparent reason, something went wrong with the machine. Close examination showed that a moth had been caught in one of the relays. The moth was removed, and the first computer had been "debugged." Since then, computer scientists have used the term **debugging** to refer to removing any errors from a system, particularly ones that were unintentionally programmed in. The use of the term has spread, and today mechanics, repairers, and students talk about debugging their respective problems.

equipped display terminals. In addition, Pascal was designed to be totally compatible with structured programming concepts.

The major disadvantage of Pascal is that it is not yet standardized. Also, the language has been criticized by some who believe that its I/O capabilities are limited.

APL

APL—short for **A Programming Language**—was developed by Kenneth Iverson in the late 1950s. Working with IBM, Iverson attempted to develop a language that would meet the needs of applied mathematics. In 1968 APL became available for use through IBM and since that time has been adopted by several businesses as their main programming language.

APL can be used in two modes. The **execution mode** allows an instruction to be keyed in, generating a response on the next line. In this mode the terminal functions much like a desk-top calculator. In the **definition mode,** a program can be read into memory and then be executed on command from the programmer.

APL is a language that is well suited to handling tables of related values, known as **arrays.** It provides a number of operations for array manipulation, logical comparisons, mathematical functions, branching operations, and other functions, which greatly simplify the programmer's task. To represent these functions, a special APL keyboard is needed (see Figure 10–13). Figure 10–14 illustrates a program written in APL.

Advantages and Disadvantages APL is attractive because of its powerful interactive features. It can be used to perform complex operations without requiring extensive coding. Programmers can learn the language quickly because of its free-form style and lack of formal restrictions on input and output.

APL has some disadvantages that prevent it from being as widely sup-

Figure 10–13 APL
Keyboard

ported as are COBOL and Pascal. First, it is limited to only medium and large computers because of the large amount of storage required for the compiler. Also, it is difficult to read and poorly suited to handling large data files. In addition, a special keyboard is required to enter APL statements; however, this problem has been reduced to some extent because of the current availability of low-cost terminals.

OTHER PROGRAMMING LANGUAGES

There are many other programming languages from which to choose. For example, ALGOL (short for **ALGOrithmic Language**), one of the first languages to implement features in support of structured techniques, is very popular in Europe for scientific and mathematical applications. C, a language developed by Bell Labs, combines many features of high-level languages with the hardware-level capabilities of assembly languages, yielding a language that is both user oriented and machine efficient. APT (short for **Automatically Programmed Tooling**) is used primarily in manufacturing applications requiring the cutting of patterns. One additional language—Ada— is discussed here in greater detail because of its growing importance. Other languages of current interest are listed in Table 10–1.

Ada

The Ada language (not an acronym, but named after Ada Augusta Byron, Countess of Lovelace, the daughter of the poet Lord Byron and supporter of Babbage's research—see Chapter 2) deserves special mention because of the importance it already has begun to have in the computing community. Sponsored by the U.S. Department of Defense (DOD), which in the early 1970s began to see the need for a single primary programming language to be used in embedded applications, Ada has been developed with more care than any previous language. **Embedded applications** are those using a computer as part of a larger complex of electronics and mechanics, generally in the role of a control system. Such applications are characterized by a critical need for reliability; by complexity; and, frequently, by the use of separate **host** and **target** computers. The host

```
    ∇EXERCISE[□]∇
    EXERCISE
[1]   ⋒ THIS PROGRAM CALCULATES THE NUMBER OF CALORIES BURNED FOR
[2]   ⋒ A GIVEN TIME SPENT BICYCLING, RUNNING, AND SWIMMING
[3]   I←0
[4]   TOTALTIME←0
[5]   TOTALCAL←0
[6]   LOOP: I←I+1
[7]   →(I>3)/OUT
[8]   ' '
[9]   'ENTER ACTIVITY:'
[10]  ACTIVITY←□
[11]  'ENTER MINUTES OF ACTIVITY:'
[12]  MINUTES←□
[13]  TOTALTIME←TOTALTIME+MINUTES
[14]  →(∧/ACTIVITY='BICYCLING ')/BIKE
[15]  →(∧/ACTIVITY='RUNNING ')/RUN
[16]  →(∧/ACTIVITY='SWIMMING ')/SWIM
[17]  BIKE: CALORIES←MINUTES×8.2
[18]  TOTALCAL←TOTALCAL+CALORIES
[19]  'CALORIES USED BICYCLING = ';CALORIES
[20]  →LOOP
[21]  RUN: CALORIES←MINUTES×19
[22]  TOTALCAL←TOTALCAL+CALORIES
[23]  'CALORIES USED RUNNING = ';CALORIES
[24]  →LOOP
[25]  SWIM: CALORIES←MINUTES×11.4
[26]  TOTALCAL←TOTALCAL+CALORIES
[27]  'CALORIES USED SWIMMING = ';CALORIES
[28]  →LOOP
[29]  OUT: ' '
[30]  'TOTAL MINUTES OF EXERCISE = ';TOTALTIME
[31]  'TOTAL CALORIES USED = ';TOTALCAL
    ∇
```

```
                    EXERCISE

ENTER ACTIVITY:
BICYCLING
ENTER MINUTES OF ACTIVITY:
□:
    45
CALORIES USED BICYCLING = 369

ENTER ACTIVITY:
RUNNING
ENTER MINUTES OF ACTIVITY:
□:
    20
CALORIES USED RUNNING = 380

ENTER ACTIVITY:
SWIMMING
ENTER MINUTES OF ACTIVITY:
□:
    30
CALORIES USED SWIMMING = 342

TOTAL MINUTES OF EXERCISE = 95
TOTAL CALORIES USED = 1091
```

Figure 10—14 APL Program

Table 10—1 SOME OTHER PROGRAMMING LANGUAGES

ADAM	GPSS	LOTIS	PROLOG
AESOP	GRAF	MAD	SIMSCRIPT
BASEBALL	ICES	MAP	SNOBOL
CLIP	IDS	MATHLAB	SPRINT
COGO	IT	NELIA	STROBES
DIALOG	JOSS	OCAL	TRAC
DYANA	JOVIAL	OPS	TRANDIR
FACT	LISP 2	PAT	TREE
FLAP	LOLITA	PENCIL	UNCOL
FORMAC	LOGO	PILOT	UNICODE

is generally a conventional computer with elaborate software available, and the target system functions with little or no software support. Typically, an embedded application is developed and tested on the host system and then implanted in the target computer, where it must execute independently (without any user interaction).

The special demands to be placed on this proposed language led the DOD to publish a series of increasingly detailed requirements for the language and to sponsor a competition among vendors submitting language specifications. In 1979 a proposal from the French Cii-Honeywell-Bull was accepted as the basis for Ada. This language and its three major competitors in the selection process were all Pascal based, but all contained features needed in the large, ultrareliable embedded systems anticipated by the DOD.

Ada's primary features are those of Pascal; in addition, it contains characteristics that support the separate compilation of modules, or "packages," to be used in large programs; capabilities for concurrent execution of multiple modules in a single computer; extremely powerful features for handling errors detected during execution; and, perhaps most important of all, provisions for machine-independent operating-system linkages.

Although only a few Ada compilers have yet been validated (certified by the DOD as meeting all the processing specifications of the language), the activity in support of this new language is extensive. Textbooks have been published; compilers have been developed; training courses have been designed and conducted; and numerous professional meetings have been held (with large numbers of computer specialists in attendance). Operational software written in Ada is already in use—in business data-processing as well as embedded applications. The name **Ada** has even been registered as a trademark by the DOD, meaning that the use of the name is illegal unless applied to a validated compiler.

Because Ada is so strongly supported by the DOD and other advocates, it is destined to become as important as any of the languages previously discussed. Its advantages include suitability for large applications and adherence to current software-engineering principles; its primary disadvantages relate to the size and complexity of the language, which will require a painful adjustment on the part of most programmers. It is nevertheless reasonable to anticipate that Ada will be the primary language used by professional programmers before the end of the century.

CHOOSING A PROGRAMMING LANGUAGE

A number of considerations should be weighed before choosing a programming language. First, the type of processing to be accomplished must be examined, since some languages have more powerful computational or file manipulation abilities than others. Other considerations include determining whether or not the current computer system can support the language, the possibility of equipment changes in the near future, and how frequently programs will need to be modified. The need for a fast response time is another important consideration in choosing between an interactive or batch-oriented language.

● There are three levels of computer language; machine, assembly, and high level.
● A program written in an assembly or high-level language is a source program, which must be translated into an object program by a language translator.
● The language translator for a high-level language is a compiler, whereas the translator for an assembly language is an assembler.
● An interpreter, used instead of a compiler, reads and executes one statement from a source program at a time.
● Batch-oriented languages can be categorized as being either machine oriented, procedure oriented, or problem oriented.
● With an interactive programming language, a programmer can communicate directly with the computer in a conversational manner.
● When choosing a programming language, a number of considerations are made, with one of the main considerations being the type of application to be solved.

1. Describe the three levels of computer language.
2. What is the difference between an assembler program and a compiler program?
3. How does an interpreter program process source statements? List an advantage and a disadvantage of this method of translation.
4. How does a pseudocompiler differ from an interpreter?
5. What is the difference between a batch-oriented language and an interactive language?
6. List two languages that are procedure oriented and two that are machine oriented.

7. What are mnemonics, and which language or languages use them?

8. Which language is used in 80 percent of all government and industrial programming today? List some advantages and disadvantages of this language.

9. Why is FORTRAN not well suited for business data processing?

10. Which language combines the best features of FORTRAN and COBOL? Why is it not as popular as was anticipated?

11. What is a problem-oriented language? Give an example of such a language.

12. List two examples of interactive languages.

13. Which interactive language can be used in an execution mode or a definition mode?

14. What are the benefits to programming in a high-level language as opposed to assembly or machine language?

15. List some considerations that must be weighed before choosing a programming language.

OPERATING SYSTEMS

LEARNING OBJECTIVES

After studying this Chapter, you will be able to do the following:

☐ Describe the purpose and functions of operating systems.
☐ Distinguish between the different types of operating systems.
☐ List and describe some of the programs making up an operating system.
☐ Explain multiprogramming and its benefits as well as limitations.
☐ Describe multiprocessing and the different multiprocessing arrangements.

Chapter 11

For a computer to function properly and perform the tasks submitted by programmers, it must contain an operating system. Without an operating system, the programmer would be forced to be nearly as familiar with the internal circuitry and construction of the computer as was the original systems designer. This chapter will discuss the different types of operating systems, as well as describe the various subsystems that make up an operating system. Also included in this chapter is a discussion of two complex techniques supported by operating systems: multiprogramming and multiprocessing.

OPERATING SYSTEMS

When computers were first developed they were able to perform only simple and often repetitive tasks. It was neccessary, however, for computer operators to perform numerous manual functions, such as readying input and output devices, determining the order in which jobs would be run, and continually monitoring computer functions once the system began operation. As is characteristic of most human beings, the operators were not immune from making errors. In addition, the interruptions of processing for manual operations caused extensive time delays. Although computer speeds were steadily increasing, the speed of human operators remained constant. As a result, the time required to complete individual jobs was not noticeably improved.

As technology continued to progress, the complexity of computer applications began to increase. To cope with many different types of problems, it became necessary to develop some means of allowing a system to utilize its resources as efficiently and effectively as possible. By the 1960s, to accomplish these objectives, operating systems were developed. An **operating system** is a collection of programs used by the computer to manage its own resources and operations. These programs function as a control system allowing the computer to perform its tasks independent of most human intervention. Thus, the cost and time required to complete processing are greatly reduced.

Functions of Operating Systems

Operating systems range in complexity from very simple systems that manage only a few simple functions to quite complex systems that manage numerous complicated tasks. In general, the more sophisticated the computer system, the more complex the operating system software needed to manage all facets of computer use.

An important function common to all operating systems is their function as an interface between the user and the bare machine. For example, an applications programmer can issue simple system commands to the operating system, which in turn directs the hardware in performing the specific tasks. This provides a simple method for the computer user to enter and execute instructions, via the operating system, without requiring detailed knowledge of internal operations. Figure 11–1 depicts the conceptual relationship between operating system, user, and hardware.

An operating system can perform numerous other important functions. One such function is simply allowing the computer to perform input and output operations without human intervention. It is also possible to allow several programs to share computer resources and to resolve conflicts when, for example, more than one program requests access to the same record in main storage at the same time. In addition, operating systems perform a number of user services, such as providing access controls, security controls, and write protections (to prevent the user from accidentally erasing valuable data). The operating system also can keep track of all resource usage so that user fees can be determined and the efficiency of CPU utilization can be evaluated.

The scheduling of jobs on a priority basis is another useful function of an operating system. More than one program can be submitted to the computer at the same time, but one job may require more execution time than another, or the output from one program may be needed

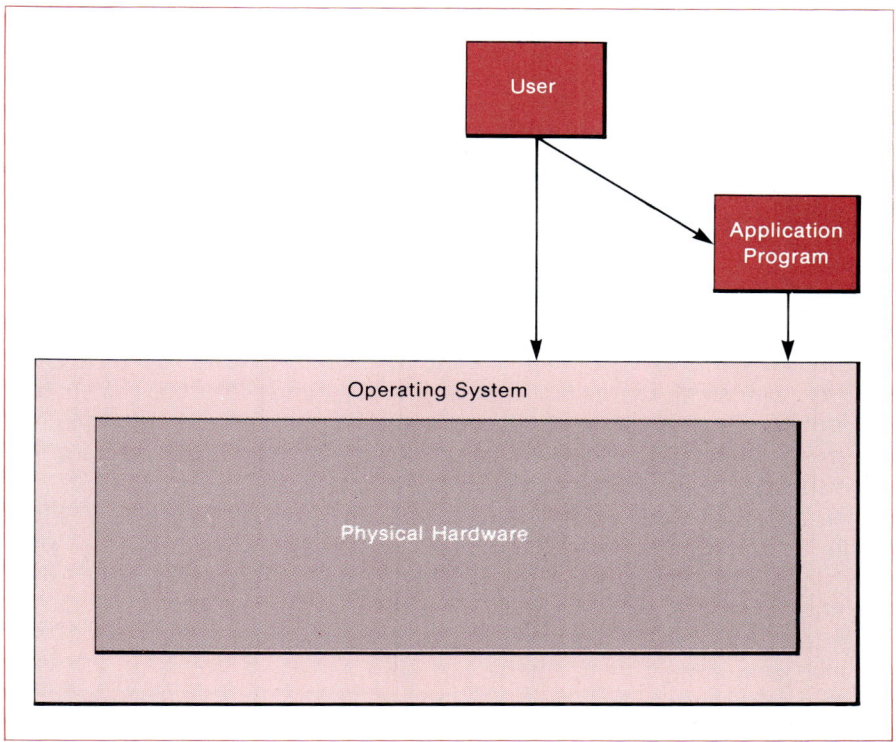

Figure 11–1
Operating System Relationships

**Operating Systems
for Business**

One of the problems in using a
microcomputer for business is that
many of the operating systems that
come with microcomputers are simply
not designed for the full range of
business applications. The solution to
this is to substitute a broader
operating system. In the past, this
created another problem: the manuals
for the systems on the market are
designed for computer scientists, not
business personnel. Thus, businesses
were presented with a great range of
useful applications, but they had no
idea of how to implement any of
them.

This situation is changing. With the
new emphasis on user-friendly
systems, it was only a matter of time
before businesses were provided with
a user-friendly operating system.

Taking into account the business
perspective, Select Information
Services has designed a tutorial
operating system—Teach-M. Teach-
M's manual explains in great detail
how to implement the business
applications without also providing
much useless information that could
confuse the business user. The
manual is written in easy-to-
understand language. It begins with a
definition of the operating system that
is tailored to the business user: "An
operating system is much like an
office manager. Office managers set
up filing systems, organize and
reorganize them, move them around,
and give us information from and
about them."

This is quite an improvement from
the mechanical hardware approach of
the past. After all, a system can never
be cost effective until the business it
serves figures out how it works.

much sooner than that from others. A system of priorities can be established based on considerations such as required processing time and the
expected need for the output.

Types of Operating Systems

The earliest operating systems were known as **single-job systems,** since
they permitted only one job at a time to be executed by the computer.
Data typically was entered from a card reader, and output was sent to a
line printer. Both of these devices operate very slowly in comparison to
the speed of the CPU. The major limitations of executing only one job
at a time, however, were that the CPU and I/O devices were idle a large
percentage of the time, and job execution was strictly sequential. Time
delays resulted from the requirement that operators set up before running the next job. Such systems are characteristic of today's microcomputers.

Improvements in system performance were realized when secondary
storage devices such as magnetic tape and disks were improved. These
I/O devices now operate at speeds somewhat closer to that of the CPU
and primary memory. A second type of operating system then was developed that would allow more than one job to be submitted to the

computer at the same time. These systems are known as **batch,** or **stacked-job, operating systems.** In this processing environment, several small, inexpensive computers would copy several input jobs from card readers to input batch tapes, which then could be transferred quickly into the CPU. The stacked-job operating system directs the processing of one job after another in a continuous stream and then copies output batch tapes to the line printer. Set-up time thus is reduced, and operators are able to perform other tasks. Figure 11–2 illustrates the flow of a job through a batch system.

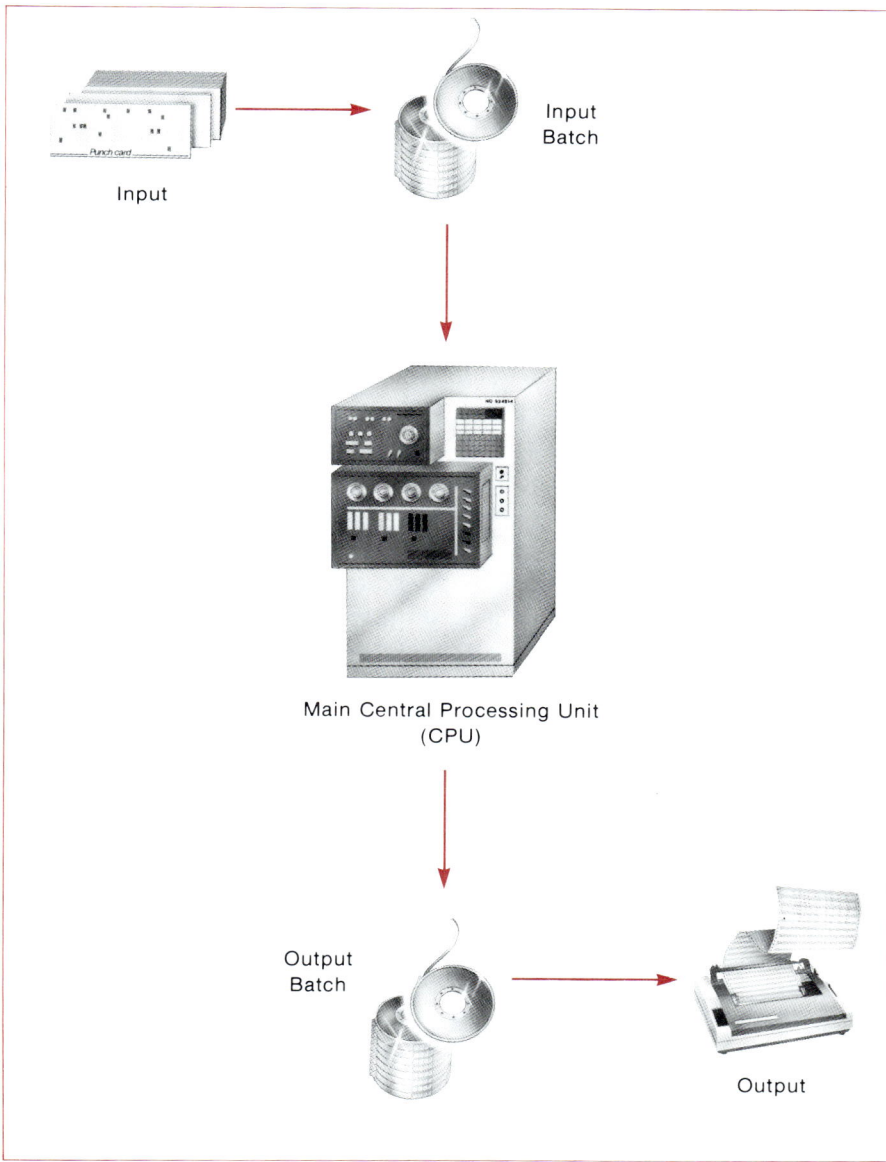

Figure 11–2 Batch Processing

Input

Input Batch

Main Central Processing Unit (CPU)

Output Batch

Output

Although the first batch systems were faster than the earlier single-job systems, they still ran jobs sequentially. As a result, short jobs could wait a long time to be processed if placed behind long jobs. Also, there were delays in receiving the printed output of the first jobs, since a batch tape was not available until the entire batch had executed. Manual delays in mounting tapes were also a problem with these early batch systems.

The next major improvement in operating systems provided for spontaneous requests for system resources without using the card reader and line printer. This task was accomplished by introducing **real-time operating systems** that interact with users via on-line terminals. All input and much output goes directly to and from the individual user at such a terminal. Instead of submitting programs with numerous instructions written on cards or tape, the user can type simple single-statement commands on the terminal. This mode of interaction is also called **interactive, demand,** or **conversational,** since the computer generally will respond instantaneously with the required information. Data is stored on a direct-access storage device (DASD) to provide this capability (see Figure 11–3).

Many operating systems today provide for both batch and real-time applications simultaneously. These systems direct the processing of a multijob stream but also respond to inquiries or **interrupts** (hardware-generated transfers of control to the operating system under special circumstances) from on-line terminals in direct communication with the CPU. A system of establishing priorities in terms of order of execution also is provided, as discussed earlier, so that programs are executed in the most efficient sequence.

COMPONENTS OF OPERATING SYSTEMS

An operating system, as described earlier, consists of a series of programs that allow the computer to perform specific functions. These programs work together in a team effort to maximize the efficient allocation of computer resources and to insure that CPU idle time is kept to a minimum. Operating system programs are stored outside of primary storage on an auxiliary device known as the **system residence device.** The most commonly used storage devices are magnetic tape (tape operating system, or TOS) and disk (disk operating system, or DOS), disk being much more commonly used. Most operating systems today use either hard magnetic disk or floppy disk to store operating system programs.

Generally, the more complex the operating system, the more programs or subsystems it contains to allow a number of different functions to be performed. Despite the variance in complexity that can exist from one operating system to another, two types of programs are fundamental to most systems. **Control programs** oversee system operations and perform such tasks as I/O, scheduling, handling interrupts, and communicating with the computer operator or programmers. **Processing**

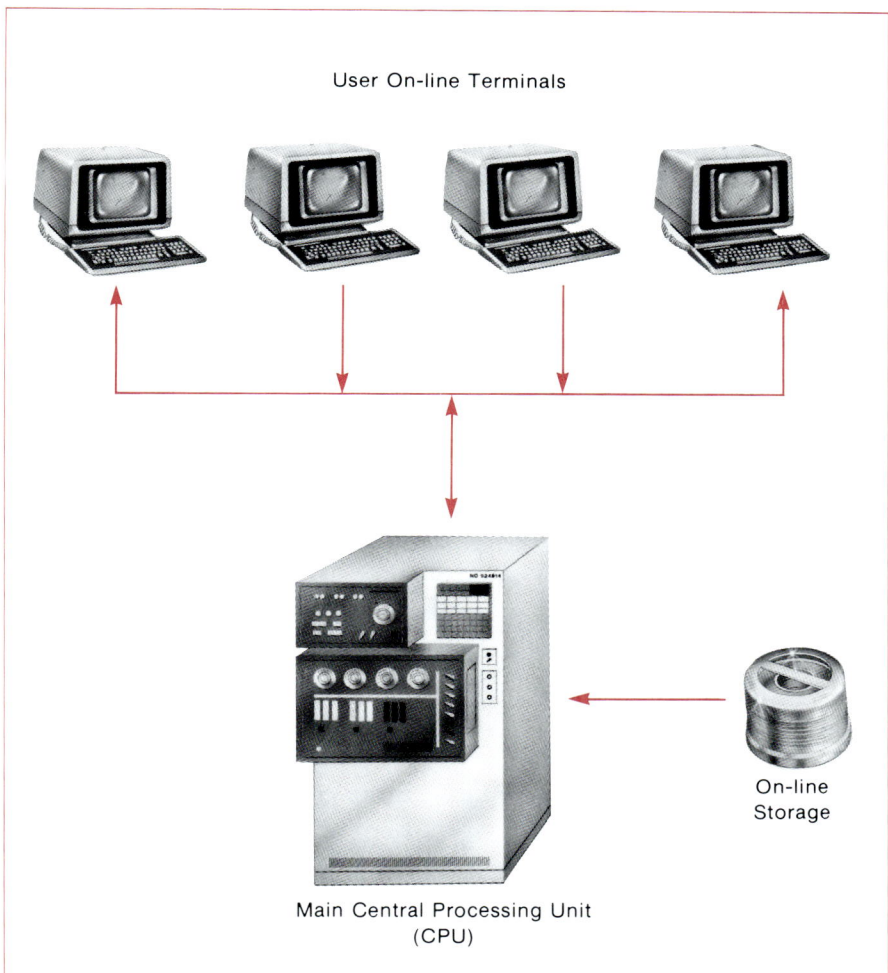

Figure 11–3 Real-Time Processing

User On-line Terminals

On-line Storage

Main Central Processing Unit
(CPU)

Note: The term **real-time** sometimes is used more rigorously than in this context to describe applications in which system response is necessary in an immediate time frame to control performance (for example in-flight control of a space vehicle).

programs are executed under the supervision of control programs and are used by the programmer to simplify program preparation for the computer system.

Control Programs

The major component of the operating system is the **supervisor program.** This control program (also called the **monitor** or **executive program**) coordinates the activities of all other parts of the operating sys-

CP/M

Control Program for Microcomputers (CP/M) was the ticket to success for a small company called Intergalactic Digital Research. Intergalactic has since changed its name to Digital Research Corporation, and CP/M has cornered the microcomputer market.

CP/M, an operating system, was written by Gary Kildall in 1973 while he was working as a consultant for Intel Corporation. When Intel decided to use a different operating system, Kildall and his wife, Dorothy McEwen, decided to market CP/M on their own.

They began by selling CP/M to computer hobbyists for seventy dollars. They have since taken over the Number 1 spot in supplying operating systems to computer companies. CP/M compatible programs can be used on the Commodore 64, Hewlett-Packard's HP-86, the Advanced Personal Computer by NEC Information Systems, Inc. (a subsidiary of Nippon Electric Company, Ltd.), the Xerox 820, the Apple II, the DEC VT 180, and the IBM Personal Computer. Altogether, there are over three hundred CP/M-compatible systems on the market.

One of the reasons so many companies are using CP/M is the large amount of supporting software available. As of 1983, over one thousand software programs were designed for use on CP/M systems.

tem. Each time the computer is put into use, the supervisor is the first program to be transferred from the system residence device into main storage. This process is known as **initial program loading,** or **bootstrapping.** Typically, the bootstrapping process consists of either hardware or system software resident in ROM (permanent Read-Only Memory) reading in a small bootstrapping program, which in turn reads in the supervisor program. During this process, only the most frequently used programs, known as **resident routines,** are brought into primary storage. Other, less frequently used supervisor programs, known as **transient routines,** remain in auxiliary storage with the other operating system programs.

Not all of the operating system programs are brought into memory at one time. The main reason this is not done is that too much memory space would be required, which then would limit the size and number of applications programs that could be executed. Supervisor routines call for the nonresident (transient) programs when required and load them into main storage. When these programs have accomplished their tasks, they are sent back to the system residence device by the supervisor until needed again. The supervisor also schedules I/O operations; allocates channels to I/O devices; and sends messages to the computer operator indicating the status of a particular job, error conditions, and other forms of communications.

A second control program is known as the **job control program,** which translates job control language (JCL) into machine language. The JCL, supplied by the programmer, identifies the beginning of a job and the specific program to be executed, describes the work to be done, and indicates the required I/O devices. This important information serves as the communications link between the programmer and the operating system. The JCL can be executed by the computer only after it has been translated into machine code by the job control program.

Processing Programs

The second type of program found in the operating system makes program preparation and execution much simpler for the user. These programs are known as **processing programs.** The major processing programs contained in the operating system are the language translators, linkage editor, library programs, and utility programs.

As described in the last chapter, most applications programs are written in high-level languages, since these languages are much easier and less time consuming to write than are assembly or machine languages. However, to be executed by the computer, these English-like instructions must be translated into machine code. A **language-translator program** translates a program written in a language other than machine language into a series of 1s and 0s. Once this translation has taken place, the **source program,** which is the user's version of the program, is converted to an **object program,** which is machine executable. The source program also is retained for modification and maintenance purposes.

Each of the languages discussed in Chapter 10 has its own individual language-translator program. When a particular program is to be executed, the programmer must specify in the JCL the language in which the program is written. The job control program, which interprets the JCL, then conveys this message to the supervisor program. The appropriate language-translator program is then brought into memory from the system residence device by the supervisor program. After the applications program has been translated into machine code, the language-translator program is no longer needed, so it is sent back out to auxiliary storage. Some language-translator programs require a large amount of space in memory; thus, certain programming languages cannot be executed on small computers with limited memory size.

After the applications program has been translated into an object program, it too can be sent out to the system residence device until it is called for execution by the supervisor program. To load the object program from auxiliary to primary storage for execution, a **linkage editor** and loader are needed. The linkage editor assigns appropriate main storage addresses to each byte of the object program and incorporates standard I/O and error-handling routines into the program.

Another type of processing program that can be found within an operating system is either user written or manufacturer supplied. These programs, known as **library programs,** perform various frequently needed functions. Instead of the programmer being required to write the series of instructions needed to perform a certain function, a library program can be called into main storage to accomplish the necessary tasks. In this way, built-in programs can be linked with applications programs to fulfill program requirements. A **librarian program** manages the storage and use of library programs by maintaining a directory of programs in the system library. Procedures for adding and deleting programs also are contained in the system library. Currently, much attention is being given to reusable **software components** maintained in libraries.

Utility programs are another type of processing program. A number of utility programs can be included in the operating system to perform various specialized tasks for the user. For example, when it is desirable to transfer data from one storage medium to another—such as from cards to tape, tape to tape, tape to disk, and so on—a utility program can be run that will transfer the data in the appropriate format. In this way the user is relieved of the need to retype the data to the new device. A significant amount of time may be saved, and back-up copies of data can be easily created with these programs.

Other utility programs, known as **sort/merge programs,** are used to first sort records in a specific order. For example, records in a transaction file stored on magnetic tape would be sorted in the same sequence as those on the master file requiring updating. Multiple tapes already in the same sequence can also be merged through the use of a sort/merge program to create a new consolidated file. Statements in the JCL specify the need for these programs, which are then brought into memory as requested. Figure 11–4 illustrates the various subsystems of operating systems.

Additional Software

Operating system programs can be written by systems programmers or purchased as standard packages from software firms. In the last few years, certain operating systems have become standard within various products (for example, UNIX for minicomputers and CP/M for microcomputers). These operating systems can be used on more than one vendor's system, thus making these systems compatible. When the same operating system is used on different machines, data can be exchanged back and forth. For example, many unlike systems such as microcomputers, minicomputers, and mainframes can send messages to each other through electronic mail networks.

The popularity of standardized operating systems can be attributed to their ease of use and flexibility. Once the standard operating system has been purchased, other subsystems can be added, providing additional capabilities such as word processing or more complex applications. It is also possible on some computers to implement more than one operating system. For example, one operating system can handle simple applications and offer easy, or "user-friendly," interaction for the inexperienced user. In addition, a more sophisticated system may be included to handle the more complex applications that would be required by the experienced user.

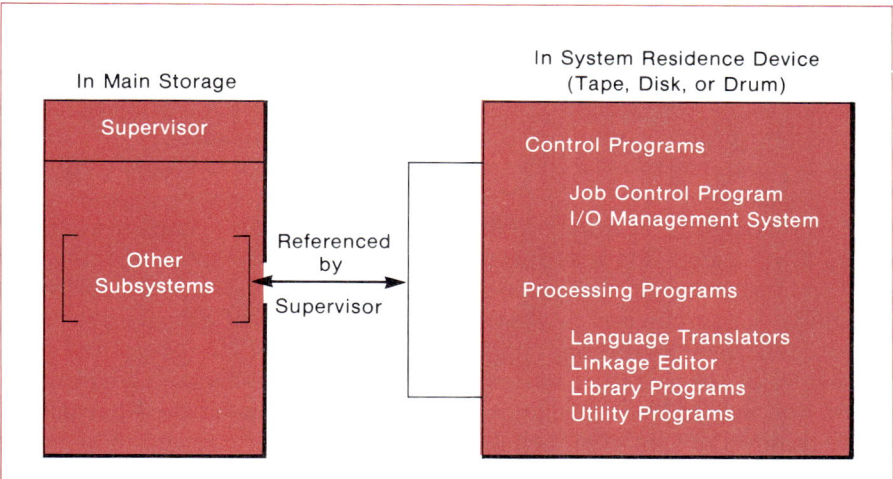

Figure 11—4
Operating System in Main Storage and System Residence Device

In Main Storage

Supervisor

Other Subsystems

Referenced by

Supervisor

In System Residence Device (Tape, Disk, or Drum)

Control Programs

Job Control Program
I/O Management System

Processing Programs

Language Translators
Linkage Editor
Library Programs
Utility Programs

MULTIPROGRAMMING

The CPU operates at speeds much faster than those of I/O devices. For the CPU to execute instructions in a program, they first must be placed within primary storage; if an input device is slow in providing these instructions, the CPU is kept idle. Similarly, during execution of a program, when instructions call for data to be printed, the CPU must wait until output operations have been completed before continuing with the next executable instruction in the program.

To keep the CPU and I/O devices as busy as possible, a technique known as **multiprogramming** was developed. The basic idea behind this process is to have several different programs in primary storage at the same time. One instruction at a time will be executed in a program until an input or output operation (or interrupt) is reached. The I/O device, being much slower than the CPU, can be managed by a channel, thus freeing the CPU to begin execution of another program. The execution of the first program thus is suspended temporarily during an interrupt, and a second program is begun. When the second program also requires input or output, control is returned to the first program, enabling it to resume processing. A rotation from one program to another occurs so quickly that it seems that programs are executing simultaneously, but they are in fact executing **concurrently** (over the same period of time). By executing programs concurrently, the CPU runs only one program at a time, while (ideally) other programs are having some type of input or output operation being performed.

Multiprogramming greatly improves the efficiency of a system, yet it also increases system complexity. One problem that has to be solved is how to keep one program separate from another. This is solved through the use of **memory regions** or **partitions** to prevent one concurrently running user from interfering with another or with the operating system. A region is a storage area of variable size for a program, whereas a partition is a storage area of fixed size. Keeping programs in the correct region or partition is known as **memory management** or **memory protection.**

A second problem that occurs with multiprogramming is the scheduling of programs to establish a means for deciding which program will be executed first, which second, which third, and so on. One method involves assigning a priority to each program. In a time-sharing environment, users at on-line terminals executing programs interactively with the computer would be given highest priority, since response time should be instantaneous to waiting users. The highest-priority programs are loaded into **foreground partitions** and are called **foreground programs.** Most time-sharing systems also allow programs to be submitted in a batch mode. These programs are assigned to **background partitions,** since they do not involve user interaction; they are referred to as **background programs** (see Figure 11–5). Since foreground programs have the highest priority, control is sent from one high-priority program to the next when interrupts occur. Only when there are no foreground programs requiring execution will a background program gain control.

For large systems with numerous foreground and background programs, scheduling is not a simple task. More than one program with the same priority may require CPU resources at the same time. In this case, the operating system may direct control to the program that has been in main storage the longest. In other systems, the principle of "last come,

Figure 11–5
Foreground and Background Programs in a Multiprogramming Environment

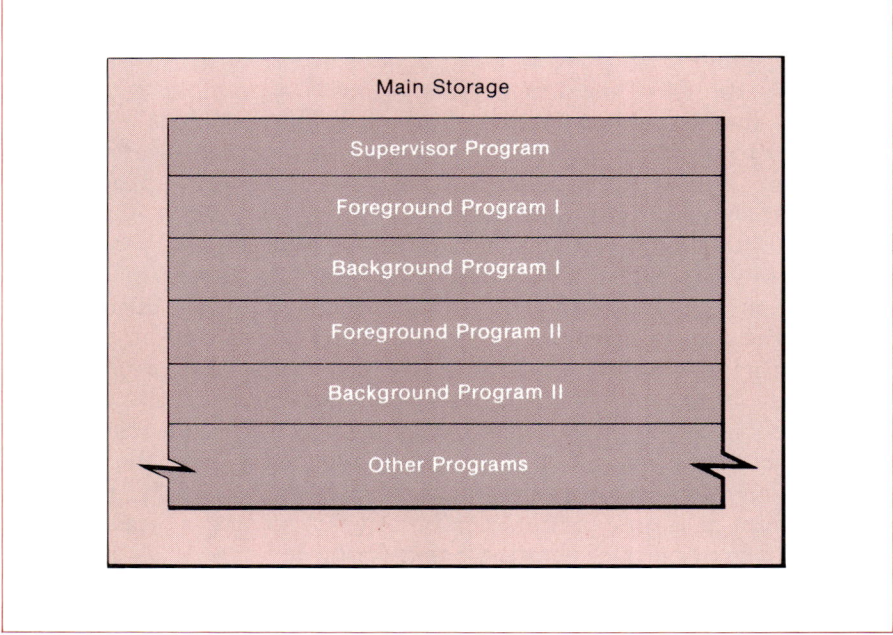

Main Storage

Supervisor Program

Foreground Program I

Background Program I

Foreground Program II

Background Program II

Other Programs

Future or Fact?

Science fiction precedes fact by a steadily narrowing margin. Take, for example, the car named Kit on the television show "Knight Rider." Kit is a car that monitors itself, watches the road, and tells its driver when it needs gas or oil. Is Kit just science fiction?

Yes and no. The ability to reason that is assumed in Kit's conversational tone is not possible with today's technology. However, everything else is fact. Since 1981, all General Motors cars have been equipped with Computer Command Control, a system that observes and controls engine operation to limit the amount of exhaust emissions. Datsuns now on the market come with computers that tell their drivers (via computerized voices) to turn off the headlights, fasten their seatbelts, and so on. And today's Honda Accord provides a

display of the car on the dashboard. If the taillights are not working or the trunk is left open, the display flashes that information to the driver.

We also have the technology to provide each car with computerized maps and hook our car computers to our home computers. We even could have the car's computer hooked to the highway patrol's computer to keep us advised of such things as speed limits and road conditions.

All of these concepts are already possible. Unfortunately, they are not yet cost effective. You could buy a car very much like Kit today, but it would cost a few hundred thousand dollars. Keep in mind, though, that ten years ago you would have paid three hundred dollars for a calculator that you can buy today for under ten dollars. If computerized cars follow the same trend, we may see the "Kit cars" on the road sooner than we think.

first served" is sometimes used to allow the most recent input to be entered, or priority can be given to I/O-intensive programs to keep peripherals as busy as possible. The ideal system gives preference to foreground programs without totally ignoring background programs.

Another problem encountered in multiprogramming was how to separate the output from several concurrently executing programs using a single line printer. This task was accomplished through a technique known as **spooling** (for **simultaneous peripheral operations on-line**). Execution begins on the first program until an interrupt occurs, for example, an output operation. While output is printed on the line printer, control already has been sent to a second program. As described earlier, the next program also will execute until it too has an input or output operation. If, in this example, the second program also requires data to be printed, a spooling program intervenes and writes the output to a secondary storage device, such as a disk. In this way output from different programs will be kept separate. After the programs have completed execution, the printer-destined output from different programs recorded in separate locations on the disk will be printed correctly on the line printer.

VIRTUAL STORAGE

The ability of programs to be executed concurrently under multiprogramming increases system efficiency, since resources are utilized more fully. There are limitations to this technique, however. First, each partition must be large enough to hold an entire program. If programs are very lengthy, the number of programs that can reside in primary storage will be limited.

Another limitation of this approach is that all the instructions of a program are required to be resident in primary storage even after they are no longer required. Memory space is not used efficiently, since it is occupied by data and instructions that may be used infrequently within a program or not at all. In the past, programmers have had to spend a great deal of time in an effort to limit the size of programs to conform to available memory space.

In an extension of multiprogramming known as **virtual storage,** not all parts of a program must be simultaneously in primary memory for the program to execute. It is necessary that only a section at a time be resident in memory, allowing unneeded portions to be kept in secondary storage. Numerous large programs can be accommodated by bringing only part of the program in at a time and then sending it back out to secondary storage once execution has been completed. This approach provides the illusion of a very large, almost limitless primary memory space.

Under virtual storage, programs are stored on a DASD such as a magnetic disk. When data or instructions are brought into primary storage, they are said to be in **real storage;** while they are located on the DASD they are referred to as being in **virtual storage.** The process of exchanging data or instructions from virtual storage to real storage and vice versa is known as **swapping.**

The majority of virtual storage systems are implemented through either **segmentation** or **paging.** Under segmentation, programs are divided into logical segments of varying size. For example, one segment may consist of a subroutine, whereas another would consist of statements located within a loop. The operating system software allocates storage space according to the size of these logical segments. In this way memory space is not wasted, since variably sized storage spaces can accommodate segments of differing sizes.

Paging, in contrast, does not consider the logical divisions of a program but instead involves breaking programs into equal sections, or **pages.** Each page is the same size, and main storage is divided into areas of equal size, known as **page frames,** to contain these pages. Figure 11–6 illustrates virtual storage and swapping in multiprogramming.

Virtual storage is beneficial, since it extends the storage capacity of primary storage without increasing its size. More and longer programs thus can be executed concurrently in a multiprogramming environment. There are several disadvantages to virtual storage, however. For instance, significant on-line auxiliary storage is required in addition to a highly sophisticated operating system. Also, extensive memory manage-

"Credit" Cards for the Poor?

Management reformers are pointing their fingers now at the horse-and-buggy ways that food stamps, welfare aid, and Medicaid are being handled at the user's level. Food stamps, for example, still are doled out in packets that look like play money. Besides being cumbersome and expensive to print and distribute, the stamps are easy vehicles to abuse. They can fall into the wrong hands and be used for the wrong purposes. The reformers say that recipients of government aid would be better off—as would the government—if the aid were given in the form of individual plastic cards with computer memory chips. Only the person for whom the card was designated could use it, since a personal code would have to be punched in for each use. This would activate the memory chip to then specify what goods or services were due the user.

ment is needed to allow one part of a program to be swapped for another without errors occurring.

A problem that can occur with virtual storage is a phenomenon known as **thrashing.** This situation arises when a page or segment forces the replacement of another page or segment before it has actually been executed. As a result, operating system overhead (time spent in systems management rather than problem solving) is increased substantially through time spent correcting such a problem. If virtual storage is implemented carefully, however, and primary memory space is adequate, thrashing can be avoided. Much study has been devoted to algorithms for determining which page is to be swapped out of storage to accommodate an incoming page.

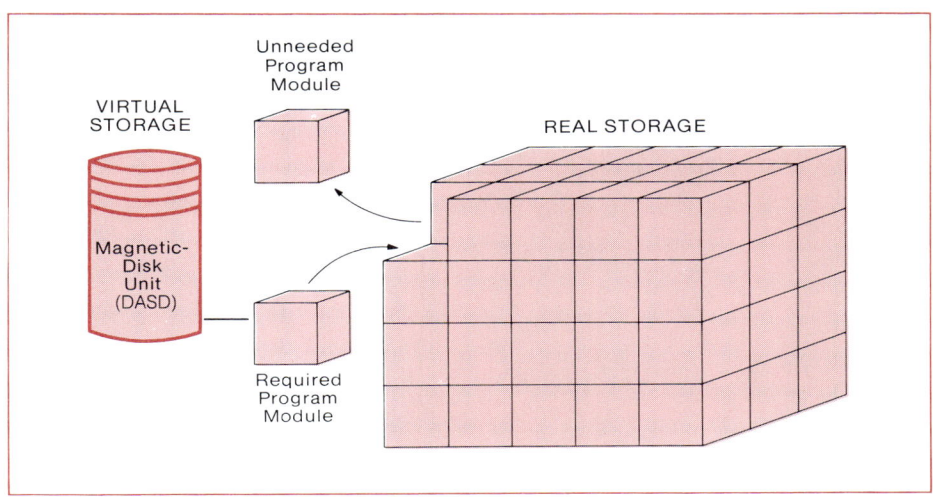

Figure 11—6 Virtual Storage and Swapping

MULTIPROCESSING

As described in the "multiprogramming" section, one CPU can execute parts of a program until an interrupt occurs where there is an input or output operation; execution then begins on a second program. Although the process of switching from one program to the next occurs quite rap-

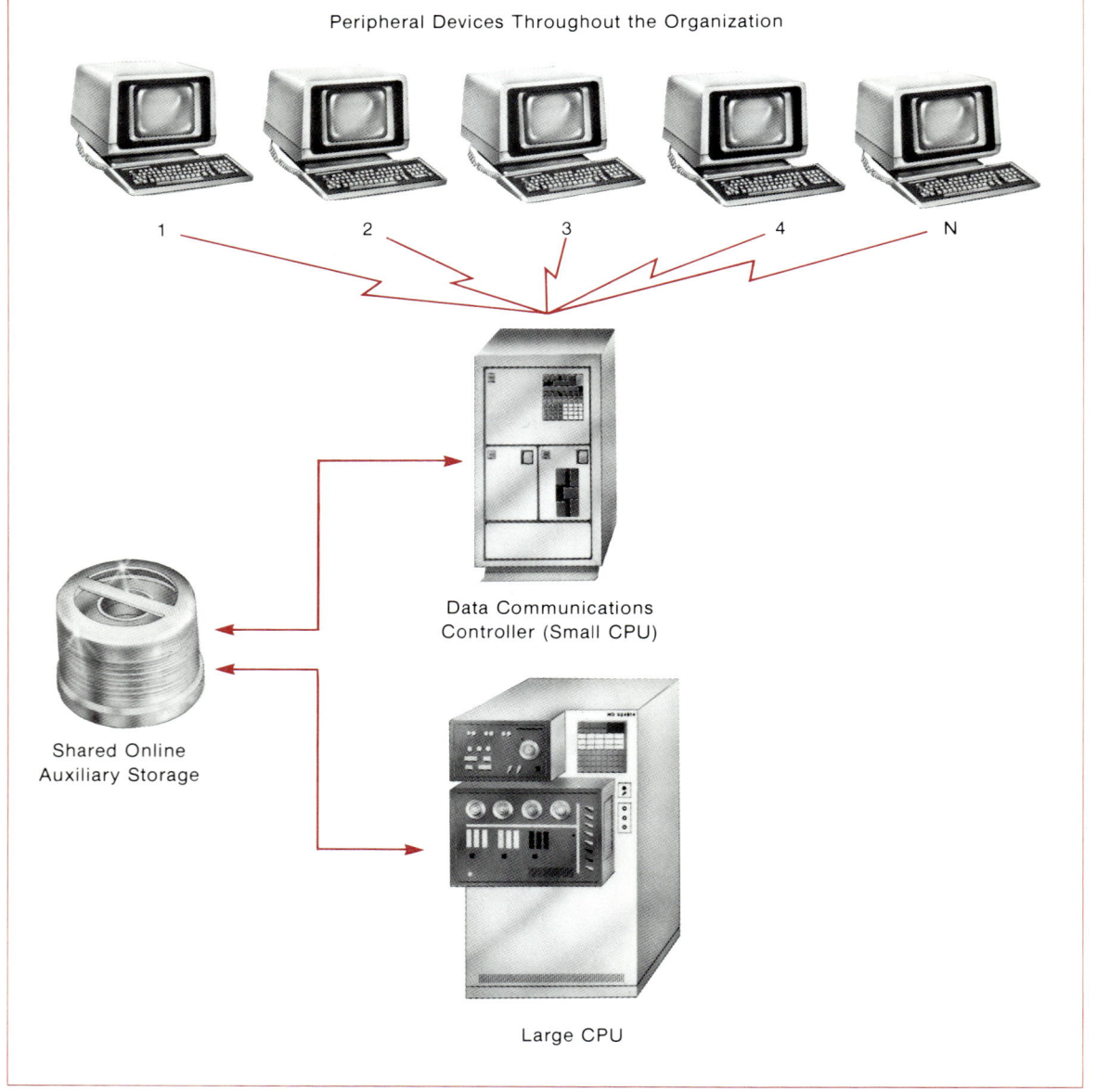

Peripheral Devices Throughout the Organization

1   2   3   4   N

Data Communications
Controller (Small CPU)

Shared Online
Auxiliary Storage

Large CPU

idly, the CPU can be slowed down when many interrupts occur. This situation led to the use of two or more CPUs working together in a **multiprocessing** arrangement to provide truly simultaneous execution of more than one program.

Under multiprocessing, multiple CPUs can share the same memory space, or each can have its own separate storage. Modules from the same program can be executed, as well as instructions contained within separate programs.

Some of the more common multiprocessing arrangements involve the combination of a large system with one or more smaller systems. For example, a small system such as a minicomputer can interface between the user and the large CPU and perform a number of tasks such as editing data, scheduling, and maintaining files. In this way, the large CPU is relieved of such duties and instead can concentrate on more sophisticated operations. The small CPU is referred to as a **front-end processor** in this configuration, which is shown in Figure 11–7.

One large CPU also can control several specialized I/O processors or channels. In turn, these devices each control one or more I/O devices and, with direct-access capability, require little attention from the main CPU. In this arrangement, the interrupt overhead of the main CPU is reduced significantly.

In another multiprocessing arrangement, a small CPU can be used for maintaining a data base. The small CPU, referred to as a **back-end processor,** is linked between the large CPU and the data base stored on DASDs. The small CPU will access specified items in the data base and update them as required.

When processing requirements are extremely great, multiple large

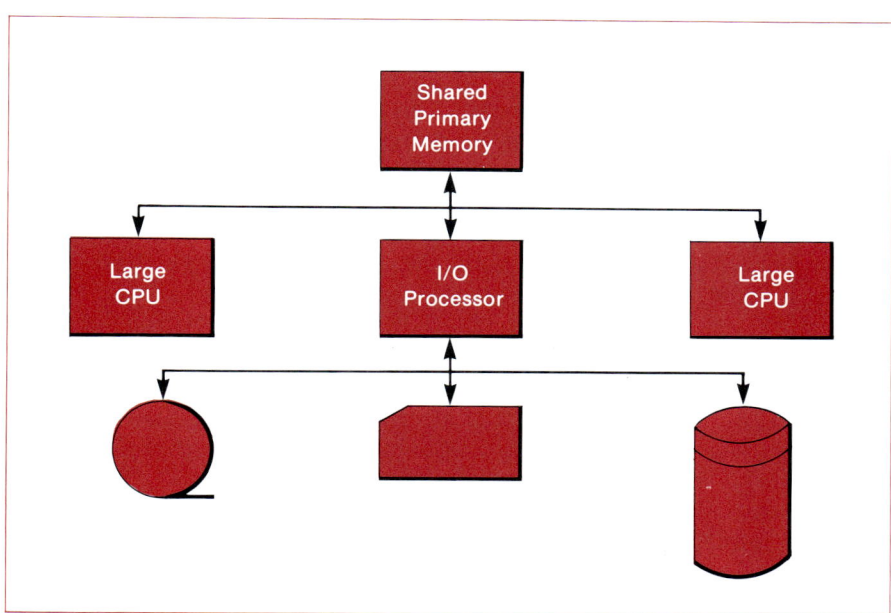

Figure 11—8 Large Multiprocessing Arrangement

CPUs can be linked to work in a coordinated effort. These systems can share the same memory space or have their own individual memory. In addition, each CPU can be dedicated to a specific task, such as just handling I/O operations, handling on-line requests only, performing only batch processing, and so on. An example of a multiprocessing arrangement where one CPU is dedicated to just I/O operations is illustrated in Figure 11–8.

The use of multiprocessing configurations has become more and more popular because of the decreasing prices of computers, especially microprocessor systems. Coordinating the efforts of several CPUs, however, requires highly sophisticated software and careful planning. The benefit from this effort is a system with greater capabilities than can be realized with a single CPU system. In addition, the need to maximize the utilization of a single CPU is lessened to some extent. The current status of multiprocessing is best represented in **distributed systems,** which will be discussed in the next chapter.

● An operating system allows a computer to handle many different problems by providing the computer with the capability of managing its own operations.

● An operating system acts as an interface between the user and the bare machine. It allows the user to enter instructions and the computer to execute them without requiring user knowledge of detailed computer operations.

● There are three types of operating systems: single-job; batch, or stacked-job; and real-time operating systems. Most operating systems today are a combination of batch and real-time systems.

● An operating system consists of control programs and processing programs. The more complex the operating system, the more programs it will contain.

● Operating system programs can be written by systems programmers or purchased as standard packages. Different types of computers that have the same operating system are compatible.

● Multiple programs can be executed concurrently through a technique known as **multiprogramming.**

● Programs in a multiprogramming arrangement are loaded into either foreground or background partitions, depending on their priority.

● Virtual storage is an extension of multiprogramming in which only the parts of a program to be executed are brought into main storage at one time.

● Virtual storage can be implemented through segmentation or paging. Segmentation involves breaking a program into logical divisions, whereas paging involves breaking a program into equal-sized divisions.

● Multiple CPUs can be linked to work in a coordinated effort. This arrangement is known as **multiprocessing.**

● In multiprocessing, different CPUs can share the same memory space or have their own individual memory. Each CPU can be dedicated to a specific task as well.

1. Discuss the purposes of developing operating systems and the functions these systems perform.

2. List and describe the different types of operating systems.

3. Where are operating system programs stored, and why are they stored in this location?

4. What are the purposes of JCL? Which control program translates the JCL?

5. List and describe two types of processing programs.

6. Why have standardized operating system packages become so popular?

7. Why was multiprogramming developed?

8. What is the difference between programs executing simultaneously and programs executing concurrently?

9. Distinguish between a foreground partition and a background partition.

10. When will control from one program be sent to another program to begin execution, and how can the output from different programs be kept separate on the same line printer?

11. Explain virtual storage. What advantages does this approach have over multiprogramming?

12. What is the difference between real storage and virtual storage?

13. Distinguish between implementing virtual storage systems through segmentation and through paging.

14. What is multiprocessing? When would it be more advantageous to implement a multiprocessing arrangement rather than a multiprogramming arrangement?

15. Describe two common multiprocessing arrangements.

PART IV

SYSTEMS

TELE-COMMUNICATIONS AND DISTRIBUTED COMPUTING

LEARNING OBJECTIVES

After studying this chapter, you will be able to do the following:

☐ Understand and define the concepts and techniques involved in the transmission of data.
☐ Define and discuss the functions and the types of equipment that make data communications possible.
☐ Explain the concept of a computer network, and discuss some of the more popular architectures.
☐ Define *distributed computing,* and provide examples of its use.
☐ Define a *satellite-based network.*

Chapter 12

INTRODUCTION   **Data communications** is the electronic transmission of data from one location to another. In recent years the number of organizations requiring information systems using geographically dispersed people and equipment has been growing. To accommodate the transfer of data, communications facilities such as telephone systems are being used with data-processing equipment. This is referred to as **teleprocessing** or **telecommunications.**

The physical link or medium that is used to carry data from one location to another is a **communications channel.** It allows remotely located I/O devices to communicate with the computer. Telephone lines are a frequently used type of communications channel.

COMMUNICATIONS CHANNELS

Message Transmission

The transmission of data over communications channels can take one of two forms: analog or digital. **Analog transmission** is the transmission of data in continuous wave form. Voice signals transmitted over telephone lines are converted to wave form, making telephone lines a medium for carrying analog signals. Most of the communications lines produced for use today are designed to carry analog signals. This is largely due to the type of communications lines provided by American Telephone and Telegraph (AT&T), the largest provider of communications services.

The other way of transmitting data, using distinct on and off states, is called **digital transmission.** Here the data is represented in the same form as it is in a computer (see Figure 12–1).

If computers represent data in digital (on/off) form, we might well ask how data can be sent via an analog line. First, the data must be converted from the digital form in which it is stored to analog (wave) form before it is transmitted. The process of translating digital data to analog form is called **modulation.**

On the receiving end the opposite of the original problem then exists—there is data in analog form but a computer that works with digital forms. The solution is to reconvert to a digital signal, a process called **demodulation.** The device that can accomplish both modulation and demodulation is called a **modem** or a **data set** (see Figure 12–2). The word **modem** is an acronym for **MOdulator-DEModulator.**

A common form of modem uses an **acoustic coupler** such as that shown in Figure 12–3, which requires that the telephone handset be

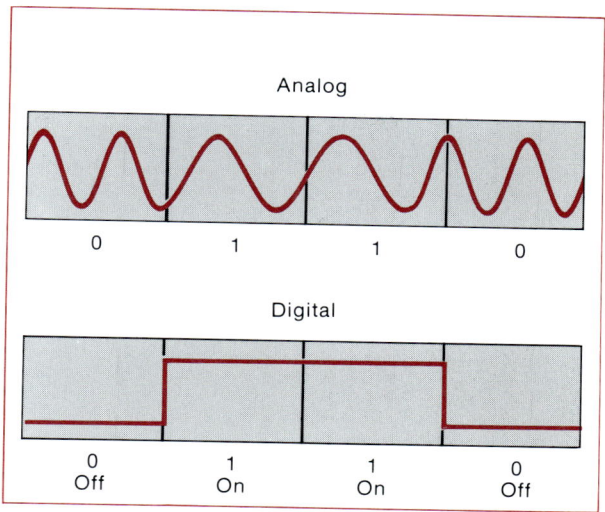

Figure 12–1 Analog Versus Digital Transmission

placed in a special cradle that converts bit-generated sounds into wave forms. An increasingly popular modem design couples directly into the telephone line (see Figure 12–4), eliminating handset use for data transmission.

Unlike analog transmission, digital transmission requires no conversion of data, because the computer stores and accepts data in digital form. Because no conversion is involved, the time required to send a message is less. Another advantage of digital transmission is that it results in fewer transmission errors than does analog transmission. Digital transmission thus allows an exchange of large amounts of data faster and more reliably than analog transmission. As technology advances, it is safe to say that digital probably will become the predominant means of data transmission.

Figure 12–2 Signal Conversion Process

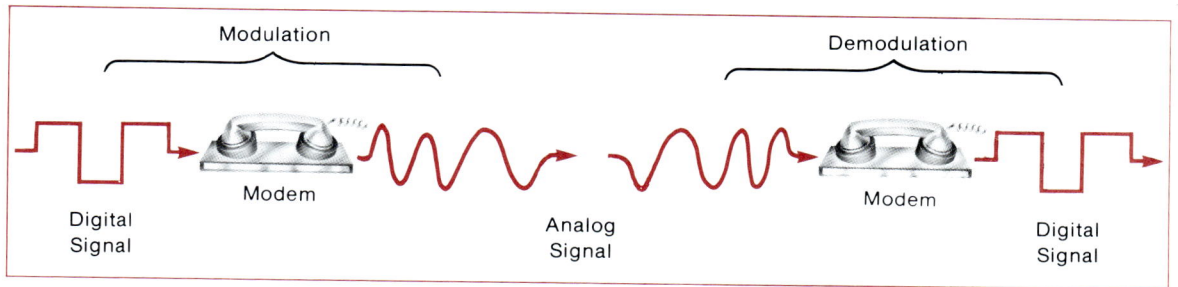

Figure 12–3 Acoustic Coupler Modem

Grades of Transmission

The rate or speed at which data can be transmitted across a channel is determined by the **grade,** or **bandwidth,** of the channel. There are three grades of channels: narrow-bandwidth channels, voice-grade channels, and broad-band channels. A **narrow-bandwidth channel** typically transmits data at a rate of 45 to 90 bits per second. An example is telegraph channels. **Voice-grade channels** can transmit at rates from 300 to 9,600 bits per second. A telephone line is a voice-grade channel. **Broad-band channels** can transmit data at rates of up to 120,000 bits per second and so are suitable for applications requiring high-speed transmission of large amounts of data. Examples of broad-band channels include coaxial cables, microwaves, and laser beams.

Figure 12–4 Direct Connect Modem

COMPUTERS IN BUSINESS AND INDUSTRY

Businesses require meaningful information to make decisions. To meet these demands, computers are used to generate information and automate processes. The following pages illustrate the uses of computers in a variety of applications.

1. Technical innovations such as a hand-held computer capable of recording extensive sales data have enabled the Fountain Sales Department of The Coca-Cola Company to increase efficiency in meeting the needs of its food service customers.
2. Santa Fe's Network Management Center monitors the flow of information from the central computer center in Topeka to a network of over 4,000 CRT's on the railroad.
3. Sporting goods stores are taking advantage of the effectiveness computers offer in recording sales and inventory of merchandise.

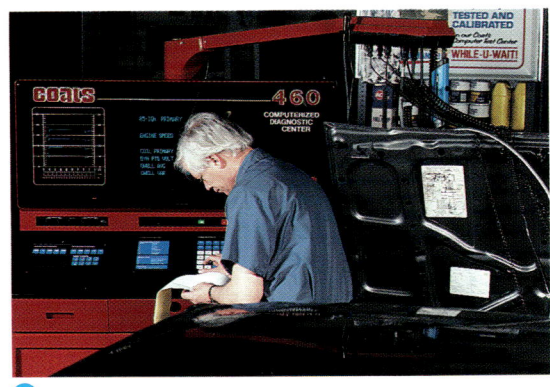

Business and Industry—continued. **4.** The new *Coats* computerized diagnostic center fills part of the growing need for accurate, inexpensive diagnosis of engine-related problems of automobiles and other vehicles. **5.** "Intergraph" graphics work station used for automated mapping of gas and electric service facilities. **6.** Computers are essential for airline reservations. **7.** Holiday Inn headquarters Memphis Reservation Center. **8.** Quotron's Financial Information Services provides users with instant access to stock, bond, option, and commodity quote services.

9. Process computers aid rail freight classification yard operation linking yards with central computer for advance train transit information. **10.** AccuRay 1180 MICRO Paper Machine control system monitors and controls the complex process of making paper from wood fiber and water. **11.** Pacific Gas & Electric uses one computer to monitor plant perimeters and print-out plant status and alarm status. Another computer controls turbine generator speed and load. **12.** U.S. Steel's computer—control console in control room of Lorain Works 10″ Bar Mill.

Business and Industry—continued. **13.** Data is being displayed to an electric dispatcher on a terminal connected to one of five computers of the Northern California electric power company's dispatch computer system. The dispatch system is, in turn, linked to twelve remote computers throughout the Northern California system to provide power control of hydroelectric and fossil fueled plant. **14.** To help assure the quality of dishwashers manufactured at GE's Kentucky appliance plant, assembly-line data are fed into a computer to aid inspectors in spotting deficiencies. **15.** The manufacture of fiberglass insulation used to conserve energy and increase the heating/cooling efficiency in residential homes is controlled by a minicomputer/microcomputer combination system manufactured by AccuRay Corporation. **16.** An operator uses an electronic reader to scan a menu of drafting symbols, selects the appropriate symbols, and the drawing appears above the keyboard.

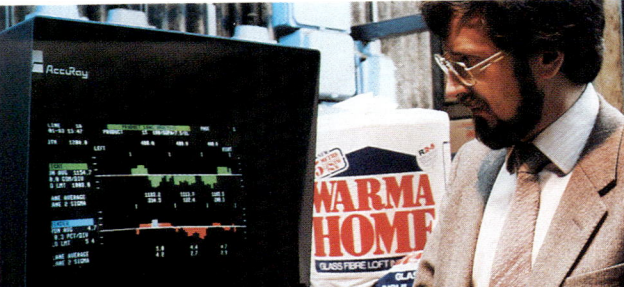

Modes of Transmission

The transmission of data may be handled in one of three basic modes: simplex, half-duplex, or full-duplex modes (see Figure 12–5). In a **simplex** channel, data can travel in only one direction on the line. A terminal transmitting via a simplex channel can either send or receive, but it cannot do both. This mode is of limited usefulness for data communications.

A **half-duplex** channel allows data to be transmitted in both directions but in only one direction at a time. A terminal transmitting by a half-duplex channel, then, can send and receive, but not at the same time. Most telephone networks operate in half-duplex mode.

The **full-duplex** mode allows data to be transmitted in both directions at the same time, so a terminal using this mode can send and receive simultaneously. Full-duplex capability in traditional channels requires double the wiring needed for half-duplex capability.

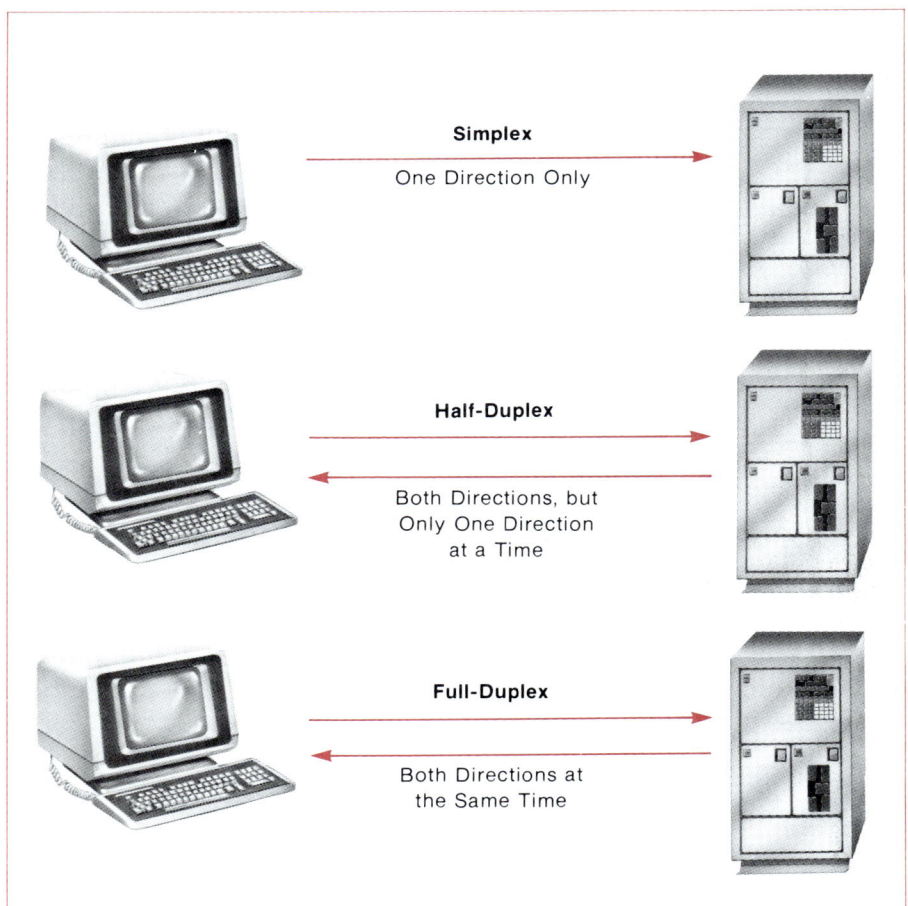

Figure 12–5 Channel Transmission Modes

Simplex
One Direction Only

Half-Duplex
Both Directions, but
Only One Direction
at a Time

Full-Duplex
Both Directions at
the Same Time

There are two methods of transmission: asynchronous and synchronous. **Asynchronous transmission** is the process whereby characters are sent at any time convenient to the transmitting or receiving device. It is also referred to as **start-stop transmission,** since the transmission is synchronized by a start-stop bit. There are three common codes used to transmit characters asynchronously.

Baudot is a five-bit code with thirty-two possible combinations. A shift code (shifting from a code for numbers to a code for letters and special characters) makes it possible to code sixty-four combinations. The unit of measurement for this code is called a **baud.** One baud per second is equivalent to one pulse or code element per second. Baudot uses five bits for a character plus a start and stop bit. With asynchronous transmission, the receiving device (terminal, computer, and so on) controls the flow of data: When it signals it is ready, data is sent; data transmission is stopped when the device signals it is not ready. Transmission speeds frequently are referred to as **baud rates.**

The second type of code used to transmit characters asynchronously is the **binary coded decimal (BCD)** method. It is similar to Baudot, but a six-bit code is used instead of a five-bit code. A third method is the **American Standard Code for Information Interchange (ASCII).** This code uses seven or eight bits per character.

Synchronous transmission is the process whereby whole blocks of characters are transferred in a timed sequence. It allows for a higher volume of data to be transferred through the channel but requires more sophisticated equipment than does asynchronous transmission. Synchronous transmission is normally used where the transmission rate exceeds two thousand bits per second.

TYPES OF COMMUNICATIONS CHANNELS

There are three major types of communications channels: wire cable (telegraph lines, telephone lines, and coaxial cable), microwave, and fiber optics.

Wire cable is presently the most common form of communications channel. Data is transmitted in analog form. Advantages of using wire cable include the low initial investment required because of the availability of already existing cable networks, as well as the standardization of the technology. There are some disadvantages, such as the problem of electrical interference and the fact that in some cases—if the users are separated by such things as mountains or long distances—cumbersome physical links may be needed.

Microwave is also an analog type of transmission channel. However, unlike wire cable, microwave is sent through the atmosphere in a way similar to radio or television transmissions. Microwave must be transmitted in a straight line between two points. It also may be used with satellites that have been placed in a geosynchronous (rotating at the same speed as the earth) orbit approximately 22,300 miles from the equator. Such satellites appear stationary from the vantage of earth stations. For example, by using only three appropriately positioned satellites, data can be sent or received between any land-based stations.

Microwave transmission has some distinct advantages, including relatively error-free transmission; a high degree of flexibility, because there is no need for a physical link between transmission points; and potential cost benefits as compared with wire cables for large amounts of data transfer.

However, microwaves must be transmitted in a straight line between two points, requiring the use of repeater towers (that boost and redirect signals) for long distances or rough terrain. The high initial costs of ground stations and satellites are another disadvantage.

A relatively new form of technology is **fiber optics,** which employs digital transmission. Light impulses are sent down clear, flexible tubing measuring approximately half the diameter of a human hair. These tubes are grouped together inside a cable that is about one-tenth the diameter of wire cable. Data can be transmitted much faster with fiber optics than with other technologies.

With fiber optics, data can be handled without conversion to analog form; data can be transmitted at high rates with few errors; the small size and flexibility of fiber optics tubing allows easy installation; and fiber optics are not affected by electrical interference. However, light impulses tend to lose signal strength over distance, and repeaters are needed to read and boost the incoming light pulses. Fiber optics, however, have demonstrated high reliability.

LINE MANAGEMENT

There are two principal types of line, or channel, configurations: point to point and multidrop (see Figure 12–6). In a **point-to-point configuration,** each terminal is connected directly (has a **dedicated line**) to the computer. A disadvantage of this type of configuration is that a single terminal is usually not active enough to keep the line busy. The **multidrop configuration** alleviates this problem by connecting several terminals to the same line. In a multidrop configuration, only one terminal can transmit at a time; however, more than one terminal can receive messages from the computer simultaneously. This configuration increases the efficiency of line usage and thus reduces line costs.

Line Control

In multidrop configuration, two methods are employed to prevent more than one terminal from using the line at a time: polling and contention.

When **polling** is used, the computer asks each terminal if it has a message to transmit. If the terminal has a message, it is directed by the computer to send it. After the message has been sent, the computer asks

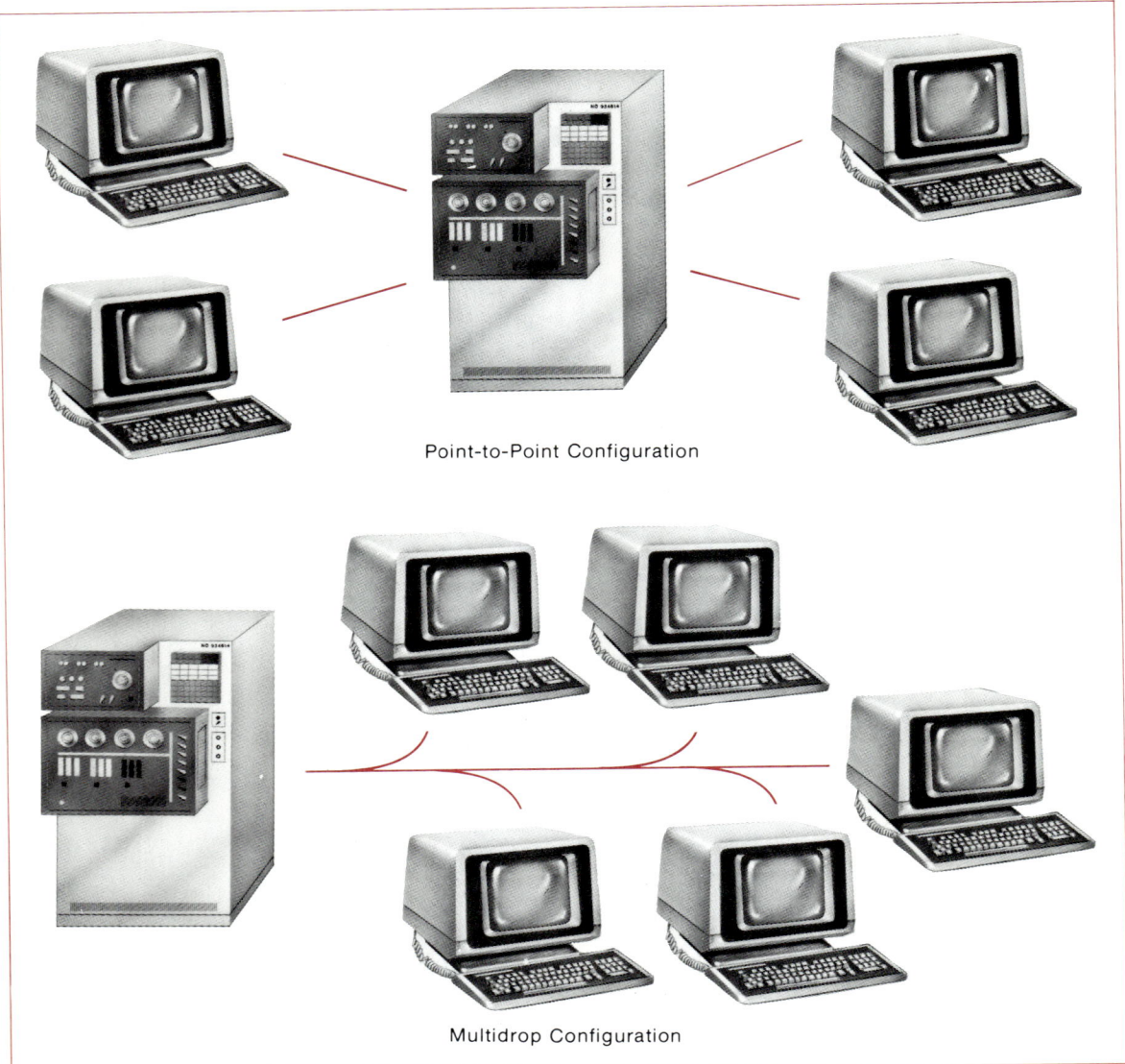

Point-to-Point Configuration

Multidrop Configuration

Figure 12—6 Point-to-Point Versus Multidrop Line Configurations

the next terminal if it has a message to transmit. The computer continues polling each terminal in turn until all the terminals on line have had an opportunity to transmit; then it begins the process again. A major disadvantage associated with polling is that if a particular terminal does not have any messages to send, the processor sits idle during polling, and valuable processor time is wasted.

Contention is the method of line control that attempts to overcome this problem. The focus of contention is on the terminal end. Each terminal monitors the communication line before sending its message. If

Telesecurity

As telecommunications become commonplace in the future, there will be greater emphasis placed on "telesecurity," the security of telecommunications. Although networks were designed to allow legitimate users to communicate with public data bases and each other, they are increasingly being exploited by illegal users to gain access to classified material, free computer time, or "just beat the system."

One former student at San Jose State University used its computer system for such a long list of crimes that he finally was arrested and expelled. In addition to peering over people's shoulders to steal their passwords and destroying other student's files, he also used the TALK program on the school's network to get between seven thousand and eight thousnd dollars worth of free telephone calls. (Besides assorted calls to places across the United States, he called Sweden, Iran, and the People's Republic of China.) The student also accessed the computer system at MIT, adding countless hours of game playing to the already outrageous telephone bill.

The frightening fact is that this student is not alone. As networks flourish, so do individuals determined to abuse them. Some of them even form "user groups" dedicated to abusing the networks. Time and time again, tests have shown that there are no secure networks. However, there must be in the future. Telesecurity may very well determine the future of telecomputing.

the line is free, the terminal sends its message; if it is busy, the terminal will wait a set period of time (perhaps one or two seconds) and then try again. This process is repeated until the line is free. A major disadvantage of this method is that one terminal may tie up a multidrop line for long periods of time, not allowing other terminals to get their messages through.

Data Transmission Control

As was mentioned earlier, during data transmission the modem at the sending end takes the digital signal and modulates it into an analog signal. At the receiving end another modem receives the analog signal and demodulates it back into digital (binary) form.

The modem, not knowing exactly when to expect the data, must be given some type of signal warning it that data is being sent. This gives the modem time to get itself aligned and "in synch" with the incoming signal. Special characters, called **message characters,** provide this warning. They are placed in front of and behind the data to mark the beginning and end of the message.

With asynchronous transmission, each character of data must be surrounded with message characters. As a result, more total bits must be transferred than would be necessary if the synchronous method were used. The synchronous method only requires a single set of start- and end-message characters per block of data, thus permitting more characters to be sent per second (see Figure 12–7). Whereas synchronous transmission is faster, it has the disadvantage of requiring a more complex and expensive modem than does asynchronous transmission.

Transferring data between devices also involves an exchange of prearranged signals, referred to as **handshaking.** These signals, in combination with a prearranged pattern of message characters, define the rules to be followed for exchanging data over a communications line. What these exact rules are depends on the computer manufacturer, the telephone company, and the other related devices (for example, the front-end processor or modem) that make up the computer system. **Protocol** is the specific set of rules governing handshaking and message characters.

Line-regulating Devices

Multiplexers, concentrators, and **programmable communications processors** are devices that allow more peripherals to be connected to the host computer at a lower cost; they relieve it of many of the necessary housekeeping and control functions required to coordinate the network components, thus allowing more efficient use of the CPU time.

Multiplexers A single terminal generally will not use a communications channel to its full capacity. Multiplexing data can create more economical use of the channel. It works by combining the input from several terminals into a single input stream, allowing data from all these terminals to be transmitted over a single channel, usually a voice-grade channel (see Figure 12–8). At the receiving end a similar unit or the CPU itself separates the individual data inputs for processing.

A multiplexer will use one of two basic techniques to multiplex data: frequency division multiplexing or time division multiplexing. The first

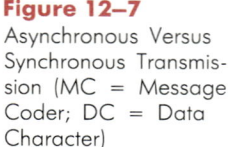

Figure 12–7
Asynchronous Versus Synchronous Transmission (MC = Message Coder; DC = Data Character)

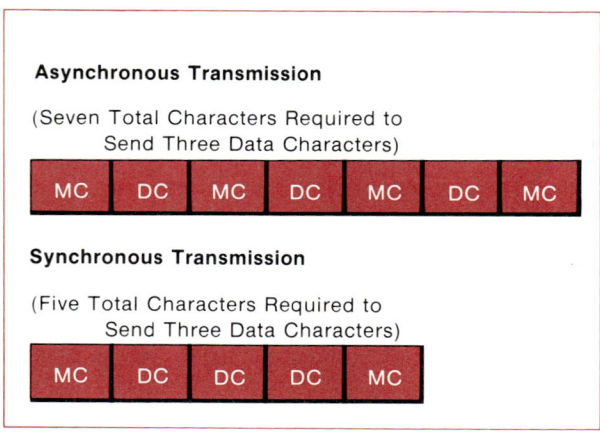

Asynchronous Transmission

(Seven Total Characters Required to Send Three Data Characters)

| MC | DC | MC | DC | MC | DC | MC |

Synchronous Transmission

(Five Total Characters Required to Send Three Data Characters)

| MC | DC | DC | DC | MC |

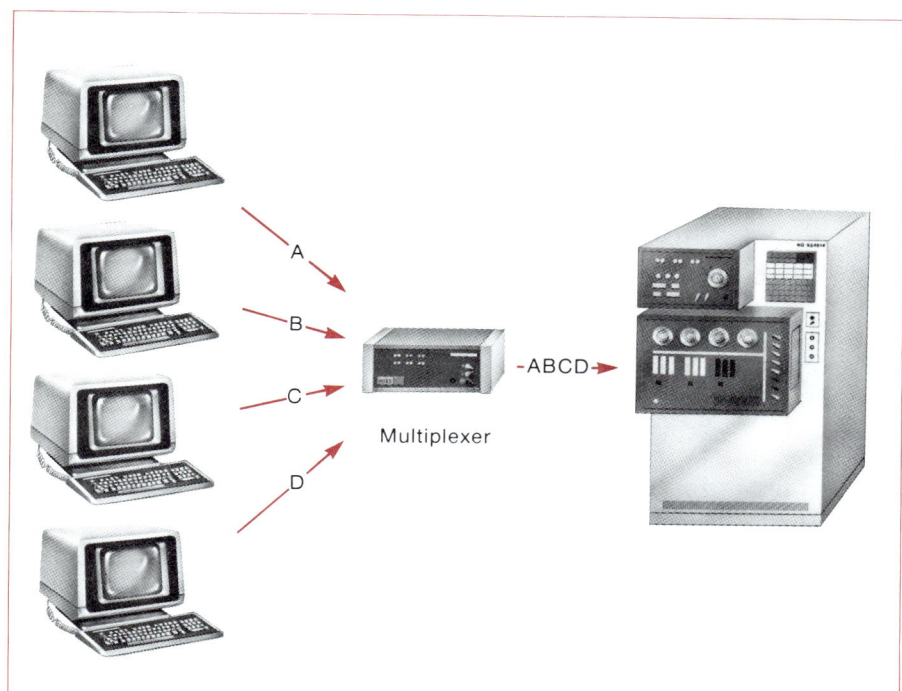

Figure 12—8 System with Multiplexer

step in **frequency division multiplexing (FDM)** is to have a modem convert the digital signal from each terminal into an analog signal. Each analog signal is allocated its own portion of the frequency of the available channel. This frequency will be unique to the terminal from which the signal originated. These signals then are combined and transmitted over the communications channel. On the receiving end a similar device will demultiplex the individual signals. This is accomplished by a set of filters, each designed to detect a particular frequency. The analog signal then passes through a modem, where it is demodulated back into a digital pulse signal. The tuning mechanism of a radio receiver selectively filters frequencies other than the desired station.

In **time division multiplexing (TDM),** the multiplexer continuously samples digital inputs from each terminal, one by one, for a fixed time period (generally expressed in nanoseconds). There are two types of TDM: **bit interleaved** and **byte interleaved.** In bit-interleaved TDM, the sampling time per input corresponds to the amount of time used to designate a bit. In byte-interleaved TDM, it corresponds to the amount of time used to designate a byte. The signal then is time compressed (adjusted to the speed of the TDM) and placed in a time slot in the TDM output signal.

If a system has a number of low-speed terminals or is geographically dispersed with fewer than sixteen channels, FDM is the method typically used. The TDM method should be used if the system has a transmission rate of 2,400 bits per second or more or if a large number of channels are used.

Concentrators   A concentrator allows data from only one terminal at a time to be transmitted over a communications channel. The concentrator polls each terminal, one at a time, to see if it has any messages to send. Provided there is a free channel, the first terminal ready to send or receive data will get control of the channel and will maintain control of it for the length of the transaction (see Figure 12–9). The use of a concentrator relies on the basic assumption that not all terminals will be ready to send or receive data at a given time. Where transactions occur simultaneously, each terminal must wait its turn based on a first-in, first-out system.

Programmable Communications Processors   When the total number of peripherals, the volume of data transmission, or both surpass a certain level, computer throughput is reduced significantly. This happens because the CPU must devote more of its time to such functions as executing interrupts, moving data into and out of storage, and performing other necessary housekeeping functions. A programmable communications processor is a device that relieves the CPU of many of these tasks, which can take up as much as half the processing time of the host com-

Figure 12–9 System with Concentrator

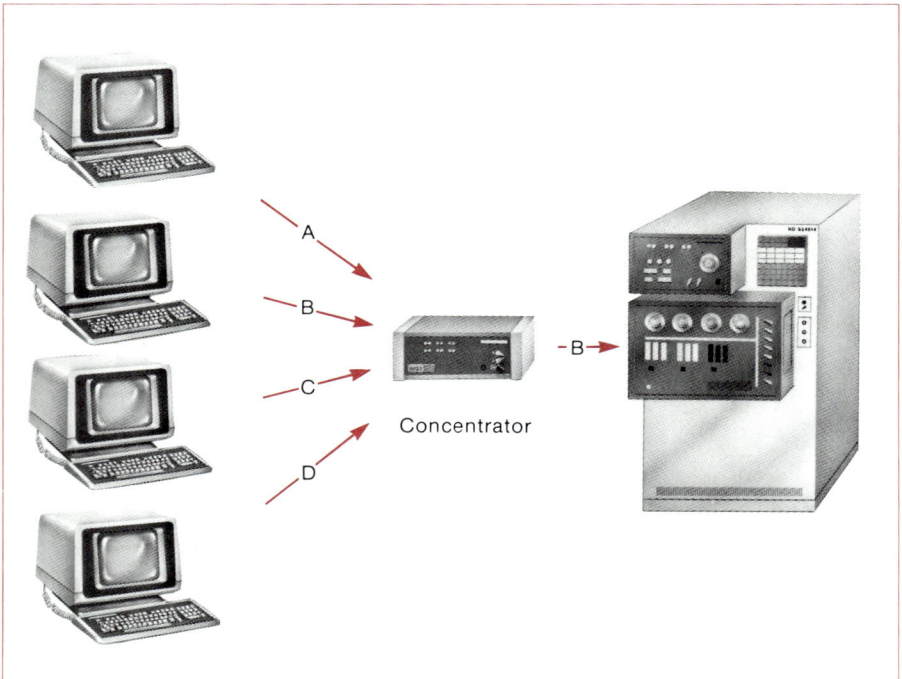

PULSE Banking Network

The PULSE banking network electronically links four hundred banks and savings and loans via four hundred automated teller machines (ATMs) in Texas and Louisiana. For example, if a customer of the First National Bank of Dallas (a member of the PULSE network) is in Austin and wants to withdraw one hundred dollars from a checking account, he or she can do so by dropping by any ATM hooked up to the PULSE network. The customer simply inserts a plastic "debit" card into the ATM (just as he or she would in Dallas)

and punches in the request and a personal four-digit identification code. The code is recognized by the Austin bank computer, which relays the transaction to the PULSE network's Houston switching center. From there it is routed via leased telephone lines to the Dallas bank's computer. In Dallas, the usual checks are made to determine if the cardholder has sufficient funds to cover the withdrawal. The Dallas bank computer then sends an OK back through the same channels to the ATM, which then dispenses the money. The elapsed time for the entire transmission is only six seconds.

puter. The programmable communications processor can perform these functions with fewer steps and simpler software than the host CPU. It reduces direct processor time costs, programming costs, and debugging time.

Communications processors typically are used for **message switching** and **front-end processing.** In message switching, the processor's principal task is to receive messages and route them to the appropriate destinations. A front-end processor also performs more sophisticated operations such as validating transmitted data and preprocessing data before its transmission to the central computer.

NETWORKS

The development of the data communications channels just discussed has made possible the development and widespread use of computer networks. A **computer network** is the linking together of CPUs and terminals via a communications system. A network allows users at different locations to share files, devices, and programs.

Networks may be local or remote. A **local-area network (LAN)** operates within a well-defined and generally self-enclosed area such as a small office building. The communication stations are usually linked by cable and are generally within one thousand feet of each other.

Remote networks (also called **wide-area networks**) cover large, geographically dispersed areas. Communications between stations usually occurs via standard telephone lines, a dedicated telephone line, or microwave relays. Because of the prohibitive costs, remote network use is generally restricted to large corporations.

Network Architecture

All networks comprise two basic structures: nodes and links. A **node** refers to the end points of a network and consists of CPUs, printers, VDTs, and other physical devices. **Links** are the transmission channels that connect the nodes. Nodes and links can be arranged in a number of ways. Some of the more common structures include star, ring, hierarchical, and distributed networks (see Figure 12–10).

The **star network** requires that all transactions go through a central computer before being routed to the appropriate network node. The idea is to create a central decision point to facilitate work load distribution and resource sharing. A major disadvantage with the star configuration is that the system is exposed to single-point vulnerability: if the host computer fails, none of the others can communicate with each other.

A **ring network** consists of a number of CPUs connected by a single transmission line. Unlike in the star, in a ring configuration data can bypass a malfunctioning CPU without disrupting operations throughout the network.

A **hierarchical network** (also called a **tree network**) is a more sophisticated approach that divides an organization's needs into multiple levels, each receiving different levels of computer support. The system consists of a network of small computers that feed into a large central computing complex. It can be a relatively inefficient configuration, however, since a node at the lower end of one branch has to traverse all levels of the network to communicate with a node at the lower end of another branch.

A **fully distributed network** is one in which every set of nodes in the network can communicate directly with every other set of nodes through a single communications link. Each local system has its own processing capabilities. The designation **distributed network** is used for both fully distributed and partially distributed arrangements. A distributed network places computers in a number of locations but does not necessarily place control or the administrative and technical resources required to operate them in the same location. When the control and resources also are distributed (to individual locations or administrative units within the organization), it is referred to as **distributed computing.** In common use, however, the distinction between a distributed network

The Case of the APB (Automated Perverted Bulletin)

There is at least one woman in Florida who is not singing the praises of computers. More likely, she is singing songs of freedom after having been incarcerated in jails and a mental hospital for more than two months because of "computer error." Police had issued an APB (All Points Bulletin) for Jo Ann Hammock on bad check charges when they encountered Janette Elaine Cammock and took her into custody because of what they called "bizarre" behavior. When they ran her name through the statewide computer network, it confirmed that—despite a difference in name and physical description— she was the person on the wanted list. After two months, Cammock was able to convince the police of their error. The computer still is not sure.

and distributed computing has been blurred, with both terms generally being used to describe any system where the computers, although physically dispersed, are all interconnected.

DISTRIBUTED COMPUTING

As has been mentioned, dispersing data-processing resources to individual locations or administrative units within an organization is referred to as **distributed computing.** This is opposed to a centralized approach, in which all data-processing resources are in a common physical location and administrative unit within the organization. Figure 12–11 shows an organization with a centralized structure of data-processing resources and a second organization with a distributed structure of data-processing resources.

In a distributed computing system, the personnel, such as data-processing and systems development people, are located physically and administratively within the user functions—for example, a payroll department or sales department in a company. Users may even perform many of their own data-processing tasks.

The hardware also is located in each user area and is tailored to user requirements. However, software in a distributed system is developed in the same way it is in a centralized system: it comes from computer vendors, outside sources, or in-house development.

With a distributed system, data is collected, stored, and processed to fulfill the requirements of both the specific user area and other user areas. For example, data may be collected, stored, and processed for both the production department and the marketing department. The developments in microcomputer and data communications technologies have allowed for a more efficient and cost-effective flow of data from computer to computer.

Figure 12—10
Common Network Architectures

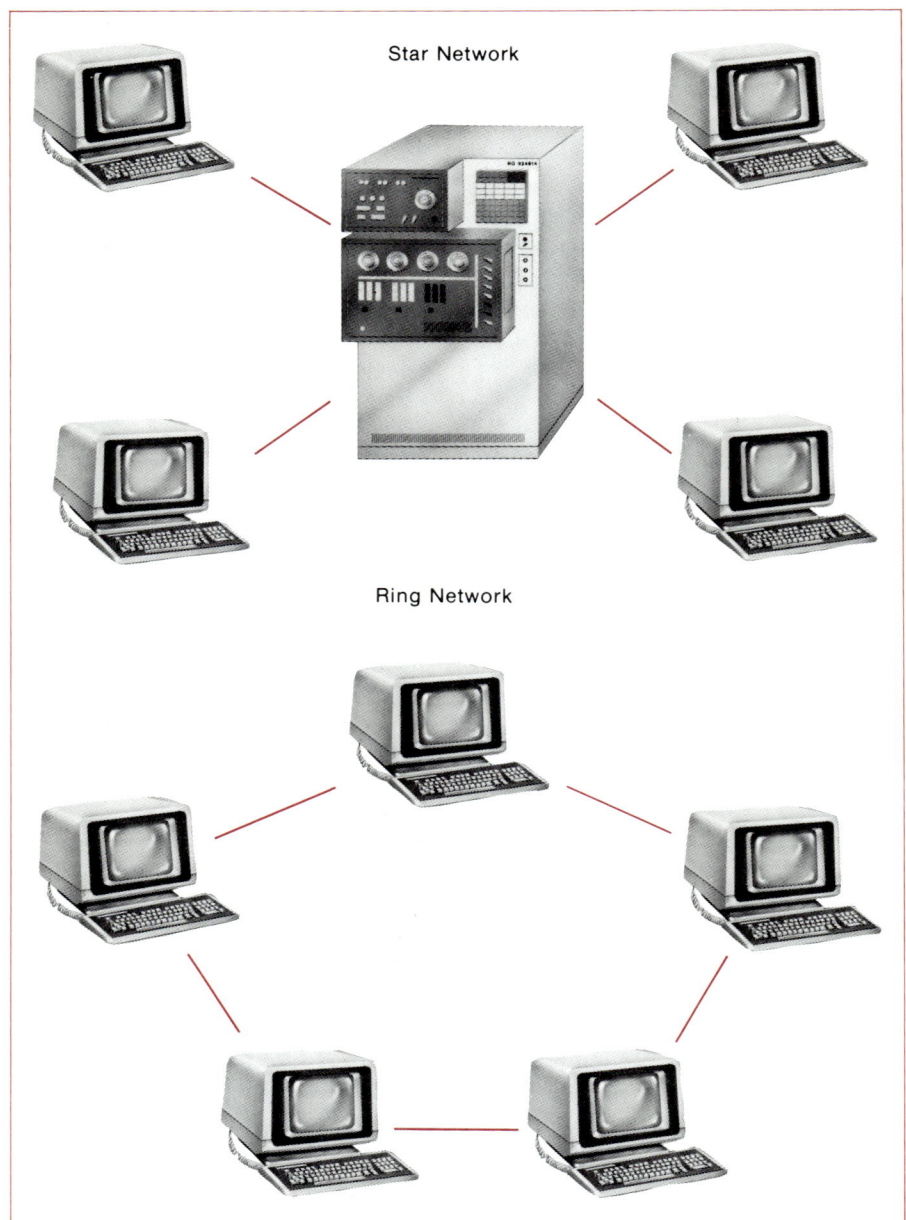

Star Network

Ring Network

There can be a number of advantages to employers' using distributed computing: It is easily adaptable to organizations characterized by diversity in management style, diversity in service or output, or geographical diversity; it gives the users responsibility and authority over their own data-processing needs, which permits a more flexible approach to solving individual user needs; and it provides job enrichment by allow-

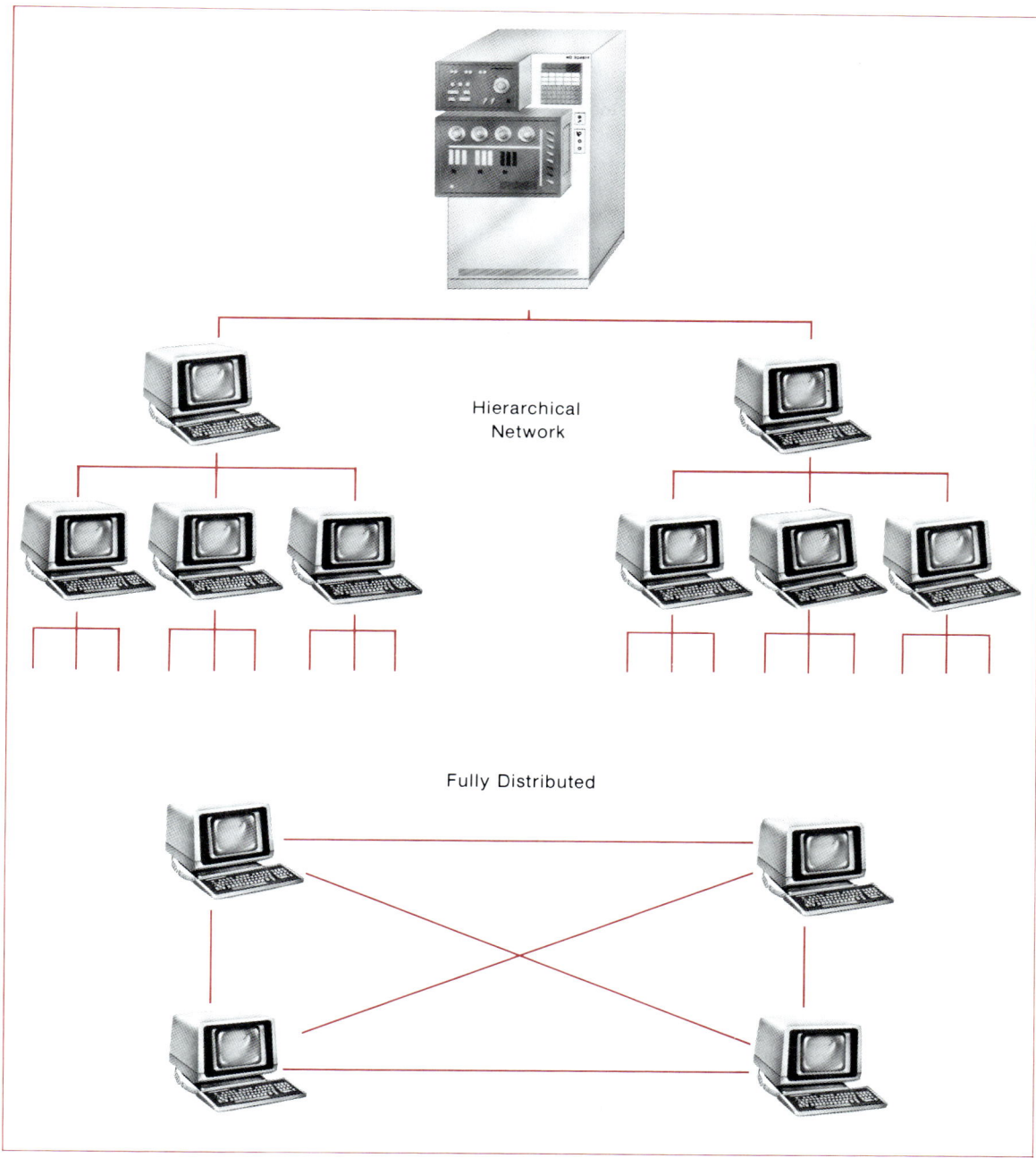

Figure 12–10 A

ing individuals to share or split responsibilities. In addition, each user's data-processing facility can be more easily managed because of its relatively small size and its simplicity.

There are also certain disadvantages associated with distributed computing. It requires much effort in planning and coordination to prevent

Figure 12–11
Centralized Versus Distributed Computing Approach

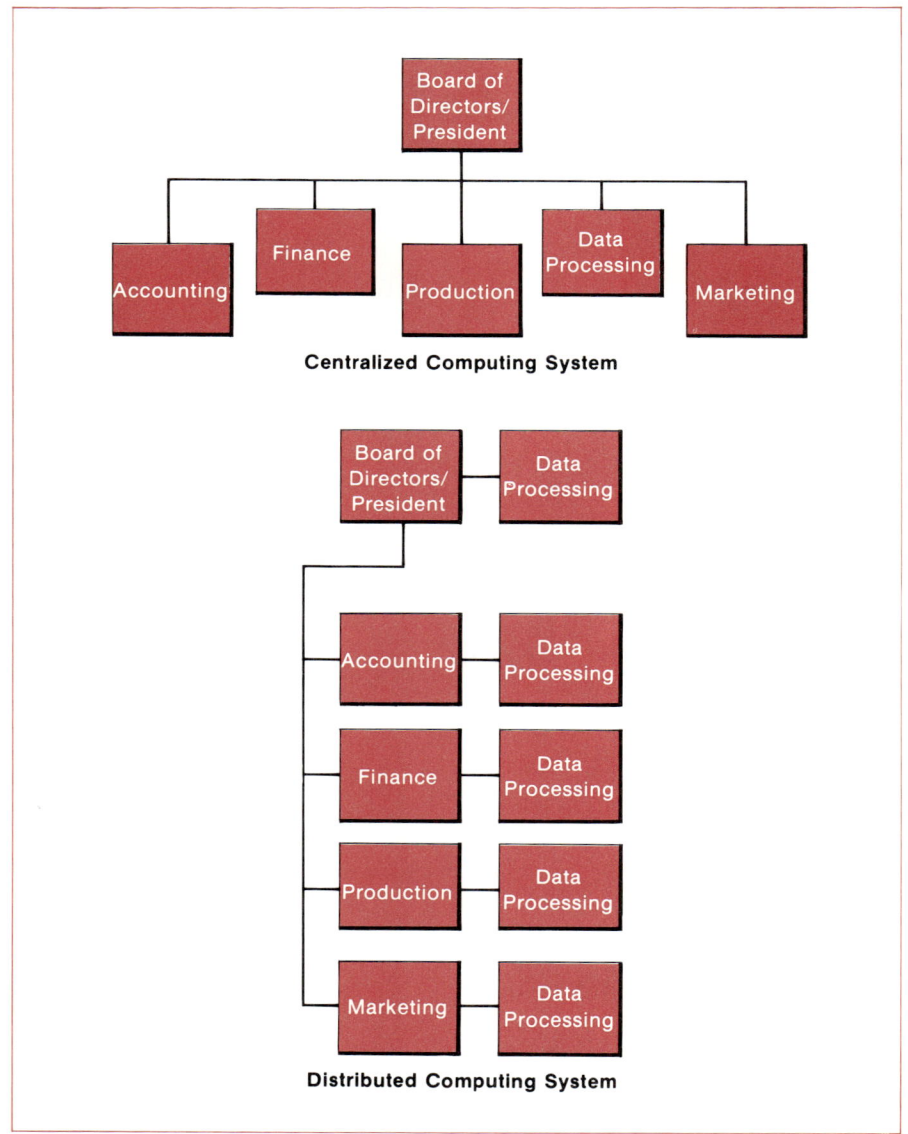

or minimize suboptimization and fragmentation in the development of the overall information system. Also, it often requires redundant resources (equipment, data files, and personnel).

Despite these drawbacks, many organizations are using a distributed computing approach successfully. The Bank of America in California is an excellent example. It has set up a distributed computing facility (DCF) to handle the communications between the branch banks and the IBM host computer located in the data-processing center. There are

1,200 branch banks and 200 automated teller machines (ATMs) in California, in addition to 223 branches, affiliates, subsidiaries, and representative offices around the world.

For the locations to communicate with each other, an extensive communications network was built. Two data-processing centers—one in Los Angeles and the other in San Francisco—provide the major support for the system and are connected to each other via communications channels. Figure 12–12 diagrams the DCF at San Francisco. The DCF at the Los Angeles location is similar.

The system begins at the branch banks, where the terminals are connected by coaxial cable to a control unit also located in the branch bank. The control unit communicates via telephone lines to the minicomputers located at the DCF. Customer transaction data then is passed from each minicomputer to the host computer via six high-speed digital lines. Using the DCF allows the bank to keep up-to-the-minute account balances for every customer.

There are eight independent hardware modules in the DCF system, each of which handles only a portion of the full customer data base. The system is designed so that if any module goes down, another module can immediately take over its customer file; thus, teller access is not interrupted.

Bank of America also has a network of ATMs that are connected to the DCF via telephone lines. The digital signals from the ATMs are converted to analog by a modem and then sent to the DCF, where another modem demodulates the analog signal to a digital signal and feeds it into a control unit. The control unit sends the data to a programmable communications processor, which then routes it to the host computer.

The Bank of America is an example of a private network developed for a single organization. There are also several multiorganizational distributed computing networks. One is the Advanced Research Projects Agency (ARPA) of the U.S. Department of Defense. This network uses approximately fifty computers ranging in size from minicomputers to supercomputers. They connect about forty universities and research institutions throughout the United States and Europe.

A remote network is not the only way in which distributed computing can be used. Many large and small firms have begun to realize the benefits associated with local-area networks (LANs). An LAN connects computers and peripherals in an unbroken computing circle, allowing them to speak to each other efficiently, as well as share common information, massive storage vaults, and peripherals.

A well-planned LAN can increase department efficiency, result in better-informed individual managers, and decrease downtime on printers, disk drives, and modems. This all translates into substantial monetary savings for a corporation. Local-area networks have allowed individuals and corporations to become more productive through the sharing of data. Sharing leads to a more efficient use of data and can be worth money to a firm. The only way data can be shared efficiently between computers is via LANs.

A basic LAN includes five components:

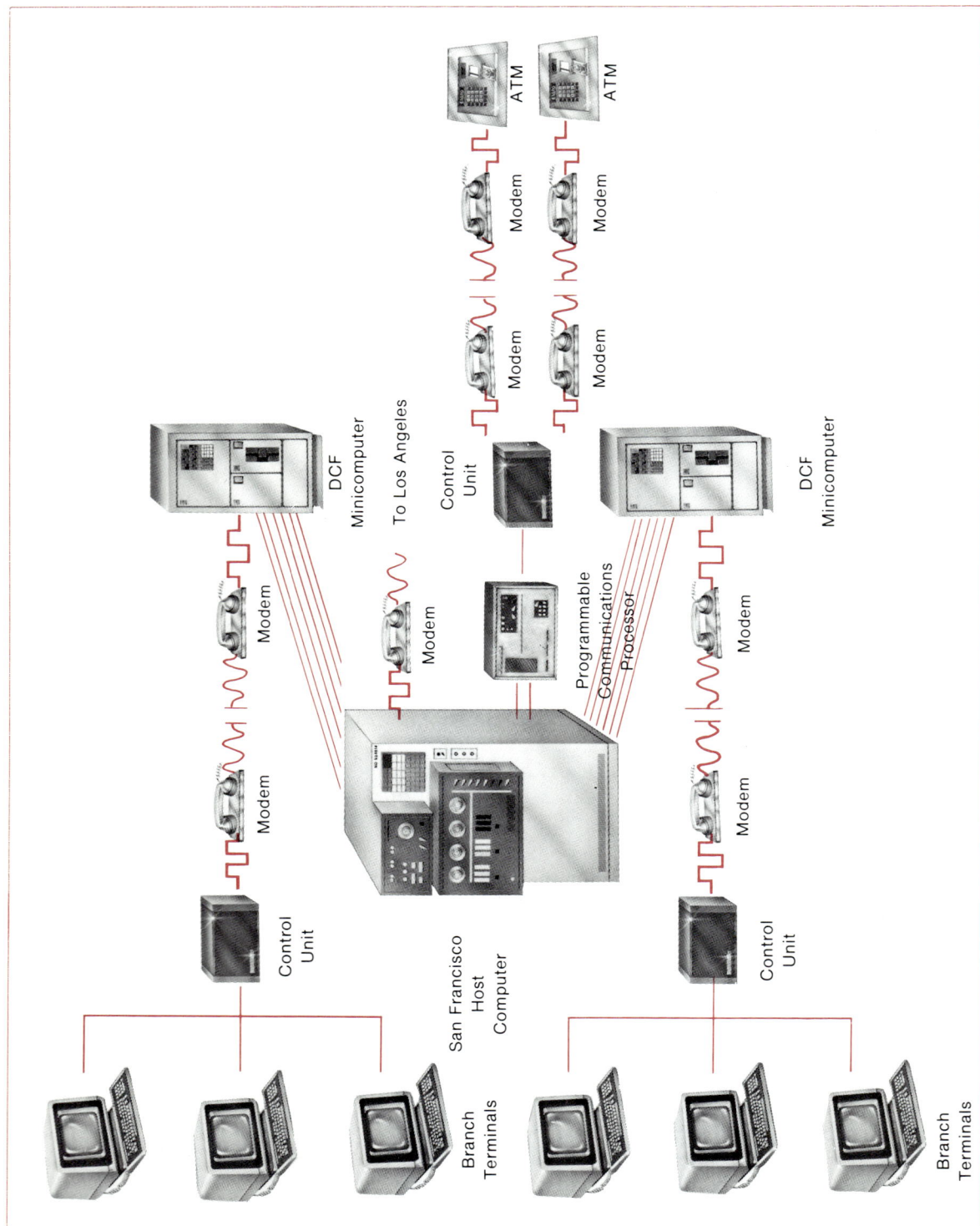

Figure 12-12 Bank of America Distributed Computing Facility (DCF)

1. The hardware (computers and peripherals).
2. The network interface (usually an expansion card that plugs into the hardware).
3. The network master controller (either a chip on the expansion card, a hard disk drive, or a dedicated computer).
4. The network server (usually a hard disk drive containing both the software that fuels the LAN specifically and the programs available to network users).
5. The wiring.

An excellent example of the varied uses of an LAN using microcomputers can be found at the cardiology department at the Los Robles Regional Medical Center in Thousand Oaks, California. Its network consists of seven IBM PCs using a Nestar Plan 4000 LAN (the software and other hardware needed to establish the network). The network consists of a computer in the cardiology office, the technicians' office, the catheterization laboratory, and the vascular laboratory, as well as one in each of three doctors' offices. The computer in the cardiology office runs the patients' information file; the catheterization laboratory computer takes the information from the catheter recorder, does physiological calculations, and keeps an inventory of supplies; the technicians' office computer is used for word processing, making spreadsheets, and keeping personnel records; and the vascular laboratory computer keeps a patient data base. The other three computers are used by three private physicians who are located at the center. Their computers are used to maintain billing and insurance records, to keep their patient data bases, to do word processing, and to look into the cardiology offices' data base if information is needed on a patient in the cardiology unit.

All the software is stored on a 137-megabyte hard disk drive and can be called up by any work station (a terminal), giving each user access to a wide variety of data and programs and permitting manipulation of the data in any way desired.

Some of the more popular microcomputer network packages that can be purchased are listed in the following paragraphs.

OMNINET, by Corvus Systems, is compatible with the Corvus concept, Apple II, IBM PC, DEC LSI-11, and TI Professional microcomputers. It allows up to sixty-four work stations to be linked together over a maximum distance of four thousand feet using twisted-pair wiring.

PLAN 4000, by Nestar Systems, Inc., is compatible with the Apple II, Apple III, and IBM PC. This network allows up to sixty-four work stations over a maximum distance of up to 20,000 feet using coaxial baseband cable.

ARCNET, by Datapoint Corporation, is compatible with Datapoint computers. In addition, the Tandy Corporation has announced that Radio Shack Model 16 and Model II computers will soon support ARCNET. It allows up to 255 computers to be linked together over a distance of up to 20,000 feet using coaxial baseband cables.

Information Services

Personal computers, along with networks and data bases, can be used to research vast amounts of information. As of 1983 there were over one thousand informational services scattered throughout the United States and Canada.

The following are just a few of the information services available:

□ AGNET—agricultural information.
□ BAMBAM—Bookline Alert: Missing Books and Manuscripts.
□ BIOETHICSLINE—information on areas of heated ethical debates in biology (for example, euthanasia, abortion, and so on).
□ CANCERPROJ—cancer research information.
□ COFFEELINE—international information on all aspects of coffee.

□ COMMODITY—stockbroking data.
□ ENERGYNET—research on energy organizations and experts.
□ EXCEPTIONAL CHILD EDUCATION RESOURCES—abstracts of articles on the education of handicapped and gifted children.
□ HORSE—thoroughbred pedigree data base.
□ INFORMART—general research.
□ MEDAB—Middle East Database.
□ MEDLINE—medical data base.
□ MONEY MARKETS—treasury reports.
□ SSIE—Smithsonian Science Information Exchange (abstracts of current research projects in the sciences).
□ WESTLAW—legal data base.
□ UTOPIA—antique and rare book information source.

The Xerox Corporation developed ETHERNET in an attempt to create a universal networking standard. It allows up to 1,024 work stations to be linked over a distance of 8,000 feet using a coaxial baseband bus network. Because ETHERNET's architecture and topology are not proprietary, a number of separate distributors sell ETHERNET-compatible products. One such product is ETHERSHARE, by 3Com Corporation. It is compatible with the IBM PC and soon will be compatible with Apples.

A new network just reaching the market is APPLENET, which is compatible with all Apple computers. It uses a bus configuration and allows work stations to be linked over a maximum distance of eight thousand feet.

Some microcomputer networks also can be tied into a mainframe. For example, IBM recently introduced a 3600 system, which replaces the 3400 system and can interact with the IBM PC, therefore allowing a network of PCs within one organization to be directly connected to the 3600 mainframe.

The master controller is the brains of the network. It acts as a traffic manager to route data between the hardware components and to detect and prevent any binary collisions. For example, if one computer on the network is currently using a printer and another one is ready to send data to the same printer, the master controller will hold up the data from the second computer until the first computer is finished with the printer.

Two recent major developments made the use of local-area networking with the microcomputer very popular. The first was a switch from twisted-pair cables to **coaxial baseband wiring,** which is approximately one-third the cost of twisted pair, can transmit information more quickly, and offers the possibility of eventually retrofitting the network with **broadband coaxial wiring.** Broadband coaxial wire can carry a host of data, voice, and broadcast messages simultaneously and is expected to be the wiring of choice in the future.

The second development concerned the method in which a network's topology (geometric structure) is configured. The first networks used a star configuration. The master controller (usually a hard-disk drive) was located in the middle of the equipment, and data was dispersed from the center of the star to its arms. This type of configuration resulted in slow communications, because all instructions and commands had to be cleared and approved by the hard disk drive before they could go any farther.

Most networks now use the bus topology. In a **bus network,** each computer plugs into a single cable that runs from work station to work station and must have its own interface. The interface is typically a card plugged into an expansion slot of the computer that contains both the hardware and the protocol software to allow access to the network. All the hardware in the network issues instructions independently, and the master controller's task is simply to direct the data traffic up and down the length of the wiring (see Figure 12–13).

A major advantage of networking microcomputers, as compared with using stand-alone minicomputers or mainframes, is that each time the network is expanded, the power of the system increases through the addition of more memory, another peripheral, or more storage capacity. However, in a system of stand-alone minicomputers or mainframes, each time a new user is added to the system (that is, each time a new dumb terminal is installed), the overall computing power of the system degrades. Because the demands on the system increase but its power does not, the whole system is slowed down.

Some drawbacks still exist with networking microcomputers, however. They can cover only a limited distance—usually less than a mile—to make up the entire computing circle, and different types of computers cannot easily communicate on the same LAN. Despite these disadvantages, the LAN appears to be one of the major trends in the future of personal computing.

Networks are not limited to just business applications. A number of organizations currently provide services to the personal computer owner. One of these is The Source, a network offered by the Source Telecomputing Corporation, a subsidiary of Reader's Digest. The Source provides instant access to over one thousand information and communications services and can be accessed over local telephone lines.

Another popular network is CompuServe Information Service. Like the Source, CompuServe offers a large number of information and communications services that are easily accessed over local telephone lines.

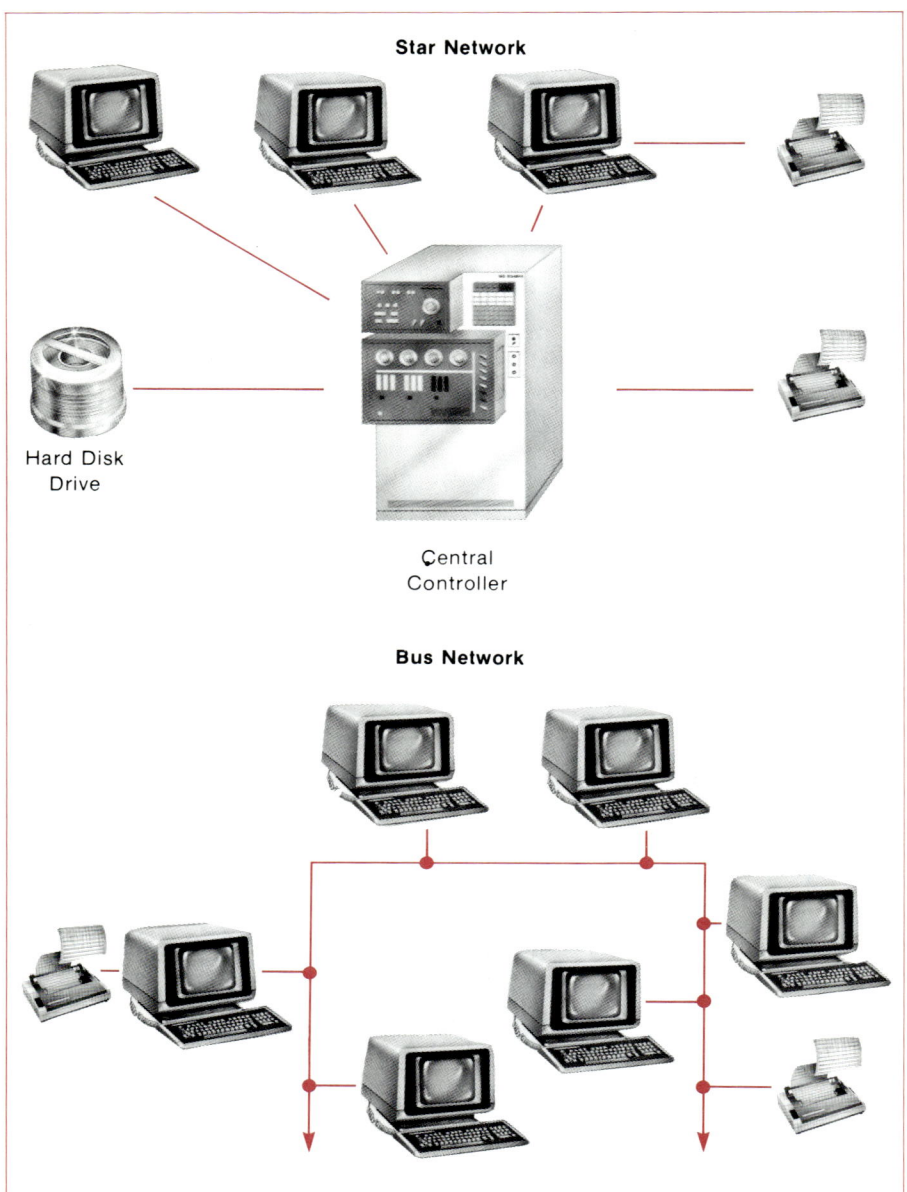

Figure 12–13 Star Versus Bus Networks

SATELLITE SYSTEMS

A **satellite-based network** uses orbiting satellites and earth stations to extend the range of communications channels. An **earth station** includes a dish-shaped receiving device and the necessary processing facility. Satellites were first used for voice and television transmission but currently are being used for business applications as well. Large organizations that are geographically dispersed can use satellites to save time and money in the transfer of voice and data. Satellite communications, while being a cost-effective method for large companies, is not cost effective for small and medium-sized organizations because of the large initial investment in equipment that is required. Existing land-based networks offer smaller firms a much more cost-effective alternative.

For those who can afford it, satellite systems have the advantage of being able to transmit data using a wide bandwidth. As a result, more data can be transmitted at faster rates than with narrow-bandwidth channels like telegraph lines or voice-grade channels such as telephone lines. Also, the capability of data transmission from a multitude of locations adds to the effectiveness of satellite use.

The International Telecommunications Satellite Consortium (INTEL-SAT), an international organization with approximately one hundred member nations on six continents, is a satellite communications system. The U.S. representative to INTELSAT is the Communications Satellite Corporation (COMSAT), which was chartered by Congress in 1962. INTELSAT now has several generations of satellites in use, forming a global communications system that accounts for the majority of all long-distance international communications.

A number of domestic satellite systems also operate in the United States. Satellite Business Systems (SBS) is a joint venture between IBM, Aetna Life and Casualty Insurance Company, and COMSAT; it provides digital transmission services at very high speeds. Others are RCS American System, Western Union's Westar System, American Telephone and Telegraph System, and American Satellite Company.

SUMMARY POINTS

● Data communications is the electronic transmission of data from one location to another.

● The transfer of data using communications facilities such as telephone systems in combination with data-processing equipment is referred to as teleprocessing or telecommunications.

● A communications channel is the physical link or medium that is used to carry data from one location to another.

● Analog transmission is the transmission of data in continuous wave form.

● Digital transmission is the transmission of data as distinct on and off states.

● Modulation is the process of converting data from the digital form in which it is stored to analog (wave) form before transmitting it. Demodulation is the reverse conversion—from analog to digital.

● Modems are devices that accomplish both modulation and demodulation.

● The grade, or bandwidth, of a channel determines the rate at which data can be transmitted. The three grades of channels are narrow-bandwidth channels, voice-grade channels, and broad-band channels.

● The three basic transmission modes are simplex, which allows data to travel in only one direction on the line; half duplex, which allows data to be transmitted in both directions, but in only one direction at a time; and full duplex, which allows data to be transmitted in both directions at the same time.

- Asynchronous transmission is the method of data transmission whereby characters are transmitted at any time convenient to the transmitting or receiving device. Three common asynchronous codes are Baudot, binary coded decimal (BCD), and the American Standard Code for Information Interchange (ASCII).
- Synchronous transmission is the method of data transmission by which whole blocks of characters are transferred in a timed sequence.
- The three major types of communications channels are wire cable, microwave, and fiber optics.
- The two principal types of line configurations are point to point (where each terminal is connected directly to the computer) and multidrop (where several terminals are connected to the same line).
- Polling and contention are two methods of line control used to prevent more than one terminal from using the line at a time.
- Message characters are special characters placed in front of and behind data to mark the beginning and end of the message.
- Handshaking is the exchange of prearranged signals between devices that are transferring data.
- Protocol is the specific set of rules governing handshaking and message characters.
- A multiplexer combines the input from several terminals into a single input stream, allowing data from all these terminals to be transmitted over a single channel. Two basic techniques are used to multiplex data: frequency division multiplexing (FDM) and time division multiplexing (TDM).
- A concentrator polls each terminal in turn to see if it has any messages to send. It allows data from only one terminal at a time to be transmitted over a communications channel.
- Programmable communications processors are devices that relieve the CPU of many tasks. They perform functions such as message switching (receiving and routing messages) and front-end processing (validating transmitted data and preprocessing data).
- The linking of CPUs and terminal devices via a communications system is referred to as a computer network. There are two types of computer networks: local-area networks (LANs), which operate within well-defined and generally self-enclosed areas; and remote (wide-area) networks, which cover geographically dispersed areas.
- All networks comprise two basic structures: nodes, which are the end points of a network and consist of CPUs, printers, and other physical devices; and links, which are the transmission channels that connect the nodes. These nodes and links can be arranged in a number of configurations, including star, ring, hierarchical, and distributed networks.
- Distributed computing refers to the dispersing of data-processing resources to individual locations or administrative units within an organization.

• A satellite-based network uses orbiting satellites and earth stations to extend the range of communications channels. It transmits data using a wide bandwidth, which results in more data being transferred at faster rates. This can be a cost-effective method for large organizations but not for small and medium-sized firms because of the initial cost involved.

REVIEW QUESTIONS

1. Describe analog and digital transmission of data. Which do you see as being the more desirable method? Why?

2. What is a modem, and what is its function in a data communications system?

3. Name and describe the three grades of channels, giving an example of each.

4. Describe the three basic transmission modes.

5. What is the difference between asynchronous and synchronous transmission?

6. Discuss what you see as the advantages and disadvantages of each of the three major types of communications channels: wire cable, microwave, and fiber optics.

7. What are the two principal types of line configurations?

8. What is the purpose of polling and contention, the line control methods? Describe how each works.

9. What are message characters, and why are they important in data transmission?

10. Define handshaking and protocol.

11. Describe the purpose of multiplexers, concentrators, and programmable communications processors.

12. Define a computer network, and distinguish between a local-area and a remote network.

13. Describe the following network architectures: star, ring, hierarchical, and distributed networks.

14. Define the term distributed computing.

15. What advantages and disadvantages do you see with using a satellite-based communications network?

16. Describe a bus network.

DATA DESIGN AND FILE STRUCTURE

LEARNING OBJECTIVES

After reading the chapter, you will be able to do the following:

☐ Understand the difference between physical and logical files.
☐ Name and give examples of three logical data structures.
☐ Describe three methods of linking data elements and records together within a file.
☐ List the two types of logical records that can be used in a data file and their advantages and disadvantages.
☐ Name the two methods of accessing a data file and the circumstances for which each method is best.
☐ Describe the three file structures discussed (sequential, index sequential, and direct access), as well as the method or methods of accessing each structure.
☐ Describe why a data base management system currently is preferred over traditional data file organizations.

Chapter 13

INTRODUCTION

The way in which data elements are organized within a data file (data design) and the manner in which the data file is organized (file structure) are very important issues relating to computer data files. The issues of data design and file structure must be resolved prior to implementation of any computerized data-processing system. *Data design* refers to the way in which independent data elements are grouped or linked into logical records and how these records are combined into data files of related records.

The manner in which data files are structured pertains to the logical organization of the data file. The type of logical record desired and the method used to access the data in the file are the primary determinants of *file structure.* File structures include (1) sequential file organization, (2) index sequential file organization, and (3) direct-access file organization. The concepts of data design and file structure will be discussed in greater detail throughout the chapter.

DATA DESIGN

Physical and Logical Files

Within any information-processing system—whether manual or computerized—there exists a way in which the data is logically organized, as well as a physical means of storing the data. The data can be logically organized according to last name, account number, policy number, and so on, and it can be physically stored in files in a four-drawer filing cabinet. The **physical design** of a file, therefore, relates to the particular medium on or in which the data is stored and is independent of the logical design of the data. In a manual information-processing system the storage media can consist of such items as file folders, filing cabinets, ledgers, index cards, and journals. In a computerized system the storage media may include magnetic tape, magnetic disks, and punched cards.

The **logical design** of files relates to the way in which the independent elements of data are grouped to create a file. The grouping of these elements of data is done in a way that attempts to model relationships as they exist in the real world. For example, the name of a person using city water is grouped with his or her billing address, usage, and rate to create a logical record. The logical record then is grouped with other customer records to obtain a file of city water customers. The grouping of this data concerning city water customers is independent of any particular storage media; at this point the data could be recorded manually on a sheet of paper or stored in a computer. The logical design of a file, therefore, is independent of physical storage considerations. The remainder of the chapter is devoted to the logical design of data and the logical organization of files for use with computers.

Logical Data Structures

Data elements can be related to one another in a computer file in a number of ways. These relationships, referred to as **data structures,** represent the ways in which data elements can be linked logically. The three most common data structures are the **hierarchical, network,** and **relational structures.**

Hierarchical Data Structures The hierarchical, or tree, data structure represents the situation in which one primary data element may have numerous secondary data elements linked to it at a lower level. The primary data element is referred to as a **parent.** A parent may have any number of children related to it; however, each child can have only one parent. Each point on the hierarchical tree is referred to as a **node,** and a node without a downward link is considered a **terminal node.**

A general example of a hierarchical structure is shown in Figure 13–1, and Figure 13–2 is an example showing the relationship between the various data elements of a retail customer's charges by department. These examples show the relationships between various data elements at a number of levels within the hierarchical structure.

Network Data Structures The network, or **plex,** data structure is similar to the hierarchical data structure in that a parent can have any number of children related to it; however, within the network structure a child can be related to more than one parent. Therefore, any data element can be linked to any other data element within the structure.

Within the network data structure, the hierarchy of data elements that exists in the hierarchical structure is lost. The relationships of the

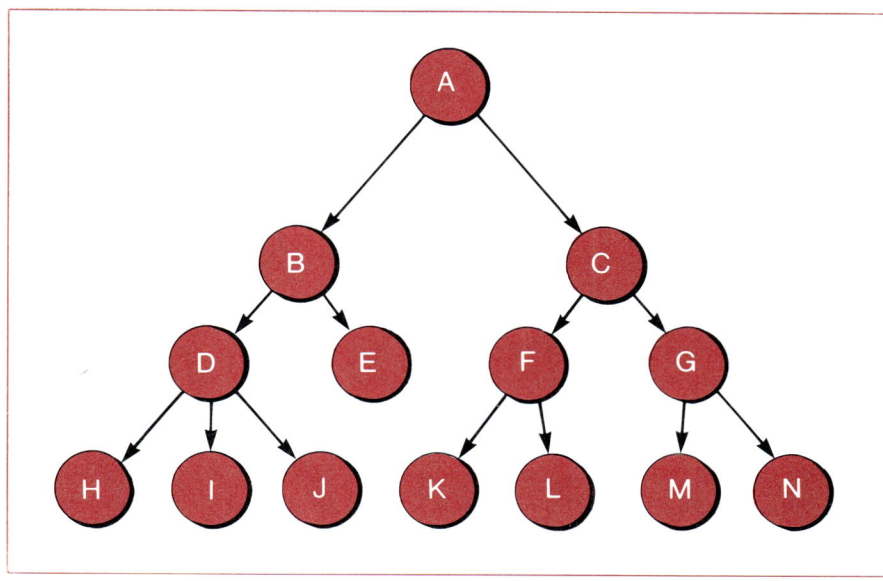

Figure 13–1
Hierarchical Data Structure

Figure 13–2
Hierarchical Data
Structure for Retail
Charges

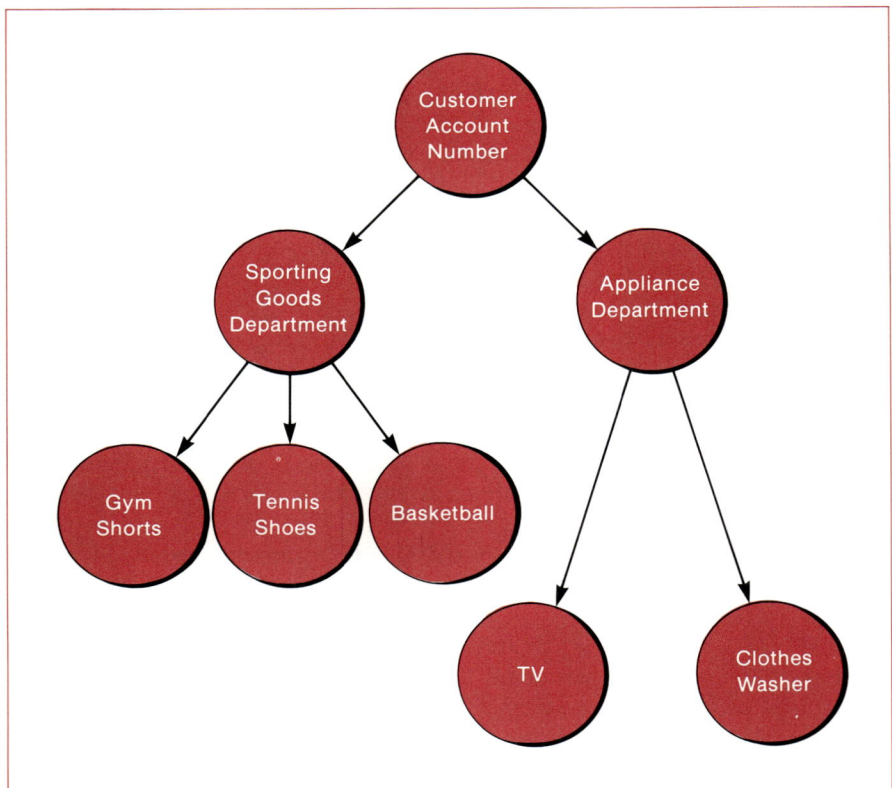

data elements in the network structure do not necessarily have to flow downward. Data elements at a lower level can be related to data elements at a higher level, with the relationship going upward rather than downward. Figure 13–3 is a general example of a network data structure, and Figure 13–4 shows the possible relationship between data elements of a file representing customers and the products they have ordered from a warehouse.

Relational Data Structures A relational data structure relates the data elements by what can be thought of as a two-dimensional table. This structure differs from the hierarchical and network data structures, because the elements of the table can be accessed using a mathematical representation of the table location holding the data element. The data elements are stored in a table having a given number of rows and columns. To access the data, the user simply indicates the row and column numbers where the data element is stored. Table 13–1 represents a relational data structure of customers, their addresses, and their charge account balances. Conceptually, the rows represent records and the columns, fields or data elements. An **entity** is described by a row, which contains values of **attributes** relating to that entity.

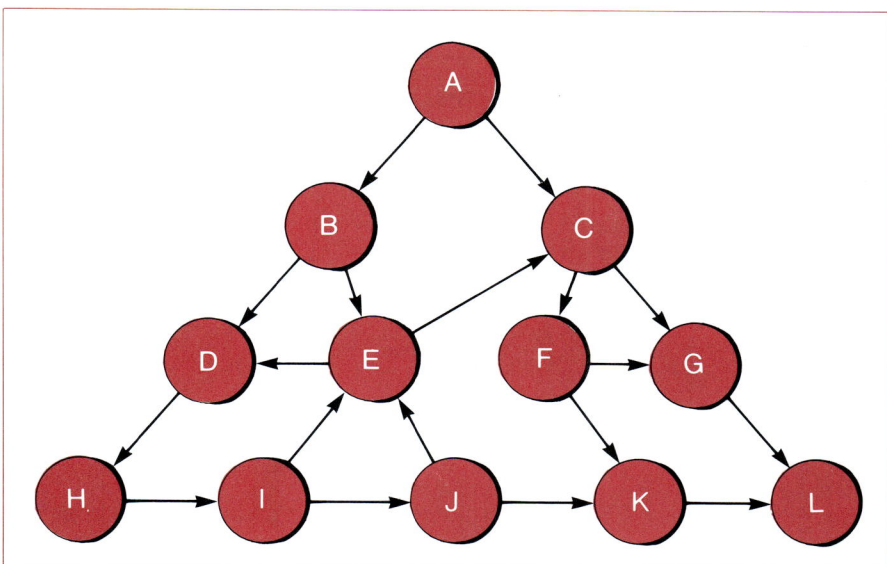

Figure 13–3
Network Data Structure

The relational data structure is commonly used in higher-level computer programming languages that allow the use of tables (COBOL) and the use of arrays (BASIC). An array is a sequence of related data items, all addressed by a common name and differentiated only by a numeric position (index or subscript). In many cases the tables or arrays are filled with the data elements at the beginning of the program so that they can be accessed by mathematical notation later in the program. In Table 13–1, for example, John Jones's account balance may be accessed by the mathematical subscript (2, 5). John Jones's account balance, therefore, is in Row 2, Column 5 of the table.

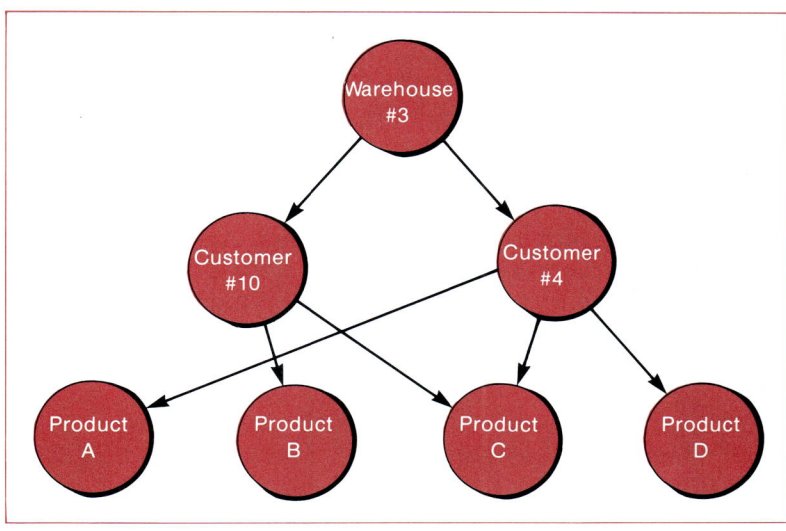

Figure 13–4 Data Network Structure for Customer Orders

TABLE 13–1 RELATIONAL DATA STRUCTURE

	Columns/Fields/Attributes				
	Name	Address	City	Zip Code	Account Balance
Rows/Records/ Entities	Smith, Sam	450 First	Toledo	43420	55.64
	Jones, John	29 Eighth	Dayton	43002	463.39
	Doe, Dan	54 Court	Canton	44709	0
	Mann, Mary	16 Mill	Akron	44805	234.00

Logical Data Organization

Pointers and Chains Some method of linking data records together within a file is required. This linkage may be either physical or logical. For example, we may want to keep the data in physical customer account number sequence; to permit this structure, we would sort our data records—each containing a customer account number field—into ascending order according to this field. The customer account number, in this case, is used as the **key,** or field on which we base the sorting and accessing of this sequential file. In another situation we might wish to keep our file logically in customer account number sequence without the requirement that we physically sort it into that order. In such a case we might add an extra field to each record, which would serve as a **link** or **pointer** to the next record in logical sequence (which might not be positioned in close physical proximity to the current record). This additional field, then, contains no data describing the current record but rather contains the address on the DASD of the next record to be processed in customer number order. A file structured in this fashion is called a **linked list.**

In some cases a link or pointer is used not to show a sort sequence, but merely to associate records with a common value in one field. This use of a link field, called **chaining,** can increase the speed of file searching when a common characteristic or field value is sought. Multiple chains may connect records in a file; a typical customer order record, for example, could have one chain based on the customer account number (logically grouping all orders made by a single customer) and one on the department number from which the order is made (logically grouping all purchases without regard for customer account number). The use of multiple-link fields permits multiple logical structures within a file to have a single physical structure. In other words, a link or chain field must exist for each logical grouping desired for the file. Figure 13–5 shows a file of customer order records containing one link or pointer field relating to customer account number. Three chains are illustrated—one for each of the repeated customer account numbers in the file. An asterisk is used to indicate the end of a chain.

Computer at the Fair

To most people, the county and state fairs that line the autumn countryside with their endless exhibits of crafts, home canning, and prize vegetables, fruits, and livestock are the last symbols of old-fashioned living. However, the computer has now shown itself useful even in these rural affairs. At the Saginaw (Michigan)

Fair, for example, computers help keep the thousands of exhibits straight (in a bookkeeping sense), speed up the registration process, compile lists of entrants and winners, print out judging sheets, and make out exact checks to the winners. So far, though, the computer has not been drafted to spin cotton candy or clean out the stables.

Lists

Simple Lists. Table 13–2 illustrates a file without pointers (a **simple list**); to group records by common characteristic (such as city) or to place them in sequence by record number, sorting would be necessary. Both of these logical relationships, however, can be represented without sorting if appropriate pointer fields are added, as Table 13–3 shows.

Figure 13–5 Pointers and Chains

Record Number	Customer Account Number	Item Number	Quantity	Amount	Pointer
1	15	402	2	5.50	5
2	4	104	1	75.50	4
3	9	26	4	10.00	*
4	4	206	2	65.50	8
5	15	10	1	15.75	6
6	15	606	2	26.30	*
7	10	306	1	115.25	9
8	4	807	10	10.50	10
9	10	15	25	100.65	*
10	4	456	1	15.60	*

- - - - - - - - - Chain for customer account number 4.
· · · · · · · · · · · Chain for customer account number 10.
——————— Chain for customer account number 15.

Table 13–2 SIMPLE LIST

Record Number	Name	Address	City	Zip Code	Account Balance
10	Smith, Ann	27 Eighth	Toledo	43420	45.60
5	Jones, Mary	222 Mill	Dayton	43002	115.80
23	Doe, Fred	114 Court	Akron	44805	465.60
47	Mann, John	345 S. Main	Toledo	43421	15.75
15	Toth, Al	16 Williams	Toledo	43420	89.80
18	Krum, Lori	75 First	Canton	44709	455.00
27	Lewis, Mark	109 Capitol	Columbus	42801	110.80

Linked Lists. Files structured as linked lists are frequently used in applications requiring sequential access but demanding update efficiency over sequential processing efficiency. No re-sorting of the file is necessary when insertions are made; only pointers need to be updated. Pointer modifications also accomplish logical deletion of records no longer needed. If, for example, Record 18 were to be deleted from the file shown in Table 13–3 it could maintain its physical position in the file but be ignored if the record number pointer in Record 15 were changed to 23.

Ring Lists. A slight variation in a linked list converts it to a **ring list.** This variation involves merely replacing the asterisk in the pointer field of the last record with the address of the first record in the list or chain. This arrangement permits access to the beginning of the list from any point within the file. As Table 13–4 shows, rings can be developed from both sequence pointers and chain pointers.

If a file organized in ring list fashion is to be updated, the process of updating its record pointers is more difficult. To make this process

Table 13–3 SIMPLE LIST WITH ONE CHAIN POINTER (FOR CITY) AND ONE SEQUENCE POINTER (FOR RECORD NUMBER)

Record Number	Name	Address	City	Zip Code	Account Balance	City Pointer	Record Number Pointer
10	Smith, Ann	27 Eighth	Toledo	43420	45.60	47	15
5	Jones, Mary	222 Mill	Dayton	43002	115.80		Start 10
23	Doe, Fred	114 Court	Akron	44805	465.60		27
47	Mann, John	345 S. Main	Toledo	43421	15.75	15	*
15	Toth, Al	16 Williams	Toledo	43420	89.80	*	18
18	Krum, Lori	75 First	Canton	44709	455.00		23
27	Lewis, Mark	109 Capitol	Columbus	42801	110.80		47

Computers in Advertising

Computers cannot create effective advertising campaigns—not yet, anyway. However, they can make life easier for those who do. Microdata Corporation has created a software system, AD PAK, which is specifically designed for advertising agencies. The package is made up of eight primary service modules: accounts payable, accounts receivable, payroll, general ledger, production expenses/materials, labor/time keeping, traffic, and mailing list management. This combination, says Microdata's vice-president for marketing and sales, will give management "immediate access to information necessary to control and manage virtually every agency operation."

somewhat easier, the first record of the ring usually contains some additional symbol identifying it as such. A procedure similar to that mentioned in the "Linked Lists" section of the chapter can be used to update data files containing both simple and ring lists.

Inverted Lists. **Inverted lists** differ from simple and ring lists in that an index is created that relates the common characteristic being searched for and the record number. One index is created for each characteristic requested. An index can be created for each of the characteristics within the data file (a fully inverted list) or for only selected characteristics (a partially inverted list).

An example of a partially inverted list is given in Table 13–5. The indexes created are based on requests concerning the characteristics *last name* and *city*. Since indexing takes additional storage space, it is not unusual that more storage is required for the indexes than for the actual data itself. In this case, sufficient space must be allocated in a file for the creation of the desired indexes.

Table 13–4 RING LIST

Record Number	Name	Address	City	Zip Code	Account Balance	City Pointer	Record Number Pointer
10	Smith, Ann	27 Eighth	Toledo	43420	45.60	47	15
5	Jones, Mary	222 Mill	Dayton	43002	115.80		10
23	Doe, Fred	114 Court	Akron	44805	465.60		27
47	Mann, John	345 S. Main	Toledo	43421	15.75	15	5
15	Toth, Al	16 Williams	Toledo	43420	89.80	10	18
18	Krum, Lori	75 First	Canton	44709	455.00		23
27	Lewis, Mark	109 Capitol	Columbus	42801	110.80		47

Table 13-5 PARTIALLY INVERTED LIST

Characteristic	Record Number
Last name:	
Smith	10
Jones	5
Doe	23
Mann	47
Toth	15
Krum	18
Lewis	27
City:	
Toledo	10, 47, 15
Dayton	5
Akron	23
Canton	18
Columbus	27

Inverted lists are very helpful in speeding the search of data for certain characteristics, but they are of little use in the generation of reports using the majority of the characteristics within the data file. Inverted lists, therefore, are of the greatest use when large files are searched for a small amount of data. The process of creating indexes allows the user to access data without reading the entire file.

FILE STRUCTURE

A number of factors must be considered prior to the selection of a file structure. Such factors as the type of logical records to be used in the file, the methods used to access the data in the file, and the desired organization of the file determine the final structure of the file.

Logical Records

Prior to determining the final structure of the data file, the **logical records** that will be contained within the file must be defined. Within the logical record, the **data fields** and their lengths must be defined. The data fields then are combined to form the logical record. **Unique keys** must also be chosen from the data fields of the record so that each record can be uniquely identified.

Fixed-Length Records
After it has been determined which data fields will be contained in the logical record and which data field or fields will be the key or keys, it is necessary to determine whether the records will

Info Centers

Many people are troubled by the question of which microcomputer to buy. Even after they sit down and decide for certain which applications they want to accomplish, the wide range of microcomputers available is confusing and difficult for the new user to sort through. For this reason, a new type of consulting agency is springing up across the country—the info center.

Info centers specialize in helping new users select the microcomputers best suited to their needs, wants, and pocketbooks. Many of the info centers are small offices located within larger corporations. For example, Security Pacific Bank in Los Angeles has had an info center since 1970. (Note that the microcomputer was not even available until the late 1970s; earlier than that, info centers specialized in helping businesses find the right minicomputers and mainframe computers.) Many other major corporations today have info centers, including Atlantic Richfield Oil Company (ARCO), Union Carbide, Lockheed, Northrop, Chase Manhattan, and North American Philips. Some of these info centers within corporations provide information for employees only, whereas others service walk-in customers from all sectors as well.

be of fixed or variable length. **Fixed-length records** are easier to design and work with in a data file; however, depending on the particular application, fixed-length records can create several problems.

The data field containing an individual's name can create a severe problem for some applications. In a fixed-length record format it is necessary to assign a maximum number of characters (bytes) to each of the data fields in the record. It is important, therefore, that each of the fields be given enough character spaces to handle any of the data that may be stored in the field. In the case of the name data field, the number of available characters can become a critical issue. For exmple, for legal purposes it may be mandatory that an individual's full name be printed on any documentation; thus, sufficient characters must be allocated to handle any possible name without truncation. However, when a fixed-length record is stored in the data file, the maximum number of characters specified in the record are stored whether the positions are occupied or not. This situation leads to wasted space within the data file and is the reason variable-length records are becoming more widely used.

Variable-Length Records **Variable-length records** are designed such that a maximum number of characters is still specified for a particular data field; however, before the record is stored on the file, a process known as **data compression** takes place to eliminate unused character positions. Although the maximum allowable characters for a data field will be larger in a variable-length record, the total storage used in a data file with variable-length records is significantly reduced because of data compression.

Table 13–6 demonstrates the use of fixed-length records as opposed to variable-length records. Note the advantage of being able to use fifty characters for the name data field in the variable-length record versus thirty characters in the fixed-length record. Also note the total amount of storage, in characters, used by each type of record.

Although they provide the best use of available storage, variable-length records are not always the most efficient. Also, not all software systems allow for the use of variable-length records; therefore, fixed-length records are the best alternative in many instances (again, depending on the application).

Methods of File Access

The manner in which the data will be retrieved from the file is also an important consideration in trying to determine the best file structure. Depending on the need for data relative to the time available, it can be retrieved either through batch file access methods or on-line file access methods. The type of retrieval desired will be a key factor in determining the structure of the data file.

Batch File Access In **batch file access** methods, all transactions to be processed are accumulated for a given period of time and then processed all at once. The period of time for which the transactions are held may be eight hours, twenty-four hours, or a length determined by some log-

Table 13–6 FIXED-LENGTH VERSUS VARIABLE-LENGTH RECORDS

Account Number	Name	Address	City	State	Zip Code	Balance
4056-6	Leatherman-Smith, Jacquelyn	12 First St.	Ann Arbor	MI	48105	564.39

Data Field	Available Characters		Characters Used		Value Stored	
	Fixed	Variable	Fixed	Variable	Fixed	Variable
Account Number	6	6	6	6	4056-6	4056-6
Name	25	40	25	27	Leatherman-Smith, Jacquel	Leatherman-Smith, Jacquelyn
Address	30	40	30	12	12 First St.	12 First St.
City	15	20	15	9	Ann Arbor	Ann Arbor
State	2	2	2	2	MI	MI
Zip Code	5	5	5	5	48105	48105
Balance	8	8	8	6	564.39	564.39
	91	121	91	67		

ical point in the information-generating process such as the end of work shifts or the closing of accounting records for a month.

These methods imply that there is not a strong need for completely current information at all times. In the case of a delivery route, the orders to be delivered may be processed at the end of the working day prior to the day of delivery. Customer orders, therefore, are accumulated until they can be processed at the end of the day.

On-Line File Access **On-line file access** methods provide the ability to retrieve updated information at any time. Environments that need correct information at any time include inventory control, airline reservations, and banking. The information contained within the data file must be updated at the same time the transaction takes place to insure the accuracy of the information.

The methods by which the data is accessed in the data file are critical to the file structure, because different access methods require different file structures. If a data file is to be accessed using batch access methods, the file may be structured using **sequential file organization.** If an on-line access method is used, an **index sequential file organization** or a **direct-access file organization** must be used.

Logical File Organizations

Sequential File Organization Data files that are organized sequentially generally are used in a system using batch access methods. The files are organized based on a key value chosen for the record, and the data records are sorted in an ascending or descending order, according to the value of the key.

The transactions that have been accumulated for application to the data file must be sorted in the same sequence as the data file itself. The data file can be accessed only in the specific order in which it has been sorted (according to the value of the key). Should a transaction be out of order, the processing of the file would stop. Any additions or deletions made to the file must not disrupt the sequence of the file. A sequential file has a common logical and physical structure, which is represented by magnetic tape as a file storage medium.

Index Sequential File Organization Index sequential files are also dependent on a key within the data records. When an index sequential file is created, an index also is created that contains information relating the key values to the record locations within the data file. An index sequential file can be accessed either sequentially or through direct-access methods.

In an environment where it is desirable to process transactions using batch-processing methods and retrieve information using direct-access methods, index sequential data files can serve a dual purpose. Index sequential files, therefore, have a built-in flexibility that is not available with either sequential or direct-access file organization. Index sequential files must, of course, use DASDs.

Direct-Access File Organization Direct-access file organizations utilize the data record key differently than do the sequential or index sequential file organizations. The data record key provides the only means of accessing data within a direct-access file organization. The data records are stored in the data file in no apparent order; for the user to access a given data record, the desired key value must be equal to the record key value being sought.

The data record that is being sought is retrieved according to the key value, thereby preventing the reading of any records prior to or after the desired record. Usually, a mathematical process called **randomizing** or **hashing** is applied to the record key, yielding a storage address. At file creation time, this address determines where the record is recorded; at

Table 13—7 THE THREE PRIMARY FILE ORGANIZATION METHODS

Sequential File
(sorted by Employee Number)

Record Position	Employee Number	Last Name	Initials		Salary
1	032	Martin	A	C	425
2	067	Stein	B	F	380
3	130	Chavez	P	E	500
4	174	Powers	R		450
5	258	Emerson	L	C	295
6	290	Jones	C	T	360
7	305	Fields	S		420
8	367	Parker	P	D	380
9	422	Goldman	I	N	440
10	488	Weiss	T	L	610
11	529	Roberts	N	P	520
12	592	Gomez	J	F	375
13	641	Chang	S	L	400
14	679	Breck	H	M	420
15	723	Thomas	R	P	235
16	763	Harper	T		380
17	807	Smith	L	L	450
18	854	Ellis	V	M	425
19	892	Roth	A	P	425
20	936	Jones	R	O	440

Index Sequential File

(Records will be in same positions as in sequential file; indexes are shown for a DASD with a capacity of five records per track.)

Track Number	Highest Key
1	258
2	488
3	723
4	936

Table 13–7 (cont.)

Direct-Access File

(Records will be allocated among 23 possible record locations; the three extra positions are provided to reduce the likelihood that multiple records will hash to the same address or position. A record's location will be determined by dividing the Employee Number field by 23, adding 1 to the *remainder* from the division, and using the result as the location in which to place the record. If the location already contains a record, the next empty location will be used. Retrieval is accomplished by repeating the division-remainder hashing process. File contents are shown as they would be developed from the sequential file above.)

Record Position		Employee Number	Last Name	Initials		Salary
1		529	Roberts	N	P	520
2	(empty)					
3		807	Smith	L	L	450
4		854	Ellis	V	M	425
5		763	Harper	T		380
6		258	Emerson	L	C	295
7		305	Fields	S		420
8*		488	Weiss	T	L	610
9		422	Goldman	I	N	440
10		032	Martin	A	C	425
11		723	Thomas	R	P	235
12	(empty)					
13		679	Breck	H	M	420
14		174	Powers	R		450
15		290	Jones	C	T	360
16		130	Chavez	P	E	500
17		936	Jones	R	O	440
18		592	Gomez	J	F	375
19		892	Roth	A	P	425
20	(empty)					
21		641	Chang	S	L	400
22		067	Stein	B	F	380
23		367	Parker	P	D	380

---

*The hashed address for Employee Number 488 was 6, but position 6 had been previously filled by Employee Number 258. The next position, 7, had also previously been filled (by Employee Number 305); therefore position 8 was used to store Employee Number 488. Such a situation is described as a *synonym, collision,* or *hash clash.*

retrieval time, it determines where it is sought. (See Appendix B for a discussion of randomizing techniques.)

This method of accessing data is much more efficient than searching a data file or indexes until the appropriate record is found. Direct-access file organization is very useful where timeliness and accuracy of data are critical. The booking of seats on commercial airline flights is one application where the use of direct-access file organization is common.

Data Publishing

If the current market is any indication, the great money-makers in the future computer market may come in paperback rather than on floppies. And major publishers are betting their bankbooks on those paperbacks.

The scale of money to be earned in the field is phenomenal. In 1983 alone, big-name publishers advanced millions of dollars to would-be computer book authors. Simon & Schuster advanced $600,000 to the staff of **PC World** (a magazine for IBM Personal Computer owners) for a ten-volume series of computer books.

Harper & Row advanced the same amount to the editors of **InfoWorld** (a weekly computer magazine) for a six-volume series of reviews on computer hardware and software.

Even so, the truly amazing price would have to be that given to Stewart Brand. Based on a twelve-page outline of a book projected at only two hundred pages, Doubleday advanced Brand $1.3 million dollars. His book, **The Whole Earth Software Catalog,** will be a collection of software recommendations gathered with the help of small information network users.

Up-to-the-minute availability of accurate information about available flights and seats is critical to the operation of this business.

A definition of the application, the application's needs, and the timeliness of accurate data are critical factors in determining the method used in accessing the necessary data and, finally, in determining the structure or organization of the data file. Sequential files are useful in applications which involve high **activity** (frequent use of a large percentage of the records in the file). Direct-access organization is preferred for files with low activity. Index-sequential organization provides the capabilities of both other structures at an added overhead cost. Table 13–7 shows a sample file of twenty records organized in each of these ways. One additional file structure, **partitioned organization,** merits mention. This structure is used to divide a large file into subfiles, each of which can be identified by a name. Multiple programs stored on the same microcomputer diskette constitute a partitioned file.

Data Base Management Systems (DBMSs)

The explanations of the previous logical file organizations stated that the type of application in which the data file is to be used is a key factor in determining the appropriate file organization. History has shown a functional division of applications within the field of data processing. Until recently, data processing was characterized by functionally oriented data file designs. For example, the accounting department would maintain a data file containing customer information necessary to the functions performed by accounting. The order-processing area of a company would maintain a data file containing customer information necessary to the functions performed in order processing. This approach was extended to all functional areas of the organization.

This practice causes a duplication of much information common to all functional areas of the company. Such data elements as customer name, account number, and address may be duplicated in the data files within each of the various functional areas. If the customer's address needs to be changed, it has to be corrected in a number of separate data files.

Recently, however, an attempt has been made to overcome the idea of functionalizing the data files of an organization. The concept, referred to as a **data base management system (DBMS),** creates a centrally maintained and controlled data base, or file, that may be accessed by the different functional areas of an organization. The goals of a DBMS are to minimize data redundancy, provide the ability to update a data element in only one location, and solve the problem of trying to acquire data from multiple related but separate data files for consolidation into one report.

With DBMSs have come a number of problems concerning such things as who owns the data, who may have access to the data, and who may alter the data within the data base. In an attempt to resolve these problems, many organizations have created a position in their organizational structure referred to as the **data base administrator.** This individual oversees the operation and use of the company's data base and resolves the conflicting needs of users.

The current move, therefore, is away from the functional data files of the past to DBMSs. If managed properly, the data base concept should allow a much more efficient use of both computer and human resources.

- The logical design of a file consists of the manner in which the data elements of a file are grouped together.
- The physical design of a file relates to the particular medium on which the data is stored.
- Data elements can be logically linked together in a data file using hierarchical, network, or relational data structures.
- Data can be organized to help speed inquiries by using pointers, chains, and lists.
- The factors to be considered when designing a data file are (1) the type of logical records to be used in the file, (2) the methods used to access the data in the file, and (3) the desired organization of the file.
- Batch file access methods require the accumulation of transactions for processing at one time.
- On-line file access methods provide the ability to retrieve data and update data at any time.
- Batch access methods are generally used in conjunction with sequential organizations.
- Direct-access file organizations are generally accessed using on-line access methods.

● Index sequential files can be accessed using either batch or on-line file access methods.
● Data base management systems (DBMSs) have been designed to overcome redundancy of data and provide simple methods of updating data used by more than one functional area of an organization.

1. What is the difference between logical and physical files?
2. How does a hierarchical data structure differ from a relational data structure?
3. What is chaining?
4. What is the advantage of chaining?
5. How does a ring list differ from a simple list?
6. What two disadvantages of fixed-length records are discussed in the chapter?
7. Are variable-length records always preferred to fixed-length records? Why or why not?
8. What are the two most common methods of accessing a data file?
9. What three logical file organizations are discussed in the chapter?
10. What is the advantage of index sequential files versus direct-access files?
11. Using an organization with which you are familiar, describe how a DBMS could assist in that organization's information processing.

SYSTEMS ANALYSIS AND DESIGN

LEARNING OBJECTIVES

After studying this chapter, you will be able to do the following:

☐ Understand the role and function of a systems analyst.
☐ List the steps of the systems life cycle.
☐ Explain how and why a systems analysis and design project is initiated. Explain the purpose of a feasibility study.
☐ List and describe the sources used to gather data and the tools used for data analysis.
☐ Understand why it is important for the analyst to design several alternatives, and discuss the tools that help the analyst design these alternatives.
☐ List and describe the implementation specifications required during the detailed system design step.
☐ List and discuss the factors considered during the implementation step.
☐ Understand the reasons for the maintenance step and why it is an ongoing process.

Chapter 14

INTRODUCTION   Chapter 3 presented you with a very brief introduction to systems analysis and design, and it outlined the steps in the systems life cycle. We now will expand on each one of these steps. Before beginning our discussion of systems analysis and design, it is appropriate to describe the person who actually accomplishes the analysis and design: the systems analyst.

SYSTEMS ANALYST

When a systems-related problem arises that requires intervention from outside the functional user area, a **systems analyst** is called upon to find a solution. The systems analyst is the key person around whom steps of the **systems life cycle** revolve. The analyst must be able to perform a number of functions, including the following:

- Working with the user to help determine information needs.
- Collecting and analyzing data about the existing system to determine the effectiveness of current processing methods and procedures.
- Planning and designing new systems, recommending changes to existing systems, and participating in the implementation of suggested changes.

The success of any analysis and design project depends heavily on the abilities of the analyst. In general, the analyst must possess good communications skills (both oral and written), a sharp analytical mind, a high level of creativity, and the ability to work with and coordinate activities between many levels of interested parties. The ability to communicate clearly, persuasively, and concurrently with a user group, the technical professions, and management is one of the analyst's most important characteristics. Because the analyst typically has much more latitude in methodology than does the programmer, this individual needs breadth in capabilities more than he or she needs the programmer's technical depth. A good systems analyst has many possible approaches from which to pick, and the resulting systems vary dramatically in form.

The analyst should know the firm that needs the problem solution, its goals and objectives, and the products and services it provides. This person also should be familiar with the organizational structure of the company in order to proceed through the proper channels of authority within the organization. Even though "going through channels" at times may seem like the long way around, it will prove to be the better approach. It gains respect and confidence from management and probably will elicit better cooperation from subordinates, who know that their supervisor has given permission for them to meet with you.

The systems analyst should also be well acquainted with data-processing methods, current hardware, and the programming languages that will be used. In the past, most systems analysts have come up from the ranks of programmers. In many firms the programmer and the analyst are the same person, usually carrying a job title of programmer/analyst.

Recently, however, this tradition of programmers becoming analysts has begun to change with the realization that the qualities that make a good programmer do not necessarily produce a good analyst and vice versa. Whereas systems analysts today may not be expected to begin their careers as programmers, it is still important that they be familiar with programming. A major portion of the analyst's job entails writing system specifications that the programmer must transform into computer code. The analyst's knowledge of programming will help in creating system specifications that will be easy for the programmer to understand and work from.

SYSTEMS ANALYSIS AND DESIGN

Our approach to systems analysis and design is based on the systems life cycle. As Chapter 3 explained, the steps of the systems life cycle are as follows: (1) problem definition, (2) feasibility study, (3) systems analysis, (4) general system design, (5) detailed system design, (6) implementation, and (7) maintenance. In a structured environment, each step of the cycle must be completed and approved by management, the user, or both before the next step is undertaken. The first step we will look at is problem definition.

PROBLEM DEFINITION

There are basically four reasons for initiating a systems analysis and design project: in response to (1) a problem in the system, such as tardy or erroneous reports; (2) new requirements, such as new governmental regulations; (3) changes in technology, such as the introduction of a new process that becomes essential to remain competitive; or (4) the need for broad system improvements because of a change in business activity, such as the introduction of a major new product.

For the **problem definition** stage to begin, someone—either the user, management, or perhaps even the analyst—must recognize a problem. Once the problem has been recognized, the user, management, and analyst sit down together and reach an agreement on the nature of the problem and whether it is severe enough to warrant further investigation.

Once an agreement has been reached, the analyst prepares a written statement outlining the nature and scope of the problem and the objectives of the analysis and design process. This statement is then reviewed—ideally by both management and the user group. It is important that the analyst communicate the interpretation in writing, because people generally respond more to something they see in print. A written document allows the reader to review thoroughly and question points that might be misunderstood or overlooked in an oral presentation. This allows both the user and management to insure that the analyst's understanding of the problem is the same as theirs.

At this stage the analyst is asked to give management a rough estimate of the costs of the project, as well as an accurate assessment of both the cost and the time schedule for the next step in the systems life cycle—the feasibility study. The estimation process is probably the analyst's most demanding task. Once the basic scope and objectives have been formally agreed upon, the analyst proceeds to the feasibility study.

FEASIBILITY STUDY

During the **feasibility study,** the analyst attempts to discover if there is a feasible solution to the problem and, in fact, if the problem is even worth pursuing at all. It is a miniature study of the entire analysis and design process.

Initially, the analyst tightens up the system scope and objectives that were formulated during the problem definition phase. The analyst again presents these to the user to insure that the parties involved have not drifted apart in their understanding of the nature and scope of the problem. Once this has been done, the analyst can estimate the costs of the system more accurately, allowing for a more accurate cost/benefit analysis to be performed.

A cost/benefit analysis is an integral part of this and most of the following steps. A systems analysis and design project is an investment for the firm and, as with any other investment, management expects to realize either a reduction in costs or an increase in benefits. The bottom line in most organizations is profit; if the systems analysis and design project is not going to improve that figure, management will invest its funds elsewhere. There are exceptions to this, however, such as government regulations that require the development and implementation of systems that may not be profitable.

The feasibility study, in summary, must address several types of feasibility. These generally are defined as follows:

1. **Technical feasibility.** Can current technology meet the requirements of the proposed system?
2. **Economic feasibility.** Are the organizations's financial resources sufficient to support the development and operation of the proposed system?
3. **Operational feasibility.** (This might better be called **social** or **political feasibility.**) Do the realities and constraints under which the organization functions permit the introduction of the system?
4. **Time-related feasibility.** Can the system be developed within the schedule required or dictated by management?
5. **Legal/ethical feasibility.** Does the proposed system violate any statutes or codes of professional practice?

COMPUTERS IN THE WORKPLACE

Office automation is expected to grow significantly in the next decade. Technology has replaced the traditional manual methods of office routines with word processing, electronic mail, teleconferencing, and electronic information retrieval and filing. Computers in the workplace are not limited to the secretarial staff; many professionals and managers are experiencing the benefits of automated process.

1. Reporters use word processing equipment to write and edit stories.
2. Computers are used in the newspaper business for a variety of functions. Here, a permissions editor inventories and records information on photographs that will be reprinted in the publication.

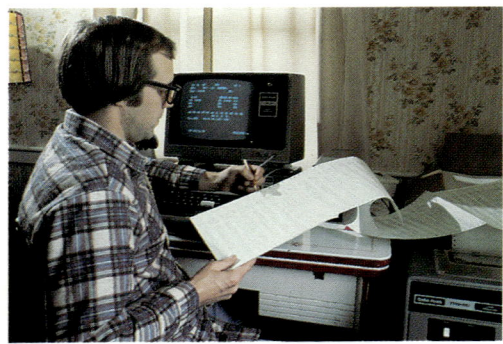

3

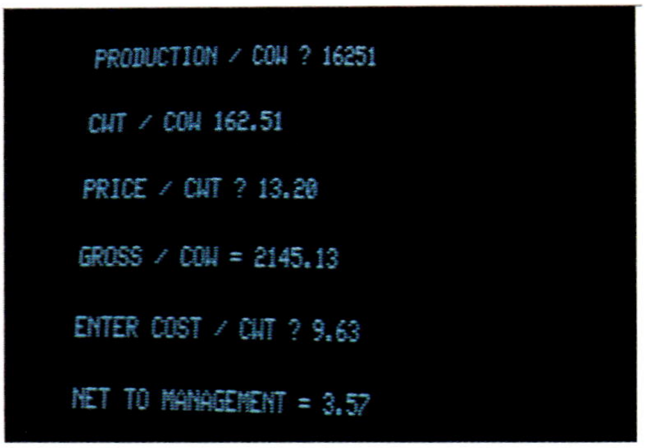
PRODUCTION / COW ? 16251
CWT / COW 162.51
PRICE / CWT ? 13.20
GROSS / COW = 2145.13
ENTER COST / CWT ? 9.63
NET TO MANAGEMENT = 3.57

4

5

6

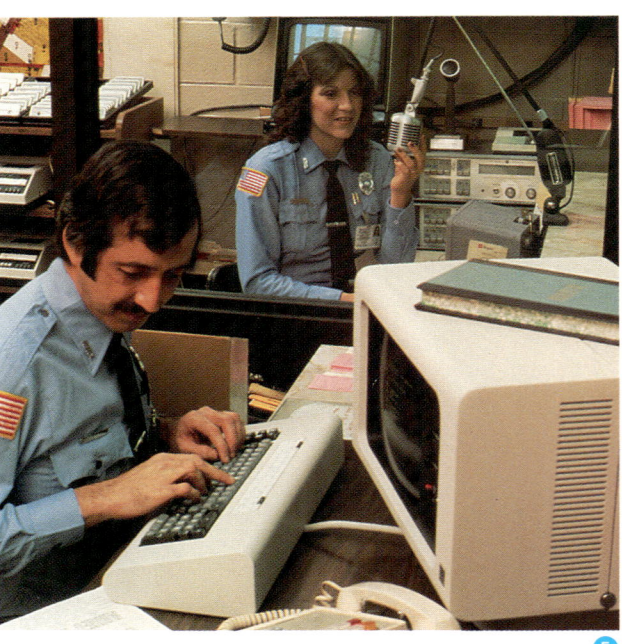

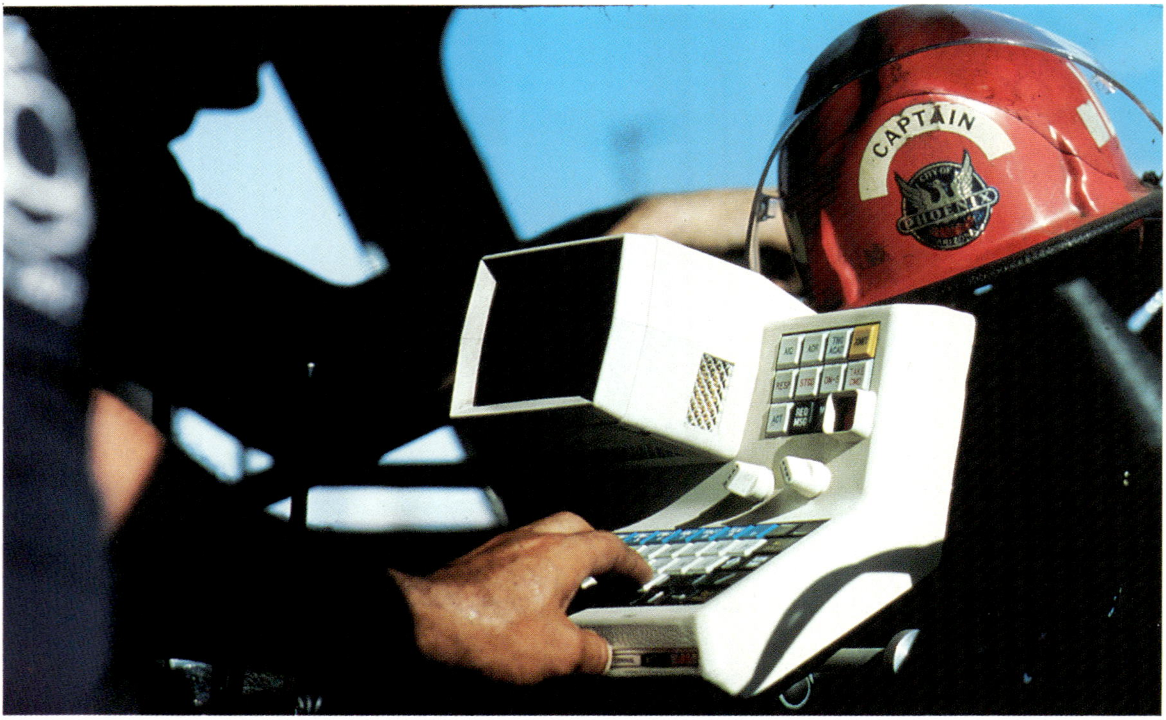
CAPTAIN
PHOENIX

Computers in the Workplace—continued.
3 and 4. This farmer examines a printout giving information on his dairy operation. **5.** Police officers use computers to keep track of arrest records, car and gun registrations, and fingerprint files. These automated processes enable instant access for urgent situations. **6.** Graphic computer terminals installed in fire trucks improve fire departments' ability to respond to emergencies. **7.** With electronic mail capabilities, the traditional methods of hand-delivering memorandums and physically mailing correspondence may be accomplished electronically via telephone lines. **8.** Office workers can produce typeset output that is more readable and memorable than word processor output. Compugraphic computerized phototypesetting equipment is used by publishers, printers, and advertising agencies as well as by businesses.

7

8

9

Computers in the Workplace—continued. **9.** Bell Labs' Picturephone® meeting service, using a digital network combining satellite and land-based facilities, provides a two-way, full-color video, voice and data transmission between specially-equipped meeting rooms. **10.** The office automation effort of Thelen, Marrin, Johnson and Bridges, a major San Francisco law firm, uses Informatics software on Wang mini computers. **11.** Portable computers, such as this one by Hewlett Packard enable professionals to process information away from the office.

10

11

12. Bell Labs' service representatives use computers to access customer billing records and generate customer service orders.
13. Genesco uses computer technology to improve customer service. At an online order entry station, the operator can immediately notify the wholesale customer of stock availability, or she may enter the order to fill the request. **14.** A public relations manager and his secretary learning how to use a newly-installed Wang word processor at The Gillette Company.

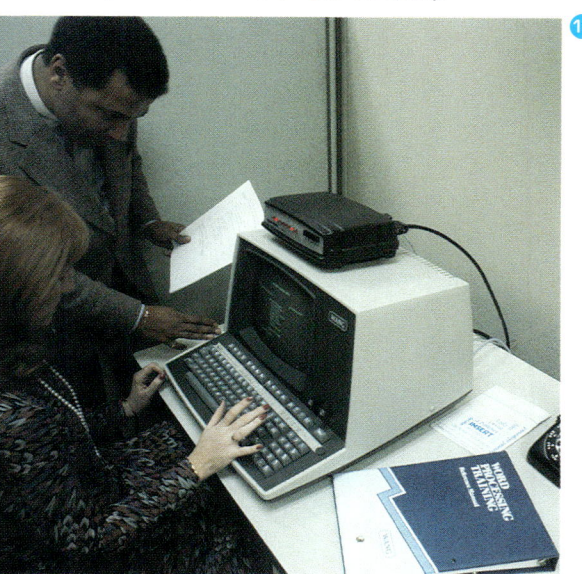

Computers in the Workplace—continued. **15.** The workplace is already experiencing the effects of office automation from the physical environment to the changes in individual job roles. **16.** Here, an office worker accesses one of the databases available from The Source. **17.** With Nestar's PLAN 4000™ (Personal Local Area Network) each user has the power of his or her workstation, plus the availability of network mass storage, communication facilities, and printers. **18.** Right from the planning and development stage, Nixdorf Computer designers work in close association with industrial physicians and ergonomicists. A few examples of Nixdorf ergonomic design are: 1) swivel swan neck to accommodate various height requirements and ease physical strain and 2) flat, detachable keyboards to suit individual needs. **19.** Radio Shack TRS-80 Personal Desktop computer serves as a versatile, multi-purpose workstation in the office.
20. Eastman Kodak Company's new Kodak KAR-4000 information system is designed for job streams where users typically process between 1,000 and 7,000 documents per day.

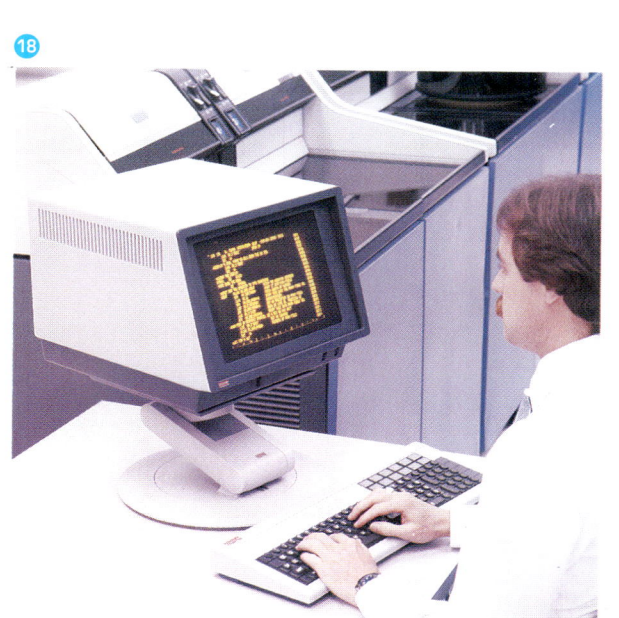

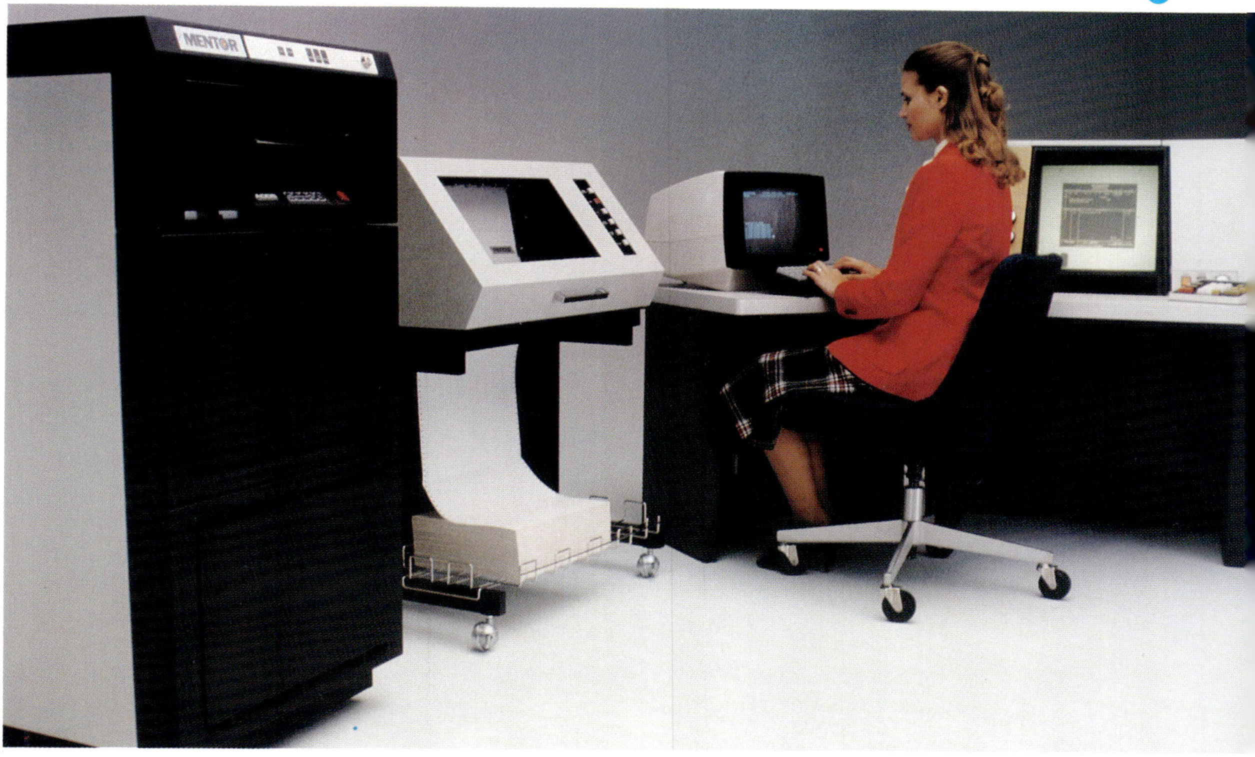

Computers in the Workplace—continued. **21.** This office information system combines word and data processing along with a company-wide communications network. **22.** This office computer system, Wang Alliance 250, integrates data, word, audio, and image processing. The proliferation of office information systems such as these, and the impact they're making in the business world, opens a wide-range of career possibilities for people with business and data processing skills.

Computers Go to the Dogs

Actually, computers go to the dog owners. Dog food purchasers are receiving a total of 1,100 Commodore personal computers. The computers are being given away as part of the Lucky Dog Supergame sponsored by the makers of Alpo dog food, the Allen Products Company. The game can be played using game cards available in specially marked packages of Alpo dog food.

Why computers and dog food? Suprisingly enough, Alpo's senior product manager, Tyrone Allen, explains that research has shown that the percentage of video game players among dog owners is 38 percent higher than among the general population. In addition, Allen says, "They're [personal computers are] the hottest thing going as far as consumer marketing is concerned."

The results of the feasibility study are communicated to both management and the user in a formal presentation. At this point the project is subject to one of four management decisions: (1) terminate the study; (2) postpone the study until a later date; (3) fix the problem immediately if the solution is simple; or (4) approve the immediate continuation into the next step, systems analysis.

SYSTEMS ANALYSIS

Upon approval of the feasibility study, the analyst is ready to begin the **systems analysis.** This step involves two principal tasks: **data gathering** and **data analysis.**

Data Gathering

The first thing the analyst needs to do is gather data—now in much greater quantity and detail than during previous phases of the study. The types and amount of data gathered are based on the system scope and objectives, which were precisely defined in the feasibility study. The analyst has two general sources of data available: internal and external.

Internal Sources Internal sources are sources available within the organization. There are four principal sources of internal information: written documents, questionnaires, interviews, and observations. The analyst may use all or any combination of these, depending on the circumstances.

Written Documents. Written documents include system flowcharts, procedure manuals, formal reports, or any other written documentation concerning the system. The analyst should be thoroughly familiar with all relevant documentation concerning the existing system; this will give the analyst credibility and avoid wasting a client's valuable time with questions answered in existing documents.

Questionnaires. Questionnaires have the potential for being a very useful tool, provided the analyst understands the possible drawbacks. They can be used to economically cover a large group, and they allow anonymity of respondents, thereby encouraging truthfulness. There are, however, some potential problems. Some questionnaires may never be returned; some people may not want to take the time, others just may not want to commit anything to writing, and those who do reply may tend to submit biased answers. Furthermore, the questions should be designed so that the answers will be short, even to the point where the respondent merely has to check a box. Questions that require long answers are best left to the interview process. The analyst should do a little research on proper techniques before attempting to construct a questionnaire.

Interviews. Personal interviews can be a very valuable source of data. Even the most skilled analyst will find some questions or ambiguities remaining after a survey of existing documentation, procedures, and so on. To answer these questions and fill in the gaps, the analyst must approach people who are directly involved in the system and conduct interviews. The following paragraphs outline the interview approach an analyst should take.

The analyst should properly prepare for each interview. Being prepared will avoid wasting the interviewees' time and will help build good rapport. The analyst should begin by formulating a clear idea of what he or she intends to gain from the interview, then select the individual or group who can best answer the questions.

A list of questions should be developed as a guide. However, the analyst may find that the questioning will lead to a fertile area of information that was not anticipated. If this happens, the analyst should pursue the information. The list of questions is meant only to be a guide. Once the interviewee is no longer saying anything of value, the analyst can refer to the list of questions to get the interview back on track.

When scheduling interviews, the analyst should keep in mind that he or she is asking people to give up valuable time and should offer to schedule the session at the interviewees' convenience. Consideration of this type generally will bring more respect and cooperation.

After the interview, the analyst should summarize all notes and key ideas and arrange for the interviewees to review what has been written. This provides a good opportunity to resolve any misunderstandings and builds goodwill with the interviewees. Minor problems might be cleared up by telephone; otherwise, a follow-up interview might be needed.

Observations. An analyst can go into the organization and observe first-hand how the various functions are performed. This can be a valuable

Olympian Microcomputer

Very few people realize that one of the major coaches for the 1984 Olympic Game Ski Team was a microcomputer. Actually, the microcomputer, an Apple II, was more adept at graphics than pep talks. Used in the U.S. Olympic Committee's biomechanical laboratory in the Sports Medicine Division located in Colorado Springs, the microcomputer coach proved to be quite valuable.

The microcomputer coach was programmed to watch athletes during their performances, analyze the digitized results of those performances, and use the results to instruct the athletes on how to improve their performance in the future. The microcomputer coach was especially well suited to detect subtle changes in posture or movement that were difficult to pinpoint with the human eye. Of course, the digitized versions of the athletes' performances also were stored for later analysis and instruction.

method of identifying informal systems that exist within the organization.

The analyst operates as an agent of change, and change generally invokes fear and distrust in many people. Behavior and work patterns may change markedly by the presence of the analyst. Normally, the analyst will return many times until he or she has become a familiar sight and stops drawing much attention.

External Sources Potential external sources of data include periodicals, books, brochures, product specifications from manufacturers, interviews (conversations) with customers and suppliers, and contacts with companies that have developed similar information systems. External sources can be especially valuable if any potential outputs of the proposed system directly affect these customers, suppliers, or both.

Data Analysis

After collecting all needed data, the analyst must analyze it. The analyst must organize and integrate this data to gain a proper perspective of what is currently being done in the existing system. The major question in this portion of the analysis is, Why are things being done as they are? The analyst needs to investigate whether there are better ways of accomplishing what is being done or if, in fact, the system is needed at all.

The analyst uses a variety of tools to analyze the data. These include (1) data flow diagrams, (2) data dictionaries, (3) grid charts, and (4) decision logic tables. These important techniques are explained here, but by no means are they the only tools available to the analyst.

Data Flow Diagrams A **data flow diagram** is a graphic representation of a logical model of a system. It is independent of hardware, software, data structure, or file organizations. As such, a data flow diagram serves as an excellent communication tool that can be understood by both technical and nontechnical users.

The data flow diagram uses four basic symbols (see Figure 14–1). A square is used to define a source or destination of data. A process that transforms data is represented by a rectangle with rounded corners. An open-ended rectangle is a data store (data that is at rest), and an arrow signifies a data flow (data in motion).

Data flow diagrams are used to describe what happens rather than how it happens. Thus, there are usually a number of simplifying assumptions made. Figure 14–2 illustrates the use of a data flow diagram to give a high-level view of the information flow involved in a pari-mutuel betting system (a type of betting system used by most horse-racing tracks).

Data Dictionaries Words can have different meanings to different people. A **data element** is a field or unit of data that cannot be further broken down, for example, employee number, employee last name, and hourly pay rate. Within an organization a given data element may be defined quite differently from one group or individual to the next. To avoid possible misunderstandings or interface problems, a data dictionary should be developed. A **data dictionary** provides information on the definition, structure, and use of each data element an organization uses.

Grid Charts A **grid chart** (sometimes called a **tabular chart**) summarizes the relationships among the various components of a system. Table 14–1 illustrates a general example of a grid chart indicating which department uses which document.

An I/O chart is a particular type of grid chart that specifies the rela-

Figure 14–1 Data Flow Diagram Symbols

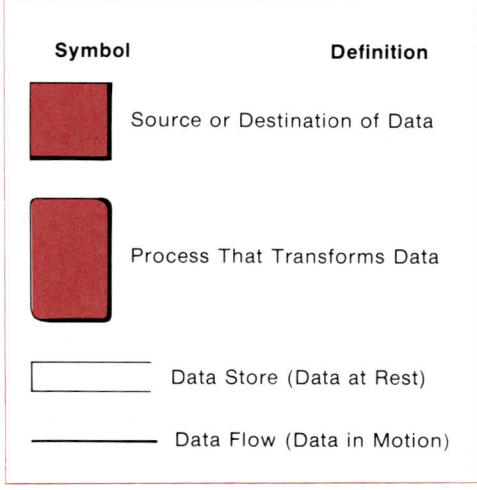

Symbol	Definition
	Source or Destination of Data
	Process That Transforms Data
	Data Store (Data at Rest)
	Data Flow (Data in Motion)

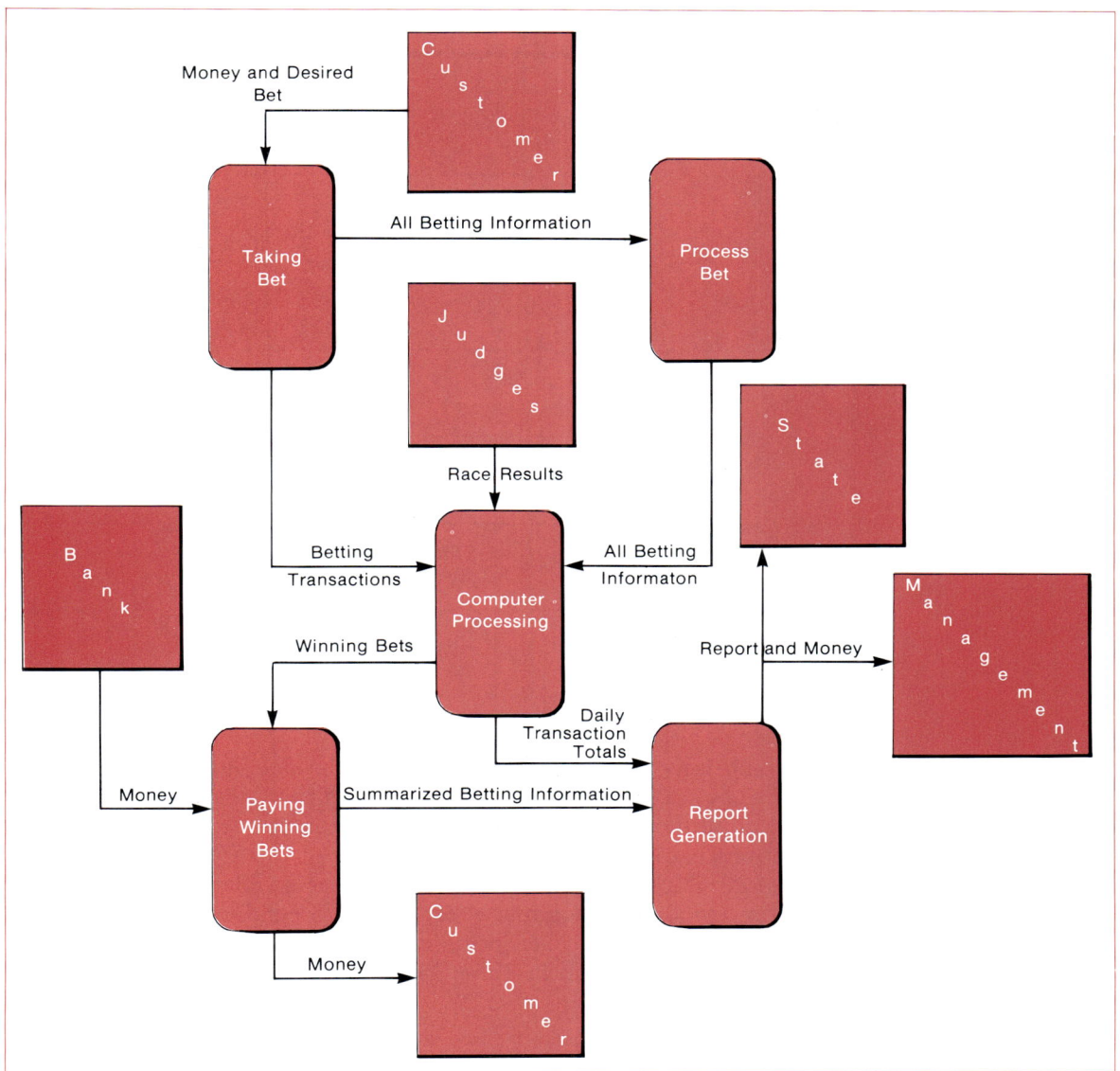

Figure 14–2 Data Flow Diagram: Pari-Mutuel Betting System

tionships between system inputs and outputs. It is used to identify sub-systems—those parts of the system that may be relatively independent.

Decision Logic Tables A **decison logic table** (or **decision table**) is used to identify the actions to be taken for a given set of circumstances. It is an aid in the decision-making process. The logic of the table is based on the following principle: If this condition is met, then take this action. A general example of a decision logic table is shown in Table 14–2. The upper left portion of the table describes the possible conditions, and the lower left portion indicates the possible actions to be taken. The appli-

Table 14–1 GRID CHART

Document \ Department	A	B	C	D	E
1		X	X		X
2	X	X			
3		X	X		
4			X	X	
5	X			X	X
6				X	X

cable conditions are marked in the upper right side of the table, and the actions to be taken are indicated by marks in the lower right portion. A vertical column containing an instance of conditions and their associated actions is called a **rule.**

Decision tables are used to clarify the decision logic involved in determining appropriate actions where multiple conditions exist. A simplified decision table for accepting or rejecting a systems analysis and decision project is shown in Table 14–3.

Table 14–2 DECISION LOGIC TABLE

Heading	Rule Numbers				
	1	2	3	4	5
Possible Conditions			Applicable conditions		
Possible Actions			Actions to be taken		

Table 14–3 DECISION LOGIC TABLE FOR SYSTEM SELECTION

Proposed System		Rules			
		1	2	3	4
Conditions	Required by law	Y	N	N	N
	Reduced costs		N	Y	N
	Increased benefits		N	N	Y
Actions	Accept	X		X	X
	Reject		X		

The analyst first determines the conditions that must be considered. In the example in Table 14–3 these conditions are as follows:

- Is the system required by law?
- Will the system reduce costs?
- Will the system increase benefits?

Following this, the actions that can take place must be considered:

- Accept the project.
- Reject the project.

In Table 14–3, **Y** means yes, **N** means no, and **X** indicates an action to be taken. The example would be read as follows:

- **Rule 1.** If the system is required by law, then accept the system.
- **Rule 2.** If the system is not required by law, does not reduce costs, and does not increase benefits, then reject the system.
- **Rule 3.** If the system is not required by law, does reduce costs, but does not increase benefits, then accept the system.
- **Rule 4.** If the system is not required by law, does not reduce costs, but does increase benefits, then accept the system.

Systems Analysis Report

The final step in the analysis phase is the submission of a **systems analysis report** to management. This report should include the following:

- A restatement of the scope and objectives of the systems analysis.
- A data flow diagram of the current system that outlines the logical system and highlights any problem areas.
- A summary of constraints imposed on the existing system and any assumptions made.
- A preliminary report on alternative solutions that currently appear feasible.
- A cost/benefit analysis outlining the resources and capital that will be required to modify the existing system or design a new one. It should include a detailed, carefully prepared projection of the time and costs of the next step—general system design.

The systems analysis report assures management and the user that the analyst really understands the problem and seems to be heading in the right direction to solve it.

Again, we come to a crucial point in the systems life cycle. If management does not decide to continue, the system will die here. Management approval permits the analyst to proceed to the general system design step.

GENERAL SYSTEM DESIGN

During the analysis stage, the analyst focuses on what has to be done to solve the problem. After determining this, the analyst proceeds to the **general system design,** where the focus is on determining, in a general outline, how the problem might be solved. In this stage the analyst determines the logical design that must precede the physical or detailed design.

Evaluation of Organizational Constraints

Before the analyst proceeds to the development of alternative designs, he or she must understand the organizational constraints. These might include budgetary constraints, the political environment, unions, governmental regulations, and so on. It would be foolish, for instance, for the analyst to design a system that could not possibly be financed with the firm's existing budget. This process is a repetition of selected steps in the feasibility study described earlier—but with more information available.

Alternative Designs

Usually the analyst is asked to develop several alternative solutions to the problem. This requirement forces the analyst to analyze and compare a number of different options rather than just pick one and move on.

Space Chips

Engineers who design chips for use in the space program have more to worry about than their earthbound colleagues. Computer chips intended for space are subject to a certain type of malfunction that cannot be tested for on the ground.

These special computer chip malfunctions are caused by the cosmic rays and energized protons that float around in space. When either a cosmic ray or an energized proton comes into contact with the sensitive area of a computer chip, it can change the contents of that chip. Such a change could possibly endanger an entire mission.

A new project is being researched to allow scientists to complete tests for this type of malfunction. The project is called the Chemical Release and Radiation Effects Satellite (CRRES) and represents a joint effort between the National Aeronautics and Space Administration (NASA), the Navy, and the Air force. Flight tests are scheduled to start in 1985, when the satellite will begin to monitor abnormalities and changes in chip function while analyzing the environment of space.

This research probably will not completely eliminate chip malfunctions in space. However, it is expected to decrease the probability of their occurrence by examining those malfunctions in the environment that causes them.

The primary input document used is the data flow diagram created in the analysis stage. From this, the analyst outlines a series of possible automation approaches and uses these to suggest physical implementation strategies. For example, the analyst might develop one alternative using a manual system and a second using a computer. The computer-based system might be developed into several alternatives, one using batch processing, another using interactive processing, and so on.

As a minimum requirement, management usually requires at least three options: a low-cost "bare bones" solution that provides only those features that are absolutely needed; an intermediate-cost solution that adds some additional features that are nice; and a higher-cost "Cadillac" solution that gives the user everything asked for. Each alternative identified should be documented with a system flowchart, a list of physical components, a cost/benefit analysis, and a schedule.

System Flowchart The analyst must start to convert the logical model into a physical model. At this point specific details are not desired; what is needed is an overview. Symbols are used to represent each component in the system and form a **system flowchart.** Figure 14–3 shows each of these symbols.

Figure 14–4 shows a simplified payroll process in system flowchart form. (The continued use of time cards justifies the use of punched cards in the 1980s for payroll applications.)

Figure 14–3
Symbols for System
Flowcharting

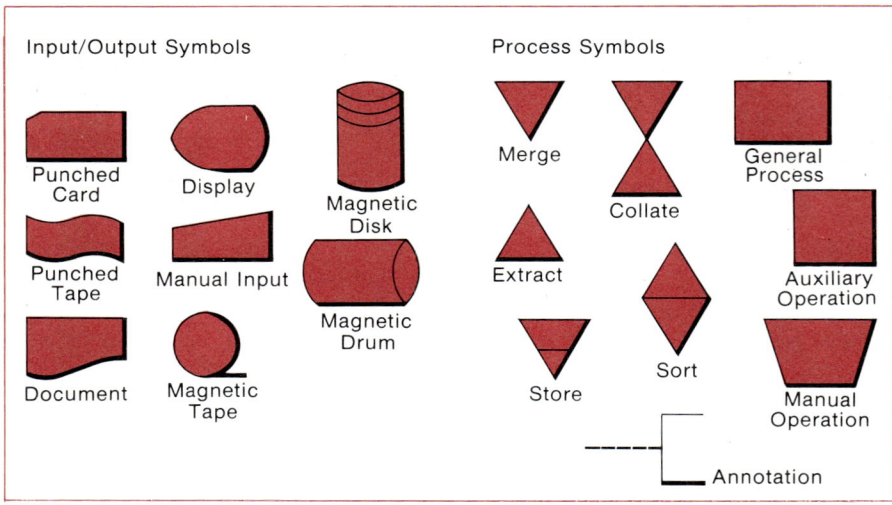

Physical Components The analyst must determine what type of physical components each of the alternatives will require. For example, the general hardware requirements, such as the type of computer needed (for example, mainframe, minicomputer, or microcomputer, printers, terminals, and so on, must be identified. No specifics are identified at this time.

Cost/Benefit Analysis As with the preceding step in the systems life cycle, a cost/benefit analysis is performed and presented to management. This is a crucial stage in the development of the system. As we move into the detailed system design stage, costs will begin to accelerate (see Figure 14–5). The system, as noted before, is an investment for management; as with any investment, management is concerned with realizing some benefit or reduction in costs.

Scheduling Two of the more popular methods used in project management for scheduling complex activities are the Program Evaluation and Review Technique (PERT) and the Critical Path Method (CPM). The key to both PERT and CPM is the project network, which provides a graphic picture of the logical steps in a project, showing sequences and interrelationships. This helps break down a large, complex project into smaller, manageable parts (see Figure 14–6). A schedule is required for each alternative approach to help management in the evaluation process.

The example of a PERT network diagram in Figure 14–6 shows the relationships of eight **events** or milestones (circles) and the **activities** (lines) that link them. Precedence and succession are illustrated, as is a **critical path,** or route through the network that must be optimized if the schedule for the entire project is not to slip. The critical path (the bold sequence of lines representing Activities A-B, B-D, D-E, E-G, and G-H) represents the longest path through the network, based on the du-

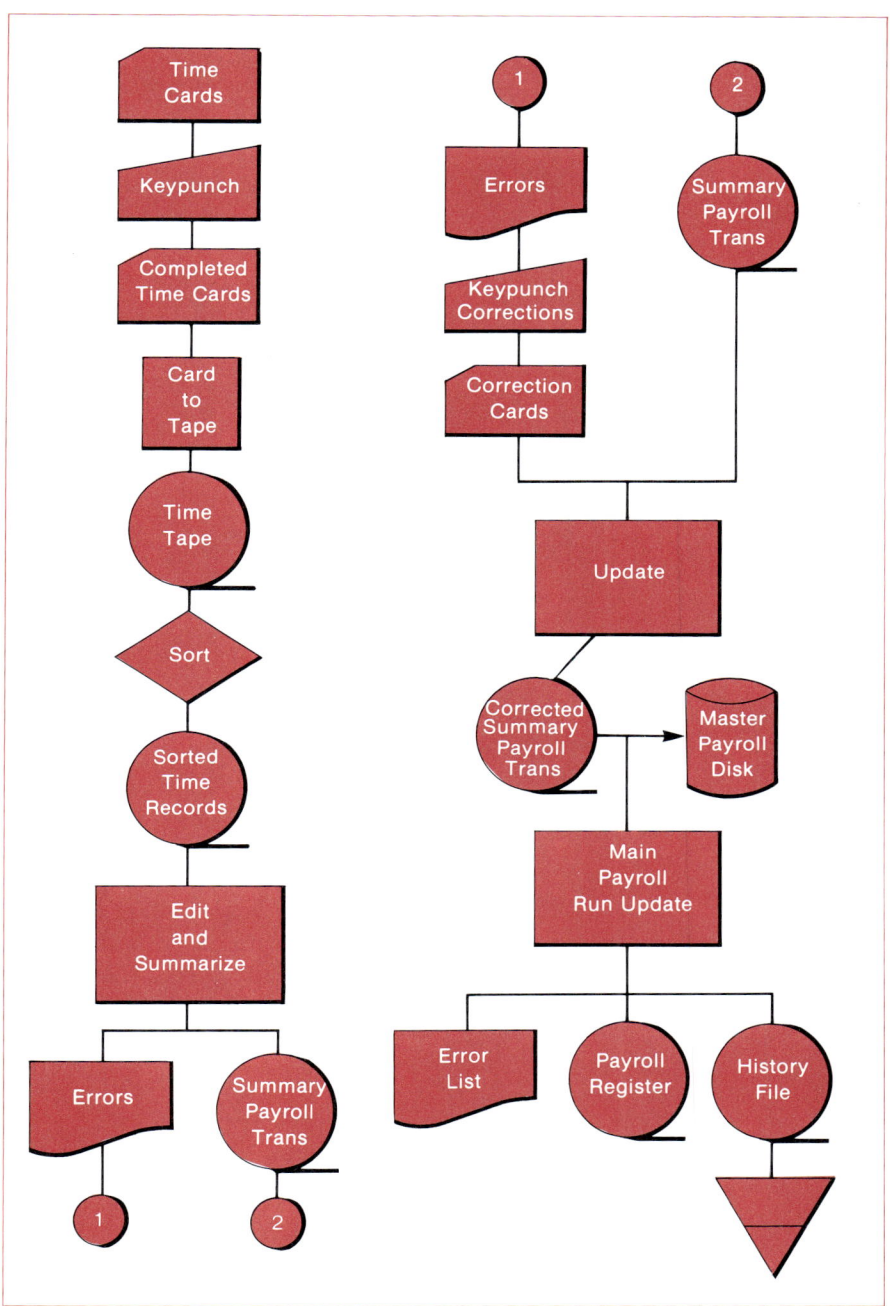

Figure 14—4 System Flowchart: Payroll Processing

Figure 14–5 Relative
Costs of System Steps

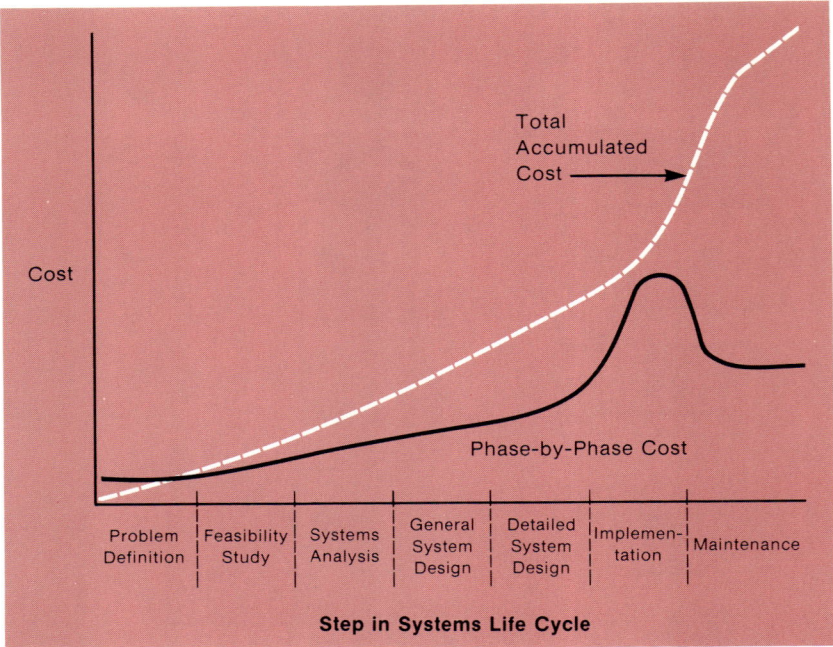

ration of each activity as listed above the activity lines. An activity cannot begin until all preceding activities leading to its initial event have been completed. For example, Activity G-H cannot begin until Activities D-G and E-G both are finished.

General System Design Report

The **general system design report** is presented to management after the analyst has completed the general system design for each of the required alternatives. The report should contain, as a minimum, the following:

Figure 14–6 Pert
Network Diagram

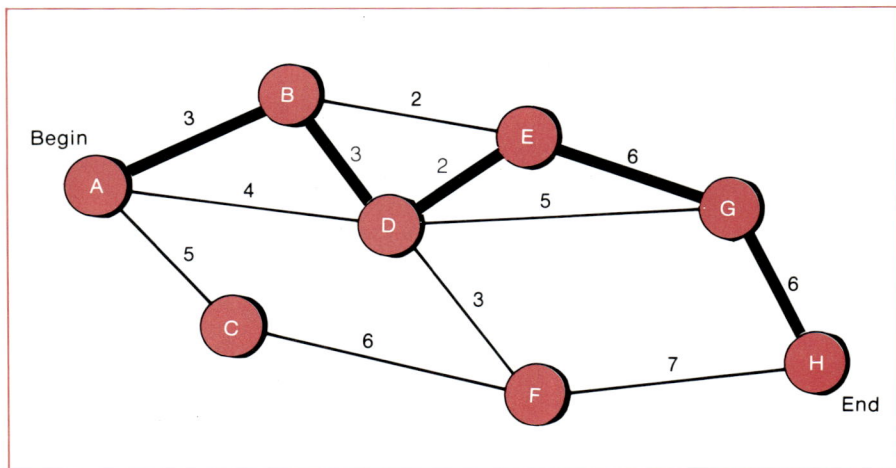

- A restatement of the scope and objectives.
- Several alternatives, each supported by a systems flowchart, a list of physical components, a cost/benefit analysis, and a schedule.
- The analyst's recommendation of an alternative.

Management then reviews the report and decides either to terminate the project or to continue to the next phase. If a decision to continue is made, management (ideally in conjunction with the user) will select an alternative to be developed in the detailed system design phase.

DETAILED SYSTEM DESIGN

During the general system design phase, the general or logical system structure was mapped out. The types of programs needed were determined (although no consideration was given to how they would be written); the general nature of hardware was suggested (although specifics were not given); and so on. In the **detailed system design** phase, the analyst's attention is directed to developing the implementation specifications of the system. These include defining the following: output requirements, input requirements, file and data base requirements, system processing, system controls and backup, an implementation schedule and cost estimate, and a detailed system design report.

Output Requirements

Before deciding the inputs of the system, the analyst must know the output needs of the user. This entails knowing the types of reports (summary, exception, and so on) that will be needed and the types of information these will contain. The medium on which each report will be created also must be determined (CRT terminals, hard copy, and so on). Once the medium has been determined, the analyst designs the necessary screen layouts, report layouts, or both (see Figure 14–7).

Input Requirements

Now that the specific output requirements are known, the analyst will be able to determine the types of input data needed to produce the desired output. The analyst must be concerned with how the input is to be collected. Will the data be gathered at one location and transferred to another? If so, forms will need to be designed to insure that the correct data in the correct form will be used. Another option might be to gather data at its source using the computer (source-data automation). No matter how or where the data is collected, there should be some means of editing it to check for the reasonableness of the data. For instance, if the order quantity for a particular part averages around 100 units per week and an order for 100,000 parts comes in, the user should be alerted to verify the data.

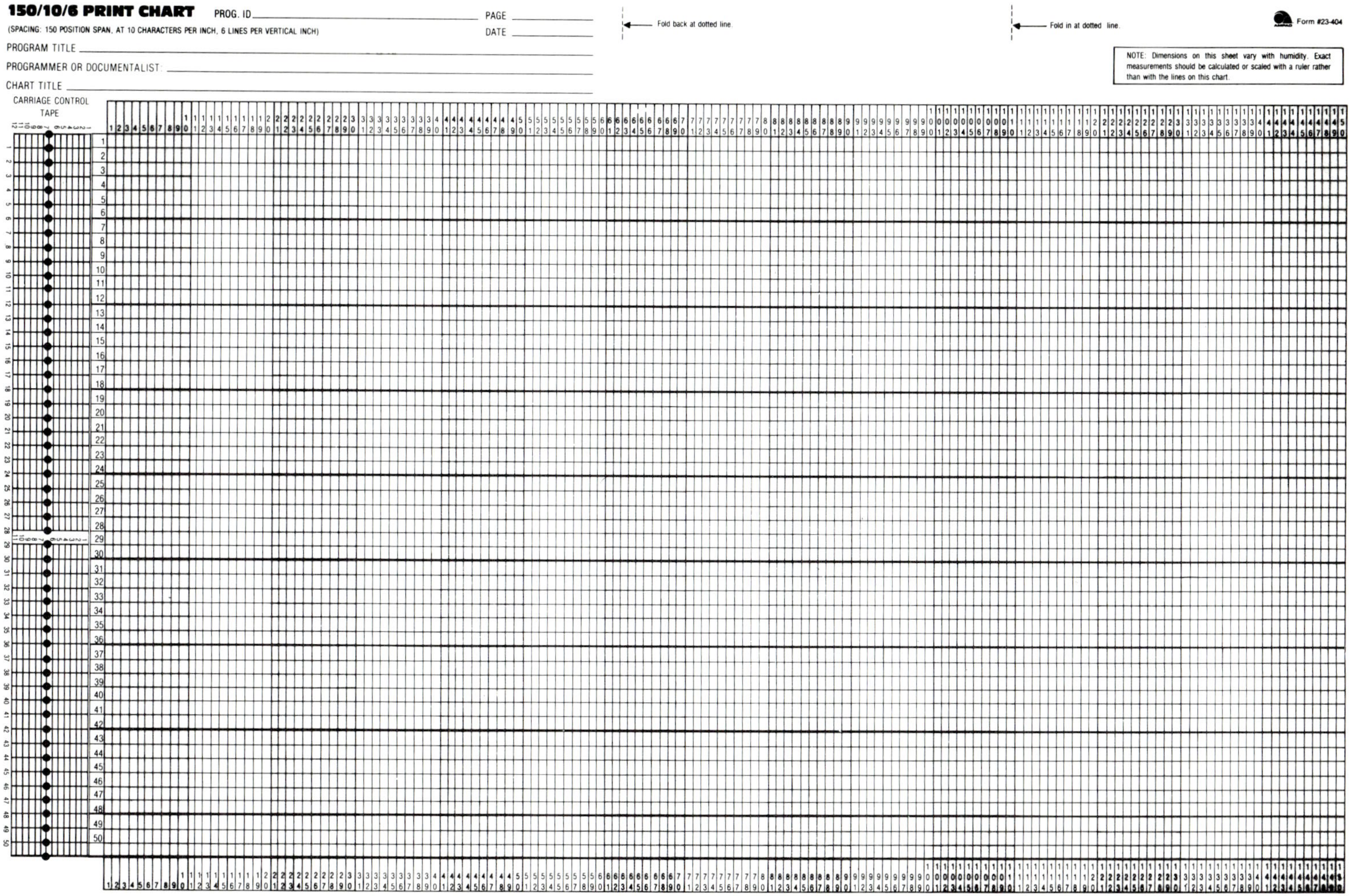

Figure 14-7 Screen or Report Layout Form

File and Data Base Requirements

Once the input content and sources have been determined, the next step is to decide how this data will be organized once it has been collected. A record layout form is a helpful tool used to describe the formats of records making up data files. There are also a number of possible file organization alternatives, including sequential, direct, and indexed. Consideration also must be given to how data will be accessed (for example, sequentially on magnetic tape or randomly on disk), as well as to whether data will be maintained on separate files or integrated into an existing data base.

System Processing

The analyst must develop detailed system flowcharts to show the flow of data in the new system. The flowcharts help the analyst determine whether or not the necessary information is getting to the appropriate user, if there is redundancy of data, if any data is being generated that is not needed, and so on. The scope of some systems analysis and design projects can become so large that it is easy for these problems to occur. The detailed system flowcharts put the whole system in perspective for the analyst, so problems of this sort can be detected. Programming specifications, often including detailed logic flowcharts or pseudocode, are an important element developed during this step.

System Controls and Backup

To protect the integrity of the data, appropriate controls must be instituted to insure that data is entered, processed, and output correctly. Input must be controlled to insure accurate conversion of data from source documents to a form that can be processed by machine. Backup copies of all important files should be made regularly and stored in an off-site location. Controls are also necessary to prevent fraud and tampering with the system.

Implementation Schedule and Cost Estimate

A schedule must be outlined for the next phase—implementation. This gives management an idea of the time involved in getting the new system running. As always, management is also interested in the cost and will require the analyst to submit a detailed cost estimate for the implementation step.

Detailed System Design Report

The final action in this step is to present management with a **detailed system design report.** The detailed system design report should contain the following:

- A brief restatement of the problem.
- A cost/benefit analysis.
- An explanation of the detailed design.
- An implementation schedule.

This is the final decision point before the actual implementation of the system begins. Management now must decide whether to reject the design or to accept it and commit the time and funds necessary for the implementation of the new system.

IMPLEMENTATION

In the **implementation** step, the system designed by the analyst is physically created. Any programming specifications must be coded, debugged, and documented. The hardware must be selected, ordered, and installed. Operating procedures must be drawn up. Personnel need to be trained to use the new system. A test plan must be created, followed by a formal system test involving all components and procedures. If the test is satisfactory, conversion from the old to the new system takes place. Finally, auditing procedures must be drawn up to evaluate the system's performance.

Programming

At the heart of any computerized system are the computer programmers. If the systems analyst is not the programmer, he or she must be able to communicate clearly and precisely the detailed programming specifications. The ability to do so will help avoid the time and expense involved in reprogramming.

In some instances, the analyst and the programming department may want to evaluate some of the packaged software that is available. If a package can be found that is compatible with and easily adaptable to the system, it could save considerable time and money that otherwise would be expended in developing in-house programs. Developing the programs in structured, independent modules will make system maintenance and modification much easier to accomplish (review Chapters 8 and 9).

Hardware Selection

In the detailed system design step, the analyst specified the types of hardware that would be needed to implement the system. In the implementation step, the specific brands and models are selected, ordered, and installed. The analyst must consider such factors as cost, vendor support, and future expandability of the hardware components.

Computer Criminals

Officials have been putting a great deal of thought into devising ways to stop computer crime. Unfortunately, "computer criminals" are no easier to spot than any other kind of criminal. However, they may be easier to stop. One authority on this exotic brand of outlawry says that job-related frustrations are more likely to make a computer criminal than any set of personality traits. In particular, programmers who feel they have been cheated of a program's rights or not properly rewarded often will sabotage the program. That being the case, he adds, management must find out if employees are disgruntled with their work and, if they are, why.

Crime stopping then becomes a matter of easing the frustration. "No matter how tight the controls," the authority says, "any computer system can be defeated. Believe me, they all have their loopholes." People on the inside of the system will have no difficulty seeing through these loopholes (especially because they are generally the ones who programmed them into the system in the first place).

Personnel Training

Along with the new system come new ways of doing things. The analyst must thoroughly document each aspect of the new system. How is the data to be gathered? In what form will the data need to be when it is entered into the system? How are the output documents distributed? What can the user expect from the system? Questions like these need to be clearly answered and documented to insure the efficient and effective operation of the system.

Two documents that need to be prepared for training purposes are the user's manual and the operator's manual. The **user's manual** is directed at general management, staff personnel, line managers, and other operating personnel. It instructs them in the particular functions they are to perform, as well as in what they can expect the system to do for them. The **operator's manual** is directed at the computer personnel who run the programs. It contains instructions on how to run the programs, including how to prepare input data, load and unload files on auxiliary storage devices, handle problem situations, and so on.

Training may take place in large or small groups, in a classroom environment, or on the job. Each approach has distinct advantages and disadvantages. Whatever the chosen route, personnel training and education are essential to successful system implementation.

System Testing

Before conversion to the new system, it must be thoroughly tested and debugged. The first step is to test all the programs. Each module of the complete applications program used is tested to insure that the input, processing, and output operations perform the desired function. Next, the modules are integrated, and the complete applications program is tested as a whole.

System testing begins upon successful completion of program testing. It involves checking all the applications programs that support the system, all clerical procedures, data processing, and data storage and retrieval methods.

Two common methods of system testing (also used in program testing) are desk checking and processing test data. **Desk checking** is the process of mentally running through the logic used to perform a particular function to determine its correctness. **Processing test data** involves using data that was previously processed on the old system and checking the earlier results to see if they match the new system output. If they do, the new system is functioning properly. Once the performance of the new system is found to be satisfactory, conversion of the old to the new system begins.

Conversion

Replacing the old system with the new one is a process called **conversion.** We will examine four of the possible approaches to system conversion. In most situations some combination of these methods is used.

Parallel conversion involves running both the old and the new systems side by side until the new system proves itself. Once the bugs have been worked out of the new system and confidence has been gained, the old system is shut down. Running both systems at once, however, can be quite costly.

Pilot conversion involves implementing the complete system in only one area, such as one production line. Once the system has proved itself there, it is extended to the rest of the organization.

Phased conversion differs from pilot conversion in that it involves implementing only one segment of the system at a time. Each segment is thoroughly tested and debugged before the next is implemented.

Crash (direct) conversion is a high-risk method, because it involves the immediate discontinuation of the old system. If problems should arise in the new system, the organization has nothing to fall back on. This approach requires that extreme care be taken in both the planning and testing of all system components. It is, however, the least costly method (if it works!).

Auditing

Once the new system is up and running, the organization needs some means of evaluating the system's performance. Management and the systems staff need to know if the system is meeting its original objectives. A formal audit or postimplementation review is necessary to remedy problems—major or minor—that invariably prevent a new system from satisfying all needs of the users. The auditing process can be conducted by the systems analyst or by an independent evaluation team.

The final results of the evaluation usually lead to modifications or improvements in the new system.

Security also plays an important part in the audit. The conscientious analyst will have incorporated an audit trail in the system to trace data back to its source. This will help locate the source documents in the event that any data is tampered with once inside the system. Protecting the integrity of the data is a full-time job.

MAINTENANCE

The development process has been completed, and the system is up and running. The final stage is that of **maintenance;** it is an ongoing process during the rest of the system's life. Its objective is to keep the system functioning at an acceptable level. Any problems that slipped through system testing and auditing are addressed here, as is any required updating in programs or procedures. A well-designed system should be adaptable to change.

In time, major changes that require redesign of the system may become necessary. When this happens, the entire systems life cycle is repeated. Change seems to be the only constant in information systems, and keeping systems responsive to these changes is a never-ending process.

SUMMARY POINTS

- The systems analyst is the person responsible for the analysis, design, and implementation of information systems. The analyst is the bridge that links user groups, technical professionals, and management.
- Problem definition is the first step in the systems life cycle. Here the nature and the scope of the problem are defined, along with the objectives that the analysis and design are intended to meet.
- There are four basic reasons for initiating a system analysis and design project: (1) to respond to a problem in the system, (2) to meet new requirements, (3) to accommodate changes in technology, and (4) to make broad system improvements.
- The feasibility study is the second step in the systems life cycle. During this step the analyst attempts to discover if there is a feasible solution to the problem and whether or not the problem is worth pursuing.
- A cost/benefit analysis is a quantitative form of evaluation that determines benefits and costs associated with achieving the benefits.
- Systems analysis is the third step in the systems life cycle. It involves data gathering and data analysis of the old system.
- In the data-gathering portion of the systems analysis, the analyst has two general sources of data. Internal sources are those found within the organization. The four principal sources of internal information are written documents, questionnaires, interviews, and observations. External sources are those found outside the organization.
- General system design is the fourth step in the systems life cycle. In this stage the analyst defines a number of alternative solutions. Each alternative is documented with a system flowchart, a list of physical

components, a cost/benefit analysis, and a schedule. The analyst presents the alternatives to management, along with a recommendation of the alternative considered most feasible.

● Detailed system design is the fifth step in the systems life cycle. In this step the analyst develops the specific implementation structure of the system. This includes the output requirements, input requirements, file and data base requirements, system processing, system controls and backup, and an implementation schedule and cost estimate.

● Implementation is the sixth step in the systems life cycle. It involves the actual physical creation of the system. Included in this step are: programming, hardware selection, personnel training, system testing, and auditing.

● The seventh and last step in the systems life cycle is maintenance, an ongoing process during the rest of the system's life. The objective is to keep the system functioning at an acceptable level.

REVIEW
QUESTIONS

1. Identify three functions of a systems analyst. What are some of the skills and abilities required by the analyst to successfully execute these functions?

2. What does the word structured imply in the term structured systems analysis and design?

3. What are the steps in the systems life cycle?

4. Give four reasons why a systems analysis and design project might be initiated.

5. What are the major objectives of the problem definition stage?

6. Why is it important to have the systems analyst communicate findings in writing?

7. What two questions are the focus of the feasibility study?

8. What are the two principal tasks in the systems analysis stage? What are the two general sources of data available to the analyst?

9. Name and briefly describe the four internal sources of data.

10. On what questions does the data analysis portion of the systems analysis stage focus? Name four of the tools available to the analyst for this purpose, and briefly explain each.

11. What is the purpose of the general design step?

12. Identify and briefly discuss six areas in which the analyst must develop implementation specifications during the detailed system design step.

13. What is the focus of the implementation step?

14. Define conversion. List and discuss the four methods of conversion discussed in the chapter.

15. What is the focus of the maintenance step? What benefits do you think using a structured approach in the systems analysis and design steps has on the maintenance step?

16. Pick an area of application with which you are familiar. Define a new (or revised) systems requirement and play the role of the systems analyst by documenting systems life cycle activities with the appropriate charts, tables, and narrative. Include alternative solutions.

MANAGEMENT INFORMATION SYSTEMS

LEARNING OBJECTIVES

After studying this chapter, you will be able to do the following:

☐ Define a management information systems (MIS), and know how it relates to the different levels of decision making in a typical organization.
☐ Present and define the four basic MIS design structures.
☐ Define a data base, and tell how a data base management system (DBMS) is used to facilitate access and control of the data base.

Chapter 15

INTRODUCTION   The basic purpose of management is to make decisions, whether these decisions are top-level strategic decisions, middle-level tactical decisions, or low-level operational decisions. The key to any decision is supplying the appropriate manager with correct and timely information.

In the past, these information needs often were satisfied manually, resulting in incorrect, overlooked, or late information. Recently, however, managers have begun to realize the potential of the computer to generate information to support decision making. A system with such a focus has come to be known as a *management information systems (MIS)*. An MIS is a formal information network that uses computers to provide information for decision making. Its purpose is to provide each manager with appropriate and timely information.

LEVELS OF MANAGEMENT USING THE MIS

The type of information needed varies greatly with the level of decision making required. Within any organization there are typically three levels of management, each tasked with a different level of decision making. Figure 15–1 depicts the three levels.

Managers at each level require some form of decision-oriented information; however, because the nature of decisions varies greatly between each level, the types of information each requires is different. This poses a major difficulty when designing an MIS, since the system must be able to provide the appropriate information to each level of management.

Top-Level Management

Managers at the top level are concerned with **strategic decision making.** These decisions are future-oriented and involve a great deal of uncertainty. One of the main functions of top-level management is to establish organizational goals and determine the strategies needed to achieve

Figure 15–1 Levels of Management

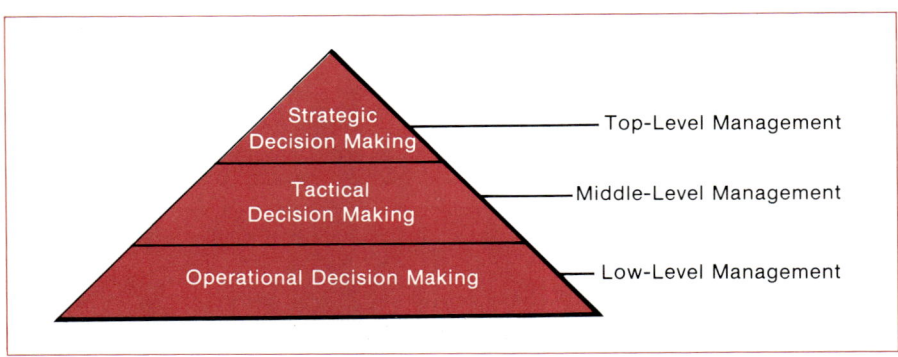

Information Specialists

In the near future, MISs will be restructuring the corporate ladder—that is, at least according to Joseph Izzo, president of JIA Management Group, Inc., a Santa Monica, California, consulting firm. Izzo claims that the information revolution will change the face and the background of tomorrow's executive aides. This is because a new profession is emerging, that of the information specialist.

Information specialists will be invaluable to company executives. They will be responsible for condensing the great mounds of information output by the company's computers and presenting executives with only the information they really need for decision making.

It is fairly well known that most executives make 80 percent of their decisions based on a core 20 percent of the available information. It will be the job of information specialists to provide executives with that essential 20 percent. To prepare for this, the information specialists probably will have an MBA degree and definitely will have an aptitude for synthesizing information.

these goals. These managers must also be ready to make decisions about events that happen unpredictably. To accomplish these tasks, top-level managers need ready access to historic information and an analysis of data trends for the business as a whole, and they must be prepared to handle the unpredictable events that can occur. The MIS must be able to produce on-demand reports that can effectively integrate information about the currect situation.

The top level is where MISs typically have fallen short of their goals. Strategic decision making involves problems that are nonrepetitive, characterized by uncertainty, and capable of having a significant impact on the organization. Attempting to define the information needed can be an extremely difficult task. A well-designed MIS may not present a definitive answer, but it can be an extremely valuable aid to top management.

Middle-Level Management

Once top-level managers have determined the specific strategies to be employed, it is the responsibility of the middle-level managers to implement them. This involves **tactical decision making.** A major portion of a middle-level manager's job focuses on control and short-run planning. Activities performed by the middle-level manager include formulating budgets, making short-term forecasts, and scheduling production. To meet the needs of the middle-level manager, the MIS must supply summary reports that are timely enough to allow the manager to react appropriately to changing conditions in the business environment.

Middle-level decisions, or tactical decisions, rely heavily on internal information and on rapid processing and retrieval of data. Decisions at the tactical level generally have a weekly or monthly time frame. At this level, a well-designed MIS can easily supply the manager with the appropriate information needed.

Low-Level Management

Low-level managers are concerned with day-to-day operations and **operational decision making.** They must make operating decisions to insure that specific jobs get done. Their major function is to control the results of the specific jobs to insure that they are in line with the overall company objectives. Low-level managers are also responsible for implementing corrective actions when necessary.

At the low level, decisions are generally routine and well defined. The necessary information can be supplied evenly through normal administrative data-processing activities, including activities such as the preparation of financial statements, recording the shipping backlog, and other routine record keeping. Figure 15–2 shows a comparison of the three levels of management decision making.

KINDS OF DECISION-ORIENTED REPORTS

Each level of management has different information requirements; therefore, an MIS must be able to supply several types of reports to meet the needs of each level. Four typical reports used are scheduled reports, exception reports, predictive reports, and demand reports.

Figure 15–2
Comparison of the Three Levels of Decision Making (Typical Profile)

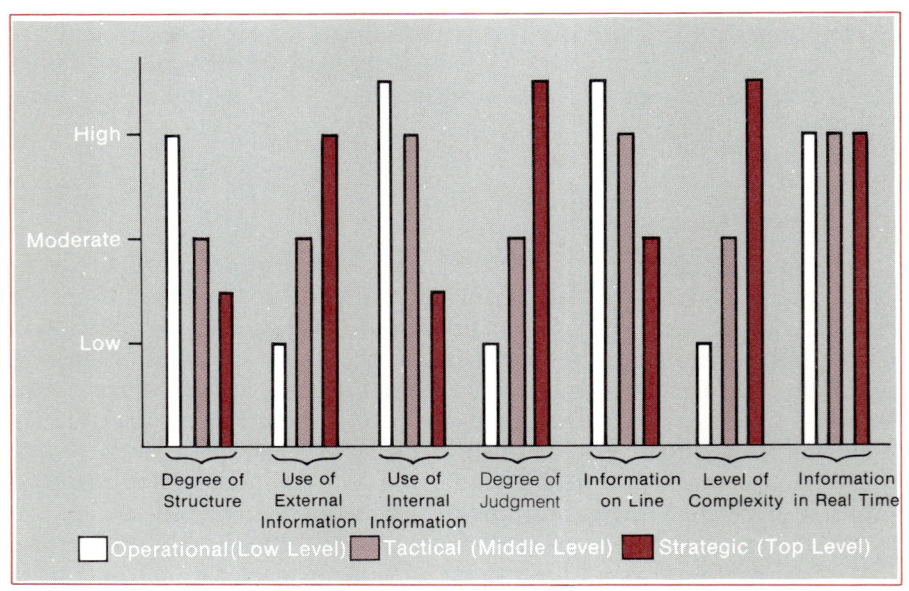

Scheduled reports are produced routinely and have a wide variety of users. Because of the number of users accessing these reports, the scope tends to be fairly broad; each report generally contains more information than is required by an individual user. **Exception reports** alert management to abnormal situations that require special attention. They are referred to as **action-oriented management reports.** Whenever the results of a component of the system deviate from the expected results by more than the predetermined limits, an exception report is generated. **Predictive reports** use decision models to project future results that are useful for planning. They are used for tactical and strategic decision making. By manipulating the variables in the models, managers can see the results to "What if?" kinds of queries. **Demand reports** are used mainly in strategic decision making to provide responses to unanticipated queries. As the name suggests, they are produced only upon request.

EFFECTIVENESS OF AN MIS

Having a MIS does not guarantee that all of management's decisions will be appropriate. However, if the MIS has been properly designed, it can be an invaluable aid in the decision-making process. A major problem in designing an MIS is determining what information management needs. The analyst who develops the MIS must rely on the users to communicate their information needs. Unfortunately, many managers lack an understanding of what information they truly need; as a result, they request everything the computer can supply them. This results in information overload, a concept addressed earlier. In this situation, the manager is presented with so much information that it is difficult to determine what is needed; as a consequence, important facts are often overlooked.

Decision making at any but the most elementary levels (for example, determining fixed order quantity) is something the computer is incapable of doing, because it has no intuitive capability. An MIS, however, can help the manager by supplying and integrating essential data for the decision process if the proper care and effort are put into its development.

DECISION SUPPORT SYSTEMS

A **decision support system (DSS)** is used to assist managers in decision making for relatively unstructured tasks. It differs from an MIS: An MIS is associated with systems that emphasize structured or routine decisions, and a DSS emphasizes less-structured or nonprogrammable decisions.

In a DSS, the computer is an analytic aid to decision making: the DSS makes no attempt to automate the manager's tasks or impose solutions. A DSS is simply a management planning tool that provides the information that supports the decision-making process. It allows managers to evaluate multiple alternatives and ask "What if?" questions for a given set of circumstances. Managers still make the decisions, but DSS reports allow them to make the decisions with greater confidence in the effectiveness and quality. A DSS relies heavily on packaged software in the **management science** discipline (that is, simulation, modeling, and quantitative data analysis).

DESIGN ALTERNATIVES

An analyst designing an MIS has a virtually unlimited number of possible designs to choose from. Organizational philosophy, along with other factors (such as budgeting constraints), will help narrow the range of possibilities, but the task can remain monumental. There are four basic MIS design structures: centralized design, hierarchical design, distributed design, and decentralized design. We will talk about these as separate entities, but they should be looked at as points along a continuous range of design alternatives rather than as separate, mutually exclusive options. As might be expected, these MIS designs usually parallel the structure of the organizations they serve.

Centralized Design

In a **centralized design,** a separate, autonomous electronic data-processing (EDP) department is set up to provide data-processing facilities for the whole organization. The EDP department has responsibility for and control of all program development, as well as all equipment acquisition. Portions of the organization located in other areas can use the centralized equipment through remote access via a communications network. The centralized design uses a common data base that permits authorized users to access information. Figure 15–3 depicts a centralized design.

The centralized approach has a number of advantages. It presents economies of scale, eliminates redundancy and duplication of data, and results in efficient utilization of data-processing capabilities. Certain disadvantages are also associated with the centralized approach. Response to a particular decision can be slow, since priorities are assigned based on overall organizational needs. Many managers are also reluctant to relinquish authority to a centralized EDP group, preferring instead to control their own data-processing needs.

Hierarchical Design

A **hierarchical** (or, more precisely, a group/division) **design** is characterized by relatively autonomous operating units within an organization, each having segmented responsibility and decision-making authority. Figure 15–4 illustrates this design. The design provides each group with the appropriate computer power to accomplish its goals. This requires

Wholesaling Made Easier

Thanks to Management Systems Division (MSD) of Columbus, Ohio, many of the risky variables and costly delays have been removed from wholesaling. In a stripped-down way, the system works like this. Say a stock clerk in a supermarket notices that all or most of an item has been sold and that more of the item is needed quickly. The clerk enters a reorder for the item via a calculatorlike keyboard. This flashes the information to MSD computers in Columbus, where the order is registered in all the appropriate accounting records and then automatically transmitted to the supplier of the item. The supplier boxes, bills, or back orders the item and ships it directly to the requesting supermarket. The item will show up in the wholesaler's accounting and managing reports within hours—and the profit will have been made, even though the wholesaler never actually laid hands on the requested item.

varying levels of support for each management level. At the low level, support is minimal because of the technical nature of the work. The middle level requires more information processing to support managerial decisions and will require more extensive support. The greatest amount of support is required by top-level managers, because the information they need requires much greater processing and storage capabilities. This design differs from the decentralized design by the presence of a top-level data processing function.

Distributed Design

The **distributed design** borrows a little from each of the previously described approaches. Independent operating units are identified as they

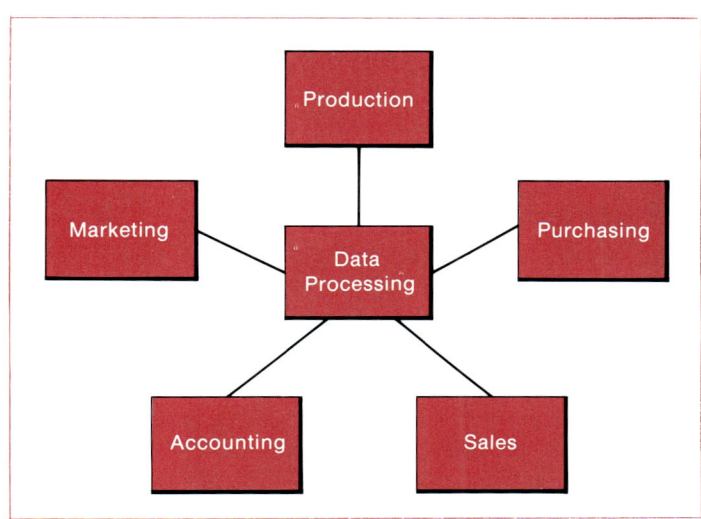

Figure 15–3
Centralized Design

Figure 15–4
Hierarchical (Group/
Division) Design

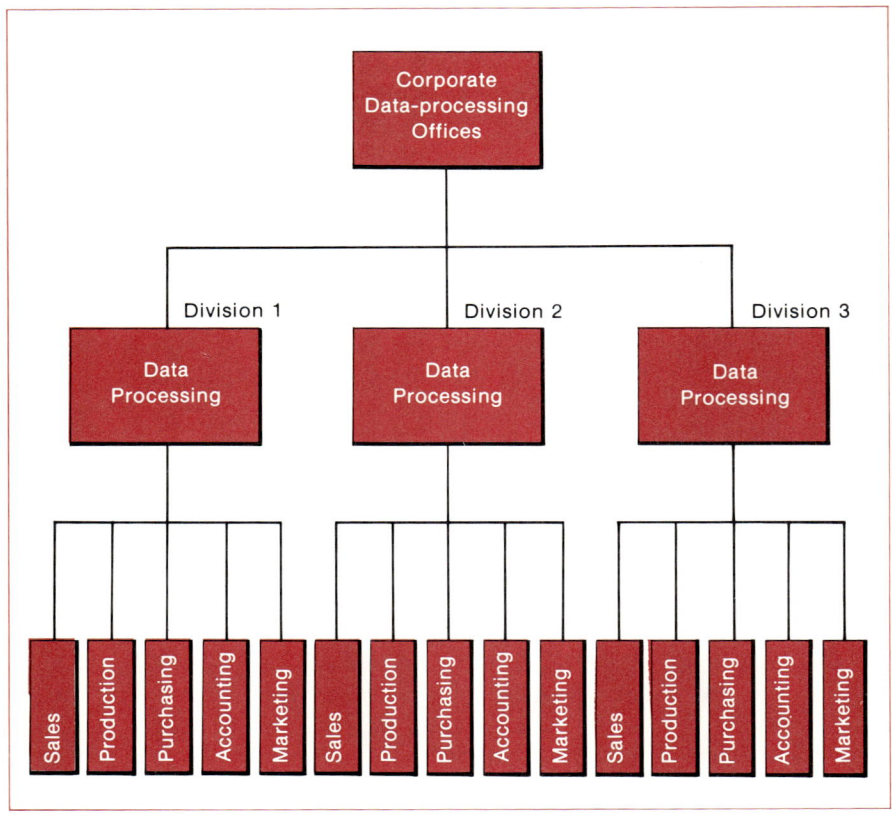

are in the hierarchical approach, but the distributed approach also recognizes the benefits of central coordination and control. To implement this approach, the organization is divided into the smallest activity centers requiring computer support. This division may be based on organizational factors, geographical location, functional operations, or a combination of these factors. In many cases, if the distributed sites are in communication with each other, all the centers will use a standardized class of hardware, share a common data base, and have a coordinated systems development. Figure 15–5 shows an example of a distributed design approach.

Decentralized Design

The **decentralized design** breaks an organization into relatively autonomous operating units. Each unit is given authority and responsibility for computer support. In most cases, there is no central point of control. The managers of each operating unit are given complete authority for computer operations. They are each responsible for acquiring hardware, developing software, and making personnel decisions in the respective

Ali

Chips are finding their way into practical applications. In West Germany an innovative combination of in-car and roadside microprocessors is telling drivers which exit to take to reach their destination, the best route to take, and even the number of kilometers to the next gas station.

The new system, called Ali, has cost the West German government eight million dollars and currently encompasses a hundred-kilometer network of roads. At the point of departure, drivers enter their

destinations into in-car processors, which send signals to roadside processors as the cars travel down the road. The roadside processors look up the route and relay this information back to the in-car processors. The drivers then can concentrate on driving and merely follow the route given.

If this experimental project is successful, the government will decide whether to install Ali guidance systems nationwide. The cost for such a project would be $200 million; it would take about five years to build.

units. Because each system is dedicated to a particular operating unit, the decentralized approach tends to be very responsive to user needs. This type of design can prove to be expensive to maintain because of the amount of redundancy of data required. Since communication between units is limited or nonexistent, there is also a problem of data integrity: what gets changed or updated in one unit may not be changed in another unit.

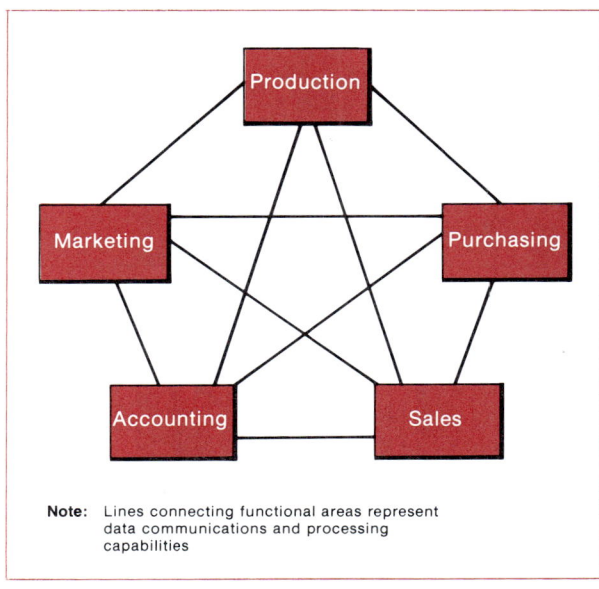

Figure 15–5
Distributed Design

This design is typically used only where an existing organizational structure supports decentralized management. Figure 15–6 shows an example of a decentralized design.

DATA BASE SYSTEMS

Prior to the introduction of the integrated systems approach, each department in an organization maintained its own separate data files and collected its own input. This led to much duplication of effort and data integrity problems. As a solution to these problems, MISs were installed that used some form of standardized data storage.

Data in an MIS needs to be stored in a fashion that will allow it to be accessed by multiple users for a variety of applications. Establishing a **data base** (introduced in Chapter 13) is an effective means of accomplishing this. A data base is a grouping of data fields structured to fit the information needs of multiple functions of an organization. In a data base, data is independent of any one application and is grouped and organized according to its inherent characteristics and relationships. Multiple departments can use data organized in this fashion, avoiding duplication of files by each department. Efficiency is also increased, because when a particular item is to be updated, the change only needs to be made once rather than multiple times, as is the case with separate files. When all data is integrated at a central location, the entire organization can obtain the results of updating at the same time. A data base also provides greater flexibility in responding to information requests that before would have required accessing several departments' individual data files.

Figure 15–6
Decentralized Design

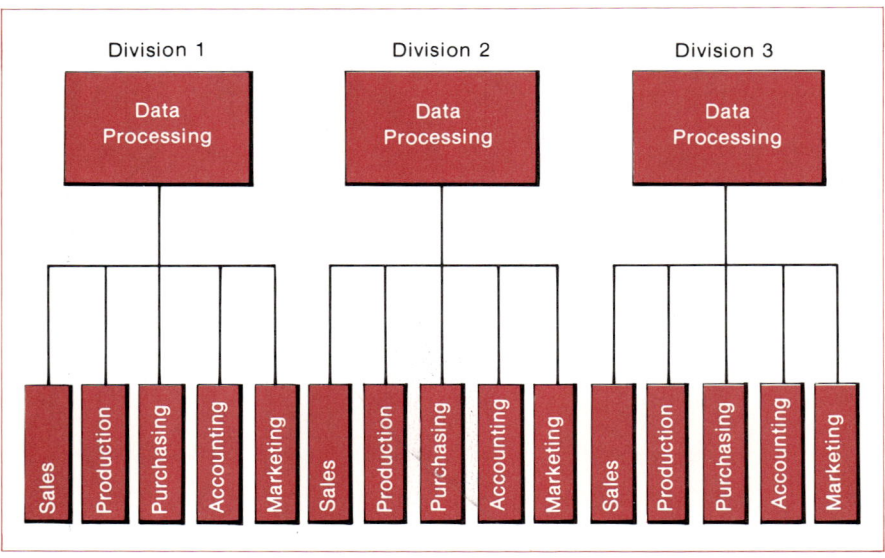

DATA ORGANIZATION

As Chapter 13 stated, there are two basic approaches to the design of data for a data base: physical design and logical design. Physical design refers to how the data is kept on storage devices and how it is accessed. Logical design deals with how data is viewed by applications programs or individual users. The systems analyst and **data analyst** are responsible for the logical data design. The data analyst's job is to analyze the relationships of data in the data base. The goal of this function is to attempt to model the real-world relationships that exist among data items. Logical records should be designed before it is determined how the data will be physically stored. To keep the designs separate, a separate department—typically, the **data administration department**—is assigned the responsibility of maintaining the data base.

A logical file may extend across more than one physical file, and one physical file may contain parts of several logical files of data. In the situations described in Figure 15–7, the structure of the data is said to be **transparent** to the user (i.e., not apparent to the user).

DATA BASE MANAGEMENT SYSTEMS

To properly use a data base, an organization must develop or acquire the detailed data-handling capabilities necessary for manipulating the relevant data. In-house development of such a system is extremely costly and time consuming. As an alternative, a number of **data base management systems (DBMSs)** are available. A DBMS is a set of programs that makes the data in the data base readily available to the three principal users: the programmer, the operating system, and the manager (or other information user).

A DBMS permits the physical data independence mentioned earlier. This physical data independence permits the physical layout of data files to be altered without necessitating changes in applications programs. This capability is desirable, because the user can simply refer to specific data that the program processes rather than require knowledge of the physical structure of the file.

The DBMS simplifies the user's task of accessing information from the data base by providing a set of language commands designed for this purpose. By allowing the sharing of common data, it also effectively eliminates most instances of data redundancy.

A DBMS comes equipped with many features to facilitate and control its operations. These features deal with data access, identification, security, concurrency, and backup and recovery. These are necessary, because a data base will typically be accessed by a wide variety of users having different skill levels and access authorizations.

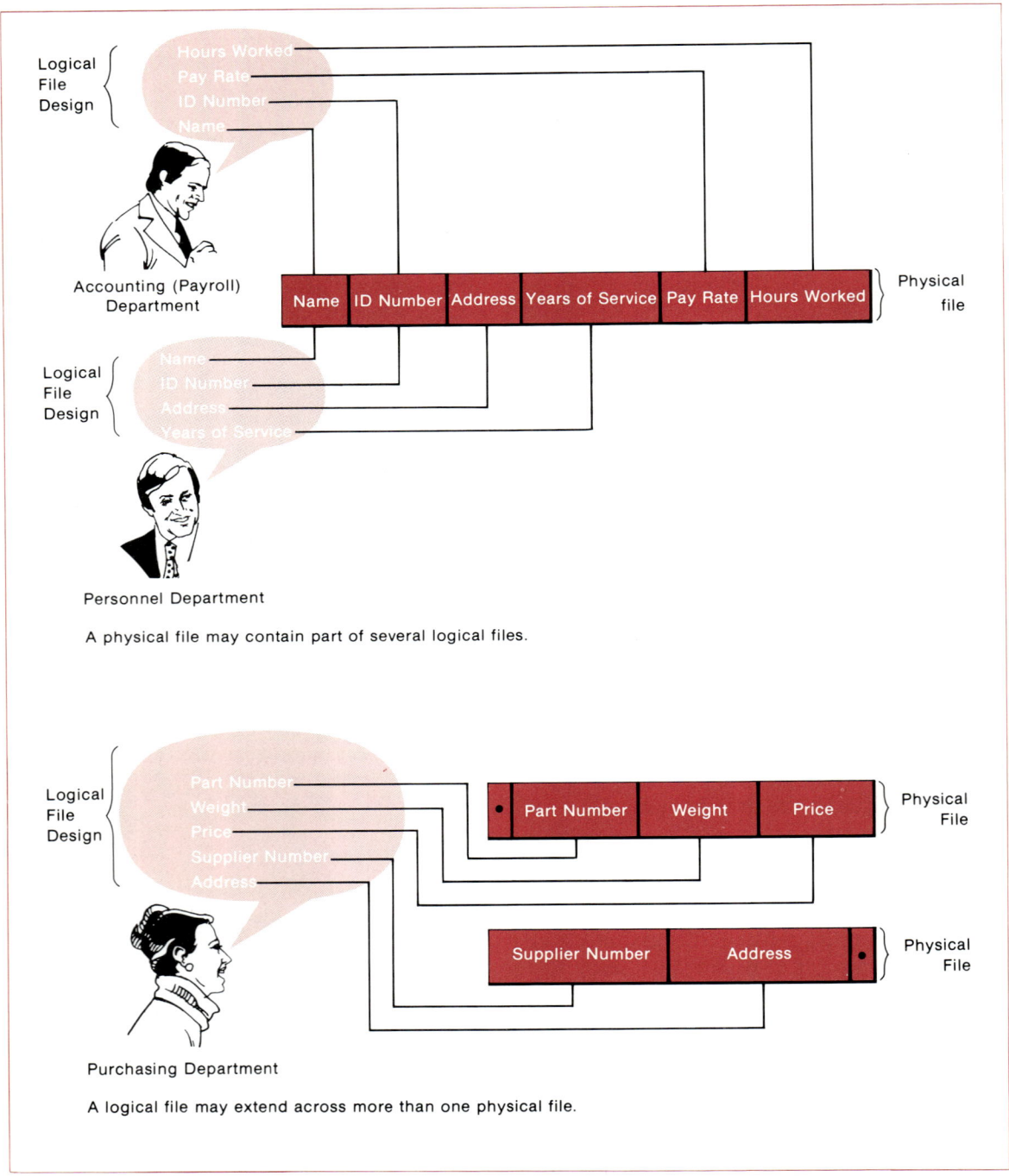

Figure 15–7 Logical and Physical File Design

Microcomputers on the Farm

Today's farm requires a great deal of record keeping, updating, and calculating, and computers are moving in to help. Farmers use personal computers to analyze profits, keep health records on livestock, and calculate a variety of other factors.

Farm-oriented software has been slow in coming. Even programs written especially for farmers often must be modified to reflect the differences between farms. One of these programs is the least-cost feed program. This program takes into account up to one hundred feed ingredients and tells the farmer the most economical and nutritional combination. Another useful package is IBM's Dairy Cow and Herd Health Management System. Large farms also use their computers to handle payrolls and help with crop management.

Data Access

One feature of a DBMS is access to the data base. Three dimensions are the method, mode, and type of data base access:

● **Method of access.** A user may direct the DBMS by two methods. The first is by using a computer **host language** such as COBOL, FORTRAN, or BASIC that is understood by the host computer. This method is not very suitable for most managers and nonprogramming personnel, so query languages have been developed to simplify the process. A **query language** is one composed of special English-like statements that are easily understood by nontechnical personnel.
● **Mode of access.** A DBMS can be accessed through one of two modes—batch or interactive—depending on the urgency of the information needed.
● **Type of access.** The types of data base access are classified as either static or dynamic. A static request is one that is routine, whereas a dynamic request is one that is made in response to the ad hoc needs of users.

Identification

A second feature of a DBMS involves how data is identified by the user to the DBMS. Data identification can be done by sequential processing, direct processing, or attribute identification:

● **Sequential processing.** The most basic and least used method, sequential processing, involves starting at the beginning of the data base and reading the records in sequence until the desired data is located. To use this method, all the data must be ordered, and all data records must contain the same data fields.

- **Direct processing.** Direct processing discriminates among records by using unique keys supplied by the user. Each key is connected by an algorithm to a physical storage location, which thus allows only the desired data records to be processed (see Appendix B).
- **Attribute identification.** Identification by attribute involves identifying data by certain field contents. This method allows a user to access all records that contain the specified data value. For example, an employer might want to access the records of all employees who have access to classified data. By using this method, only those employees whose records contain the desired data value (or range of values) would be processed. (A query for such a retrieval might appear as follows: SELECT EMPLOYEE-NAME, EMPLOYEE-NUMBER FROM PERS-DATA WHERE CLEARANCE = 'CONFIDENTIAL' OR 'SECRET' OR 'TOP SECRET'.)

Security

How the security of a data base is maintained is a third feature of a DBMS. A data base typically contains large amounts of data that are important and valuable to an organization or other users. A major problem facing most—if not all—users of data bases is how to protect that data from unauthorized users and accidental or intentional destruction or alteration. A DBMS attempts to minimize these problems by employing passwords, logs, edit checks, and encryption:

- **Password.** The most common of these techniques is the password. A user must enter the correct password into the system before being allowed to access data. A number of different passwords may be used in a system, each allowing access to only one particular part of the data base. After accessing specific data, the user may be required to enter an additional password to alter or delete the data.
- **Log.** Whenever a user accesses or modifies any portion of the data base, a log is automatically generated. The log includes such items as the date, time, user identification, program name, location, and access type. The log then can be examined periodically to help alert management to any suspicious activity.
- **Edit checks.** Edit checks prevent the unintentional modification of data by validating the accuracy of data entering the system. They include, among others, reasonableness, range, and character type checks.
- **Encryption.** Encryption of data protects it from being tapped by an illegal line and from being accessed by programs outside the system. Encryption is the scrambling or coding of data.

Concurrency

A fourth feature of a DBMS is the prevention of **concurrency,** which occurs when two or more users access and attempt to modify the same data at the same time. This can cause problems in data integrity (consistency and correctness), since neither user realizes the other also is updating the data. The two techniques employed by a DBMS to prevent concurrency are lockout and notification:

● **Lockout.** Data currently being examined by a user is not available for access by any other user until the current user is finished with it; a **lockout** is created.
● **Notification.** The DBMS notifies users that previously retrieved data has been modified by other users.

Backup and Recovery

The final feature of a DBMS that we will examine concerns backup and recovery of data. To provide for a backup, data is copied (dumped) from its normal storage medium to a secondary storage medium. Another method of backup involves maintaining a log file of all data base modifications. The DBMS records the changes in the log file (which may contain the data before the change, after the change, or both).

This log can also be used to create a clean version of the data. If the log contains the data after the changes were made, the data base can be dumped back into the system, and the system can be restarted using this restored data base.

Some of the most popular DBMSs include the following: ADABAS, supplied by Software AG of North America for large IBM and IBM-compatible processors; IDMS, supplied by Cullinane Corporation for large IBM processors; IMS, supplied by IBM for large IBM processors; SYSTEM 2000, supplied by Intel Systems Corporation for large IBM, CDC Cyber series, and Univac 1000 series processors; and TOTAL, supplied by Cincom, which is available for more types of processors than any other DBMS.

SUMMARY POINTS

● A management information system (MIS) is a formal network using computers to provide information for decision making.
● A typical organization consists of three levels of decision making. Top-level management is concerned with strategic decisions; middle-level management is concerned with tactical decisions; and low-level management is concerned with operational decisions.
● An MIS can fairly easily supply low- and middle-level managers with the appropriate information, but MISs usually have fallen short of their goals for top-level management.
● An MIS must supply several types of reports to satisfy the needs of each level of user. Four of the most common types of reports are scheduled reports, exception reports, predictive reports, and demand reports.
● An MIS does not guarantee that a manager's decisions will be appropriate; however, it can be an invaluable decision aid.
● A major problem in designing an MIS is determining what information management needs.
● A decision support system (DSS) differs from an MIS in that an MIS

is associated with systems that emphasize structured or routine decisions, whereas a DSS is used to assist in relatively unstructured tasks.

● There are four basic design structures to consider when designing an MIS: centralized, hierarchical, distributed, and decentralized. Most organizations use some hybrid of these designs.

● A data base is a grouping of data fields structured to fit the information needs of multiple functions of an organization.

● The two faces of data design for a data base are physical design and logical design. Physical design refers to how data is physically stored in storage devices and how it is accessed. Logical design refers to how data is viewed by applications programs or individual users.

● A data base management system (DBMS) is a set of programs that makes the data in a data base readily available to its users. It allows users to simply refer to specific data the program needs rather than have to pay attention to the physical structure of the file.

● A DBMS has a number of operational and control features that deal with data access, identification, security, concurrency, and backup and recovery.

REVIEW QUESTIONS

1. What is an MIS? What is its goal?

2. Identify the three levels of management, and discuss the types of decisions that are typically made by each.

3. Why have most MISs fallen short of their goals in supplying appropriate information to top-level management?

4. Name and describe four typical reports produced by an MIS.

5. Will having an MIS guarantee that management's decisions will be appropriate? Why or why not?

6. What is a DSS? How does it differ from an MIS?

7. Discuss the four basic design structures of an MIS.

8. What is a data base? What are some of its advantages over maintaining separate data files?

9. Define the two basic approaches to the design of data for a data base.

10. What is a DBMS?

11. Define the methods, modes, and types of data base access that are associated with a typical DBMS.

12. Discuss the three methods by which a user can identify data to a DBMS.

13. List and discuss the four techniques used to protect a data base from unauthorized use, accidental or intentional alteration, or accidental or intentional destruction.

14. What is meant by the term concurrency? What are the techniques used to protect the integrity of data?

15. What are some of the ways in which a DBMS allows for backup and recovery of the data base?

PART V

COMPUTER IMPACT

COMPUTER SYSTEMS

LEARNING OBJECTIVES

After reading this chapter, you will be able to do the following:

☐ List the four major categories of computer systems.
☐ Define *word length,* and understand its significance in determining a computer's capabilities.
☐ Describe a bus, and understand its significance in determining a computer's capabilities.
☐ Understand and be able to discuss the general differences and similarities between the different classes of computers.
☐ Describe a micromainframe.

Chapter 16

INTRODUCTION   It is difficult to compare the computer industry with any other industry in existence today. The computer industry is a dynamic and unique one, because it is so closely tied to changes in technology. While the prices of most other products are increasing, prices of computers are decreasing. In fact, a person who purchases a computer today can receive more computer power at less cost than was possible less than a year ago. Since technological improvements constantly are being made, this trend probably will continue.

THE COMPUTER INDUSTRY

There is a broad range of machine sizes and capabilities from which to choose in selecting a computer system. It is becoming increasingly difficult, however, to distinguish among the different classifications of systems. The four major categories of computer systems are *supercomputers*, *mainframes*, *minicomputers*, and *microcomputers*, but there may be considerable overlap from one category to another in terms of size, cost, and capabilities. In the past, the larger a system was, the faster and more powerful it would be; however, today this is proving not to be true in many cases. Characteristics other than physical size must be examined to determine a system's power.

Word Length

One such distinction is made on the basis of word length and the overall size of primary memory. **Word length** is determined by the number of bits of information that can be stored in each memory location and that consequently can be manipulated by the CPU at one time. For example, a computer with an eight-bit word length can have up to eight bits in each memory location; in other words, it can represent numbers up to 256 (2^8). Usually more than one byte will be accessed and linked in processing, but additional time is spent in doing so. Thus, with longer word lengths—such as sixteen or thirty-two bits—more bits can be accessed at one time from a single location, and, in turn, processing time is faster for a given set of data. In addition, the more room a computer has in RAM, the more addressable primary storage it will have and the less time it will spend bringing data in from secondary storage. As described earlier, it is possible to store 64K (65,536) bits or even 256K (262,144) bits on a single chip. In the future, millions of bits probably will be stored on each chip, thus decreasing the size and cost of memory even more, while at the same time increasing speed.

Buses

Another difference between computers is the type of buses used. A **bus** can be thought of as an electronic pathway on which data must travel to go from one part of the computer to another (for example, from primary storage to the ALU or from the ALU to an output device). Buses differ in terms of address width, which is equivalent to how many bits can be transferred from an individual memory location. They also differ in how data is transmitted—in one direction at a time or in opposite directions at one time—to different locations in the computer. The larger the number of buses in a system and the greater the capabilities of each bus, the larger the amount of data that can be transferred simultaneously. The overall transfer speed from one point in the computer to another thus will increase, which in turn accelerates the overall processing speed.

Peripherals

Another distinguishing feature among computers is the number and type of peripherals that can be attached and the number of users who in turn can share computer resources. Generally, the larger the system, the more capabilities it will have for accommodating multiple users and complex applications.

Vendor and software support is another area that can differ among the four major categories of computers. Small systems generally have the least vendor support, whereas larger systems typically offer the most. This characteristic is beginnning to change, however, because of the ever-decreasing cost of hardware. Most computer manufacturers are beginning to see software and service as areas that can not only compensate for decreased hardware revenues, but also can generate high profits.

Whatever the major differences are or will be between one type of computer and another, the computer industry will remain a highly competitive one. Not only must vendors compete with those selling products in the same product class; now they also must compete with products in different classes with similar capabilities. For example, many of the high-end (highest cost) microcomputers now have capabilities that rival the low-end (lowest cost) minicomputers. An organization may use computers of varying sizes and capabilities that may be manufactured by several different vendors. Whatever the criteria may be for a particular user, the main objectives today in selecting one system over another are usually price, performance, and ease of use.

SUPERCOMPUTERS

Supercomputers, also referred to as **maxicomputers** or **monster computers,** are the largest, fastest, and most expensive computers in existence today. Only about forty of these powerful systems have been installed worldwide since the early 1970s.

Supercomputer Characteristics

Since the development of the first commercially sold computer, the UNIVAC I, the speed of large-scale computers has doubled nearly every two years. In addition to increased processing speeds, vast improvements in memory space capacity have been made. The most recent supercomputers have the capability of performing 100 million calculations per second and storing up to 4,194,304 sixty-four-bit words within memory.

The great improvements in speed and internal storage are due primarily to the steady decrease in size of microelectronic circuits. One of the earliest supercomputers, the ILLIAC IV, was the first large-scale computer to use silicon chips rather than iron alloy doughnut-shaped cores to store memory contents. Each chip had the capacity to store 256 bits, with the total machine memory capacity equivalent to 131,072 sixty-four-bit words. The ILLIAC IV was installed in 1972 at the Ames Research Center of the National Aeronautics and Space Administration (NASA), where it successfully solved some of the most difficult aerodynamic problems ever attempted by a computer.

Current Supercomputer Families

Today only two families of supercomputers are in operation or available for sale. One was built by Cray Research, Inc., and is called the CRAY-1 (see Figure 16–1). The first CRAY-1 was installed in 1976 at the Los Alamos Scientific Laboratory in New Mexico. Since then, nearly forty CRAY-1s—including one located at the Lawrence Livermore Laboratory in California for top-secret nuclear weapons research calculations—have

Figure 16–1 CRAY-1 Computer System

Computer Failure Avoidance

A computer gone haywire is not the nightmare of science fiction writers only. Businesses dread the prospect so much that some have installed spare computers as a backup system—always at great expense. Their thinking has been that the cost of a second (backup) system would be less than what they would lose if the computer actually went out of action. For example, Eastern Airlines says it could lose as much as twenty thousand dollars a minute in bookings if its computer went down. Nowadays, even some computer manufacturers are building "subsystem redundancy" into their computers. This provides an automatic second line of defense against malfunctioning. Other manufacturers, however, are looking to improved wiring and more complex ICs to make sure that the first breakdown never occurs.

been put into operation. The other supercomputer in existence today is the CYBER-205, developed by Control Data Corporation. The first CYBER-205 was purchased by the Meteorological Service of the United Kingdom. Several other CYBER-205s have been acquired for government, university, or private industry use. Two oil companies recently purchased CYBER-205s for solving complex petroleum and engineering computations.

Both the CRAY-1 and the CYBER-205 have a selling price of between ten million and fifteen million dollars, depending on the amount of fast memory, the type of peripherals, and other desired options. These supercomputers are designed to process long data words consisting of sixty-four bits and have a primary memory capacity of 4,096 bits per chip, or, as mentioned earlier, over four million words of sixty-four bits each. The cycle times (which is the time required to perform one addition) of the CYBER-205 and the CRAY-1 are 20 and 12.5 billionths of a second (nanoseconds), respectively. The longer cycle time of the CYBER-205 is due to the fact that it is much larger than the CRAY-1. Both machines pack a large amount of circuitry into a small space to minimize the distance that electricity must travel. (Electrical current in a theoretically resistance-free environment travels at the speed of light, which is 11.784 inches per nanosecond. In some machines, this becomes a speed consideration.) As a result, these supercomputers generate high levels of heat and must be kept cool by compressed Freon refrigerant that runs through special cooling channels.

Supercomputers can execute multiple program steps simultaneously rather than one at a time, as other types of computers do. It is estimated that during the next five years, one hundred to two hundred supercomputers will be sold worldwide to be used in applications involving meteorology, aerodynamics, seismology, nuclear physics, and new areas requiring high-speed calculations.

MAINFRAMES

The popularity of mainframes was highest in the 1960s, when the emphasis in computer technology was on building larger and faster central computers to handle all the processing needs of an organization. Mainframes are still used by large organizations with high processing requirements; however, the trend is more toward smaller systems such as minicomputers and microcomputers, which allow for decentralized or distributed processing (see Figure 16–2).

Mainframe Characteristics

Differing sizes and capabilities characterize the **mainframes** that are marketed today; however, these systems have certain common features that distinguish them from other types of systems. First, mainframes have longer word lengths (usually either twenty-four, thirty-two, thirty-six, forty-eight, or sixty-four bits). Thus, it is possible to access more data at one time than is possible with eight- or sixteen-bit minicomputers or microcomputers.

Mainframes also have faster processing speeds than smaller systems. The modular construction of memory is one reason for this increased speed. If memory is divided into three modules, for example, it is possible to have simultaneous access to data stored in each of these modules. In this way, three times as much data can be accessed and brought into memory at the same time. As is true of most minicomputers, dif-

Figure 16–2
Mainframe

The Sting

The high stakes—and high risks—involved in computer supremacy surfaced with a vengeance in June 1982, when three Hitachi Ltd. executives were arrested for attempting to buy trade secrets about IBM computer technology from an FBI agent masquerading as an industrial spy. The buying and selling of scientific secrets is almost commonplace, but what set this one affair apart from hundreds of others was the relatively high corporate rank of the executives involved. Not only did it demonstrate the degree to which one company may go to gain an edge over a competitor; it also pointed out how easily a subtle international trade war can explode into an open one.

ferent parts of the mainframe are linked through separate buses, which also contribute to increased processing speeds.

The speed of mainframes is commonly measured in terms of millions of instructions per second (MIPS). The VAX 780, a popular mainframe developed by Digital Equipment Corporation (DEC), for instance, can handle one MIPS. The current limit of mainframe memory capacity is sixteen megabytes (a megabyte equals approximately one million bytes—actually, 2^{20}, or 1,048,576, bytes), and some of the medium or small mainframe systems have space for as little as one-half megabyte. Mainframes also use more secondary storage than minicomputers, since applications usually involve large amounts of data. In addition, the operating system is generally very large and sophisticated, adding to the need for additional primary and secondary storage space.

Mainframe Purchase Considerations

The cost of a mainframe ranges between $200,000 and $1 million or more. The purchase of a mainframe involves considerations other than just the cost of the system, however. Although today's mainframes are much smaller than those developed a few years ago, the computer, along with its peripheral devices, still may take up a sizable space. Considerable thought must be given not only to the location of the system, but also to the security protections that will be installed to guard against fire, flood, or other types of disaster. Mainframes cannot be plugged into standard electrical outlets, as minicomputers and microcomputers can. Special transformers, sometimes costing several thousands of dollars, are required to generate the necessary electrical power. Despite the small size of mainframes due to LSI technology, the computer—along with its numerous printers, CRTs, disk drives, and other peripheral devices—still can generate a considerable amount of heat. Special air-conditioning systems therefore must be installed, not only to provide for the comfort of operators, but also to insure that the system operates accurately and avoids the problems caused by severe temperature increases.

As mentioned earlier, the operating systems of mainframes are more sophisticated than those of smaller computers. The system usually handles both batch mode and direct-access processing in a variety of languages. Software can be provided that allows for both multiprogramming and multiprocessing, as described in Chapter 10. Since hardware is becoming one of the least expensive components of the total system, more emphasis is being placed on developing a variety of software packages and services that will be made available to the user. For example, very powerful software systems, such as CICS, IMS, or OSVS, can be acquired for several thousands of dollars. A wide variety of application packages also is available that provides such capabilities as industrial and manufacturing control, business and financial forecasting, payroll and human resources management, and numerous other applications.

Mainframe Vendors

Several large and relatively stable general computer manufacturers are major competitors in the mainframe market segment: IBM, Burroughs, Amdahl, National Cash Register (NCR), Control Data Corporation (CDC), Sperry Univac, DEC, and Honeywell. There are foreign competitors as well, such as Hitachi from Japan and West Germany's Nixdorf Corporation. The mainframe market is highly competitive because of the trend toward smaller, less-expensive microcomputers and minicomputers. Smaller systems that are less costly and more "user friendly" than large computers can be substituted in many instances for mainframes.

In an effort to gain a competitive edge in the computer market, Intel Corporation, the forerunner in silicon chip technology, has developed a microminiaturized mainframe referred to as a **micromainframe.** The CPU of the computer consists of three tiny silicon chips small enough to fit on a fingertip. The total system is as powerful as a medium-sized mainframe at about one-tenth the size and cost. The system is designed to handle numerous functions in addition to those characteristic of the larger-sized mainframes. One of the most distinguishing features is the micromainframe's ability to perform different tasks simultaneously. For example, the micromainframe can send and store messages, handle electronic mail, or control different types of robots or machines—all at the same time. The micromainframe is still in its beginning stages of development, although it is expected to become more user friendly and thus more popular in the near future.

MINICOMPUTERS

The **minicomputer** was introduced in the late 1960s to perform special-purpose industrial and factory tasks. This type of computer was smaller

COMPUTERS IN MEDICINE

Advances in medical research and treatment have been made possible through computer technology. Computerized equipment is used extensively in the health care field for laboratory testing and analysis, clerical and administrative procedures, computer-assisted diagnosis, and life support and information retrieval functions.

1. Patients at Parkland Memorial Hospital in Dallas, Texas, are admitted with the aid of computer terminals that record patient information, type of medical problem, etc. These computerized patient records are part of the modern Patient Online Information System (POIS) developed at the large trauma hospital. **2.** Medical testing is made easier with computers. **3.** Computers are used extensively in the health-care profession. Large amounts of patient information can be stored (such as medical history and test results) and then retrieved.

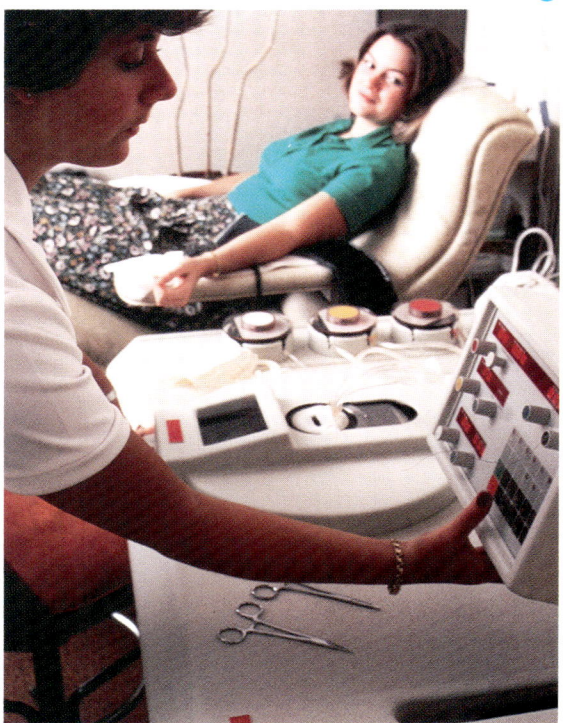

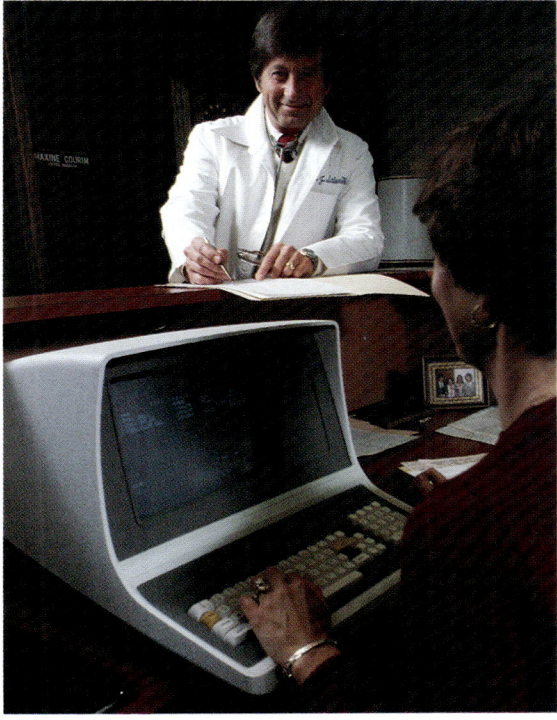

*Computers in Medicine—
continued.* **4.** Medical
administrators review
computerized patient
information (financial
and insurance
information, personal
data, and the patient's
medical information).
5. GTE's Medical
Information Network
Service offers
physicians and medical
researchers a wide
variety of information.
Such information
includes: drug
information services,
disease and diagnostic
services, educational
services, business and
professional services,
and general medical
information and
literature. **6.** Computers
assist the local
pharmacist.

7. Computers are used in laboratories for storage and analysis of specialized tests. **8.** After data has been entered into the computer from special chemical tests, information is printed out. **9.** Here, a special system tracks and measures blood flow through the brain enabling physicians to diagnose blood flow impairments in the brain; it discloses the area and the extent of the damage.

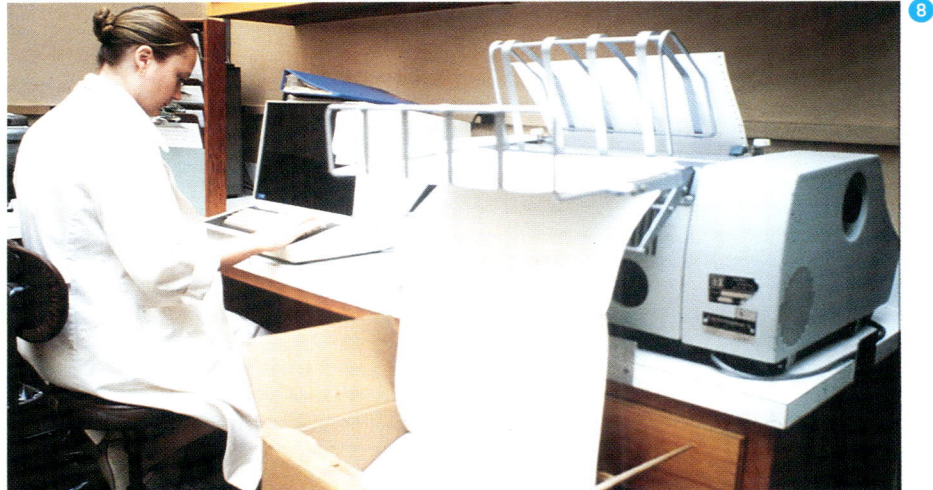

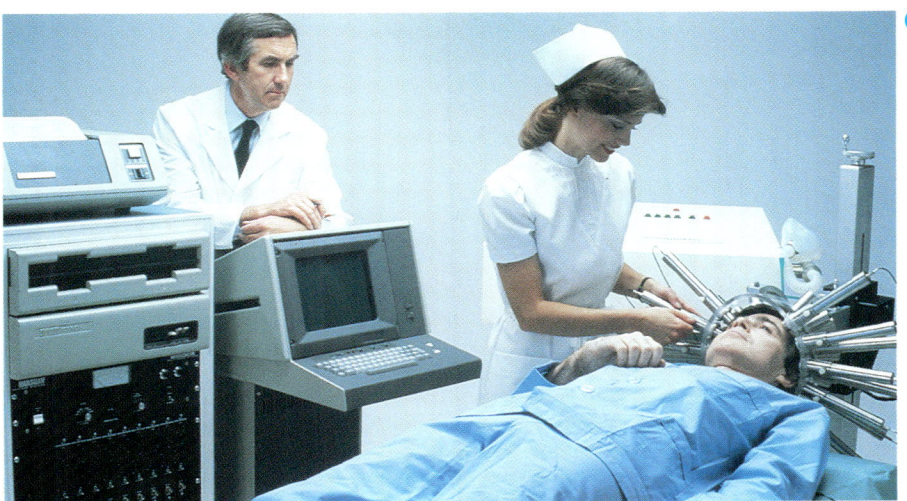

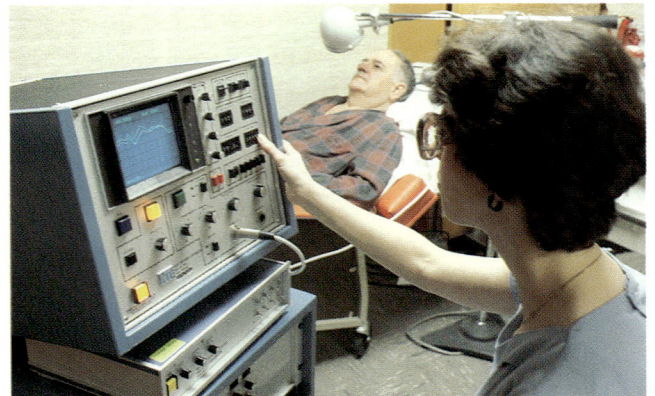

Computers in Medicine—continued.
10. Equipment similar to that in the intensive care units is used to monitor patient's in the Sleep Disorder Clinic. Patients with sleep disorders are monitored for several evenings to determine whether the disorder is physiological or psychological. **11.** A physician reviews a CT scan of the brain. Eyes and the nose can be seen at the top of the scan. **12.** Through the use of brain CT scans and special tests, brain activity can be seen. This high magnification scan shows activity in the cortex (the outer layer of brain tissue).

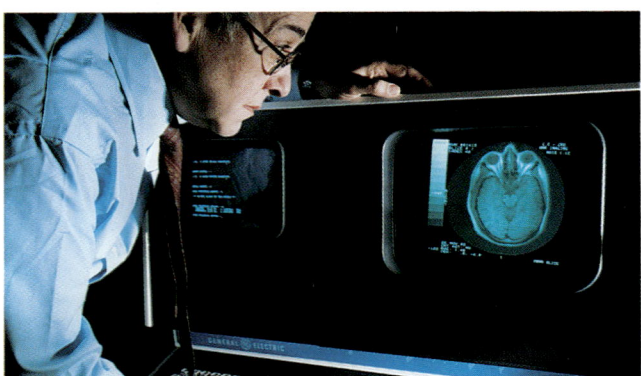

13. A computerized cell analysis machine is used in a medical laboratory. This machine locates and identifies cells from a tissue sample. **14.** This special system has capabilities for both heart and blood vessel imaging. The system is mobile and is easy to use with existing x-ray systems. **15.** A radiologist views a computerized image and reviews a printout of information regarding the image.

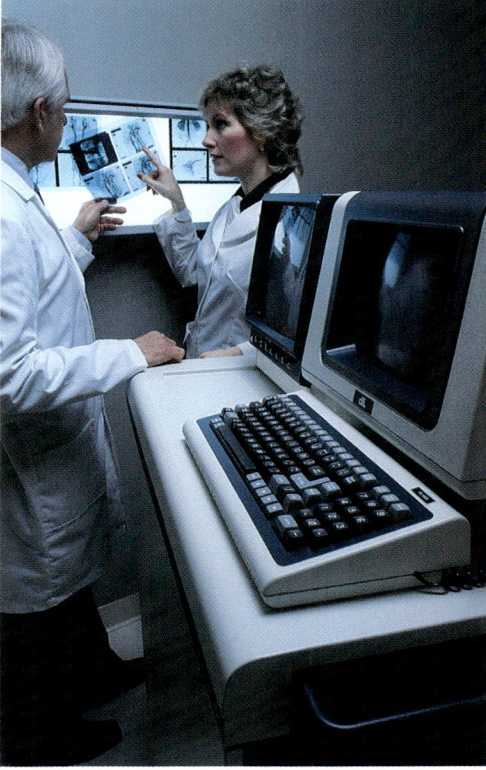

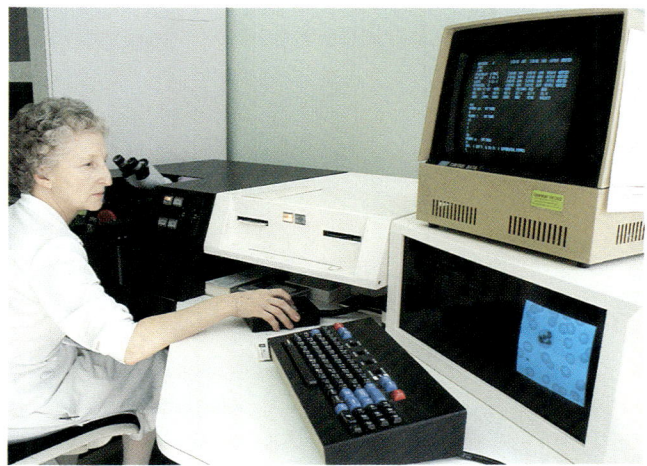

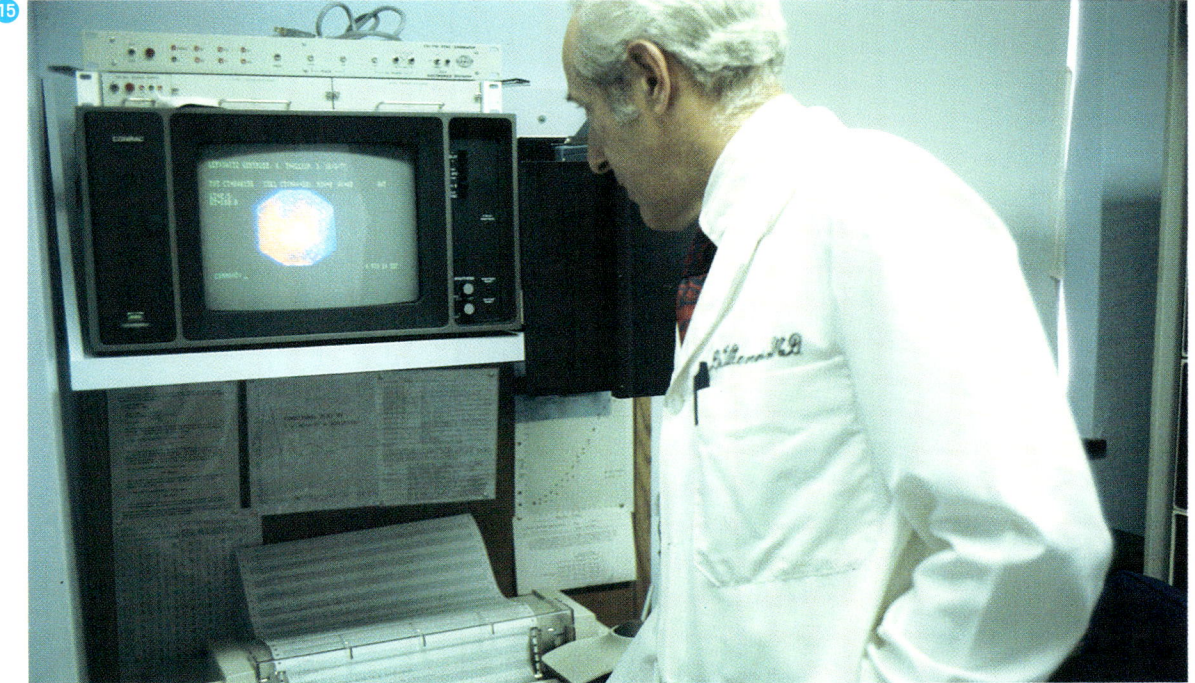

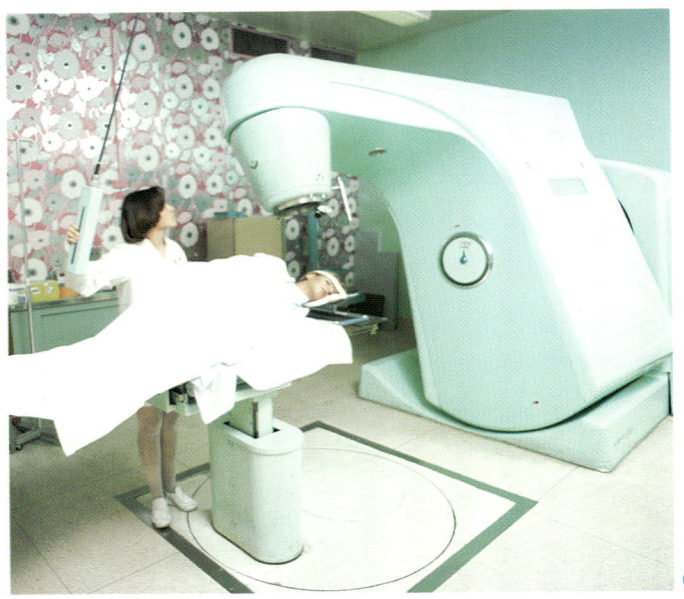

Computers in Medicine—continued. **16.** The linear accelerator performs radiation treatment on a cancer patient. One of the advantages of the linear accelerator is the accuracy with which the radiation fields can be defined. The equipment allows more precise definition of the dosage area so that the tumor receives a larger percentage of the dosage, with minimal effect on healthy tissues. **17.** An instrument which uses light to analyze blood is used in an intensive care nursery; it is used to determine the risk of brain damage to a jaundiced baby. This instrument produces the results that are at least 10 times faster and far easier than comparable blood chemistry measurements.

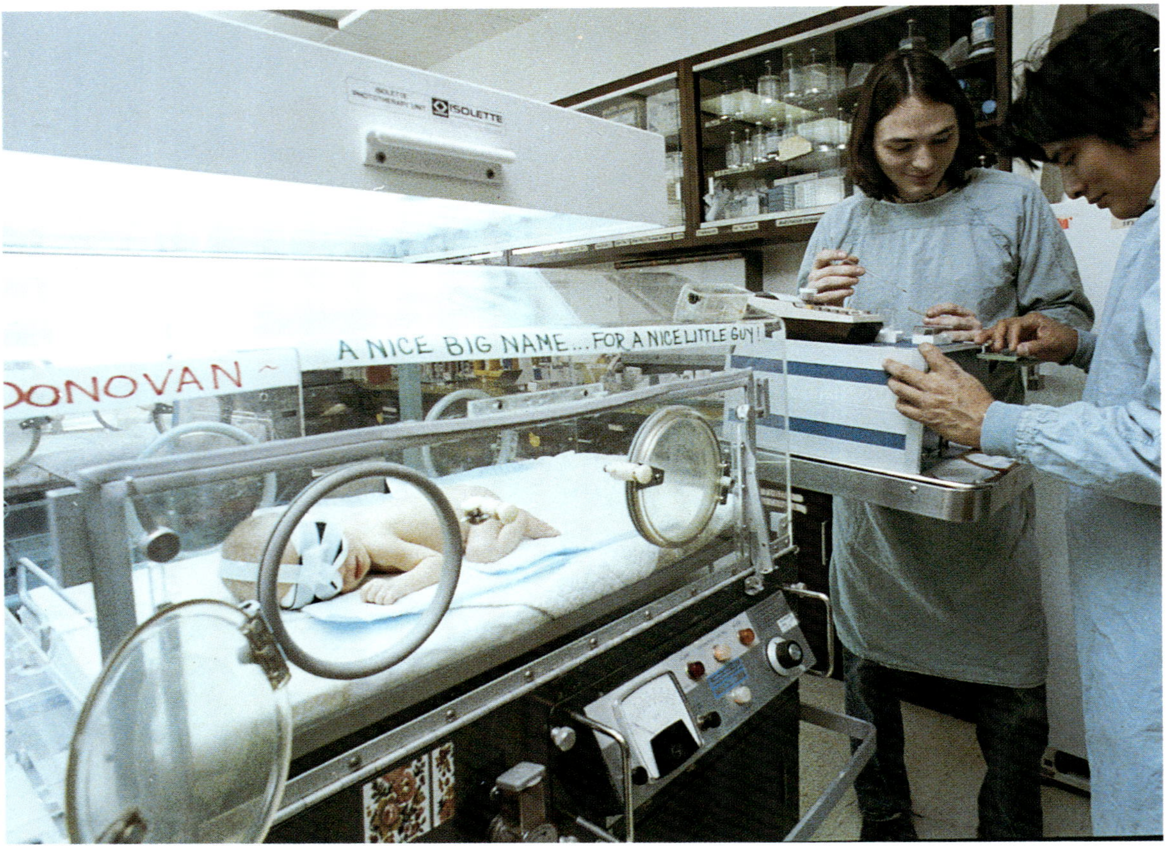

18. This portable monitor allows patients to continue normal daily activities while blood pressure and heart rate are measured and recorded throughout the day. This information is stored in computerized form for subsequent display and analysis by a physician. **19.** In the Heart Lab at Parkland Memorial Hospital, Dallas, Texas, cardiologists can visualize the pumping heart through a computer assisted procedure. The images produced on a CRT show the heart in action, which can help reveal cardiac problems before they materialize into life-threatening attacks.

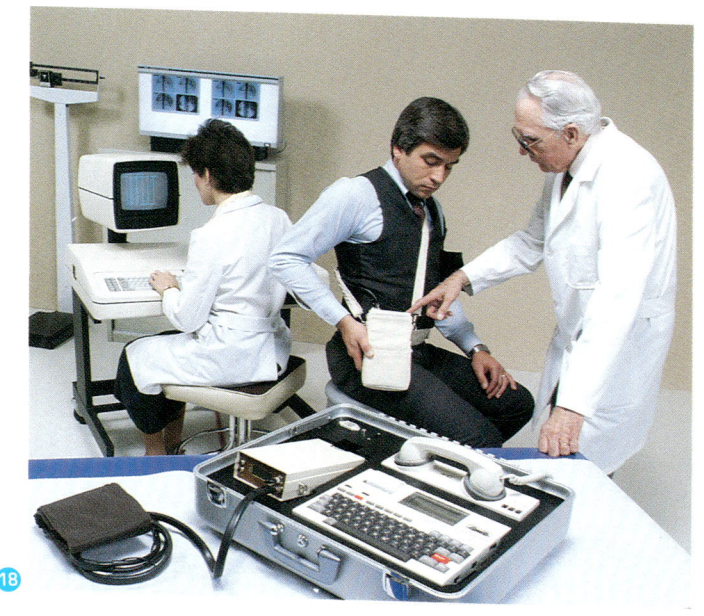

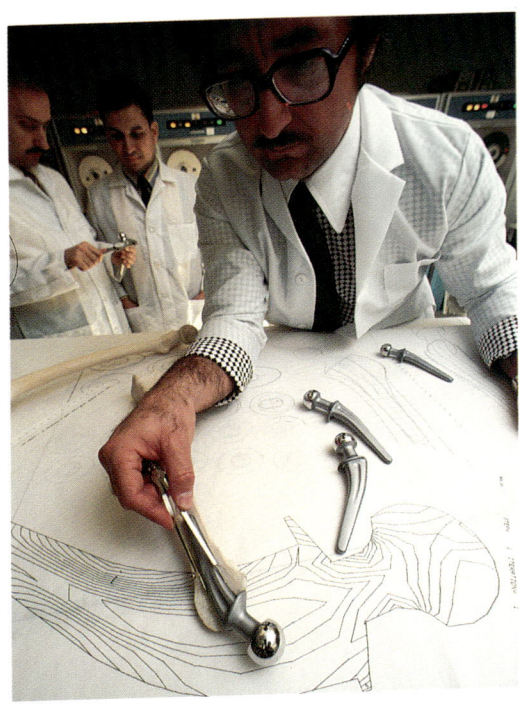

Computers in Medicine—continued. **20.** This hip prosthesis (an artificial hip bone) was designed by a computer to maximize resistance to stress. **21.** With the "computerized stimulation and feedback system" developed by Dr. Jerrold Petrofsky at Wright State University, Nan Davis, a WSU student paralyzed from the waist down, has taken several steps. The computer is used to control electrical signals to Nan's leg muscles causing them to contract.

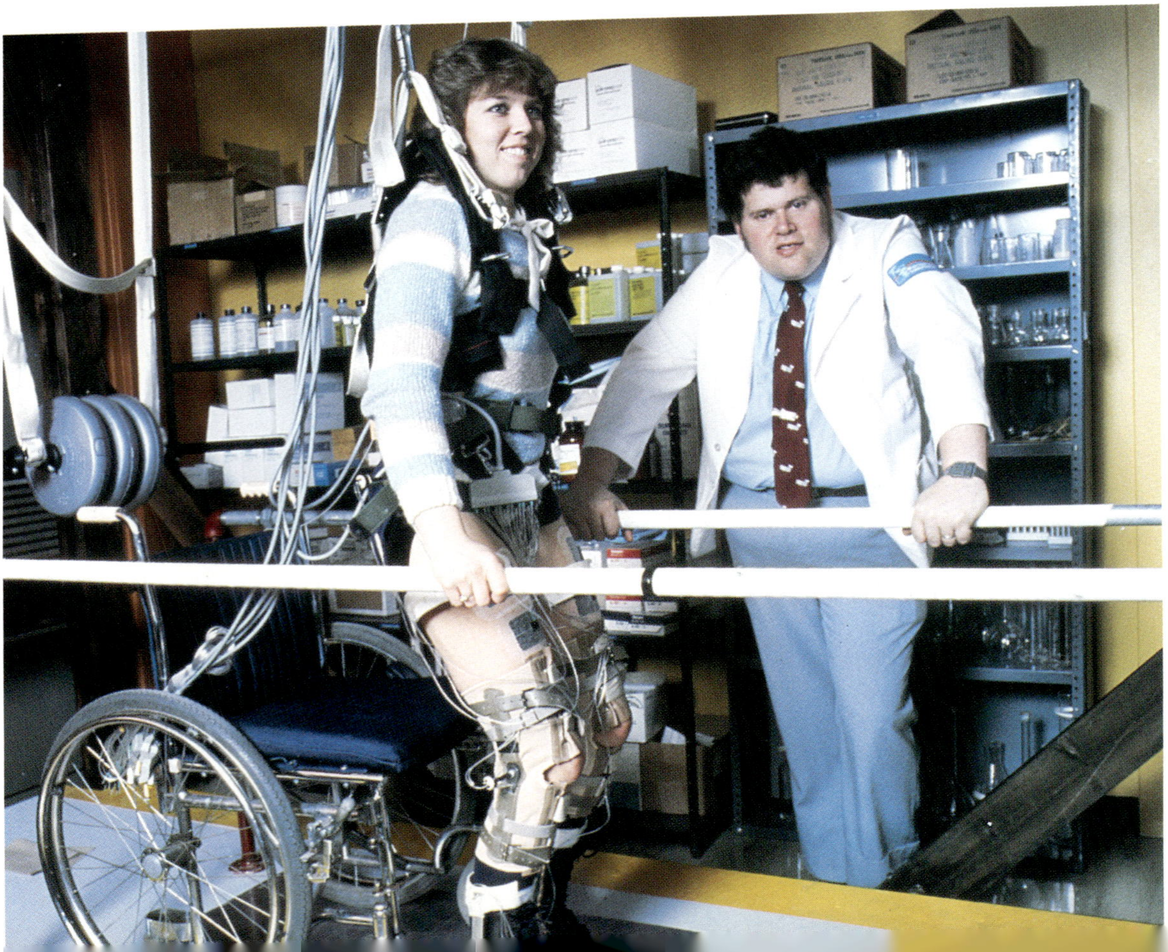

than the larger and more powerful mainframes and, thus, was referred to as a "mini," or "minimal," computer (see Figure 16–3). Some of the most common business-oriented peripheral devices could not be used with the earlier minicomputers. It was not possible, for example, to attach card readers, high-speed printers, or magnetic tape and disk drives.

Until 1972, the major applications utilizing minicomputers involved control, such as directing machine tools or maintaining constant temperatures. During this period, the microcomputer was developed and began to replace the minicomputer in such applications. The minicomputer then evolved into a more general purpose machine. Improvements were made that allowed the system to be used in many other areas, thus making it more versatile.

Minicomputer Characteristics

Today's minicomputers accommodate peripheral equipment such as CRT terminals, disks, tapes, and printers; minicomputers are generally very simple to connect to other systems as well. Because of their small size, minicomputers do not require their own computer room, but instead are placed in the individual departments in which they are used. Expensive air-conditioning and electrical arrangements are not required, since these computers generate little, if any, heat during operation and need only be plugged into a standard electrical outlet. Most data is entered by users via a CRT as transactions occur rather than through submission of jobs in a batch run. In this way, the minicomputer provides the capability of updating files interactively with the user in real-time processing.

The cost, speed, storage capacity, and other characteristics of different types of minicomputers can vary greatly. Some of the high-end microcomputers are not powerful enough to be exact replacements for low-end minicomputers, but they may be adequate and less costly substitutes for them. By the same token, high-end minicomputers are com-

Figure 16–3
Minicomputer System

petitive with low-end mainframes, so the distinction between various types of computers,—minicomputers, microcomputers, and mainframes—is becoming increasingly blurred.

Minicomputer Hardware

In general, most minicomputers have greater storage capacity and higher processing speeds than microcomputers. Word lengths are usually sixteen bits, although the high-end microcomputers now use thirty-two-bit words. The size of memory that can be addressed directly is expanded from 65,536 characters in sixteen-bit systems to over four billion characters with thirty-two-bit word length. Another reason for increased speed with minicomputers is that they use separate buses to connect parts of the system rather than use common buses, as microcomputers do. For example, one bus would be used to link memory with one input device, and another bus would join memory and the control unit. In this way, it is possible to avoid time delays resulting from waiting to access a single available bus.

The cost of a minicomputer typically ranges between about fifteen thousand and twenty-five thousand dollars; an additional expense commonly is added for periodic maintenance. More languages, such as assembly language, RPG, and full versions of COBOL, are available on minicomputers than on microcomputers because of the additional memory space. Whereas the microprocessor in a microcomputer is contained on a single chip, the processor of a minicomputer consists of several chips.

The instruction set of a minicomputer is generally more complex than that of a microcomputer. Microprograms stored in chips within read-only memory (ROM) and containing the instructions needed to control system functions generally are supplied by the manufacturer. Additional chips can be added to expand the system's capabilities. It is also possible to implement multiprogramming with minicomputers, since the operating systems are more sophisticated than those of microcomputers.

Minicomputer Software and Peripherals

More expensive peripherals, such as high-speed tape drives, 14-inch Winchester disks that can hold billions of bytes within secondary memory, and additional high-speed printers, can be attached to minicomputer systems. In addition, minicomputers tend to have better software support than microcomputers, since they have been available longer. A current disadvantage of minicomputer software, although probably only temporary, is that it is vendor specific and therefore less flexible than packaged microcomputer software. A microcomputer developed by one manufacturer can accommodate packaged software developed by numerous other vendors as long as it has the appropriate microprocessor and

The Microcomputer Stretch

Users of microcomputer systems have long noticed that people who spend too much time at their terminals experience tired backs and necks and eyestrain. Generally, they feel restless and fatigued. What they need to do is stretch and exercise a few of those strained muscles.

Now microcomputer users can do just that. They can exercise those muscles, and they can do it without leaving their terminals. Verbatim, the world's largest manufacturer of floppy disks, and fitness expert Denise Katnich have produced an exercise floppy.

"Tone up at the Terminals" is an exercise routine contained on a floppy disk. It can be used right at the terminal and concentrates on exercises designed to relieve back and neck strain and eyestrain. Altogether, the disk contains twenty exercises that require little space and no training on the part of the user.

type of operating system. Some of the more powerful microcomputers are even able to accommodate minicomputer software. To remain competitive with microcomputers, minicomputer vendors must incorporate more flexibility in the software made available to users.

The minicomputer market has experienced tremendous growth since DEC introduced the first minicomputer, the PDP-2, in 1965. Numerous competitors have since entered the market; among them are Data General, Honeywell, Hewlett-Packard, Texas Instruments, Wang, and IBM (to name just a few). Although DEC still remains the leader, other competitors are steadily gaining, among them such international corporations as Fujitsu and Hitachi, both Japanese companies. The high growth rate of the market appears to be stabilizing, so companies in this segment are beginning to concentrate on more efficient production and other capabilities, such as software servicing, in their efforts to remain profitable.

MICROCOMPUTERS

Technological advances leading to increased capabilities and falling costs have bolstered the widespread use of the microcomputer. Its present uses range from "home" applications, such as budgeting family finances, to the creation of distributed computing networks.

The prefix **micro** should be interpreted not in terms of capability, but rather in terms of physical size and cost. Typical microcomputers today can outperform the mainframes of a decade ago; because of their low cost and portability, they have contributed to the widespread use of distributed computing systems.

Microcomputer Characteristics

A closer look reveals some of the main features that distinguish microcomputers from large computers. First and foremost is the physical size of the computer. As the name **microcomputer** implies, these computers are small enough to fit nicely on a desk. Recently, portable microcomputers have been introduced that can be transported easily from one location to another, some small enough to be tucked away in a briefcase.

The cost of a microcomputer is significantly lower than that of larger computers, ranging anywhere from several thousands of dollars for a system such as the IBM PC to under fifty dollars for systems such as the Timex/Sinclair. Figure 16–4 shows some of the popular microcomputers.

Microcomputers should not be confused with microprocessors. A microprocessor is the integrated circuits (ICs) etched on a chip and enclosed in a protective casing (see Figure 16–5). Microprocessors are used not only in microcomputers, but in calculators, microwave ovens, automobiles, and a host of other devices. They are the heart of a microcomputer, but the computer proper consists of both the microprocessor CPU and the associated RAM and ROM memories. When speaking about a microcomputer, most people also mean the peripheral devices such as monitors, printers, keyboards, and the like.

Architectural Evolution of Microcomputers

Technological advances constantly increase the capabilities of microcomputers; however, a clear separation still exists between the computing power of microcomputers and minicomputers. One of the reasons for this is the word size that the computers can use. Most of the microcomputers available have eight-bit words; however, the sixteen-bit words found on the IBM PC are becoming the accepted standard. Most mainframes have word sizes ranging from twenty-four to sixty-four bits. Having a smaller word size results in microcomputers' having a slower processing time, since they cannot access as much data at one time.

The number and sophistication of the buses found in microcomputers are lower than in larger computers. The buses in most larger computers can transport data in both directions simultaneously. Microcomputers, however, transmit data in only one direction at a time (similar to half-duplex transmission in a data communications system), resulting in delays while a bus completes transfer to one part of the computer before another transfer can be made.

The internal memory of a microcomputer is also smaller than that of larger computers. The typical microcomputer comes equipped with anywhere from 4K to 64K bytes, and some can be upgraded to 512K or more through the addition of additional memory boards. Because their primary memories are small, microcomputers require secondary storage media; these greatly decrease processing speed.

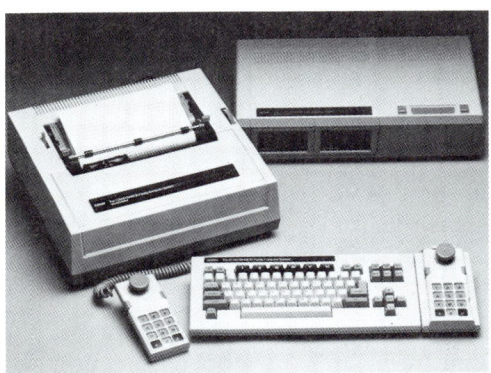
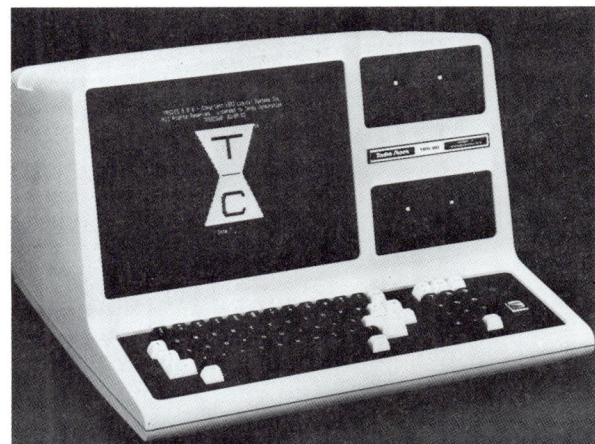

Figure 16–4 Some Popular Microcomputers

One advance has been the development of **cache memory** for micro-computers, a feature previously available only for minicomputers and larger computers. Cache memory allows the microprocessor to access more than one instruction from secondary storage and leave the extra data in the cache (a small, very fast addition to primary storage) until

Computers in Every Library, Hotel, Shopping Center, Airport . . .

One of the many effects of the computer revolution has been a renewed interest in libraries. Librarians across the country agree that it is nearly impossible to keep the computer books on the shelves. However, many libraries are keeping more than just books about computers.

Coin-operated computers are becoming a common sight in today's libraries. Part of this craze is due to Kim Cohan, a young entrepreneur in California. In 1981, at age seventeen,

Cohan bought a coin-operated microcomputer and installed it in the Malvern Ark Public Library. The venture was so successful that he dropped out of college and formed Micro Timesharing, Inc. By 1983 Cohan's company had made the coin-operated computer systems available to over 1.7 million library members and was no longer able to keep up with the orders. Other companies soon joined in the market. In addition to use in U.S. public libraries, these companies see a growing market for coin-operated computers in hotels, shopping malls, airports . . .

ready for use. This eliminates the time that the microprocessor spends waiting for data from disk.

Because microcomputers have had such a dramatic impact on the ways in which computers are being used and on who uses them, the entire next chapter will be devoted to discussing some of their characteristics. Advances continually occur; microcomputers soon may rival in power even the most powerful minicomputers. Some of what the future may hold is discussed next.

Figure 16–5
Microprocessor on a Chip

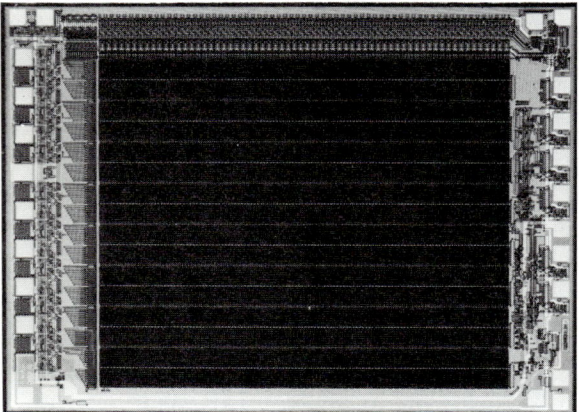
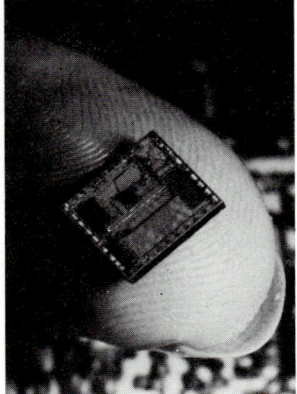

A FIFTH GENERATION?

In an effort to gain a competitive edge in the international computer market, Japan currently is engaged in extensive research to develop what it refers to as a fifth generation of computers. Although its success is thought to be unlikely by many major computer companies in the United States, the new technology, Japan promises, will be more humanlike. Fifth generation machines will use AI and, ideally, will be able to "think" and communicate somewhat like humans.

The fifth generation computers will not be programmed in the conventional manner. Instead of requiring programmers to outline specific steps, these machines will be able to determine how to solve a particular problem on their own. These computers, in fact, will have "common sense." The language chosen for programming fifth generation computers is known as **PROLOG** (for **PROgramming in LOGic**). This language was chosen because of its ability to express not only equations, but also logical relationships found between objects.

Fully backed by the Japanese government in addition to eight large Japanese firms, the project is not expected to yield its first substantial results until the 1990s. In the United States, a few companies—DEC, Xerox, Texas Instruments, and Hewlett-Packard—have begun to do serious work in AI, but on a much smaller scale than the Japanese. Whether or not the fifth generation of computers as envisioned by the Japanese will ever become a reality remains to be seen; in the meantime, however, computers will continue to become simpler and more economical to use.

● The four major categories of computer systems are supercomputers, mainframes, minicomputers, and microcomputers.

● Word length is the number of bits of information that can be stored in each memory location and, consequently, manipulated by the CPU at one time.

● A bus is an electronic pathway on which data travels from one part of the computer to another.

● Price, performance, and ease of use have become the main criteria selecting a computer system.

● Supercomputers, also referred to as *maxicomputers* or *monster computers*, are very expensive systems capable of processing very large amounts of data and performing millions of calculations per second. They are used primarily by large organizations and government agencies that have to support large data bases and complex calculations.

● Mainframes come in a wide variety of sizes and capabilities. They have faster processing speeds, have more memory, and allow the connection of a greater number of peripherals than do smaller systems. They typically are used by large organizations with extensive processing requirements.

● Minicomputers are smaller and have less processing power than mainframes; however, some high-end minicomputers now are capable of competing with some low-end mainframes.

● Microcomputers take their name from their compact size and low cost. They have made the use of computers feasible in small businesses and homes. Advances in technology have been steadily increasing microcomputer capacity while keeping both their size and cost at a minimum.

REVIEW QUESTIONS

1. Define word length. Is it important?
2. What significance does word length have on the overall processing speed of a computer?
3. What is the significance of having a larger amount of RAM in a computer?
4. Define a bus.
5. How does a bus affect the overall processing speed of a computer?
6. Describe the characteristics of a supercomputer.
7. Describe the characteristics of a mainframe.
8. Describe the characteristics of a minicomputer.
9. Describe the characteristics of a microcomputer.
10. What is a micromainframe?
11. Do you agree that there is a fifth generation of computers? Why or why not?
12. What are some uses of supercomputer systems? Of mainframes? Of minicomputer systems? Of microcomputer systems?
13. How have recent trends in the computer industry affected computer vendors?
14. What factors should a prospective buyer of a computer system consider before deciding to purchase a particular class of computer?
15. Discuss some typical uses for each class of computer.

MICROCOMPUTERS AND PERSONAL COMPUTING

LEARNING OBJECTIVES

After reading and studying this chapter, you will be able to do the following:

☐ Know what is meant by the terms *personal computer* and *home computer*.

☐ Describe and discuss the basic hardware of a personal computer, and identify important hardware-buying considerations.

☐ Understand the importance of the type of operating system used by a particular computer.

☐ Discuss some applications of the personal computer.

Chapter 17

INTRODUCTION

The previous chapter presented some of the characteristics that distinguish microcomputers from minicomputers, mainframes, and supercomputers. This chapter will elaborate on some of the microcomputer's characteristics and discuss some important considerations for purchasing a microcomputer.

We have all heard of *personal computers* or *home computers*. Many people interpret these terms as meaning small size and low cost. To some extent this is true, but *personal* really refers to the fact that the user has direct access to and control over that computer. Users can update, edit, or completely change what is being done with the computer whenever they wish. The user has *control;* this differs from the institutionalized control found in many organizations, where even if users have access to computing power, how and when they can use it are generally restricted. In the institutionalized control case, users typically must adapt to the program rather than adapt the program to fit their particular needs.

HARDWARE

This survey of personal computers will begin with a discussion of some of the associated hardware: microprocessors, memory chips, secondary storage devices, VDTs, keyboards, and printers. It also will look at some of the extras that are available, such as light pens and joysticks, plus a few of the hardware cards that can be installed to enhance the computing power of a machine.

Microprocessors

The first piece of hardware—and the most important we will consider—is the microprocessor chip, which contains the CPU. The CPU is the "brain" of the computer—the place where all the work takes place (the calculating, comparing, manipulating, and controlling). All this is done extremely quickly, approaching speeds of millions of instructions per second. (Consider that the typical CPU in a microcomputer is about half the size of a thumbnail!) Different types of microprocessor chips are used in the various personal computers (see Table 17–1). These include the Intel 8080, Zilog Z-80, Motorola 6800, and Synertek and MOS Technology 6502. These particular types are distinguished by many variations. The basic difference between them is in their instruction sets, that is, in the number of different types of instructions that can be executed and the speed at which their execution takes place.

Because the CPU executes instructions so fast, some sort of memory must be available—as in larger machines—where the instructions can be accessed easily by the computer in order to make efficient use of its capability. Memory is directly connected to the CPU of the microcomputer. It is the place where instructions and data are stored or accessed

Table 17-1 POPULAR COMPUTERS AND MICROPROCESSOR CHIPS USED

Computer	Microprocessor Chip	Word Length
Apple II Plus and IIe	6502	Eight bits
Apple III	6502A	Eight bits
Atari 400 and 800	6502	Eight bits
Commodore 64	6510	Eight bits
Commodore VIC 20	6502A	Eight bits
IBM Personal Computer	8088	Sixteen bits
Osborne 1	Z-80A	Eight bits
Sinclair ZX81	Z-80A	Eight bits
Texas Instruments 91/4A	TI 9900	Sixteen bits
TRS-80 Model III	Z-80	Eight bits

by the CPU. Memory also can contain the results of the execution of instructions by the CPU. This type of memory, usually implemented in chips like the microprocessor itself, generally is referred to as **random-access memory,** or **RAM.** The typical microcomputer has anywhere from 4K bytes of RAM to an average of around 64K; in some, such as the IBM XT, the standard is 128K internal memory. Many vendors, as well as outside manufacturers, supply memory boards that can be plugged directly into one of a personal computer's slots to increase its RAM capacity. The standard minimum for these hardware boards typically is 64K of RAM; they usually can be upgraded to 256K, although as much as one megabyte can be added to some. Figure 17-1 shows an example of an add-on memory board.

A second type of memory found in microcomputers is **read-only memory,** or **ROM.** This type of memory cannot be written to (recorded in) and cannot be used for storing user instructions or data. The ROM can only be read; it is installed by manufacturers to perform specific tasks. For example, the BASIC language in some personal computers comes hard wired in ROM chips. In this case, no disk has to be read in order to load BASIC, and valuable RAM space is not used to store the language. The CPU and its memory chips (both RAM and ROM) make up what is known as the computer proper. All other hardware devices, such as printers, VDTs, and so on, are peripherals. Each of the various brands of personal computers contains a CPU and memory, but the type and number of peripherals available can differ greatly.

Secondary Storage Devices

Personal computers generally use two types of secondary data storage: cassettes and floppy disks. Others are available, including hard disks and microfloppies, but today their use is limited.

Most low-cost personal computers have cassettes readily available for use. It is not necessary to buy a special unit; almost any home audiocas-

Figure 17–1 Add-on
Memory Board

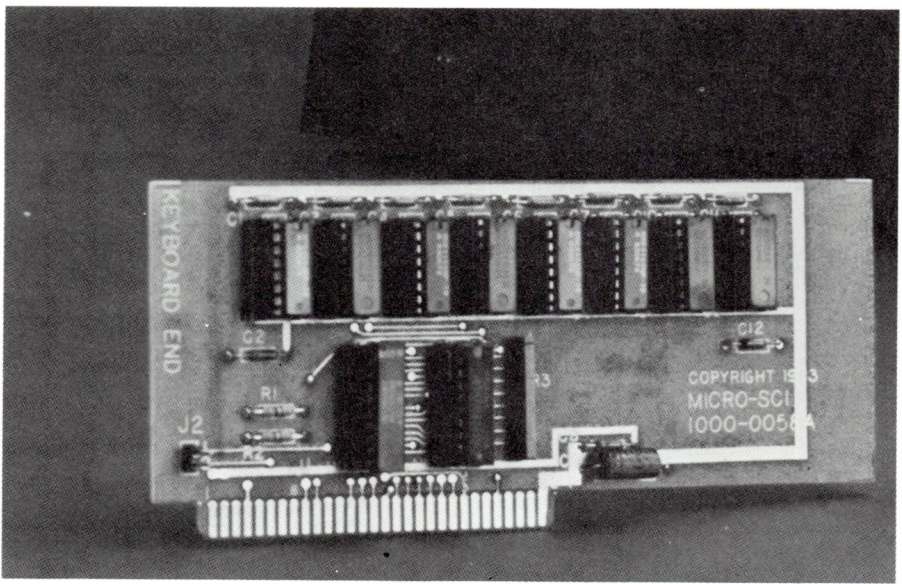

sette unit will work. Some cheaper cassette units, however, may not
have a constant tape speed and could cause some data retrieval problems. Cassettes are a low-price option that the user may find acceptable
for temporary storage of short programs and data that is suitable for
sequential access. However, loading cassettes into memory for long programs or for large amounts of data manipulation becomes tedious. This
is because of the relative slowness as compared with other peripheral
storage media and the fact that programs and data must be stored and
accessed sequentially. A tape counter is highly recommended to help
keep track of the location of particular programs and data stored on cassette tape and thereby reduce search time.

The most widely used form of secondary storage on personal computers today is the floppy disk, or diskette. Floppies overcome the drawbacks of cassette tapes, but at a higher price. A single disk can hold
relatively large chunks of programs and data, and it can access them
randomly at many times the speed of magnetic tape. Floppies are available in two standard sizes: 8 inches and 5¼-inches (see Figure 17–2). A
new 3-inch microfloppy disk recently was introduced but applications
software for this diskette is still very limited, and standard formats remain to be developed. Floppies now have storage capacities ranging from
approximately 100K to 1 megabyte (one million bytes) for 5¼-inch disks
and from 125K to 1.2 megabytes for 8-inch disks. However, an increase
in storage capacity can be expected to push the upper boundaries even
further in the near future.

Data on a floppy disk is stored as magnetized spots in tracks, which
are addressed by track number and sector number. A standard 8-inch
disk contains seventy-seven tracks and twenty-six sectors, whereas a
minifloppy disk (5¼ inch) has thirty-five tracks and eighteen sectors.

Computing Genealogy

Family computing has taken a new turn and now is computing families. Since the airing of the television miniseries based on Alex Haley's book *Roots,* more families have become interested in tracing their roots.

One of the most useful tools for a genealogist is a personal computer. It can be invaluable for storing the mounds of information unearthed in the research. For example, one man found forty-five thousand relatives dating back to the 1600s on a single branch of his family tree. Without a computer, cataloging even minor information on that one line would be a monstrous struggle with paperwork.

Many other uses for computers in genealogy are being projected for the future. Howard Nurse, president of a genealogy software firm called Commsoft, points to the fantastic possibilities. "Most of us will see the day when a computerized family history can be more than just statistics and a limited biography. Pictures, voices, images, and wisdom from the past will become part of it."

Within the floppy disk itself, data storage can take a number of formats. These include single-sided/single-density, single-sided/double-density, double-sided/single-density, and double-sided/double-density. **Double-sided** indicates the system's ability to use both sides of the disk. **Double-density** means that the system permits doubling the disk capacity no matter how many sides are used.

Figure 17–2 8-Inch and 5¼-Inch Floppy Disks

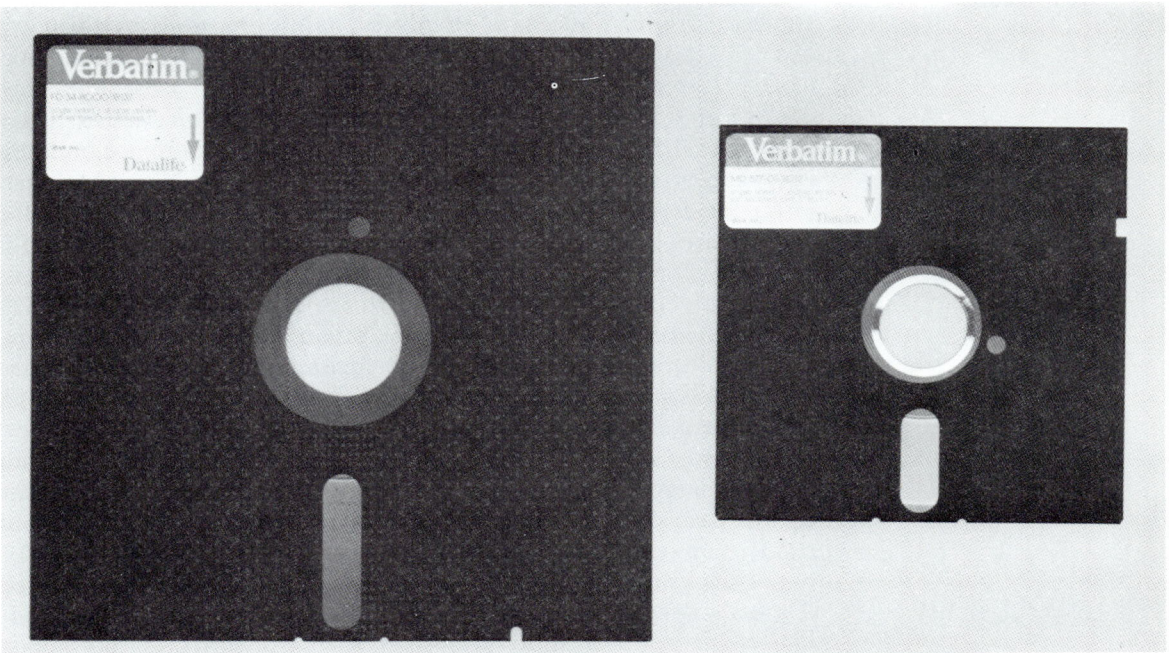

The device used to read and write data on a floppy disk is the **disk drive.** An individual disk drive is not universally compatible with all personal computers. Each is configured for a certain brand or brands of computer. The basic function of all disk drives, however, is the same. The floppy disk is inserted in a slot in the drive, and the door is closed to bring the read/write head in contact with the disk. The read/write head actually rests right on the surface of the disk. When the drive is activated, it spins the disk (the part located inside the protective casing) at very high speeds, performing read or write functions as instructed.

In many personal computers, the disk drive is physically separate from the computer and usually is placed on top of or beside the computer. More commonly, however, the disk drives are integrated in the body of the computer, as is the case with the IBM PC, the Lisa from Apple, and current Radio Shack TRS-80s.

Although floppies are adequate for most applications, some personal computer users may have greater storage requirements than are provided for by even the largest-capacity floppy disks. Many personal computing systems now allow the use of hard disks (generally packaged in a cartridge, which includes both the disk and the read/write mechanism). Hard disks offer, in addition to more storage capacity, greater speed in accessing data. The cost of a hard disk, while continuing to decrease, still remains a prohibiting factor for most users. A hard disk on a microcomputer system, however, does not preclude the use of floppy disks. Floppies still are needed to enter new programs or data into the computer and to create backup copies of programs or data.

Recent advances in data storage technology have introduced two new types of storage devices: optical (laser) disks and RAM chips that act like disk drives. The optical disks, which are even faster than hard disks, have a capacity equivalent to about 1,735 average books per side; however, optical disks now are limited in that they cannot be erased or rerecorded.

Inputting data from any type of disk is relatively slow compared with the speed with which the microprocessor can manipulate that data. The RAM chips are an attempt to close that gap. At this time, RAM chips are the only type of memory device that can approximate the speed of a microprocessor chip. They are available as hardware boards that plug into the same slot as would the disk drive and, to the computer, are indistinguishable from a disk drive. One drawback, however, is that RAM chips require a continuous power supply; therefore, battery backup units are recommended to prevent losing data in a power failure. Periodically transferring data onto a backup floppy disk also is recommended so that valuable data will not be lost.

The appearance of optical disks and RAM chips suggests that new technologies are continually being developed. As a result, we can expect increases in both the amount of data that can be stored on a given medium and the speed at which that data can be retrieved. The future may see floppy disks' becoming as obsolete as magnetic tape cassettes are becoming now. New techniques of data storage greatly enhance the efficiency of personal computers and open up many new possible applications.

Video Display Terminals

A VDT permits the user to see the transactions occurring between computer, peripherals, and user. It may be a standard television set (as is usually the case with lower-cost personal computers), or it may be a unit specially built for use with the computer. Black and white or color displays are available for VDTs; the choice of a unit is a function of user needs and budget. To use a color VDT (frequently called a **color monitor**), the computer must incorporate hardware capable of generating colors. Many of the newer personal models come equipped with color capability. If this feature is not part of the system, it usually can be incorporated by adding a plug-in color/graphics board. Good color and graphics are not restricted to expensive models; many lower-priced personal computers, such as the Atari 400 and 800 and the Commodore VIC 20, have exceptional color and graphics capabilities. Video display terminals also are called **cathode-ray tubes** (CRTs)—more properly the name of the electron beam tube, which actually is the display portion of the terminal.

An important factor in the selection of a VDT is the resolution of the screen. **Resolution** is the maximum number of positions (horizontally and vertically) that can be used in generating characters and graphics. For example, a low-resolution screen might contain only 32×64 positions, whereas a high-resolution screen might have 128×256 positions. These positions are called **pixels.** The higher the resolution, the better the quality of graphics. On high-resolution terminals, diagonal lines and curves appear smoother and more natural. With personal computers used for word processing, a high-resolution screen forms characters that are sharper and easier to read, reducing possible eye strain and fatigue problems.

Keyboards

The selection of a keyboard is one area that many buyers overlook. However, a wide variety of differences can be found. Most keyboards closely resemble the conventional typewriter in both appearance and function, although the layout of some can be quite different. If a user is familiar with a particular keyboard layout and plans to do a large amount of word processing or make other heavy use of the keyboard, the user would be wise to examine computers that offer that particular layout.

Most keyboards include special function keys and numeric keypads along with the standard character keys. Some keyboards, such as the one on the Commodore VIC 20, have multiple capabilities for each key. For example, a typical key might include uppercase and lowercase letters, as well as a choice of graphic characters. The availability and ease of use of various keyboard functions is an important factor to consider. Different physical types of keyboards can be found. There are the standard tactile types (permitting users to feel the keys moving under their fingers), such as those found on the Apple and the IBM PC. Models such as the Atari 400 and the Timex/Sinclair have a pressure-sensitive mem-

Figure 17–3
Pressure-sensitive
Membrane-Covered
Keyboard

brane-covered keyboard (see Figure 17–3). This type of design, although not suitable for large amounts of data entry, protects the keyboard from spills and other forms of contamination. Such keyboards are appropriate for computers used by younger children or for environments in which dust and other damaging substances may be present. The IBM PCjr keyboard requires no cable to connect it to the CPU; the user merely "aims" it at the processor, and it communicates with infra-red signals.

Printers

For most applications, a printer is necessary. There are a number of printer designs from which to choose. The two general types of printers are impact and nonimpact (thermal). The most common type used with the typical personal computer system is the impact printer. Impact printers come in two categories: dot matrix printers and full-font printers. Dot matrix printers are probably most frequently used by personal computer owners. They form characters by printing a matrix of dots. Full-font printers use fully formed characters, giving typewriter-quality printouts; they are more expensive than dot matrix printers. Some printers and specialized printing devices such as plotters (devices which actually "draw" on paper) can enhance output by displaying charts, graphs, and complex curves and shapes in a multitude of colors (see Figure 17–4). Many of today's dot matrix printers contain microprocessors and can easily be programmed for such features as underlining, italics, boldface, and double-width characters.

The user should consider a number of other features when selecting a printer. These include the restriction to uppercase letters only (as can be the case with lower-priced printers) or the availability of both uppercase and lowercase letters. This flexibility becomes an important consideration if the computer is intended to be used for word processing. Other considerations include proportional versus strict column spacing, single sheet versus continuous forms feed, and the ability to accept various sizes of paper.

Computerized Birth Control

Personal computing has been host to an array of obscure applications almost from its very conception. Now it appears that conception has become one of these obscure applications.

Edmond Desjacques, a Swiss architect, has designed the world's first contraceptive computer. Bioself 101, as his creation is called, works on the rhythm-temperature theory of fertility. The computer is shaped like an egg and works very simply. Every morning the women places the Bioself 101 into her mouth and waits for the beep. The beep indicates that her temperature has been taken and recorded. Each month when her period begins, she presses a button on the device, and the time is recorded. The Bioself holds two months worth of data and uses it to compute fertile and infertile periods. Having completed the calculations, the device operates much like a traffic light: it flashes green and red lights to signal fertile and infertile times. The devices sell for about fifty dollars each and have been on the market in Geneva and Montreal since late 1983.

Additional Devices

The hardware previously discussed includes the devices typically found on the average home computer. There are also a number of other hardware devices of interest. The joystick and the mouse (trackball) are two popular devices used to control the cursor movement (see Figure 17–5). Inside each are a number of contact points, each generating a particular voltage. Contact is made by moving the devices in the specified manner. The resultant voltages then are interpreted by the computer, and the cursor (the current point of access to the VDT screen) is moved in the appropriate direction. The more contact points, the finer control the user has over the cursor's movement (but the more expensive the device).

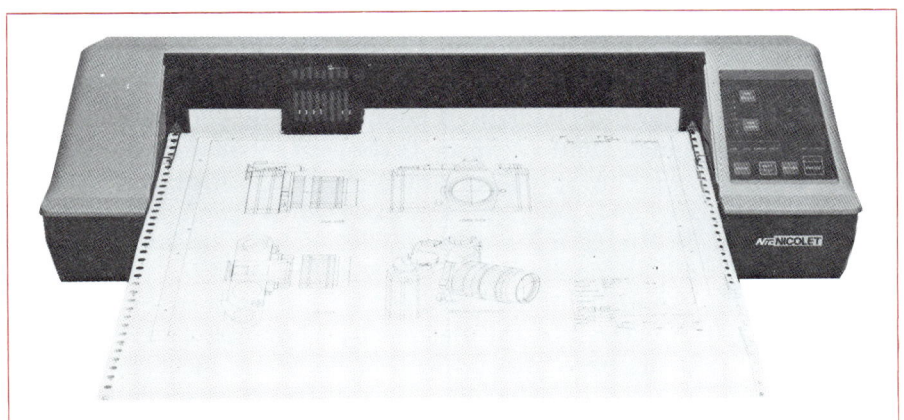

Figure 17–4 Pen Plotter

Figure 17–5 Joysticks

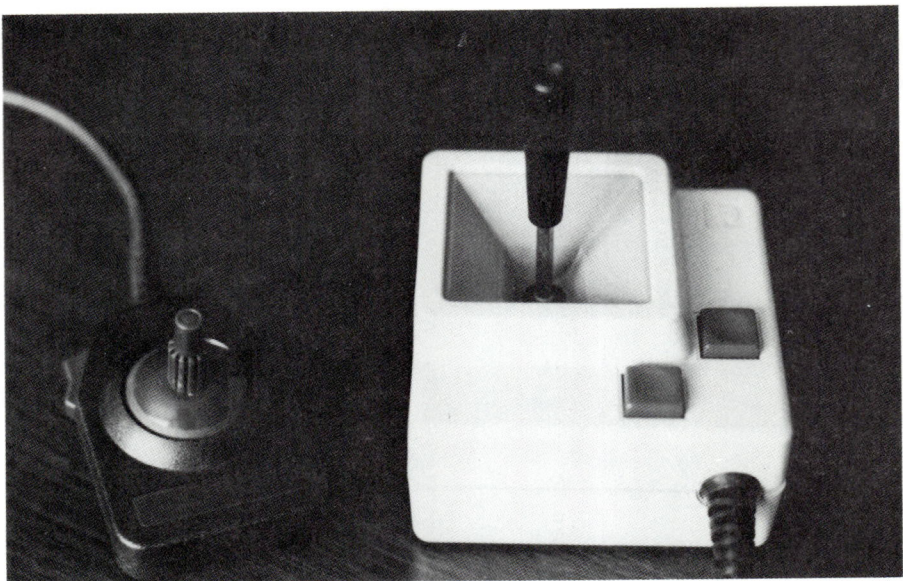

The light pen is becoming more popular on personal computer systems. This is a pen-shaped device that is connected to the computer. At its tip is a photoelectric cell that can detect voltages and thereby determine the screen position at which it is pointed. It can be used to enter or manipulate data directly from the screen rather than via the keyboard (see Figure 17–6).

Spatial digitizers and speech I/O systems are other interesting devices. Spatial digitizers allow users to record the x, y, and z coordinates of any three-dimensional object and store that information in the computer. This is done by using an armlike appendage to trace the object's shape (see Figure 17–7).

Speech I/O systems recently have begun to make significant advances. There are two types: voice entry (input) and voice synthesis (output). A **voice-entry system** will "understand" a voice command (instruction). There are systems available that can accomplish this, but the vocabulary they understand is still very limited. **Voice synthesis** refers to computer reproduction of a human voice. Again, although progress is being made, we are still far from realizing a computer with a vocabulary equal to HAL's in the movie **2001: A Space Odyssey.** Considering all the variables involved in giving speech meaning (such as accents, inflections, tone of voice, slang, and double meanings of words), it should be apparent that the task of creating a computer capable of understanding or speaking effectively is monumental.

There are also a number of hardware printed circuit boards (cards) that can be plugged directly into the inside of a computer to enhance its capabilities. Two of these already have been mentioned: the add-on memory board and the color-graphics board. Others include **spoolers,** (devices that allow the user to continue working on a microcomputer

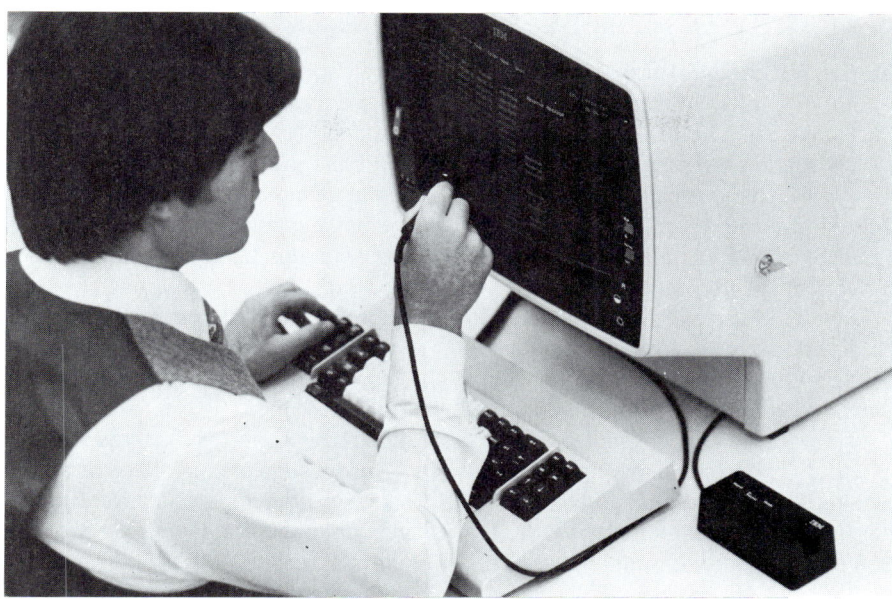

Figure 17-6 Light Pen

while its printer is being used) and devices that actually increase the processing speed of the microprocessor. It is even possible to buy cards that will essentially turn one computer into another computer. For example, a card known as Quadlink, by Quadram, adds a microprocessor to the IBM PC that allows it to function just like an Apple II or Apple IIe. No reformatting of disks is needed.

Figure 17-7 Spatial Digitizer

Model Makes Millions

Until 1981 Sue Currier was a New York model. Today, she is a New York millionaire. Currier made her money marketing a friend's software for the Timex/Sinclair 1000, a ninety-nine-dollar microcomputer.

At the time she started, there was no outside software for the Timex/Sinclair 1000 available in the United States. All the market had to offer was the software put out by Sinclair. That is where Currier came into the picture. An Australian friend asked her to help him market his software. She invested one thousand dollars in her friend's idea and set up a mail order company, Softsync, from her apartment.

The money was obviously well spent. Since then, Softsync's product line has expanded from the original two programs to include twenty programs. Softsync also has outgrown Currier's apartment. The company now has nine full-time employees and several part-timers. Best of all, Softsync was expected to gross over one million dollars in 1983.

Success stories like Softsync's shows microcomputer software to be a model business. Or maybe a model's business?

SOFTWARE

The first thing to consider before buying a personal computer is its intended use. Potential users should analyze their needs to determine exactly what they want their computer to do. Once this has been determined, they should survey the available software to determine what is available that can do the job. Only after this has been done will users want to consider hardware (which is, after all, merely a vehicle for the execution of software). Approaching the purchase of a personal computer in this way will save users much frustration and anxiety such as discovering that the computer purchased cannot or does not have the software available on the market to do what is wanted. However, the best approach to choosing a personal computer does not stop there. Future applications may be hard to judge now, so an important consideration is what type of operating system to choose.

Operating Systems

Since applications software runs only on particular operating systems, the user must make sure that the operating system has a variety of applications software available from which to choose. To review, an operating system is the group of programs that takes care of all the details involved in controlling computer hardware and internal operations. Some common operating systems are the Apple-DOS, Radio Shack's TRS-DOS, Microsoft's MS-DOS, and Digital Research's Control Program for Microcomputers (CP/M). There now are many software packages for the Apple, Radio Shack TRS-80, and computers that run on CP/M operating systems. For other computers, the choice is more limited; however, software for the IBM PC and the Commodore 64 is appearing very rapidly.

Digital Research's CP/M, it appears, may become an industry standard. The future is still relatively uncertain, however, as competing control programs, such as Microsoft's MS-DOS, battle for their place in the market. At present, CP/M will run on more models of microcomputers than any other disk operating system available. It was developed for the 8080 microprocessor, but versions are now also available for use on the 8085, Z-80, and the new 8086 and 8088 sixteen-bit microprocessors. CP/M has been renamed CP/M-86 for the version used on the 8086 and the 8088 (sixteen-bit) microprocessors and CP/M-80 for those versions used on the 8080, Z-80, and 8085 (eight-bit) computers. In trying to stay on top, Digital Research recently made available Concurrent CP/M. This operating system gives a microcomputer many of the features previously available only on mainframes, such as the ability to run two or more programs at once.

Because CP/M is compatible with such a large number of microcomputers, software manufacturers have flooded the market with applications software for CP/M, making it a good choice. There still may be hope for the user who has purchased a computer with an operating system that will accommodate little applications software. Many systems easily can add a version of CP/M, either by being retrofitted with a CP/M board or by using a CP/M software package. Table 17–2 lists some of the most popular microcomputers that can run CP/M.

Applications Software

Any microcomputer, regardless of type or cost, is only as good as the applications software available for it. Software packages are available for

Table 17–2 SOME POPULAR MICROCOMPUTERS THAT CAN RUN CP/M

CP/M-80

Apple IIe
Commodore 64
DEC VT 780
Hewlett-Packard HP-86, HP-87, and HP-125
NEC-8000
North Star Advantage
Osborne 1
Radio Shack TRS-80 Models I, II, and III
Xerox 820

CP/M-86

IBM Personal Computer and PCjr

all types of applications, including business, home, and educational uses. With the ever-growing numbers and kinds of places that sell software, users may find themselves a bit bewildered about where to go to find out what is available. Fortunately, there are clearinghouses, such as Sof-search, that provide this information.

A number of sources exist for purchasing software. Some of the larger publishing and distributing firms include Peachtree Software, Inc., Lifeboat Associates, and Personal Software, Inc. Computer specialty stores and mail order firms also are possible sources.

Some good rules of thumb when purchasing software are as follows: Users should (1) ask to see a demonstration of the program to make sure it meets specified needs; (2) check to see if the program is user friendly (features English-like commands); (3) be sure the program is supplied with easily understandable documentation; and (4) if possible, talk to people who have used the program.

When purchasing a software package, the user easily can tell which computer it runs on: the packages are clearly marked as to the type of machine, the memory required, and any peripherals required or recommended for the package use.

PERSONAL COMPUTER APPLICATIONS

Personal computers have become very popular in areas from business to home to education. There seems to be no end to their possible applications. The most common applications of these machines (other than games)—and areas of high competition for vendors of packaged software—are probably word processing, electronic spreadsheets, and data base management.

Word processing (more appropriately called **text processing**) permits the user to generate, revise, restructure, and print documents with great flexibility and efficiency. Some sophisticated word-processing packages include spelling checkers and software to facilitate the addressing and tailoring of many similar letters to different individuals, giving each recipient the illusion that the letter was developed for him or her alone.

Electronic spreadsheet programs give the user a powerful tool for analyzing alternatives (usually financial) and revising these alternatives with an automatic "ripple effect" of changes throughout the budget or financial plan. The fundamental structure of these programs is a matrix, each cell of which is given a meaning and relationships to other cells. Quantities then are entered in these cells and manipulated; the program "remembers" the linkage of these cells and automatically makes associated changes in other cells when a related one changes in value. This structure provides a powerful financial modeling capability, permitting the user to construct different scenarios with great ease.

The **DBMSs** for microcomputers are more rudimentary than those available for mainframes, but they are still important tools for users. They permit data to be stored and retrieved based on logical relationships and related field values rather than on physical file structures. As

Dictionary on Disk

With the rapid growth of word processing has come a proliferation of computerized dictionaries: Chextext, Magic Words, Proofreader, Easy Spell, Electric Webster, Perfect Speller, Spell Star, Sensible Speller, Super Spellguard, and Spell. All the programs are designed to catch spelling errors. Some of them correct the errors, while others suggest possible spellings. Their vocabularies range from ten thousand to eighty-five thousand words, and most allow the user to add new words to their memories.

The spelling programs work by checking words in the text against the words in their memories. When a match is not found, the programs report a possible error. The only major flaw with the programs is that they do not catch errors in grammar. For example, if you typed *for* instead of *four* or *to* instead of *two*, no error would be reported.

Many people have noted that spelling programs actually improve their spelling by showing them their mistakes again and again.

the secondary storage capacity of microcomputers increases—through increased floppy disk capacity and the growth in the use of hard disks— sophisticated techniques for the management of large data files become more essential to the effective use of these systems. Data base management software provides a means of implementing these techniques.

Within the business environment, personal computers are being incorporated to help increase the efficiency of managers by allowing them their own personal work stations at which they can collect, obtain, and analyze data in ways that previously would not have been possible. Microcomputers are beginning to find acceptance in the corporate world, although they generally were regarded with mistrust and skepticism when first introduced. It has been suggested that the entry of major mainframe and minicomputer vendors such as IBM, Hewlett-Packard, and Xerox into the personal computer field has led to the general acceptance and credibility of the microcomputer.

In the business world, microcomputers are adopted through a number of different approaches. Some cautious companies are installing personal computers in stand-alone modes only, with no access to remote computer facilities. This approach avoids the potential problems of on-line use, such as data integrity and data security. Others have allowed limited access to remote computer facilities, with most microcomputers being used for stand-alone applications such as financial analysis, spreadsheet preparation, and so on. Some companies, however, have approached microcomputers with a more open and decentralized approach, structuring them in a hierarchy of mainframes, minicomputers, and microcomputers so that they can be linked using the same data base. The linking of mainframes and personal computers allows managers at various levels to communicate among themselves or pass information easily up and down the organizational structure. Mainframes typically still are used to manipulate large data files, whereas microcomputers enable such applications as inventory analysis to be executed at the manager's desk. One of the factors that has most severely limited the incorporation of microcomputers into a first-rate distributed system has been the slow pace of software package development. The rate of software package development, however, has begun to accelerate as microcomputers have become more common in business. The issue of data control is also a major problem that remains to be solved.

We have seen that microcomputers have been used in business to set up communications networks between individual work stations, but these networks are not limited to business applications alone. Networks established by and for individuals with shared interests are cropping up all over the United States. These so-called electronic mail systems, or bulletin boards, allow individuals to exchange a wide range of information. There are also many services commercially available to subscribers. Some of the largest are the Source, Dow Jones, and CompuServe, Inc. These firms offer huge data bases with all sorts of information, including stock and bond reports, sports reports, medical news, tax advice, theater listings, major newspapers, weather reports, and much more. These computer network services constantly are increasing their services and the amount of information available to the personal computer user.

Within the home, personal computers are finding a variety of uses. Many users are happy with just the traditional applications such as checkbook balancing, family budgeting, and games, but many more have put their creative genius to work at new applications. In some homes, computers now wake up the occupants in the morning and start the coffee, control the lights and heat, activate the sprinkler system to water the lawn, and provide security for the home. Homes and businesses also are being combined. Many executives can now work from their homes using a personal computer that can tie into the system at work. This process is referred to as **telecommuting.**

There also has been a big push recently for personal computers in education. Many schools now have at least one computer for the students to use, and some have many more. Educational software for the home is starting to find a larger audience as parents and children alike discover the potential for learning that the personal computer holds. If all this is any indication of consumer interest, we can expect to see the personal computer soon become an integral part of everyday life. Microcomputers are here to stay.

- The terms personal computer and home computer suggest small size and low cost, but they also refer to the fact that the user has ready access to and control over a computer.
- The basic CPU difference between microcomputers is in the number

of different types of instructions that can be executed and the speed at which this execution takes place (that is, in their instruction sets).

● The CPU, along with RAM and ROM chips, make up the computer proper; all other hardware devices, such as disk drives, printers, and so on, are referred to as peripherals.

● The two most popular types of secondary storage for microcomputers are cassettes and floppy disks. Others include hard disks, microfloppies, optical (laser) disks, and RAM chips.

● A disk drive is a device that can read and write data on a floppy or hard disk.

● A video display terminal (VDT) is a device used to visually display transactions that are occurring between the computer and the users. It can be a standard television set or a specially built unit.

● Resolution is the maximum number of positions on a VDT (horizontally and vertically) that can be used in generating characters and graphics.

● There is a wide variety of keyboard layouts from which to choose. Two physical classes of keyboards are tactile (permitting users to feel the keys moving under their fingers) and pressure-sensitive membrane-covered keyboards.

● The two general types of printers are impact and nonimpact. Impact printers typically are used with microcomputers. Impact printers are of two types: dot matrix and full-font printers.

● The joystick and mouse (trackball) are devices used to control cursor movement.

● A light pen is a device containing a photoelectric cell that can detect voltages; it is used to enter or manipulate data directly from the screen.

● A spatial digitizer is a device that uses an armlike appendage to trace and record the x, y, and z coordinates of any three-dimensional object and to store that information in the computer.

● Two types of speech I/O systems are voice entry (which "understands" a voice command) and voice synthesis (which reproduces a human voice).

● A personal computer's capabilities can be enhanced by a variety of available hardware cards.

● The type of operating system a personal computer uses is important, because applications software is designed to run only on specified operating systems.

● The CP/M operating systems today run on more models of microcomputers than any other disk operating system.

● Personal computers are finding their way into business, education, and the home.

REVIEW QUESTIONS

1. What is meant by the terms personal computer and home computer?

2. Describe the CPU of a personal computer. How do CPUs differ from computer to computer?

3. What is the significance of the amount of RAM and ROM to the overall processing speed of a computer?

4. What are the two most common secondary storage devices for personal computers? Describe each.

5. Identify and discuss three other forms of secondary storage.

6. What is a disk drive? Describe its basic operation.

7. Describe and define the purpose of a VDT.

8. What is resolution? Why is it an important consideration when buying a VDT?

9. Describe the two different physical types of keyboards.

10. What are the two general types of printers? Identify and describe the categories of the type most commonly found in use with personal computers.

11. Define the following devices, and give an example of the type of applications that might use them: joystick and mouse (trackball), light pen, spatial digitizer, and speech I/O system.

12. Why is it important to know what operating system a personal computer uses?

13. What is CP/M? Why is it significant?

14. What are some of the ways in which personal computers have affected you?

15. Using your imagination, suggest some uses for a personal computer.

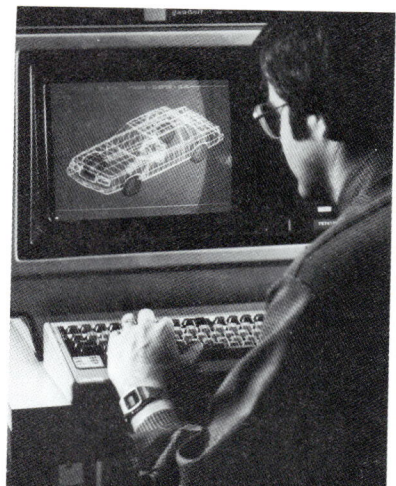

CAREERS IN COMPUTING

LEARNING OBJECTIVES

Having carefully assimilated this material, you will have learned the following:

☐ What positions are available in data processing and what skills and education are required for these positions.
☐ What positions are available in systems development.
☐ The difference between types of programmers (for example, applications, systems, and maintenance programmers) and how these differences affect the skills and education required.
☐ What careers are available in the area of data base management.
☐ The potential for management positions in all levels of data processing.
☐ Traditional and centralized placements of data-processing departments within overall company structures.
☐ The need for continuing education once a person has a job.

Chapter 18

INTRODUCTION   Career opportunities in computers and data processing are greater today than ever before. Rapidly changing technology demands various types of computer-related skills, creating new jobs and positions in the ever-expanding computing field. The U.S. Department of Labor (DOL) predicts that by 1990 there will be more than two million people in the United States working with computers. (Programmer annual job openings through 1990 are projected to be 21,200; systems analysts, 21,200; data entry and computer operators, 46,200.)

Will these jobs ever become obsolete? "Not in this decade," claims U.S. Regional DOL Commissioner Samuel M. Ehrenhalt in an article in the *New York Times*. "Growth in computer use—and computer-related jobs—will continue into the 1990s, he predicted. And if it slows down, he said, those trained in computer technologies will be needed to program and maintain the coming generation of technology—robots."

THE CAREER PATH

Data-processing Operations Personnel

Data-processing operations personnel, although not considered professionals, are seen by management as important in the effective use of an organization's computer resources. Positions in data-processing operations are librarian, computer operator, data-entry operator, and remote terminal operator.

The **librarian** classifies, catalogs, and maintains files and programs stored on cards, tapes, disks, and diskettes (see Figure 18–1). This person also transfers backup files to alternate storage sites, weeds out old files, and supervises the periodic cleaning of magnetic tapes and disks. The librarian is vital to the organization, because he or she is actually a guardian of the stored data and programs. To become a computer librarian, an individual does not need a college degree. The person in this position should have some knowledge of basic data-processing concepts, as well as clerical record-keeping skills.

The **computer operator** is the individual who works most directly with the computer. This employee sets up the equipment for particular jobs; mounts and removes tapes, disks and diskettes; and monitors the operation of the computer (see Figure 18–2). The computer operator should be able to identify operational problems and take appropriate corrective actions. People working at this job must have computer technical know-how and be able to communicate effectively with users. A college degree is usually not a requirement for the computer operator. Training is available through technical schools and junior colleges, but most operators receive on-the-job training as apprentice operators.

A **data-entry operator** transcribes data into a form suitable for computer processing. A keypunch operator uses a keypunch machine to

Figure 18—1 Data Processing Library

transfer data from source documents to punched cards, and operators of other key-entry devices transfer data to magnetic tape or magnetic disk for subsequent processing. Like computer operators, data-entry operators do not need a college degree. Usually, on-the-job training is provided for new operators. Typing or keying skills, however, generally are required for this position.

Figure 18—2 Computer Operator

A **remote terminal operator** also is involved in the preparation of input data. This person is located at a remote site, probably some distance from the computer itself. The data is entered into the computer directly from the location at which it is generated.

Changes in data-processing technology are affecting some jobs in computer operations. The demand for keypunch operators will continue to decline. However, as the use of computers continues to grow, especially in small businesses, the demand for computer-operating personnel should remain strong.

Systems Development Personnel

Programmers   Moving up the scale of computer jobs, **programmers** represent the first level of professional responsibility. At this point on the scale, the educational requirements are more stringent. Programmers usually need a two-or four-year college degree. In specialized areas, additional course work is required.

Generally, three types of programming are done in an organization: applications, maintenance, and systems programming. People working in any of these areas should possess the following basic skills:

- A knowledge of general programming methodology and an understanding of software and hardware.
- Analytic reasoning ability.
- Creativity and discipline to develop new problem-solving methods.
- A craftsperson's pride in a well-built product.

An **applications programmer** writes programs that tell the computer how to process data to solve specific problems (see Figure 18–3). Applications programmers also test, debug, document, and implement programs. Additional requirements and skills are needed for business data-processing and scientific applications programmers. A person in business data processing must apply the capabilities of the computer to problems such as customer billing and inventory control, know the objectives of the organization, and have a basic understanding of accounting and management science. A scientific applications programmer works on scientific or engineering problems that require complex mathematical solutions, so this programmer needs a basic knowledge of science or engineering. (Some jobs in scientific programming require graduate degrees.)

A **maintenance programmer** changes and improves major programs. To be effective, a person in this position needs considerable programming experience and analytic reasoning ability.

A **systems programmer** is responsible for creating and maintaining system software. Systems programmers develop utility programs; maintain operating systems, data base packages, compilers, and assemblers; and are involved in decisions concerning additions and deletions of hardware and software. Because of their knowledge of operating systems, they offer technical help to applications programmers. A systems

Figure 18–3 Applications Programmers

Computer Intern

Some computer departments in companies offer internships to college students. This type of program is beneficial to both the student and the company. The intern receives valuable on-the-job training, and the company hopes to employ a worker who is already knowledgeable about its computer operations.

Dave Armbrust was enrolled in such a program at Nationwide Insurance in Columbus, Ohio. Today he is an applications programmer with that company—a position he accepted because of his familiarity with the job. Armbrust now is working with a systems development team. Along with his programming job, he is enrolled in an extensive training program at Nationwide. His immediate career goal is to become a programmer analyst. Because Armbrust enjoys the technical aspects of the computer operation (the interface between personnel and machines), he hopes to advance to the position of technician manager in the future.

programmer should have a background in the theory of computer language structure and syntax, as well as detailed knowledge of the hardware and software in use.

Within an organization, a programmer's chances for advancement are usually good. The career path for an applications or systems programmer often leads to the position of systems analyst. With the necessary background in communications and leadership skills, it also can lead to a managerial position.

Systems Analysts The key person in a computer operation—who analyzes, designs, and implements a formal information system—is the **systems analyst** (see Figure 18–4). Acting as a link between the user and technical personnel such as programmers, machine operators, and data base specialists, the systems analyst evaluates current processing methods and procedures, designs new systems, and recommends changes to existing systems. (The systems analyst's role in the department becomes more important as the cost of designing, implementing, and maintaining information systems rises.)

The systems analyst should have the following:

● General knowledge of the organization—its goals, objectives, and structure.
● Organizational and creative skills.
● Ability to communicate with all personnel.

The systems analyst's function is typically one step above the programming function; however, many of the requirements of a good systems analyst are at odds with those of programming positions. Systems analysts must be more concerned with the end user than with the computer.

Figure 18—4 Systems Analyst

The minimum requirements for a job as a systems analyst generally include work experience in system design and in programming, as well as some specialized industry experience. Analysts seeking jobs in a business environment should have a college degree with background in business management, accounting, economics, computer science, information systems, or data processing. An MBA degree or some graduate study is often required. For work in a scientifically oriented organization, a college background in the physical sciences, mathematics, or engineering is preferred.

With the continued growth of management consulting firms and computer services organizations, along with the increasing use of minicomputers and microcomputers, the U.S. DOL estimates the growth rate in systems analyst jobs to be 37 percent by 1990.

Data Base Specialists Data base specialists design and control the use of an organization's data resources. As a key person in the analysis, design, and implementation of data structures, a **data base analyst** plans and coordinates data use within the system, working with the user or systems analyst to analyze the interrelationships of data, define physical data structures and logical views of data, design new data base systems or recommend changes to existing ones, and eliminate data redundancy.

A data base analyst needs technical knowledge of programming and system methodologies. For people planning physical data base structures, a background in systems software is important. Educational requirements for a data base analyst position are a college degree with course work in computer science, business data processing, and DBMS design.

The career path of data base specialist often leads to the position of organizational **data base administrator (DBA).** This management-level

Jack Dacre's Job

Jack Dacre is one of the many disabled people who are back in the work force because of the computer. Dacre, a paraplegic, utilizes the splint he normally wears to support his arm. With an extension piece on that splint, he is able to key in on the computer terminal.

Dacre completed three years of college before an automobile accident in 1965 left him almost totally disabled. Six years later he was able to get a degree in business administration. For a period of time, Dacre was employed at a rehabilitation center. When his job

was phased out, Dacre heard of a course being offered by the Central Ohio Rehabilitation Center (CORC), a division of Goodwill Industries. After testing and screening, Dacre was accepted into a CORC computer class. With a business background, the switch to computing was easy.

Today Dacre has a feeling of independence because of that computer training. He is able to work at Battelle Memorial Institute in Columbus, Ohio, which is completely accessible for the handicapped. He is working with a team of applications programmers and a systems analyst in the financial end of Battelle's operation.

individual controls all the data resources of the organization. In this position, a person must develop a dictionary of standard data definitions (so all records are consistent); design data bases; maintain the accuracy, completeness, and timeliness of data base backup and recovery; insure effective communications between analysts and users; and direct analysts, programmers, and system users in how to best use data bases. To handle these responsibilities, a data base administrator must have a high level of technical expertise, as well as good communications skills and leadership—all developed through experience.

Demand is strong for data base specialists. The trend toward data base management is increasing the need for people with the technical knowledge to design data base–oriented applications systems.

Software Engineers A **software engineer** is a specialist whose concern is increasing the efficiency and effectiveness of computer software (see Figure 18–5). This individual requires an educational background in computer science, generally at the graduate level. The software engineering function evolved as computer specialists were faced with software systems of increasing size and complexity. Concerns of software engineers include programming techniques, project management, documentation, software reliability, portability of software between computer systems, and the methodologies that differ for small and large programming projects.

MANAGING INFORMATION SYSTEMS

Managers of information systems generally require advanced degrees and a minimum of five years' experience or an equivalent combination.

Figure 18–5
Software Engineer

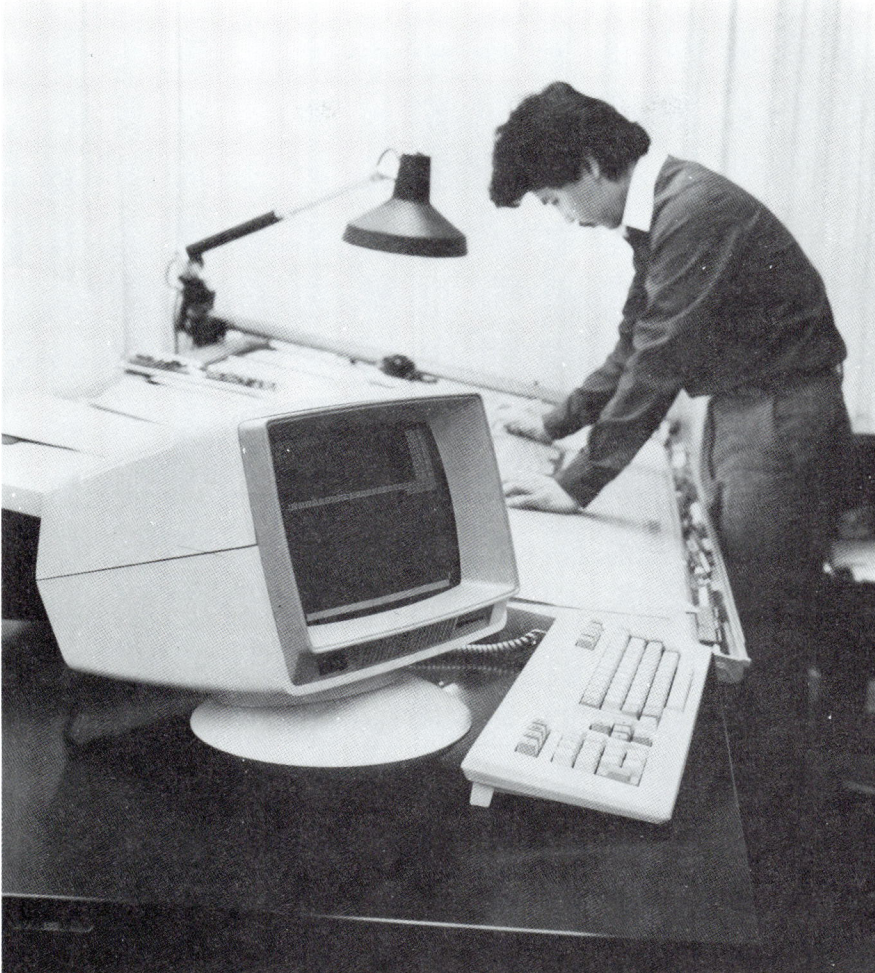

Along with strong management skills and the ability to work independently, managers must have the necessary skills to evaluate personnel, report budgeting progress, and supervise project management.

Organization of Data Processing

With the increasing importance of current information to many companies, data-processing operations have been elevated in the companies' organizational structures. The extensive use of computers in firms has moved the computing function from its original location to an area that best services all departments.

Figure 18–6 shows two organization charts for a typical manufacturing firm, each with a different location for the EDP department. Figure 18–6a shows the traditional location. This is satisfactory only if the other functional areas do not demand extensive use of computer capa-

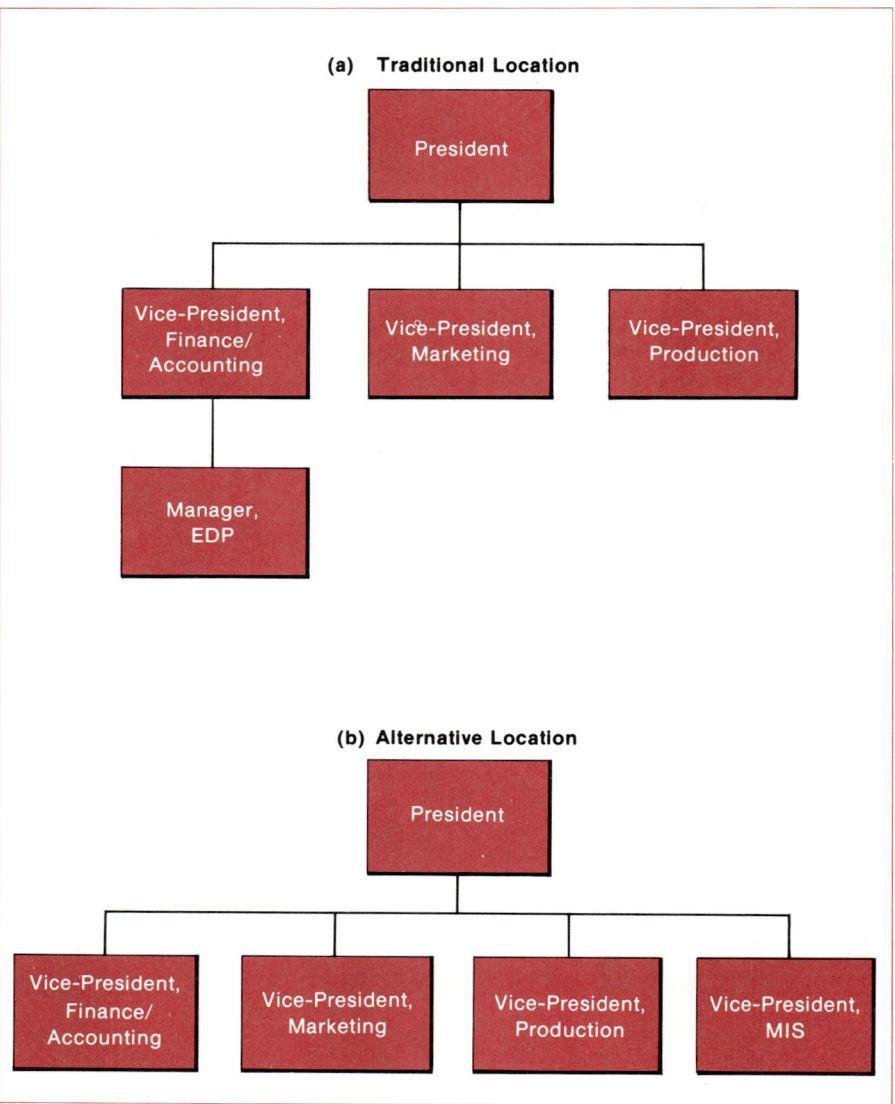

bilities. Unless the processing needs of the accounting and finance department are great, the computer is not used to its full potential.

Figure 18–6b shows an alternative structure that elevates the data-
processing operations to a position reflecting a corporate-wide scope. At
this status, the EDP department's name often is changed to the management information systems (MIS) department. The independent status of
the MIS department insures all functional areas that they will get service and that their particular information requirements will be integrated to meet organizational goals.

Free-lancing Analyst

Hollis Vail is a self-employed systems analyst living in the suburbs of Washington, D.C. As a computer free-lancer, he works out of his home and spends his days trying to make government agencies and other organizations function more smoothly.

Currently he is working on a research project for the U.S. Geological Survey with eight other people scattered all over North America—in California, Colorado, Virginia, Missouri, and Canada. Vail and the other project members get in touch by hooking their computers, via Telenet phone lines, to a central computer at the Geological Survey's offices in Reston, Virginia. By using Telenet—a long-distance network designed to carry messages between terminals and computers—they avoid long-distance telephone charges.

From the comfort of his home work station, Vail receives and sends reports, taps into extensive files of information stored on computers, and does his letter writing and filing electronically. Vail sees home computers as a way to allow many professional people to work where they like to work, be it center city, suburb, or remote hamlet.

The MIS department's internal structure varies in organizations. The most common structure is by data-processing function: systems analysis and design, programming, and computer operations. Another structure emphasizes project assignments. Analysts and programmers work on specific projects in teams that include personnel from user departments. As projects are completed, teams are restructured, and team members are assigned to new projects. This approach is called a **matrix structure.**

Managing Systems Development

Projects in data processing must be completed within reasonable time schedules. That job is the responsibility of the **systems development manager,** who monitors the total systems development cycle.

A manager can use various formal network techniques, such as the Program Evaluation and Review Technique (PERT) and the Critical Path Method (CPM), for project planning and control (see Chapter 14). To use such techniques, the manager must break the project into distinct activities, determine the sequence in which the activities are to be performed, and establish a time estimate for each activity. A scheduling chart then can be designed.

A good manager monitors the progress of a project by comparing estimated completion times with actual times. If delays occur, the reasons behind them must be identified and corrective actions taken.

Managing Computer Operations

Companies demand efficient use of their computers in return for the large sums of money spent on the purchase of the systems' CPUs and peripheral devices. The **manager of computer operations** is responsible for monitoring the efficiency, scheduling, and assignment of operators. In addition, this individual must maintain the equipment and strive for a high degree of reliability.

When a user requests a change in computer processing, it is this manager's responsibility to control how the changes are to be made. It is also his or her job to keep computer operations running smoothly while the changes are being made.

Better systems can be achieved if the manager sees that (1) changes do not interrupt computer use for other users, (2) all changes are documented, and (3) processes are audited to see if all users are following the procedures.

Information System Managers

The person responsible for planning and tying together all the information resources of the firm is the **information system manager** (see Figure 18–7). An information system manager must have leadership capability and good communications skills. To achieve organizational goals, this person must organize the physical and human resources of the department and devise effective control mechanisms to monitor progress.

The position at the highest level of the scale is the **MIS director.** This person should have at least two years of extensive management experience, as well as advanced knowledge of the industry and competence in all technical, professional, and business skills.

Figure 18–7
Information System
Manager

Invasion of the Robots

U.S. Regional Department of Labor Statistics Commissioner Samuel M. Ehrenhalt predicted that growth in computer use—and computer-related jobs—would continue into the 1990s. He further stated that if the growth slowed down, those trained in computer technologies would be needed to program and maintain the coming generation of technology—robots.

That new generation is here. Norman L. L. Naidish of Revlon, Inc., claims robots are arriving in large numbers on the doorstep of U.S. industry. Naidish feels that robots could replace one million workers in the United States in the hard goods and electrical industries if the technology in use today were applied. About five thousand robots are now in use in the United States, or about 0.3 percent of potential, stated Naidish.

Although robots are unpopular with industrial workers, they are looked upon favorably by U.S. industry, especially now that those in operation are proving themselves in full-time, profitable use. (Currently Japan has over 10,000 robots in operation and is producing around 7,500 more each year—five times the output of U.S. robot makers.

Will robots eventually replace workers? Many experts feel it's inevitable. They see a future where robots will be used in repetitive and hazardous work. People will still be working, but they will be doing only those jobs requiring intelligence. For example, somebody will have to design, build, and maintain all those robots.

Managing an MIS is a challenging job. It involves overseeing an integrated and yet diverse set of people and machines. No matter how sophisticated the MIS, success in using it can be achieved only through its acceptance by users at all levels of the organization.

CAREER GROWTH—LEARNING BEYOND THE DEGREE

For people with their eyes on advancement, learning should be an on-going process. In the computer world this is especially true. With rapid changes in computer technology, career-minded people must keep abreast of the latest information about computers.

Many organizations realize the value of this attitude and provide on-the-job training for their workers. Others encourage workers to enroll in classes at local colleges, attend conventions and exhibitions relating to computers, and join professional associations. By becoming a member of either a local or nationally affiliated professional association, people can become involved in workshops and seminars sponsored by that organization. Being a member also enables people to meet others with like interest. Such personal associations can provide a useful career network for job-seeking individuals.

Professional Organizations

Current professional associations include the following:

- The American Federation of Information Processing Societies (AFIPS) represents member societies on an international basis and also disseminates knowledge of these.
- The Association for Computing Machinery (ACM) is the largest scientific, educational, and technical society of the computing discipline. The ACM has established Special Interest Groups (known as SIGs) to address the wide range of interests in the computing field. For example, SIGSMALL is concerned with small computers; SIGPLAN, with programming languages; SIGCSE, with computer science education; SIGBDP, with business data processing; and SIGCPR, with computer personnel research. The ACM supports student chapters in colleges and universities.
- The Data Processing Management Association (DPMA) is one of the largest worldwide organizations serving the information-processing and management communities. Through its efforts to promote and develop educational and scientific inquiry in the field of data processing and data-processing management, DPMA sponsors college student organizations interested in data processing.
- The Association for Systems Management (ASM) informs its members of the rapid growth and changes occurring in the field of systems management and information processing.
- The Institute of Electrical and Electronics Engineers Computer Society (IEEE/CS) is a group subordinate to an organization traditionally concerned with electrical engineering. The IEEE/CS is a large group that has gained recognition and membership through its support of software engineering and its conferences and tutorials in many areas of current interest.
- The Institute for Certification of Computer Professionals (ICCP) is a nonprofit organization that concerns itself with professionalism and certification in the computing discipline. Evolving from early certificate programs sponsored by the DPMA, the ICCP is supported by eight constituent societies that participate in the development and maintenance of professional credentials. The organization currently sponsors certification programs in data processing (CDP) and computer programming (CCP). A certification in systems analysis (CSA) is under development. Individual memberships in the Association of the ICCP (AICCP) are available to certificate holders.
- Women in Data Processing (WDP) encourages both male and female membership. Prospective WDP members should be interested in promoting the placement and advancement of women in data processing.

Publications

Currently there are many computer publications. Among the most popular are the newspaper **Computerworld** and the magazines **Datamation,**

Popular Computing, Byte, and **Microcomputing.** Most of these are available at newstands. Other publications, including association journals and magazines pertaining to specific areas in computer operation, can be found through college libraries.

- Career opportunities in computers and data processing are greater today than ever before. Growth in computer-related jobs will continue into the 1990s.
- Data-processing operations personnel are important to the effective use of an organization's computer resources. Those positions—librarian, computer operator, data-entry operator, and remote terminal operator—generally do not require a college degree.
- Programmers (applications, maintenance, and systems programmers) represent the first level of professional responsibility. These jobs often require stringent educational preparation. An applications programmer writes programs that tell the computer how to process data to solve specific problems. A maintenance programmer changes and improves major programs, and a systems programmer is responsible for creating and maintaining system software. The employment forecast for programmers is excellent.
- The key person in a computer operation—who analyzes, designs, and implements a formal information system—is the systems analyst. The growth rate in systems analyst jobs is estimated to be 37 percent by 1990.
- Data base specialists design and control the use of an organization's data resources. The career path of a data base specialist often leads to the position of organizational data base administrator (DBA).
- The DBA, who holds a management-level position, controls all the data resources of the organization. The need for people with the technical knowledge to design data base–oriented applications systems is increasing.
- With the increasing importance of current information to many companies, the data-processing function has been elevated in the organizational structure. The extensive use of computers in a firm has moved computing from its original location in the organization chart to an area where it reflects the appropriate corporate-wide scope. At this level, the department's name often is changed to the management information system (MIS) department. The internal structure of the MIS department varies in companies.
- Managers must oversee an integrated, yet diverse, set of people and machines. The systems development manager monitors the total systems development cycle. This person must see that projects in the data processing department are completed within reasonable time schedules.
- A manager of computer operations is responsible for monitoring the efficiency, scheduling, and assignment of operators.
- Information system managers are responsible for planning and tying together all the information resources of the firm. The position at the

highest level of the scale is the MIS director. This person should have at least two years of extensive management experience, as well as advanced knowledge of the industry and competence in all technical, professional, and business skills. Managers at this level generally require advanced degrees and a minimum of five years' experience or an equivalent combination.

● No matter how sophisticated the MIS, success in using it can be achieved only through its acceptance by users at all levels of the organization.

● In the computer world, learning should be an ongoing process. Career-minded people must be alerted to rapidly changing computer technology. This can be achieved by on-the-job training, enrolling in classes, attending conventions and exhibitions, joining professional associations, and reading computer publications.

REVIEW QUESTIONS

1. Name three types of programmers, and describe their jobs.

2. In what location is the EDP department in most companies' organizational structures today?

3. What job in a computer installation demands the most workers?

4. What position is at the highest level of the computer job scale?

5. Why is an information system manager's job a challenging one?

6. What are the two internal organizational structures of an MIS?

7. On the career path, what position follows a programmer?

8. How can a worker keep abreast of computer technology?

9. How can successful MIS use be achieved?

10. What people are involved in a project assignment?

11. The demand for what computer-related positions continues to decline?

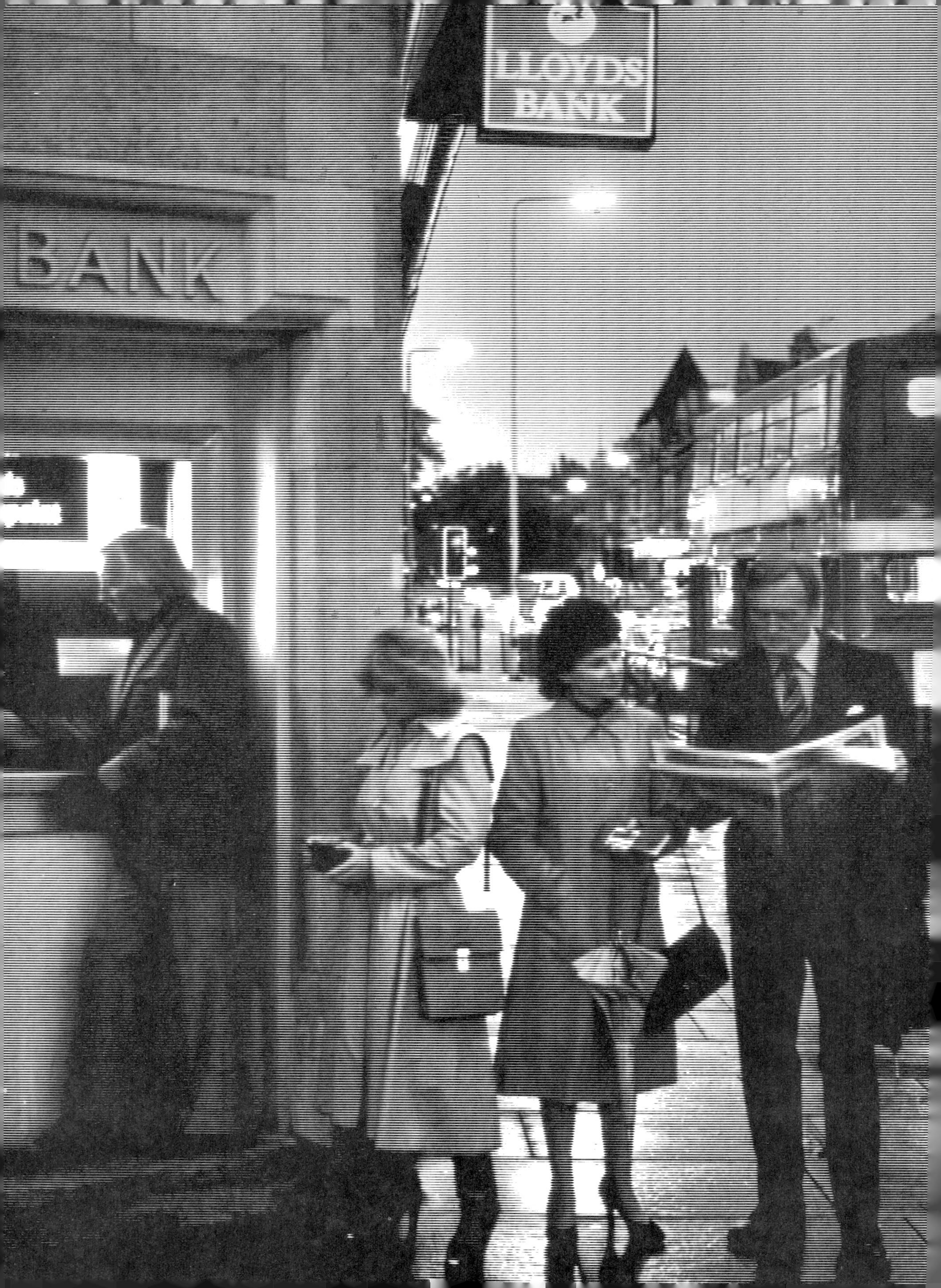

LLOYDS
BANK
BANK

SOCIETY

LEARNING OBJECTIVES

As you read and study this chapter, you will learn the following:

☐ How computers are being used to speed up and make more efficient the transactions, services, and record keeping of the banking industry.
☐ How businesses use computers to facilitate their production, inventory, and selling processes.
☐ How the government keeps track of information necessary to its functioning with computers.
☐ How computers are used to enforce—and, sometimes, to break—the law.
☐ How science and medicine are being advanced by the use of computers.
☐ How computers are being used as educational and religious tools.
☐ How computers can bring us the arts and entertain us.

Chapter 19

INTRODUCTION   In many ways, computers are becoming part of our society—more often and in more ways than are immediately recognizable—and as a result, part of our everyday lives. As computers become a greater part of our society, they have a greater impact on each of us individually and personally. This chapter aims to give a closer view and a greater appreciation and understanding of that impact.

COMPUTERS—A GROWING PART OF THE EVERYDAY WORLD

On her way home from work, Mary stops at her bank. It is too late for the bank to be open, so she uses the automated teller machine (ATM) located on the outside of the building by inserting her plastic card into the appropriate slot. She punches in the amount of money she wants, the ATM gives it to her, and then it returns her card. She knows she can get money from the ATM at any hour of the day or night.

At the grocery store, Mary selects her items and takes them to the checkout counter. There, the cashier passes what looks to Mary like a magic wand over the product, and the price of the item flashes on a miniterminal. (In some stores, a computer-synthesized voice will recite the price as well.)

Next, she stops at the pharmacy, where she has a prescription filled. In her car, Mary listens to the weather forecast on the radio. Once at home, she gets to work on her income tax return. And that night after supper, she listens to her children tell her about things that sound foreign to her—video games and, most incomprehensible of all, a televisionlike screen with a keyboard that is helping them learn their traditional reading, writing, and arithmetic.

Mary does not realize that all these aspects of her life—as well as many others—are being touched, affected, and even changed by computers. To her, computers are part of a strange, foreign, science fiction–type world. She believes she has no connection with them.

All of us, like Mary, have many aspects of our lives affected by the computer, even if those effects are not readily obvious. Like Mary, we may not even realize that our lives are being affected—even as they are—by computers, a growing and important part of society.

COMPUTERS IN BANKING AND BUSINESS

Can you imagine the difficulty of handling all the information that banks must process every day—with only ledger books and pencils? Check processing, loan records, deposit records, account balances, savings club and investment information—banks must keep all this information up to date daily. With the growth of banks and the numbers of

Traveling Microcomputers

Microcomputers are becoming a common item of carry-on luggage at airports around the United States as computer enthusiasts take their vacations. Briefcase, or "portable," computers are the fad now, and these easily are transported to and from vacationlands. Why take a computer on vacation? Enthusiasts use them for planning itineraries and calculating such activities as travel expenses.

While traveling with a microcomputer, there are certain things to watch. Never let the airport personnel x-ray disks and cassettes—it may randomly rearrange data. X-raying a computer is inadvisable, if for no other reason than that some microcomputers will set off airport security alarms. As a final precaution, protect a traveling microcomputer from humidity, sea air, and sand. Thus, you can take it to the shore, but you should not take it to the beach.

people and companies using them, computers have become essential to the functions of the banking business. In fact, every banking institution across the country uses computers in some way.

Computers not only enable banks to keep up with the incredible amounts of information and figures they must process, but also to provide more customer services and make banking easier, quicker, and more efficient. For example, an ATM like the one Mary used can often be found on the outside walls of bank buildings, in supermarkets, at airports, or on college campuses. Some banks have even located these ATMs inside shelters in shopping center parking lots. Using an ATM is very easy and often more convenient than actually going inside the bank. Transactions can be made at any time of the day or night, be it 11:00 P.M. or 3:00 A.M. Banking customers place a plastic card, with their account number on it, in the appropriate slot of the ATM; by simply pushing a series of buttons, they can make withdrawals, deposits, and other transactions automatically—and all because of the computer.

Other transactions can be handled for individuals—without their ever having to worry about them. This concept is known as **electronic funds transfer (EFT).** For example, paychecks or portions of paychecks can be deposited directly into an employee's account each month by the employer. On certain dates, payments for utility and credit card bills, for example, can be transferred automatically from savings to checking accounts. It may seem that EFT takes place magically, but it does not. It is made possible by computers.

The use of EFT will grow in the future, as, no doubt, will another concept—home banking. As more and more consumers begin to purchase and use home computers, banking from the home will become more desirable and more feasible. In fact, in early 1982 nearly one dozen such major projects were being tested and were in operation across the United States. A recent survey by Payment Systems, Inc., showed that home banking is the home computing two-way service most desired by the U.S. consumer.

Banks also are using computers more often—and in more ways—to meet not only their customers' needs, but theirs as well. For example, the Chase Manhattan Bank recently implemented a worldwide credit information network. This network will serve as a data base for generating management information worldwide while providing the company with word and data processing. This computer system saves the bank time, paperwork, and money usually spent on international credit approval.

Like banks, businesses and manufacturers must process much information daily. Computers help speed up and control the processing of growing amounts of business information and transactions that, without computers, would take vast amounts of time to sort, process, and store. Businesspeople use computers for control of inventory levels, billing customers for services and products, calculating payroll and taxes, paying for inventory and supplies, reporting decisions made by managers, and other business functions.

Customers also may find that their dealings with businesses are being affected by computer-generated transactions. In other words, not only are customer billings by businesses handled by computer; cash transactions also are often controlled by a behind-the-scenes computer. For example, the Universal Product Code (UPC), a standardized bar code used by the computer to identify products and their manufacturers, can be found on most items in retail stores.

Along with point-of-sale (POS) terminals, the UPC makes purchasing an item quicker and easier for the customer and easier to keep track of for the business. A POS terminal closely resembles a typical cash register; however, its potential is greater, and its work is controlled by a computer. The clerk at the POS terminal passes an optical scanner, which may look like a wand, over the UPC (or passes the UPC over a counter-mounted scanner). The scanner, programmed to read the code, interprets the code, which then is looked up in the computer's file, from which the product's name and price are retrieved. The computer then records the transaction and provides the item name and price printed on the receipt. Because the POS terminal can keep track of the product's name and price in the computer file, it is very useful for quickly and efficiently updating inventory levels and calculating sales figures at the end of a business day or week. (See Figure 19–1.)

The computer also helps businesses to increase their manufacturing productivity. Computers help businesses' routine scheduling of workers or shipping of products, inventory control, control and scheduling of machinery, and labor accounting. A manufacturer can even meet future demands, using a more complex system known as **materials requirement planning (MRP)** to figure out what raw materials will be needed and when.

As costs for computer equipment continually decrease, small businesses as well as larger companies can afford the benefits of computers; there are computer programming packages that keep track of accounts receivable and accounts payable, payroll, taxes, and billing operations.

Figure 19–1 NCR POS Terminal

Entrepeneurs—or individuals who start and operate their own small businesses—now can install complete accounting systems on micro-computers.

Businesses and their branches can be connected by computer lines. Airlines, travel agencies, and hotels can use computer networks to process reservations.

Not only do computer systems keep business operations going, some even help companies to manufacture products. Engineers and technicians can use **computer-aided design (CAD)** to input their requirements for a product design and receive a computer-generated picture of that product (see Figure 19–2). Then, with the calculations used to generate the CAD designs, engineers can use **computer-aided manufacturing (CAM)** to make the products (see Figure 19–3).

Some manufacturers, such as DuPont, Merck, Sharp & Dohme, and McDonnell-Douglas are already using CAD-CAM innovations. However, the greatest and most exciting possibilities of CAD-CAM design and production lie in the immediate future (see Chapter 20).

Figure 19–2
Computer-Aided Design

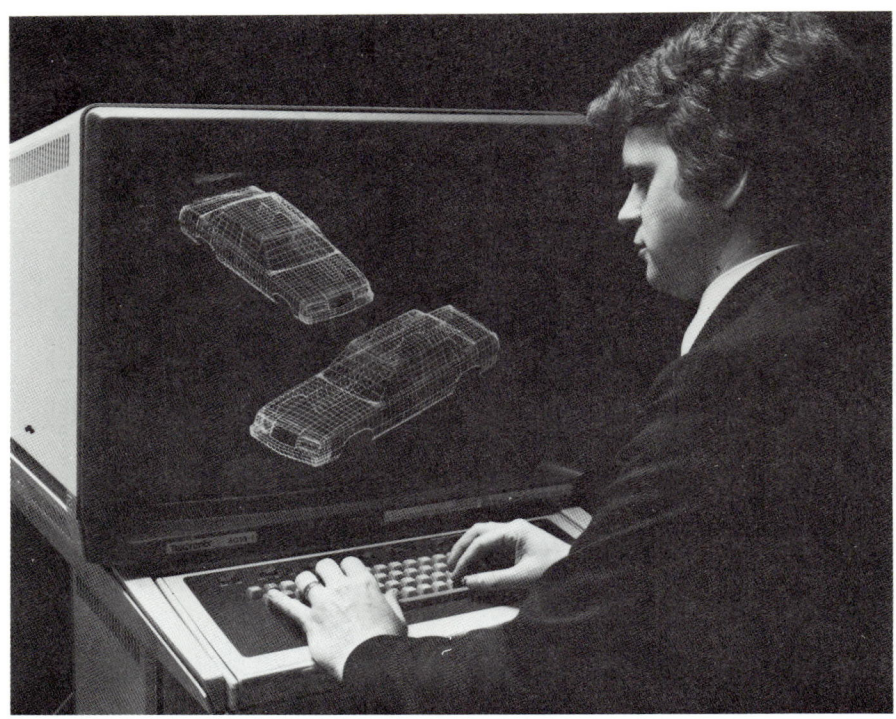

Figure 19–3
Computer-Aided Manufacturing

COMPUTERS IN GOVERNMENT AND MILITARY APPLICATIONS

Considering the vast amounts of information the U.S. government must process about its population, it is not surprising that the federal government is the largest computer user in the United States today. Many government agencies use computers to collect, process, and store information about U.S. citizens. In fact, one of the earliest computers was developed to meet the demands of processing the large amounts of information resulting from the census of a growing population (see Chapter 2).

Another major user of computers is the Internal Revenue Service (IRS). Each year, any person who makes over a minimum income (and all businesses and corporations) must file tax returns to the government. Without the computer, years would be required to process only one year's tax returns. Computers monitor returns, record information, and thus speed up the time needed to process the millions of tax returns. The computer also can randomly select returns for auditing and perform some of the necessary preliminary operations. This reduces the number of manual operations required for audits, thus increasing the number of audits that the IRS can perform each year.

The government agencies that protect the environment's future use computers. For example, the Department of Health and Human Services predicts and controls the effects of industrial waste in U.S. rivers and streams with computers, which determine the amounts of oxygen and chemicals in the water and provide information about how well the rivers can sustain life. Computers also can aid in determining the causes of water pollution by analyzing the contents of water and then suggesting ways of cleaning it up. In much the same way, the causes and effects of air pollution can be determined by computers used by the Environmental Protection Agency. As the movement toward stronger pollution control laws continues, computer use in finding ways to protect the environment is becoming increasingly important.

The U.S. government also uses computers to determine and forecast weather. Large computers process complicated mathematical equations from data such as air pressure, wind velocity, temperature, and humidity collected from weather stations around the world. Forecasters can use the results given by computers at their locations to predict the next day's weather.

Computers are of increasing importance in military applications. High-level officials in the armed forces often make decisions with the aid of computer-generated information, and the military also uses computers to transmit data.

A network of twenty communications satellites transmits data from all over the world to military computer centers. The North America Air Defense Command near Colorado Springs, Colorado, maintains a huge data base, which accepts data from radar and satellite equipment positioned throughout the world. The data can be quickly updated and retrieved at a moment's notice, calculating, for example, the position of rockets and missiles within several seconds after they are launched. In case of attack, the computer can signal and perform necessary actions appropriately (see Figure 19–4).

Military planners use computers to practice making decisions in life-like situations, such as war, before the real situation might occur. Such simulation saves the government millions of dollars, since it does not have to pay for or provide actual equipment for the practice of important military skills. For example, computers can be used to simulate tanks. The user sits in a compartment similar to the one in an actual tank and "fires" by pushing buttons at the "targets" on the screen. The computer then provides the user with a critique of the performance. Such computer simulation is similar to the video games found in arcades.

COMPUTERS IN LAW AND PRIVACY

Computers Used to Enforce Laws

Law enforcement agencies—for example, both the Federal Bureau of Investigation (FBI) and the Central Intelligence Agency (CIA)—use computers to effectively enforce the law, store information, plan operations, and track criminals. The National Crime Information Center uses a national network of computer terminals for keeping track of police and law enforcement information. State computers are hooked into the system at the National Crime Information Center. The police then can access this information from remote police station terminals connected

Figure 19–4 Interior view of Command Post Area of Strategic Air Command (SAC) Headquarters

Filing Fingerprints

Now fingerprint computers are being used to help law enforcers trace criminals from fingerprints left at the scene of the crime. Printrak, one such new system developed by Rockwell International, records and encodes minutiae, the ridge endings and splits on a print, and then stores that data. When examiners try to identify a print—even if it is just a fragment or is barely visible—they can conduct a high-speed computer search that results in a listing of suspects whose fingerprints most resemble those found at the scene of the crime.

As many fingerprint collections are becoming unmanageably large, this system could dramatically aid law enforcers in solving crimes. For example, as of 1981, the FBI headquarters in Washington, D.C., had 173 million sets of ten fingerprint cards—and it received twenty-five thousand new fingerprint cards to identify each day.

Experts anticipate that someday police may be able to search fingerprint files from terminals in their patrol cars after taking electronic fingerprint impressions of a suspect.

to the state computers. This system is very useful for local police as they seek information about stolen property, criminals, and criminal records.

Computer-based dispatch systems also aid police in getting to the scene of a crime more quickly than before computers. Operators can get information to the dispatchers much more quickly. Some such systems also, at the request of the terminal operator, can give detailed information about a call, such as the units dispatched, the times they were sent and arrived, and when the call was cleared.

Court systems use computers to find citizens qualified for jury duty; schedule judges, lawyers, defendants, and witnesses for court; and record information used during a trial, generate reports about the trial, and report the activities of a case. Innovations with microcomputers have advanced to the point where lawyers now can carry portable computers containing their clients' files and information that are capable of being tied to larger home-base computers.

Computer Crime

Unfortunately, the computer also can be used for criminal purposes. Estimated losses from computer crime to "high tech crooks" range from two billion dollars to more than forty billion dollars per year. Financial and other personal gains are the motivations for illegally using or manipulating data; such crimes are hard to detect or prevent. Both public and private businesses and groups exert considerable effort trying to reduce their vulnerability to these crimes. Knowing and understanding how computer crimes have been committed, it is hoped, will help the computer programmer develop methods to prevent abuses of new systems.

Computer security—or preventing computer crime—rests on protecting the actual computer and keeping unauthorized people from using the computer facilities. However, the growing number of telecommunications facilities makes criminal access to computer installations easier, even though the criminal may be miles away from the base computer. For example, $10.2 million was illegally transferred—via the telephone—from Security Pacific Bank in California to a Zurich bank account. The money later was used to buy $8.1 million worth of diamonds from the Soviet government.

Privacy

All these crimes seem far removed from the average person. However, computers play an increasing part in daily life, and as more and more individuals choose to use home computers, privacy becomes an important issue. Privacy means that all individuals have control over their own personal information—information that relates directly to their lives. With computers, however, people seldom realize that personal information about them is being gathered—or that with computers, it is possible to compile lists of people from widely scattered data that would be difficult to bring together manually. Such information could determine whether or not a person can receive services, privileges, opportunities, or benefits from credit, education, medical care, and employment facilities.

Main concerns over the proper protection of privacy are these:

- Whether too much personal information is being collected and stored in computer files.
- Whether organizations are increasingly using these files to make decisions about individuals.
- Whether much of this data is relevant to the purposes for which it was collected.
- Whether the standards of accuracy, completeness, and currency of the data are high enough.
- Whether the data is stored securely enough.

Often people feel that their individual privacy is being sacrificed to the age of computers; however, institutions—both private and public—are able to run more smoothly and efficiently by using computers. The privacy concerns of individuals must be balanced with the institutions' operational needs for information. Furthermore, privacy laws passed since the early 1970s protect the individual's right to privacy. The Freedom of Information Act of 1970 was passed so that individuals could gain access to data that federal agencies have about them. It was passed because of the government's potential ability to keep its proceedings away from public scrutiny.

The Fair Credit Reporting Act of 1970 is the only significant federal law that attempts to regulate how private organizations handle their

Robots for the Handicapped

Engineers at the Palo Alto Veterans Administration Center in California are working on an electronically controlled, computer-programmed remote robot arm to help the handicapped. The robot, responding to a computerized voice-recognition system, will help handicapped people do things they previously could not have done easily, or even at all, such as turn the pages of a book, pick up eating utensils, or move a small object.

The handicapped person who will use the robotic arm will program it by verbally describing a series of instructions, which will be stored in the robot's computer memory and given a name. The robot will be programmed to recognize and respond to only the voice of the user; when he or she says the task name, the robotic arm will carry out the task—from start to finish.

The engineers are working on not only making the robotic arm mobile, but on giving it sight as well. In the not-too-distant future the robot, mounted with a video camera on a mobile device, could be programmed to move around the user's home while the user watches the robot's movement on a television monitor and gives the robot voice commands. The robot could be ordered, for example, to bring a book from a bookshelf or to get a snack from the refrigerator and bring it to the user. By 1988 the inventors of this computer-programmed robotic arm hope this robot will have made the leap from fiction to helping the handicapped in real life.

information about individuals. This law is intended to keep lending institutions that use computers from committing privacy violations. Individuals have the right to see credit data about themselves and to challenge and correct erroneous data. On a state level, legislation that basically strengthens the protection of the Fair Credit Reporting Act of 1970 has been introduced to regulate the information activities of organizations outside the government.

The most sweeping legislation to protect an individual's privacy was signed into effect on January 1, 1975—the Privacy Act of 1974. This act protects the privacy of those about whom the federal government keeps information and provides the following assurances:

- Individuals must be able to know what information government agencies are keeping on them and how they will use it.
- Individuals also must be provided with a method to correct or change information that they know is incorrect.
- Individuals must consent to information collected for one purpose being used for another purpose.
- Any organization that creates, maintains, uses, or disseminates personal information must insure its reliability and take precautions to prevent its abuse.

Although criticized for not reaching to state and private institutions, the act was an important move toward protecting individual privacy rights. Other laws, such as the Education Privacy Act (which regulates access to computer-stored grades and behavior evaluations) and the Right to Financial Privacy Act of 1978 (which limits the government's access to the customer records of financial institutions) have continued that move.

COMPUTERS IN SCIENCE AND MEDICINE

Computer innovations have supported many rapidly developing innovations in science and medicine, as well as facilitated hospital processes. Computers also have been put to use in scientific and hospital laboratories (see Figure 19–5).

Computers are useful in hospitals for making easier even the most routine—but necessary—information processing required. For example, computers can organize, evaluate, and retrieve the data needed for the proper diagnoses of patients and can plan and control hospital operations such as routine billing and payroll, monitoring patients, and training personnel. Computers also can fulfill many clerical and administrative functions in hospitals:

Figure 19–5
Computers Used for
Scientific Testing

- Record keeping of money received for services and paid to employees.
- Patient billing, storing and retrieving records and information, and monitoring conditions.
- Personnel payroll and accounting.
- Scheduling beds, facilities, and equipment.

Computers are useful for specialized patient needs. For example, Ohio State University hospitals have two computerized nutrient data base systems that can assess individual patients' nutritional needs and then plan menus. The university is teaching other hospitals, researchers, and private companies how to use these facilities.

As a diagnostic tool, the computer can save doctors time, which they then can spend personally with patients rather than in the laboratory. **Computer-assisted diagnosis** can be performed by technicians and paramedics trained to use computer equipment. Multiphasic centers use computers to compare the results of electrocardiograms; X-ray, blood, hearing, incision, and blood pressure tests; and height and weight measurements to sets of predetermined standards developed by physicians. Multiphasic diagnosis is important for preventive health care (see Figure 19–6).

Computers also are being used to "question" patients about their medical histories. Patients answer the questions by pointing with a light pen to the correct answer on the televisionlike VDT screen. For example, appearing on the screen may be a question about whether or not the patient has a family history of diabetes. If the patient points to no, the

Figure 19–6 The MEDLINE database is an important research tool available to health personnel.

computer asks the next question. If the patient points to yes, the computer asks more about the patient's family history of diabetes. Such a computer-automated method of keeping a patient's medical history, again, saves the doctor valuable time that can be spent with patients needing more immediate attention. Furthermore, the system simplifies updating the history, as well as transferring the information to a doctor in another city if the patient moves.

Computers occupy an important, exciting, and growing place in the future of medicine and science. Already researchers are looking for—and finding—ways that computers can be used to help the handicapped. Computerized systems may not only aid the handicapped but, through computerized biostimulation feedback, actually enable the paralyzed to move again.

COMPUTERS IN EDUCATION AND RELIGION

Used as an instructional tool, the computer can bring further richness, individualized instruction, potential for practicing with knowledge gained, and efficiency to education and religion. Computers were first brought into the classroom during the 1960s as automated flash cards. Now **computer-assisted instruction (CAI)** can, for example, supplement the teacher with drills, exercises, enrichment or remedial material, and tests (see Figure 19–7). In one application, multiple-choice questions appear on the computer screen. If the student answers correctly, the computer goes to the next question; if the student answers incorrectly, the

Figure 19–7 The PLATO® Computer-Based Education System.

Video Games Hit the Streets

About the size of two telephone booths, the shelter on the corner of the street houses two video games. Does this sound like a video game addict's fantasy? The booth-sheltered street-corner video games in reality are known as Video Outposts and are being promoted by Playtime International. Video Outposts are open twenty-four hours a day and are sheltered from vandalism, rain, and up to fifty-mile-per-hour winds.

Most video games are found inside stores, where often too many video game players can cause store owners a few problems, say Video Outpost promoters. In contrast, Video Outposts can be fixed to a concrete sidewalk or to the outside of a building, thus saving shop owners from some headaches of inside games. And because the Video Outposts are highly visible, the video games draw business from people who have never played a video game.

computer tries to steer the student to the correct answer. Students can get immediate gratification from computerized instruction, because they can work with computers on a one-to-one basis and get instantaneous feedback. Students' learning can be aided by computers on any topic—geometry, spelling, music theory, sales, history, and, of course, computer programming. Teachers also find computers useful in developing teaching plans and course curricula, creating and individualizing lessons, recording students' progress and grades, and grading tests.

The U.S. Department of Education estimates that twenty-two thousand—or one out of every four—schools in the United States have at least one microcomputer or computer terminal for instructional purposes. That estimate is further broken down to 50 percent of all secondary schools, 14 percent of all elementary schools, and 19 percent of all other types of schools (vocational, special education, and elementary and secondary combined).

Predictions forecast that school systems may purchase as many as 150,000 microcomputers per year by 1985. In Florida, officials hope all state schools up to the college level will be linked via computer network systems by 1986.

Why is there so much interest in bringing the computer as a learning tool to the schools? Students clearly benefit from interacting with computers to learn. Slow learners, as well as fast-paced students, can learn at their own pace without the frustrations of being held back or pushed too fast.

On the college level, computers also have a growing place in the classroom. All students at Drexel University in Philadelphia now are required to purchase their own personal computers. The same is true at Carnegie-Mellon University in Pittsburgh, and, as microcomputer prices continue to drop, may become common at private universities. This approach helps to ease the scarcity problem of computer resources on most campuses.

The study of computers themselves has reached a boom level. Computer textbooks began to be published just over twenty years ago, when there were only a few dozen. Today, computer textbooks number around three thousand, and that number includes only textbooks written for computer science courses—not textbooks on the applications of computers to science and other classes. Computer study has even extended to summer camps, some of which focus almost exclusively on computer-related topics. (See Figure 19–8).

Computers are finding their way into religion as well. The King James Version of the Bible, for example, is now available for home computers on eight small, plastic disks. Chicago's Institute for Computers in Jewish Life keeps track of Jewish history, traditions, ceremonies, and holidays via computer.

Churches have begun using microcomputer systems to keep track of records on their congregations and for bookkeeping tasks. Bible study cassettes for home computers are available, providing lessons on the ability to search the New Testment for specific types of scriptures, such as those on love, sin, or evil. Computers also are being used by Bible researchers and scholars. Parish Secretary (PARSEC), which was coauthored by a Catholic priest, and Automated Church Transaction System (ACTS) are examples of computer packages designed specifically for churches to keep track of collections, fund-raising activities, and memberships.

The Mormon Church, or the Church of Jesus Christ of Latter-Day Saints, has used computers since February 1981 in four of its temples in

Figure 19–8
Computer Camp

COMPUTERS IN THE ARTS AND LEISURE

The many potential uses of computers are now surfacing in the arts. Graphics capabilities have been refined and a new classification of art—computer art—has emerged (photograph No. 1). Similarly, computer-generated music and sound effects are being recognized for their unique features. The applications of computer technology for computer-generated special effects, choreography, animation, and museum exhibits are also being adopted by the entertainment field.

1

2. Sample of color graphics work done on the Symbolics 3600.
3. "Aurora," by Richard Katz. **4.** "Three Atoms," courtesy of Greg Abram, University of North Carolina at Chapel Hill.

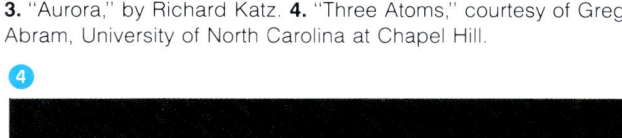

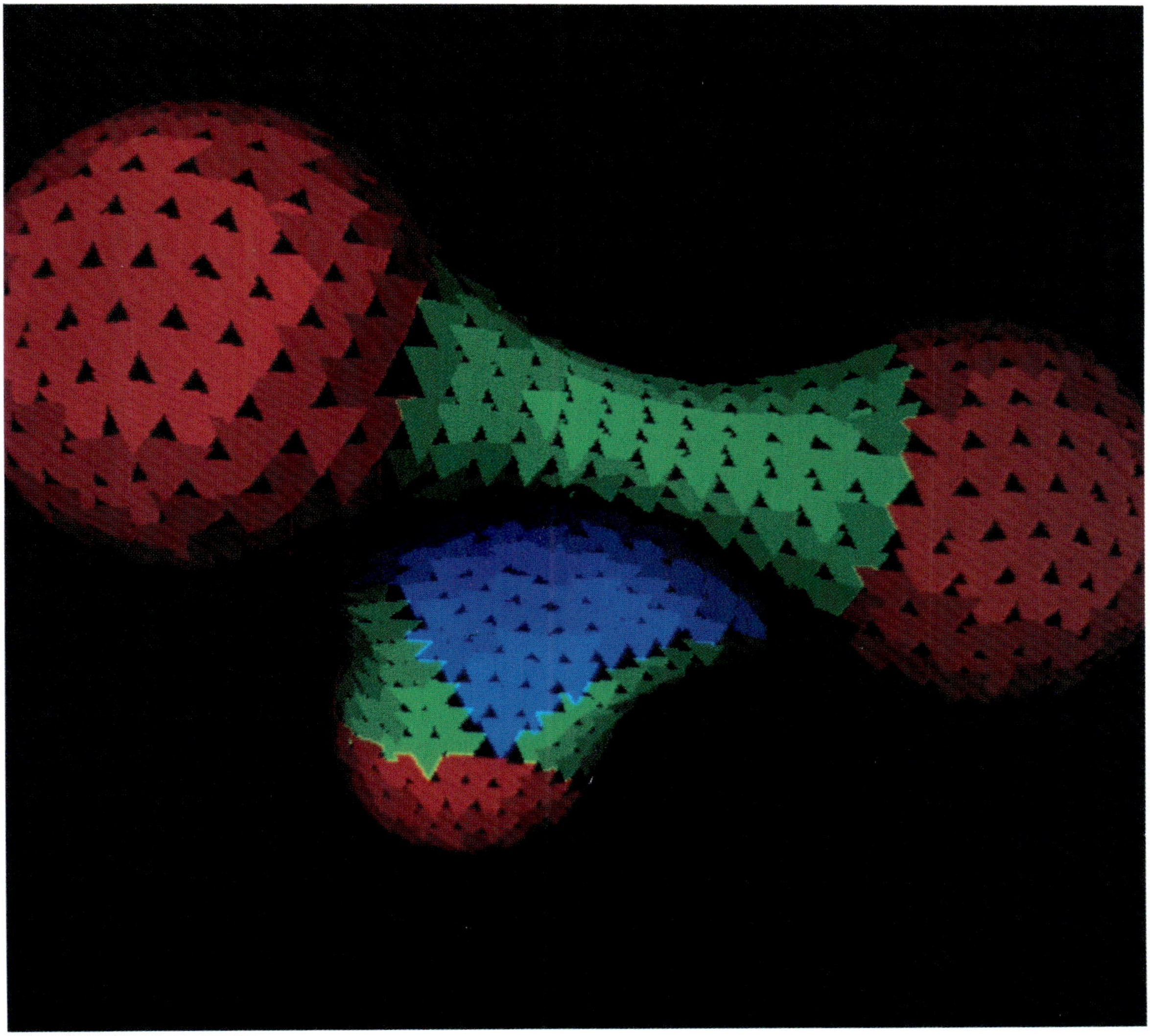

Arts and Leisure—continued. **5.** By feeding mathematic and geometric instructions into a computer, this artwork was produced by a Bell Laboratories scientist. **6.** *Recollections.* In this Artist-In-Residence piece by Ed Tannenbaum, a video image of the visitor is digitized, artificially colored and projected onto a screen. Four or five different coloring patterns are cycled through the exhibit every 2—3 minutes.

7. Freehand illustration on the Aycon/16 series display computer using the optional graphics™ art brush system, a system designed specifically for today's graphic artist. **8.** Computer-assisted graphics help animators to create cartoons in a fraction of the time it would take to draw each frame. **9.** The film industry relies on computers for creating special effects in motion pictures. Computers had an active role both on and off screen during the making of *War Games*.

7

8

9

Arts and Leisure—continued. **10 and 11.** By using a microcomputer and a video display screen, choreographers may combine the best aspects of written and visual recording techniques. **12.** A microcomputer music system. **13.** Computer programmed robots at Pizza Time Theatre franchises entertain patrons. **14.** Walt Disney Productions' computerized Audio-Animatronics® enables voices, music, and sound effects to be synchronized with lifelike movements of three-dimensional objects ranging from birds to humans.

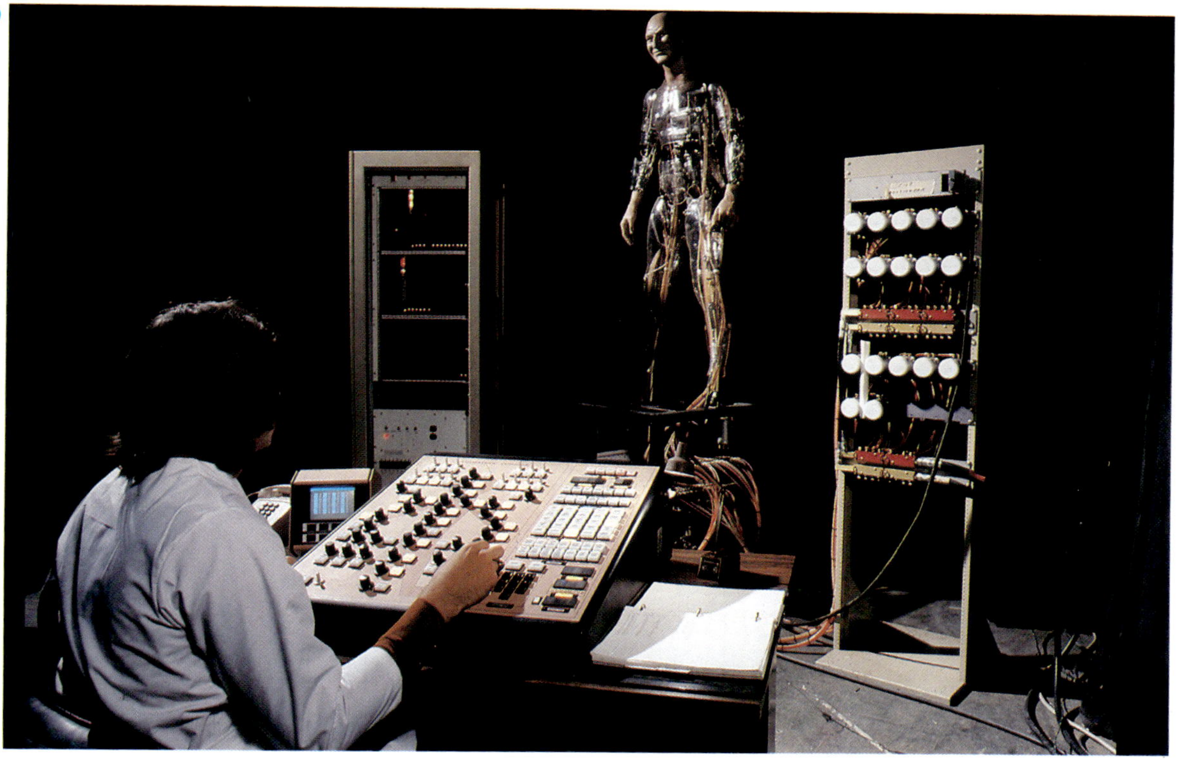

Arts and Leisure—
continued. **15.** Shown
here is the editing room
for NBC television in
Burbank, California.
16. Strand Century's
Light Palette Control
Console allows complex
lighting changes to be
programmed in advance
and played back exactly
as recorded, or modified
for the immediacies of
live performance.

15

16

Utah and in one in Atlanta to perform the ordinances of baptism and marriage, for example. The Mormon Church recently has expanded the computer network system to include all twenty-two Mormon temples in the country.

COMPUTERS IN THE ARTS AND ENTERTAINMENT

Almost everyone is familiar with computerized video games, and most have played them at one time or another (see Figure 19–9). Now such games are "out on the street," more available than ever to the population. Video games are not the only way computers are becoming a part of the arts and entertainment. More and more newspapers are being

Figure 19–9 Video Games

written and formatted via the computer. Animated films are produced through computer animation—more quickly than by traditional methods of manual animation, its proponents say, and with greater capabilities for fantastic, awesome animated effects.

Computers also are being used to create new sounds in music. Electronic music and synthesizers have become increasingly popular. Computer hardware has been designed to produce sounds to feed stereo systems, synthesizing sounds of the pipe organ, the clarinet, and even a perking coffee pot or chiming clock. Software has been designed to create music, with a four-octave range, using such hardware. A computerized drum machine can electronically simulate sounds of drums, tom-toms, and cymbals. As a tool for the study of music theory, the computer offers the musician greater flexibility than traditional methods have permitted. (See Figure 19–10.)

The capabilities of computer hardware to maintain and store information are being recognized as useful for art museums. For example, as mentioned earlier, the National Museum of Canada maintains an on-line computer catalog of over thirty-five million artifacts from 152 of its member museums. Nearly all 250 member museums are expected to be on line eventually.

Computer graphics are being used to create unusual and interesting "computer art." Also, artists can use computers to simulate traditional art forms—for example, using an electronic pen and tablet for input while watching a reflection of their work as they create it on a televi-

Figure 19–10
Computer-Aided Music
Theory

Figure 19–11 The Study of Human Motion by Computer

sion monitor screen. Graphics are also useful in the analysis of dynamic processes for artists and others. (See Figure 19–11.)

The use of computers in the arts reflects the versatility of computers—reaching beyond science and technology into all aspects of life.

● Banking institutions use computers both to aid the banking customer in making quick and easy transactions at automated teller machines (ATMs) and to facilitate their own transactions as well.

● Computers are a vital part of the business world and offer businesspeople such innovations as the Universal Product Code (UPC) and point-of-sale (POS) terminals to help keep track of accounts, transactions, and inventory.

● Computer-aided design (CAD) and computer-aided manufacturing (CAM) are increasingly implemented by manufacturers both to create and to produce marketable items.

● The military finds the computer useful to provide video simulations so that military personnel can practice their targeting and shooting skills more readily. This saves the military millions of dollars.

● Government agencies, such as the Internal Revenue Service, the Environmental Protection Agency, weather bureaus, and others, use computers to more quickly and efficiently process the vast amount of information necessary to run the government.

● Police, the FBI, and the CIA find the computer useful for tracking criminals and keeping records. Court systems and lawyers also use computers.

● Computer criminals sometimes find the computer useful for gaining and misusing computer-stored information. Therefore, the government has passed several laws to protect the individual from misuse of personally sensitive computer data.

● The computer is useful in hospitals and medical research to diagnose, prescribe treatments, and keep track of all the many pieces of medical data about individual patients.

● Students find computers useful for drilling exercises, reinforcement, and individually paced learning. School administrators and teachers find computers useful for keeping records on students, recording and calculating grades, and planning lessons. Software packages are available for these educational purposes.

● Keeping track of a church congregation's attendance, participation, and offerings is made easier by software packages specially designed for these tasks. Computers also can be useful for church lessons, religious history and research, and church ceremonies.

● Computers can be used to expand the work capabilities of artists in areas such as animation, painting, and music.

REVIEW QUESTIONS

1. Name three ways in which banking institutions use computers.
2. How do retailers use the UPC and POS terminals?
3. Define CAD. Define CAM. Why are these important in businesses?
4. In what ways does the military use computers to help sharpen its combative potential?
5. Describe how three government agencies use computers.
6. Discuss how computers sometimes are used in computer crime.
7. How do law enforcement agencies such as police, the FBI, and the CIA use computers to solve and prevent crimes?
8. Name and discuss at least three laws that have been brought into effect to help protect the individual's right to privacy.
9. Explain how hospitals can use computers to keep track of patients and their records.
10. Give examples of how computers are being used to diagnose, treat, and in some cases, overcome illnesses and handicaps.
11. How can students use computers to learn about many different subjects?
12. How can teachers use computers to teach many different subjects?
13. Describe how computers are being used in churches.
14. Are computers and the arts really opposites? Argue that they are not, giving at least three examples to support your argument.
15. Name five ways in which you can observe how computers directly affect your own life.

20

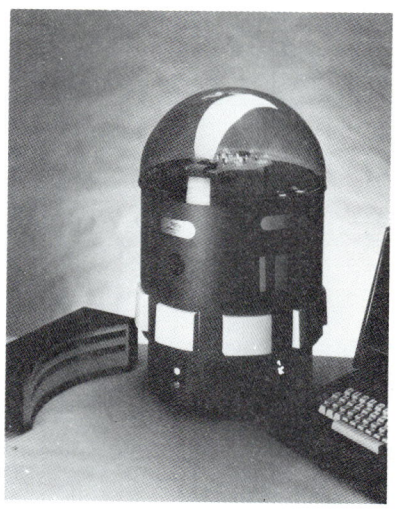

THE FUTURE

LEARNING OBJECTIVES

After carefully reading this chapter, you will have a good idea of the possibilities for computers in the future. Specifically, you will examine the following:

☐ New developments to come in computer hardware, such as Josephson technology and biochips.

☐ The components of tomorrow's automated office.

☐ The applications and possibilities for industrial robots.

☐ Coming developments for domestic or personal robots.

☐ The basic concepts underlying artificial intelligence (AI).

Chapter 20

INTRODUCTION   The computer revolution came with little warning and exploded into action. In the span of a few short decades, the computer has moved out of the realm of science fiction and isolated laboratories and into the everyday world.

Having examined the history of computers, their workings, and their impact on today's society, we are ready to examine their possibilities for the future. These future developments will include new trends in hardware, the integration of office automation, the proliferation and advancements in industrial robotics, the development of practical personal robots, and the coming of a new age of reason in AI.

Proper study of these areas will insure that the continuation of the computer revolution will not be composed of random explosions that scatter effects and ideas as humanity is carried along by the aftershock. Instead, the changes will be carefully planned and manipulated. Humanity will occupy the control seat instead of just being along for the ride.

HARDWARE TRENDS IN THE FUTURE

The trend since the beginning of computer history has been for computer hardware to become smaller, more efficient, and faster at handling data input and producing data output. Because efficiency and speed are essential for the growing amounts of information to be handled by computerized data manipulation, the trend of the future will be in the same direction—toward computers that are increasingly compact, efficient, and speedy. Two major branches of new technology may lead the way to this hardware breakthrough: Josephson technology and biochips.

Josephson Technology

The development of the large-scale integrated circuit formed of silicon has brought monumental changes to the computer industry. Now research is being done on **Josephson technology,** also called the **Josephson Junction.** Named after the British Nobel laureate Brian Josephson, of Cambridge University, it may replace the silicon chip in the relatively near future.

The Josephson technology works in the following manner. Metal alloys are cooled to temperatures near absolute zero (-273.15 degrees Celsius, or -459.67 degrees Fahrenheit). At this cold temperature, all molecular motion stops (see Figure 20–1). This causes the metals to lose their otherwise normal resistance to the flow of electricity and become superconducting. Two metals that are superconducting at this temperature are put together in a thin sandwich. Electrons from a current source are shot through the sandwich, triggering the conducting device. This entire process is carried out at close to absolute zero.

Stringy Floppies and Wafer Drives?

The major emphasis in microcomputer technology has always been price. The microcomputer has earned its place in history by offering affordable computing to the average person. This has caused fierce price wars between manufacturers and a keen sense of value among consumers.

Another result of this emphasis on price will be the introduction of new technologies to improve the speed of inexpensive machines without doubling their price. One of the problems with inexpensive computers has been that they generally are equipped with cassette tape systems for secondary storage. These tapes are very slow, and users often spend frustrating amounts of time waiting for their programs to be read. Floppy disks are much faster, but a floppy disk drive can cost up to five times as much as the inexpensive computers.

New technologies are evolving that will fill this gap, giving users a happy medium—both in time and price. The devices, called *stringy floppies* and *wafer drives*, were developed by Exatron and Unitronics, respectively. They both use a continuous-tape cartridge and are expected to become widely used in the future as inexpensive alternatives to disk drives.

Obviously, the use of Josephson technology will make computer operations much more speedy and efficient than they are today. Josephson Junction devices are very small and very fast. The smaller the junction, the faster it is. One such device (made by Bell Laboratories) is only one thousand angstrom units square. (An angstrom is one ten-millionth of a millimeter.) These devices are so small that the electronic switches occur in one-trillionth of a second (one picosecond).

Figure 20–1
Josephson Technology

Biochips

In the past several decades, computer memory capacity has grown an average of 35 percent each year, and the space required for that memory has shrunk by a factor of 800 since 1953. The future trend will be for memory to continue decreasing in size while increasing in its capability to retain more and more information. If this trend continues at the current rate, by the year 2078, a single computer will be able to store the same amount of information as sixteen thousand human brains.

We might wonder if someday these machines, with such great capacity, may evolve into living matter. Perhaps they will not have to; they already may be composed of living matter. Research currently is being conducted on what scientists are calling **biochips.** When perfected, biochips will be organic microchips. They will be built from protein and manufactured by genetically engineered bacteria. Futuristic as the approach may seem, the reasoning is laced with logic. As Forrest Carter of the Naval Research Laboratory in Washington, D.C., said, "We anticipate the day when they [computer circuits] will approach the size of molecules. Wouldn't it make more sense to use the molecules themselves?" Carter sees this organic computer of the future storing ten million times as much information as today's computers in the space of a single cubic centimeter. It is also expected that such a bioprocessor would not only store data, but also transfer and manipulate it at even greater rates of speed and efficiency than is possible with the silicon chip or Josephson technology.

Biochips will not be used in the near future. Scientists are still working on creating that first "simple" molecular switch—the biological equivalent of the transistor. This switch will turn molecules in a bacterium on and off by switching hydrogen molecules directed by electricity. These switches will represent the binary 0s and 1s and will enable the biochip to calculate. In this way, the process will be the same as the one used now, different only in that the medium will be organic rather than silicon. Some researchers feel that the breakthrough for the molecular switch may be here by the time this book is published. In any case, it will be a great many years before scientists have perfected the bioprocessor or biochip.

Once the bioprocessor has been perfected, its implications will be incredible and nearly unlimited. The biochip could easily grow and reproduce itself. It could process data three-dimensionally in the way the living brain does. Not only could biochips be used in computers; they could interact with the human nervous system as implants restoring sight to the blind and hearing to the deaf, as well as enhance the human capacity for memory.

The development of the biochip will bring with it a great number of ethical questions, the least of which may be whether the end product is an organic machine or a mechanized organism. It is alive? What about the people who have their memories enhanced with such a thing? How will our society react to them? How should society react to them? These will be just a few of the questions that will arise with the use of the biochip.

THE AUTOMATED OFFICE

Just as the new technology will affect the way computers work, new and integrated applications of this technology will affect the way people work. Because we live in a postindustrial, service-oriented society, one of the places this effect will be most evident will be in the office of the future.

The office of the future will be sleek, efficient, and automated. We already are seeing the beginnings of this. Teleconferencing, electronic mail, ergonomics, and networking are just components. The final product will integrate all these processes and more, producing the optimum atmosphere for productivity.

Teleconferencing is a major step toward the office of the future and represents state-of-the-art communications. Teleconferencing enables executives and salespeople in different cities to hold conferences without the time constraints of travel (see Figure 20–2). Officials at the home office of a New York–based company can confer with their Chicago subsidiary without leaving their company. This is possible if both buildings have two-way satellite antennae on their roofs, a requirement highlighting the disadvantages of teleconferencing. Two-way satellite antennae are very expensive. Unless a company is planning to hold a great many teleconferences, the cost of installing the equipment is prohibitive.

Of course, a company would want to try out teleconferencing a few times before investing in all that equipment. Or perhaps the company likes the idea of teleconferences, but it is not planning to hold many of them. In that case, a teleconference would call for a trip to the telephone company's facilities. This type of teleconferencing can cost several thousand dollars an hour and create a problem with company security, because telephone company officials must monitor the sessions.

There is another major problem with teleconferences: they tend to ignore the human factor. For example, Avon, Inc., was a forerunner in the use of teleconferences, but Avon now is cutting back on teleconferences. Officials claim that the teleconferences lack the personal interaction and creativity of on-location conferences.

Designers see the human factor as a major element of the office of the future. One reason for this is the attention given lately to ergonomics, the study of the relationship between humans and machines. Study in this area has indicated that there are many ways in which the office can become more compatible with humans.

The first component of the office to be redesigned for human use will be the computer itself. Inevitably, the computer will be as essential to the office of the future as the telephone is to the office of today. Therefore, it should be designed for optimum use—taking the user into account. In computer redesign, the first area tackled should be the terminal. Today's terminals take up too much space on the desk. One remedy might be to adopt the swivel arm feature of Wang's new Professional Computer. This arm holds the computer several inches above the desk. Work space on the desk is saved, and the only space lost at all is the three inches required for the clamp that holds the arm in place. In ad-

Figure 20–2
Teleconferencing

High-Speed Fax

Japan holds the reins on the growing high-speed photo facsimile (fax) machine market, but the fastest such device is the French-made CIT-Alcatel. Japanese fax machines—some of which can be linked to word processors, computers, and message-storing units—can transmit a standard page in less than a minute. The French fax, however, can transmit a page in three seconds. Such speed, with the auxiliary capabilities, foreshadows increased competition with regular mail service. In the future, as the cost of these machines drops, they may even completely replace the postal and air express industries for printed materials.

dition, the arm allows the office worker to push the computer out of the way when it is not needed.

An even better idea would be a flat, folding terminal. Such a terminal (without the folding option) has been available for almost fifteen years. It is called a **flat plasma display screen** and has not caught on yet because of its high cost. However, mass production easily could change that.

Naturally, the display itself should be a soft light that is easy to read and easy on the eyes. One suggestion has been a liquid crystal display (LCD) much like the displays on most digital wristwatches. The traditional QWERTY keyboard probably will be eliminated. It has been known for a long time that there are more efficient ways of arranging the letters for maximum typing speed. One of those ways undoubtedly will be adopted, perhaps the Maltron Keyboard proposed by Malt Keyboard Dynamics, Inc. The keyboard will fold into the display for easy storage and an uncluttered desk.

But aren't we taking a few things for granted? Will we have desks? Will we still be typing? It would be much easier simply to talk to the computer. Surely it will be able to understand us in the future. Great progress is being made in the area of vocal input. And desks? Desks are used mainly to store papers. Will there be any papers in the office of the future? There may not be. Word processing, electronic mail, and the proliferation of computer terminals are eliminating the paper-based office.

Word-processing systems allow people to write, edit, insert, delete, and rearrange text (see Figure 20–3). They enable users to change a manuscript many times without retyping. They save time in the office, and time is money.

Electronic mail is an extension of word processing. It allows text to be transferred from one word processor to another in a different office, building, or city. Using electronic mail, text is transmitted at high speeds over telecommunications facilities. Because the mail is received immediately and stored, it helps businesspeople avoid the problem of

Figure 20—3 Word
Processing System

"just missing" each other's calls. There are two basic types of electronic
mail in use; teletypewriter systems and facsimile systems. Teletypewriter systems transmit text in character strings. Facsimile systems transmit a "picture" of the entire page of text. Although electronic mail can
be used across the country, it often is used in local-area networks
(LANs), systems of computers and peripherals in connected buildings
and offices that are linked electronically.

Unfortunately, electronic mail is still a very expensive form of communication, and many people that others wish to contact may not have
a terminal at their disposal. An inexpensive alternative to electronic
mail is an electronic message system called **Voice Store and Forward
(VSF).** VSF is a relatively inexpensive service that is offered for a
monthly rate and requires only that the users have push-button telephones. VSF changes voices into digital form and stores them in the
computer at the VSF company. Receiving parties then can retrieve calls
at any time simply using their telephones. This is an excellent alternative to electronic mail, but it probably will fade away as more offices
become automated and electronic mail becomes less expensive because
of increasing demand.

Reprographics, or computer typesetting, is another facility available
in the automated office. It is very useful for companies that do any publishing, such as newspaper offices. A reprographics system is a computer
connected to a typesetting machine. The document or text is prepared

and edited on the word processor. All formats are specified, such as titles in boldface type, certain words in italic type, and so on. The final text then is printed on film "repro" paper, already having been electronically typeset and ready for the printer.

All these systems and others will be available in the truly automated office. The only major technological problem to be overcome is that of compatibility. Today's offices contain most of the machinery necessary to be called truly automated offices. Unfortunately, these machines have not been made so that they can communicate with each other. Word processors made by Company X cannot talk to word processors made by Company Y, and so on. In the future, all office machinery will communicate with all other office machinery. This theoretically will enable all office personnel to spend their working time tending to the really important aspects of the business rather than the paperwork.

INDUSTRIAL ROBOTS

Like the office of the future, the factory of the future also will be automated. Industrial robots already are taking their places in assembly lines around the world. Today's industrial robots are basically mechanical arms that are bolted to the floor and equipped with either pneumatic, hydraulic, or electrical power systems (see Figure 20–4). They have limited "sight" and/or "hearing" capabilities and, for the most part, are built for a single function.

The production of industrial robots began in the 1960s, but the world was not yet ready for them. Production was slow, and profit was nonexistent. Robots that cost sixty thousand dollars to build sold for only twenty-five thousand dollars. Industry was not ready for industrial robots until 1974. From that point, the market exploded. Unimation, the world's largest industrial robot manufacturer, watched sales soar from eight million dollars in 1974 to thirty-five million dollars in 1980. The demand for robots had finally caught up to the supply. That demand is expected to keep growing by 30 to 40 percent a year, with worldwide sales for 1990 projected at over three billion dollars. It is no wonder that General Electric, IBM, and General Motors all have formed robotics divisions.

Part of the reason that the demand for industrial robots has expanded so dramatically is that manufacturers and employees are beginning to realize what these robots can do. Although many employees still fear being replaced by robots, they are seeing first-hand that this is usually not the case. It is true that one of the uses of robots is on multiple-shift jobs where one robot can replace several employees for cost effectiveness. More often, though, robots are used in dangerous jobs where employees could be injured or killed. Robots work with dangerous fumes, toxic chemicals, and other materials in jobs that their human counterparts would prefer not to do. They are replacing human workers in boring, repetitive jobs where absenteeism is excessively high. Robots are also used in tiring jobs where it is obvious that employees perform

Figure 20—4
Industrial Robots

poorly later in the day because of fatigue. Problem areas where product damage and operator error are high are also prime candidates for robot automation.

As the applications of industrial robots continue to expand, the capabilities of these robots also will expand. We are quickly coming to the goal of roboticists. They see, in the future, a totally automated factory completely run by robots, with only a few token humans for routine maintenance and supervision. This future factory may be here more quickly than we had anticipated. In Japan the already designed prototype is slated to open in 1984. An automated factory in Italy is planned to be running by 1990.

PERSONAL ROBOTS

Very few dreamers could imagine a future without robots. We envision a society filled with metallic, pseudohuman slaves that follow us about and wait on us constantly.

Today we are seeing the beginning of that society. Personal robots are finally on the market. To be sure, those offered now are very primitive, boiled-down versions of what is to come, but they are definitely a start.

In the early 1980s, the first domestic robots were introduced. Mostly designed for computer hobbyists, they are expensive, clumsy, and very limited in function and capability. One of these robots is **HERO 1**—

A Candlelight Dinner

The effects of computers on society are already profound. They are helping with everything from marketing techniques to making dinner.

How does a candlelight dinner sound? Romantic? There is a robot specially designed to prepare just this. A one-armed, stationary robot, built for quadriplegics, was developed at the Veterans Administration Rehabilitation, Research and Development Center in California. The specially developed robot has a fifty-seven-word vocabulary. Upon human voice command, the robot opens a refrigerator, removes a TV dinner, places it in a microwave oven, and starts the oven. It then lights a candle, extinguishes the match, removes the dinner, and places it on a table.

How is that for service? And remember, this is only a candle's reflection of what will be possible tomorrow.

short for **Heath Educational RObot.** HERO 1 is twenty inches high and gleaming metal. This robot sports a mechanical arm that allows the robot to manipulate small objects and carry up to five pounds. HERO can make you a martini or patrol the house for burglars while you are away. The problem is the things that HERO cannot do. HERO cannot wash the dishes, vacuum the rug, make the bed, wash the car, mow the lawn, and so on. HERO cannot do anything without being programmed by an outside source—that is, through a separate home computer—and the robot cannot do anything that requires lifting or pushing more than five pounds. This puts most of the things that people would like a robot to do in the category of things that HERO cannot do. As far as helping around the house, HERO is not very useful. One of the few things the robot is programmed to say is "I don't do windows."

However, HERO is a first generation robot. Like the first generation computers, first generation anythings do not generally do much. They show us where our mistakes are and what we need to work on.

In addition to HERO, there are several other domestic robots on the market. GENUS is one, and GENUS also does not do windows. GENUS does vacuum, though. A beater brush attachment can be inserted under GENUS's "feet" so that while it is wandering about the house, it is picking up dust and lint. Otherwise, GENUS does not do much that HERO does not do. Perhaps it should be more accurately said that GENUS also cannot do the same things that HERO cannot do. In addition, GENUS is much more expensive. HERO costs about $1,500 in kit form or $2,400 if the buyer perfers to have it preassembled. GENUS costs between $5,000 and $8,000. (For some reason the manufacturers cannot seem to make up their minds.)

What HERO and GENUS--and their Androbot friends **TOPO** and **B.O.B.,** short for **Brain on Board** - - (see Figure 20–5) are doing while

Figure 20–5 Personal
Robots

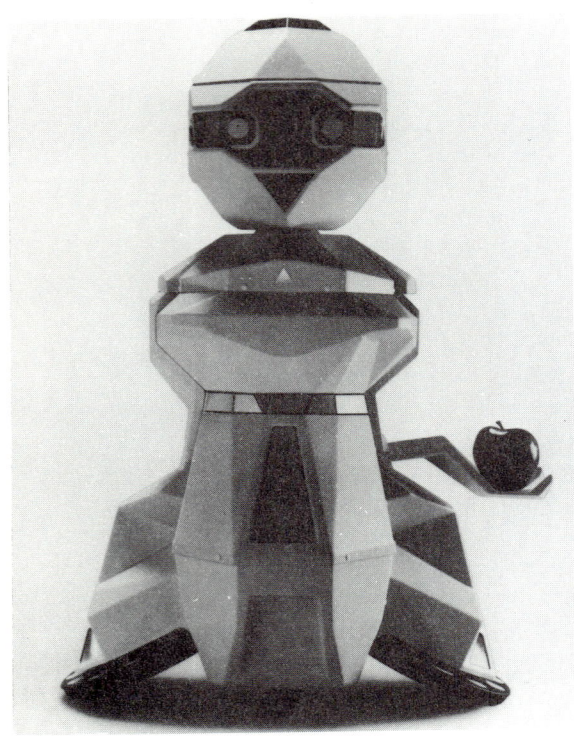

TOPO

B.O.B.

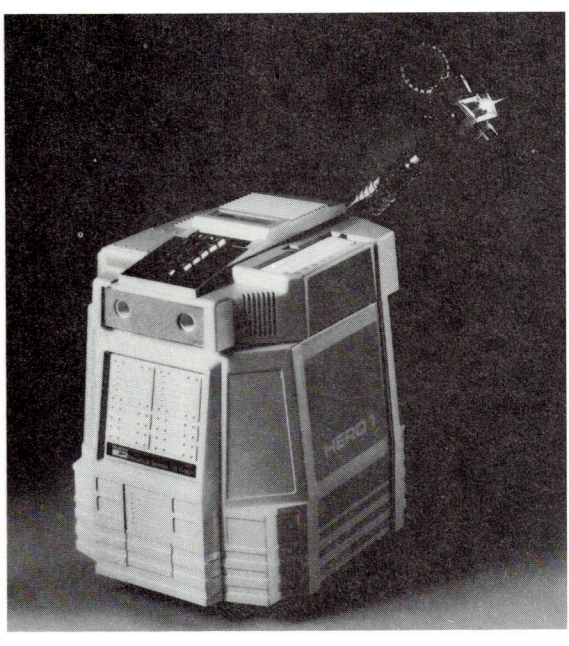

Hero 1

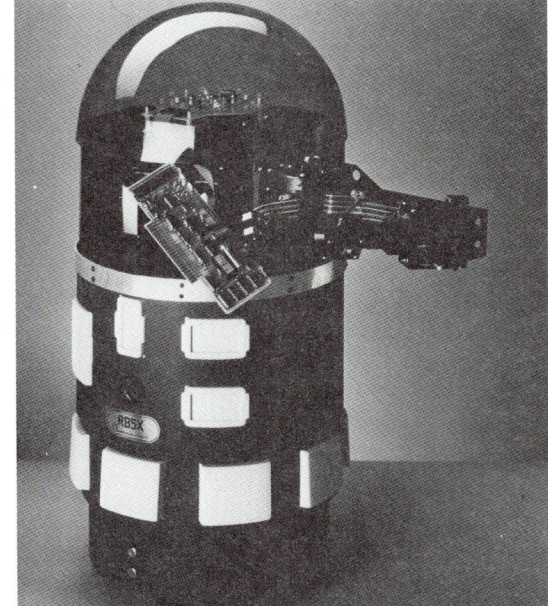

RB5X

they are not doing windows and dishes is working out some of the problems that are specific to personal robots. One of these problems is mobility. Unlike industrial robots, home robots are not clamped to the floor. If they are going to be of use around the house, they must be able to wander about freely. This involves traveling from room to room, preferably through the door and not through the walls. This also means avoiding obstacles such as coffee tables, other furniture, pets, and children. This seems almost a silly notion, but people seem to forget that the circles on the "faces" on the robots are not eyes, but cameras. It is very difficult to teach a robot to recognize visual images. The system of sight and understanding that people use constantly and take for granted is not easily mimicked. In addition, the camera presents a two-dimensional version of the world, yet robots must use that information to function in a three-dimensional setting. Depth and distance are difficult to include in a sight system based on camera images, yet they are essential for a functioning mobile robot (see Figure 20–6).

Some other problems dealing more with AI (and the current lack thereof) will be covered in the next section. Assuming then, for the present, that robots will develop the AI necessary for them to function properly as slaves to humanity, other matters will need to be taken into consideration. If these machines are taught to think, might it not occur to them that they are a bit smarter than people are? Might they then discover that they really have no use for people?

In anticipation of such responses, perhaps it would be best if we followed the fiction of Isaac Asimov and instilled a code of ethics into our machinery. Perhaps we could simply use the code Asimov developed in **I, Robot** (Gnome Press, 1951):

1. A robot may not injure a human being, or, through inaction, allow a human being to come to harm.
2. A robot must obey the orders given it by human beings except where such orders would conflict with the First Law.
3. A robot must protect its own existence as long as such protection does not conflict with the First or Second Law.

Will that work? Already, one of Japan's robots has violated the highest and most sacred of these Three Laws of Robotics. On July 4, 1981, an industrial robot in Tokyo crushed its controller to death. Obviously, the action was not malicious or intentional. Today's robots simply do not have the ability to make such decisions. But will tomorrow's? Can we simply program a robot not to harm a human being and expect it to listen? What if the robot reasons, "I am more intelligent than human beings. Therefore, my reasoning is more correct. Intelligent beings always do the correct thing. Humans are not being correct. They fight each other and destroy the balance of life on this planet. It would be better for the planet if they were eliminated." What would we do with such a robot, or an army of such robots?

Naturally, the argument seems silly. We are worrying about things that are so far off in the future that it is difficult even to visualize them.

Figure 20—6 ODEX,
the First Walking Multi-
function Robot

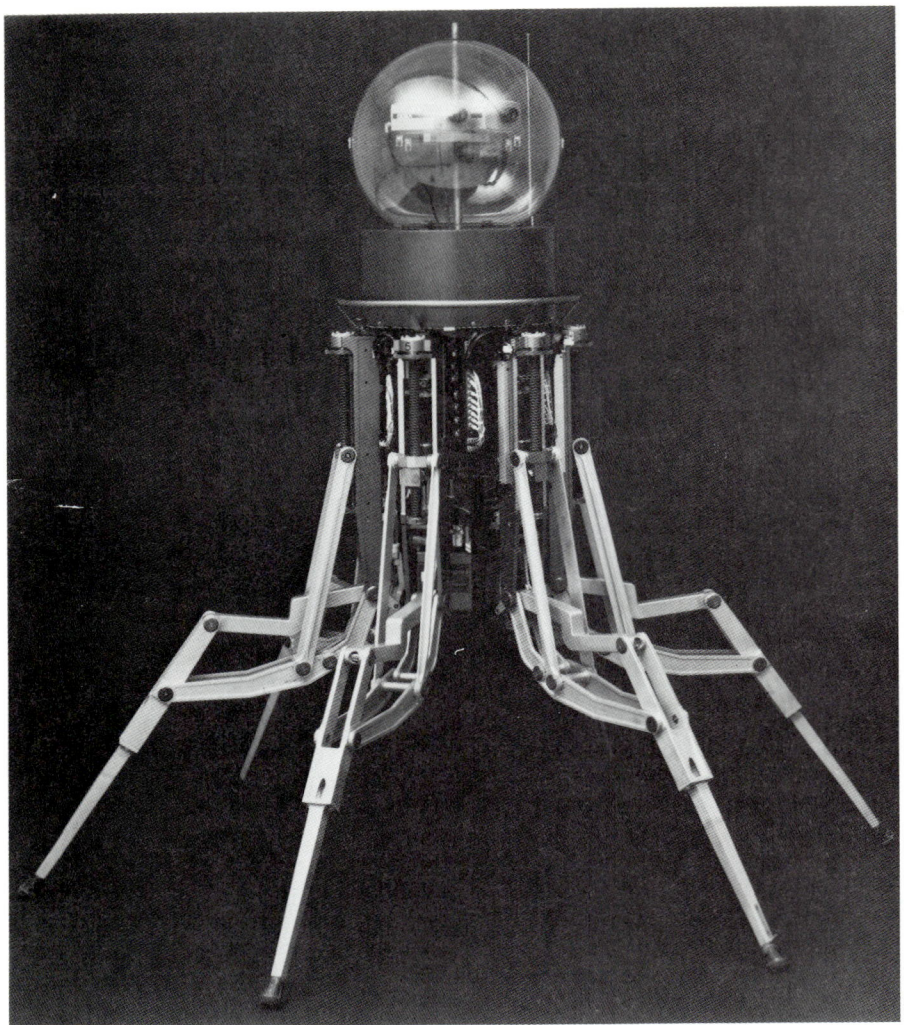

However, would it not be better to work out every possibility for disaster before the possibilities become reality? If, along with giving these machines AI, we can program them with a code of ethics, we could avoid many unpleasant possibilities in the future.

Of course, before we can program their ethics, we must give them common sense, greater freedom of movement, and, naturally, the ability to do windows.

ARTIFICIAL INTELLIGENCE

Before computers in robot form can become the mechanical slaves envisioned by science fiction, they will have to be able to better commu-

2001 in 1992

Japanese computer specialists are working on what they call a fifth generation computer that will revolutionize global communications. Its designers, Hozumi Tanaka and his colleagues at Electro-Technical Laboratory outside Tokyo, claim that the system will approach the intelligence level of HAL, the computer in **2001: A Space Odyssey.**

In addition to executing spoken commands, the system will be equipped with state-of-the-art artificial intelligence. That AI will enable the computer to make inferences, search through information to decide what is important, and even help to program itself.

Perhaps the best part of the computer will be its ability as a translator. Already its prototype can translate between Japanese and English with a hundred-word vocabulary. The final product, which will be finished by 1992, will translate between several languages with a 100,000-word vocabulary and will produce translations that are 90 percent accurate.

What about the other 10 percent? That should not be any problem either—they are teaching it to learn from its mistakes.

nicate with and understand people. First, this will involve perfecting voice input and output. Processing will become faster and less complicated for people when they can simply tell their computers what they want them to do. There have been significant advances in this area, but the major problem is speed. IBM has designed a typewriter that takes dictation, but it is excruciatingly slow. The machine works perfectly, and its transcriptions are accurate. Unfortunately, it takes the machine over one hundred minutes to transcribe thirty seconds' worth of dictation. Obviously no threat to secretaries at the present time, the machine is at least a start, and time surely will improve its efficiency.

Once computers are capable of understanding voice input more quickly, they must be taught to understand figures of speech. Many times humans do not actually say what they mean; what they vocalize is a figurative analogy. Such concepts are beyond the understanding of today's computers and cause large errors in logic when they are not explained. This was made clear in the laboratory of Roger Shank. Shank is chairman of the computer science department at Yale University and is well known for his work in AI. His computer produces summaries and conclusions from the information it is fed. Linguistics poses a major problem in his area. In one specific instance, the computer was fed the newspaper headline "Pope's Death Shakes U.S." The computer concluded that there had been an earthquake. Obviously, if computers are to communicate with human beings in the way that C-3PO and R2-D2 conversed with Luke Skywalker in the **Star Wars** series, either humans must be taught to speak with greater precision or computers must be taught to interpret figurative phrases.

Figure 20–7 Marvin
Minsky and Robot

After the problems with linguistics have been conquered, computers will have to be taught the basics of logic. They will learn inductive and deductive reasoning. They will learn to make value judgments. Most important, they will learn to make decisions based on what is termed **common sense.** This is the most difficult aspect of instilling machines with AI. Without common sense, however, computers will never be able to mimic the thought patterns of people—and that is the goal of AI.

The major problem with AI today is that experts cannot agree on how human beings make decisions based on common sense. Even the two founders of the field cannot agree. Marvin Minsky (see Figure 20–7) and John McCarthy are the founders of AI research. Minsky and McCarthy founded the MIT Artificial Intelligence Laboratory in 1957. McCarthy, who coined the term **artificial intelligence,** then moved on and founded a similar laboratory at Stanford in 1963. Both men agree that the most important part of AI is teaching the computer commonsense reasoning. What they disagree on is the method of doing this.

To both men, common sense is aligned with the ability to recognize exceptions. The example they usually give is "Birds can fly." This statement is usually true unless the bird is a penguin, you are holding the bird's feet, or the bird is dead. Those are all specific exceptions where the statement "Birds can fly" is no longer true.

In ordinary programming logic, machines would have to be programmed to test for the existence of each possible exception every time the term bird was encountered. Obviously, that is not the way humans think. If we thought about every commonsense assumption or decision we made—either by testing for exceptions or consecutively checking our memory for additional information—we would never decide anything.

To advance AI, then, the machine must be taught to make the type of commonsense decisions that humans make consciously without having every possible situation programmed in or consecutively searching for information. One way to do this would be with Minsky's Framing Concept. Minsky claims that when we encounter a situation or a key concept, we form a frame. This frame is the dominant concept under which we operate. For example, in this case, the frame would be birds in general. Associated with this dominant frame would be subframes covering such things as exceptions, egg laying, feathers, and so on. Minsky's concept, then, is based on associative functions.

McCarthy, in contrast, bases his theory on assumptions. The machine should simply assume that general facts such as "Birds can fly" are true unless something prevents them from being true. In other words, the machine would be expected to assume that such a statement were true unless it were given a specific reason explaining why it should not be true. This resembles the way humans operate. Most of the time we work on assumptions and trust, assuming that birds can fly unless we are given a specific reason why a particular bird cannot fly. In this way, McCarthy's reasoning is very similar to formal logic.

Although both theories are valid, the fact remains that neither man has yet determined how a machine can be endowed with commonsense capabilities. Both realize that true AI is still a long way in the future. However, neither doubts that someday and somewhere we, or most probably our descendants, will witness a world with intelligent machines.

CONCLUSION

Through studying the possibilities, it becomes apparent that the future of computers and high technology will be dynamic and ethically explosive. As computers develop agility and the ability to reason, they become more and more a species unto themselves. Will they become our masters or our slaves? Will we, as Asimov wrote in **I, Robot,** be forced to instill in our machines an ethical code to protect ourselves? What are the implications of applying such things as human ethics to inanimate machinery?

However, will the computers of the future be truly inanimate? For centuries human beings have placed themselves above all other creatures for their ability to reason and make value judgments. However, with the dawn of AI and reasoning structures, we will be programming these things into our machines. Although true AI (the ability to mimic the human thought process) is still very far in the future, what will we do when the time arrives? Will not those machines be human by our own definition—"beings" capable of thought and decision making previously attainable only by human intelligence?

Some of these questions, of course, seem too removed from reality to be of much significance now. People's greatest fear at the present time is that the computer will take over—not in the sense of ruling human beings, but by making them obsolete, inadequate, and unnecessary. Factory workers fear being permanently displaced by robots. Scholars wonder what use they will be when more information can be more easily stored, more accurately retrieved, and more quickly synthesized by machine.

Of course, people still will be building the machines and programming them. They still will be in charge of the fundamental decisions.

Or will they? Today in Japan a system is being created that is claimed will help to program itself. The ICs that form the core of all computer systems already are being built using CAD/CAM. Would it not be possible for the computers of the future to design, build, and program their replacements?

This future of endless question marks is still far removed from today's reality. However, the time for questions such as these is long before we find answers that we do not want or cannot cope with.

SUMMARY POINTS

● The future trend in computer hardware will be to continue toward smaller, faster, and more efficient machines. Two areas being researched as possible hardware developments are Josephson technology and biochips. Josephson technology involves cooling metal and then sandwiching thin strips that are electrified and become superconducting. Biochips will be organic circuits composed of protein produced by genetically engineered bacteria.

● The automated office of the future will take today's office systems and integrate them for compatibility. Tomorrow's automated office will include word processing, reprographics, electronic mail, data processing, and the entire array of technology working together in an atmosphere that has been designed with the human factor in mind to constitute history's most productive workplace.

● Industrial robots will be used in larger numbers than ever before. New developments in robotics will produce robots with better "vision," and the capabilities of the machines will increase.

● Today's personal robots will be replaced by more useful and capable versions that will possess sufficient artificial intelligence (AI) to truly serve their human masters.

● The computers of tommorrow will be equipped with AI that will enable them to communicate freely with human beings. They will be able to understand vocal commands, reason through problems, and make decisions based not only on facts, but on common sense as well.

1. What is Josephson technology?
2. What are some possible uses for biochips for which silicon chips would not be suitable?
3. What are the components of an automated office?
4. What is reprographics? What is it used for?
5. Explain electronic mail.
6. What is an industrial robot?
7. What types of jobs are industrial robots being used for?
8. What is the difference between electronic mail and VSF?
9. List five problems with the personal robots currently on the market.
10. List three developments that would make personal robots more practical and enable them to do more for their human masters.
11. Why does linguistics pose a problem in AI research?
12. In what ways do you think the mass production of personal robots would affect society?
13. If you had a personal robot, what are some of the things you would like it to do?
14. What do you think will be the most significant development in computer science in the next decade?

APPENDIX A

NUMBERING SYSTEMS

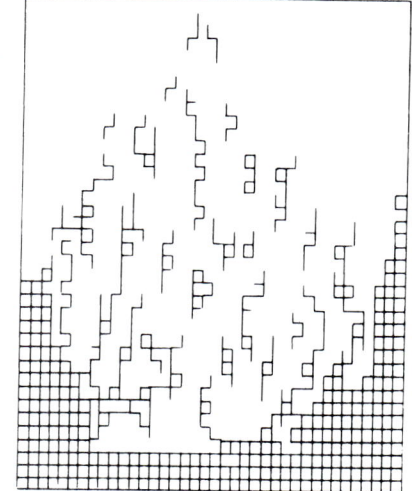

POSITIONAL CONCEPTS

General Rules

The class of numbering systems discussed here is called **positional notation.** This includes the familiar decimal, or base 10, system, as well as any numbering system that conforms to the three rules in the following list. It does not include such numbering systems as the tally system (which does not accord value to the *position* of a number or digit, but only to its face value) or the Roman numeral system (which does not use place value consistently). It does include the systems most commonly used with computers: binary, octal, and hexadecimal.

Any system that meets the requirements of the following three rules can be properly called a **positional notation numbering system:**

1. Each positional notation numbering system is developed around a **base** or **radix**—a value that indicates the following:

   a. The number of unique symbols (digits) that may be used in the system. These digits will range in value from 0 to (base − 1).

   b. The **positional** or **contextual multiplier** for each digit position in a number (b^p in Rule 3).

2. The value of a multidigit number is the sum of the positional or contextual values of its digits.

3. The positional or contextual value of any digit can be determined from the following formula:

   $$\text{Value} = db^p,$$

where d = the face value of the digit, b = the value of the base, and p = the number of positions d is to the left of the units (low-order) digit.

Decimal Example

Let us use these rules to evaluate a number in the decimal system. This process may seem somewhat self-evident because of our deep familiarity with decimal values, but try to follow the concepts to evaluate 7158_{10}. (Here the subscript 10 indicates a decimal, or base 10, number.)

Using the formula from Rule 3 to evaluate the leftmost digit, 7 (also called the **higher-order digit**), we have the following:

$$d = 7$$
$$b = 10 \qquad \text{Or } 7 \times 10^3 = 7000$$
$$p = 3$$

Evaluating the 1 in the same way, we have the following:

$$d = 1$$
$$b = 10 \qquad \text{Or } 1 \times 10^2 = 100$$
$$p = 2$$

In the same way, the 5 is evaluated:

$$d = 5$$
$$b = 10 \qquad \text{Or } 5 \times 10^1 = 50$$
$$p = 1$$

Finally, the rightmost digit, 8 (also called the **low-order** or **units digit**), is evaluated:

$$d = 8$$
$$b = 10 \qquad \text{Or } 8 \times 10^0 = 8$$
$$p = 0 \text{ (Any value raised to the power 0 equals 1.)}$$

To calculate the value of the four-digit number, sum the four positional values:

$$7000 + 100 + 50 + 8 = 7158$$

(back to where we started, because we are working in a familiar numbering system). What we really have accomplished is a reinforcement of the fact that in any positional notation numbering system, the units digit is multiplied by $base^0$, the next position to the left by $base^1$, the next by $base^2$, and so on. In the decimal system these positions become the familiar units, 10s, 100s, and so on.

New Numbering System

Now let us create a new numbering system (base 5) according to our three elementary rules. A base 5 system, as indicated by Rule 1, would legitimately make use of only five unique digits: 0, 1, 2, 3, and 4. A value expressed in base 5 notation as 134_5 would be evaluated for conversion to the decimal system as follows, according to Rule 3:

$$
\begin{aligned}
(1 \times 5^2) + (3 \times 5^1) + (4 \times 5^0) &= \\
(1 \times 25) + (3 \times 5) + (4 \times 1) &= \\
25 \quad + \quad 15 \quad + \quad 4 \quad &= 44_{10}
\end{aligned}
$$

The study of computers typically makes use of three numbering systems other than decimal: binary (base 2), octal (base 8), and hexadecimal (base 16).

THE THREE COMPUTER-RELATED SYSTEMS

Binary Numbering System

Binary is the only numbering system actually used inside computers; it is used because the on (1) and off (0) states of the computer's electronic components make it a logical and reliable means of data representation. The two other computer-related numbering systems—octal and hexadecimal—are convenient shorthand notation forms for the binary system. Both octal (which is infrequently used with contemporary machines) and hexadecimal follow the three elementary rules, however.

According to Rule 1, the only two permissible digits are 0 and 1. These are called **bits,** or **binary digits**. In the formula db^p, the only possible values for d are 0 and 1; consequently, the positional multiplier of a digit will be added to the total when $d = 1$ and ignored when $d = 0$. For example, the binary number 1011001_2 is evaluated as follows:

$$
\begin{aligned}
(1 \times 2^6) + (0 \times 2^5) + (1 \times 2^4) + (1 \times 2^3) + (0 \times 2^2) + (0 \times 2^1) + (1 \times 2^0) &= \\
(1 \times 64) + (0 \times 32) + (1 \times 16) + (1 \times 8) + (0 \times 4) + (0 \times 2) + (1 \times 1) &= \\
64 \quad + \quad 0 \quad + \quad 16 \quad + \quad 8 \quad + \quad 0 \quad + \quad 0 \quad + \quad 1 \quad &= 89_{10}
\end{aligned}
$$

Starting from the rightmost, or low-order, digit (bit position), the positional values in binary—rather than the units, 10s, 100s, 1,000s, and so on used in decimal—are units, 2s, 4s, 8s, 16s, 32s, 64s, and so on.

The following are the positional values as they would appear in a number:

$$
\begin{aligned}
&128 \; 64 \; 32 \; 16 \; 8 \; 4 \; 2 \; 1 \\
\text{or} \quad & \\
&2^7 \; 2^6 \; 2^5 \; 2^4 \; 2^3 \; 2^2 \; 2^1 \; 2^0
\end{aligned}
$$

As in the decimal system, of course, there is no limit to the number of digits that can appear in a number.

Octal Numbering System

The octal numbering system employs the value 8 as the base or radix. Its primary use is as a shorthand representation form for binary numbers in machines that use a six-bit byte as the unit of information (a common byte size in machines of the 1960s and before).

According to Rule 1, the permissible digits in an octal number are 0, 1, 2, 3, 4, 5, 6, and 7.

The value 2734_8 would be evaluated as follows:

$$
\begin{array}{rcl}
(2 \times 8^3) + (7 \times 8^2) + (3 \times 8^1) + (4 \times 8^0) &=& \\
(2 \times 512) + (7 \times 64) + (3 \times 8) + (4 \times 1) &=& \\
1024 \quad + \quad 448 \quad + \quad 24 \quad + \quad 4 &=& 1500_{10}
\end{array}
$$

Place values are units, 8s, 64s, 512s, and so on. Positional values as they would appear in an octal number are as follows:

$$
\begin{array}{cccccc}
32768 & 4096 & 512 & 64 & 8 & 1 \\
\end{array}
$$

or

$$
\begin{array}{cccccc}
8^5 & 8^4 & 8^3 & 8^2 & 8^1 & 8^0
\end{array}
$$

Hexadecimal Numbering System

The hexadecimal numbering system employs the base 16. This is the first base larger than 10 described here. The hexadecimal system is used in contemporary computer systems as the standard method of representing binary values compactly in systems using the eight-bit byte as the standard unit of information. As will be shown later, the use of hexadecimal notation to represent binary notation reduces the number of digits required by a factor of 4.

Referring back to Rule 1, we see that there must be sixteen different individual symbols or digits used with hexadecimal notation (frequently called **hex**). The symbols used to represent decimal values above 9 are the letters *A* through *F*, with meanings of 10 through 15, respectively. The value $2B7E_{16}$ would be evaluated as follows:

$$
\begin{array}{rcl}
(2 \times 16^3) + (B \times 16^2) + (7 \times 16^1) + (E \times 16^0) &=& \\
(2 \times 4096) + (11 \times 256) + (7 \times 16) + (14 \times 1) &=& \\
8192 \quad + \quad 2816 \quad + \quad 112 \quad + \quad 14 &=& 11134_{10}
\end{array}
$$

Representation Summary

The following table gives the values equivalent to the decimal values 0 through 15 in each of the three computer-related numbering systems introduced. Leading 0s may be eliminated from the representation in any numbering system; they are shown here for reasons of conversion simplicity:

Decimal	Binary	Octal	Hexadecimal
0	0000	00	0
1	0001	01	1
2	0010	02	2
3	0011	03	3
4	0100	04	4
5	0101	05	5
6	0110	06	6
7	0111	07	7
8	1000	10	8
9	1001	11	9
10	1010	12	A
11	1011	13	B
12	1100	14	C
13	1101	15	D
14	1110	16	E
15	1111	17	F

CONVERSION BETWEEN BINARY, OCTAL, AND HEXADECIMAL SYSTEMS

There is a special relationship between the binary, octal, and hexadecimal systems, because the base for each is a power of 2: for binary, 2^1; for octal, 2^3; and for hexadecimal, 2^4. From the table in the preceding section you can see that any single octal digit can be represented by three binary digits; likewise, any single hexadecimal digit can be represented by four binary digits. Because each successive position in a binary number (moving to the left) represents the next higher power of 2, and because $2^3 = 8$ and $2^4 = 16$, we can directly convert a binary value to its octal equivalent by beginning at the low-order digit and marking off groups of three bits. When this has been done, we can directly convert each group of three bits to its single octal equivalent. The resulting octal digits will have a value equal to that of the original binary number.

Examples: Given the binary value 1011100, we can mark it off as follows:

001/011/100.

(Note that we can add leading 0s). This equates to $1/3/4_8$. Using the three fundamental rules, we can see that the binary and octal numbers both equal 92_{10}.

It is equally easy to convert from octal to binary notation. Given the octal value: 6/4/2/7, we can directly convert to binary:

110/100/010/111.

What is the decimal equivalent of these two values?

The conversion process between binary and hexadecimal notation is similar, except that the ratio of bits to hexadecimal digits is 4 to 1. Again, we must start from the rightmost digit of the binary value if we wish to convert it to hexadecimal notation. Using the binary value in the immediately preceding example, 1101/0001/0111 can be directly converted to $D/1/7_{16}$ Therefore, $110100010111_2 = 6427_8 = D17_{16} = 3351_{10}$.

It is again easy to go the opposite direction and substitute groupings of four binary digits for each hexadecimal digit we wish to convert. Thus, B/2/A becomes 1011/0010/1010.

The 3-to-1 ratio of binary to octal digits and the 4-to-1 ratio of binary to hexadecimal digits are the reasons that octal and hexadecimal values are used to represent bytes of six and eight bits, respectively. Two octal digits typically are used to represent the bit structure of a six-bit byte; two hexadecimal digits are used as shorthand notation for an eight-bit byte.

CONVERSION TO AND FROM DECIMAL NOTATION

Because the decimal system does not share a common root for its base with the binary, octal or hexadecimal systems, conversion to and from decimal notation requires some arithmetic. The rules differ for conversion to decimal notation and conversion from decimal notation, but they are the same regardless of the number system other than decimal that is involved.

Converting to Decimal Notation from Another Base

To convert a number to decimal notation from another base, do the following steps:

1. Multiply the high-order (leftmost) digit of the number by its base.
2. Add in the next digit to the right.
3. Multiply the sum by the base.
4. Repeat Steps 2 and 3 until the units digit has been added in. The sum is the decimal equivalent.

Examples: a. Convert 527_8 to decimal notation:

$$
\begin{array}{r}
5 \quad\quad 2 \quad\quad 7_8 \\
\times\ \ 8 \quad\quad\quad\quad\quad \\
\hline
40 \quad\quad\quad\quad\quad\quad \\
+\ \ 2 \leftarrow\quad\quad\quad \\
\hline
42 \quad\quad\quad\quad\quad \\
\times\ \ 8 \quad\quad\quad\quad\quad \\
\hline
336 \quad\quad\quad\quad \\
+\ \ 7 \leftarrow \\
\hline
343_{10}
\end{array}
$$

b. Convert 1101_2 to decimal notation:

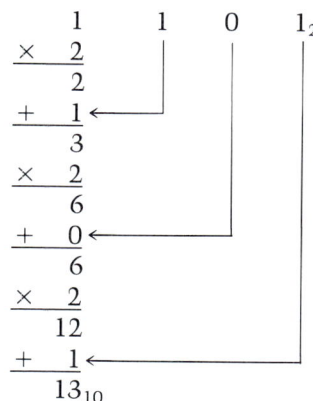

Converting from Decimal Notation to Another Base

To convert from decimal notation to another base, follow these steps:

1. Divide the decimal number by the desired base.
2. Keep the **remainder** as the units digit of the new number.
3. Divide the **quotient** from the previous division by the desired base.
4. Keep the **remainder** as the next digit to the left.
5. Repeat Steps 3 and 4 until division yields a quotient of 0; the remainder of that step will be the high-order digit of the new number.

Examples: **a.** Convert 923_{10} to hexadecimal notation:

```
16)923
 16)57            Rem.     11 (B)
  16)3      Rem.     9
    0   Rem.     3
                ↓      ↓      ↓
 Result =       3      9      B₁₆
```

b. Convert 743_{10} to octal notation:

```
8)743
 8)92                  Rem.     7
  8)11          Rem.     4
   8)1    Rem.     3
     0  Rem.     1
 Result =       1      3      4      7₈
```

READING A COMPUTER CORE DUMP

A common use of the hexadecimal number system is in the display of the contents of computer memory when a program is terminated be-

Figure A–1
Conversion of a Core
Dump

C3D6D407	E4E3C5D9	E200D5C5	E5C5D900
D4C1D2C5	D4E8E2E3	C1C5D2E2	0000F0F1
F2F3F4F5	F6F7F9F8	00005A5A	00000000

C3D6D4D7 =
$$C3 = (12 \times 16^1) + (3 \times 16^0) = 195.$$
$$D6 = (13 \times 16^1) + (6 \times 16^0) = 214.$$
$$D4 = (13 \times 16^1) + (4 \times 16^0) = 212.$$
$$D7 = (13 \times 16^1) + (7 \times 16^0) = 215.$$

Table A–1 DECIMAL EQUIVALENTS TO EBCDIC CHARACTER SET

Decimal Value	Hexadecimal Value	Character	EBCDIC Bit Configuration
193	C1	A	1100 0001
194	C2	B	1100 0010
195	C3	C	1100 0011
196	C4	D	1100 0100
197	C5	E	1100 0101
198	C6	F	1100 0110
199	C7	G	1100 0111
200	C8	H	1100 1000
201	C9	I	1100 1001
209	D1	J	1101 0001
210	D2	K	1101 0010
211	D3	L	1101 0011
212	D4	M	1101 0100
213	D5	N	1101 0101
214	D6	O	1101 0110
215	D7	P	1101 0111
216	D8	Q	1101 1000
217	D9	R	1101 1001
226	E2	S	1110 0010
227	E3	T	1110 0011
228	E4	U	1110 0100
229	E5	V	1110 0101
230	E6	W	1110 0110
231	E7	X	1110 0111
232	E8	Y	1110 1000
233	E9	Z	1110 1001
240	F0	0	1111 0000
241	F1	1	1111 0001
242	F2	2	1111 0010
243	F3	3	1111 0011
244	F4	4	1111 0100
245	F5	5	1111 0101
246	F6	6	1111 0110
247	F7	7	1111 0111
248	F8	8	1111 1000
249	F9	9	1111 1001
250	FA	!	1111 1010

cause of an error. This display is referred to as **core dump,** and its conversion from hexadecimal to decimal notation for error diagnosis can be accomplished as follows. Figure A–1 represents a portion of a core dump. (Note that a group of two characters within the dump represents one byte of information.)

Table A–1 lists the decimal equivalents to the EBCDIC character set: 195 = C, 214 = O, 212 = M, and 215 = P. Thus, C3D6D4D7 = COMP. The remaining eleven groups of eight hexadecimal characters can be converted in the same manner using Table A–1.

APPENDIX B

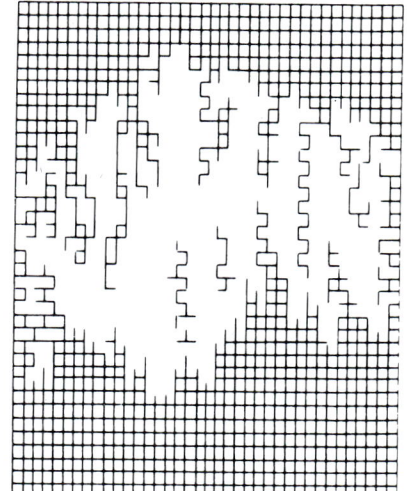

RANDOMIZING TECHNIQUES

RANDOM-ACCESS PROCESSING

Overview

As noted in the text, there are three basic types of computer file organizations used in data processing. Standard sequential file organization is designed so that each and every record within a file is read beginning with the first record each time the file is accessed. Index sequential file organizations, so named for the index of records contained within each file, can be accessed either sequentially or by random-access processing. When index sequential files are accessed randomly, the computer operating system performs the functions necessary to access a particular record within the file. Random-access, or direct-access, file organizations, however, can only be accessed randomly. The functions necessary to access a particular record within the file are contained in the program itself. The process typically used to direct the computer operating system to read a particular record is referred to as **randomizing,** or **hashing,** and is a function of the computer program written for a given application such as inventory control.

Random-access processing, therefore, provides a means of going directly to a chosen record within a file without reading any of the records prior to or after the desired record. This type of processing therefore can provide up-to-the-minute information at an efficient speed. To accommodate direct-access processing, computer files must be stored on a direct-access storage device (DASD). This type of device is usually either magnetic disk storage or magnetic drum storage.

To facilitate direct-access processing, an identifier must be chosen that will uniquely identify each record within the file. This unique identifier is called a **key** and can be, for example, a part number, a flight number, or a customer number contained in each record within the file. It is upon this key that a randomizing technique is used to create a record address identifying the location of a particular record in secondary memory.

An address can be thought of as an identifier of a unique location in computer secondary memory much the same as 1558 Main Street represents a unique location in a given city. Addresses, therefore, are used to locate a character, element of data, or record within the computer's memory. If, for example, a record were stored on a magnetic disk in the fifth cyclinder on the fourth track of the cylinder, and it were the tenth record on the track, the address representing the record might be 0050410. The computer operating system could be directed to read the record by being given the address 0050410.

Applications

As can be seen, there are a great number of applications for which direct-access processing of file contents is desirable. Such applications as inventory control, airline reservations, and bank record keeping require almost immediate updating of files containing supplies on hand, flight availability, and account balances, respectively, to operate efficiently and effectively. Without direct-access processing, the use of computers in these environments would be limited.

RANDOMIZING TECHNIQUES

The division/remainder method of randomizing is perhaps the most widely used of randomizing techniques (which also include such methods as shifting and folding). The following material will demonstrate the use of the division/remainder method on a large mainframe computer (IBM 370) and a microcomputer (Apple II).

Division/Remainder Method: Mainframe Computers

When developing a randomizing algorithm that will convert a record key to a track identifier, the user must consider the size of the file being created and the type and capacity of the DASD to be used. Tables listing the characteristics of the storage devices generally are provided by computer manufacturers. Such figures as the number of bytes per track, number of tracks per cylinder, number of cylinders per device, and total device capacity in bytes can be used in determining the size of a given file in terms of the storage device chosen.

A common problem faced when using a randomizing algorithm within a program is that of synonyms. Synonyms (also called "collisions" and "hash clashes") occur as a result of a record key value randomizing to the address of an already existing record. This occurs when different record key values randomize to the same storage address, because the number of record storage addresses allocated for the file is usually much smaller than the possible number of unique keys. (A file of 10,000 records might have keys with a possible range of 100,000,000—only a few of which are present in the actual file.) When a synonym occurs, the computer recognizes that an attempt is being made to store a record where one already exists, causing an error condition. The program then must take corrective action, such as checking the next location.

An algorithm, therefore, should be developed that will infrequently create the same value from two unique keys. One method of minimizing synonyms is that of increasing the file storage size by about 20 percent beyond what is required and creating an algorithm that will spread the records across the available storage space as evenly as possible. A division/remainder method algorithm using a prime number as the divisor and the record key as the dividend can be demonstrated as follows, assuming a file with five thousand records and 150 characters (bytes) per record:

1. Calculate the file storage size, increasing the actual file size by 20 percent to reduce the frequency of synonyms:

    $5,000 \times 1.20 = 6,000$ records
    $6,000 \times 150 = 900,000$ characters (bytes)

2. Determine the number of tracks on the DASD that will be needed to hold the file (assuming track capacity of 9,500 bytes).

    900,000 characters/9,500 characters per track = 95 tracks

If an IBM disk were to be used with a capacity of 19,000 bytes per track (double the amount used in the previous calculation), there would be a 50 percent utilization of space when the file was created. This 50 percent utilization allows for the addition of records in the future and also for the spreading of records across the range of the file.

3. Choose the prime number that is closest to, but not greater than, the number of tracks required for file storage:

    89 is the closest prime number to 95.

4. If the record key is numeric, divide it by the prime number. If the record key is alphanumeric, convert it to a numeric value and divide the resultant value by the prime number:

    4A65 = 4165
    4165/89 = 46, remainder 71

The quotient, 46, will be ignored, and the remainder, 71 will be used as the relative track address. Also note that because the largest remainder is 88, a maximum of eighty-nine tracks will be used (zero through eighty-eight).

In this case it is sufficient to give the computer operating system the track address. The entire track will be read in the search for the desired record.

Division/Remainder Method: Microcomputers

When developing a randomizing algorithm for a microcomputer using a disk operating system, a relative record address is used to access a particular record. **Relative record address** refers to the record number within the direct-access file. For example, if a file contained one hundred total records, the records would be referred to as Records 1, 2, 3, . . . , 100. When randomizing, therefore, the randomizing algorithm must create a unique whole number to act as the record location identifier.

The disk operating system begins storing the file wherever room is available on the diskette and continues until the entire file has been stored. As the direct-access file is created, the microcomputer's operating system creates a list for the file that contains information that tells the operating system where each record of the file is located on the diskette. This list would include the relative record number and its track and sector location on the diskette. A directory also is created by the disk operating system, containing such information as the file name, file type, file size, and the location of the list containing the record locations.

Since the microcomputer's disk operating system creates the file by filling any available open locations, it is not possible to allocate a given amount of space for a file and attempt to spread the records across the range of the size of the file. Also, this concept may not be possible because of microcomputer storage capacity limitations. It is possible, however, to attempt to spread the relative record numbers created by the randomizing algorithm across the range of available key values.

As was noted, it is also necessary to calculate the size of the direct-access file and determine whether the diskette capacity is sufficient to handle the file. Information regarding the capacity of the diskette is provided by the manufacturers. The standard diskette used on the Apple II microcomputer is a thirty-five-track, sixteen-sector diskette (a sector being a segment of a track). Each sector contains 256 bytes, giving a total diskette capacity of approximately 140,000 bytes. (However, the disk operating system occupies three tracks and reserves one track for the file directory, leaving approximately 125,000 bytes for the storage of user files.)

An example of a division/remainder method algorithm for the creation of a relative record number follows. The direct-access file that is to be created contains five hundred records with 120 bytes per record, and it has key values of four digits each ranging from 1000 to 9000. We will use 1002 as our example key. In this approach we will use fractions rather than remainders as the basis for calculating relative record numbers:

1. Calculate the size of the file, and determine if it can be stored on the diskette:

500 × 120 = 60,000 characters (bytes)

2. Choose the prime number that is closest to, but not greater than or equal to, the number of records in the file:

499 is the closest prime number to 500.

3. If the record key is numeric, divide it by the prime number. If the record key is alphanumeric, convert it to a numeric value, and divide it by the prime number:

1002/499 = 2.008

If the algorithm were complete at this point, the fraction that was created would have sixteen possible synonyms (all key values differing from 1002 by multiples of 499). Therefore, further calculations should be performed.

4. The result of Step 3 could be multiplied by 13 (the closest prime number to 16), and that result then could be divided by 499:

2.008 × 13 = 26.104
26.104/499 = 0.052

The quotient of 0 will be ignored, and the fraction of 0.052 will be used as the relative record number. Note that if the calculations are performed on the key of 1501, which would have been a synonym of 1002 after Step 3, the relative record number of 78 is created. This indicates that a spread of twenty-six relative record numbers occurs for approximately each five hundred key values. If a greater spread were needed, additional calculations could be performed to increase the spread of relative record numbers to key values. When a fraction in excess of 0.499 is generated, it can be reduced through division by 2 or other, more sophisticated means.

   Although an algorithm may appear to be correct initially, it may be necessary to alter it several times before all key values can be randomized to a unique identifier. General methods of developing a randomizing algorithm can be discussed and illustrated; however, it is likely that the algorithm will change from application to application, file to file, and computer to computer.

Other Techniques

Although the division/remainder method is most common, other approaches to mapping key numbers to relative storage locations may be used. **Folding** involves shortening a key by adding digits at its beginning and end to those in its middle.

Example: When there are one thousand relative record numbers and a seven-digit key, view the key as having "hinges" between its second and third and between its fifth and sixth digits:

43¦527¦18

"Fold" the first two and the last two digits by adding them in reverse order to the three internal digits:

```
   527
 + 34
   867
 +  81
   948
```

(Any carry out of the high-order position may be dropped.) The resultant relative record number is 948.

Truncating merely drops digits from one or both ends of the key. Using the same key value and truncating the two high-order and the two low-order digits, we would generate a relative record number of 527. This approach is also called **shifting.**

Other, more complex methods, such as midsquares and radix conversion, also can be used; this appendix has attempted to show only selected alternative approaches to randomizing.

APPENDIX C

FLOWCHARTING COMMON PROBLEM SOLUTIONS

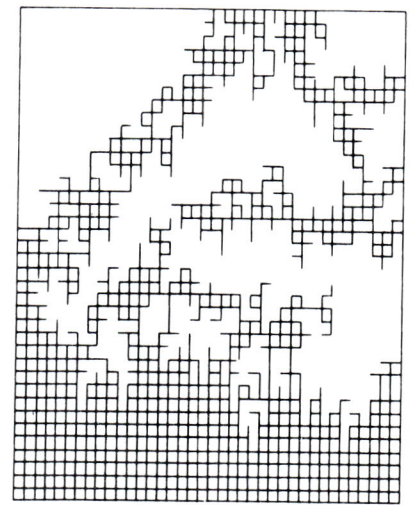

A number of problem solutions are common to many business applications. When a computer is used to solve these problems, the problem must first be clearly defined. Once the problem has been defined, a flowchart is prepared representing the problem solution. In representing the problem solution, a flowchart employs one or a combination of more than one of the four basic patterns of logic.

These basic logic patterns in a flowchart can be used to represent such common processes as using a counter within a program, searching data for certain characteristics, file sorting, accumulation of subtotals and totals, table handling, and file merging. These activities are common to many business applications; each can be considered an entire computer program or a portion of a program.

Pseudocode can be used to represent these problem solutions as well. Like flowcharting, it simply serves as a representation of the computer program logic necessary to help solve the defined problem. Flowcharts and pseudocode are differing depictions of logic patterns that can be translated into any computer programming language.

USING A COUNTER

A variable, or memory location, designated as a **counter** can be used in a program to count such things as the number of records read, the number of males or females processed by a payroll program, or the number of lines printed per page of a report. A counter can be used in a great number of ways within a program.

One important consideration when using a counter in a program is that, depending on the program logic, the counter at some time must be set to 0 (initialized). This is particularly important when the counter is contained within a loop logic pattern that is repeated more than once

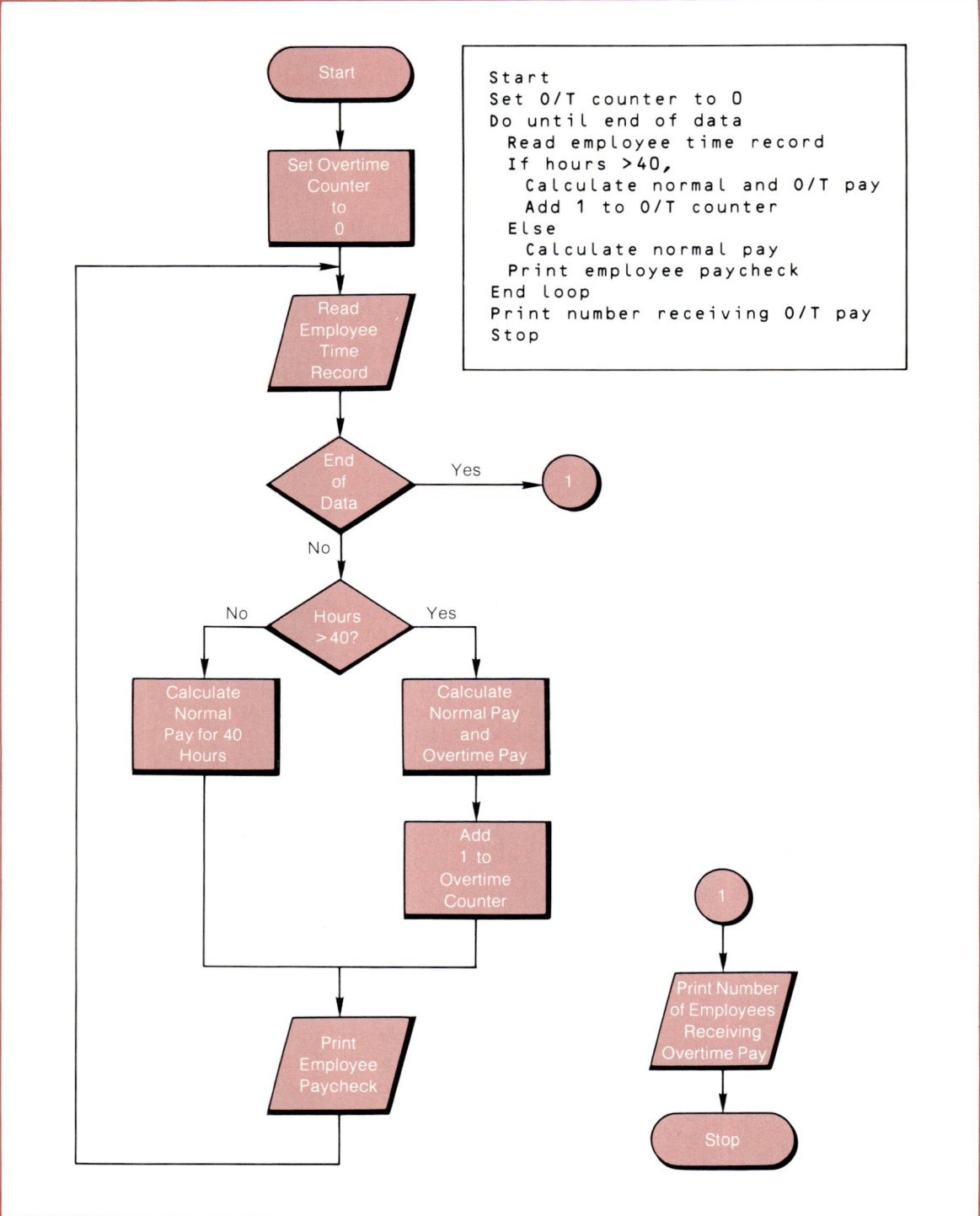

```
Start
Set O/T counter to 0
Do until end of data
  Read employee time record
  If hours >40,
    Calculate normal and O/T pay
    Add 1 to O/T counter
  Else
    Calculate normal pay
  Print employee paycheck
End loop
Print number receiving O/T pay
Stop
```

Figure C–1 Overtime Pay Eligibility

during the execution of the program. Figure C–1 shows the flowchart and pseudocode representing the logic for a counter to establish the number of employees receiving overtime pay.

SEARCHING DATA

In many instances it is necessary to read a record and then determine whether the data in the record meets certain predetermined criteria. An

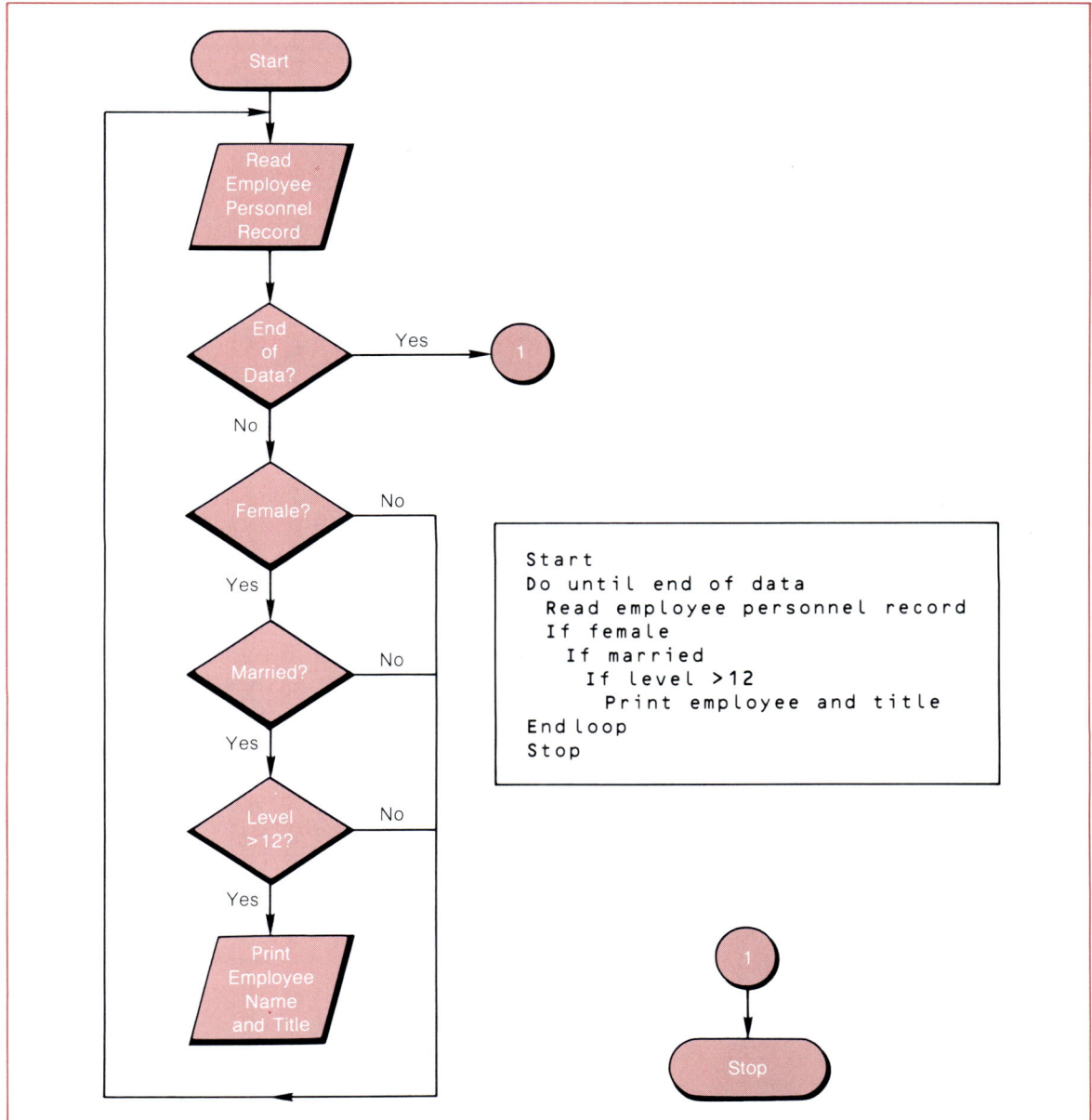

Figure C–2 Print Selected Employee Records

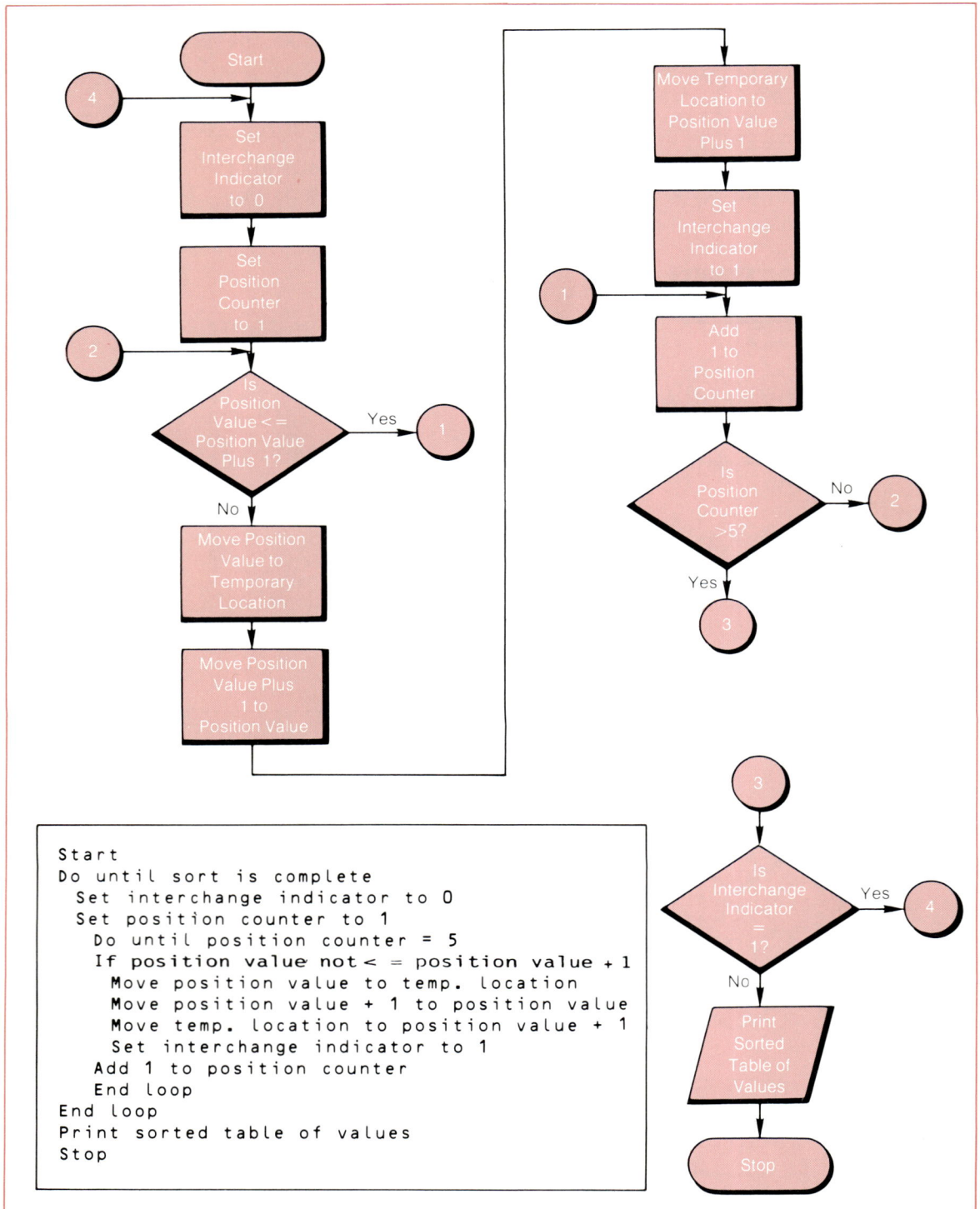

Figure C–3 Bubble Sort (Descending Order)

Position	Value	Sorted
1	15	11
2	11	12
3	12	13
4	13	14
5	16	15
6	14	16

Note = The terms **position value** and **position value plus 1** here refer to the values in Positions 1 and 2 (15 and 11) the first time; then they refer to those in Positions 2 and 3, 3 and 4, 4 and 5, and 5 and 6, in turn.

Fig. C–3 (cont.)

example of such a situation might be the need to identify all married women currently occupying positions in a corporation at the level of middle management or above. Within the corporation's scheme, the lowest middle management position is designated as a level of 13. Figure C–2 shows the flowchart and pseudocode written to accomplish a search of the corporation's personnel data to meet the criteria requested.

FILE SORTING

Often files have to be sequenced either alphabetically or by such fields as department number, customer number, or employee number before they are processed. This process of sequencing the files is referred to as **sorting.** Files that contain daily sales transactions often have to be sorted by the product number, from lowest to highest, before they can be used to decrease the store's master inventory file total amounts of units on hand.

The most common method of sorting, called a **bubble sort,** is demonstrated in Figure C–3. The bubble sort compares two adjacent values of the file and then interchanges them according to an ascending or descending order. This process is repeated until no values are interchanged. Note that the entire process is reexecuted if any interchanges occurred in the most recent pass through the data. This method of sorting is shown for its simplicity rather than its efficiency.

ACCUMULATION

Once the transaction file has been sorted, and before it is run against the master inventory file, it might be desirable to also look at the pur-

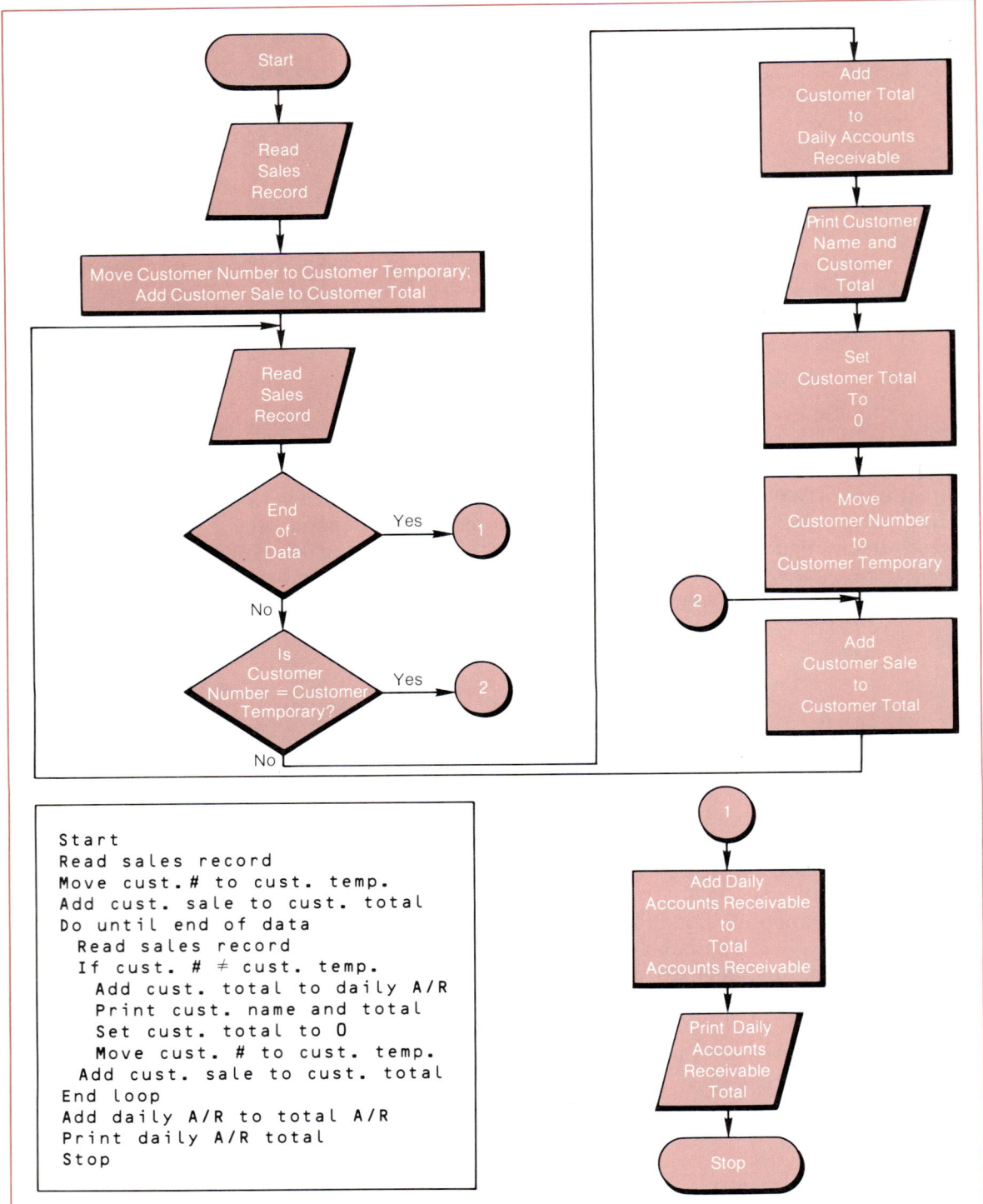

Figure C—4 Accumulating Totals From a Sorted File

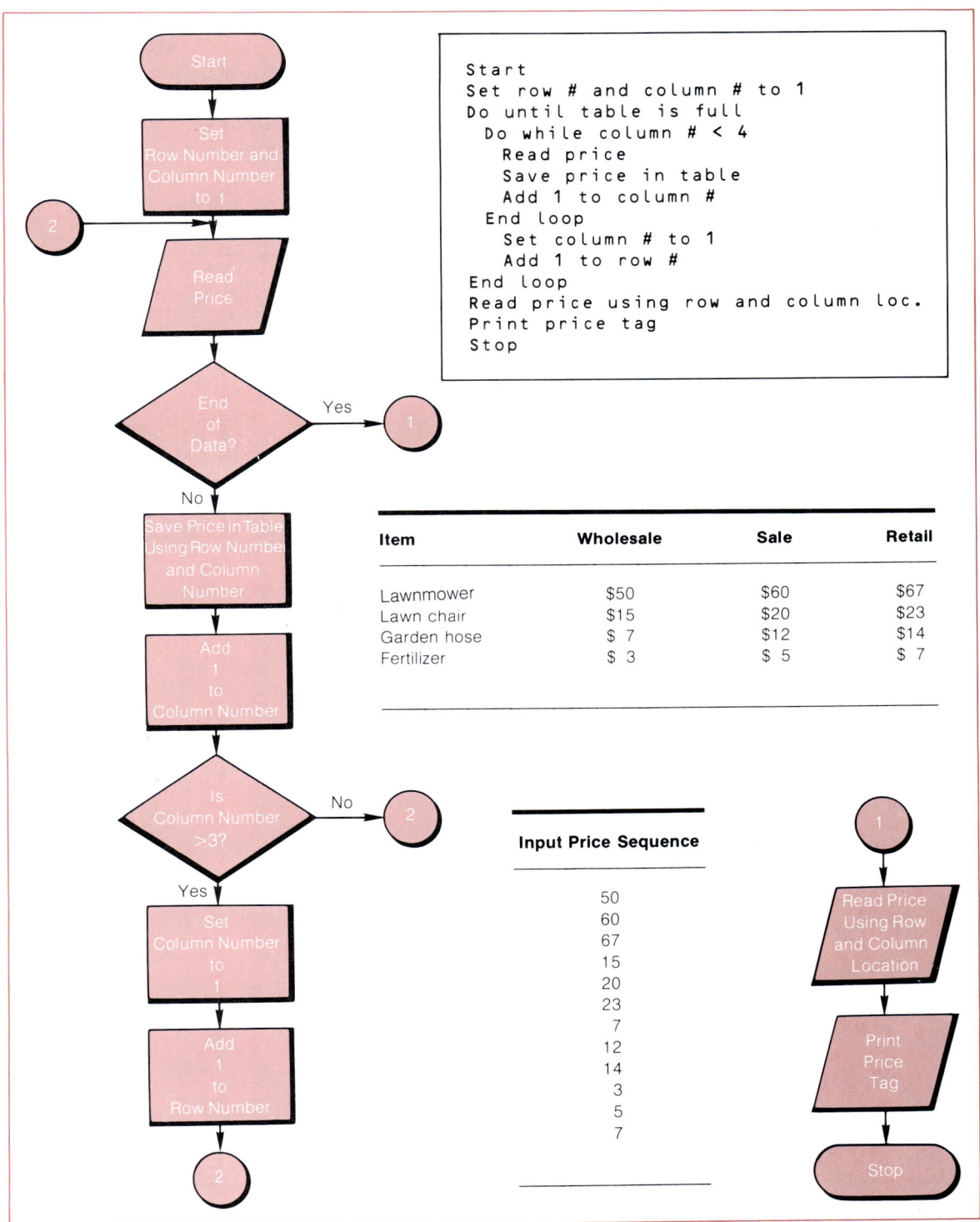

```
Start
Set row # and column # to 1
Do until table is full
  Do while column # < 4
    Read price
    Save price in table
    Add 1 to column #
  End loop
    Set column # to 1
    Add 1 to row #
End loop
Read price using row and column loc.
Print price tag
Stop
```

Item	Wholesale	Sale	Retail
Lawnmower	$50	$60	$67
Lawn chair	$15	$20	$23
Garden hose	$ 7	$12	$14
Fertilizer	$ 3	$ 5	$ 7

Input Price Sequence

50
60
67
15
20
23
7
12
14
3
5
7

Figure C–5 Price Tag Creation (Using Table Handling)

chases of each customer. If, for example, a customer made four credit card purchases in various departments throughout the store, these purchases could be summed, with the balance being added to both the customer's charge statement and the accounts receivable total for the store. This type of procedure, known as **accumulation of subtotals and totals,** is illustrated in Figure C–4.

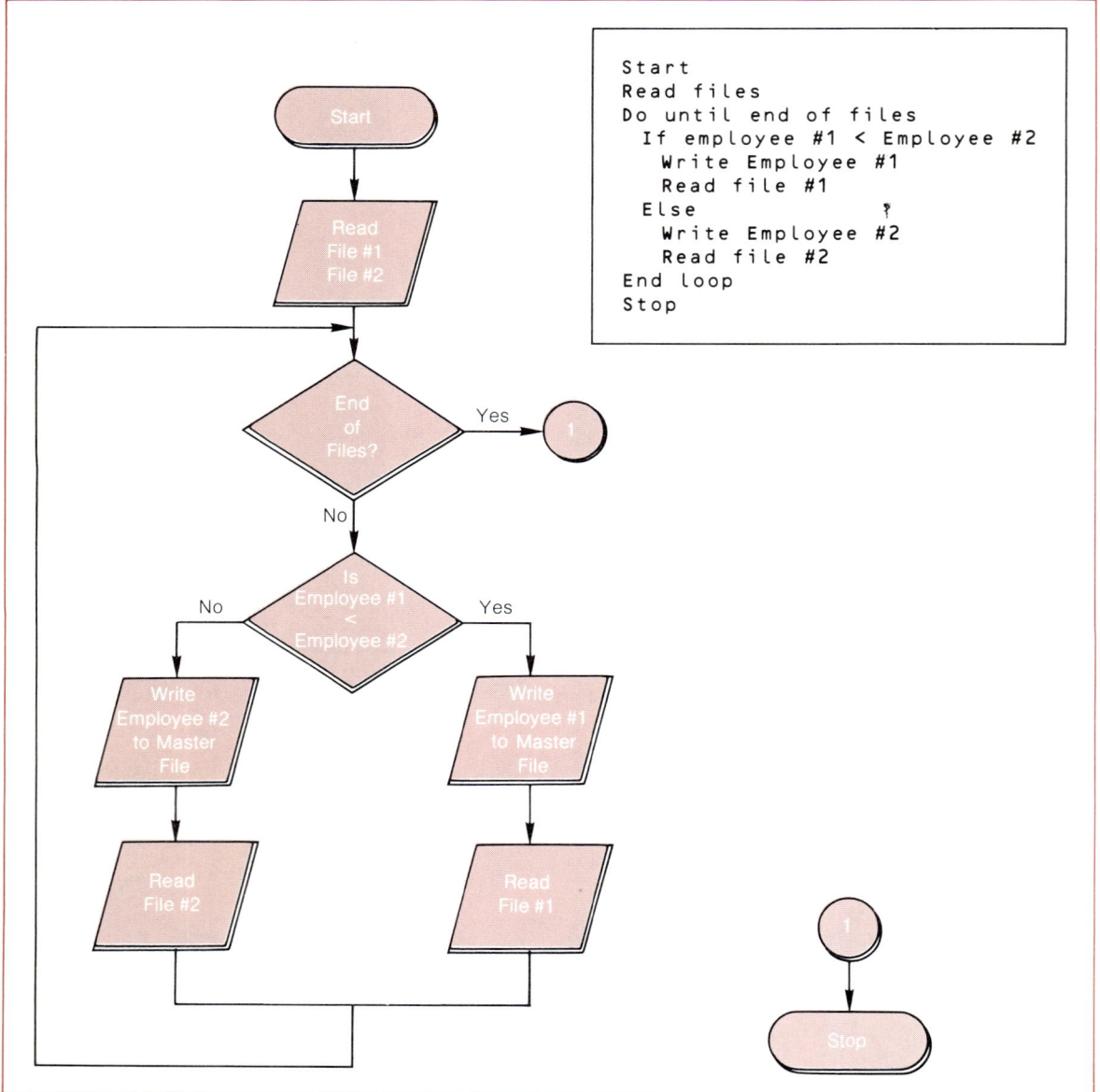

Figure C–6 Merging Two Sorted Files

TABLE HANDLING

Table handling can be used to solve a common business problem of linking two pieces of data together. Consider the situation in which each item in a department store's inventory has three prices associated with it: a wholesale price, a sale price, and a retail price. The department store uses a computerized system to print price tags and must relate an item it wishes to sell to one of the three prices to print the sales tag.

A table containing the items along the horizontal rows and the prices across three columns can be created within the computer program to accomplish the task of linking the items to the related three prices. Figure C–5 shows an example of the table after it has been created by the computer program. The figure also lists the flowchart and pseudocode showing the logic necessary to create the table and access the information in the table.

FILE MERGING

The process of file merging is accomplished by taking the contents of one file and combining it with the contents of another file in the same sequence to create a new file. This procedure might be needed in any environment where employee weekly time sheets are kept and compiled by department. It therefore would be necessary to merge the compiled data from each department into one file so that the payroll program could be run to print employee paychecks.

Prior to merging the files, it is necessary to sort the various department files by employee number in ascending order. Employee numbers are compared to each other as the combined file is created so that the employee numbers in the final file also will be in ascending order. Figure C–6 demonstrates the logic required to merge two department files into one complete file for payroll. Although not shown on the flowchart, this logic requires that when either of the two input files ends while data still remains on the other, the employee area for the completed file be set to a "dummy" value higher than the highest possible employee. This arrangement will permit the other file to be copied to completion because its remaining records will all be lower than the dummy value.

BASIC
Programming
Supplement

SECTION 1

GETTING STARTED WITH BASIC AND THE COMPUTER

OVERVIEW

A computer can do no processing without a set of instructions. These instructions are called a **program.** The rules, or syntax, that apply to the computer instructions define the computer language. The most widely used language for microcomputers is BASIC (short for **B**eginner's **A**ll-**P**urpose **S**ymbolic **I**nstruction **C**ode).

Professors John G. Kemeny and Thomas E. Kurtz developed BASIC at Dartmouth College in the mid-1960s. BASIC originally was designed for interactive programming. The feature that allowed BASIC to be used interactively was its method of translation—an interpreter rather than a compiler. Interpreters translate program statements into machine code line by line rather than a whole program at a time. Interpreters are much slower than compilers, but this lack of speed became less important as machines became faster and faster. Interpreters also take up much less space than compilers. This makes them very desirable for use in a microcomputer because of the limited memory available for programs. Because BASIC is the simplest general-purpose, interpreted language, it is the language of choice for use with most microcomputers and some larger systems.

Because BASIC is so attractive, many different versions of the language have emerged. The American National Standards Institute (ANSI) has developed a standard for BASIC, but differences can be found among different systems. This supplement will discuss features that can be found in most versions of BASIC. Color coding has been used throughout the material to assist the student. The following legend should prove valuable: Red Highlighted Statements **GREY SHADING** User Response

INTRODUCTION TO PROGRAMMING

When a set of instructions is to be developed (a **program**) in order to solve a problem or perform a task, five steps must be considered:

1. Defining the problem.
2. Designing a solution.
3. Writing the program and documenting it.
4. Entering the program.
5. Testing and debugging the program.

Defining the Problem

The first step in developing a program is to define the problem. This is a very critical stage: the more accurately the problem is identified, the easier it will be to determine a solution. The programmer must first ask, "Does this situation require a computer?" Computers are good at performing many calculations and handling large numbers of records. If it is clear that the application can benefit from the use of a computer, the situation must be analyzed in more detail.

The way to analyze a potential application (system) is to look at its outputs, inputs, and the work required to transform input into output (processing). When we define a problem, we usually specify the output we wish to develop and then determine the inputs that are necessary. For example, suppose we want some hamburger, but all we have is a pound of beef. It is then obvious that a meat grinder is required to turn our input (beef) into our output (hamburger). In this simple example, the meat grinder is analogous to a computer program. A computer program takes data and "grinds" it into some kind of information. Once we have defined a problem, we must determine what kind of program is needed to generate the desired outcome.

Suppose we wish to compute an employee's paycheck. The paycheck will be the output, and we must write a program to calculate the paycheck given the inputs—the hours worked and the wage rate. The problem is to design and write a program to calculate the paycheck.

Designing a Solution

The second part of the programming process is designing a solution. The basic logic flow for any solution is input-processing-output (I-P-O). It is important for novice programmers to learn to organize their thinking in terms of this I-P-O process. One tool to aid the programmer in designing a solution is the flowchart.

Flowcharting Symbols Flowcharts consist of symbols that represent program statements. The symbol for input or output is ▱. The symbol for processing is ▱. All programs must be finite, so there are symbols for the beginning and the end (⬭).

To design a program solution, begin with a start symbol ⬭ and connect the subsequent statement blocks with arrows. Figure I–1 shows a flowchart for the paycheck example.

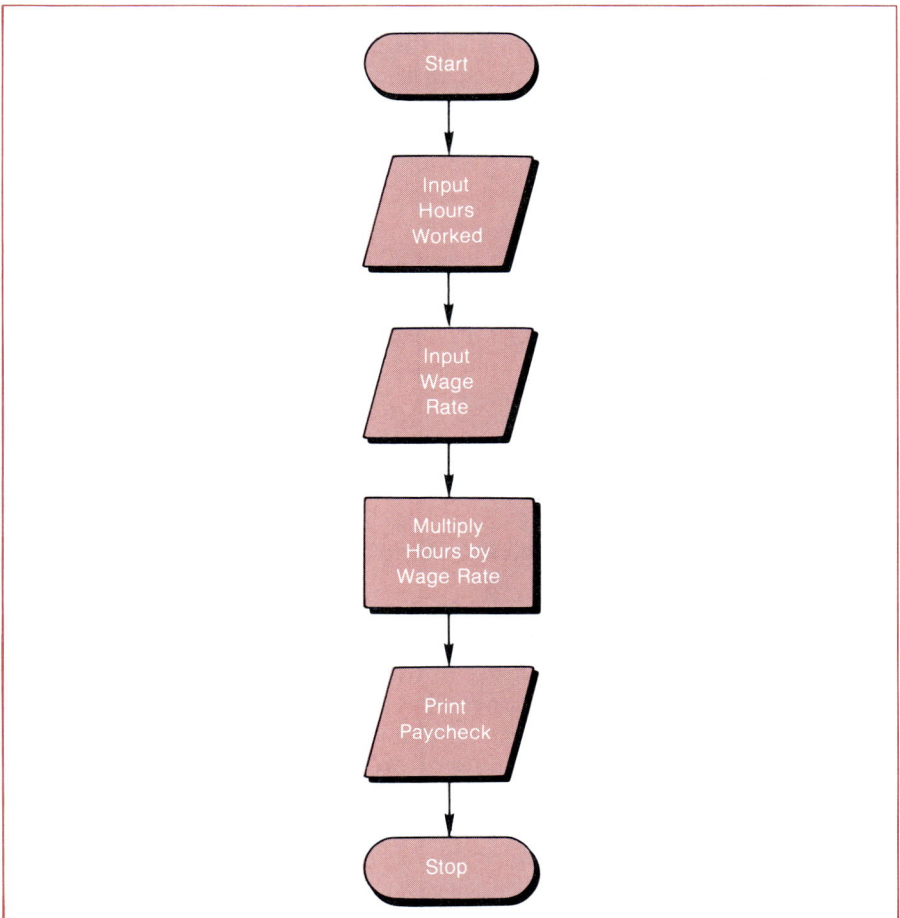

Figure I—1 Flowchart for Paycheck Program

Flowcharting the I-P-O Process From the flowchart, the I-P-O process should be obvious. We first input the hours worked and the wage rate. Next, the process is represented. Finally, the output, or the desired result, is shown. The stop symbol ⬭ designates the end of the program. In this simple example, the inputs and outputs may seem obvious, but as problems increase in complexity, the flowchart method will enhance our ability to identify the various stages of the I-P-O process.

Writing and Documenting the Program

After the solution has been designed, the program logic can be converted into a programming language form. All languages have statement types that correspond to input, output, and any kind of processing we might care to use. In BASIC, keywords such as PRINT and INPUT, as well as arithmetic symbols such as /, *, +, and −, are used to create programs.

You can see that the program in Figure I–2 closely corresponds to the flowchart design. Note that lines 10 through 30 constitute that part of the documentation that is included in the program itself.

In the program in Figure I–2, H, W, and P are called **variables.** These are pieces of data whose values may change throughout repeated executions of the program. Lines 10 through 30 provide documentation of the program with the help of the REM (remarks) statement. Lines 40 and 50 print the messages enclosed in quotation marks so that the user will know what values to enter for variables H and W; Line 60 computes P as the product of H and W; and Line 70 prints the computed pay amount, preceded by the message in quotation marks.

Entering the Program

Entering a program into the computer requires a knowledge of how to use the computer. The basic operating features of an Apple II microcomputer will be discussed here. Other models have slightly different command formats, but the principles are similar for all microcomputers.

Operating the Computer To operate the Apple II, sit down at the keyboard, and turn on the monitor (display) and the keyboard (processor). Next, place a floppy disk (diskette) in the disk drive. If the diskette does not contain a copy of the disk operating system, you must use a system master diskette to initialize the diskette.

Initializing a diskette means putting a copy of the disk operating system on a diskette. The disk operating system is the supervisory program that tells the microcomputer how to manage a floppy disk's memory. Because a microcomputer's internal memory is erased when the machine is turned off, floppy disks are a form of external memory used to keep permanent copies of programs and data. To initialize a disk, use the following six steps:*

1. Insert the system master.
2. Turn on the computer.
3. Type NEW.
4. Type in the hello program.
5. Insert the diskette to be initialized.
6. Type INIT HELLO.

Once the floppy disk has been initialized with a hello program, you can load and save programs. A hello program may be only a few print statements that identify the user. Save the program under the filename (program name) HELLO. When you see a prompt, it means you are in the Applesoft mode and can use system commands to create, store, or run your BASIC programs.

---

*Note: After each of these steps that require user data entry, the "Return" or "Enter" key must be hit to transmit the preceding data to the computer.

```
10 REM *** PROGRAM TO CALCULATE PAYCHECK ***
20 REM *** INPUTS - WAGE AND HOURS WORKED ***
30 REM *** OUTPUTS - PAYCHECK AMOUNT ***
40 INPUT "ENTER HOURS WORKED ";H
50 INPUT "ENTER WAGE ";W
60 LET P = H * W
70 PRINT "AMT OF PAYCHECK IS: $";P
80 END
```

Figure I–2 Paycheck Program

Computer Commands To create a program, type in NEW. Then type in the first line of the program. In BASIC, you must use line numbers for each separate statement.

Once you have typed in your program, you can save it on the floppy disk by typing

SAVE filename

When you wish to execute the program, type in

RUN

Whatever is in internal memory at the time will be executed. To bring a program into internal memory from diskette, type

LOAD filename

This command will read the designated program from the floppy disk into internal memory.

In addition to executing a program in memory, you can get a copy of it on the screen by typing LIST. This will print whatever program is in memory on the cathode-ray tube (CRT) screen.

If you wish to see what programs you have stored on a floppy, type CATALOG. This command will list the names of all the files you have stored on the diskette.

Here are the most common and useful system commands for the Apple; they or their equivalents will be found on any microcomputer:

NEW

RUN

SAVE

LOAD

LIST

CATALOG (On some systems, DIR or FILES is used to request a directory.)

If you want to save a program, make sure you have that program in memory. If you type SAVE filename, whatever was on the floppy under that filename will be **replaced** by what is in memory. Make sure you know what you are saving. For this and other reasons, it is always good to keep two copies of your program on separate disks.

Once you are comfortable with the computer, type in the program and the documentation. Documentation includes the comments that identify the variables (named data), input/output (I/O), and any other information that may help you or another person understand the program. Documentation should also include a concise narrative of the program's function.

Testing and Debugging the Program

The final stage of the programming process is testing and debugging the program. Once you have entered the program into main memory, you can execute it. There are two stages to testing and debugging. The first is checking the syntax (the mechanics of the program), and the second is checking for logic errors. Syntax checking is similar to checking a business letter for possible spelling, grammatical, and punctuation errors. Logic checking corresponds to determining whether the same letter communicates the intended meaning.

Checking for Syntax Errors To analyze the syntax, execute the program. If the program runs without any error messages, there are no syntax errors. If there are syntax errors, the interpreter will send messages to the screen. Figure I–3 shows a typed error message from the computer.

Common syntax errors are misspelled keywords, omitted semicolons, and arithmetic expressions with illegal (incorrect) symbols. To debug syntax, scrutinize the line in error, and refer to a manual if a statement format is in question. Syntax checking becomes very easy with experience. A trained eye can detect errors without much trouble. Once the error is evident, retype the line number and the correct statement. This replaces the bad or incorrect code.

Checking for Logic Errors The second kind of error that must be tested for and debugged is logic errors. These are more difficult to find and correct. These errors indicate that the logic of the solution design is

```
]RUN

?SYNTAX ERROR IN 40                        (Computer detects an Error at Line 40.)
]LIST 40

40 INPURE"ENTER HOURS WORKED";H            (Programmer examines Line 40 for error.)

]40 INPUT "ENTER HOURS WORKED";H           (Programmer retypes Line 40.)
```

Figure I–3 Error Message

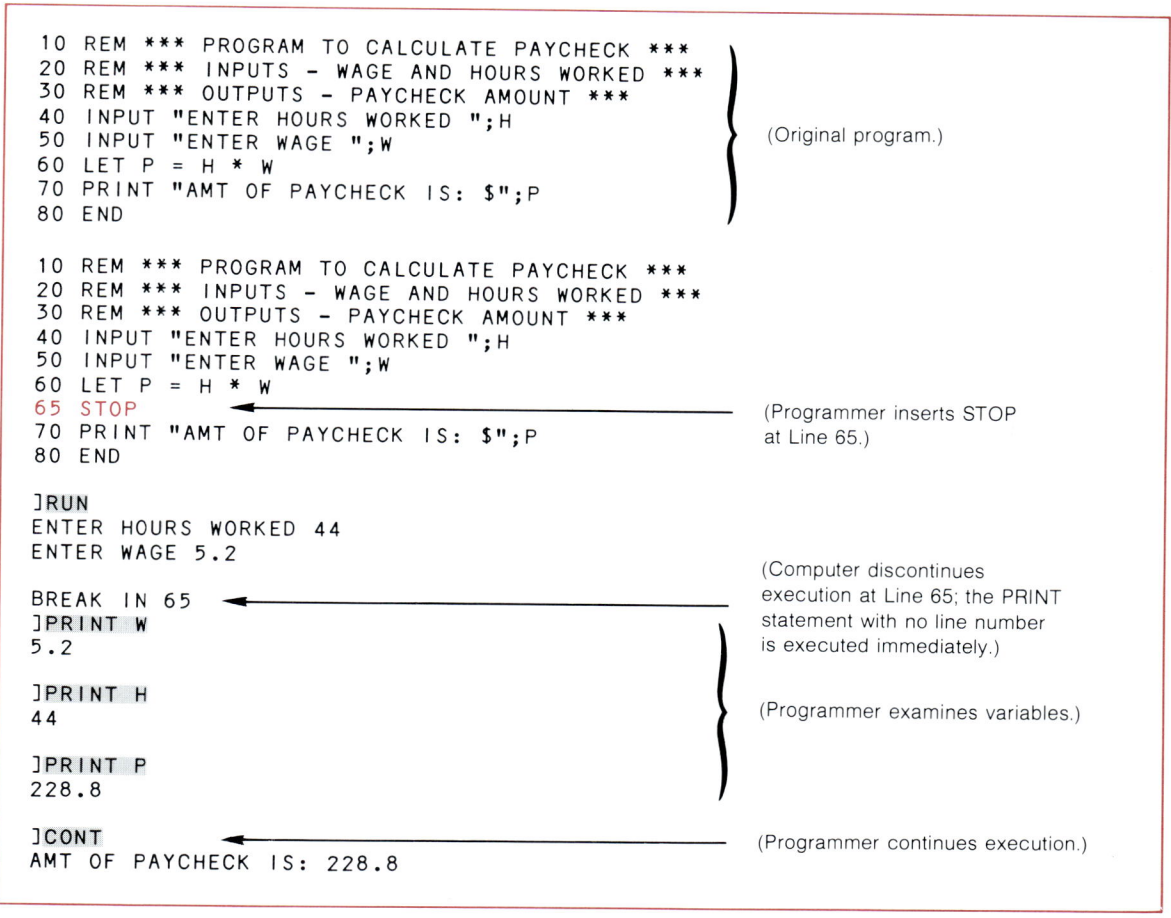

Figure I—4 Debugging Aid

incorrect. Logic errors cause the generation of output that is incorrect or inconsistent with what was expected. To debug a logic error, examine the output and see if it gives any clues as to what process may be incorrect. Maybe the sequence of instructions is incorrect, or a statement was omitted by mistake. Also, examine the inputs to verify that they are reliable. If these steps turn up no errors, you may want to trace through the program by hand. "Hand execution" should reveal what is actually happening. Another way to check what is going on during execution is to place a STOP command in the program. This will stop the execution, and you will be able to examine any variables you want in order to get an idea of where your logic failed. Figure I–4 shows a debugging aid.

1. Why is BASIC a good language for microcomputers?
2. What are three characteristics of any program or system?
3. How does a programmer get a program off a disk and into the computer?

REVIEW
QUESTIONS

SECTION II

FUNDAMENTALS

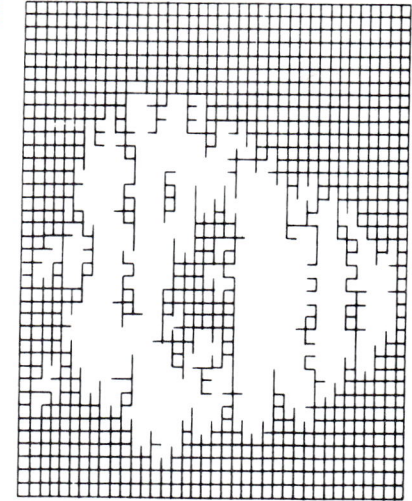

Section II introduces the most common elements of the BASIC language. Variables, constants, assignment statements, and expressions are described as they appear in BASIC. These features are present in all languages but do not use the same rules and formats. One feature that does not appear in all languages is line numbers. Because BASIC is interpreted and not compiled, BASIC needs line numbers so the computer can determine the order in which to execute the statements.

Suppose you wish to calculate the mileage your new car is getting. The output you want to arrive at is the miles per gallon, or MPG. The inputs needed to get the MPG are the miles traveled and the amount of gas consumed during a trip. In this case, the only processing involved is a simple division operation. To convert the inputs to the desired output, divide the miles traveled by the amount of gasoline used. Having determined the I-P-O process for the problem, design the corresponding flowchart (see Figure II–1).

The program steps can be seen in the flowchart solution. The next step is to convert the flowchart into BASIC statements. The BASIC program in Figure II–2 corresponds to the flowchart problem solution. It illustrates the basic elements of the BASIC language.

LINE NUMBERS

Line numbers are required for BASIC programs. They determine the order in which the statements are executed. The numbers typically can be any positive integer (whole number) from 1 to 99999. Although any increment can be used to identify line numbers, it is best to use either 10 or 100, depending on the length of the program. Increments of 10 and 100 are very readable and leave sufficient intervening values for the in-

Figure II–1 Flowchart for Mileage Program

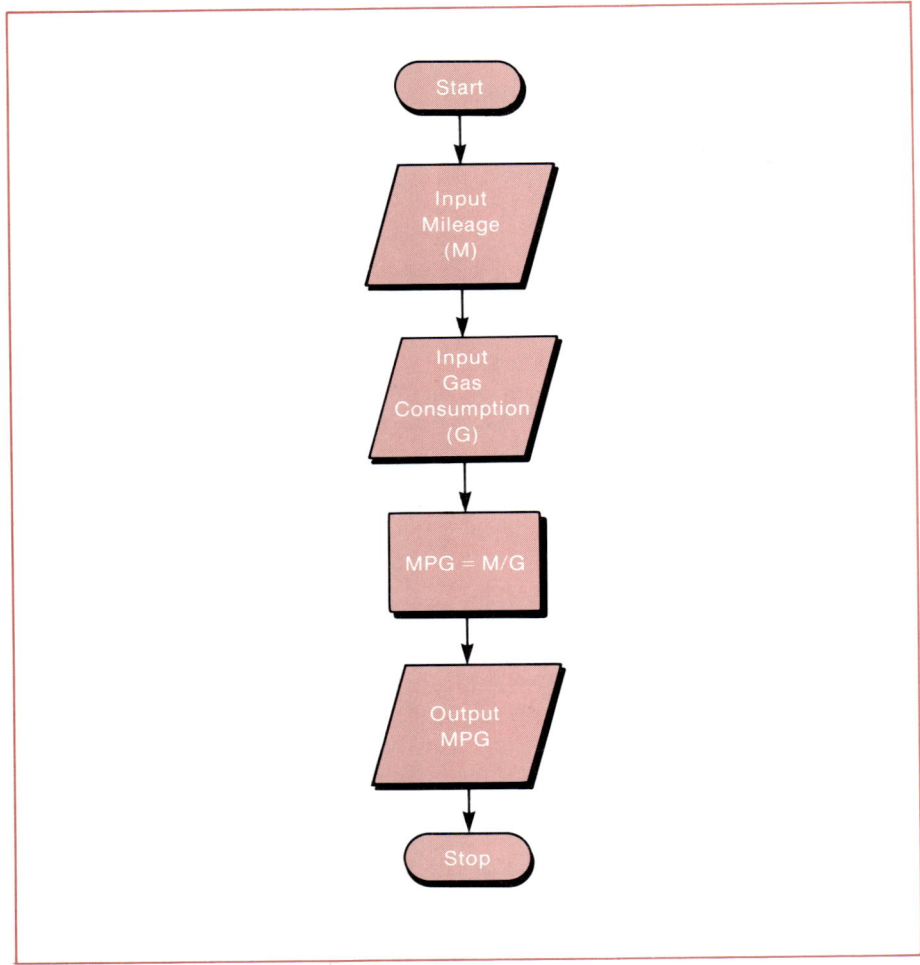

sertion of additional statements if they are needed. In the examples following, most increments of other than 10 and 100 indicate programmer afterthoughts.

Editing is a term used to describe the altering of a program. To edit a BASIC program, you must use line numbers to indicate the part of the program you are changing. It is possible to insert a new line, replace an existing line, or delete an old line. To insert a new line, load the program into memory, and type in the desired new line number and the statement. In the following segment, line 550 was added to the mileage program in this way:

```
400  INPUT "ENTER MILEAGE ";M
500  INPUT "ENTER GAS CONSUMPTION ";G
550  REM *** CALCULATE MPG ***
600  LET MPG = M / G
700  PRINT "MILES PER GALLON = ";MPG
800  END
```

Figure II–2 Mileage Program

```
100 REM *** THIS PROGRAM CALCULATES ***
200 REM *** A CAR'S RATE OF GAS CONSUMPTION ***
300 REM *** MILES PER GALLON = MPG ***
400 INPUT "ENTER MILEAGE ";M
500 INPUT "ENTER GAS CONSUMPTION ";G
600 LET MPG = M / G
700 PRINT "MILES PER GALLON = ";MPG
800 END
```

To replace a line, type in the old line number followed by the new statement. To delete a line, type in the old line number and hit the "return" key. More advanced editors that permit changes to part of a line or to multiple lines are available for microcomputers and can be found on most large systems.

In the program example, there are three statements, 100 through 300, that are not represented in the program flowchart:

```
100 REM *** THIS PROGRAM CALCULATES ***
200 REM *** A CAR'S RATE OF GAS CONSUMPTION ***
300 REM *** MILES PER GALLON = MPG ***
```

These statements are simply comments and have nothing to do with the logic of the program.

Program comments can be referred to as **documentation.** This is the way in which the programmer communicates to anyone reading the program. Comments are designated by using the REM (short for **remark**) keyword. Any statement containing a REM will be ignored by the BASIC interpreter.

REM statements may be inserted anywhere in a BASIC program. The required format for a REM statement is

line# REM comment

The blanks or asterisks are only to enhance the clarity of the comment.

CONSTANTS AND VARIABLES

Constants

There are two kinds of **constants** in a BASIC program: numeric constants and character string constants. A constant represents a value that does not change throughout the program.

Numeric Constants Both **real number** and **integer constants** can be expressed as numeric constants. Here are some examples of integers:

4   0   212   10000

Notice there is no comma in 10000; 10,000 is an invalid number format. No commas may appear in a number. Integers also may be signed. Here are some examples of signed integers:

    +4   − 10000   +579

The sign always appears to the left of the highest-ordered digit. Thus, 50+ is an invalid format. Real numbers (values containing fractions) can be represented in exponential or decimal notation. Real numbers also can be signed or unsigned. The following are examples of decimal real numbers:

    4.2   .599   1222.6   1.1005

Examples of exponential notation follow:

    7.8E + 05   2.117E − 04

This notation is used to represent large or small numbers. The E + 05 represents the number, or mantissa, 7.8 multiplied by 10 five times (E stands for 10). This is the BASIC equivalent of scientific notation, using the value following the E as the exponent of 10, or the power to which 10 is to be raised before being used as a multiplier. If a minus is present, divide the mantissa by the specified power of 10. The decimal equivalent of these numbers would be as follows:

Exponential	Decimal
7.8E + 05	780000.0
2.117E − 04	.0002117

Character String Constants A **character string constant** is any sequence of letters, numbers, and symbols appearing in quotation marks, for example,

    "BOB"

    "STATION-995"

    "BOMO-HUNTER"

Variables

Variables are symbols that identify values used in a computer program. A variable can be either of numeric or string type. Variables must be assigned values by an input statement or an assignment statement. The use of variables permits added flexibility (and reusability) to be incorporated into a program. A general solution to a problem can be written using variables; when the program is to be run, input statements can assign specific values to these variables.

Most microcomputers allow only two significant characters for variable names. This means that only the first two letters or numbers are recognized by the computer. For example, FLAG1 and FLAG2 would represent the same variable. However, F1 and F2 would represent different variables.

Each variable represents a memory location in the computer's internal memory. The BASIC interpreter designates a portion of the computer memory for program variables. The interpreter stores the value the programmer assigns to a variable at the proper memory location. A memory location value changes as the variable in the program changes. The computer keeps track of variables by location.

The first position of a variable name must always contain a letter. The following positions may contain either letters or numbers, but no other keyboard symbols (with the exception of the dollar sign, which must be the last character of a string variable name). Look at the following examples of valid and invalid variable names:

Valid	Invalid
XX	32
X2	Z*
ALPHA1	A-1
Z$	F.1

Numeric Variables Numeric values are represented by variables that contain one or more digits.

String Variables A **string variable** is a character string assigned to a variable name. String variable names have the string format designated by a dollar sign at the end of the variable name. Some examples are A$, BB$, and ZAP$. Again, on some computers, the two-character name limit—including the $—must be observed. String variables are assigned values, just as numeric variables are. For example,

```
LET M$ = "MILES PER GALLON = "
PRINT M$; MPG
```

results in the following output:

```
MILES PER GALLON = 20.5
```

ASSIGNMENT STATEMENTS

Assignment statements are statements that give a value to a variable. They can take one of two forms:

LET variable name = expression
or
variable name = expression

The keyword LET clearly defines an assignment statement and, therefore, eliminates some confusion as to the type of statement. This statement always assigns (moves) the value of the expression on the right
side to the single variable name on the left. Because it is an assignment
statement, it does not follow the normal algebraic rule of having expressions on both sides of the equal sign. Once again, the value of the
expression is actually placed in the memory location represented by the
variable name. This makes legal such statements as A = A + 1, which
means "add 1 to the variable A, and store the sum as the new contents
of the variable A."

In the program example, the statement

```
LET MPG = M / G
```

takes the value of the expression M / G and places it in the memory
location designated by the variable MPG. Other examples of assignment
statements are shown in Figure II–3.

EXPRESSIONS

Expressions are the right half of assignment statements and can take
many forms. Expressions can be a constant, a character string, a variable, or an arithmetic expression. Arithmetic expressions are combinations of numeric variables, constants, and arithmetic operators. The operators are shown in Table II–1.

String variables may not be part of an expression unless the left side
of the assignment statement is a string variable. In that case, the expression may either be another string variable or a character string.

Arithmetic expressions can be complex and contain multiple sets of

Figure II–3. Assign-
ment Statements

Assignment	Computer Execution
LET A$ = "PHYLLIS"	Character string is assigned to string variable.
LET Z = A + B	Value of variable A + variable B is assigned to the variable Z.
LET X = 5	Constant 5 is assigned to X.
LET X = Z	Memory location value of variable Z is assigned to the variable X (contents of Z are copied in variable X).
LET X = X - 1	Value of variable X is decremented by 1 and assigned to the memory location of variable X

Table II–1 ARITHMETIC OPERATORS

Operator	Function	BASIC Expression
+	Addition	A + B
−	Subtraction	A − B
*	Multiplication	A * B
/	Division	A / B
∧ (or **)	Exponentiation	A ∧ B (or A ** B)

parentheses; therefore, a precedence of operators must be defined. The order of priority follows:

1st priority: parentheses	( )
2nd priority: exponentiation	∧
3rd priority: multiplication or division	* or /
4th priority: addition or subtraction	+ or −

In evaluating parentheses, the interpreter analyzes the innermost pair first. Let us use (A + (C * 2) + 5) for an example. The expression C * 2 is evaluated first. After that, the result of C * 2 is added to A. Then 5 is added to A + (C * 2). When operators have the same precedence, the leftmost expression is evaluated first. For example, the expression

6 * 5 / 10 * 3

is evaluated

1st: 6 * 5 = 30
2nd: 30 / 10 = 3
3rd: 3 * 3 = 9

In examples of equal precedence, the order is always left to right. A more complicated example to illustrate BASIC arithmetic hierarchy follows. The expression

5 + (10 − (6 ∧ 2) * 2) / 2

is evaluated as follows:

Evaluated	New Expression	Description
(6 ∧ 2) = 36	5 + (10 − 36 * 2) / 2	Evaluate innermost first.
36 * 2 = 72	5 + (10 − 72) / 2	Multiplication has precedence within parentheses.
10 − 72 = −62	5 + (−62) / 2	Complete the evaluation of parentheses.
(−62) / 2 = −31	5 + (−31)	Division is next in precedence.
5 + (−31)	−26	Complete the evaluation.

Figure II—4 Assignment Statements in an Income Tax Program

```
100   REM  *** PROGRAM TO CALCULATE ***
110   REM  *** INCOME TAX ***
120   LET I = 30000.0
130   LET TX = .22
140   LET ITX = I * TX
150   LET T$ = "YOUR INCOME TAX = $ "
160   PRINT T$;ITX
170   END
```

Figure II—4 shows a program that illustrates BASIC assignment statements. The program calculates how much income tax a person would have to pay on earnings of $30,000. The variable I is assigned the person's income, and TX is assigned the tax rate of 22 percent. The arithmetic expression I * TX is evaluated, and its value is assigned to ITX. For output, the character string "YOUR INCOME TAX = $" is assigned to the string variable T$. Notice the first $ designates a string variable. The output of this program is

```
YOUR INCOME TAX = $  6600.00
```

REVIEW QUESTIONS

1. Evaluate the BASIC expression 5 * 6 ∧ 2 + (4 * (5 − 3) + 1. List each operation sequentially.
2. Indicate if the following variables are valid or invalid, and tell why: 1A, AA, AB$, 3$, and X945.
3. Explain what a variable is and how a computer uses variables.
4. Write two BASIC statements to assign the value 10 to the variable X.
5. Write a BASIC statement that assigns any character string to a string variable.
6. Write a BASIC statement that assigns any expression to a numeric variable.

SECTION III

INPUT AND OUTPUT STATEMENTS

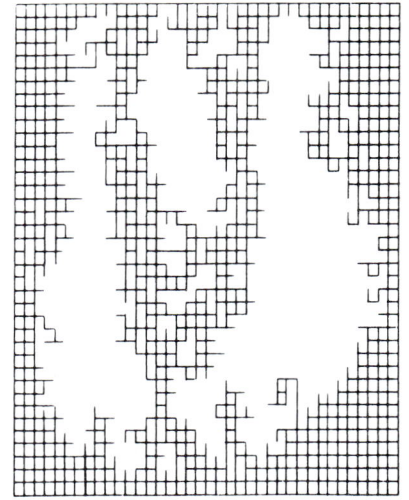

An important part of any programming language is its input and output functions. This is the way a language reads data into, and writes it out from, a computer's internal memory. BASIC uses the keywords INPUT and READ/DATA to designate input statements. Output statements use the keywords PRINT, TAB, and PRINT USING. To enter small amounts of data, assignment statements can be used.

Program Problem

A gold dealer would like a program that calculates the price of a quantity of gold. Figure III–1 is a program that will determine the dollar amount of a gold transaction.

After the initial comments, two assignment statements are needed to enter the amount of gold in ounces and the current price per ounce of gold. Lines 120 and 130 assign the data to variables. Line 140 processes the data. Lines 150 and 160 output the results with headings in a formatted style. This section will discuss other ways to enter data and how to use BASIC output features effectively.

Figure III–1 Gold
Program

```
100    REM  *** PROGRAM TO CALCULATE THE ***
110    REM  *** DOLLAR VALUE OF GOLD ***
120    LET G = 8.5
130    LET P = 320.00
140    LET CAMT = G * P
150    PRINT "OUNCES","PRICE","COST"
160    PRINT G,P,CAMT
170    END
```

OUTPUT

PRINT Statement

The PRINT statement is the command that is used to output information to a CRT, line printer, or other output device connected to a computer. The PRINT statement format follows:

line# PRINT expression

We know that an expression can be a constant, variable, character string, or arithmetic expression. The following example illustrates the various ways a PRINT statement can be used:

```
400 INPUT "ENTER MILEAGE ";M
500 INPUT "ENTER GAS CONSUMPTION ";G
600 LET MPG = M / G
700 PRINT MPG
800 END
```

The output follows:

```
ENTER MILEAGE 230
ENTER GAS CONSUMPTION 10
23
```

Using the miles-per-gallon example, we can see how a variable is printed. By using the PRINT statement with a character string, we can make the output more meaningful:

```
400 INPUT "ENTER MILEAGE ";M
500 INPUT "ENTER GAS CONSUMPTION ";G
600 LET MPG = M / G
650 LET M$ = "MILES PER GALLON = "
700 PRINT M$;MPG
800 END
```

The output follows:

```
ENTER MILEAGE 230
ENTER GAS CONSUMPTION 10
MILES PER GALLON = 23
```

By using a character string and a variable together, it is possible to make the output more comprehensible. Notice the semicolon separating the two variables in the PRINT statement in Line 700. By using a semicolon, we can string variables together to format output. Printed character strings lose their quotation marks. Another use of character strings is for column headings. When lists of information are to be printed, it is good to use column headings to identify the variables being listed. The gold program is used as an example:

```
100   REM    *** PROGRAM TO CALCULATE THE ***
110   REM    *** DOLLAR VALUE OF GOLD ***
120   LET G = 8.5
130   LET P = 320.00
140   LET CAMT = G * P
150   PRINT "OUNCES","PRICE","COST"
160   PRINT G,P,CAMT
170   END
]RUN
OUNCES           PRICE           COST
8.5              320             2720
```

In the example before this one, a semicolon merely separated the variables to be printed. In this case, the commas indicate that the strings should be printed in a predescribed program format. Each string constant will start at evenly spaced columns. On most computers, these columns are separated by 14 to 15 positions.

Arithmetic expressions also can be printed directly without the user's having to assign their value to a variable. In the miles-per-gallon example, the statement

```
600 PRINT M / G
```

would be equivalent to the following two statements:

```
600 LET MPG = M / G
700 PRINT MPG
```

The computer evaluates the expression M / G and then prints it out just as if it were printing a variable.

PRINT statements without variables or expressions also can be used to leave blank lines between lines of output:

```
100 PRINT
110 PRINT
```

These statements will generate two blank lines.

BASIC Display Formatting

To control the appearance of the output, the PRINT statement can be used with either commas or semicolons. When commas are used, the variables will be printed in the predetermined format zones. Each computer has its own number of spaces per zone. The Apple has a zone width of sixteen spaces, whereas the IBM Personal Computer (PC) and TRS-80 have zone widths of fourteen spaces. The IBM PC and TRS-80 also allow an extra space for signed numbers, whereas the Apple does not. When designing the display format required, check the specifications of the machine you are working on, and plan accordingly.

Commas Examine the following program segment:

```
120 LET BW = 162.0
130 LET H$ = "BODY WEIGHT ="
140 PRINT H$,BW
150 END
```

The resulting output is as follows:

	Zone 1			Zone 2		Zone 3
	1	5	10	15	20	
Column						
	BODY WEIGHT =				162	

Each variable is printed in a new zone, as dictated by the comma. If Line 130 were changed:

```
130 LET H$ = "YOUR LEAN BODY WEIGHT = "
```

the output would change as well:

	Zone 1			Zone 2		Zone 3
	1	5	10	15	20	
Column						
	YOUR LEAN BODY WEIGHT =					162

Since the variable H$ is longer than the sixteen-character width of the zone, the computer prints the entire string value and skips to Zone 3 for the second variable.

The programmer could purposely skip a zone by using one of two techniques. The first is enclosing a space in quotation marks, and the second is adding two commas with nothing between them. For example, for

```
130 LET H$ = "BODY WEIGHT = "," ",BW
```

```
130 LET H$ = "BODY WEIGHT = ",,BW
```

the resulting output (from either statement) would be

```
BODY WEIGHT                              162
```

Another technique using the comma is to end a PRINT statement with a comma, as is shown in the following examples. This will cause the output of the next PRINT statement to appear on the same line as that of the previous statement. For

```
10 PRINT "JOHN SMITH",
20 PRINT "AGE","22"
```

the output is

```
]RUN
JOHN SMITH        AGE                 22
```

Semicolons Semicolons cause variables to be displayed in successive spaces, not zones. Because of this, variables may run together and be hard to read. For example, the statement

```
10 PRINT "J.SMITH";"AGE";"22"
```

has the following output:

```
]RUN
J.SMITHAGE22
```

To get around this problem, the programmer should enclose spaces within the character string:

```
10 PRINT "J.SMITH ";"AGE  ";"22"
```

The output would be this:

```
]RUN
J.SMITH AGE  22
```

A PRINT command ending with a semicolon prevents the carriage return from being advanced and continues printing on the same line. For example,

```
5 PRINT "NAME: ";
10 PRINT "J.SMITH ";"AGE  ";"22"
```

has this output:

```
]RUN
NAME: J.SMITH AGE  22
```

TAB Function

TAB allows the programmer more control over output than commas or semicolons do. The BASIC format for TAB is

```
line# PRINT TAB(expression);variable
```

TAB determines the column where the computer will begin printing the variable. The expression (variables, constants, or arithmetic expression) is evaluated, and the printer moves that number of spaces over from the margin. For example,

```
PRINT TAB(5);"BODY WEIGHT = ";TAB(20);BW
```

has this output:

Column	Zone 1			Zone 2		Zone 3
	1	5	10	15	20	
		BODY WEIGHT =			160.2	

Semicolons must be used in conjunction with the TAB function. If commas are used, the output will be displayed in the preformatted zones. Commas take precedence over TAB declarations. For example,

```
PRINT TAB(5),"BODY WEIGHT = ";TAB(20),BW
```

has this output:

Column	Zone 1			Zone 2		Zone 3
	1	5	10	15	20	
		BODY WEIGHT =				160.2

Notice that the output ignored the TAB parameters and defaulted to the zones as indicated by the commas.

When using TAB, the TAB expression must proceed in value from left to right. The programmer cannot request the printer to back up and print a variable. For example, the printer cannot go to Column 25 for the variable B and then back up to Column 15 to print C.

PRINT USING Statement

Another technique for added formatting control is the PRINT USING statement. The PRINT USING statement is not available on many microcomputer versions of BASIC. It is not implemented for the Apple II, for example, but is available for the IBM PC. It is an extension of standard BASIC. The PRINT USING format is

```
line# PRINT USING "control characters";expression list
```

The control characters define the output format for the variables in the expression list. Some control characters for the IBM PRINT USING statement are shown in Table III–1. The slash marks indicate that an alphanumeric character string will be used. The number of spaces between the marks specify the length of the string.

The program in Figure III–2 illustrates the use of the PRINT USING statement. It also incorporates additional language features (READ/DATA, GOTO, and IF statements) that will be presented later. The use of a colon between statements permits the programmer to enter multiple related statements on a single line, as shown in Line 50.

The PRINT USING statements in Lines 90, 93, and 96 all describe the format for the output of the program. The first PRINT USING state-

Table III–1 Control Characters

Control Character	Function
\ \	Alphanumeric character string indicator
#	Numeric field indicator
$$	Dollar sign generator
+, −	Sign generator
!	String truncation indicator (truncates to one character)
&	Character string print indicator

ment is used to define the string field for the items purchased. The spaces separating the slash marks denote the character length of the string variable. Any string longer than the prescribed length will be truncated. The next two PRINT USING statements define numeric fields. The control characters allow us to format the output in a way

```
10 REM *** PROGRAM TO ILLUSTRATE PRINT USING ***
20 PRINT
30 PRINT
35 LET B$ = "ITEMS PURCHASED              PRICE            SALES TAX"
40 PRINT B$
50 PRINT : PRINT
60 READ A$,X
70 IF A$ = "END" THEN GOTO 140
80 LET Y = X * .06
90 PRINT USING "\                    \";A$;
93 PRINT USING "         ##.##";X;
96 PRINT USING "         ##.##";Y
99 GOTO 60
100 DATA TOASTER,27.5,BLENDER,15.45,DRILL,21.95,BLANKET,9.90
110 DATA KNIVES,34.99,FAN,29.99
115 DATA END,1
140 END

]RUN


ITEMS PURCHASED              PRICE          SALES TAX


TOASTER                      27.50           1.65
BLENDER                      15.45           0.93
DRILL                        21.95           1.32
BLANKET                       9.90           0.59
KNIVES                       34.99           2.10
FAN                          29.99           1.80
```

Figure III–2 Sales Tax Calculation Program

that represents monetary amounts. Using these statements gives the programmer more control over the spacing, length, and data type of the output.

COMPUTER INPUT

Now you know how to get information out of the computer in attractive and readable ways. To obtain reliable output, reliable input methods are needed. This section will explain how to get data into the computer for processing. One way you have seen is through assignment statements. This is fine for entering constants or character strings, but what if you had to enter five hundred pieces of data? Five hundred assignment statements would necessitate quite a large and cumbersome program. The INPUT and READ/DATA functions are faster and more convenient ways to put data into a computer.

INPUT Statement

BASIC is an interactive language, so you can enter data while executing a program. Typically, programs will be run with different data every time. If assignment statements were used, you would have to retype the program every time you changed the data. The INPUT statement can be used to assign data interactively while the program is executing. The INPUT statement format is

```
line# INPUT variable list
```

The variable list is any number of variables separated by commas. INPUT statements are used to enter data while the program is in execution. To see how they are used, examine the program to calculate the value of gold:

```
100    REM  *** PROGRAM TO CALCULATE THE ***
110    REM  *** DOLLAR VALUE OF GOLD ***
120    LET G = 8.5
130    LET P = 320.00
140    LET CAMT = G * P
150    PRINT "OUNCES","PRICE","COST"
160    PRINT G,P,CAMT
170    END
```

We can replace the assignment statements by INPUT statements:

```
120 PRINT "ENTER QUANTITY AND PRICE"
130 INPUT G,P
```

When the program is executed, the PRINT statement will display the message, and the prompt (?) will appear on the screen, requesting a user response:

```
]RUN
ENTER QUANTITY AND PRICE
?22
??512.0

OUNCES          PRICE           COST
22              512             11264
```

In this example, one question mark is used as the prompt character for the first variable, two, for the second. On some computers only a single question mark would be displayed for each. Both variables could be entered on a single line, for example, ?22,512.0

The machine interrupts execution and waits for the user to respond by typing in the two values requested. The user must type in data that matches the type of variable. If the user tries to enter characters when the INPUT statement is anticipating a numeric variable, the interpreter will display an error message and request another entry:

```
]RUN
ENTER QUANTITY AND PRICE
?W3                         (Invalid response)
?REENTER                    (Error: nonnumeric value)
?WER                        (Invalid)
?REENTER                    (Error: nonnumeric value)
?33                         (Valid)
??512
OUNCES          PRICE           COST
33              512             16896
```

Once the data has been entered and accepted, the user presses the "Return" key, and the program continues its exection. The great advantage of this statement is that it allows the user to change input values each time the program is run. Here are three different executions:

```
]RUN
ENTER QUANTITY AND PRICE
?10
??543.00
OUNCES          PRICE           COST
10              543             5430

]RUN
ENTER QUANTITY AND PRICE
?20
??670.00
OUNCES          PRICE           COST
20              670             13400

]RUN
ENTER QUANTITY AND PRICE
?120
??389.00
OUNCES          PRICE           COST
120             389             46680
```

Another helpful feature of the INPUT statement is the use of a prompt. The INPUT statement allows a message to be inserted before the variable list. The format is line# INPUT character string;variable list

A semicolon must be used to separate the prompt from the variable list. In the gold example, lines 120 and 130 could be replaced by the following single line:

INPUT "ENTER QUANTITY AND PRICE";G,P

The message will appear when the data is to be entered into the computer.

READ and DATA Statements

The READ statement allows the programmer to enter data via a list of constants that he or she supplies in the DATA statement. These two statements must be used together. The formats are

line# READ variable list
line# DATA constant list

Both lists are separated by commas. The number of variables declared in a program using READ statements must correspond to the number of constant values supplied.

The READ statements are inserted wherever the program requires data. When the computer encounters a READ statement, it will search for a DATA statement and read the first value that has not been used. For subsequent variables in the READ statement, the corresponding data values will be read into the program. The number of variables must match the number of constant values supplied. Also, the types of data values must correspond to the variable type, or an error will follow. The following program illustrates how the READ/DATA commands work in an application that prints a student name and grade point average (GPA) developed from three equally weighted grades (G1, G2, and G3):

```
30 PRINT : PRINT
40 READ N$,G1,G2,G3
50 LET GPA = (G1 + G2 + G3) / 3
60 PRINT N$,"GPA = ";GPA
65 PRINT
70 READ N$,G1,G2,G3
80 LET GPA = (G1 + G2 + G3) / 3
90 PRINT N$,"GPA = ";GPA
100 DATA "J.K. RAYNO",2.3
110 DATA 2.9,4.0,"JOSE WASHINGTON"
120 DATA 3.5,4.0,1.9


]RUN


J.K. RAYNO        GPA = 3.06666667

JOSE WASHINGTON   GPA = 3.13333333
```

1. How are commas and semicolons used in PRINT statements?
2. What is the major advantage of using the INPUT statement?
3. How does a READ/DATA statement assign values to variables?
4. Write a program to calculate the average speed for a car trip using the INPUT statement.
5. Write a program to calculate the average cost of food bills using READ/DATA statements. Use at least three food bills for the DATA statements.

SECTION IV

PROGRAM CONTROL

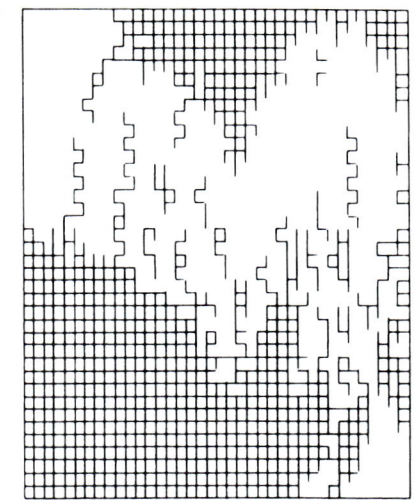

In BASIC programs, the line numbers tell the computer the order in which the statements are to be executed. Until now (with a minor exception in Figure III–2), all the example programs executed statements sequentially from the first to the last lines. However, many times a sequential order is not desirable. It may be necessary to execute a group of statements more than once or in an order other than that dictated by the line numbers. To change the sequential execution, control statements are needed. Control statements allow the programmer to control the sequence of execution. The control statements that will be examined are GOTO, IF/THEN, and ON/GOTO.

PROGRAM PROBLEM

Suppose you wish to design a program to balance your checkbook. Deposits and withdrawals vary from month to month, so the program must be able to handle any number of transactions. There most likely will be more than one check to process, so some repetition is necessary in the program. The ability to repeat calculations is one of the greatest assets of a computer and can be accomplished by using a loop.

    The flowchart in Figure IV–1 shows the program design to solve the checkbook problem. Notice the program flow arrows for a loop starting with the INPUT statement, traveling through processing, and returning to the very same INPUT statement. This execution cycle, or loop, can be repeated as many times as the programmer likes. Also note that there is a flow line that leads out of the loop. This is the means by which the programmer can terminate the loop execution.

    Constructing a loop in BASIC is done with control statements. The loop processes checking account transactions until there are no more entries. In Figure IV–2, Lines 50 through 100 print the beginning balance

Figure IV–1
Checking Account
Flowchart

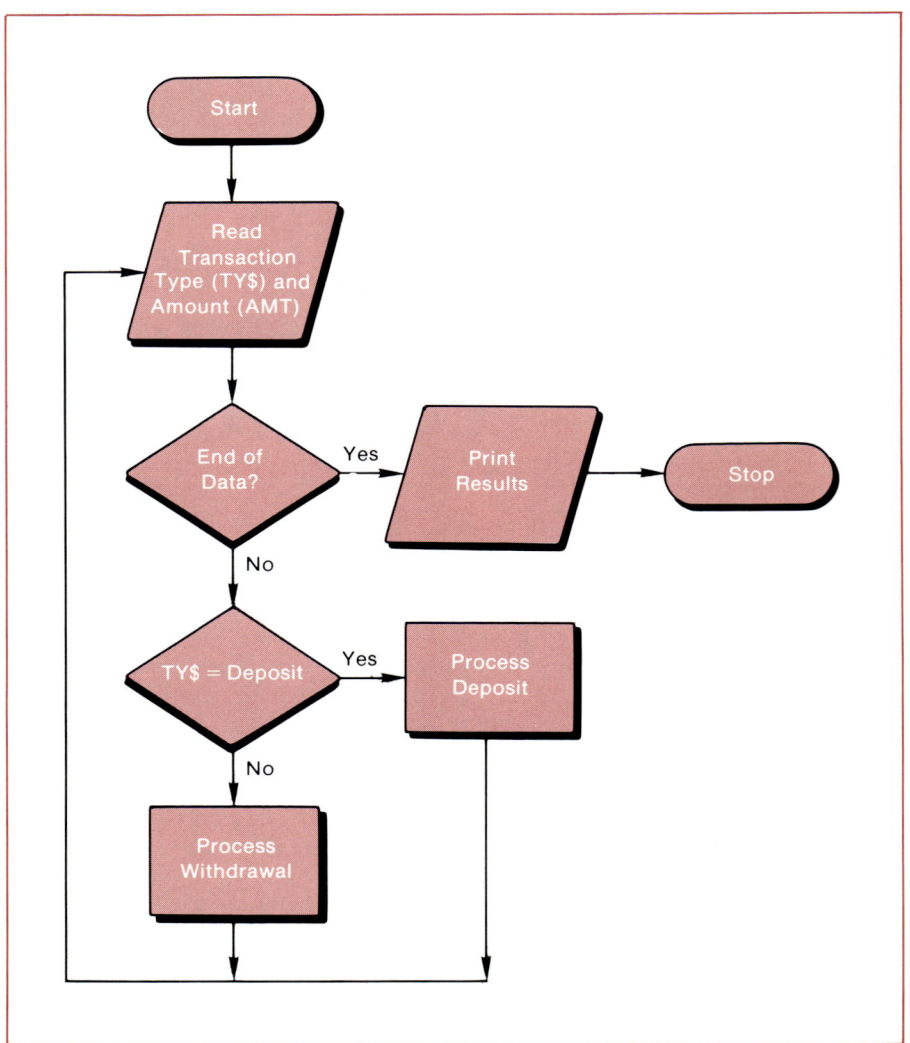

and the headings for the transactions. The main loop begins at Line 110. The program control returns to this point every time a new check or deposit transaction is required. The GOTO statements at Lines 180 and 210 both return control to Line 110. Once a transaction has been processed, the program returns to get more data.

There are two IF/THEN statements. The IF/THEN statement at Line 130 will direct program control out of the main loop if there is no more data to be read in. The IF/THEN statement at Line 140 directs control to either the deposit or withdrawal processing statements. Notice that the IF/THEN statements offer two alternative routes of program control: to the specified line number if the equality tested for is present, and to the next line number in sequence if it is not.

Figure IV–2 Program
Using Control Transfer

```
 50 REM *** UPDATE CHECKING ACCOUNT ***
 55 REM *** VARIABLES ***
 60 REM *** TY$ - TRANSACTION TYPE ***
 61 REM ***   B - BALANCE ***
 62 REM *** AMT - AMOUNT OF TRANSACTION ***
 63 REM *** SUM1,SUM2 - TOTALS ***
 65 LET SUM1 = 0
 67 LET SUM2 = 0
 70 INPUT "ENTER BALANCE: ";BALANCE
 75 PRINT
 80 LET B = BALANCE
 90 PRINT "TRANSACTION","AMOUNT"
100 PRINT
110 READ TY$,AMT
120 PRINT TY$,AMT
130 IF TY$ = "END" THEN GOTO 230
140 IF TY$ = "DEPOSIT" THEN GOTO 190
150 BALANCE = BALANCE - AMT
160 LET SUM1 = SUM1 + AMT
180 GOTO 110
190 BALANCE =BALANCE + AMT
200 LET SUM2 = SUM2 + AMT
210 GOTO 110
220 PRINT : PRINT
230 PRINT "BEGINNING BALANCE = ";B
240 PRINT
250 PRINT "ENDING BALANCE = ";BALANCE
260 PRINT
270 PRINT "TOTAL DEPOSITS = ";SUM2
280 PRINT
290 PRINT "TOTAL WITHDRAWALS = ";SUM1
300 DATA DEPOSIT,123,WITHDRAWAL,34.5
310 DATA WITHDRAWAL,12.75
320 DATA WITHDRAWAL,45.90
330 DATA DEPOSIT,20.0,END,0

]RUN
ENTER BALANCE: 279.55

TRANSACTION    AMOUNT

DEPOSIT        123
WITHDRAWAL     34.5
WITHDRAWAL     12.75
WITHDRAWAL     45.9
DEPOSIT        20
END            0


BEGINNING BALANCE = 279.55

ENDING BALANCE = 329.4

TOTAL DEPOSITS = 143

TOTAL WITHDRAWALS = 93.15
```

Note: Versions of BASIC that analyze only the first two characters of a variable name for uniqueness would not distinguish between SUM1 and SUM2.

GOTO STATEMENT

To create computer programs that will accomplish a wide variety of tasks, it is necessary to control the sequence in which the computer executes program statements. All computer languages supply this flexibility with branch instructions that cause program control to be transferred from one statement to another. In BASIC, the GOTO statement is the primary instruction for branching. Normally, when a statement has completed execution, control will go to the next line number (sequential execution). However, if a GOTO statement is used, control will branch to the line number specified by the GOTO statement and resume sequential execution at that point. The format for the GOTO statement follows:

line# GOTO transfer line#

This statement is unconditional and is restricted only by the limits of the program. The GOTO statement is unconditional because without exception, the machine will transfer control whenever it encounters a GOTO statement. The GOTO statement must transfer control to a line number within the program, or an error will result. Because of the great flexibility and power of the GOTO statement, programmers can make a program as complex as they want, with control being transferred to many different places. Complex programs may be ingenious, but they have been found to be counterproductive. A complex program is difficult to maintain. Another person may find it impossible to alter or even understand the code. A more structured approach to program design is desirable. The GOTO statement can be used indiscriminately, but it also can be used to create orderly, structured control transfers that represent logical program design. Structured control will be examined in the next chapter.

Suppose we had a hundred numbers and wished to divide them all in half. Try to write a program to do this without a GOTO statement. It might look something like Figure IV–3. This ridiculous program would be over three hundred statements long. It would be easier to use a calculator.

However, if we could use a GOTO statement, the program would be simple (see Figure IV–4). In this program the GOTO statement will cause repeated branches to Line 100 until a 999 is entered, which will cause the program to transfer control to the end of the program and out of the loop.

Note the loop in the flowchart in Figure IV–5. Program control will go around and around, processing all the data until the loop terminates.

IF/THEN STATEMENT

The IF/THEN statement is a conditional statement: **If** a condition is true, **then** perform a statement; **if** that condition is false, **then** do not

```
100  INPUT  X
110  LET  X  =  X  /  2
120  PRINT  X
130  INPUT  X
140  LET  X  =  X  /  2
150  PRINT  X
160  INPUT  X
170  LET  X  =  X  /  2
180  PRINT  X
190  INPUT  X
200  LET  X  =  X  /  2
210  PRINT  X
       •
       •
       •

2970  INPUT  X
2980  LET  X  =  X  /  2
2990  PRINT  X
3000  END
```

Figure IV–3 Ridiculous Program

perform that statement. The IF/THEN statement is like a fork in the road. If the condition of a given expression is true, then you go down one road. If that condition is false, then you go down the other one. For example,

```
150  IF  A  =  B  THEN  GOTO  200
160  A  =  A  +  1
```

Figure IV–4 More Efficient Program

```
100  INPUT  X
110  IF  X  =  999  THEN  GOTO  150
120  LET  X  =  X  /  2
130  PRINT  X
140  GOTO  100
150  END

]RUN
?34
17
?55
27.5
?145
72.5
?67
33.5
?144555
72277.5
?345555
172777.5
?999
```

Figure IV–5
Flowchart for More Ef-
ficient Program

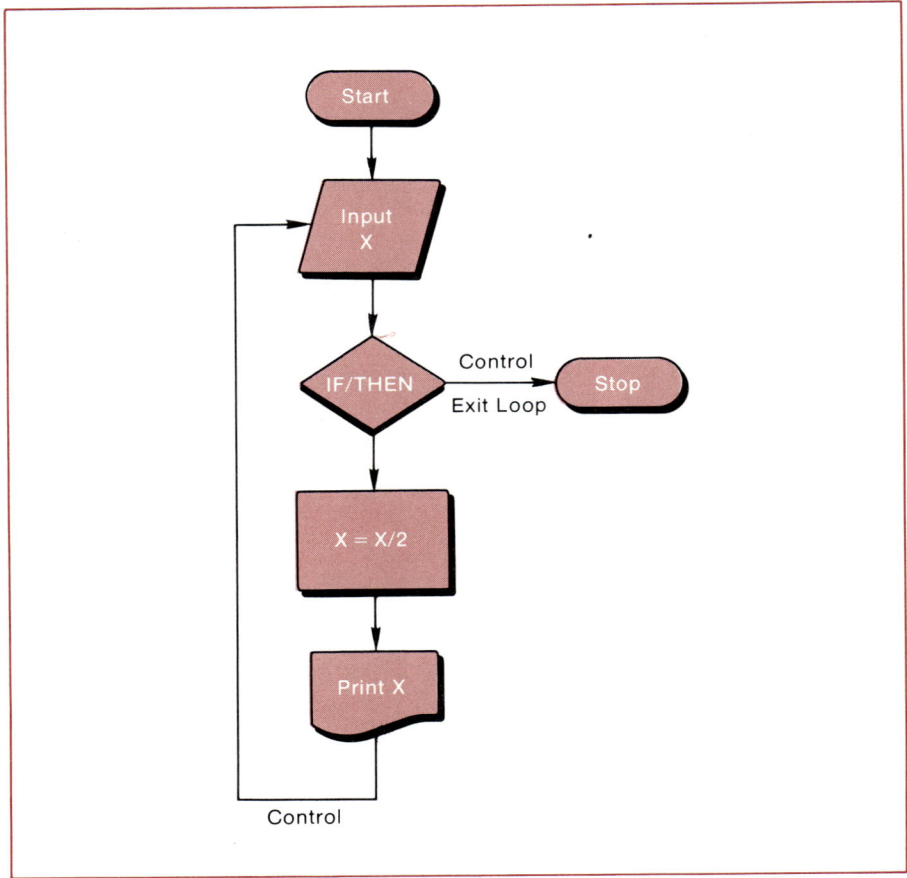

This IF/THEN statement functions in the following way. If the condition A = B is true, then branch to Line 200. If the condition A = B is false, then ignore the GOTO statement, and perform the next sequential statement (Line 160)*:

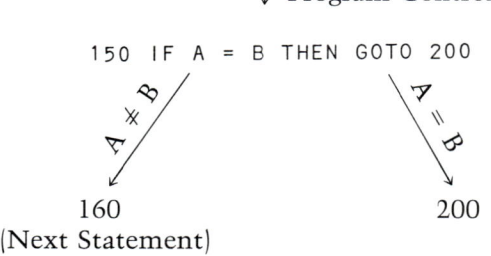

*Note: Some versioins of BASIC require that a true condition branch to a line number by using either THEN or GOTO, but not both.

Table IV–1 BASIC RELATIONAL SYMBOLS

Operators	Meaning	Boolean Expression
<	Less than	C < 5
>	Greater than	D > 10
=	Equal to	A$ = "YES"
< >	Not equal to	C < > B
< =	Less than or equal to	X ≤ 100
> =	Greater than or equal to	Y ≥ A + B

The format for the IF/THEN statement follows:

IF expression relational symbol expression THEN statement

The expression following the IF clause is called a **Boolean expression.** It tests the condition of the relationship between two expressions with the help of **Boolean operators.** Boolean operators are commonly called **relational symbols** and also are used in algebra (see Table IV–1).

Once evaluated, a Boolean expression can reflect only one of two possible values or conditions. Either it is true or it is false. When the computer encounters an IF/THEN statement, it evaluates the Boolean expression; if the condition is true, the computer executes the THEN part of the statement. If the Boolean expression is false, the computer will skip over the THEN part and go on to execute the next statement. The statement following the THEN clause can be any BASIC statement. Figure IV–6 shows some IF/THEN statements.

In the last example in Figure IV–6, the IF/THEN statement was combined with a GOTO statement. These two statements form a conditional transfer statement. Remember, the GOTO statement alone is an unconditional transfer statement, because it always will transfer control. The IF/THEN statement tests a condition; if it is true, the GOTO statement will be executed, and the program control will be transferred.

Figure IV–6 IF/THEN Statements

```
IF A = B THEN A = A + 1
IF A > 5 THEN INPUT "ENTER NEW VALUE";A
IF B < C THEN PRINT B
IF A <= 10 THEN GOTO 220
```

Boolean Expression	Conditional Statement
IF A = B	A = A + 1
IF A > 5	INPUT "ENTER NEW VALUE";A
IF B < C	PRINT B
IF A <= 10	GOTO 220

Conditional transfer is an important component in designing loops, because we need to test a condition each time around the loop to see if it is time to exit from the loop. We can exit from a loop when the condition of an expression is true.

The IF/THEN statement is used whenever one of two alternate actions needs to be performed. The checking account example uses two IF/THEN statements. The flowcharts in Figure IV–7 illustrate the alternate directions the program control can go. The diamond shape is used to represent the IF/THEN statement. Notice that the character strings can be evaluated in a Boolean expression just like any numeric variable or constant.

The technique of inserting a key value into data to indicate when to exit a loop is called **using a trailer value.** To use a trailer value, construct an IF/THEN statement that tests for the trailer value. For example, we used "END" in the checking account program and 999 in the division-by-two program. When "END" or 999 was encountered, the GOTO statement was executed, and the loop was terminated. Another way of keeping track of loop execution is through the use of a counter. To use a counter, the programmer must do three things: first, initialize a variable to 0; second, construct an IF/THEN statement to test whether the counter variable is equal to the number of times the loop is to be

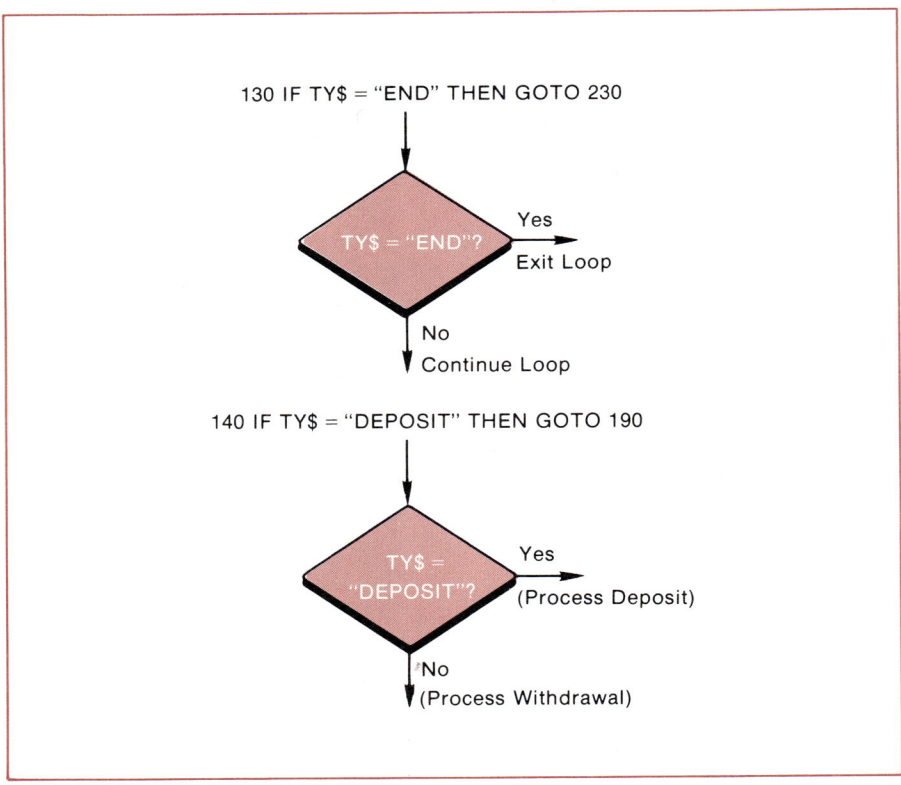

Figure IV–7 Structure of IF/THEN Statements

130 IF TY$ = "END" THEN GOTO 230

TY$ = "END"?

Yes
Exit Loop

No
Continue Loop

140 IF TY$ = "DEPOSIT" THEN GOTO 190

TY$ = "DEPOSIT"?

Yes
(Process Deposit)

No
(Process Withdrawal)

executed; and third, increment the variable each time through the loop.

Suppose we wish to execute a loop five times. Examine the flowchart and statements in Figure IV–8. The counter variable, C, will be equal to 0 the first time around the loop, equal to 1 the second time, and so on until it equals 5. When C = 5, the IF/THEN statement will be true, and program control will be transferred outside of the loop.

MULTIPLE CONDITIONAL TRANSFER

With the IF/THEN/GOTO statement, we saw a way in which program control could go in one of two directions. Suppose the programmer has five different functions to perform. These functions may be multiplying

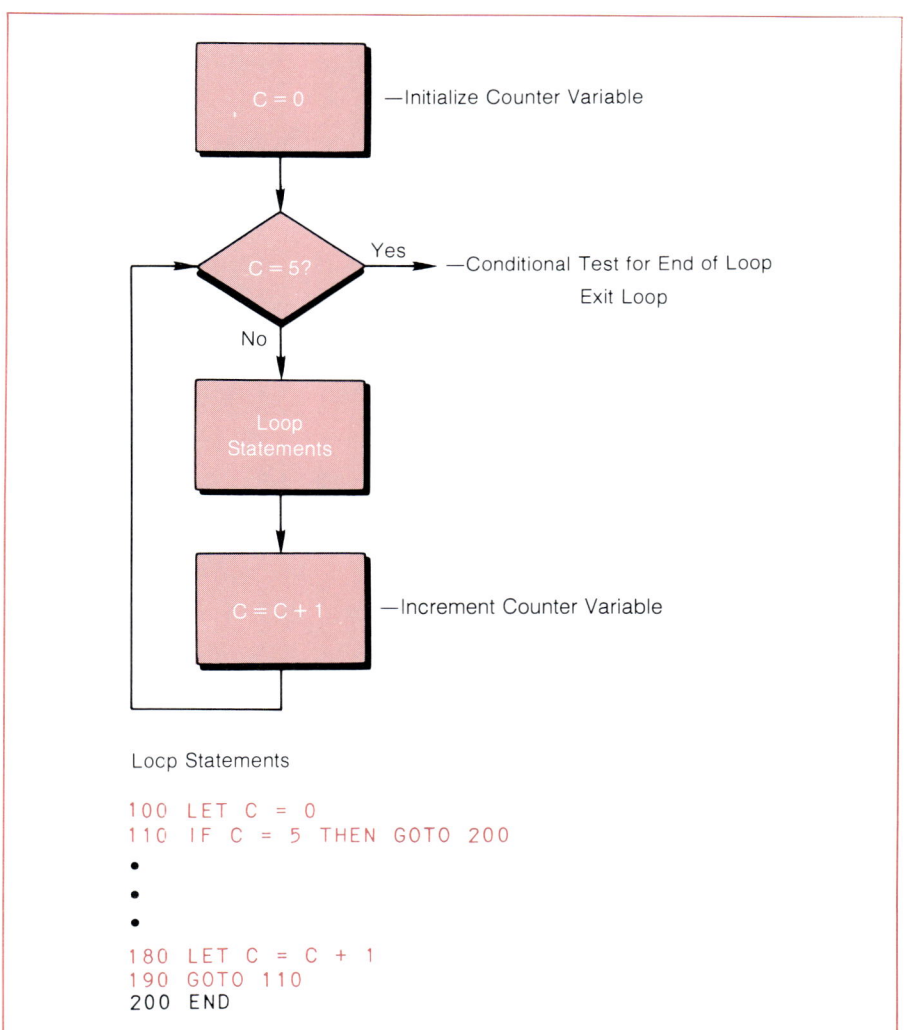

Figure IV–8 Loop Flowchart

two numbers, printing a sum, inputting a value, or any other process that is possible in BASIC. If the program design calls for a multipath decision to be made, the ON/GOTO statement can be used. The format for ON/GOTO is

line# ON expression GOTO line#1, line#2, . . ., line#n

When the computer encounters an ON/GOTO statement, it evaluates the expression and reduces it to an integer. If the expression equals 1, control is transferred to the first line number; if the expression equals 2, control is passed to the second line number; and so on. If an expression evaluates to an integer that is greater than the number of line num-

Figure IV–9 Structure of a Simulated Case Statement in BASIC

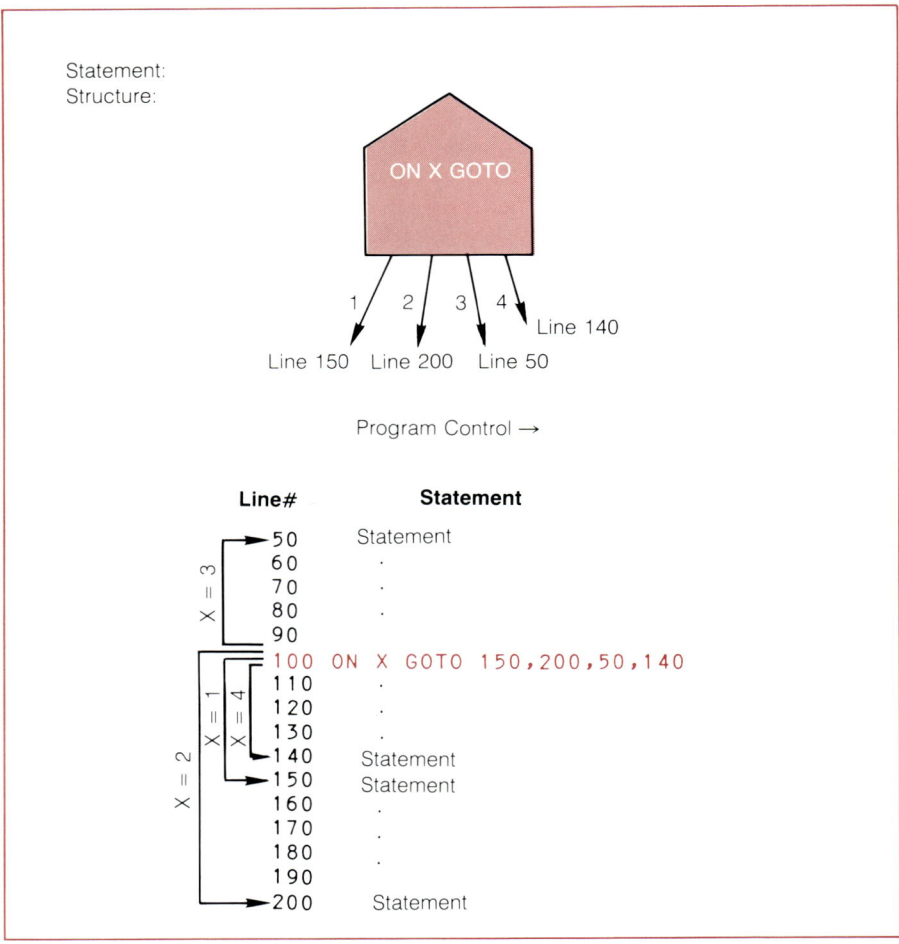

Note: If the values 1 through 4 are the only correct values, Line 110—immediately following the ON statement—should be either the first statement of an error routine or a GOTO statement that will branch to such a routine.

```
 10 REM *** PROGRAM TO COUNT COLLEGE STUDENTS BY CLASS ***
 20 REM *** VARIABLES ***
 30 REM *** NAME$ = STUDENT NAME ***
 40 REM *** CLASS = CLASS DESIGNATION (1-4 FOR FRESHMAN - SENIOR) ***
 50 REM *** FRCT,SOCT,JRCT, AND SRCT ARE COUNTERS FOR EACH CLASS ***
 60 FRCT = 0
 70 SOCT = 0
 80 JRCT = 0
 90 SRCT = 0
100 READ NAME$,CLASS
110 IF NAME$ = "END" THEN GOTO 280
120 ON CLASS GOTO 150,180,210,240
130 PRINT "INVALID CLASS DESIGNATION = ";CLASS
140 GOTO 100
150 LET FRCT = FRCT + 1
160 LET C$ = "FRESHMAN"
170 GOTO 260
180 LET SOCT = SOCT + 1
190 LET C$ = "SOPHOMORE"
200 GOTO 260
210 LET JRCT = JRCT + 1
220 LET C$ = "JUNIOR"
230 GOTO 260
240 LET SRCT = SRCT + 1
250 LET C$ = "SENIOR"
260 PRINT NAME$,C$
270 GOTO 100
280 PRINT:PRINT
290 PRINT "CLASS","COUNT"
300 PRINT "FRESHMAN",FRCT
310 PRINT "SOPHOMORE",SOCT
320 PRINT "JUNIOR",JRCT
330 PRINT "SENIOR",SRCT
340 DATA SMITH,3,PARKER,2,RODRIGUEZ,4
350 DATA STEIN,2,BRADLEY,1,OLSON,3
360 DATA MILLER,1,ADAMSON,4,FLYNN,1
370 DATA BAKER,2,KAHN,1,ELLIS,1
380 DATA SCHULTZ,2,END,0
999 END

]RUN
SMITH           JUNIOR
PARKER          SOPHOMORE
RODRIGUEZ       SENIOR
STEIN           SOPHOMORE
BRADLEY         FRESHMAN
OLSON           JUNIOR
MILLER          FRESHMAN
ADAMSON         SENIOR
FLYNN           FRESHMAN
BAKER           SOPHOMORE
KAHN            FRESHMAN
ELLIS           FRESHMAN
SCHULTZ         SOPHOMORE

CLASS           COUNT
FRESHMAN         5
SOPHOMORE        4
JUNIOR           2
SENIOR           2
```

Figure IV–10 Use of the ON Statement in a Program

bers listed, control automatically will be passed to the next sequential statement and bypass the GOTO statement. Examine the statement and control structure in Figure IV–9, as well as the program in Figure IV–10.

Program control can go in four ways. The statement in Figure IV–9 would be equivalent to four IF/THEN statements. Figure IV–10 gives a typical example of how the ON statement might be used in a program to count college students by class. These examples illustrate how the conditional statements introduced in this section provide the programmer with computational power and flexibility.

1. What is the difference between a conditional and an unconditional transfer?
2. In what situation would it be better to use an ON/GOTO rather than an IF/THEN statement?
3. What problem is created by having too many GOTO statements?
4. Write a program to read in a hundred numbers and keep a running total. Print out the result.
5. Write a program to read in a hundred numbers. Keep separate running totals of the negative and positive numbers. (Hint: Use an IF/THEN statement to determine the sign of each number.)
6. Modify the program in Figure IV–4 so that a legitimate value of 999 could be correctly handled.

SECTION V

STRUCTURED PROGRAMMING IN BASIC

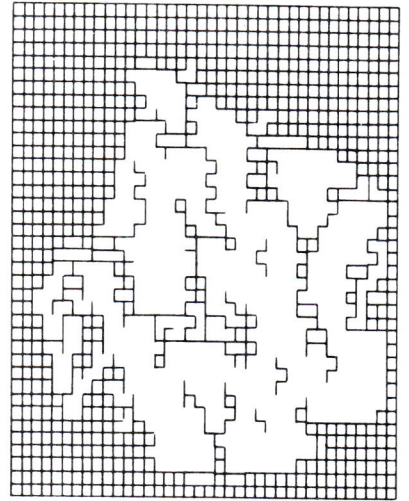

To develop efficient, well-designed programs, the programmer must build a certain amount of order into the code. The order is defined by the control structures used in the program, as well as the degree of modularity. **Modularity** is the partitioning of functions into distinct program segments. Every program has certain functions that it must perform. Structuring separates the functions so that they are easier to identify and understand. To increase the modularity of programs, subroutines are needed. **Subroutines** are small programs within a program that can be called on to perform a certain function whenever it is needed. With subroutines and the more advanced control structures introduced in this section, better programs can be created.

PROGRAM PROBLEM

The program in Figure V–1 demonstrates a few of the control structures this section will examine. This program calculates a student's GPA and the mean GPA for the class. To accomplish these two functions, we need one control structure within another. This is commonly referred to as an **inner loop** and an **outer loop.** The outer loop is a conditional iteration of statements. The condition is whether or not there are any more students to process. This loop also keeps a running total of the number of students and their scores. The inner loop begins on Line 130. This loop is a controlled iteration. The BASIC statement for controlled iteration is a FOR/NEXT statement pair. It is controlled because we know how many times the loop is to be repeated or iterated.

Figure V–2 illustrates the two control structures for the program in Figure V–1. The inner control loop, in red, is completely contained by the outer loop, in blue. Nesting of control structures within one another is a very useful programming technique.

```
10 REM *** GRADE EVALUATION PROGRAM ***
20 REM *** VARIABLES ***
30 REM *** C1 - CLASS SIZE ***
40 REM *** S2 - TOTAL CLASS GRADE POINTS ***
50 REM *** N$ - STUDENT$ NAME ***
60 REM *** C - COURSES FOR CURRENT STUDENT ***
70 REM *** GP - GRADE POINTS FOR CURRENT STUDENT (AVERAGE) ***
80 REM *** S1 - TOTAL GRADE POINTS FOR CURRENT STUDENT ***
85 REM *** G - INDIVIDUAL COURSE GRADE ***
90 LET C1 = 0 : LET S2 = 0
100 INPUT "ENTER NAME, # OF COURSES: ";N$,C
105 PRINT
110 IF N$ = "999" THEN GOTO 210
120 LET C1 = C1 + 1 : LET GP = 0 : LET S1 = 0
130 FOR I = 1 TO C
140    INPUT "ENTER COURSE NAME AND GRADE: ";N$,G
150    PRINT
160    LET S1 = S1 + G
170 NEXT I
175 PRINT
180 LET GP = S1 / C : GOSUB 225
185 PRINT "STUDENT GPA = ";GP
190 LET S2 = S2 + GP
195 PRINT : PRINT
200 GOTO 100
210 LET GP = S2 / C1 : GOSUB 225
215 PRINT : PRINT
220 PRINT "CLASS AVERAGE = ";GP
222 STOP
225 LET GP = INT(GP * 10 + .5) / 10
230 RETURN
240 END

]RUN
ENTER NAME, # OF COURSES: ART STILL,3

ENTER COURSE NAME AND GRADE: C.S. 100,2.5

ENTER COURSE NAME AND GRADE: MATH 105,3.75

ENTER COURSE NAME AND GRADE: ART HISTORY,2.25


STUDENT GPA = 2.8


ENTER NAME, # OF COURSES: JOE TREW,4

ENTER COURSE NAME AND GRADE: BUS.AD. 234,3.0

ENTER COURSE NAME AND GRADE: ACCOUNTING 112,2.0

ENTER COURSE NAME AND GRADE: MATH 231,4.0

ENTER COURSE NAME AND GRADE: P.E. 111,2.5


STUDENT GPA =  2.9


ENTER NAME, # OF COURSES: ? 999, 1



CLASS AVERAGE =  2.9
```

Figure V–1 Structured Program

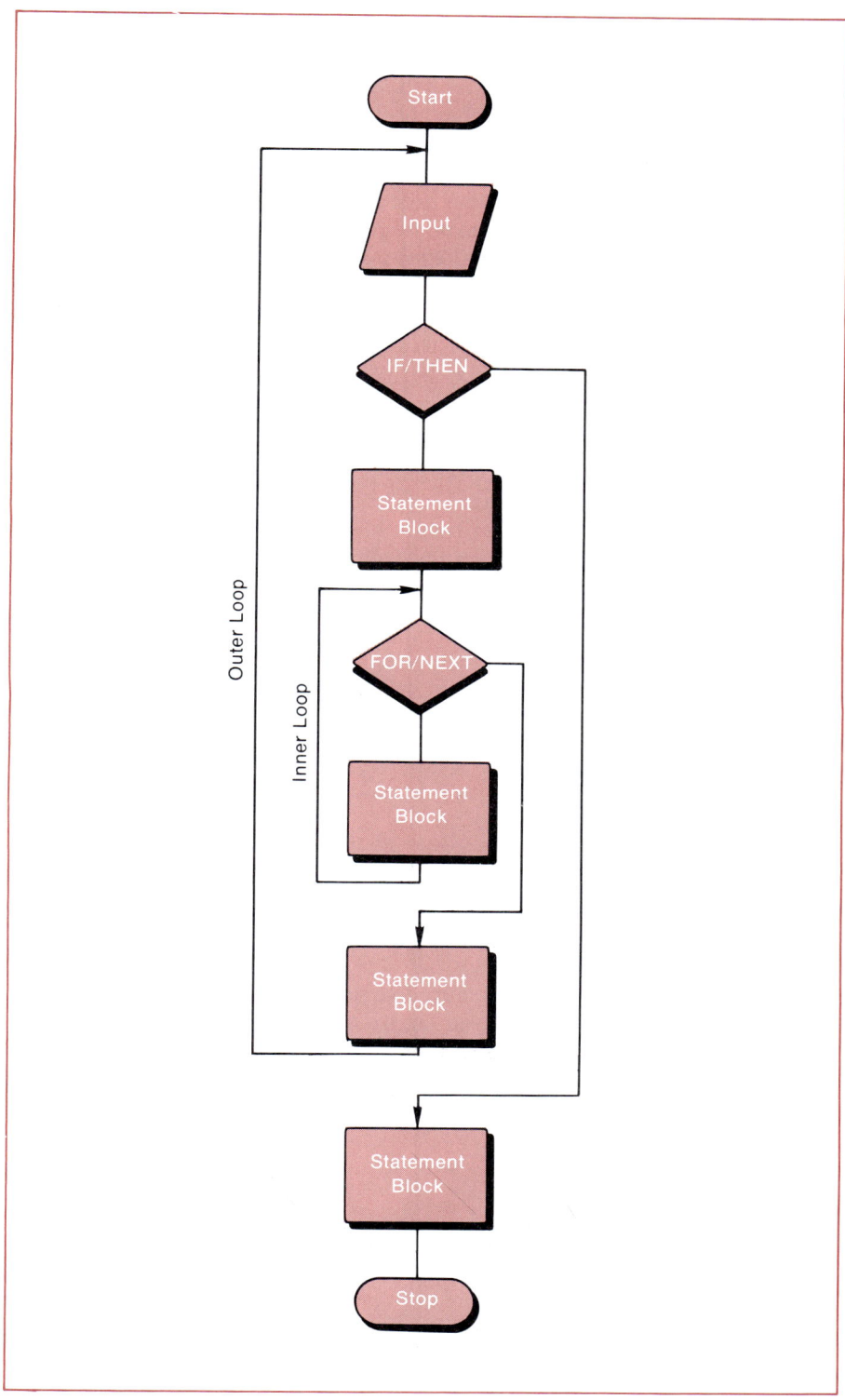

Figure **V–2** Program Control

BASIC CONTROL STRUCTURES

We already have examined the control statements GOTO, ON/GOTO, and IF/THEN/GOTO. Two other useful control statements are IF/THEN/ELSE and FOR/NEXT. Using these five control statements, the programmer can create logical, noncomplex program structures that accomplish the required functions. Three kinds of structures are available: sequence, iteration, and alternation. **Sequence** consists of one statement after another without branching. **Iteration** is a group of statements repeated a number of times (a loop). **Alternation** is a structure that allows branching in two or more directions based on the condition of the variable. There are alternate routes program control can take.

Sequential Statement Lists

Sequential program statements represent the simplest kind of program structure. Sequential statements form blocks of code, which are the basis for the program design. We already have noted how program control is passed from one line number to the next after each statement is executed:

```
100    INPUT X,Y
200    LET X = X / 2
300    LET Z = X * Y
400    PRINT "X","Y","Z"
500    PRINT
600    PRINT X,Y,Z
700    END

]RUN
?4
??7
X                      Y                      Z

2                      7                      14
```

This group of statements is executed sequentially; therefore, we can refer to it as a **statement block** (see Figure V–3).

Figure V–3 Sequence of Statements Referred to as a Statement Block

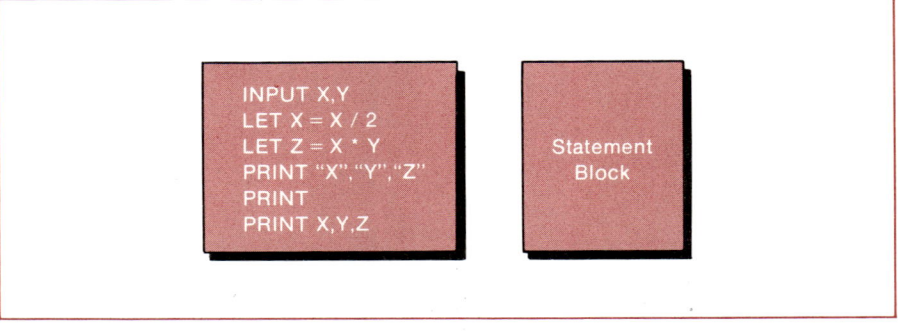

```
INPUT X,Y
LET X = X / 2
LET Z = X * Y
PRINT "X","Y","Z"
PRINT
PRINT X,Y,Z
```

Statement Block

In a statement block, control is passed from one line to the next with no control transfer statements. Statement blocks are the building blocks of a structured program. Since control is so well defined, we can put blocks together to design the type of program that is needed. Figure V–4 shows how three statement blocks can be used to build the three basic types of control structures.

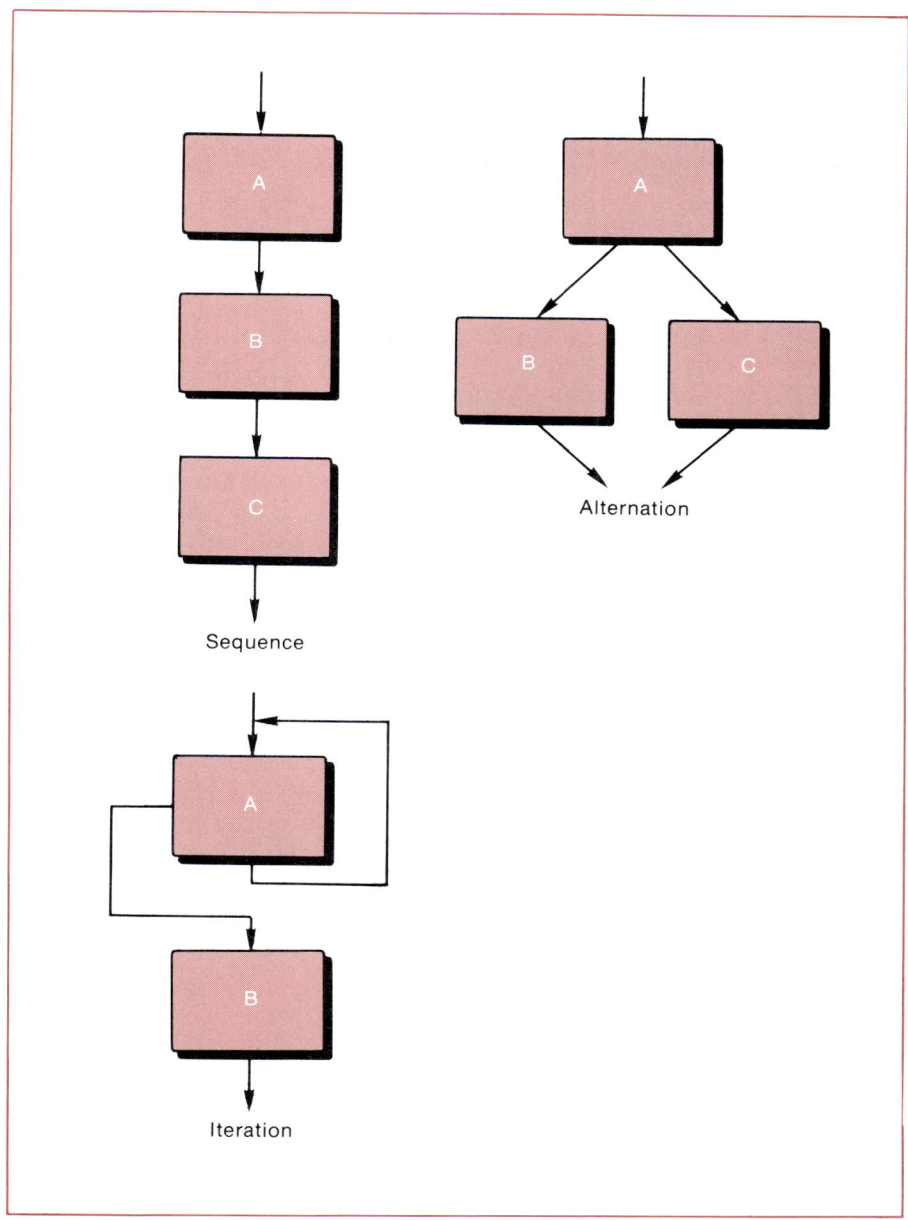

Figure V–4 Control Structures

The different ways the blocks can be arranged is determined by the control statements used. A good program design may use any combination of these three structure types. The programming problem will determine the program design.

Iteration

The dictionary defines **iteration** as "the act of repeating." This is precisely what iteration structures tell the computer to do—repeat. The purpose of an iterative structure is to explicitly define what statements are to be repeated and how many times the repetition is to occur.

Controlled Iteration In BASIC, the FOR/NEXT statement pair is used in controlled loop structures. The format is

```
line# FOR variable = initial expression TO terminal expression STEP value
line# statement list
  .
  .
  .
line# NEXT variable
```

The STEP keyword indicates the increment by which the loop variable will be altered each time through the loop. The STEP value may be omitted, in which case the value will default to 1. Some example statements are shown in Figure V–5. The statement block between the FOR and NEXT statements will execute until the loop variable is equal to the terminal expression. Each time through the loop, the computer automatically will increment the loop variable (see Figure V–6).

Figure V–6 shows how the loop variable, I, is automatically changed. I is incremented each time through the loop. When I = 10, the loop is terminated, and the output is discontinued. The FOR/NEXT pair automatically tests the value of the loop variable and the termination value each time through the loop. The diagram in Figure V–7 illustrates the FOR/NEXT statement pair structure and the transfer of control within it.

In the FOR/NEXT loop, the STEP clause allows the programmer to control the amount by which the loop variable is incremented. Figure V–8 is an example. In this short program, we can see that the loop variable, I, is incremented by 5 rather than 1. The STEP value also can be a negative number if we wish the loop variable to be decremented each

Figure V–5 FOR Loop Structure

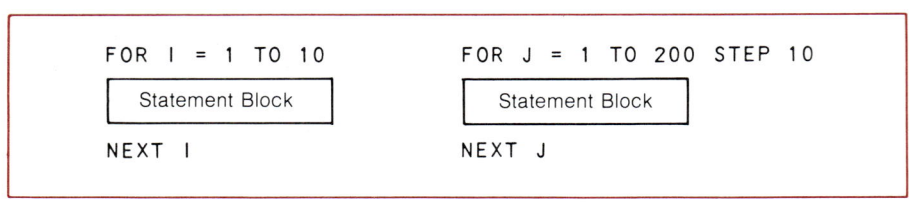

```
100 FOR I = 1 TO 10
200    PRINT "LOOP VARIABLE = ";I:PRINT
300 NEXT I
400 PRINT "*** LOOP TERMINATED ***"
500 END

]RUN
LOOP VARIABLE = 1

LOOP VARIABLE = 2

LOOP VARIABLE = 3

LOOP VARIABLE = 4

LOOP VARIABLE = 5

LOOP VARIABLE = 6

LOOP VARIABLE = 7

LOOP VARIABLE = 8

LOOP VARIABLE = 9

LOOP VARIABLE = 10

*** LOOP TERMINATED ***
```

Figure V–6 Program Illustrating Loop Variable

time through the loop; Figure V–9 shows this. In these two statements, the loop variable will be decremented by either 1 or 10. When a negative STEP value is used, the initial expression must be larger than the terminal expression, or an error will result. For example,

```
FOR I = 10 TO 20 STEP -1
```

is an invalid FOR statement.

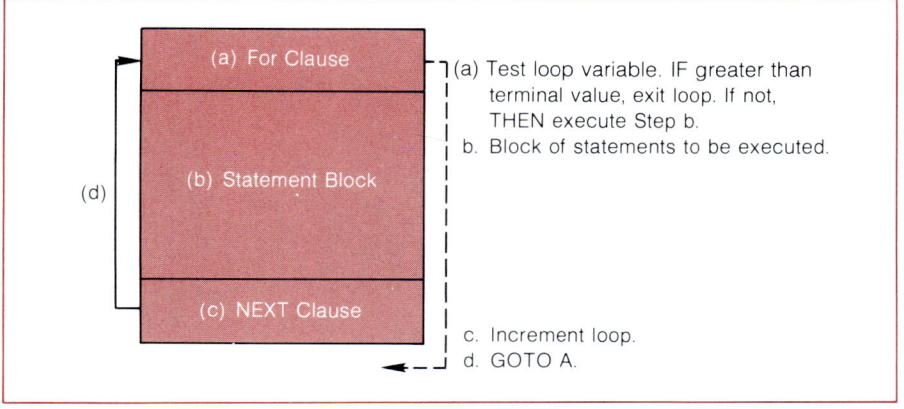

Figure V–7 Structure Function of FOR/NEXT Statement Pair

Figure V–8 Using a
Step Value

```
100 FOR I = 5 TO 25 STEP 5
200    PRINT "LOOP VARIABLE = ";I
300    PRINT
400 NEXT I

]RUN
LOOP VARIABLE = 5

LOOP VARIABLE = 10

LOOP VARIABLE = 15

LOOP VARIABLE = 20

LOOP VARIABLE = 25
```

The terminal, initial, and STEP values also may be variables in a FOR/NEXT statement pair. Using variables, we can vary the number of iterations and the loop variable increments each time the program is run (see Figure V–10). In this short program segment, the loop will be executed K times. The programmer controls the number of iterations by inputting different values for K.

Figure V–9 Negative
STEP Value

```
FOR I = 10 TO 1 STEP -1
NEXT I

FOR I = 100 TO 10 STEP -10
NEXT I
```

Figure V–10 Variable
FOR/NEXT Loop

```
100 INPUT K
200 FOR I = 1 TO K
300    PRINT "LOOP VARIABLE = ";I
400 NEXT I

]RUN
?3
LOOP VARIABLE = 1
LOOP VARIABLE = 2
LOOP VARIABLE = 3

]RUN
?5
LOOP VARIABLE = 1
LOOP VARIABLE = 2
LOOP VARIABLE = 3
LOOP VARIABLE = 4
LOOP VARIABLE = 5
```

```
INPUT J, K, L
FOR I = J TO K STEP L
•
•
•

NEXT I
FOR I = (J + 5) TO (K - 5) STEP L
•
•
•

NEXT I
```

Figure V–11 Control
Variables in FOR/NEXT
Loop

Other valid FOR/NEXT statement pairs are shown in Figure V–11. In these statements, the programmer has complete control over the loop. Any valid BASIC expression can be used within a FOR/NEXT loop. The control variables and expressions must not be changed within the FOR/NEXT block.

The loop variable in Figure V–12 is assigned the value of A; this is

Figure V–12 Bad
FOR/NEXT Loop

```
100 FOR I = 1 TO 10
200    PRINT I
300    LET A = B + C
400    LET I = A
500 NEXT I


] RUN
1
1
1
1
1
1
1
1
1
1
1
1
1
1
1
1
1
1
1
1
1
1
1
1
```

Figure V–13
Nested FOR/NEXT
Loop Structure

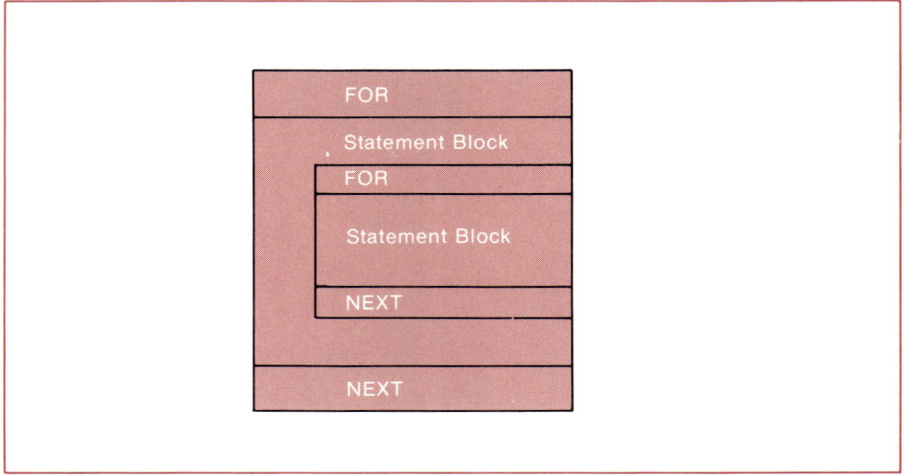

bad programming. If the loop variable is modified, execution will not proceed as intended. In this case, an infinite loop occurred.

Putting a FOR/NEXT structure within the statement block of another FOR/NEXT loop is called **nesting.** Figure V–13 illustrates a nested FOR/NEXT structure. Figure V–14 shows the BASIC statements for a nested FOR/NEXT structure. This is a more complex control structure. Each time through the outer loop, the inner nested FOR/NEXT loop is repeated until completion. Then control is passed to the outer loop, the outer loop variable is incremented, and the outer loop is executed again. In the example shown in Figure V–14, the statements of the inner loop will be executed fifty times.

As we can see in Figure V–15, each time the outer loop is executed, the inner loop will be processed three times. Nested structures can be very valuable for processing lists in which one element must be held constant until another element has been processed. This will be discussed in a later section.

Figure V–14
Nested FOR/NEXT
Loop Statements

```
FOR I = 1 TO 5
   •
   •
   •
   FOR J = 1 TO 10
      •
      •
      •
   NEXT J
   •
   •
   •
NEXT I
```

```
100 FOR I = 1 TO 4
200    FOR J = 1 TO 3
300       PRINT "INNER LOOP VAR = ";J
400    NEXT J
500    PRINT
600    PRINT "OUTER LOOP VAR = ";I
700    PRINT
800 NEXT I

]RUN
INNER LOOP VAR = 1
INNER LOOP VAR = 2
INNER LOOP VAR = 3

OUTER LOOP VAR = 1

INNER LOOP VAR = 1
INNER LOOP VAR = 2
INNER LOOP VAR = 3

OUTER LOOP VAR = 2

INNER LOOP VAR = 1
INNER LOOP VAR = 2
INNER LOOP VAR = 3

OUTER LOOP VAR = 3

INNER LOOP VAR = 1
INNER LOOP VAR = 2
INNER LOOP VAR = 3

OUTER LOOP VAR = 4
```

Figure V–15
Execution of Nested
FOR/NEXT Loops

Conditional Iteration With the FOR/NEXT statement pair, we saw how to design a structure where the number of repetitions is controlled by using a loop variable and a range of expression values. Iterative statements also may be of the conditional variety. In this type of structure, a statement block will be executed while the condition or a key expression is either true or false. Conditional iteration appears in the more structured languages like Pascal and PL/I in the form of WHILE DO or REPEAT UNTIL statements. These statements are not available in BASIC, but they can be simulated very easily. In BASIC, more statements are required to build a conditional loop, but the results are the same.

Suppose the programmer wishes to execute a group of statements while the variable, X, is less than 10. The structure in Figure V–16 should be used. The statement block will be executed anywhere from zero to an infinite number of times, depending on the control variable, X. The advantage of this structure over the FOR/NEXT structure is that the loop variable can be modified within the statement block. The condition of the loop variable, X, will determine whether or not the state-

Figure V–16
Conditional Structure

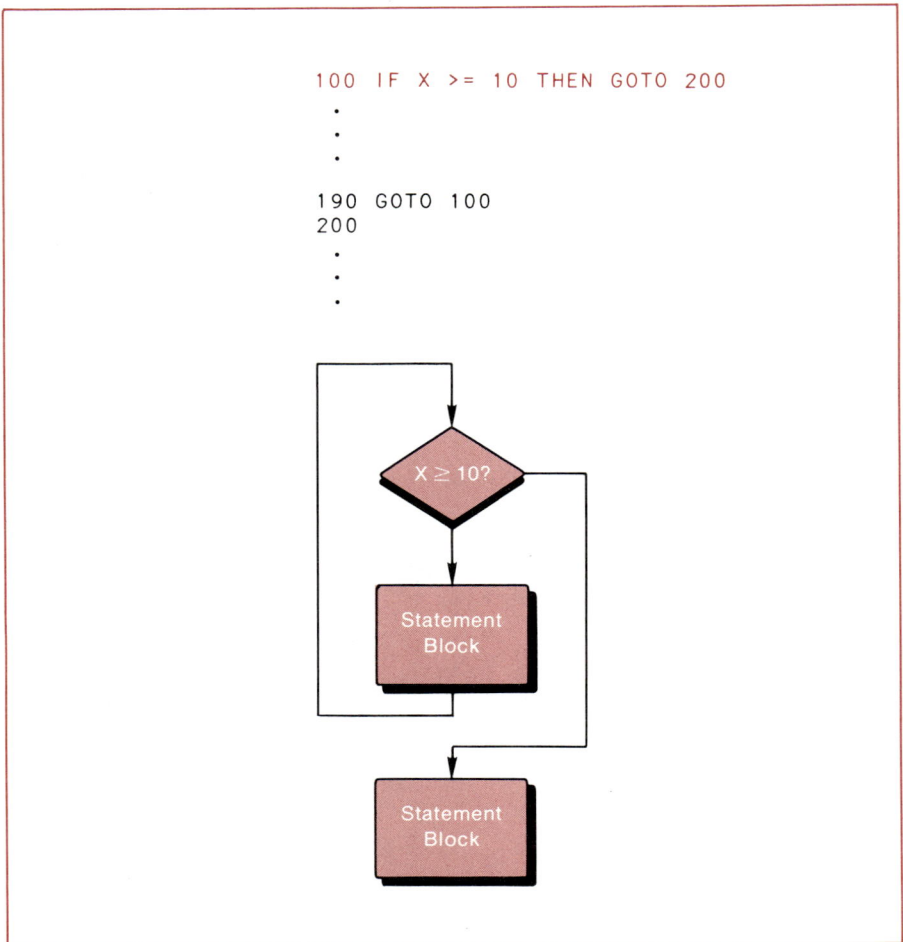

```
100 IF X >= 10 THEN GOTO 200
      .
      .
      .
190 GOTO 100
200
      .
      .
      .
```

ment block will be executed. The GOTO statement at Line 190 insures that this condition will be tested each time through the loop.

The program in Figure V–17 demonstrates the use of a conditional loop in a manner used also in previous examples. The structure is defined by the IF/THEN statement at Line 130 and the GOTO statement at Line 170. The statement block (Lines 140 through 160) will be executed until the condition, C = 999, is true. When this expression is true, the GOTO 180 will be executed, and the loop will be terminated.

The flowchart in Figure V–18 illustrates the program structure for the program in Figure V–17. This structure can be used whenever a group of statements is to be repeated while a condition is true. In this case, the program will calculate the cost and tax of a number of books until a 999 data entry is encountered by the conditional statement. The processing is repeated until the condition for termination has been satisfied. The value of this structure lies in the fact that the program can run

```
100 REM *** PROGRAM TO CALCULATE ***
105 REM *** BOOK PURCHASE TOTALS ***
110 T = 0
115 PRINT "COST","SUBTOTAL"
120 READ C
130 IF C = 999 THEN GOTO 180
140 TX = C * 0.06
150 T = T + C + TX
160 PRINT C,T
170 GOTO 120
180 PRINT : PRINT "TOTAL PURCHASE = ";T
190 DATA 23.5,33.9,16.7,14.99,22.5,999


]RUN
COST                SUBTOTAL
23.5                24.91
33.9                60.844
16.7                78.546
14.99               94.4354
22.5                118.2854

TOTAL PURCHASE = 118.2854
```

Figure V–17
Program Illustrating a
Conditional Loop

using a data set of any size. If a FOR/NEXT statement pair or controlled iteration had been used, the number of data items would be predetermined by the loop variable.

Alternation

Alternation is the control structure that allows for alternate paths to be executed by the computer. In the last section we examined the IF/THEN and ON/GOTO statements. These statements permit branching based on the condition of an expression. Figure V–19 illustrates the IF/THEN and ON/GOTO structures.

IF/THEN/ELSE Statements IF/THEN statements are very useful in creating conditional loops. Two other powerful control statements are the IF/THEN/ELSE and the ON/GOSUB (a variant of ON/GOTO) statements. The IF/THEN/ELSE statement is a variation of the IF/THEN statement available in many microcomputer versions of BASIC. The IF/THEN/ELSE statement provides the programmer with a way to specify two alternate statements to be executed.

Recall that the IF/THEN statement will execute the THEN clause if the accompanying Boolean expression is true. If it is false, the next sequential statement will be executed. The IF/THEN/ELSE statement works in much the same way. If the Boolean expression is true, the THEN clause will be executed and the ELSE clause ignored. If the Boolean is false, the ELSE clause will be executed and the THEN clause will be ignored.

Figure V–18
Program Structure

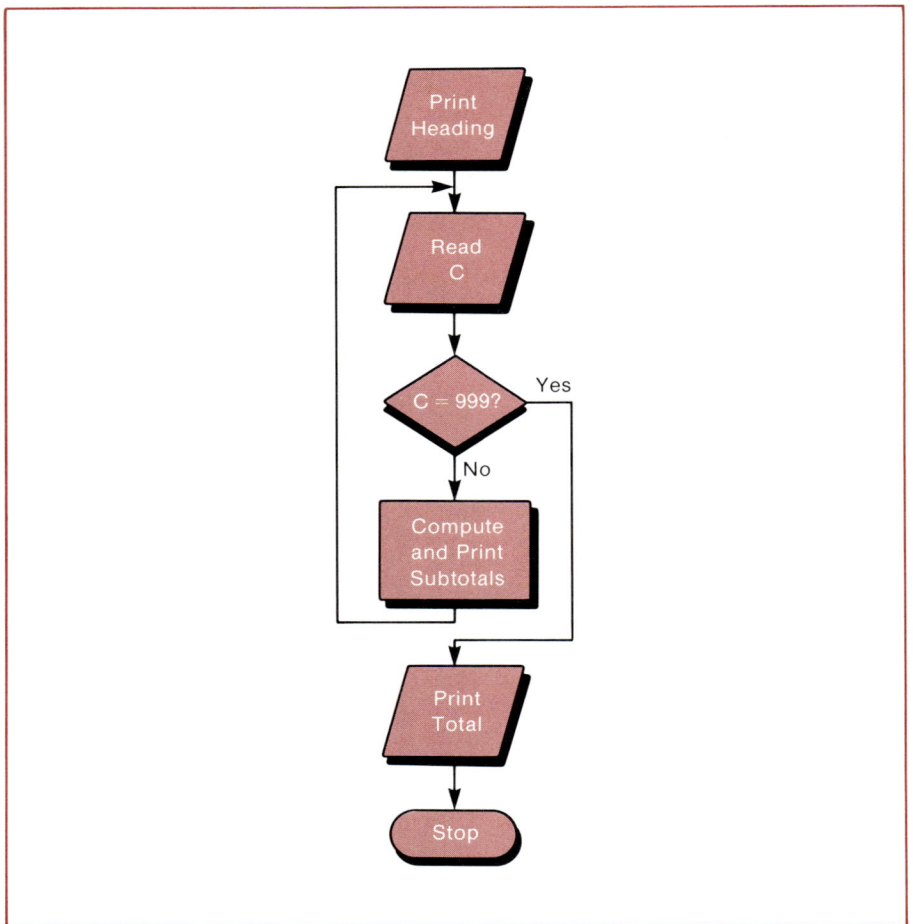

The two statements in Figure V–20 are examples of IF/THEN/ELSE statements. The format for the IF/THEN/ELSE statement is IF (Boolean expression) THEN (statement) ELSE (statement).

In Figure V–21 we can see the fork in the road, or the alternate control paths. The advantage of the IF/THEN/ELSE statement is the way in which the next sequential statement is handled. In the IF/THEN statement, the next statement becomes one of the alternate statements to be executed, and therefore it will be executed unless the THEN clause contains a GOTO. In the IF/THEN/ELSE statement, there are two alternate clauses, and one or the other may be executed, but not both. Either the THEN clause or the ELSE clause is executed. This allows the programmer to design programs with a more well-defined transfer of program control.

A good example of when to use an IF/THEN/ELSE statement is the checking account example in Part IV (see Figure V–22). The program design is well tailored to fit the IF/THEN/ELSE statement because there

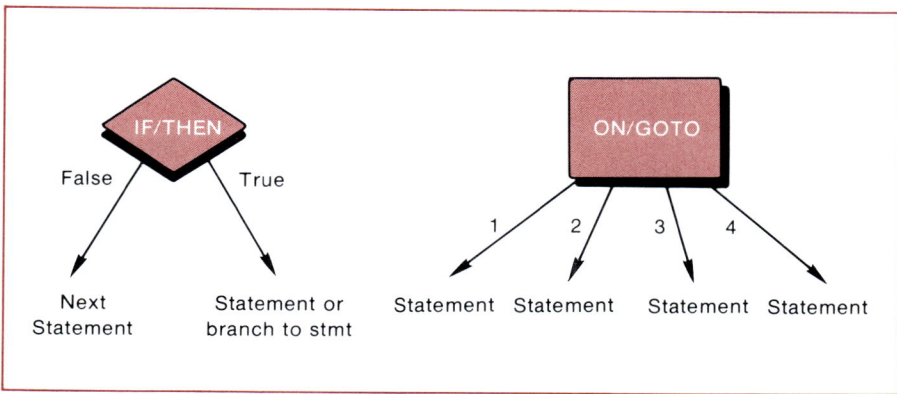

Figure V–19 Alternation Structures

are two program control paths that are mutually exclusive. Either we process a check withdrawal or a deposit; a transaction cannot be both.

Figure V–23 shows the problem logic. Control transfer is easy to follow, and the logic is not complex. There is one further refinement that we could make in this example:

```
IF TY$ = "DEPOSIT" THEN GOSUB 200 ELSE GOSUB 150
```

The GOSUB statement is the way BASIC calls subroutines. Subroutines increase modularity and thus increase the degree of structure in the program.

GOSUB Statement   The format for the GOSUB statement is

```
line# GOSUB line#
```

The GOSUB statement works much like a GOTO statement in that it transfers control to the line number following the keyword GOSUB. That line number is the first line of the subroutine. The subroutine statements are terminated by a RETURN statement. The computer will branch to the subroutine after executing a GOSUB statement and execute all the statements until it reads a RETURN statement. At this point, control will be transferred to the line following the original GOSUB statement. This structure permits the subroutine to be entered from different points within the main program and to return control to the statement immediately following the most recently executed GOSUB statement.

Figure V–20 IF/THEN/ELSE Statements

```
100 IF X > 5 THEN A = B + 10 ELSE A = B + 20


100 IF Y = Z THEN GOTO 290 ELSE GOTO 200
```

Figure V–21 IF/THEN/
ELSE Structure

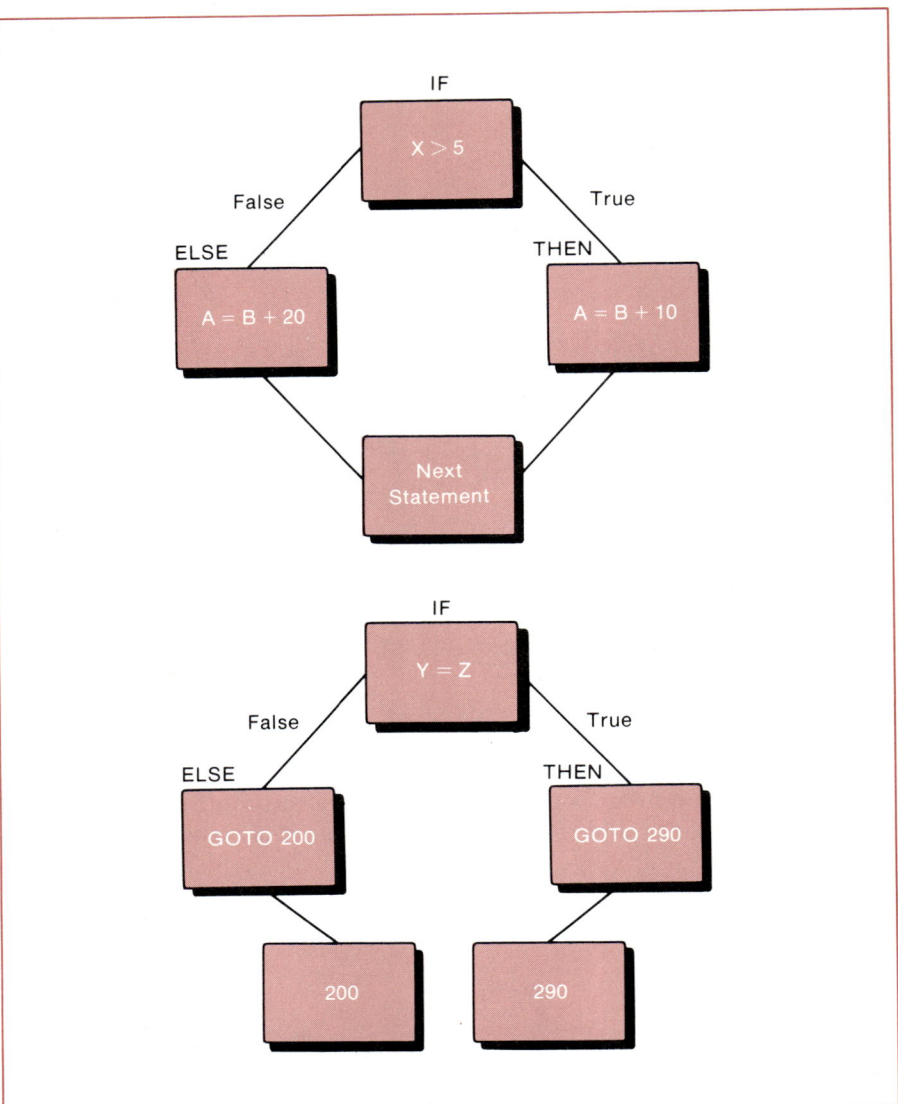

Figure V–22 Illustration of Alternate Selections

```
100 INPUT TY$,C
110 IF TY$ = "DEPOSIT" THEN GOTO 150 ELSE GOTO 200
        .
        .
        .
150 BALANCE = BALANCE + C
160 PRINT "DEPOSIT = ";C
        .
        .
        .
200 BALANCE = BALANCE - C
210 PRINT "WITH = ";C
```

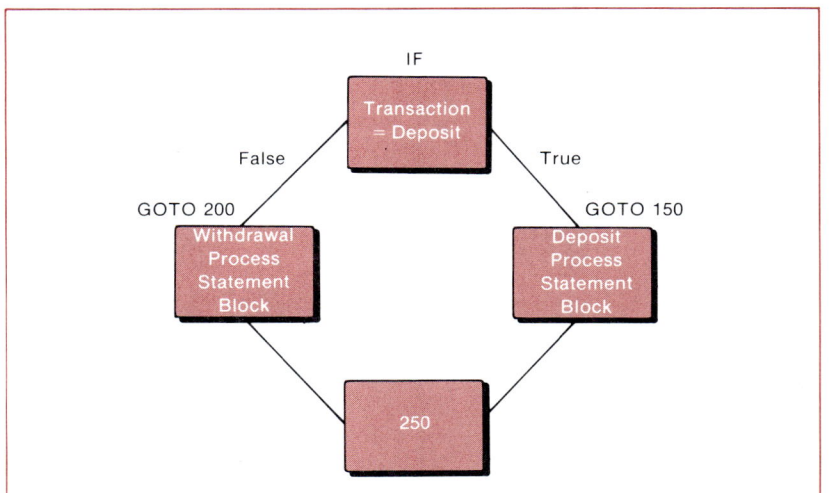

Figure V–23
Alternate Control Structure

The GOSUB statement at Line 100 of Figure V–24 will cause a jump to Line 200. Lines 200 through 230 will be executed, and the RETURN statement will cause program control to jump back to line 110. Figure V–25 shows the difference between a GOTO and a GOSUB statement. With a GOSUB statement, control is returned to the GOSUB statement rather than to the next sequential statement, as would be the case with a GOTO statement.

The GOSUB statement increases program modularity, because it can be used to avoid repeating program statements throughout a program. If a function must be repeated four times in a program, GOTO statements can be used to branch to the statements that perform the process. The problem is that control will not return to the point of the branch. The GOSUB statement allows branching to a routine and returning again so that processing can continue.

The program in Figure V–26 illustrates the use of subroutines. Sup-

```
100 GOSUB 200
110
       .
       .
       .
200 A = B
210 PRINT "A";A
220 PRINT "B";B
230 RETURN
       .
       .
       .
```

Figure V–24 GOSUB
Statement

Figure V–25 Control Transfer in GOSUB versus GOTO Statements

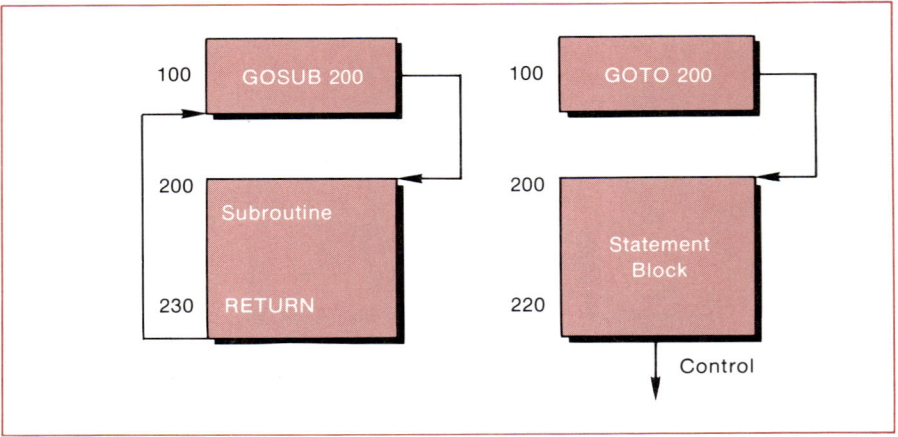

Figure V–25 Control Transfer in GOSUB versus GOTO Statements

pose you are doing a report on groups of people and would like to get some simple statistical information about their age, income, and weight. The structure of the program in Figure V–26 delegates each function to a statement block or a subroutine. The GOSUB statement allows you to minimize the repetition of statements, and this further enhances program modularity. The GOSUB statements in Lines 240, 270, and 300 would have to be replaced by the lengthy statements in Lines 400 through 430 if this subroutine capability were not available.

This example also introduces the notion of **functions.** (Here the term is used more precisely than in previous appearances). A function is pre-defined process that is executed when its name—used in much the same way as a variable name—appears in the program. A function always yields, or returns to the program, a single value. The functions used in Figure V–26 are SQR, which computes the square root of the expression in parentheses that follows the SQR (Line 410), and INT, which yields the integer (whole number) portion of the expression in parentheses fol-lowing it (Lines 420 and 430). The INT function is used here for the purpose of restricting the fraction size in the mean and standard devia-tion to one decimal position. Functions will be discussed more thor-oughly in Section VII.

Figure V–27 shows how simple the logic design for this program is. The data is read in and totaled. Then each population variable is as-signed the subroutine variables, and the subroutine is called upon to calculate the standard deviation and the mean. Once all the processing has been done, the results are printed out. Notice how program control is returned to the point of departure after each GOSUB subroutine call. Without the subroutines, you would have to repeat the statistics pro-gram segment or end up with a complex program full of unnecessary GOTO statements. The GOSUB statement is a very useful tool for de-signing structured programs; it also can be used in the form of the ON/ GOSUB statement.

```
10    REM   PROGRAM TO ANALYZE POPULATION
20    REM   DEMOGRAPHICS.
30    REM   VARIABLES - A: AGE
40    REM              I: INCOME
50    REM              W: WEIGHT
60    REM              X: SUM OF DATA
70    REM              X2: SUM OF X-SQUARES
80    LET A1 = 0: LET A2 = 0: LET I1 = 0
90    LET I2 = 0: LET W1 = 0: LET W2 = 0
100   READ N$
110   IF N$ = "999" THEN  GOTO 230
120   READ A,I,W
125   PRINT N$; TAB( 15)A; TAB( 25)I; TAB( 33)W
130   LET A1 = A1 + A:A2 = A2 + A ^ 2
140   LET I1 = I1 + I:I2 = I2 + I ^ 2
150   LET W1 = W1 + W:W2 = W2 + W ^ 2
200   LET N = N + 1
220   GOTO 100
230   LET X = A1: LET X2 = A2
240   GOSUB 400
250   LET AS = SD: LET AM = XM
260   LET X = I1: LET X2 = I2
270   GOSUB 400
280   LET IS = SD: LET IM = XM
290   LET X = W1: LET X2 = W2
300   GOSUB 400
310   LET WM = XM: LET WS = SD
315   PRINT "      **********    **********"
316   PRINT : PRINT
320   PRINT "MEAN VALUE"; TAB( 15)AM; TAB( 25)IM; TAB( 33);WM
330   PRINT
340   PRINT "STAN. DEV."; TAB( 15)AS; TAB( 25)IS; TAB( 33)WS
350   PRINT
360   PRINT "SAMPLE SIZE = ";N
380   GOTO 450
400   LET XM = X / N
410   LET SD =  SQR ((1 / N) * X2 - XM ^ 2)
420   LET SD =  INT (SD * 10 + .5) / 10
430   LET XM =  INT (XM * 10 + .5) / 10
440   RETURN
450   DATA  "J.SMITH",22,14500,145
460   DATA  "J.JOHNSON",34,22500,189
470   DATA  "M.KEENE",19,46700,105
480   DATA  "B.BOONE",32,30000,178
490   DATA  "S.MITCHELL",28,10500,123
500   DATA  "V.JONES",24,44000,111
510   DATA  999,1,1,1
520   END


]RUN
J.SMITH         22          14500   145
J.JOHNSON       34          22500   189
M.KEENE         19          46700   105
B.BOONE         32          30000   178
S.MITCHELL      28          10500   123
V.JONES         24          44000   111
     **********     **********


MEAN VALUE    26.5      28033.3 141.8

STAN. DEV.     5.3      13713.9 32.2

SAMPLE SIZE = 6
```

Figure V–26 Program Illustrating Subroutines

Figure V–27 Structure
Chart

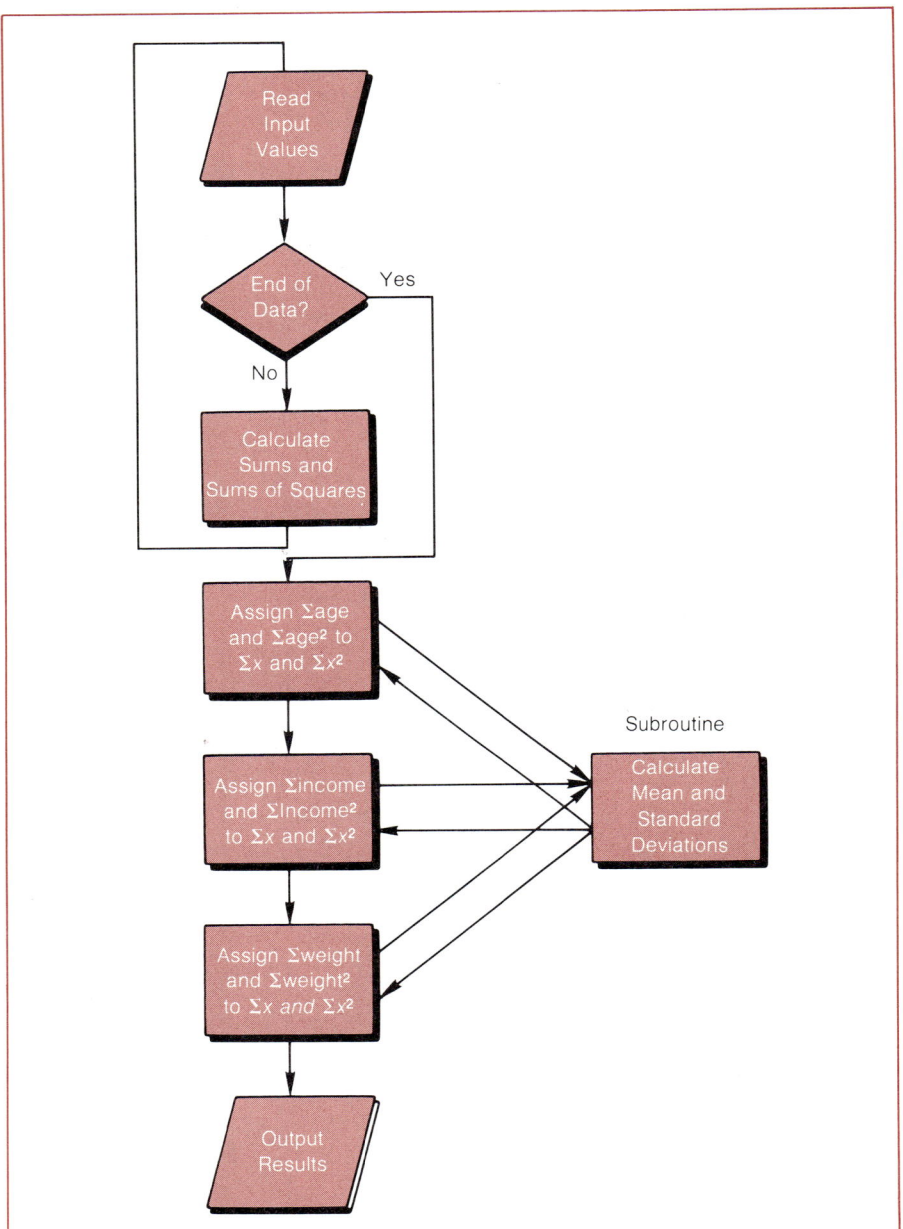

Multiple Alternation

Many structured languages use a CASE statement for multiple branch
statements. The CASE statement allows the programmer to set up multiple subroutines that will be executed if a certain condition is met.
Each case (subroutine) is represented by an order. In BASIC, the ON/

GOSUB statement represents the CASE or multiple alternation statement. The form is

line# ON expression GOSUB line#1,line#2

The ON/GOSUB statement works like an ON/GOTO statement, except the control returns to the line following the ON/GOSUB statement once the subroutine is executed.

In Figure V–28, if X = 1, the subroutine at Line 200 will be executed; if X = 2, the subroutine at Line 250 will be executed; and so on. In all cases, program control will return to the statement after the GOSUB statement.

GOSUB statements are useful if we have a subroutine that needs to be executed at different parts of the program. If we have multiple subroutines that may need to be executed, the ON/GOSUB statement provides us with the power to accomplish this in a neat and structured fashion.

A structure chart for a program using the GOSUB statement is shown in Figure V–29; another using the ON/GOSUB statement is shown in Figure V–30. Notice that the ON/GOSUB statement will allow three different subroutines to be used between each statement block. This increases the functionality of the program without increased complexity or loss of modularity.

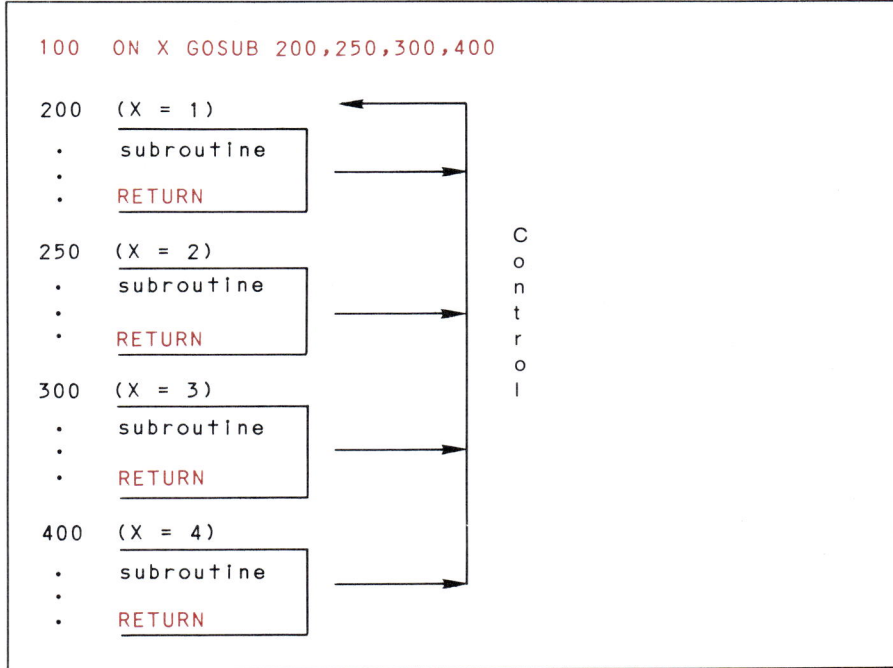

Figure V–28 Control Transfer in an ON/GOSUB Statement

Figure V–29 GOSUB
Structure (Subroutine
Calls)

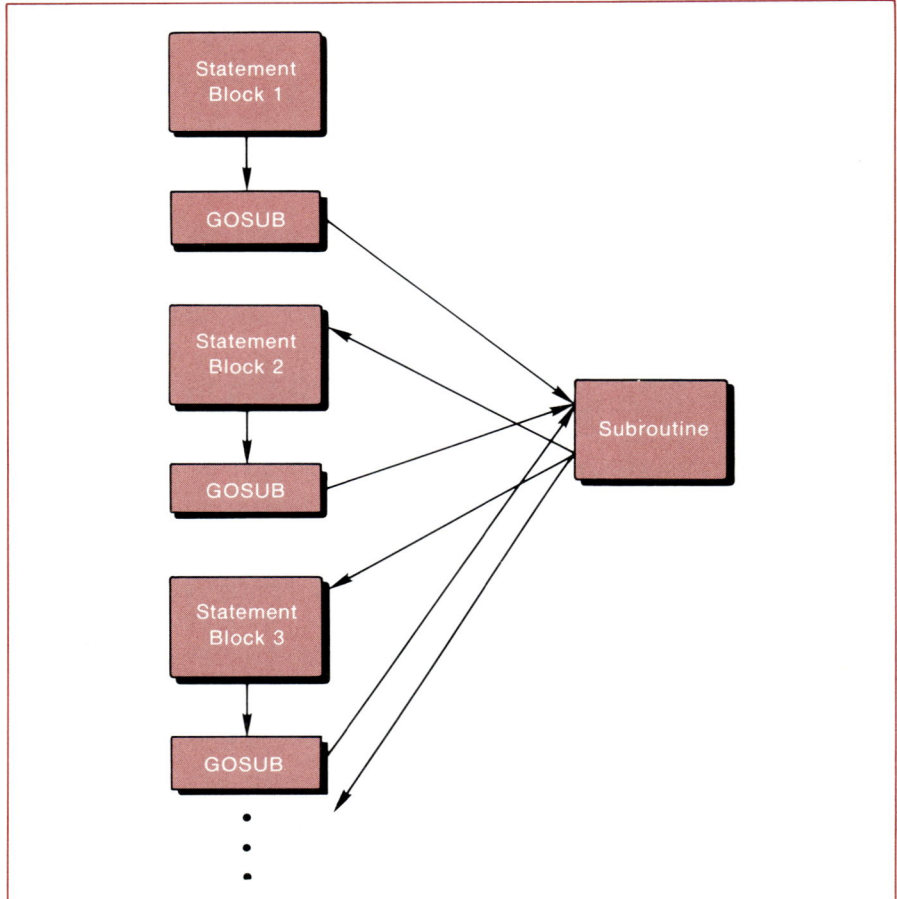

We have used the term **structured programming** in both the title and
the contents of this chapter. Because of certain limitations in BASIC,
we more realistically should use a term like **semistructured** or **partially
structured programming.** Regardless of the terminology used, application of the concepts in this chapter should lead to better, more logical,
and more understandable programs.

REVIEW
QUESTIONS
1. What are statement blocks, and how are they used in structured programming?
2. What is the difference between a conditional and a controlled iteration?
3. What are the advantages of using GOSUB statements and subroutines?

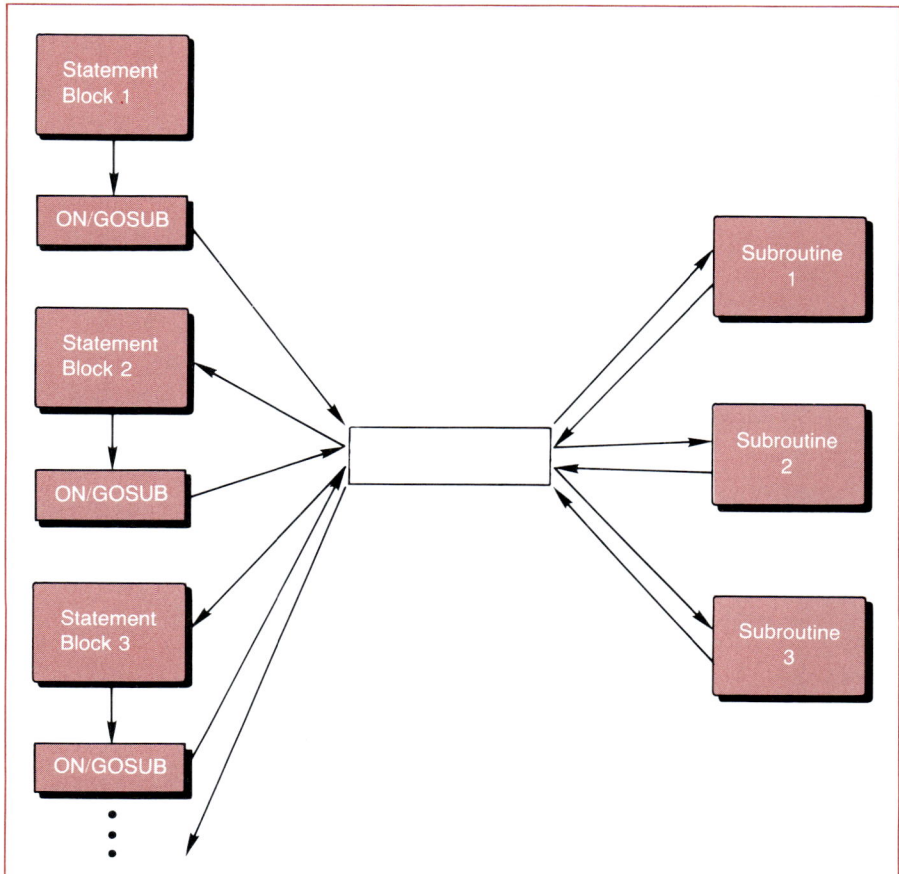

Figure V–30
ON/GOSUB Structure (Multiple Alternate Subroutine Calls)

4. Write a program to read in three numbers and calculate the average. There are ten groups of three numbers.

5. Write the same program as in Question 4, but for any number of input items.

6. Write program routines to calculate the average of three numbers, the sum of three numbers, and the range between the highest and lowest numbers. Input any amount of number groups, and use GOSUB statements to call the routines. Print out the information in a formatted style with headings.

SECTION VI

BASIC DATA STRUCTURES

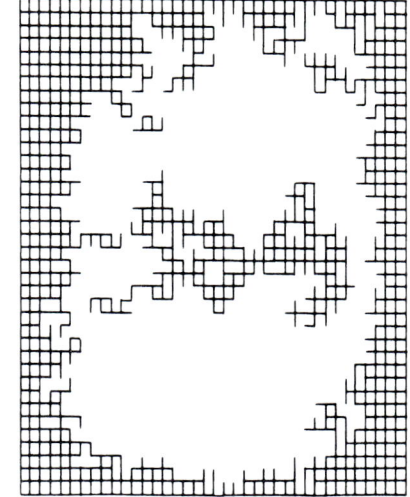

Until now, all the program values have been represented by single variable names. In many cases, pieces of data will be related to each other in one way or another. For example, if a student has five different grades, the grades are related to each other because they were received by one person. If a grocer has two hundred different product names, the products all are related because they are sold at that one store. Most computer problems have to deal with groups of related data rather than nonrelated values. To process these groups, data structures are used. Data structures provide a way to group data together and access it using a common variable name. BASIC and most programming languages do this with **arrays.** The following program problem illustrates the use of arrays in BASIC.

Program Problem

Imagine you are a Little League manager and would like to post weekly batting averages for your nine starters. You can use arrays to store the groups of data. There will be nine names, nine at-bat totals, and nine hit totals. These values can be grouped together for processing by using arrays.

The program in Figure VI–1 uses four arrays. FOR/NEXT loops are used to read in the data, process it, and print it out. The following section will examine how to use arrays to create better programs.

ARRAYS

An array is an order or arrangement of items. In computers, an array is an arrangement of values. We know that an individual value is given a variable name that represents a memory location. An array of values is given a variable name that represents several consecutive memory locations. Each memory location in an array is indexed using a subscript. Array variables take the following format:

    variable name(subscript)

The variable can either be a string or numeric variable. The programmer also can declare the number of elements in an array using the DIM statement, which assigns a size (dimension) to the array. The format is

    line# DIM variable(number of elements)

Examples of DIM statements are shown here:

    100 DIM A(10) (Will allocate ten memory locations to A.)
    100 DIM N$(5) (Will allocate five memory locations to N$).
    100 DIM C1(25) (Will allocate twenty-five memory locations to C1.)

Figure VI–2 illustrates an array with ten elements. The ten slots represent ten memory locations that can hold values. At any one time we can store ten different numeric values in Array A.

We can assign values to array variables with the help of array subscripts (Figure VI–3). The subscript attached to the array name indicates which element we are using. The subscript can be a constant or any other BASIC expression. For example,

    A(B + 2)
    A(M * N)
    A(L)

are all legal array subscripts. For values $I = 5$ and $J = 2$, the assignments shown in Figure VI–4 will be made.

The BASIC interpreter first evaluates the array subscript and rounds it to an integer value. It then assigns the value to the array element indicated by that subscript value. If the subscript is 1, the array element 1 is used; if the subscript is 2, the array element 2 is used; and so on. Figure VI–5 demonstrates the elements of the following string array N1$ being assigned values:

    10 DIM N1$(5)

```
10 REM ** PROGRAM TO CALCULATE BATTING AVG
20 REM ** USING ARRAYS
30 DIM N$(9)
40 DIM AB(9)
50 DIM H(9)
60 DIM BA(9)
70 FOR I = 1 TO 9
75    PRINT "ENTER NAME,AB,HITS"
80    INPUT N$(I),AB(I),H(I)
90 NEXT I
110 FOR I = 1 TO 9
120    BA(I) = H(I) / AB(I)
130 NEXT I
140 PRINT "NAME"; TAB( 10)"AB"; TAB( 15)"HITS"; TAB( 20)"BATTING AVERAGE"
145 PRINT
150 FOR I = 1 TO 9
155    BA(I) = INT (BA(I) * 1000 + 0.5) / 1000
160    PRINT N$(I); TAB( 10)AB(I); TAB( 15)H(I); TAB( 20)BA(I)
170    S1 = S1 + AB(I):S2 = S2 + H(I)
180 NEXT I
190 S3 = S2 / S1
195 S3 = INT (S3 * 1000 + 0.5) / 1000
200 PRINT : PRINT
210 PRINT "TEAM BATTING AVERAGE = ";S3
220 END


]RUN
ENTER NAME,AB,HITS
?SMITH
??22
??5
ENTER NAME,AB,HITS
?JONES
??32
??9
ENTER NAME,AB,HITS
?JOHNSON
??22
??7
ENTER NAME,AB,HITS
?RUTH
??27
??11
ENTER NAME,AB,HITS
?FELLER
??26
??4
ENTER NAME,AB,HITS
?LANE
??34
??12
ENTER NAME,AB,HITS
?GORMAN
??21
??5
ENTER NAME,AB,HITS
?NIMS
??18
??4
```

continued

```
ENTER NAME,AB,HITS
?KING
??25
??14
NAME      AB    HITS BATTING AVERAGE

SMITH     22    5     .227
JONES     32    9     .281
JOHNSON   22    7     .318
RUTH      27    11    .407
FELLER    26    4     .154
LANE      34    12    .353
GORMAN    21    5     .238
NIMS      18    4     .222
KING      25    14    .56

TEAM BATTING AVERAGE = .313
```

Figure VI–1 Program Using Arrays

Subscripts index string arrays just like numeric arrays. Only the values are different.

Input/Output and Arrays

To use arrays, we must assign data to the various array elements. Iterative loops work very well with arrays. Using a FOR/NEXT loop is an effective way of repetitively reading data into or printing it out of an array. Figure VI–6 shows a program segment that will assign values to an array with five elements. The FOR/NEXT loop will increment I

Figure VI–2 Physical Representation of an Array

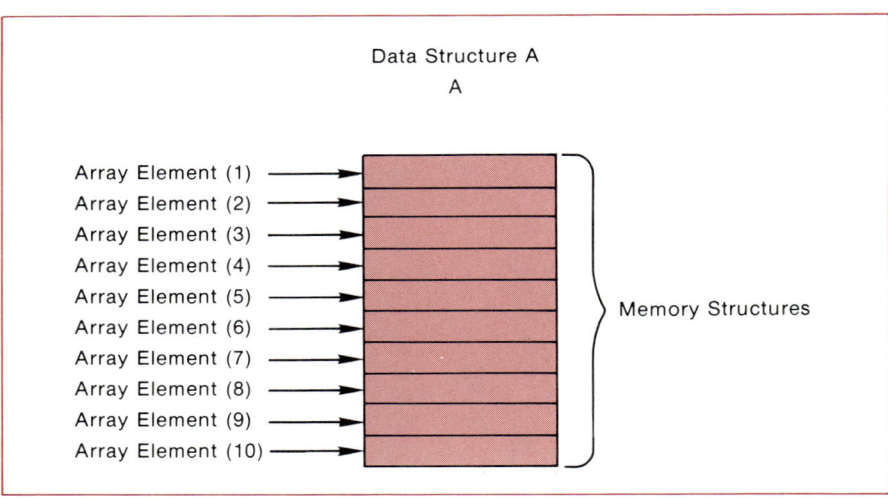

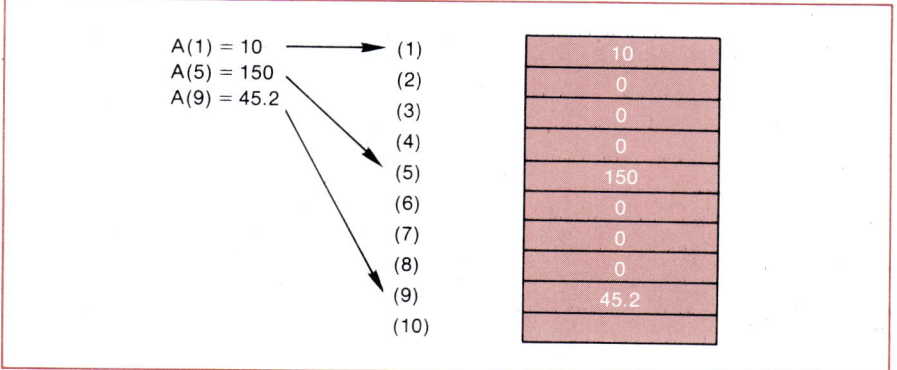

Figure VI–3
Assignment of Values to an Array (Constants as Subscripts)

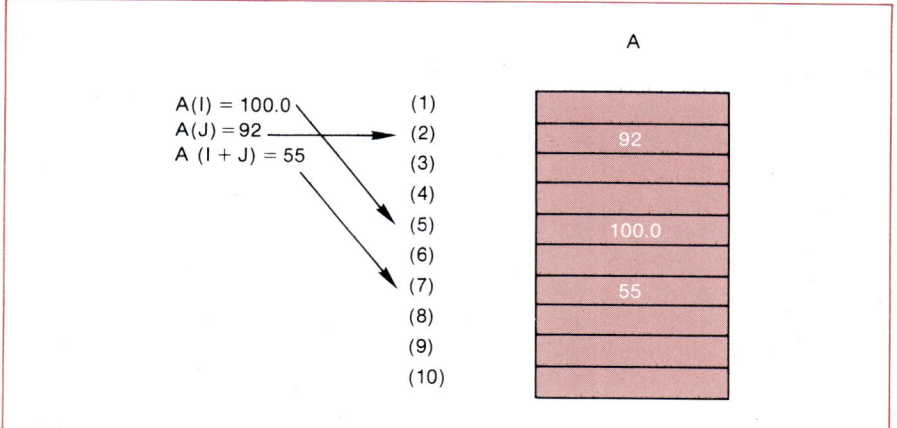

Figure VI–4
Assignment of Values to an Array (Variables as Subscripts)

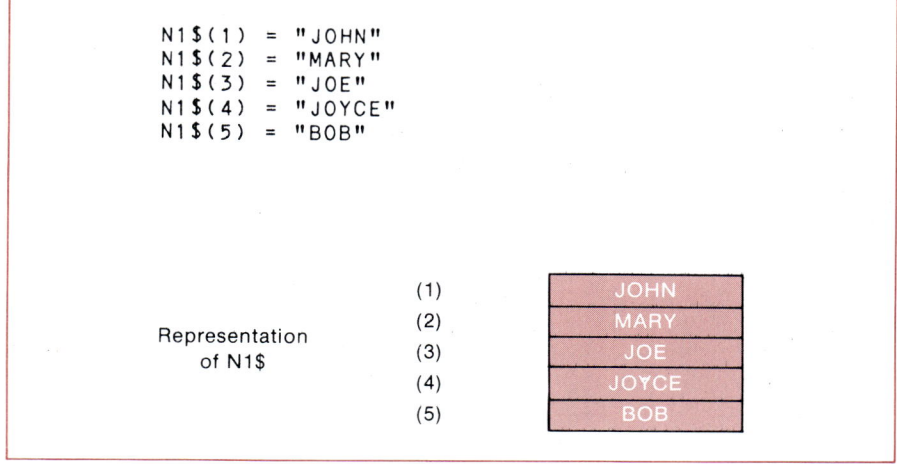

Figure VI–5
Assignment of Character Values to a Sting Array

Figure VI–6 Array
Input Segment

```
10 DIM A(5)
20 FOR I = 1 TO 5
30    INPUT A(I)
40 NEXT I
```

through each subscript of the array. This will assign values to each successive array element.

If we wish to print out all the array elements, the same technique can be applied (see Figure VI–7). When printing out array values, the FOR/NEXT loop increments the array subscript each consecutive time. Figure VI–7 shows that each time the index changes, another value is printed out.

Processing with Arrays

Arrays can be used for calculation and data manipulation in the same way variables can. Any arithmetic expression can be used with array variables. Because arrays contain many values, some kind of loop must be used to do repetitive processing.

The program in Figure VI–8 demonstrates the use of arrays. In this program there are three arrays. Arrays A and B are used to store the data that will be processed. This is accomplished with the first FOR/NEXT loop. The second FOR/NEXT loop does the arithmetic processing. Array C is used to store the new values and keep running totals.

Array elements can be processed just like regular variables. The advantage is that the values will remain in the arrays and can be used over and over. In a large program this is very advantageous, because access to data may be required in different places for different reasons. When data has been placed in an array by means of assignment, READ, or INPUT statements, subsequent references to the array can be made without repeating such commands (unless the values are destroyed by program statements).

TWO-DIMENSIONAL ARRAYS

Many times in programming, a simple array will not suffice to represent the information that is present. In that case, a more complex structure may be required. In BASIC, two-dimensional arrays are used to represent more complex groupings of data. Figure VI–9 shows the difference between a one-dimensional array and a two-dimensional array.

Figure VI–7 Array
Output Segment

```
10 DIM A(5)
20 FOR I = 1 TO 5
30    PRINT A(I)
40 NEXT I
```

```
10  DIM A(10),B(10),C(10)
20  REM PROGRAM TO ILLUSTRATE USE
25  REM OF ARRAYS
27  T1 = 0
30  FOR I = 1 TO 10
35    READ A(I),B(I)
40  NEXT I
50  FOR I = 1 TO 10
60    C(I) = 2 * A(I) + B(I)
70    T1 = T1 + C(I)
80  NEXT I
90  FOR I = 1 TO 10
100   PRINT "ARRAY C-INDEX-";I;" = ";C(I)
110 NEXT I
120 PRINT "TOTAL = ";T1
130 DATA 150,140,10,60,40,36,88,3,15,10
140 DATA 2,55,4,77,46,13,15,19,22,49
150 END

]RUN
ARRAY C-INDEX-1  = 440
ARRAY C-INDEX-2  = 80
ARRAY C-INDEX-3  = 116
ARRAY C-INDEX-4  = 179
ARRAY C-INDEX-5  = 40
ARRAY C-INDEX-6  = 59
ARRAY C-INDEX-7  = 85
ARRAY C-INDEX-8  = 105
ARRAY C-INDEX-9  = 49
ARRAY C-INDEX-10 = 93
TOTAL = 1246
```

Figure VI–8 Program Illustrating Multiple Array Manipulation

The format for declaring a two-dimensional array is

line# DIM (number of rows, number of columns)

In our example, the array A(3) has only one column, and it has three rows. This array could be declared A(3,1), but the 1 is not necessary. The second array, A(3,2), declares three rows also, but it has two columns. This creates a 3×2 table or matrix. Figure VI–10 shows which element will be accessed by which subscripts. Rows are referenced by the first subscript, and columns are referenced by the second subscript.

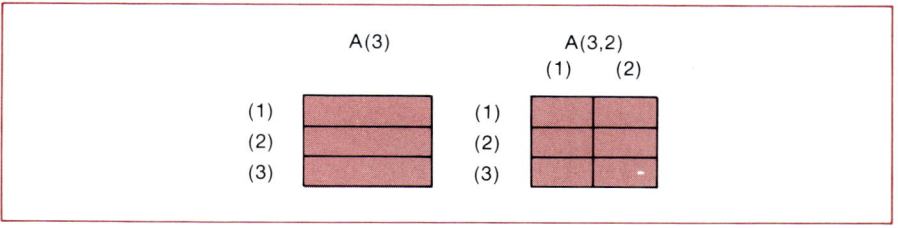

Figure VI–9 One-Dimensional Versus Two-Dimensional Array

Figure VI–10
Representation of Two-Dimensional Array Subscripts

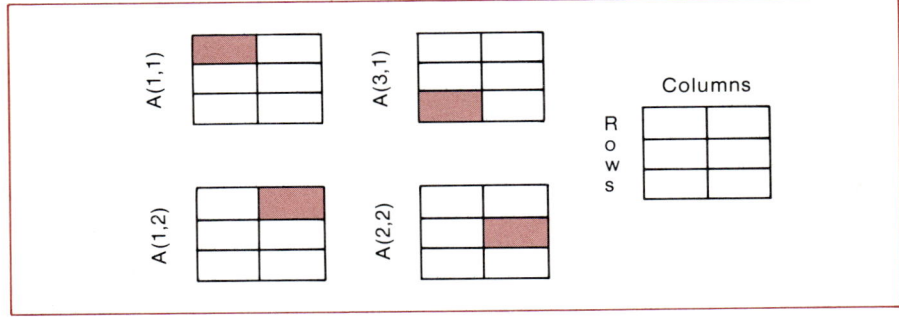

Two-dimensional arrays are used to group arrays of relevant data together. For instance, if we wanted a data structure to store the height, weight, and age of a group of twenty people, it would be simple (see Figure VI–11). The 20 × 3 array in Figure VI–11 contains sixty elements. There are twenty rows and three columns. If we used Column 1 for height, column 2 for weight, and Column 3 for age, the table might look like Figure VI–12.

Figure VI–11 Two-Dimensional Array

DIM (20,3)

	Column	1	2	3
Row 1				
2				
3				
.				
.				
.				
20				

Figure VI–12 Two-Dimensional Array

A(20,3)

Column 1 Height	Column 2 Weight	Column 3 Age
70	150	22
59	105	15
65	130	31
.	.	.
.	.	.
.	.	.
72	180	19

The separate array N$ in Figure VI–13 is needed to hold the names, because string variables and numeric variables cannot be stored in the same array. If we wanted to access Smith's weight, we would use A(2,2). The subscript (2,2) points to the second row and the second column. If we wanted to use Duke's age, we would use A(20,3). This index points to the twentieth row and the third column.

Two-Dimensional Array Input/Output

Recall that FOR/NEXT loops can be nested. To read and print out two-dimensional arrays, we must use two nested FOR/NEXT loops to process the rows and columns. The program in Figure VI–14 will process the age, height, and weight matrix.

The first nested FOR/NEXT loop works in this fashion: The outer loop variable represents the row subscript, and the inner loop variable represents the column subscript. The outer loop starts at I = 1 and then executes the inner FOR/NEXT loop. While the inner loop is executed, I remains at 1, and J (the column subscript) goes from 1 to 3. Figure VI–15 shows the nested FOR/NEXT loops.

Data is read into the array elements (1,1), (1,2), and (1,3). Once J equals 3, the inner loop is completed, and control returns to the outer loop. The outer loop will increment I to 2. The row variable I now is pointing at the second row, and control once again is passed to the inner loop. I remains at 2, and data is read into the array elements (2,1), (2,2), and (2,3). Row 2 is completed, and control once again passes to the outer loop. This process will repeat until all the rows are filled.

To output the information in the array, a FOR/NEXT loop is used to step through the array. For each row element, there are three PRINT array variables—one for each column entry.

Processing Two-Dimensional Arrays

Two-dimensional arrays can be processed just like regular one-column arrays. Totals can be kept for groups of data, or individual elements can be arithmetically manipulated or transferred. The key feature of two-dimensional arrays is that either rows, columns, or both can be added to get sum totals for groups of information.

	N$(10)
Row 1	Jones
2	Smith
3	Andrews
.	.
.	.
.	.
	Duke

Figure VI–13
String Array

Figure VI–14
Program Using Two-
Dimensional Arrays

```
10 DIM A(10,3)
20 FOR I = 1 TO 10
30    FOR J = 1 TO 3
40       READ A(I,J)
50    NEXT J
60 NEXT I
70 PRINT "AGE","HEIGHT","WEIGHT"
73 PRINT : PRINT
75 FOR I = 1 TO 10
80    PRINT A(I,1),A(I,2),A(I,3)
85 NEXT I
90 DATA 22,66,134,25,71,155,33,67,167
100 DATA 15,64,112,21,69,153,41,72,189
110 DATA 19,67,105,20,68,110,31,60,100
120 DATA 21,67,122
130 END

]RUN
AGE                HEIGHT              WEIGHT


22                 66                  134
25                 71                  155
33                 67                  167
15                 64                  112
21                 69                  153
41                 72                  189
19                 67                  105
20                 68                  110
31                 60                  100
21                 67                  122
```

To process either a row or a column, one subscript must be held constant with an outer loop while the other subscript is incremented through the span of the array. To add up a row of data, the program in Figure VI–16 could be used. Assume we have a 10 × 4 array representing ten students and their four grades for the quarter. The short program in Figure VI–16 will add up each row and allow us to arrive at the average grade for each student. To add up all the grades by column, particularly if all grades in each column are for the same course, simply reverse the loops.

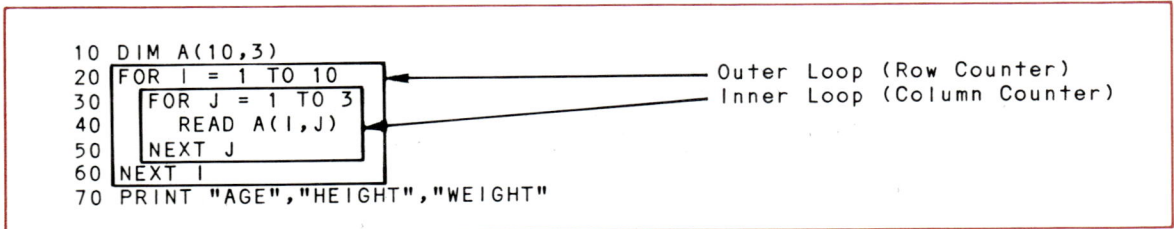

Figure VI–15 Nested FOR/NEXT Loops

```
100 DIM G(10,4)
110 FOR I = 1 TO 10
120    SUM = 0
130    FOR J = 1 TO 4
140       SUM = SUM + G(I,J)
150    NEXT J
160    SUM = SUM / 4
170    PRINT "GRADE AVG = ";SUM
180 NEXT I
```

Figure VI–16
Segment That Processes a Two-Dimensional Grade Array by Student

The segment in Figure VI–17 totals the columns. To process a row or column, design an outer FOR/NEXT loop and an inner loop whose variable matches the subscript of the row or column you wish to total.

To total all the array elements, do not reinitialize the variable that keeps the totals. This will keep a running total. Figure VI–18 shows a program segment that will sum up all the array values. It does not matter which variable is the inner or outer loop counter, because all the array elements must be added, and the order they are accessed is not important. You must make certain, however, that the value of the row subscript (first subscript) does not exceed the row dimension in the DIM statement and that the value of the column subscript (second subscript) does not exceed the column dimension.

```
100 DIM G(10,4)
110 FOR J = 1 TO 4
120    SUM = 0
130    FOR I = 1 TO 10
140       SUM = SUM + G(I,J)
150    NEXT I
160    SUM = SUM / 10
170    PRINT "GRADE AVG = ";SUM
180 NEXT J
```

Figure VI–17
Processing a Two-Dimensional Grade Array by Course

```
100 DIM G(10,4)
110 LET SUM = 0
120 FOR I = 1 TO 4
130    FOR J = 1 TO 10
140       LET SUM = SUM + G(J,I)
150    NEXT J
160 NEXT I
170 PRINT "CLASS AVERAGE = ";SUM / (I * J)
```

Figure VI–18
Processing a Two-Dimensional Grade Array by Class

ARRAY POINTERS

When using a data structure, we must know what array elements are currently being used in our program. In the previous examples we have used a FOR/NEXT loop to sequentially process an array. The FOR/NEXT loop automatically uses an array pointer (counter variable) to keep track of the array element currently being processed. If we have a ten-element array and want to read in ten values, the FOR/NEXT loop is used. For example, after the FOR/NEXT loop in Figure VI–19 has executed six times, I, the loop variable, will equal 7 and point to the next available array space. The FOR/NEXT loop variable actually is behaving as an array pointer that always indicates the position of the slot being accessed.

Pointers are very helpful tools in programs, because data structures can become very large and would be impossible to manage without index aids. If a FOR/NEXT loop is not being used, programmers must construct their own array pointers. Consider the problem of a cafeteria manager who wants to write a program to process the amount and cost of meat purchases for the year. The program would require two data structures for beef and chicken. It also would need array pointers, because the purchases are recorded by date and cannot be read in sequentially with FOR/NEXT loops. Figure VI–20 illustrates a program that processes meat purchases with the use of arrays and pointers. In this program the pointers allow us to process two arrays at random intervals without losing track.

Figure VI–21 shows how data would be stored in the data structures. The pointers J and K indicate the next empty array space. In this way we can add items to the chicken array and not lose our place in the beef array. The pointers are incremented any time an addition is made to an array. Once the information has been read into the arrays, the pointers help in setting up FOR/NEXT loops to print and process the data. The pointer becomes the terminal expression of the FOR/NEXT loop, because it tells us how many array elements are filled and thus how many are to be processed. Since the pointer indicates the next **empty** array element, the FOR/NEXT loop terminal expression should be pointer − 1. This will give us the number of items we wish to print out.

Figure VI–19

Illustration of an Array Pointer

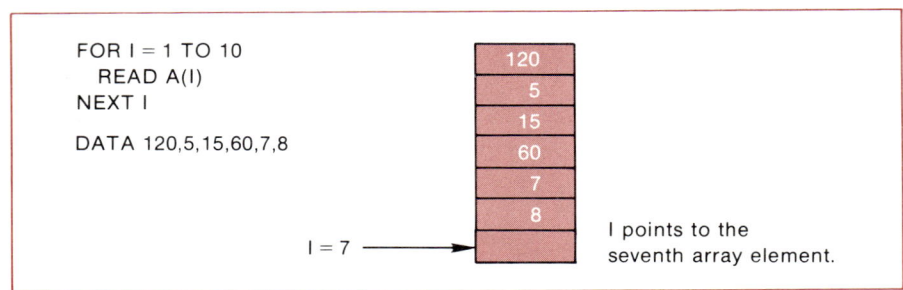

```
FOR I = 1 TO 10
    READ A(I)
NEXT I

DATA 120,5,15,60,7,8
```

I = 7 → I points to the seventh array element.

```
10    REM   ** PROGRAM TO RECORD MEAT PURCHASES
20    REM   ** AND CALCULATE TOTALS.
30    REM
40    REM   USES ARRAY POINTERS
50    REM   J-POINTER INTO BEEF ARRAY
60    REM   K-POINTER INTO CHICKEN ARRAY
70    DIM B(20,2),C(20,2)
100   LET J = 1: LET K = 1
110   INPUT "ENTER B FOR BEEF, C FOR CHICKEN, Q TO QUIT: ";TY$
120   IF TY$ = "Q" THEN   GOTO 300
125   PRINT : PRINT
130   IF TY$ = "B" THEN   GOSUB 200
140   IF TY$ = "C" THEN   GOSUB 250
150   GOTO 110
200   INPUT "ENTER LBS: ";B(J,1)
210   INPUT "ENTER COST: ";B(J,2)
220   LET J = J + 1
230   RETURN
250   INPUT "ENTER LBS: ";C(K,1)
260   INPUT "ENTER COST: ";C(K,2)
270   LET K = K + 1
280   RETURN
300   PRINT : PRINT
310   PRINT "NUMBER","LBS","COST"
320   PRINT
330   FOR I = 1 TO J - 1
340   PRINT I,B(I,1),B(I,2)
350   LET S1 = B(I,1) + S1: LET S2 = S2 + B(I,2)
360   NEXT I
370   PRINT : PRINT "# OF BEEF PURCHASES: ";J - 1
380   PRINT "TOTAL COST: ";S2
390   PRINT "TOTAL LBS: ";S1
400   PRINT "AVG PRICE: "; INT ((S2 / S1) * 100 + .5) / 100
410   PRINT : PRINT
420   PRINT "NUMBER","LBS","COST"
425   PRINT
430   FOR I = 1 TO K - 1
440   PRINT I,C(I,1),C(I,2)
450   LET S3 = S3 + C(I,1): LET S4 = S4 + C(I,2)
460   NEXT I
470   PRINT : PRINT "# OF CHICKEN PURCHASES: ";K - 1
480   PRINT "TOTAL COST: ";S4
490   PRINT "TOTAL LBS: ";S3
500   PRINT "AVG PRICE: "; INT ((S4 / S3) * 100 + 0.5) / 100

]RUN
ENTER B FOR BEEF, C FOR CHICKEN, Q TO QUIT: B


ENTER LBS: 15
ENTER COST: 35.6
ENTER B FOR BEEF, C FOR CHICKEN, Q TO QUIT: C


ENTER LBS: 20
ENTER COST: 13
ENTER B FOR BEEF, C FOR CHICKEN, Q TO QUIT: C
```

continued

```
ENTER LBS: 33
ENTER COST: 59
ENTER B FOR BEEF, C FOR CHICKEN, Q TO QUIT: B


ENTER LBS: 22
ENTER COST: 46
ENTER B FOR BEEF, C FOR CHICKEN, Q TO QUIT: C


ENTER LBS: 21
ENTER COST: 19
ENTER B FOR BEEF, C FOR CHICKEN, Q TO QUIT: Q


NUMBER              LBS                 COST

1                   15                  35.6
2                   22                  46

# OF BEEF PURCHASES: 2
TOTAL COST: 81.6
TOTAL LBS: 37
AVG PRICE: 2.21


NUMBER              LBS                 COST

1                   20                  13
2                   33                  59
3                   21                  19

# OF CHICKEN PURCHASES: 3
TOTAL COST: 91
TOTAL LBS: 74
AVG PRICE: 1.23
```

Figure VI–20 Program Illustrating Array Pointers

SORTING AN ARRAY

Groups of data usually must be ordered in some fashion. The order in which the data is collected may not be the order needed to accomplish some task. Arrays provide useful ways to group data. Once the data has been collected in an array, it is easy to write a program to sort the data in some order.

One example of data that could be sorted is an array of names. The two arrays in Figure VI–22 contain identical values, yet the second array's values are ordered alphabetically. Computers are excellent tools for sorting data, especially when there are hundreds or thousands of items in a list.

There are many ways to sort lists of data, but the easiest (if not the most efficient) way is the bubble sort. If a teacher has fifteen test scores and wishes to sort them so that the highest score comes first and the lowest comes last, the bubble sort program in Figure VI–23 could be

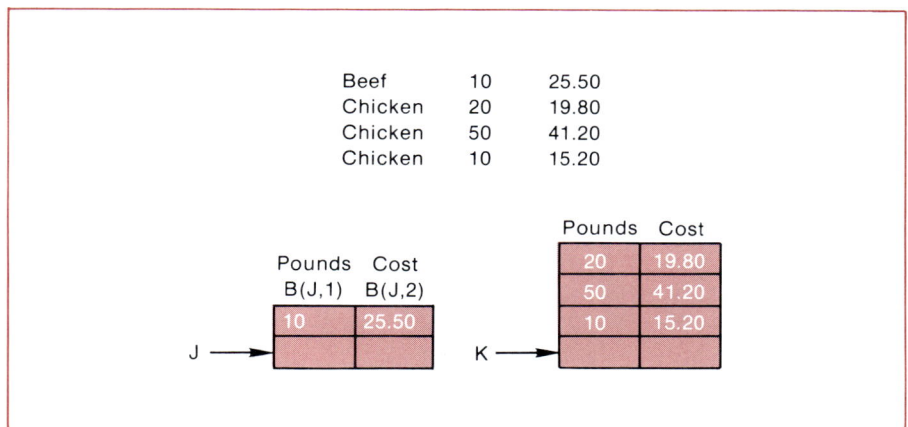

Figure VI–21 Data Structures and Pointers

used. The program reads the data into an array in a random order. Once the data is in the array, the list can be processed using a FOR/NEXT loop. Within the FOR/NEXT loop, two consecutive array values are compared using an IF/THEN statement. If the higher-subscript location contains the higher value, the values are swapped and the loop continues. If the lower-array element has a higher value, we increment I (the loop variable) and continue the loop. This has the effect of bubbling any high values to the top of the array. The variable FL is a flag that is set to 1 when any two values are swapped. When FL remains at 0, we know that no swaps have occurred during our last scan of the data, and the grades are sorted in the order that we desire. The FL variable will cause the FOR/NEXT loop to continue execution until the sorting is completed. It would be easy to sort the grades in the other direction by reversing the > = comparison at Line 200 to < =. This would bring the low values to the top of the array. If the process appears complex to you, step through the program with only five data values.

MATRIX COMMANDS

A previous section discussed two-dimensional arrays. These arrays are in fact matrices, and there are special BASIC commands to manipulate matrices. Matrix mathematics and I/O can be performed with the matrix commands.

Figure VI–22

Array N$	Array S$
Jones	Abbott
Smith	Dolin
Abbott	Enderle
Martin	Jones
Dolin	Martin
Enderle	Smith

Figure VI–23 Sort
Program

```
100 REM PROGRAM TO SORT CLASS
105 REM GRADES USING ARRAYS
110 DIM G(20)
120 PRINT "***UNSORTED GRADES***"
130 FOR I = 1 TO 15
140    READ G(I)
150    PRINT G(I)
160 NEXT I
170 PRINT : PRINT
180 FL = 0
190 FOR I = 1 TO 14
200    IF G(I) >= G(I + 1) THEN GOTO 250
210    TEMP = G(I + 1)
220    G(I + 1) = G(I)
230    G(I) = TEMP
240    FL = 1
250 NEXT I
260 IF FL = 1 THEN GOTO 180
270 PRINT : PRINT
280 PRINT "***SORTED GRADES***"
290 PRINT
300 FOR I = 1 TO 15
310 PRINT G(I)
320 NEXT I

]RUN
***UNSORTED GRADES***
87
99
67
78
77
80
91
70
65
94
81
80
85
90
74


***SORTED GRADES***

99
94
91
90
87
85
81
80
80
78
77
74
70
67
65
```

Matrix/Input/Output

The MAT keyword is used to read in or print out matrix data. The format follows:

INPUT

```
line# MAT READ matrix name
line# MAT INPUT matrix name
line# MAT PRINT matrix name
```

The MAT statement is equivalent to the nested FOR/NEST loop we used to insert or print data from two-dimensional arrays. The following statements perform input for a 3×3 array:

```
DIM A(3,3)
MAT INPUT A
```

These two lines correspond to the following program segment:

```
05 DIM A(3,3)
10 FOR I = 1 TO 3
20    FOR J = 1 TO 3
30       INPUT A(I,J)
40    NEXT J
50 NEXT I
```

A READ can replace the INPUT keyword to accomplish an input task. To print out information, we can use

```
MAT PRINT A
```

which is equivalent to

```
10 FOR I = 1 TO 3
20    FOR J = 1 TO 3
30       PRINT A(I,J)
40    NEXT J
50 NEXT I
```

The MAT PRINT statement is similar to a PRINT statement in that if the statement ends in a comma, the data will be printed on the same line.

Matrix Math

Multidimensional arrays or matrices are useful for storing large amounts of data. Matrices also can be treated as separate entities, and mathematical functions can be performed with them. BASIC allows the

Figure VI–24
Matrix Addition

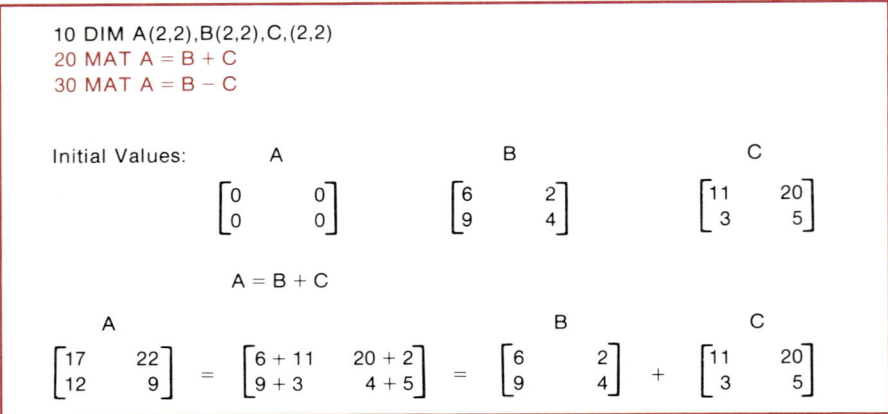

```
10 DIM A(2,2),B(2,2),C,(2,2)
20 MAT A = B + C
30 MAT A = B − C
```

Initial Values:

$$A = \begin{bmatrix} 0 & 0 \\ 0 & 0 \end{bmatrix} \quad B = \begin{bmatrix} 6 & 2 \\ 9 & 4 \end{bmatrix} \quad C = \begin{bmatrix} 11 & 20 \\ 3 & 5 \end{bmatrix}$$

$A = B + C$

$$A = \begin{bmatrix} 17 & 22 \\ 12 & 9 \end{bmatrix} = \begin{bmatrix} 6 + 11 & 20 + 2 \\ 9 + 3 & 4 + 5 \end{bmatrix} = \begin{bmatrix} 6 & 2 \\ 9 & 4 \end{bmatrix} B + \begin{bmatrix} 11 & 20 \\ 3 & 5 \end{bmatrix} C$$

user to add, subtract, and multiply matrices. BASIC also enables the user to assign one matrix value to another, initialize a matrix, create an identity matrix, transpose a matrix, or take the inverse of a matrix.

Matrix Addition and Subtraction To add or subtract matrices, the number of dimensions of the two must be equal. For example, Arrays A(3,4) and B(3,4) can be added, but Arrays A(3,2) and B(3,1) cannot. The statements needed to add and subtract arrays are shown in Figures VI–24 and VI–25. Figure VI–25 uses the same initial values and program segment as Figure VI–24.

Matrix Multiplication Multiplication is a more complex operation. The number of columns of the first matrix must equal the number of rows of the second. The dimensions of the product matrix will equal the number of rows in Matrix 1 and the number of columns in Matrix 2. An example can be seen in Table VI–1

To actually multiply two matrices, use the statements in Figure VI–27. The result is derived by multiplying Row A of Matrix 1 times Columns C and D of Matrix 2, then multiplying Row B of Matrix 1 by Columns C and D of Matrix 2. Each element is multiplied and then added together to get one element of the product matrix.

To multiply an entire matrix by a constant (scalar multiplication), use the statement in Figure VI–27. Each element is multiplied by the value in parentheses.

Figure VI–25
Matrix Subtraction

$A = B − C$

$$A = \begin{bmatrix} -5 & -18 \\ 6 & -1 \end{bmatrix} = \begin{bmatrix} 6 - 11 & 2 - 20 \\ 9 - 3 & 4 - 5 \end{bmatrix} = \begin{bmatrix} 6 & 2 \\ 9 & 4 \end{bmatrix} B - \begin{bmatrix} 11 & 20 \\ 3 & 5 \end{bmatrix} C$$

Table VI–1 MATRIX MULTIPLICATION (DIMENSIONS)

Matrix 1		Matrix 2		Product Matrix
(2 × 3)	*	(3 × 2)	=	(2 × 2)
(1 × 5)	*	(5 × 3)	=	(1 × 3)

Assignment of Matrix Value Matrices can be initialized to 0, 1, or the identity form, or they can be assigned the value of another matrix. Consider the matrix DIM A(3,3). Initialize it to 0 as follows:

```
MAT A = ZER
```

$$\begin{bmatrix} 0 & 0 & 0 \\ 0 & 0 & 0 \\ 0 & 0 & 0 \end{bmatrix}$$

Initialize the matrix to 1 as follows:

```
MAT A = CON
```

$$\begin{bmatrix} 1 & 1 & 1 \\ 1 & 1 & 1 \\ 1 & 1 & 1 \end{bmatrix}$$

N **Matrix 1 (L)** **Matrix 2 (M)**

$$\begin{bmatrix} X & X \\ X & X \end{bmatrix} = \begin{matrix} A \\ B \end{matrix}\begin{bmatrix} 2 & 5 & 4 \\ 3 & 1 & 2 \end{bmatrix} \times \overset{\begin{matrix} \mathbf{C} & \mathbf{D} \end{matrix}}{\begin{bmatrix} 1 & 2 \\ 4 & 1 \\ 2 & 3 \end{bmatrix}}$$

$$\begin{bmatrix} (2 \times 1) + (5 \times 4) + (4 \times 2) & (2 \times 2) + (5 \times 1) + (4 \times 3) \\ (3 \times 1) + (1 \times 4) + (2 \times 2) & (3 \times 2) + (1 \times 1) + (2 \times 3) \end{bmatrix} = \begin{matrix} A * C & A * D \\ B * C & B * D \end{matrix}$$

Figure VI–26 Matrix Multiplication (Elements)

MAT C = (2) * A

$$C = 2 \times \begin{bmatrix} 2 & 5 & 4 \\ 3 & 1 & 2 \end{bmatrix}$$

$$C = \begin{bmatrix} 4 & 10 & 8 \\ 6 & 2 & 4 \end{bmatrix}$$

Figure VI–27 Scalar Multiplication

Create an identity matrix as follows:

$$\text{MAT A = IDN} \qquad \begin{bmatrix} 1 & 0 & 0 \\ 0 & 1 & 0 \\ 0 & 0 & 1 \end{bmatrix}$$

Assign another matrix value to A as follows:

$$\text{MAT A = B} \qquad \overset{\textbf{A}}{\begin{bmatrix} 4 & 5 & 2 \\ 3 & 1 & 0 \\ 1 & 1 & 2 \end{bmatrix}} = \overset{\textbf{B}}{\begin{bmatrix} 4 & 5 & 2 \\ 3 & 1 & 0 \\ 1 & 1 & 2 \end{bmatrix}}$$

B must be of the same dimension as A.

Matrix Transposition and Inversion   The transposition of a matrix is the same matrix with its rows and columns switched. For example, a 2×4 matrix becomes a 4×2 matrix. If we have a 2×3 matrix, C is

$$\begin{bmatrix} 5 & 9 & 10 \\ 3 & 40 & 1 \end{bmatrix}$$

and we use the following transpose command:

    10 MAT C = TRN(D)

the resulting 3×2 matrix, D, would be

$$\begin{bmatrix} 5 & 3 \\ 9 & 40 \\ 10 & 1 \end{bmatrix}$$

The dimensions of C and D must be inverted.
   The inverse of a matrix is the matrix that will produce the identity when multiplied with the original matrix:

   A × Inverse A = Identity matrix.

To get the inverse of A, use the following statement:

    10 MAT B = INV(A)

$$\begin{bmatrix} -2 & 1 \\ 1.5 & -.5 \end{bmatrix} = \begin{bmatrix} 1 & 2 \\ 3 & 4 \end{bmatrix}$$

The inverse matrix is very useful for solving systems of linear equations and other mathematical applications.

1. Suppose you have an array with ten elements. Write a program to input ten values into that array and then print them out.

2. a. Write a similar program that will input and output a 10 × 3 data structure. Use nested FOR/NEXT loops.

   b. Perform the same I/O function using matrix commands.

3. Write a program to sort the following list of ten names alphabetically. (**Hint:** Use character string functions to compare the name values.)

Jones
Abbott
Barnes
Ewing
Drexler
Simpson
Allen
Mullah
Dawkins
Borden

SECTION VII

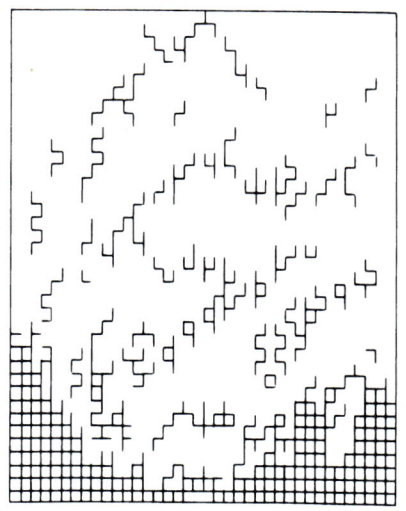

BASIC FUNCTIONS AND FILE PROCESSING

Functions are programming statements that perform certain tasks for the user. These tasks can be either mathematical or useful in manipulating character strings. Many functions predefined by BASIC are called **library functions.** BASIC also offers programmers the ability to define their own functions. This section will examine both these functions and the use of files in BASIC programs.

Mathematical Functions

Eleven mathematical functions are found in most BASIC libraries. Table VII–1 lists them. The format for a function is

    function name(argument)

Whenever the function is to be used, the programmer writes the name of the function followed by the argument (variable or expression) upon which he or she wishes the operation to be performed. The function will return a value that can be used just like any variable or constant value.

Trigonometric Functions

In trigonometry there are many functions useful in mathematical applications. Sine (SIN), cosine (COS), tangent (TAN), and arc tangent (ATN)

Table VII–1 LIBRARY FUNCTIONS

Function	Purpose
SIN(X)	Trigonometric sine function; X in radians
COS(X)	Trigonometric cosine function; X in radians
TAN(X)	Trigonometric tangent function; X in radians
ATN(X)	Trigonometric arc tangent function; X in radians
LOG(X)	Natural logarithm function
EXP(X)	e raised to the X power
SQR(X)	Square root of X
INT(X)	Greatest integer less than or equal to X
SGN(X)	Sign of X
ABS(X)	Absolute value of X
RND(X)	Random number between 0 and 1

are all trigonometric functions that can be used in BASIC. These functions are used to convert the angles (measured in radians) of a triangle into numeric values that are defined by the trigonometric function being used. BASIC converts these values, which are commonly found as fractions, into decimal numbers.

Exponential Function

The exponential functions available in BASIC are LOG(X), EXP(X), and SQR(X). The EXP(X) function calculates the constant e raised to some power of X. The constant e is useful in calculating rates of decay and compound interest. It is used in any situation where the rate of change is related to the present value of the variable.

LOG(X) is the inverse of EXP(X). The natural logarithm of X is the power to which e is raised to produce X. SQR(X) is the square root function. If we want to determine the square root of a number, we use the statement

```
10 Y = SQR(X)
```

The value of Y will be equal to the square root of X.

Other Useful Functions

In computer applications, it may be necessary to use integers (whole numbers) in some situations. The integer (INT) function will return a number in the integer form for any given identifier. For example, INT(5.6) would be equal to 5.

Notice in Figure VII–1 that the INT function does not round off the number to the nearest whole number. The function always rounds the

Figure VII–1
Rounding Function

```
10   LET Y =   INT (5.6)
20   PRINT "Y = ";Y
30   PRINT

]RUN
Y = 5
```

number off to the left (to the lower algebraic whole number). Remember that for negative numbers, the left is the lower numeric value. For example, INT(−2.1) will be equal to −3. The INT function can be used to round numbers to tenths, hundredths, or whatever precision is desired.

If we have a real number, 5.1698, the following statements would return rounded numbers to the variable Y:

Statement	Decimal Precision	Result
Y = INT(X * 10 + .5) / 10	10s place	5.2
Y = INT(X * 100 + .5) / 100	100s place	5.17
Y = INT(X * 1000 + .5) / 1000	1,000s place	5.170 (prints as 5.17)

Notice that the factor of 10 that is multiplied by the variable X determines the precision of the rounding. To round to the 10s place, multiply and divide by 10; to round to the 100s place, use 100; and so on. The number of decimal fraction digits will be the number of zeros in the multiplier and divisor.

Two functions that operate on the sign of a number are the sign (SGN) and absolute value (ABS) functions. The SGN function will return a value for 1 for a positive number, 0 for zero, and −1 for a negative number. It is convenient to use the SGN function for checking whether data is positive or negative.

The ABS function returns the absolute value of an argument. The absolute value of a number is the positive value of any real number:

X	ABS(X)
− 10	10
5	5
0	0
− 20.1	20.1

The absolute value is useful to determine the deviation of the value of one number from another number without concern for whether the difference is positive or negative.

The random number generation (RND) function is used to generate random numbers within a certain range. For example, RND(10) will return a number from between 0 and 10 in a randomized order. Random numbers are very useful in computer programs. Many games require random numbers to simulate the rolling of dice or other random events. Other applications can be found in science and mathematics.

USER-DEFINED FUNCTIONS

If you want to use a mathematical function that is not in the BASIC library, you can create your own by using the user-defined (DEF) statement. The format is

line# DEF FN function name(argument) = expression

To name the function, you must use FN followed by any letter. Once a function has been declared, it can be recalled at any time and used just like a library function. In the function in Figure VII–2, the user first defines the function. Once the function has been defined, it can be recalled and used in any manner the programmer wishes, provided it is acceptable in BASIC.

The program in Figure VII–3 utilizes a DEF function, as well as some other BASIC library functions. The user defines a function using the INT function to round off the square roots. This new function and the SQR function are used in a FOR/NEXT loop to calculate all the square roots for numbers from 1 through 25.

STRING FUNCTIONS

All the previous functions dealt with numeric fields and mathematical applications. In BASIC there are string variables as well as numeric ones, and there are string functions to assist in the processing of these variables. With these functions it is possible to compare, change, or concatenate (join) character strings. Table VII–2 lists the various string functions.

Concatenation is possible with the use of the addition symbol. To concatenate two strings, join them with "+"; Figure VII–4 is an example of concatenation.

To determine the length of a string, use the LEN function, as shown in Figure VII–5. LEFT$, RIGHT$, and MID$ functions are used to examine portions of character strings. LEFT$ and RIGHT$ must be listed with the string name and the number of characters you wish to use (see the example in Figure VII–6). LEFT$ will count eight characters from the left of the string and print them. RIGHT$ returns seven characters from the right of the string in this case. The MID$ function uses a parameter that counts off the number of characters from the left. At that

Figure VII–2 User-Defined Function

```
10   DEF   FN A(X) = (X * 0.01) + 1
20   LET Z = 95
30   PRINT   FN A(Z)

]RUN
1.95
```

Figure VII–3
Program Using
Mathematical Functions

```
100 REM PROGRAM TO CALCULATE
110 REM SQUARE ROOTS
120 DEF FN A(X) = INT(X * 100 + 0.05) / 100
125 PRINT "NUMBER","SQUARE ROOT": PRINT
130 FOR I = 1 TO 25
140   S1 = SQR(I)
150   S2 = FN A(S1)
160   PRINT I,S2
170 NEXT I
180 END

]RUN
1               1
2               1.41
3               1.73
4               2
5               2.23
6               2.44
7               2.64
8               2.82
9               3
10              3.16
11              3.31
12              3.46
13              3.6
14              3.74
15              3.87
16              4
17              4.12
18              4.24
19              4.35
20              4.47
21              4.58
22              4.69
23              4.79
24              4.89
25              5
```

point, the rest of the characters will be returned to the function. In Figure VII–7, the MID$ function causes the computer to move a pointer four characters to the right and return the rest of the character string to the PRINT statement.

All characters have ASCII code equivalents. To go from the character representation to the ASCII and back, you can use the ASC and CHR$ functions. ASC returns the numeric value of the first character in the string:

```
20  PRINT  ASC ("DOCTOR")

]RUN
68
```

CHR$ returns the character from the numeric code that is supplied:

Table VII–2 STRING FUNCTIONS

Basic String Function	Operation	Example
string 1$ + string 2$	Concatenates (joins two strings together)	"KUNG" + "FU" is "KUNGFU"
LEN(string)	Finds the length of a string	If H$ is "HELLO HOWARD," then LEN(H$) is 12
LEFT$(string,expression)	Returns the leftmost characters of a string (expression indicates how many)	LEFT$("ABCDE",2) is AB
RIGHT$(string,expression)	Returns the rightmost characters of a string (expression indicates how many)	RIGHT$("ABCDE",2) is DE
MID$(string,expression)	Starting with the character at expression returns the remaining characters.	MID$("ABCDE",3) is CDE
ASC(string)	Returns the ASCII code for the first character in the string	If A$ contains "DOG" then ASCII(A$) is 68
CHR$(expression)	Returns the string representation of the ASCII code of the expression	If CHR$(F$) > "Z" THEN 20
VAL(expression)	Returns the numeric equivalent of the string expression	X = VAL(H$)
STR$(expression)	Converts a number to its string equivalent	STR$(123) is "123"

Figure VII–4 Concatenation

```
10   LET A$ = "MAJOR "
20   LET B$ = "LEAGUE"
30   PRINT A$ + B$

]RUN
MAJOR LEAGUE
```

Figure VII–5 LEN Function

```
10   LET A$ = "COMPUTER SCIENCE"
20   LET B = LEN (A$)
30   PRINT B

]RUN
16
```

Figure VII–6 LEFT$ and RIGHT$ Functions

```
10   LET A$ = "COMPUTER SCIENCE"
20   PRINT  LEFT$ (A$,8)
30   PRINT  RIGHT$ (A$,7)

]RUN
COMPUTER
SCIENCE
```

Figure VII–7 MID$
Function

```
10   LET A$ = "COMPUTER SCIENCE"
20   LET N = 4
30   PRINT  MID$ (A$,N)

]RUN
PUTER SCIENCE
```

```
20   PRINT  CHR$ (68)

]RUN
D
```

Another possible conversion is from a character to a numeric value. The VAL function will convert a string to its numeric value (see Figure VII–8). The VAL function allows us to use a character string as we do a numeric variable. The STR$ function works the other way and converts a numeric value into a character string (see Figure VII–9). The STR$ function allows us to concatenate a real number with a character string.

Program Using String Functions

Suppose you have an organization all of whose members are recorded with the use of character string variables. Each character string includes the individual's last name followed by the date of membership. The program (see Figure VII–10) will find all members who had joined since 1980 and print their names and the date they joined. It also will check for invalid data.

The program reads in the data and then uses the LEN function to check the data for proper format length. Then the RIGHT$ and VAL

Figure VII–8 VAL
Function

```
10   LET A$ = "400"
20   LET X = VAL (A$) / 2
30   PRINT X

]RUN
200
```

Figure VII–9 STR$
Function

```
10   LET X = 150
20   LET Y$ = " DIXIE HIGHWAY"
30   PRINT  STR$ (X) + Y$

]RUN
150 DIXIE HIGHWAY
```

```
100   REM   PROGRAM TO VALIDATE AND
110   REM   PRINT OUT MEMBERSHIP DATA
120   PRINT "NAME","DATE JOINED"
125   PRINT "*****","***********"
126   PRINT
127   LET J = 1
130   READ M$
140   IF M$ = "999" THEN  GOTO 300
150   IF  LEN (M$) <  > 13 THEN I$(J) = M$:J = J + 1: GOTO 130
160   LET M1$ =  RIGHT$ (M$,2)
170   IF  VAL (M1$) < 80 THEN  GOTO 130
180   PRINT  LEFT$ (M$,8), RIGHT$ (M$,5)
190   LET X = X + 1
195   GOTO 130
200   DATA  "SMITH    02/81","JONES    06/80"
210   DATA  "HOUSTON 03/82","GERBER   05/71"
220   DATA  "BORDEN  10/67","DEAN     08/80"
230   DATA  "SOMMER01/65",999
300   PRINT : PRINT "NEW MEMBERSHIP = ";X
310   PRINT : PRINT "INVALID DATA"
320   FOR K = 1 TO J - 1
330   PRINT : PRINT I$(K)
340   NEXT K
350   END

]RUN
NAME               DATE JOINED
*****              ***********

SMITH              02/81
JONES              06/80
HOUSTON            03/82
DEAN               08/80

NEW MEMBERSHIP = 4

INVALID DATA

SOMMER01/65
```

Figure VII—10 Program Illustrating String Functions

functions are used to pick off the date and check for new members. Finally, the LEFT$ and RIGHT$ functions are used to break up the input data and print out the new members. Invalid data also is printed.

FILE PROCESSING

Many computer applications require large amounts of data. Sometimes the data cannot be accommodated by the computer's internal memory. For this reason, outside storage is needed to utilize the hundreds, thousands, or even millions of data entries that may need to be accessed by a particular program. Outside storage can take the shape of a tape or a disk. Microcomputers use cassettes, floppy disks and hard disks. The amount of data or programs that can be stored varies according to the device being used.

When a program accesses outside storage, it must use file processing. **Files** are groups of data records that are usually related. (It is wise to store related data in one file). The individual records that make up a file may be organized sequentially, randomly, or using an index. One particular file organization that is especially popular is a data base structure. A **data base** is a complex system that establishes relationships between data records that cannot be represented by simple filing systems. For our BASIC files, we will think of our data only in terms of a sequential file, that is, a file in which one record follows another in a long list of data items. The computer may access the data in a nonsequential fashion to speed up the I/O process, but our logical view of the data file is a sequential one.

A file is an organization of records, each of which is made up of fields. A telephone directory, as an example, can be considered to be one huge file of people. Each person is represented by a record containing three fields: name, address, and telephone number (see Figure VI–11). A computer disk could easily store the same information. Each record in the file would be a certain length and contain a defined amount of information broken down into fields of various lengths.

File Commands

When we use DATA statements within a program, the information is there and ready to use. When files are used, they must be **opened** by a program command before the data can be used. File commands are similar for most microcomputers. The format used to open a file on the Apple II (Apple files are called TEXT files) is

line# PRINT CHR$(4);"OPEN filename"

Opening a previously undefined file creates a new file. If a file already has been created under that filename, the OPEN command permits ac-

Record	Name	Field Address	Telephone Number
1	REED Edith D 216 Oswald		693-9168
2	Edw 6238 Reo St		865-7881
3	Edw & Phyllis 3726 Lakepointe Dr		693-7132
4	Ernest 6911 Hill AV.		865-3483
5	Floyd S 5437 Morrow Rd		535-3044
	Frank 109 Williamont Rd		476-5261
	Frank C 2613 109th St		726-7195
	Fredk & Sharon 921 Booth Av		729-4863
	G E 27 Ravine Park Village		693-7634

Figure VII–11
Telephone Book as a File

cess to that file. Once a file has been opened, it is possible to insert information into that file. This is done with a WRITE statement, followed by any number of PRINT statements. The formats are

```
line# PRINT CHR$(4);**WRITE filename"
line# PRINT expression
```

The WRITE statement notifies the computer that any PRINT statements that follow contain data that is to be placed in the specified file. To suspend the file input process, you must close the file with the following statement:

```
line# PRINT CHR$(4); "CLOSE filename"
```

After the file has been closed, PRINT statements will write data to your CRT and not to the file.

Figure VII–12
Program Using Files

```
100 REM ** PROGRAM TO ILLUSTRATE FILE
110 REM ** PROCESSING **
120 LET D$ = CHR$(4)
130 PRINT D$;"OPEN ALPHA"
140 PRINT D$;"WRITE ALPHA"
150 PRINT "A","B","C","D"
152 PRINT "E","F","G","H"
154 PRINT "I","J","K","L"
156 PRINT "M","N","O","P"
160 PRINT D$;"CLOSE ALPHA"
170 REM ** DATA IS INSERTED **
180 PRINT D$;"OPEN ALPHA"
190 PRINT D$;"READ ALPHA"
200 FOR I = 1 TO 4
210    INPUT A$(I)
220 NEXT I
230 PRINT D$;"CLOSE ALPHA"
240 REM ** DATA IS READ FROM FILE TO ARRAY **
250 FOR I = 1 TO 4
255    PRINT
260    PRINT A$(I)
270 NEXT I
275 REM ** ARRAY IS PRINTED OUT **
280 END


]RUN

ABCD

EFGH

IJKL

MNOP
```

To get data out of the file, the same sequence is used with a READ statement. First open the file, and then notify the computer that you wish to access information in the file with the following command:

line# PRINT CHR$(4);"READ filename"

Any INPUT statements that follow the READ statements will take data from the file specified and input that data into the designated program variables. To discontinue reading from the file, use the CLOSE file statement.

The program in Figure VII–12 shows how to create a file, insert data into a file, and read from a file. Lines 130 through 160 create and insert information into a file called ALPHA. The PRINT statements write the letters A through P into a file. A TEXT file called ALPHA will appear in your disk catalog. Lines 180 through 230 read the information from file ALPHA into array A$. Finally, lines 250 through 270 print out the array A$.

---

1. Write a program that will round off the following real numbers to two decimal places:

    5.1497
    6.2385
  10.451
  14.1
    2.5698
    8.9783

2. Write a program that will list the natural logarithm of all integers from 1 through 15.
3. Write a program that will create a file and read in the numbers from 1 through 10. Have the program open the file you created and print out the information.

GLOSSARY

abacus One of the earliest known computational devices; uses beads strung on wires to represent values.

access time The time required to retrieve data from memory.

accumulator A programmer-supplied storage location that maintains a running total of values during processing.

accumulator A register that accumulates the results of computations.

acoustic coupler A special cradle that converts bit-generated sounds into wave forms and then transmits the signal through a telephone handset.

action-oriented management report An exception report used to alert management to abnormal situations that require special attention.

activity Refers to the amount of use of the records in a file.

Ada A language used for embedded applications; named after Ada Augusta Byron.

address register A register that holds the address of a data item called for by a program instruction.

Aiken, Howard H. Invented the Mark I, the first large-scale digital computer.

ALGOL One of the first languages to implement features in support of structured techniques; short for ALGOrithmic Language.

algorithm A detailed design to solve a problem in a finite sequence of steps.

Amdahl, Gene Chief designer of the IBM 704 and 7030 computers; also designed the IBM System/360 series.

American Standard Code for Information Interchange (ASCII) A seven-bit standardized code used in the transmission and processing of data.

analog computer A computer in which data is represented and interpreted in a continuous wave form which is a symbolic representation of that physical data.

analog transmission The transmission of data in continuous wave form.

analytical engine A general-purpose problem-solving machine developed by Charles Babbage; very similar to the modern computer.

APL Short for A Programming Language; developed by IBM.

application package A software package designed to solve particular programming problems.

applications programmer A person who writes programs that tell the computer how to process data to solve specific problems; also one who tests, debugs, documents, and implements programs.

applications program A computer program written to solve a specific problem or accomplish a specific task.

arithmetic and logic unit (ALU) the section of the CPU that performs arithmetic computations and logical operations.

arithmetic statement A FORTRAN statement used to direct the computer in solving computations.

arrays Tables of related values.

artificial intelligence A field of inquiry, developing techniques whereby computers can be used to solve problems that appear to require imagination, intuition, or intelligence.

assembler A language translator for assembly language; a program.

assembly language Machine-oriented language using mnemonics; one step removed from machine language.

591

asynchronous transmission The process whereby characters are sent at any time convenient to the transmitting or receiving device; also referred to as start-stop transmission.

Atanasoff, John Invented the first electronic digital computer.

Atanasoff-Berry Computer The first electronic digital computer, invented by John Atanasoff and his assistant, Clifford Berry.

attributes The values of the fields or data elements relating to an entity.

audio output A type of computer output where the computer "speaks" using a voice synthesized from electronic signals.

auxiliary storage See Secondary storage.

Babbage, Charles (1791–1871) Proposed the idea for and partially built a machine that could compute the various properties of numbers, accurate to twenty digits.

back-end processor A small CPU linked between the large CPU and a data base stored on DASDs which accesses specified items in the data base and updates them as required.

background partitions The storage area where the low priority programs are placed for execution during multiprogramming.

background programs Those programs submitted in batch mode for multiprogramming; only executed when there are no foreground programs requiring execution.

Backus Normal Form A formal notation for describing the structure of a programming language.

Backus, John Leader of a team of engineers that developed FORTRAN.

bandwidth See Grade.

bar code A set of vertical bars of different widths representing a set of numbers; used in source data automation.

bar-code reader A hand-held wand reader or fixed scanning device used to read barcodes.

BASIC Beginner's All-purpose Symbolic Instruction Code; a programming language commonly used for interactive problem solving by users who may not be professional programmers.

batch file access All transactions are accumulated for a given period of time and then processed all at once.

batch mode processing The sequential reading of a transaction record and master record to create a new updated magnetic tape.

batch operating system An operating system that allows more than one job to be submitted to the computer at the same time and then processes those jobs one after the other in a continuous stream; also called stacked-job operating system.

batch-oriented programming languages Languages used to solve periodically recurring problems; includes machine-oriented, procedure-oriented, and problem-oriented languages.

baud The unit of measurement for the baudot code; one baud per second is equivalent to one pulse or code element per second.

baud rate The measure of transmission speeds.

baudot A five-bit code with thirty-two possible combinations used to represent numbers and letters for asynchronous transmission.

Berry, Clifford Assisted John Atanasoff in building the Atanasoff-Berry Computer, the first electronic digital computer.

binary coded decimal (BCD) A six-bit code used to represent numbers and letters for asynchronous transmission.

binary digit The smallest unit of information that can be represented by binary notation; represented as either a 0 or a 1. see Bit.

binary notation The use of 0s and 1s to represent the "on" and "off" electrical states which allow the digital computer to store and interpret data.

binary system The base two number system used by computers; the symbols 0 and 1 correspond to the "off" and "on" states of the computer.

biochip A futuristic process of creating organic microchips from protein and manufacturing genetically engineered bacteria.

bit Short for BInary digiT; a single binary digit; represents the smallest unit of data.

bit cell The individual electronic circuits of a semiconductor where data is located.

bit interleaved A type of time division multiplexing; the sampling time per input corresponds to the amount of time used to designate a bit.

blocked records Groups of records joined together in blocks of equal size, with each block separated by an interblock gap (IBG); also called physical records.

B.O.B. (Brains on Board) A robot developed for use in the home.

bootstrapping Also called initial program loading; the process by which the supervisor program is loaded into main memory every time the computer is put into use.

branch A logic pattern by which, depending on the result of a test condition, control can be sent to a different part of the program; this pattern is not in accordance with structured programming concepts.

broad-band channel A communication channel that can transmit data at rates of up to 120,000 bits per second; suitable for applications requiring high-speed transmission of large amounts of data.

broadband coaxial wiring Wire that can carry a host of data, voice and broadcast messages simultaneously and is expected to be the wiring choice in the future.

bubble memory The recently developed memory device that stores data in molecules located on a very thin crystal of semiconductor material; nonvolatile memory.

buffer Memory devices designed to hold electrical signals from the CPU temporarily and transfer them to the output device at the proper speed.

bugs Errors in a program.

built-in functions A built-in program that performs a specific task, simplifying the programming.

Burroughs, William Invented the first commercially successful adding machine; formed the Burroughs Adding Machine Company, a direct ancestor of Burroughs Corporation.

bursting The process of separating pages of output when continuous forms paper is used.

bus An electronic pathway on which data must travel to go from one part of the computer to another.

bus network A network in which each computer plugs into a single cable that runs from work station to work station and must have its own interface.

Byron, Ada (1815–1852) Worked with Charles Babbage on the analytical engine; discovered the concept of the loop. Known as one of the first programmers.

byte The smallest unit on which a computer operates; eight bits.

byte interleaved A type of time division multiplexing; the sampling time per input corresponds to the amount of time used to designate a byte.

cache memory A feature in computers that allows the microprocessor to access more than one instruction from secondary storage and leave the extra data until ready to use.

card reader The machine that transfers information keyed on punched cards to the computer.

cathode-ray tube (CRT) A visual display device that receives electrical impulses and translates them into a picture on a television-like screen.

census machine Invented in 1887 by Herman Hollerith to tabulate census data; used 80-column punched cards with Hollerith code.

central processing unit (CPU) The workhorse of the entire computer system; composed of three sections—the control unit, the arithmetic and logic unit, the primary storage unit.

centralized design An information structure in which a separate data-processing department is utilized to provide data-processing facilities for the organization.

chain printer An impact printer that has the character set engraved in type and assembled in a chain that revolves horizontally past all print positions; prints when a print hammer (one for each column on the paper) presses against an inked ribbon that presses against the characters on the print chain.

chaining The use of a pointer or link to associate the records of a file.

character (byte) A group of related bits representing a letter; usually eight.

character-at-a-time printer An impact printer that prints one character per stroke and completes an entire line before beginning a new line.

chief programmer team A team consisting of a small number of programmers under the supervision of a chief programmer.

chip See Silicon chip.

clustered key-to-disk A system for entering data on magnetic media; consists of several keyboards connected to a minicomputer which edits all data and then writes on a single disk.

clustered key-to-tape Consists of several keyboards connected to a minicomputer which edits all data and then writes on a single tape.

coaxial baseband wiring Cables that can transmit information more quickly and have only one-third the cost of twisted pair cables.

COBOL COmmon Business Oriented Language; a high-level programming language generally used for accounting and business data processing.

coding Converting the flowchart or pseudocode into lines of step-by-step instructions for the computer.

comment Statement inserted in a program as documentation notes; comments are non-executable and are also referred to as Remarks.

communication channel The physical link or medium that is used to carry data from one location to another.

comparison A statement that allows two items to be compared to determine whether one item is less than, greater than, or equal to another.

compiler A high-level language translator; a program.

computation Statements that specify computational instructions for the performance of arithmetic operations.

computer network The linking together of CPUs and terminals via a communicating system; allows users at different locations to share files, devices, and programs.

computer operator The individual who works most directly with the computer setting up equipment and monitoring the operation of the computer.

computer output microfim (COM) Miniature photographic images of output. Computer output is placed on magnetic tape which serves as the intput to a microfilm processor.

computer-aided design (CAD) A process by which engineers or technicians input requirements for a product design and receive a computer-generated picture of the product.

computer-aided manufacturing (CAM) A process by which computerized tasks manufacture a finished product.

computer-assisted diagnosis Using a computer as a diagnostic tool to save doctors time and assist in a speedy, accurate diagnosis.

computer-assisted instruction (CAI) Using a computer as an instructor to a student; the computer provides direct interaction with the student.

concentrator A device that systematically allocates time to different terminals for data transmission over one communication line.

concurrency Two or more users attempt to access and modify the same data at the same time.

concurrently Over the same period of time; in multiprogramming, processing of operations rotates between different programs, giving the illusion of simultaneous processing.

contention A process used in a multidrop configuration where each terminal monitors the communication line and sends its message when the line is free.

continuous forms A type of self-feeding paper that is easily separated by perforations between forms; the most common type of computer output paper in use today.

control programs Routines that oversee system operations and perform such tasks as I/O scheduling; handling interrupts, and communicating with the computer operator or programmers.

control statement A FORTRAN statement used to determine the sequence of operations.

control unit The section of the CPU that coordinates and controls all activities of the computer system.

conversational See Interactive

conversion The process of replacing the old system with the new system.

core dump Shows the contents of the memory location; aids the programmer in debugging.

crash conversion A high risk method of implementation in which the old system is immediately discontinued and replaced by the new system.

Cray, Seymour Developed large, very fast scientific computers such as the Cray-1 supercomputer, the Cray X-MP and the Cray-2.

cylinder The corresponding tracks on each surface of a disk pack.

daisy wheel printer An impact printer that uses one round disk with characters located near the ends of petal-like projections; the disk rotates until the proper

character is in position to be struck by a hammer, causing the character to be printed.

data Facts; raw information.

data analysis A principal task of the systems analysis step in which the collected data is analyzed.

data analyst A person who analyzes the relationship of data in the data base.

data base A grouping of data fields structured to fit the information needs of multiple functions of an organization.

data base administrator (DBA) The individual who oversees the operation and use of the company's data base.

data base analyst A person who plans and coordinates data use within the system.

data base management system (DBMS) A set of programs that create a centrally maintained and controlled data base that may be accessed by the different functional areas of an organization.

data communication The electronic transmission of data from one location to another over a communication channel.

data compression The process of removing unused character positions in a variable-length record.

data dictionary Provides information on the definition, structure, and use of each data element an organization uses.

data division The segment of a COBOL program that specifies all the necessary fields, records, and files.

data element A field or unit of data that cannot be further broken down.

data field The components of a logical record representing the unique related groupings of data.

data flow diagram A graphic representation of the logical model of a system.

data gathering A task of the systems analysis step requiring data to be collected from internal and/or external sources.

data structures The relationships between the data elements in a computer file.

data-entry operator A person who transcribes raw data into a form with which the computer can work.

debugging Checking and correcting errors found in a program.

decentralized design A information structure in which the authority and responsibility for computer support are placed in relatively autonomous organizational operation units.

decision logic table A table that identifies the actions to be taken for a given set of circumstances.

decision support system (DSS) A system used to assist managers in decision making for relatively unstructured tasks.

declaration A statement that defines data items used in a program.

decollating The separation of carbon paper from copies in printed computer output.

dedicated line A communication line that is used by only one terminal; it is dedicated to one terminal.

default The capability of a language to select a course of action from alternatives when one has not been specified by the programmer.

definition mode A mode in APL programming language that allows a program to be read into memory and then be executed on command from the programmer.

demand See Interactive.

demand report A report produced upon request and used in strategic decision making to provide responses to unanticipated queries.

demodulation The process of translating analog data into a digital form.

density The number of characters that can be represented in an inch of tape.

desk checking The act of reading each program instruction in the logical sequence specified, and simulating how the computer would respond in order to find errors in a program.

detail diagram A HIPO diagram that shows the greatest detail about a particular function or subfunction.

detailed listings A review of each piece of data entered and processed during a specified period of time.

detailed system design The step of the systems life cycle in which the analyst defines the implementation specifications.

detailed system design report The final phase of the detailed system design step giving management a restatement of the problem, cost/benefit analysis, an explanation of the detailed design, and an implementation schedule.

device The electronic and mechanical components necessary to transmit data between the computer and the storage medium.

diagnostics A descriptive listing of errors generated during compilation.

difference engine A machine designed by Charles Babbage to construct mathematical tables (squares, logarithms, sines, cosines, etc.) and compute the various properties of numbers; lack of technology prevented the building of a working model.

digital computer A computer in which data is represented as discrete "on" and "off" states (binary).

digital transmission The transmission of data in distinct on and off states.

direct-access file organization The data record key provides the only means of accessing data; provides the most efficient means of accessing a particular record.

direct-access storage devices (DASDs) Storage devices that can locate and read any record without having to search the entire disk; see Magnetic disk.

disk drive A device used to read and write data on a floppy disk.

disk storage Storage of data on magnetic disks; allows data to be accessed directly rather than sequentially.

distributed computing The distribution of computers as well as the control and resources required to operate them.

distributed design An information structure that identifies the existence of independent operating units but recognizes the benefits of central coordination and control.

distributed network The distribution of computers in a number of locations without necessarily placing control or administrative and technical resources in the same location.

documentation The written description of a system; includes flowcharts, major process flows, input/output forms, file designs, and a narrative.

dot matrix printer An impact printer; each character is formed by a vertical bar containing seven pins or hammers moving across a page; characters are formed within a five-by-seven or nine-by-eleven matrix. Also called wire-matrix printer.

double-density A process by which a system can double the disk capacity no matter how many sides of a disk are used.

double-sided A system's ability to use both sides of a disk.

drum plotter A graphic output device that uses a sheet of paper wrapped around a drum that rotates in either direction; a marker attached to an arm that can move from side to side and draws as the drum rotates.

drum printer An impact printer consisting of a metal cylinder that contains rows of characters engraved across its surface; one line of print is produced with each rotation of the drum.

dumb terminal A terminal with very little memory; typically used only for a specific purpose.

dump program A program run that prints out the contents of primary storage and registers in hexidecimal notation; used for debugging.

earth station A facility used in satellite-based network; includes a dish-shaped receiving device and the necessary processing facility.

Eckert, J. Presper Invented the Electronic Numerical Integrator and Computer (ENIAC), with John Mauchly.

edit check Processing statements designed to identify potential errors in the input data.

EDSAC Electronic Delay Storage Automatic Computer; the first operational computer to use the stored-program concept.

EDVAC Electronic Discrete Variable Automatic Computer; performed arithmetic and logic operations without human intervention.

electronic digital computer See Digital computer.

electronic funds transfer (EFT) A cashless method of paying for goods or services using computers to electronically adjust the accounts of the involved parties.

electronic spreadsheet program A powerful matrix structured program used for analyzing and manipulating financial data.

electrosensitive printer A nonimpact printer that uses a special metallic-coated paper; as the paper moves through the printer, tiny wires are selectively applied with voltage, burning the metal coating away; the result is black letters on silver paper.

electrostatic printer A nonimpact printer that uses special photographic paper with characters etched onto the paper using a stylus; this paper is then passed through a toner solution to develop the characters, similar to photograph developing.

electrothermal printer A nonimpact printer that uses heat-sensitive paper and creates characters by heating wires on pins in a matrix format as they pass over the paper.

element Physical part or component of a system; sometimes, a subsystem made up of its own parts.

embedded applications Those applications using a computer as part of a larger complex of electronics and mechanics, usually in the role of a control system.

encryption A method of protecting data from being tapped by an illegal line and from being accessed by programs outside the system.

ENIAC Electronic Numerical Integrator and Computer; the first operational electronic digital computer.

entity The records represented in the rows of the relational data structure.

environment division The segment of a COBOL program that identifies the type of computer, and the devices used for storage.

Erasable programmable read-only memory (EPROM) Similar to PROM in that users can permanently write their own programs into memory but they may now also erase the memory.

Estridge, Philip D. President of IBM's Entry Systems Division; in large part responsible for the success of the PC.

exception listing A report containing data that does not conform to a predefined rule.

exception report A report that alerts management to abnormal situations that require special attention.

execution mode The mode in APL programming language that allows an instruction to be keyed in, generating a response in the next line.

executive routine The controlling module of a program; the main program which accesses the subroutines when needed.

Extended Binary Coded Decimal Interchange Code (EBCDIC) An 8-bit code used to represent uppercase and lowercase letters, special characters and numbers.

external report A report designed for people external to the computer room, or even the organization.

father The tape used to create an updated tape.

feasibility study The step of the systems life cycle in which the analyst determines if a feasible solution exists to the problem.

feedback A system check which determines whether predetermined goals are being met; origin of feedback may be internal or external to the system.

fiber optics A relatively new form of technology employing digital transmission in the form of light impulses sent through clear, flexible tubing.

field One or more related characters conveying a unit of information; also known as data items, data elements, and data attributes.

file A collection of related records, usually all in the same format.

firmware Programs permanently installed in ROM; also called microprogram.

first generation computers Spanned from 1951 to 1958; first generation computers used large vacuum tubes.

fixed-length records A record format in which a maximum number of character positions are assigned; records of equal lengths.

fixed scanning device A type of bar code reader.

flat bed plotter A plotter that uses a flat tabletop to actually draw the output; markers are attached to arms that move from top to bottom and side to side over the entire paper; also called X-Y plotter.

flat plasma display screen A flat terminal designed to save space.

floppy disk A common secondary storage device; usually used for microcomputers.

flow diagram Same as flowchart;

flowchart A graphic representation of the processing that is performed in a program; also known as a block diagram or a logic diagram.

foreground partitions The storage area where the highest priority programs are placed for execution during multiprogramming.

foreground programs Those programs assigned the highest priority for execution during multiprogramming.

formal design review The process followed by a review team to determine the completeness and quality of the design with program designers; also referred to as a structured walkthrough or design inspection.

Forrester, Jay W. Devised the magnetic core.

FORTRAN FORmula TRANslation; a programming language used primarily in performing mathematical or scientific operations; first high-level language developed.

fourth generation computers First produced in 1971; characterized by monolithic semiconductor memories, self-diagnostic capabilities, and large scale integration (LSI) circuits.

FRABA Field See Transit field.

frequency division multiplexing (FDM) The technique used by a multiplexer to combine input into a single stream; the communication line is divided into different frequencies, with each terminal assigned into its own frequency.

front-end processors A small CPU that performs a number of tasks such as editing data, scheduling, and maintaining files and acts as an interface between the user and the large CPU.

full-duplex A mode of data transmission whereby data can be transmitted in both directions at the same time.

fully distributed network A network in which every set of nodes in the network can communicate directly with every other set of nodes through a single communications link.

garbage in-garbage out (GIGO) Concept explaining that the output can be no more accurate than the input.

general purpose register A register that can be used for either storage, keeping addresses, or as an accumulator.

general system design The step of the systems life cycle in which the logical design of the system is established.

general system design report The final phase of the general system design step; contains a restatement of the scope and objectives, alternative system designs, and a recommendation.

grade Also called bandwidth; the range, or width, of the frequencies available for transmission on a given communication.

grandfather The third generation of tapes usually retained for back-up use.

graphic display device A visual display device that projects output in the form of graphs and line drawings and accepts input from a keyboard or light pen.

grid chart A visual aid that summarizes the relationships among the various components of a system.

half-duplex A mode of data transmission whereby data can be transmitted in both directions but in only one direction at a time.

handshaking The process through which the rules for exchanging data over a communication line are defined for the two devices involved.

hard copy Printed output on paper from a computer.

hard disk A commonly used secondary storage device; usually used for mainframes and minicomputers, however, they are now available for microcomputers.

hard wired Connecting devices to the CPU to be the same piece of equipment.

hardware The physical devices that make up the computer system.

hashing See Randomizing.

HERO 1 (Heath, Education RObot) A robot twenty inches high with a mechanical arm that permits the manipulation of small objects.

hexadecimal number system The base 16 number system used by computers to show the contents of memory as an aid in debugging.

hierarchical design An information structure in which each level within an organization is provided with necessary computer power; responsibility for control and coordination goes to the top level.

hierarchical network Also called a tree network; a design, approach used to implement the multiple CPU concept in which an organization's needs are divided into multiple levels that receive different levels of computer support.

hierarchical data structure The situation in which one primary data element may have numerous secondary data elements linked to it at a lower level; also called tree data structure.

high-level languages Programming languages that are closer to English or mathematical notation; do not require an in-depth understanding of computer operations.

highlighting On a visual display terminal, the ability to underscore or intensify certain information, display blinking letters, or reverse the color of the letters and the background.

HIPO A documentation and design tool that describes a series of diagrams that serve as visual aids in supplementing structure charts; short for Hierachy plus Input-Process-Output.

Hoff, Ted Designed the microprocessor.

Hollerith card See Punched card.

Hollerith, Herman (1860–1929) Invented the census machine in 1887; it used punched paper cards to store data.

Hollerith code A method of data representation invented by Herman Hollerith; numbers, letters, and special characters are represented by the placement of holes in 80-column punched cards.

Hopper, Commodore Grace Murray A leader in the development of business compilers.

host A conventional computer with elaborate software available.

host language A language that is understood by a host computer when accessing a DBMS.

identification division The segment of a COBOL program that contains the program name and other optional information.

IF-THEN-ELSE See Selection.

impact printer A printer that forms characters by striking a device against an inked ribbon, causing a character to be imprinted onto the paper.

implementation The step of the systems life cycle in which the system is physically created and installed.

in-house Development of programs by permanent employees within an organization.

index sequential file organization A file organization technique that creates an index relating the key values to the record locations within the data file; capable of both sequential and direct access.

indexed-sequential access A system of file organization that uses an index which contains the disk address of each particular record.

informal design review An opportunity for selected people to study the system design documentation and make suggestions for improvement; used in the early phases of system development.

information Data that has been processed into a form that is useful to the user in making decisions.

information channel Path that the flow of information takes within an organization.

information system The methods and channels used to gather and distribute information within an organization.

information system manager The person responsible for planning and tying together all the information resources of a firm.

ink jet printer A nonimpact printer in which a spray of electrically charged ink is shot toward paper; but before reaching the paper, the ink passes through an electrical field that forms the letters.

input Data entered into the computer for processing.

input/output (I/O) statement A FORTRAN statement used to read data from or write data to an I/O device according to the instruction; a statement that permits communication between CPU and I/O devices.

instruction decoder Provides electronic signals to the control unit indicating the operation to be performed based on the instruction being decoded.

integrated circuits (IC) Electronic circuits etched on a small silicon chip less than ⅛-inch square; permits much faster processing than with transistors at a greatly reduced price; the most widely used form of primary storage; also called semiconductor memory.

intelligent terminal See smart terminal.

interactive The mode of interaction where the computer responds instantaneously with the required information; also called demand or conversational.

interactive programming language A programming language that allows a programmer to communicate directly with the computer.

interblock gap (IBG) A section of blank tape separating blocks of records.

intermediate code See Pseudocode.

internal report A report designed for limited use within the company or computer room.

interpreter A program stored in primary, or Read Only Memory that reads, interprets, and executes one statement from a source program.

interrecord gaps (IRGs) A relatively large section of blank tape separating each record.

interrupt A hardware generated transfer of control to the operating system under special circumstances.

inverted list A list that creates an index of common characteristics being searched for and the record number; best utilized when large files are searched for a small amount of data.

Jacquard, Joseph Marie Developed automated weaving through the use of coded punched cards.

job control program A control program that translates job control language into machine language.

Jobs, Steven Paul Founded Apple Computer, Inc., along with Stephan Wozniak.

Josephson technolgoy A process of cooling metal alloys to temperature to near absolute zero, causing the metals to lose their resistance to the flow of electricity.

K A symbol used to represent 1,024 bytes; used when referring to memory size.

Kemeny, John G. Developed the BASIC language; also developed the first prototype time-sharing system.

key The unique identifier or field of a record; used to sort records for processing or to locate specific records within a file.

key field A field in a record used to calculate the address of that information.

key verifier A machine used to verify the accuracy of data keyed onto punched cards.

key-to-magnetic media Allow data to be entered through a keyboard and stored magnetically on the tape or desk medium.

keypunch A machine used to record information on punched cards.

Kilby, Jack S. Introduced the integrated circuit, or silicon chip, in September 1958.

label A programmer supplied name used to refer to an instruction without having to specify the numeric address of that instruction.

language translator A program for translating a source program to an object program.

language-translator program A processing program which translates a program written in another programming language into machine language.

large-scale digital computer

large-scale integration (LSI) A miniaturization process by which thousands of transistors can be closely etched onto a single silicon chip.

laser printer A nonimpact printer where beams of light are passed through a rotating disk containing a full set of characters onto photographic paper; the paper is then developed and used to make copies.

Leibniz, Gottfried von (1646–1716) Developed a machine capable not only of addition and subtraction, but also multiplication, division, and finding square roots.

letter quality Print that is characterized by sharp, crisp, high-quality characters.

librarian An individual who classifies, catalogs, and maintains files and programs stored on cards, tapes, disks, and diskettes; the person also transfers backup files and supervises the cleaning of magnetic disks and tapes.

librarian program A program that manages the storage and use of library programs by maintaining a directory of programs in the system library.

library programs User-written or manufacturer-supplied programs that are frequently used in other programs to perform certain common functions.

light pen A pen-shaped object with a photoelectric cell at its end; used to draw lines on a visual display screen.

line-at-a-time printer A printer that can print a line of output at a time.

link See Pointer.

links The transmission channels that connect the nodes of a network.

linkage editor A subprogram of the operating system that loads the object program from the system residence device to main storage.

linked list A file utilizing pointers to maintain the sequence of the records.

logical design Relates to the way in which the independent elements of data are grouped to create a file.

logical records The records contained within a file.

loop logic pattern A logic pattern that allows a series of statements to be executed more than once within a program; requires a test condition.

machine cycle The four steps required to process a single instruction in a program.

machine language The series of 0s and 1s that represent the binary operations of digital computers; also called the language of the computer.

macroflowchart A general description of the major processing steps of a program in flowchart form.

magnetic core A type of memory internal (storage) in which tiny doughnut-shaped rings are strung on thin wires through which an electrical current passes, thus magnetizing it to represent either an "off" or "on" state.

magnetic disk A common secondary storage device; includes hard and floppy types; also known as direct-access storage device (DASD).

magnetic drums Cylindrical devices whose outer circumference contains data in tracks, each of which has a read/write head.

magnetic tape An auxiliary storage medium on which spots are magnetized to represent data; data is stored sequentially.

magnetic-ink character reader Translates magnetic ink characters into machine code.

magnetic-ink character recognition (MICR) A type of source data automation that recognizes characters by iron-oxide placed in certain sections of a matrix.

main control logic The broadest over-all description of the steps.

mainframe A full-scale computer with longer word length and faster processing speed than a small system.

maintenance The ongoing phase of the systems life cycle with the objective of keeping the system functioning at an acceptable level.

maintenance programmer A person with considerable programming experience and analytic reasoning ability whose duties include changing and including major programs.

mark sensing See optical-mark recognition.

mass storage devices High-density magnetic tapes or disks used to store infrequently used data while retaining accessability.

manager of computer operations The person responsible for monitoring the efficiency, scheduling, and assignment of operators; also must maintain the equipment.

materials requirement planning A complex system used by manufacturers to determine what and when raw materials will be needed for production.

matrix structure An internal organizational structure of an MIS department.

Mauchly, John W. Invented the Electronic Numeric Integrator and Computer (ENIAC), with J. Presper Eckert.

McCarthy, John Founded MIT and Stanford Laboratories, both artificial intelligence laboratories; created LISP; developed interactive computing at MIT: best known for his work associated with artificial intelligence.

mechanical calculator Invented by Blaise Pascal; added and subtracted numbers using a series of rotating gears.

medium The physical unit on which data is recorded; usually magnetic tape or disk.

memory dump See Core dump.

memory region A storage area of variable size used to keep programs separate during multiprogramming.

memory management Also called memory protection; the process by which programs are kept in the correct region or partition during multiprogramming.

message characters Special characters placed in front of and behind data that is transmitted to provide the receiving device with important transmission information.

micro chip A sophisticated semiconductor memory.

microcomputer A very small computer; often a special-purpose or a single-function computer on a single chip.

micromainframe A microminiaturized mainframe; as powerful as a medium-sized mainframe at about one-tenth the size and cost.

microprocessor The CPU of a microcomputer; fits on a small silicon chip.

microwave An analog type of transmission channel whereby information is sent through the atmosphere similar to radio or television transmission.

minicomputer A computer with the components of a full-size system but having a smaller memory.

miniflowchart A detailed description of one or more of the processing steps in flowchart form; several micro-flowcharts can represent one macroflowchart.

MIS director The highest level of management in an MIS. The position requires extensive management experience and advanced technical knowledge.

mnemonics Symbolic names used to specify machine operations.

modem (MOdulator-DEModulator) Also called a data set; a device that modulates and demodulates signals transmitted over communication channels.

modulation The process of translating digital data to analog form.

multidrop configuration A channel configuration where several terminals share the same communication line; only one terminal can transmit at a time, but more than one terminal can receive messages simultaneously.

multiplexer A device that combines the input from several terminals into a single input stream, allowing data from all these terminals to be transmitted over a single channel.

multiprocessing The use of multiple CPUs working together to provide simultaneous execution of more than one program.

multiprogramming A process whereby several programs are placed in primary storage at the same time, giving the illusion that they are being executed simultaneously; results in increased CPU activity time.

nanosecond One-billionth of a second.

Napier, John Developed a table of numbers to aid in multiplication and division.

Napier's Bones A table of numbers to aid in multiplication and division developed by John Napier; also called Napier's Rods.

narrow-bandwidth channel A communication channel that transmits data at a rate of 45 to 90 bits per second.

NCR paper No-carbon-required paper; eliminates the waste and mess associated with carbon paper.

network data structure Similar to the hierarchical data structure except the child may be related to more than one parent.

node Each point on the hierarchical data structure.

node The end points of a network; consists of CPUs, printers, VDTs, and other physical devices.

nondestructive read/destructive write Characteristic of memory that allows the same instructions or data to be read repeatedly without alteration or destruction.

nonimpact printer A printer that forms characters using a method other than impact, such as laser beams or heat-sensitive paper.

numeric bit The four rightmost bit positions of a six-bit BCD used to endcode numeric data.

object program A source program that has been translated into machine executable form.

on-line file access The ability to retrieve updated information at any time.

On Us Field The area on a bank check where the account number is written using magnetic ink characters.

Opel, John A chief executive officer in IBM; in large part responsible for the success of the PC.

operands The part of a machine language instruction that tells the computer which data elements the processing is to be performed on; also called addresses.

operating system A collection of programs used by the computer to manage its own resources and operations.

operation code The part of the program instruction that tells the control unit what to do; also called the op code.

operational decision making Decisions made by low level managers that are concerned with day-to-day operations.

operator's manual The instruction manual for the computer personnel explaining how to run the programs, input data, and load and unload the files of a system.

optical-character recognition (OCR) Allows recognition of characters in specific typefaces by shape.

optical disk Storage medium for films and other visual information; also called videodisk.

optical-mark recognition (OMR) Method of source data automation often used for grading exams by sensing marks made by a heavy pencil mark.

Osborne 1 A compact and inexpensive microcomputer built by Adam Osborne.

Osborne, Adam Builder of the Osborne 1 in 1982; produced an inexpensive product that was industry compatible in both hardware and software.

output Information that comes from a computer as a result of processing.

overview diagram A HIPO diagram used to show more detail about the main functions of the program illustrated in the VTOC.

P-code An intermediate code generated by a pseudo-compiler when working with Pascal.

packed decimal code A variant on EBCDIC used to represent decimal digits in four bits; permits a byte to represent two digits rather than just one digit.

pack A grouping of hard disks stacked on top of each other; a common pack size is eleven disks.

page frames Areas of equal size in main storage where pages of programs used in virtual storage systems are stored.

pages Equal sections of a program used in virtual storage systems.

paging The ability to obtain different information on a visual display terminal whereby an entirely new screen of information is displayed.

paging The method of dividing programs into equal sections used in virtual storage systems.

parallel conversion Running both the old and new system concurrently until the new system proves dependable.

parent The primary data element.

parity bit The extra bit added to a bit pattern; used for parity check.

parity check An internal form of error checking with data transmission in which the number of 1 bits in a bit pattern is determined as either being an odd or even number.

partitioned organization A file structure that divides a large file into subfiles, each identified by a name.

partitions A storage area of fixed size used to keep programs separate during multiprogramming.

Pascal, Blaise The mathematician who invented the first electronic adding machine; Pascal programming language is named after him but was developed by Niklaus Wirth in 1968.

Pascal's adding machine A machine capable of adding and subtracting, using gears, developed by Blaise Pascal in 1642.

password A technique used to safeguard system security.

periodic report A report issued on a regular basis.

phased conversion Implementing only one segment of the system at a time; after thorough testing and debugging, another segment is implemented.

phonemes Half-second recordings of voice sounds that, when properly arranged, make a computer "speak."

physical design Refers to the particular medium on or in which the data is stored.

physical records See Blocked records.

pilot conversion Implementing the complete system in only one area until it proves successful, whereupon it is extended throughout the organization.

pixels The positions on a VDT screen.

PL/I Programming Language One; a combination of COBOL and FORTRAN developed by IBM.

plotter A hard copy printer used to prepare a permanent record of drawings and charts.

point-of-sale (POS) terminal Smart terminals used for source data automation in retail sales.

point-to-point configuration A type of channel configuration where each terminal is connected directly to the computer.

pointer An additional field of a record that contains the address on the DASD of the next record to be processed.

polling A process used in a multidrop configuration where each terminal is asked in succession for data to be transmitted.

predictive report A report that uses decision models to project future results that are useful for planning.

primary storage Memory that is inside the computer itself; also known as internal storage, memory, and main storage.

primary storage unit Unit on the CPU where instructions and data are held until needed for processing; also called internal storage.

print wheel printer An impact printer with 120 print wheels, each containing 48 characters; the print wheels rotate until an entire line is in the appropriate print position, then a hammer presses the paper against the print wheels.

printer keyboard An impact printer similar to a typewriter, but controlled by a computer; a print element shaped like a golfball turns in order to strike the inked ribbon and paper to print a character.

problem definition The part of the systems life cycle that explicitly outlines the nature and extent of the problem.

problem-oriented language A language, such as RPG, which describes the problem and solution without detailing the computational procedures.

procedure division The segment of a COBOL program that contains the instructions needed to direct the computer in solving a particular programming problem.

procedure-oriented language A language that focuses on the computational and logical procedures required to solve a problem; includes COBOL, FORTRAN, and PL/1.

processing programs Routines that are executed under the supervision of control programs and are used by the programmer to simplify program preparation for the computer system

program A series of step-by-step instructions that provides a problem solution according to which the CPU processes the data.

program counter Determines which instruction is being completed and points to the location of the next instruction to be executed.

program logic The precise sequence and specification of operations to be performed.

programmable communication processor A device that relieves the CPU of many of the tasks involved in coordinating the network components.

programmable read-only memory (PROM) An alternative to ROM that permits the user to permanently write his own programs into memory.

programmer A person who writes step-by-step instructions for the computer to execute.

PROLOG The language chosen for programming fifth generation computers.

protocol The specific set of rules governing handshaking and message characters.

prototyping A methodology by which the standard steps of system development are compressed using the constriction and discussion of prototypes by the designer and the user.

pseudocode A written description of the processing steps that need to be performed within a program.

pseudocode interpreter The part of the pseudocompiler responsible for translating pseudocode into machine code.

pseudocompiler A method of language translation that first translates a program into one- or two-byte data values known as tokens.

punched card An 80-column card onto which data is recorded by punched holes in a keypunch machine; an input medium.

Q-codes Special characters that mark the beginning and end of magnetic ink character fields on bank checks.

query language A language composed of special English-like statements that are easily understood by nontechnical personnel.

random access device Magnetic disk; can selectively access recorded data without passing by all previously recorded information.

random-access memory (RAM) Storage in which programs and data can be written into and read from speedily.

random-access memory (RAM) chip The most popular of the microchips; a continuous supply of power is needed.

randomizing A mathematical process applied to the record key yielding a storage address; also called hashing.

read-only memory (ROM) Memory storage in which the computer can read data from rapidly but cannot write data to; the data or instructions are permanently wired into the computer.

read/write head The physical part of the disk pack which reads and writes on the disk.

real storage Also known as main storage or primary storage within the CPU.

real-time operating system An operating system that provides for spontaneous requests from users via on-line terminals.

record A group of related fields.

register An internal computer component used for temporary storage of data or instructions; capable of accepting, holding, and transfering that instruction or data very rapidly.

relational data structure Relates data elements in a two-dimensional table; accessed using a mathematical representation of the table location holding a particular data element.

remote network Also called wide-area network; a network that covers a large geographically dispersed area.

remote terminal A terminal located at a distance from the main computer.

remote terminal operator An individual located at a distance from the central computer who is involved in the preparation of input data.

resident routines The most frequently used routines of the supervisor program; those routines initially brought into primary storage during bootstrapping.

resolution The maximum number of positions (horizontally and vertically) that can be used in generating characters and graphics on a visual display terminal.

ring list A linked list with the last record of the file pointing forward to the first record; permits access to the beginning of a list from any point within the file.

ring network a network in which a number of computers are connected by a single transmission line in a ring arrangement.

Roach, John V. Chairman of Tandy Corporation; responsible for the release in September 1977 of the TRS-80, the first official microcomputer.

RPG A problem-oriented language; short for Report Program Generator.

rule A vertical column in a decision-logic table containing an instance of conditions and their associated actions.

run book An operator's manual.

satellite-based network A network that uses satellites and earthstations to extend the range of communication channels.

scheduled report Routinely produced reports with a wide variety of users.

scratched Erased and reused tapes.

scrolling Moving lines of information up or down on a visual display terminal.

second generation computers Made between 1959 and 1964; used solid state transistors.

secondary storage All storage devices that are not part of the CPU; magnetic tape, disks, and bubble memory.

sectors The areas of a disk divided into pie-shaped pieces.

segmentation The method of dividing programs into logical segments of varying size used in virtual storage systems.

selection A type of logic pattern that requires a test condition which results in one of two alternate paths to be followed, depending on the results of the test; also referred to as an IF/THEN/ELSE pattern.

semiconductor memory Hundreds of thousands of tiny electronic circuits etched on a silicon chip; requires a constant source of power.

semiconductors Small ceramic chips with printed circuits.

sequential file organization The files are organized in either ascending or descending order based upon the value of the key.

sequential-access storage device (SASD) See Magnetic tape.

Shockley, William Developed the transistor; awarded the Nobel Prize in 1956.

silicon chip Solid logic circuitry on a small piece of silicon used to form the primary storage of third generation computers.

silicon wafers Material upon which electronic circuits are etched to produce chips.

simple list A file without pointers.

simple sequence Sequentially executing one statement after another.

simplex A mode of data transmission where data can travel in only one direction on the line.

single-job system An operating system that permitted only one job at a time to be executed by the computer.

smart terminal A terminal with considerable memory that can perform many operations independently of the main computer.

soft copy Output that is displayed on a screen.

soft wired Connecting devices to the CPU by a set of small wires; usually storage devices.

software The programs written to control operation of computer hardware.

software engineer A specialist whose concern is increasing the efficiency and effectiveness of computer software.

software engineering A discipline that has evolved since the late 1960s in an effort to make software development more rational.

software package A standardized set of programs designed to solve a particular type of problem.

Solomon, Lester Started the microcomputer revolution; featured the MITS Altair, the first do-it-yourself computer kit in his magazine, *Popular Electronics* (now *Computers and Electronics*) in 1975.

son The newly created tape after updating.

sort/merge program A utility program used to sort records to facilitate updating and subsequent combining of files to form a single, updated file.

source document Original source of data from which that data is rewritten to enter into the computer as input.

source languages Assembly and high-level languages.

source listing A descriptive listing of program statements generated during compilation.

source program A sequence of instructions written in either assembly language or high-level language by the programmer.

source-data automation Process by which data is recorded (in computer readable form) when and where it is created.

sparse indexing Used in most indexed-sequential access systems; only the key from the last record on a track is found in the index.

specification statement A FORTRAN statement that tells FORTRAN how to interpret data from an input device and how to write data to an output device.

spooler A device that allows the user to continue working on a microcomputer while its printer is being used.

spooling (simultaneous peripheral operations online) The process whereby output is written to a high-speed recording medium (disk or tape) to be output to a slow-speed peripheral device (printer) at a later date; used in multiprogramming.

stand-alone key-to-disk device Self-contained unit with keyboard, buffer, memory, and magnetic medium.

stand-alone key-to-tape device See Stand-alone key-to-disk device.

star network A network in which all transactions go through a central computer before being routed to the appropriate network node.

start-stop transmission See Asynchronous transmission.

statements Instructions in a computer program that specify various types of operations to be performed by the computer.

storage register A register that temporarily holds data being sent to or retrieved from primary storage.

stored-program concept The storing of programs and data in computer memory; this concept distinguishes a computer from a calculator.

strategic decision making Future oriented decision that involves a great deal of uncertainty; made by top level management.

structure chart The visual representation of modules in a hierarchical manner, much like an organizational chart.

structured programming An approach to programming in which the problem is first analyzed, then the solution subdivided into smaller blocks or sections before coding; emphasis on top down design and restriction of GO TOs.

subroutine A functional step written as an independent module.

summary listing An overview of all computer activities.

supercomputer The largest, fastest, and most expensive computers in existence today; also called maxicomputers or monster computers.

supervisor program Also called a monitor or an executive; the major component of the operating system; coordinates the activities of all other parts of the operating system.

swapping The process of exchanging data or instructions from virtual storage to real storage and vice versa.

synchronous transmission The process whereby whole blocks of characters are transmitted in a timed sequence.

syntax Refers to the way rules must be followed while coding instructions, just as grammatical rules must be followed in English.

system A group of related elements that work together toward a common goal.

system flowchart A visual diagram of the system utilizing standardized symbols.

system package A software package designed to make the computer operate more efficiently.

system residence device An auxiliary storage device (disk, tape, or drum) on which operating system programs are stored and from which they are loaded into main storage.

system testing Checking all application programs, clerical procedures, data processing, and data storage and retrieval methods that support the system.

systems analysis The step of the systems life cycle involving the two principal tasks of data gathering and data analysis.

systems analysis report Presented to management as the final step of the systems analysis step; assures management of the direction and intentions of the systems project.

systems analyst A key person in computer operations who analyzes, designs, and implements a formal information system.

systems approach The approach of viewing a system as a whole.

systems development manager The person who monitors the total systems development cycle, especially project schedules.

systems life cycle An approach to systems analysis and design; cycle consisting of the following steps; 1) problem definition, 2) feasibility study, 3) systems analysis, 4) general system design, 5) detailed system design, 6) implementation, 7) maintenance.

systems programmer The person responsible for creating and maintaining system software.

systems programs Provide a computer's ability to utilize its hardware to capacity and ensure quick and efficient operations.

tactical decision making Decisions made by middle level managers that determine specific strategies to be employed.

target A computer that functions with little or no software support.

telecommunications The transmission of signals using communication facilities.

telecommuting A process by which executives can work at home using a personal computer that ties into a system at their place of business.

teleprocessing The combined use of communication facilities, such as the telephone system and data-processing equipment.

terminal A device linked in some manner to the main computer.

terminal node A node on the hierarchical data structure without a downward link.

third generation computers Produced between 1965 and 1971; made using chips made of silicon wafers upon which the Integrated Circuits were etched.

thrashing A phenomenon of a program page or segment being swapped out of real storage before it has been executed.

time division multiplexing (TDM) A technique used by a multiplexer to combine input into a single input stream; each terminal is sampled for a fixed time period.

time-sharing system A system that permits multiple independent users to interact concurrently through terminals with a central computer.

top-down design The method of organizing a solution by defining it in terms of major functions to be performed and then further breaking down these major functions into subfunctions.

touch-tone device A remote terminal used to collect and temporarily store data until that data can be forwarded to a central computer; uses tones and combinations of tones to represent characters to transmit over to public phone lines.

trace program A run of a program which lists each step of the program in the order actually executed by the computer; an aid for the debugging process.

tracks The concentric circles which make up a disk; numbered from outer track to inner beginning with zero.

Tramiel, Jack Founder and president of Commodore INternational; responsible for the presence of affordable line computers, such as the VIC 20 and the Commodore 64.

transfers of control A type of instruction which allows the sequence of execution to be altered by transferring control.

transient routines The less frequently used routines of the supervisor program; they remain in auxiliary storage during bootstrapping.

transistor A type of circuitry characteristic of secondgeneration computers; smaller, faster, and more reliable than vacuum tubes but inferior to third-generation, large-scale integration.

turnaround document Output in the form of bills, printed on thick paper or punched cards; the form is returned with payment and used as input, thus reducing the work needed to prepare data entry.

unique key The unique identifier of a record.

unit In reference to the unit record concept, the unit implies that one card should contain a single record.

unit record concept Requires that one punched card should contain one record.

UNIVAC I UNIVersal Automatic Computer; developed by J. Mauchly and J. Eckert UNIVAC I was the first commercially successful electronic computer designed for business use; the beginning of the first-generation computer.

Universal Product Code (UPC) A standardized bar code found on grocery store items.

user's manual A manual instructing management and users about the particular functions of a system and their performance requirements.

utility program A processing program that is capable of performing specialized, repeated used functions such as sorting, merging, and transferring data from one input/output device to another.

variable-length records Records stored with differing lengths.

very large-scale integration (VLSI) The ultimate miniaturization of integrated circuits with electronic circuits even more densely packed onto silicon chips than LSI.

videodisk See Optical disk

virtual storage An extension of multiprogramming in which portions of programs not being used are kept in secondary storage until needed, giving the impression the primary storage is unlimited; contrast with real storage.

visual display terminal (VDT) A terminal capable of providing output through a cathode-ray tube and, with special provisions, of transmitting data through a keyboard.

visual table of contents (VTOC) A HIPO diagram that shows the functions of the program in the most general and concise manner; much like structure chart but more informative.

voice systhesis The output portion of an I/O system; computer reproduction of a human voice.

voice-entry system The input portion of an I/O system that will understand a voice command.

voice-grade channel A communication channel that can transmit data at rates from 300 to 9,600 bits per second.

voice-recognition system An input method that recognizes spoken words.

voice-response output Same as audio output; a computer "speaks" in a voice synthesized from electronic signals.

voice store and forward (VSF) An inexpensive alternative to electronic mail; push-button phones are used to change voices into digital form and transmit the pulses to a computer where they are stored until retrieved.

volatile The characteristic of integrated circuits which requires them to have a constant source of power or all stored data will be lost.

von Neumann, John Invented the Electronic Discrete variable calculator (EDVAC); presented the stored-program concept; considered the father of flowcharting.

wand reader A hand-held bar code reader.

WATFIV An enhanced version of WATFOR.

WATFOR A subset of FORTRAN developed at the University of Waterloo in Ontario; short for WATerloo FORtran.

Watson, Thomas J., Jr. President of IBM; responsible for establishing the company's image and standard of quality.

Watson, Thomas J., Sr. Founded International Business Machines (IBM) in 1924.

Wilkes, Maurice V. Directed the building of the Electronic Delay Storage Automatic Computer (EDSAC) in 1949.

windowing On a visual display terminal, the ability to magnify certain areas of the display.

wire cable A form of communication channel over which data is transmitted in analog form; presently the most common form of communication channel.

word length The number of bits of information that can be manipulated by the CPU at one time.

word processing The manipulation of text data with flexibility and efficiency to achieve a desired output.

Wozniak, Stephen Founded Apple Computer, Incorporated, along with Stephen Paul Jobs.

xerographic printers A nonimpact printer that uses printing methods similar to a copy machine.

X-Y plotter Same as flat bed plotter.

zone bits Used in different combinations with numeric bits to represent numbers, letters, and special characters.

INDEX

Santa Fe Railway Compay. **Chapter 14** Courtesy of Quotron Systems, Inc. **Chapter 15** Courtesy of Sperry Univac. **Chapter 16** Courtesy of Cray Research, Inc. **Fig. 16-1** Courtesy of Cray Research, Inc. **Fig. 16-2** Courtesy of Burroughs Corporation. **Fig. 16-3** Courtesy of Honeywell Inc. **Fig. 16-4** Courtesy of Apple Computers, Tandy Corporation, Digital Equipment, Atari, Coleco Vision, and Commodore. **Fig. 16-5** Courtesy of Intel. **Chapter 17** Photo courtesy of Brown University. Photo by John Foraste. **Fig. 17-1** Courtesy of Micro-Sci, a Division of Standon Control, Inc.; photograph by Rich Dressler. **Fig. 17-2** Courtesy of Verbatim Corporation. **Fig. 17-3** Photo by Norma Morris. **Fig. 17-4** Photo courtesy of Nicolet Zeta Corporation, Concord, CA. **Fig. 17-5** Photo by Norma Morris. **Fig. 17-6** Reprinted by permission of International Business Machines Corporation. **Fig. 17-7** Courtesy of Chrysler Corporation. **Chapter 18** Courtesy of Chrysler Corporation. **Fig. 18-1** Courtesy of Pacific Gas and Electric Company. **Fig. 18-2** Courtesy of AT&T. **Fig. 18-3** Courtesy of Paradyne Corporation and Texaco. **Fig. 18-4** Courtesy of Apple Computer, Inc. **Fig. 18-5** Lear Siegler, Inc./Data Products Division, Anaheim, California. **Fig. 18-7** Courtesy of Santa Fe Railway. **Chapter 19** Reprinted by permission of International Business Machines Corporation. **Fig. 19-1** Courtesy of NCR Corporation. **Fig. 19-2** Courtesy of Chrysler Corporation. **Fig. 19-3** Courtesy of Burlington Industries, Inc. **Fig. 19-4** U.S. Air Force Photo. **Fig. 19-5** Photos by Bowling Green State University Photo Service. **Fig. 19-6** Courtesy of BRS College. **Fig. 19-7** Courtesy of Control Data Corporation. **Fig. 19-8** Susan Gilmore, Photographer. **Fig. 19-9** Reprinted by permission of International Business Machines Corporation. **Fig. 19-10** Photos by Bowling Green State University Photo Service. **Fig. 19-11** Gideon Airel, Coto Research Center. **Chapter 20** Courtesy of RB Robot Corporation. **Fig. 20-1** Reproduced with permission of AT&T. **Fig. 20-2** Reproduced with permission of AT&T. **Fig. 20-3** Courtesy of Lanier. **Fig. 20-4** Ford Motor Company Photo. **Fig. 20-5** Courtesy of Androbot, Inc., Courtesy of Heath Company and Photo courtesy of RB Robot Corporation, Golden, Colorado. **Fig. 20-6** Courtesy of Odetics, Inc. **Fig. 20-7** Courtesy of The MIT Museum.

Portfolio Credits

Computers in Our Homes and Daily Lives. 1. Photo Courtesy of Intel Corporation. **2.** Sony Corporation of America. **3.** Gideon Ariel, Ariel Computerized Exercisers, Inc. **4.** Gideon Ariel, Ariel Computerized Exercisers, Inc. **5.** Courtesy of Brunswick Corporation. **6.** Photo Courtesy of Intel Corporation. **7.** Courtesy of Coca-Cola Company. **8.** Courtesy NCR Corp. **9.** Photo Courtesy Compu-Home Systems, Denver, CO. **10.** Courtesy of Armstrong World Industries. **11.** Courtesy of Apple Computer, Inc. **12.** Reprinted by permission of International Business Machines Corporation. **13.** Reprinted by permission of International Business Machines Corporation. **14.** Courtesy of Digital Equipment Corporation. **15.** Courtesy of Zenith Data Systems Corp. **16.** Courtesy of AT&T, Bell Laboratories. **17.** Jay Freis, Courtesy of Planning Research Corporation. **18.** Courtesy of Commodore Computer Systems Division. **19.** Courtesy of Atari Incorporated. **20.** Courtesy of Atari Incorporated. **21.** Courtesy of Tomy Corporation. **22.** Courtesy of Commodore Computer Systems Division. **Computers in Education. 1.** Reprinted by permission of International Business Machines Corporation. **2.** Courtesy Union College—College Relations. **3.** Courtesy of General Electric, Data Communications Department. **4.** Reprinted by permission of International Business Machines Corporation. **5.** Courtesy of Control Data Corporation. **6.** Courtesy of Tektronix, Inc. **7.** Photo by Norma Morris. **8.** Susan Gilmore, Photographer. **9.** Photo shown courtesy of Radio Shack, a Division of Tandy Corporation. **10.** Courtesy of Apple Computer, Inc. **11.** John Foraste/Brown University. **12.** Reprinted by permission of International Business Machines Corporation. **13.** Courtesy of Control Data Corporation. **14.** John Foraste/Brown University. **15.** Courtesy of California Institute of the Arts. **16.** Reprinted courtesy of DIALOG Information Services, Inc. **17.** Courtesy of CL Systems, Inc. **The Chip Making Process. 1.** Courtesy of Sperry Corporation. **2.** Courtesy of AT&T, Bell Laboratories. **3.** Courtesy of Sperry Corporation. **4.** Courtesy of Sperry Corporation. **5.** Courtesy of the Perkin-Elmer Corporation. **6.** Courtesy of Intel Corporation. **7.** Courtesy of Sperry Corporation. **8.** Courtesy of Sperry Corporation. **9.** Courtesy of Electro Scientific Industries, Inc. **10.** Courtesy of Sperry Corporation. **11.** Courtesy of Sperry Corporation. **12.** Courtesy of Motorola, Inc., Semiconductor Products Sector. **13.** Courtesy of Motorola, Inc., Semiconductor Products Sector. **CAD/CAM. 1.** Courtesy of Chrysler Corporation. **2.** Courtesy of Chrysler Corporation. **3.** Courtesy of The Firestone Tire & Rubber Company. **4.** Courtesy of Fairchild Industries. **5.** Courtesy of Fairchild Industries. **6.** Courtesy of Applicon. **7.** Courtesy of Applicon. **8.** Courtesy of Calma Company. **9.** Courtesy of Cincinnati Milacron Industrial Robot Div. **10.** Courtesy of Cincinnati Milacron Industrial Robot Div. **11.** Courtesy of Bethlehem Steel Corporation. **12.** Courtesy of Paradyne Corporation. **Computers in Science. 1.** Courtesy of NASA. **2.** Courtesy of AT&T. **3.** Courtesy of the Cray Corporation. **4.** Courtesy of Odetics, Inc. **5.** Courtesy of Marathon Oil Company. **6.** Courtesy of Western Geophysical. **7.** Courtesy of Western Geophysical. **8.** Courtesy of The Perkin-Elmer Corporation. **9.** Courtesy of Los Alamos National Laboratory. **10.** Courtesy of United States Steel Corporation. **11.** Reprinted by permission from International Business Machines. **12.** Optronics International, Inc., Chelmsford, Massachusetts. **13.** Reprinted by permission of International Business Machines Corporation. **14.** Courtesy of Los Alamos National Laboratory. **15.** Courtesy of U.S. Department of Commerce, National Oceanic & Atmospheric Administration (NOAA). **16.** Courtesy of Santa Fe Railway. **17.** Courtesy of General Electric Co. **18.** Courtesy of The Perkin-Elmer Corporation. **19.** Courtesy of Apple Computer, Inc. **20.** Courtesy of Apple Computer, Inc. **21.** U.S. Department of Energy, Photos by Frank Hoffman. **Computers in Business and Industry. 1.** Courtesy of the Coca-Cola Company. **2.** Courtesy of The Atchison, Topeka, and Santa Fe Railway Company. **3.** Courtesy of Apple Computer, Inc. **4.** Courtesy of Chicago Pneumatic Tool Company. **5.** Courtesy of Pacific Gas and Electric Company. **6.** Courtesy of Sperry Corporation. **7.** Photo compliments of Holiday Inns. **8.** Courtesy of

Quotron Systems, Inc. **9.** Courtesy of Norfolk Southern. **10.** Courtesy of Brunswick Corporation. **11.** Courtesy of Pacific Gas and Electric Company. **12.** Courtesy of United States Steel Corporation. **13.** Courtesy Pacific Gas and Electric Company. **14.** Courtesy of General Electric Co. **15.** Courtesy of AccuRay Corporation. **16.** Courtesy of Burlington Northern Railroad. **Computers in the Workplace. 1.** Chicago Tribune Photo. **2.** Chicago Tribune Photo. **3.** Courtesy of U.S. Department of Agriculture. **4.** Courtesy of U.S. Department of Agriculture. **5.** Reprinted by permission from International Business Machines. **6.** Ira Wexler, courtesy of Planning Research Corporation. **7.** Courtesy of Lanier Business Products, Inc. **8.** Courtesy of Compugraphic Corporation. **9.** Reproduced with permission of AT&T. **10.** Courtesy of Informatics General Corporation. **11.** Courtesy of Hewlett Packard. **12.** Courtesy of AT&T, Bell Laboratories. **13.** Courtesy of The Gillette Corporation. **14.** Courtesy of Genesco Inc. **15.** Courtesy of Sperry Corporation. **16.** Courtesy of Source Telecomputing Corporation. **17.** Courtesy of NESTAR Systems, Inc. **18.** Photo courtesy of Nixdorf Computer Corporation, Burlington, Massachusetts. **19.** Photo shown courtesy of Radio Shack, a Division of Tandy Corporation. **20.** Courtesy of Eastman Kodak Company. **21.** Courtesy of Paradyne Corporation. **22.** Courtesy of Wang Laboratories, Inc. **Computers in Medicine. 1.** Courtesy of Parkland Memorial Hospital. **2.** Reprinted by permission of International Business Machines Corporation. **3.** Courtesy of Pfizer, Inc. **4.** The Mt. Sinai Medical Center, Cleveland, Ohio. **5.** Courtesy of GTE Telenet Communications Corp. **6.** Courtesy of Anacomp, Inc. **7.** Dr.

Armand Glassman, Department of Laboratory Medicine, Medical University of South Carolina. **8.** Dr. Armand Glassman, Department of Laboratory Medicine, Medical University of South Carolina. **9.** Courtesy of Harsahan Chemical Company. **10.** The Mt. Sinai Medical Center, Cleveland, Ohio. **11.** Courtesy of General Electric Company. **12.** Optronics International, Inc., Dr. L. Sololoff, NIH, Bethesda, Maryland. **13.** The Mt. Sinai Medical Center, Cleveland, Ohio. **14.** Courtesy of Squibb Medical Systems. **15.** The Mt. Sinai Medical Center, Cleveland, Ohio. **16.** Courtesy of American Cancer Society. **17.** Courtesy of AT&T, Bell Laboratories. **18.** Courtesy of Squibb Medical Systems. **19.** Courtesy of Parkland Memorial Hospital. **20.** © Mark Godfrey. **21.** Courtesy of Wright State University. **Computers in the Arts and Leisure. 1.** Courtesy of Los Alamos National Laboratory. **2.** Copyright 1983 Symbolics Inc. **3.** Courtesy of Vectrix Corporation, Greensboro, North Carolina. **4.** Courtesy of Vectrix Corporation, Greensboro, North Carolina. **5.** Courtesy of Bell Laboratories. **6.** Copyright, The Exploratorium, Ed Tannenbaum. **7.** Courtesy of Aydin Controls, a division of Aydin Corporation. **8.** Courtesy of Hewlett Packard. **9.** Courtesy of CompuPro. **10.** Hank Morgan/TiME Magazine. **11.** Photo by Michael J. Lopez. **12.** Jonathan Saadah—Intermedia. **13.** Photo by Jon Porter. **14.** © Walt Disney Productions. **15.** Photograph courtesy of TRW Inc. **16.** Courtesy of Strand Century, Inc.

The Life of Bismark, Private and Political: With Descriptive Notices of His Ancestry

George Hesekiel

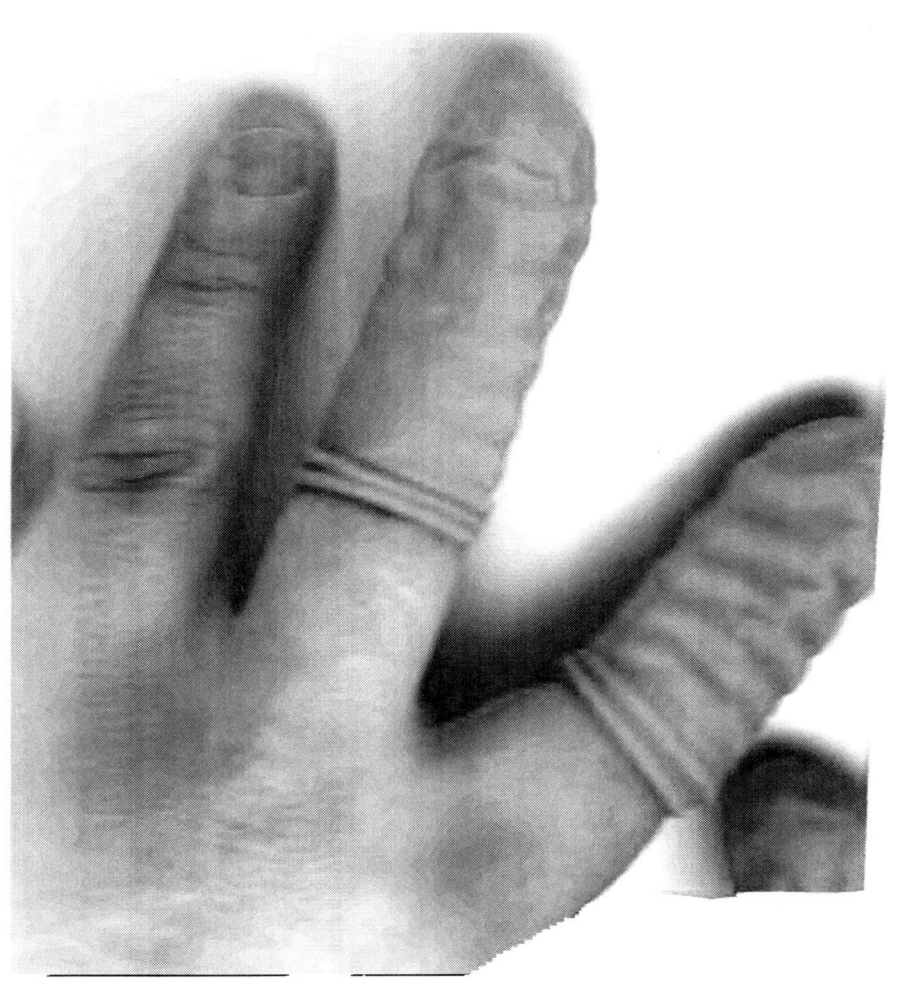